The Heath Family Engravers
1779–1878

The Heath Family Engravers

1779–1878

BY

JOHN HEATH

VOLUME 2

Charles Heath

(1785–1848)

Frederick Heath (1810–78)

Alfred Heath (1812–96)

Scolar Press

Published by
SCOLAR PRESS
Gower House
Croft Road
Aldershot
Hants GU11 3HR
England

Ashgate Publishing Company
Old Post Road
Brookfield
Vermont 05036
USA

British Library Cataloguing-in-Publication Data.
A catalogue record for this book is available from the British Library.

Typesetting by Simon Jenkins Associates

ISBN 0 85967 908 X (two volume set)

ISBN 0 85967 957 8

Printed in Great Britain at the University Press, Cambridge

CONTENTS

Volume 2 – Charles, Frederick and Alfred Heath

Introduction

THE OBITUARY NOTICES and a summary of Charles Heath's main achievements as an engraver/artist and promoter are mentioned in the introductory chapter of Volume I on the Heath engravers, which was concerned principally with the life and work of his father, James Heath A.R.A.

By way of a background to the catalogue raisonné which accompanies it, this volume deals in rather more detail with Charles Heath's activities and reputation in the distinctly different atmosphere of late Georgian and early Victorian England. Wider education, especially female education, and changing taste was leading to an ever greater appreciation of and demand for illustrated books and prints to meet the middle-class fashions of the day. This was also an age of rapid mechanical and technical development, producing market conditions which were within a few decades effectively to eliminate line engraving as a competitive artistic technique, except to some extent in the field of security printing. Meanwhile the phenomenal industry and energy which Charles Heath displayed, amidst a rising tide of fellow engravers, in striving to lead and fashion taste so as to meet the new demand, while at the same time contributing very significantly himself to technical innovations in the trade, are evidence of his style, ambition, and ability to adapt.

Unfortunately for him, the challenge proved too great, and from about 1836 he found himself increasingly over-committed and in debt. He died suddenly, and intestate, in 1848, and his estate when finally wound up in September 1852 showed assets of £808 against over £2030 owing to his creditors.[1] He was not of course the first Victorian artist and entrepreneur to end up in bankruptcy in that under-capitalised age, and though he showed himself reckless at times, the fault may not have been altogether his, but rather the uncertainties of the times and conditions then prevailing, in which only one unsuccessful publishing venture could bring about ruin.

CHAPTER 1

The Young Engraver

CHARLES HEATH WAS BORN on 1 March 1785, the second child by James Heath's common law wife, Mary Phillipson, and James' second son after George, the son of Eliza Thomas, James' wife. As a child, he would have lived with his parents at 13 Lisle Street, near Leicester Square, London until the house burnt down in 1789, and then until 1800 at 42 Newman Street: in 1791 he was baptised at St Martins-in-the-Fields. Apprenticed to his father for seven years from 5 February 1799, he would presumably have received his basic education before then at a local dame school, in much the same way as his father is assumed to have done – or even at home. At the age of 6, in December 1791, he showed early precocity (coached by his father) as an engraver, with a small etched portrait of what looks like a rather bad-tempered housemaid.

By 1802, by which time his father had entered into a publishing arrangement with the inventor Senefelder's patentee, Philipp Andre, and while he himself was only in his second year of apprenticeship, he turned his hand to lithography, known at that time in England as 'polyautography'. His portrait of a 'gypsey' (possibly a polyautograph) was exhibited at the Royal Academy in 1801, with two more in 1802.

Of these, his 'Three cupids bathing' is dated 11 February 1802, and may well have been the first example of a lithograph to be so exhibited in England; even though other well-known artists such as Benjamin West, W. Delamotte, Jean Claude Nates and Thomas Hearne had all produced lithographs dated in 1801. The first lithographic work to be published in England, the 'Specimens of Polyautography' published by Philipp Andre and James Heath in 1803 (of which no complete copy in original binding appears to have survived) may be misleading if the copy in the Victoria and Albert Museum is evidence, as although James Heath's title page is original, the 12 lithographs bound up with it (none of which are by Charles Heath) are not necessarily in the right order of production.[1] Charles Heath must have been very much involved in this new project, presumably on his father's account, using Andre's printing facilities at 5 Buckingham St, Fitzroy Square, as exemplified by his striking lithograph of 'Apollo as a Warrior' (1802), and a total of no less than 18 different lithographs produced between 1802 and 1806. When Senefelder's former assistant, G.J. Vollweiler took over the patent from Andre in 1806, he published on his own account four further parts, i.e. 36 lithographs in all, but repeating the 12 lithographs in the 1803 'Specimens of Polyautography' and including several lithographs by Charles Heath. The British Museum copy actually states 'The 3 preceding numbers [i.e. presumably the hitherto unpublished Parts 3-5] are ...designed by Charles Heath'.[2] Other lithographs of the time, including Charles' 'Pomona (Flora) with four Cupids' exhibited at the Royal Academy in 1804, were bound up in the unique volume of 400 lithographs, including a single work by William Blake dated 1807, later collected by the antiquarian Thomas Fisher, who in the *Gentleman's Magazine* for March 1808 commented, 'A drawing of Time and another of several figures by C. Heath in the manner of engraving, completely demonstrate the capacities of this invention with due improvement for some of the higher departments of the art'.

Unfortunately neither Andre nor Vollweiller were able to find a regular publisher/ dealer in London who would be prepared to back the new technique financially, and Vollweiler in turn returned to Germany in 1807 leaving the patent in abeyance.[3] As Senefelder commented in 1819: 'I am convinced that the public would have a greater number of masterly productions of the new art before them if it had been my fortune to have fallen in with an enterprising printseller who employed proper artists'. The reference is to his own stay in London in 1800/01, when he was kept under close supervision by Andre, contributing to the failure of his attempts to enlist the support of his fellow countryman and renowned London print-seller, R. Ackermann, or of the Boydells. For thereafter all Andre and his successor Vollweiler were able to do, with the help of the Heath engravers, was to interest artists, including various distinguished amateurs such as the future Louis Philippe, to try their hand out by leasing lithographic stones to them, a facility which was hardly likely to meet with much commercial success, let alone public recognition.[4] While James Heath may well have been able to help in his capacity as Historical Engraver to the King in obtaining the Royal Patent for Andre's process in June 1801, and perhaps also the patronage of the Queen and Royal princesses (which appears in the 1806 version of the 'Specimens'), and in providing contacts with well-known artists such as Benjamin West, Fuseli, Stothard and Farington, the Heaths were essentially engravers, not print dealers in the established sense. While Charles as a young apprentice took the trouble to learn the art of lithography, and to execute designs, the family resources could not at the time have been expected to go much beyond that, especially given their many other commitments. No wonder then that from 1807 until the 1820s, when Hullmandel revived it, the art of lithography in England stagnated.

Throughout his apprenticeship, Charles was living at his father's house and workshop at 15, Russell Place, Fitzroy Square, and may well have continued to do so for some years, possibly beyond 1808, the year in which he married. By 1819, no doubt by then being able to afford a house of his own, he had moved to 6 Seymour Place on the newly-built Euston Road nearby where he lived until at least 1828, before moving for the rest of his life to 24 Seymour Place North; both houses were within easy walking distance to the family firm at Russell Place and 42 Howland Street close by.

From an early age, it seems clear that Charles possessed exceptional talents, not only as a young engraver under his father's tutelage with a clearly recognisable style of his own, but as a designer/artist in his own right, and as a man of business enterprise as well. In March 1805, Farington noted in his diary that Charles Heath had passed as a student in the Royal Academy's Plaister Academy for figure drawing.[5] Although, unlike his father, he never seems to have applied later to become an Associate (perhaps because of James Heath's own difficulties with the Academy over the admission of engravers to full membership which, together with John Landseer, had come to a head between 1806 and 1813) he exhibited lithographs there until 1807; and he is also known to have been for some years in his early life a fellow of the Society of British Artists, and to have contributed drawings to their exhibitions.[6]

The precocious Charles obtained a really astonishing start to his career as an engraver when, probably while still apprenticed to his father, he was commissioned by Benjamin West, at that time President of the Royal Academy, to engrave his large painting 'Our Lord Healing the Sick' which had been paid for by subscription by the British Institute. The engraving was published in 1812, having, so it was said, taken 11 years to complete. It would seem quite extraordinary of the President to have commissioned Charles at the age of only 16 to begin the work, when there were so many other fine engravers who would have gladly competed for it. Benjamin West was related by marriage to Charles' mother Mary Phillipson, and this may well have been an underlying factor, especially as it was he, and not the British Institute who would be paying for the engraving, so that he could please himself who he employed. The choice must have caused much heart-burning, however; Farington for instance recorded on 6 July 1813: 'Sharpe, the Engraver was much mortified when Mr West gave his picture of 'Christ Healing the Sick' to Charles Heath to be engraved by him'.[7]

A remarkable letter which has survived dated March 19, 1811 from West to Sir Thomas Bernard, one of the Governors of the British Institute, sets out West's opinion of Charles as an engraver, suggesting that he may indeed have selected him on merit:

'Before I had finished the picture of Our Saviour receiving the Blind and Lame in the Temple to heal them, I spoke to Mr Charles Heath, the son of Mr James Heath, to engrave a plate in the stroke manner from it, on my own account, of the same size as Wolfe and Nelson for which I was to give him fifteen hundred guineas. My motives for making choice of this engraver were from a conviction of his superiority in drawing the human figure, as well as his taste in cutting the copper with firmness and precision, which are the requisites for an able engraver in this department of art. These essential professional powers in him, united to the energies of a mature age and ambition, all of which, under the guidance of my long experience in what constitutes excellence, I had flattered myself with these powers to give to the world a print as unrivalled as those of Wolfe and La Hogue are by Woollett. Such was the interest I then took, as I do now, in having the composition, characters and effect maintained in a print from that picture to be given to the civilised world; and as the Governors and Directors of the British Institution have given to the picture their sanction of its merits, I am the more desirous its character should be supported in a print done under their patronage. I therefore do not know of any engraver more capable of that than Mr Charles Heath. I hope yourself and the other Governors, as well as the Directors of the British Institute, will view this anxiety in me to have the print engraved with a superiority as my apology for writing this letter on the subject.

With sincerity and respect, I have the honour to be,
Dear Sir,
Your greatly obliged, humble serv't
Benjamin West[8]

Charles is believed to have eventually received 1,800 guineas for his work, while the President sold his picture to the Institute for 3,000 guineas.[9] Despite all this outlay, Farington subsequently estimated that the Institute had made 'upward of £9,300' from sales of the engraving to subscribers, thus showing a highly satisfactory profit.[10]

It is tempting to assume that it may have been on account of advances made to him by West for this engraving that Charles felt in a position to get married on 16 January 1808, two years out of apprenticeship. His bride was his first cousin, Elizabeth Petch, aged 21, whose widowed mother Amelia, who had been married to a Henry Petch, was another daughter of Thomas Phillipson, and sister to Mary.

At this stage, as a young man, Charles appears to have been interested in the theatre like his father, of perhaps a somewhat religious nature in keeping with the evangelical sentiment of the time (as some of his early engravings, notably for the Holy Bible, published in 1816 would suggest) and with philanthropic instincts towards his fellow men. He appears amongst the subscribers to Blair's 'The Grave' in 1808 for instance (along with his father), illustrated by Louis Schiavonetti to William Blake's designs, while in 1809 he was contributing towards a small pension for the poverty-stricken old engraver Tagg, whom he could have hardly known.[11] In 1814 he was appointed as a director of the newly-formed Artist's General Benevolent Institution, of which Robert Balmanno was secretary. And, if the many mock mediaeval etchings which Charles directed to illustrate that extraordinary work 'The History of the Valiant Knight Arthur of Little Britain' (published in 1814) are any guide, he must also have had a considerable interest in the romantic revival of mediaeval chivalry which was coming into fashion about this time, and influenced him when he came to promote his gift books and annuals in the 1830s.

With his father nearing retirement from the business from 1810 onwards, and his elder half-brother George showing no interest in becoming an engraver, Charles' main concern in these formative years was inevitably to build the family firm up by introducing more competitive methods, obtaining good commissions from publishers, and hiring assistants, independent engravers and part-time journeymen to help out as the work in hand ebbed and flowed. There may well have been much truth therefore in John Landseer's complaint, as registered by Farington in November 1817, that 'engraving had become a mere trade and that Heath and his son Charles had used it as such employing artists at lower prices, taking the profits and giving their names to the Plates'.[12] Twelve days later: 'He [Landseer] talked much abt the monopoly which Charles Heath held in the engraving line, by undertaking for Booksellers every kind of subject and whole commissions and dealing out the Plates to engravers at reduced prices, but still reserving a profit to Himself witht doing anything to them. This had caused Him [i.e. Landseer] to refuse work offered to Him when he was informed that Chas Heath was also engaged'.[13] Three weeks later: 'He [Landseer] spoke of Charles Heath having offered to the Booksellers Murray & Co. to have executed for them the whole of the Plates to be engraved of the Italian views drawn in Italy by Hakewill for 35 guineas each plate. Landseer and Middiman had demanded 50 guineas for each plate and they both refused to be engaged in the work shd Charles Heath be employed in it. In consequence His [i.e. Charles Heath's] offer has been refused and He is not to be employed'.[14] Landseer's rather odd attempt to get his own back on Charles is illustrated by Farington who on 16 January 1818 recorded: 'Cadell [the publisher] called to inform me that Landseer was with Him yesterday and acknowledged that he put Hay's name to the plate "View of the Dart River" having accused Heath of concealing names'.[15]

Landseer was not the only one to complain about developments in the Heath family practice. In a somewhat clumsily worded letter from William Sharp to Charles Warren dated 29 May 1810 (both were distinguished engravers, and a society for encouraging engravers was in prospect), he commented:

'The dotting engraving, in regard to the number of impressions which may far exceed 1000, and I believe be easily retouched by persons of Inferior Abilities so as to print a very large Number if the subject be a popular Subject of the day, it will prove very profitable to the Artist if he is the proprietor... Print merchants live by the Quantity as much as by the Quality and as some Mode of Engraving... being easier of execution together with that despatch frequently so necessary in Trade, gave them the prehemineince [*sic*]. The Old established Mode of Engraving which I mean... there are also Mr Robert Strange, Wollett [*sic*], Vivare, Raphael Morgan [*sic*] and others at Rome... When I look at the Impressions of these distinguished Men I see the impossibility of blending their Engravings with any other modes that have been established, neither can I see it possible that any Man to command success if his Studies are employed to imitate their Stile and manner of execution, for there is no patronage at all adequate to the trouble and time. These Great Men considered the Quality more [than] quantity... It is wellknown if a Person can get assistants and engage subjects of various sorts, Plates may be so Manufactured as to produce a large fortune. One Gentleman, an Engraver, informed Me that He has gained £20,000 only by the Labour of others during the prime of his Life, and all this was totally independent of his own labour.'

The reference here could well be to James Heath and his atelier, based on remarks probably exaggerated by Sharp, who had no atelier of his own.[16]

Another example of Charles' somewhat high-handed methods is exemplified by the ever-observant Farington whose diary for 2 April 1817 records: 'Newton [an R.A.] informed me of a very disagreeable situation in which he stood with Charles Heath the engraver respecting an engraving undertaken by Heath from a miniature portrait of Mr West painting by Newton. The impressions sent to Newton were very unsatisfactory yet Heath pressed for payment for the Plate and this day employed a solicitor to send a threatening letter to Newton. Heath having engraved the plate conditionally that Newton shd not pay for it unless he approved it. He, Newton, resolved to reject it and so informed Heath by letter'.[17] Next day: '[Newton] shewed me further correspondence with Charles Heath who had sent him a draft to accept for £157.10.0 in payment for the Plate in answer to which Newton wrote and finally rejected it, but notwithstanding what had passed wd assist Him with observations shd he determine to publish it on his own account'.[18] Next day again: 'Newton called and showed me a note he had rec'd from G. Corbould who recommended to him to compromise his dispute with C. Heath as He wd otherwise be put to an additional expense of £100 and the case wd be decided against Him; adding that George Heath, the barrister, had all the papers. Newton shewed me a statement of the case which he wd shew to his Solicitor'.[18] On 16 April: 'Newton called and shewed me a letter he had rec'd from Charles Heath to whom after touching upon the print, He sent the print and the picture, and would wait to see what the next impression would be, confident however that Heath wd not be able to make it a Plate fit for him [i.e. Newton] to publish'.[19] In fact Charles did manage to make the plate fit for publication, although it is a dark and gloomy study of the President of the Royal Academy in old age, and cannot have sold many copies. Farington seems to have heard no more about it so presumably Newton paid up in the end.

Correspondence from the Edinburgh publishers Archibald Constable (with whom Sir Walter Scott later became so heavily involved financially) introduces a rather more appreciative note, while complaining of overcharging;

'10th July 1815. Hurry of business at the end & beginning of the Year has made me rather delay writing you too long – The Frontispiece to the Encyclopaedia not being ready at the time we originally specified & which you undertook, was a great loss & disappointment to us – we were however very glad to receive it at the time we did and very well pleased with the work, but really you expect too much for it. Fifty guineas was the sum you originally mentioned and altho' that price was not actually fixed yet I could not have supposed that you would have expected so much as £21 more. The work is not *entirely* our own, and we cannot without incurring blame from others pay your demand without a remonstrance. In short I trust you will be satisfied with £63 for which you shall have our note payable at our bankers in London at 3 months date. I beg you will believe me that it is no custom of ours to *cut down* or dispute about accounts, but in the present case, the sum charged appears to me so high that I could not find myself justified in paying it without putting it before you for a reduction as I never do. Waiting your reply.' (Archibald Constable)[20]

The reply has not survived, but Charles presumably had to take his medicine and accept Constable's offer.

These examples serve to illustrate the kind of problems which Charles Heath encountered in his early years of management. He could evidently be tough, brash and occasionally unscrupulous in his dealings even though the cases on record here are perhaps little different from the sort of executive problems to be met with in everyday business. Charles was certainly no 'publishers' hack' as Bernard Adams called him rather unkindly until his 'Views in London' were engraved in 1825. He managed to play an important and very active role as the principal engraver in the family firm, and took on himself as much work as any engraver of the time could have been expected to do, earning a high reputation in consequence. As the publishers Longmans wrote to a Sir John Brierly in June 1821: 'We would recommend Mr Charles Heath as an artist most likely to do a set of plates well and in reasonable time'.[21] Longmans should have known, as they were at the time, and remained regular publishers for Charles Heath's many engraving enterprises.

A glance at his catalogue raisonné will show the quite astonishing range of publications with Heath engravings which appeared in the period between 1816 and 1825 especially, and involving in particular the publishers John Sharpe, Rodwell and Martin, Hurst, Robinson and Longmans, not to mention John Murray, Archibald Constable and Rivingtons, and at the lower end of the trade J.F. Dove, Thomas Tegg, Suttaby and several others. When it came to obtaining commissions to engrave, there is no suggestion that during this hyperactive period and even later Charles Heath exercised discrimination. This was the period which, as Iain Bain has described it, the so-called 'Legitimate' publishers (i.e. publishers of large works usually on travel or literary subjects of quality) were fighting a continuous battle with the so-called 'Pirates' such as Dove, Suttaby, Walker, Cooke and Tegg, the publishers of popular reprints in the manner originally established by John Bell in the 1770-80s in the London book trade.[22] The lure of such books with good, cheaply produced illustrations for an ever-widening more or less educated public must have been a major factor in inducing publishers to provide them, and with rising artists such as Richard Westall, Thomas Uwins, and Henry Corbould ready at hand with drawings or water colours, there was no reason why the leading firm of engravers at the time in London, as the Heaths had become, should not provide engravings to anyone. The only limitations to production would seem to have been the time it still took to produce quality engraving, and the use of copper plates which wore out all too quickly, and would then require re-engraving. On the other hand there were by the 1820s a great many capable engravers available to the Heath atelier, and with the pioneering efforts of Charles Heath and others such as Charles Warren, the problem of limited runs was solved by the introduction of hardened soft steel plates and revised techniques involving the extended use of etching in particular, which from the early 1820s revolutionised the industry. It was for security printing such as banknotes however that techniques for using engraved steel plates originated, and it is in this field that Charles Heath soon became active.

CHAPTER 2

Charles Heath's Contribution to Steel Engraving

THE AMERICAN ENGINEER AND INVENTOR, Jacob Perkins, of Newburyport, Massachusetts, is generally credited with the 'invention' of the art of steel engraving. 'Revival' would perhaps be a better description, as etching or engraving on iron or steel has been known and practised since the time of Durer in the 16th century, but had fallen into general disuse.

The genius of Jacob Perkins however lies not only in his having revived this branch of an art soon after 1805 (his first efforts actually took place in 1792, using copper-plates) but in developing his soft steel plate block, after engraving, by a hardening process, so as to produce what he called his 'check-plate', from which he could produce any number of identical steel printing plates. The process developed only slowly, but by 1805, Perkins could show that no less than 16 North American banks were using banknotes engraved by it, and in 1806 he published a pamphlet on the use of stereotype steel plates.[1] A patent on the 'check-plate' was taken out in Britain in 1806 by J.C. Dyer, an American businessman then living in England and promoting new enterprises; and it was probably about this time that contact was made with James Heath and his son Charles.

In collaboration with a local engraver, Gideon Fairman, Perkins moved to Philadelphia in 1814 and joined the firm which became known as Murray, Draper and Fairman. A real breakthrough then came for him from a contact with Asa Spencer, inventor of the so-called 'rose' engine which enabled circular designs known as 'rosettes' to be engraved on flat, convex or concave surfaces. With Spencer's aid, Perkins was able to change the whole character of the banknotes his firm was printing, and much improve their security against forgery.

Meanwhile by 1817, the Bank of England had become alarmed by the startling increase of forgeries to their banknotes; no less than 31,000 had been detected. This situation was not altogether surprising; in 1819 for instance the Society of Arts commented that there were 'no less than 10,000 copperplate engravers in the country capable of copying a Bank of England note, 9/10ths of whom were needy and many in distressed circumstances'.[2] Even allowing for some exaggeration, the problem was clearly serious, and had to be solved somehow. It was at this point that the Bank's

Commissioners offered a reward, believed to have been up to £20,000, to the originator of any scheme which could provide better security. In 1818, Charles Heath, who was by this time more or less in charge of the family firm (his father retired in 1822), showed specimens of Murray, Draper and Fairman's improved security banknotes to a Committee of the Society of Arts on forgery, while Dyer did the same to the Bank of England's Committee. The Bank's own engravers however managed to imitate some, but not all, of the most intricate machine work presented to them, and Dyer was told that the Committee were unable to 'avail themselves of the talent of that most able and ingenious artist' [either Fairman or Charles Heath were presumably meant].

Nothing daunted, Dyer proceeded to address a powerful pamphlet[3] to the Committee setting out all the advantages of the Perkins process which was described in detail, and disparaging the efforts of their main rivals for the award, Messrs Applegarth and Cowper, whose useless processes eventually cost the Bank £40,000. In his reply to the Bank's stonewalling on his earlier representations, Dyer commented: 'The Commissioners objected that when the work so imitated was shown to us, we changed our ground, and proposed to get some of Mr Heath's work which could not be imitated, thereby acknowledging after all that the security was to come from Mr Heath, and not from any work that Messrs Perkins and Fairman could execute themselves... the artists here are superior to those in America'. 'We hold it to be physically impossible in type metal, or any other composition of fusible metal in the heated state to bring up the higher styles of vignette and other copper-plate engravings and machine work, in a manner to admit of any comparison for sharpness and beauty with that which is done by steel dies and cylinders'. The interest which the new processes were arousing amongst engravers generally was evidently great, and support for them when Dyer published yet another broadside in October 1819 entitled 'Opinions and Remarks upon the means of preventing forgeries' came not only from James and Charles Heath, but from signatories which included almost all the best of them – William Holl, Charles Warren (even though in the process of developing his own tempered steel plates), William Daniell, John Pye, William Finden, William Wyon, Charles Corbould, Charles Armstrong, J.H. Robinson, Francis Engleheart, Edward Portbury, George Corbould, Rhodes, Noble, Abraham Raimbach, James Mitan, Charles Pye, Samuel Middiman, Robert Balmanno, not to mention two of the greatest engineers of their day, Mark Isambard Brunel (designer of the first Thames tunnel) and George Rennie (co-designer of the new London Bridge, now spanning Lake Tahoe in California); and also Robert Smirke the painter and Academician.

By this time Perkins himself had decided to leave Philadelphia, and, with the encouragement of the British Minister in Washington, Charles Bagot, to come to England, accompanied by Fairman and Spencer, two printers, and a mass of plant and equipment, with the intention of setting up an engraving and printing establishment 'using copper and steel plate for printing banknotes and other papers'.

It was not a question here, as has been commonly supposed, of Perkins trying to obtain the Bank of England contract for printing notes, which had always been printed in-house by the Bank anyway, but rather of competing for the award for better security engraving and printing which was on offer, with the conviction that his own process, while superior to anything anyone else could put up against it, was bound to be at a disadvantage so long as it was based in the United States. At the back of his mind he must have known that, even if he did not win the Bank's award (which would of course have carried much prestige with it, as well as money) by establishing his plant in London, he stood every chance at least of obtaining contracts for security banknotes from the many private and provincial banks in Britain, who were also having problems with the forgers.

And this is precisely what he did. New patents were taken out, and Charles Heath became a partner.[4] A prospectus issued in December 1819 refers to 'Messrs Perkins and Fairman, Inventors of the Siderographick Art (or mode of engraving on steel the most delicate and beautiful designs) having formed a partnership with Mr Charles Heath, engraver of London'. A parallel advertisement announced that their plan for using steel engraving 'was presented to the public notice as one which has stood the test of long experience, having been adopted for some years by no less than 300 banking establishments in America, without one attempt at imitation'. Apart from banknotes, the plan 'is not of less importance in objects of minor consequence, even the most trifling and minute, where elegance of design, beauty of execution and economy are held in consideration'.

In 1821, Messrs Perkins Fairman and Heath received the thanks of the Society of Arts for supplying them with details of their siderographic process for multiplying copies of engravings, particularly with a view to the prevention of forgery.[5] But in April 1821 Heath had a long interview with the Governor of the Bank of England at which he stressed the advantages of Perkins' system; after a final conversation in August, he was informed that although the Bank was open to consider further specimens, he could be given no encouragement to submit them, or to incur any further expense for the presentation of his plans'.[6] The Governor, Sir William Congreve, was a former military man, a martinet well-known for his strong anti-American feelings;[7] and he was to have the last word.

It was perhaps this disappointment that caused Gideon Fairman, who was mainly responsible for banknote design and engraving, to return to the United States when his contract ended in 1822, leaving Joshua Bacon, Perkins' son-in-law, as managing partner for many years at the firm's premises, No. 69 Fleet Street, while Perkins, the somewhat unbusinesslike but brilliant engineer went on to develop various new inventions, notably a steam machine gun, demonstrated to the Duke of Wellington with remarkable effect in 1825 (but not accepted by the War Office) in a large smithy at the back of the printing plant.[7]

Charles Heath had, as a partner, put in £1000 out of a promised £3000 in September 1819 as his share of the printing patent, and with a 14/48th share in the firm; his half-brother, George, was persuaded to loan over £4000 as well in the following year, while a near neighbour, Colonel J.E. Drinkwater, put in a further £1500 in January 1820.[8]

In October 1819, work began 'by way of experiment for C. Heath and Perkins and Fairman', and about 1820 a number of plates were made for the Commercial Bank of Calcutta – evidently the firm's first major contract. Despite all his many other preoccupations, in those early years Charles involved himself a good deal in the business of engraving banknotes for provincial banking establishments, with useful contracts which, continued until at least 1838, when such printing, in England at least, became obsolete by law. As Marcus Samuel has noted: 'Perkins country banknotes can generally be distinguished at a glance from those of other contemporary printers by the fineness of line of the steel engraving and the character of the white line engine-turned borders. The artwork was superior, many of the vignettes having been designed by Henry Corbould and engraved by Charles Heath'.[9] Extracts from two letters from Joshua Bacon, written to Charles when in Manchester in September and November 1822, illustrate the point: 'we now have 13 printers at work and I think we can find employment for 14 or 15 in the course of next week... The Roll is finished, which you saw before you left and has bitten in very deep and well... I embrace the opportunity to enclose 10 patterns made since your departure some of which requiring a great while to execute ought to be charged very high. The Blackburn Bank is secured since you left and the Sheffield have ordered drawings sent them – the business is increasing with a steady pace and every branch is crowding those employed in it exceedingly. The Guinea we have orders to finish and put to press immediately... Please remind Mr Perkins of leather for carbons' [this was used in the oven for steel hardening of plates and dies using the Perkins process].[10]

On Fairman's departure in July 1822, the firm had become known as 'Perkins and Heath', but it was in fact George Heath, the barrister in the family, who had taken over his half-brother's stake in the firm, and his name in the partnership. For bankruptcy had struck Charles Heath for the first time in April 1821, although he was not officially declared as such, as friends and relatives, probably including his father, tided him over to enable him to start up again in business in a few months' time. Meanwhile George helped to manage and represent the firm until 1829, when the name changed to 'Perkins and Bacon'. At the same time, and for many years afterwards, it is clear from the Perkins Bacon records which have survived that Charles, from his family engraving business, was in constant communication with the firm, and in effect used it as his main printing house during the 25 years during which he was, as proprietor, promoting many gift books and annuals and their numerous engravings on his own behalf.

Charles Heath's greatest achievement, though one which tends to be remembered today only by philatelists who collect classic British postage stamps, is the part he played with Perkins, Bacon and Petch (as the firm became from 1834 when Charles' brother-in-law became a partner) in assisting in the engraving of the master die, using the Perkins process in 1840, for the 1d black and 2d blue postage stamps which introduced stamps to the world. Although Perkins, Bacon and Petch had not participated in the Post Office competition for designing these stamps, their selection for this pioneering contract as engravers was logical, as they had been supplying revenue 'stamps' since 1828, and were recognised by then as being by far the most technically experienced firm in the country for this kind of security printing work.[11]

With Henry Corbould (who was also related by marriage to Charles Heath) commissioned to design the stamp, using as one of his models the 'City medal' designed by William Wyon in 1837,[12] showing in superb detail the head of the young Queen Victoria in profile, Charles and his son Frederick set to work on the steel master roller, from which all the steel printing plates were to be produced. Although due to failing eyesight, Charles left most of the engraving work to his son, the final touches were his, and when he returned the roller die to Bacon in March 1840 he accompanied it with a note which simply said: 'If this does not transfer well, nothing will.'[13] Of the 1d stamp alone, over 20,000,000 copies were subsequently printed, and the security claims put forward originally to the Bank of England in 1821 proved to be fully justified. Over 30 years were to elapse before a forgery was made that defrauded the Post Office; and it is worth reflecting how much trouble and expense the Bank might have saved itself from forgery in the 1820s and 30s had the prejudices of the by then discredited Sir William Congreve been overruled at the time, and the Perkins steel block process been adopted by the Bank's own engravers.

Charles Heath's main concern in his relations with the newly established printing firm was, as the partnership agreement of 1819 had expressly provided, 'all work not relating to banks', and it was in this field that he deserves recognition also.

As the Longman's correspondence records confirm, Charles Heath was busy in June 1820 in actually engraving his first book illustrations on steel, dated 1820, for an edition of Thomas Campbell's Pleasures of Hope, published in January 1821, and using the Perkins plate block process.[14] This was a real pioneering effort and a world first in book illustration. Charles Heath had already engraved these same four plates on copper for an earlier limited edition in 1818, but this was a popular work, and a much larger edition was in prospect probably justifying the use of steel engraving for the first time in order to obtain a longer run.

The experiment was successful; indeed without magnification it is difficult to tell the difference between the engraving on steel and the earlier engraving on copper. Charles Heath thereupon went on immediately to engrave several frontispieces to popular works of the day together with illustrating slim volumes of poetry on steel, which were to be the forerunners of the later annuals in size, if not in content. Examples include: Mavor's Spelling Book, 1821, Debrett's Peerage and Baronetcy, 1822, Pinnock's Dr Goldsmith's Histories of Greece and Rome, 1823. Bearing the legend 'C. Heath sc. Perkins and Heath Patent Hardened Steel Plate', the next substantive work engraved on steel was Campbell's Gertrude of Wyoming (plates dated 1822, and also published by Longmans); this also followed a copper-plate version with the two plates dated 1819. Two illustrations and a vignette by Charles Heath followed for Thomas Moore's 'Loves of the Angels' (1825); together with four small plates for the 1825 'Forget-Me-Not', presumably engraved in 1824 so as to meet the Christmas season. Thereafter the words 'Engraved on Steel' which first appeared on the plates for the 'Pleasures of Hope' no longer feature on plate inscriptions, as their novelty value was over.

But Charles may well have felt that he had found his real metier in executing these small prints for the new fashion in gift books and Annuals. On one of the four engravings he carried out for the 'Literary Souvenir' for 1826 for instance, its editor, Alaric Watts, commented: 'I may mention that another subject by Stewart Newton entitled 'The Forsaken' engraved by Charles Heath was so highly valued by connoisseurs for the engraver's work – it possessed I think little other value – that proofs of it before letters were purchased by Messrs Colnaghi, the printsellers, at a public sale, at a uniform price of 19/- each'.

CHAPTER 3

Charles Heath and the 'Annuals', 1825-48

THE YEARS 1825 TO 1826 must have been a traumatic period for Charles, marking major changes in his whole career. In the four months up to April 1826, no less than 59 banks and 29 miscellaneous banking establishments in Britain were declared insolvent, contributing in turn to the bankruptcy of many other firms, notably Hurst, Robinson, the publisher, and to a loss in banknote printing contracts for Perkins and Heath, in which he still had an interest as an engraver. He had only just recovered from his virtual bankruptcy in 1821 and, to meet his obligations, was forced to sell many of his books and effects at two public auctions in May/June 1826.

He had had major projects in hand in 1825, which must have cost him considerable financial loss. His 'Views in London', for instance, consisting of at least 45 out of 60 engravings, as originally planned, all of them by him, remained in effect unpublished because of Hurst Robinson's failure; it would have been 'a pioneer work in a new medium [i.e. steel engraving] and a landmark in the history of illustration'.[1] And, by February 1825, he had entered into an agreement with J.M.W. Turner R.A., with Hurst Robinson apparently taking full financial responsibility, for the line engraving of 120 water colours to be published in parts as 'Picturesque Views in England and Wales'. Hurst Robinson's bankruptcy in the following year must have been a bitter disappointment to Charles; even though by 1827 he had found another publisher in Robert Jennings, the terms were not so generous, and it looks as if Charles had to assume half the costs if the project was to continue, as Charles was evidently determined that it should (see Chapter 4).

As his father had attempted to be, Charles was equally determined at this stage to stand on his own feet, as an engraver of high reputation established especially from his engravings in Batty's 'European Scenery' series, and for Sir Walter Scott's novels and romances in 1822/3. He decided that he would do best for the family business by concentrating his efforts away from the dealer/publishing houses with whom rank and file engravers were normally obliged to do business on their terms and at their mercy. He would in future, as his own proprietor, introduce ventures involving illustrated books and their concomitant sales of prints to the public generally, using publishers on his own terms, holding copyrights, and with a printing house at his command in the form of Perkins and Heath. For this he judged correctly that the timing was right, in the realisation that, since 1823, a lucrative but still hardly exploited market lay to hand for him in the fashionable field of promoting the new wave of gift books and illustrated Annuals. He already knew the field well, having himself engraved for Ackermann's ForgetmeNot in 1825 and 1826, for S.C. Hall's 'Amulet' for 1826, and for Alaric Watts' 'Literary Souvenir' for 1826 and 1827. He saw his chance but still needed a suitable publisher, and on his terms. His personal letter to John Murray, Byron's publisher, is revealing:[2]

To John Murray esq
October 24th 1826
Dr Sir
You will perhaps be surprised at receiving this from me considering the legal measures you have been induced by false representation to institute against my business, but as it is not my intention to discuss that subject which will shortly be settled on a point of law and with which personally I have no concern, I shall proceed to the real object of this letter requesting you to consider the proposal herein contained as if it came from an entire stranger and as a mere *matter of Business.*

I have commenced a work similar to the Forget me Not and the 'Literary Souvenir' and I flatter myself that in the Embellishments if will surpass every Book hitherto published. The subjects are of such a nature that every one will sell as a separate Print, and experience has shown that Proofs enough may be sold to cover the whole or great part of the original expense. The whole ought to be ready by July in the next year. The Plates would do for a French and an American Edition. Now Sir if you would like to join me in this Speculation and would get the Literary department done as *you could* get it done, I think so splendid a work as could be brought out by our *united exertions,* and with your influence, would take the Lead in this sort of publication and we should divide annually very considerable Profit.

My motive for engaging in this and other works, is to get the *Profit* of my own Labour and Talent, as it is my intention (as far as lies in my Power) to engrave for none but such Works as I have an *Interest* in or, are entirely my *own* property.

I must again request you to consider this as a *Letter of Business* and to give me your answer as soon as possible.

I am, Sir,
Your Obt Hu. Ser.
Chas Heath
6 Seymour Place
Euston Square

P.S. I understand Mr Ackerman has sold 12,500 copies of his Forget me Not and is now printing 6,000 more. Mr Hall informed me yesterday that the subscription for the Amulet has already paid all expenses, and I know that the 'Literary Souvenir' has done the same. Messrs *Longmans* have taken four thousand. I send a Proof of the Plate I have just engraved for the Souvenir [this would have been the frontispiece to the 1827 Literary Souvenir: 'Girl in a Florentine costume of AD 1500'].

[Reply]
Wimbledon
Oct. 28. 1826
Mr Murray returns his thanks to Mr Chas Heath, for the favour of his tempting proposal, and regrets to add that there are many reasons which prevent him engaging in it.

Mr Murray returns the portrait, which Mr Chas Heath was so obliging as to send to Mr M. to look at & which he thinks very beautifully engraved.

This reply was not altogether surprising, as John Murray II had suffered heavy financial loss in the first half of 1826, after putting £26,000 into the ill-fated journal 'The Representative' (suggested by the young Disraeli), and can have been in no mood for another speculative venture, as Charles should have known. He may also have been wary of engaging with Charles again, bearing in mind his reactions when, in 1818, Charles had wished on him yet another edition of Byron's Poems, with engravings, even though this turned out profitably.[2] The legal process referred to was probably the action brought by him to court in 1830 arguing against the engraver's traditional custom of retaining twelve proof copies of every print commissioned, which he could then sell to the detriment of the publisher; an action which Charles lost.

Charles thereupon fell back on Hurst, Chance, as the revived Hurst, Robinson had become, who at the end of 1827 duly published the first edition of his 'Keepsake', which was to prove for a while a remarkable success.

The 'Keepsake', the first of the Annuals which Charles promoted until his death, and which included 'Heath's Picturesque Annual' (1832-45) and 'Heath's Book of Beauty' (1833-49) among a number of others, lasted until 1857, with Longmans as its publisher from 1832. By then, edited mainly by literary ladies and social hostesses such as Mrs Norton and the Countess of Blessington (and later her niece Miss Power), it had outlived all its rivals, many of whom sprang up from 1829 onwards, some surviving only one issue or two, in the face of fierce competition and a dwindling public, with a market thoroughly over-supplied and rising costs.

This period of Charles' career is perhaps best worth illustrating through the eyes of his contemporaries directly, some of whom such as Hall, Watts and Allan Cunningham (of the 'Anniversary' of 1829) were very much Charles' competitors, yet still manifested considerable respect for his activities, especially for the high standards of engraved illustration which he managed to maintain throughout.

To set the scene, John Britton and John Ruskin, both writing in hindsight years later had some general observations both as seen by the trade and by the general public as regards the Annuals in that long vanished period – the 'age of sentiment' of the new middle class as it has been called, or the 'age of sentimentality' as it became – as follows:

'A history of this literary family – The Annuals – would embrace much curious anecdote, biography and exposition of art and artists: of professional and amateur authors; of trade, manufacturers and commerce, of fashion, fame and frivolity; and last though not least, the fluctuation and caprices of taste and *ton*. The Annuals which were so popular and profitable to a Heath and a Fisher [i.e. the Drawing Room Scrap Book] twenty years ago [i.e. ca.1829] are now superseded and a totally different and new species has now been introduced by Messrs Longman and Co. and by Virtue in which topography, history, travels and substantial literature are the basis'.[3]
John Britton

'Then [i.e. ca.1830] the simple family circle looked forward with chief complacency to their New Year's gift of the Annual in a delicately printed, lustrously bound and elaborately illustrated octavo volume, representing after its manner the practical and artistic inspiration of the age... The ancient Annual was written by meekly minded persons who felt that they knew nothing about anything, and didn't want to know more... even the most retiring of its authors expected to be admired not for what he had discovered but for what he was... They and all the less known, yet pleasantly and brightly endowed spirits of that time are suddenly as unintelligible to us as the Etruscans – not a feeling they had we can share in.'[4]
John Ruskin

For rather more detail of the rise and fall in the fashion for the Annual, the various comments made in their autobiographies by Charles Knight (author/publisher), Henry Vizetelly (engraver and publisher), S.C. Hall, Alaric Watts, R.R. Madden (biographer of the Countess of Blessington), and Allan Cunningham (art critic) are particularly apposite:

'What were then called 'The Annuals' were introduced to England by Mr Ackerman in his 'ForgetmeNot' of 1822. Alaric Watts followed with his 'Literary Souvenir', Samuel Carter Hall started the 'Amulet' for the especial use of 'serious persons'. In 1827, I was asked to edit 'Friendship's Offering'. It was an enterprise hastily entered upon by Messrs Smith and Elder, late in the season, and I had to obtain pictures for engraving, secure contributors, and see the book through the press in two or three months...

'New Annuals started up in the next and few following years, among the best of which was 'The Anniversary' by Allan Cunningham, who had it in his power to make as good a book of this sort as could be produced, from the esteem with which he was regarded by the best writers and the best artists [The Anniversary lasted for only one

year, due to the bankruptcy of the publisher, John Sharpe, in 1829]. There were Keepsakes and Gems and Bijous; but these delicate flowerets of the literary hotbed had a brief existence. They did more for arts than letters. They had set a great many people scribbling, who would never have dreamt of committing the sin of rhyme without such excitements, and they had compelled some of those who write well to adopt a style anything but vigourous and original. They were perhaps right, and so were the editors and publishers. It was a period in which, except for a few rare instances, mediocrity was essentially necessary to great literary success'.[5]
Charles Knight

'[Ackermann's] success produced crowds of imitators, many of which speedily outstripped the original in the quality of their literary and more especially their pictorial contents. In their palmy days the 'Keepsake', 'Books of Beauty' and the like sold in their tens of thousands at high prices and yielded royal revenue. Portraits of society beauties were as much sought after when they were only to be obtained in guinea volumes as they are now, when scattered broadcast by sixpenny and penny journals.

'For these annuals the services of the ablest artists and engravers were eagerly sought, and a hundred pounds or more were paid for a steel engraving merely a few inches in size. Although 'Annual' editors relied mainly on writers with titled names, efforts were occasionally made to secure contributions from authors of the highest standing. Moore used to boast of having rejected an offer from C. Heath, the engraver, of 600 guineas for a short poem for the 'Keepsake'; whereat Lockhart contemptuously remarked that it was doubtful which was the greater fool of the two; Heath who made the offer or Moore who refused it.

'At length the time came when the crowd of annuals, with their delicately finished steel and copperplate engravings were superseded by works less fugitive in character and illustrated by high class engravings on wood, the lead in publishing which was taken by one or two Paris houses, and notably that of Leon Curnier.'[6]
Henry Vizetelly

'The public, when these productions were novel and numerous, and in their zenith as to cost and beauty, paid for the elegant works in question, according to an estimate I made at the time, £100,000 per annum. First came ForgetmeNot (1822) then Friendship's Offering (1823) then Literary Souvenir (1824-5) – a great advance – then Hall's Amulet, Winter's Wreath and Keepsake: 17 issued in 1829 alone.

In their earlier years the Annuals were all bound up in tinted paper and enclosed in a case. Paper yielded to silk in which the majority of them soon made their appearance; then followed morocco, leather and velvet. The public were startled at finding elegant books full bound in morocco – for the binding of which they had been accustomed to pay nearly as much as the cost of the whole work – illustrated by exquisitely engraved prints from paintings by artists of the highest celebrity, any one of which would previously have been valued at the charge demanded for the series, and containing prose and poetry written for the several publications by leading and popular writers of the age.

Until the Keepsake entered the field, all Annuals were published at 12/-. The Keepsake was an experiment at a guinea... the letter press was wretched in proportion yet the trial was a successful one: and the next year Charles Heath, the proprietor, amended the mistake into which he had fallen and obtained the cooperation of several of the best authors of the age and country. His expenses for the literary portion of this second volume amounted to no less than £1600'... a Landscape Annual was conceived by Mr Charles Heath'... the Book of Beauty was a new and happy idea' 'Previous prints were tawdry coloured daubs'... 'They were displaced by engravings after the choicest works of our British painters, executed in such a manner as to educate the eye and give employment to the mind'... 'They have been sneered at as literary toys. That is not just; as compared with the Christmas issues of today [1883] they were of very great excellence. No such engravings as they contained are now produced; while the literary contents, principally tales and poems, are of pure gold compared with the tinsel of the modern magazine'.[7]
S.C. Hall

'In truth the 'Keepsake' is below expectation and mine is above it. Great names do not always produce great works and so it has happened in this case. If the 'Keepsake' sells 25,000 copies then it will have expended £11,000; or if it sells 16,000 copies only, and that is the sum printed, the expense cannot be near that sum. But round numbers sound well, and the public ear is gratified by swaggering accounts of lords hired and large sums expended'.[8]
Allan Cunningham (Editor of 'The Anniversary', 1829), letter to Leitch Ritchie, 22 November 1828

'The most dangerous competitor of this time was the 'Keepsake' established in 1827 by Mr Charles Heath, the eminent engraver under the editorship, at first, of Mr Harrison Ainsworth, and afterwards for some years of Mr Frederic Mansel Reynolds, son of Frederic Reynolds, a wellknown dramatist of his day [and close friend of Charles Heath's father, James].[9]

'The Landscape Annual deserved to be eminently successful. The idea was taken up by Mr Charles Heath of the Keepsake who in 1833 [sic. actually 1831/2] established the 'Picturesque Annual' under the editorship of Leitch Ritchie, a popular and agreeable writer, who was sent abroad by the proprietors to visit the various places of which drawings for this work were made by Turner... The influence of these annuals was eminently healthful and refining, highly conducive as they were to the awakening and stimulating among the great mass of the middle classes especially in the country, of the taste for landscape art in England.'

It occurred in the year 1835 [actually in 1832/3] to Mr Heath that an annual, the engravings in which should consist exclusively of beautiful women of the aristocracy would be likely to be acceptable to a large section of the public; and the 'Book of Beauty' edited by the Countess of Blessington [the first editor for 1833 was actually 'L.E.L.' (Laetitia Landon)] was the result... it became so much a fashion that a lady of rank regarded the introduction of her portrait into the 'Book of Beauty' as indispensable as her presentation at St James' or her marriage at St George's... The Book of Beauty ultimately succumbed to the weight of embellishments thus imposed upon it by the fashion.[10]
Alaric Watts

'In leather trappings some appear
While others silk reveal
And most like knights of other days
Are armed with plates of steel.

The lordly 'Keepsake' lauds himself
And all is 'vain enough'
But 'neath his silken garb there peeps
A garb of common stuff.

In vain it boasts its gaudy hues
By men of rank drawn out
That all his contributions are
Rank nonsense, none can doubt.

Now from the 'Heath' a band arise
An amazonian train
The Book of Beauty leads them forth
For conquest on the *plain.*'
Thomas Hood's 'Battle of the Annuals' (ca. 1833/4) [11]

'Her name is eternally before the public; she produces those gorgeous inanities called 'Books of Beauty', and other trashy things of the same description, to get up which all the fashion and beauty, the celebrity and talent of London, are laid under contribution. The most distinguished artists and the best engravers supply the portraits of the prettiest women in London, and these are illustrated with poetical effusions of the smallest possible merit, but exciting curiosity from the notoriety of their authors; and so, by all this puffing and stuffing, and untiring industry, and practising on the vanity of some, and the good nature of others, the end is attained.'[12]
Charles Greville (on Lady Blessington) ca. 1835

'There is a 'large weak plate' of a woman who 'pats a greyhound or weeps into a flowerpot or delivers a letter to a bandy-legged page'. Opposite is a song perhaps entitled "The Forsaken One of Florence" by L.E.L. or Miss Mitford or Lady Blessington about 'water-lilly, chilly, stilly, shivering beside a streamlet, plighted, blighted, love benighted, falsehood sharper than a gimlet, lost affection, recollection, cut connexion, tears in torrents, true love token, spoken, broken, sighing, dying girl of Florence'. The 'Keepsake' was the best of these series.[13]
W.M. Thackeray

'The greatest and first promoter, in his day, of illustrated annuals was Charles Heath'... Mr Charles Heath had, like the Findens, entered on the publication of periodicals illustrated by him, and with the same unfortunate result. He excelled in small plates, and in his hands that sort of artistic talent exhibited in the embellishment of annuals reached their highest perfection'.[14]
R.R. Madden

'On my return from Clifton last week, I find on my table the 'Book of Beauty' and the 'Keepsake'. So anxious are some of my lady friends to read them that I had only time to look at what came from the pen of those I most value and regard. Are you quite resolved to close the 'Book of Beauty' for ever? I am among the many who hope it will not be so.'[15]
Walter Savage Landor to Lady Blessington, November 23 1846

'In 1848 Heath died in insolvent circumstances, heavily in debt to Lady Blessington to the extent nearly of £700... His failure had taken place six or seven years previously. From that time the prosperity of the Annuals was on the wane and Lady Blessington's receipts from them became greatly reduced... the public were surfeited with illustrated annuals. The taste for that species of literature had died out. The perpetual glorification of beauty had become a bore. The periodical poems sung in honour of the children of the nobility ceased to be amusing'.[15]
R.R. Madden

'I am most concerned to hear you have been so serious a loser by Mr Heath's death. But I wish at least that the Annuals may be continued by someone. They satisfy an elegant want of so large a part of the community that I do not think they can be suffered to drop and sincerely and earnestly hope you may get satisfactory terms from some publisher of capital and enterprise.'[16]

Some samples of press and periodical comment on Charles Heath's productions in the field of gift books and Annuals may help to round off the critical scene at the time. It will be noticed that while the literary content seems invariably to evoke the most scathing criticism, the illustrations and Charles Heath's contribution to them, by contrast, produces mainly the highest praise. An element of partisanship, not to mention exaggeration, seems to be common to both.

The 1828 Keepsake: 'Most assuredly this brilliant Christmas visitor is transcendent in its graphic illustrations. They are indeed extremely beautiful, and who can wonder at this, when the greater part of them are from the eminent graver of Mr Charles Heath and the whole under his immediate superintendence. Every specimen from his hand is replete with the exquisite touches of his masterly style; and there is not one of the whole collection which is unworthy of preservation in the choicest portfolio of taste.'
The Gentleman's Magazine, December 1827

Heath's Picturesque Annual, 1832: 'The Picturesque Annual is evidently an imitation of the Landscape Annual whose third appearance was noticed with due commendation in our last. It is a splendid but rather costly production.'
The Gentleman's Magazine, December 1831

'The Book of Beauty!' How talismanic the sound! how seductive the name! how calculated to mislead the soberness of impartial judgment or blunt the arrows of just criticism... Though Heath's name is pompously put forth 'ad captandum' there is not a single engraving of his own execution and the only merit to which he can lay claim is the activity he has shown in adapting the portraits which were accidentally in possession of his different friends to the stories concocted by Miss Landon... On the whole however the work may be considered a pleasing display of female beauty more splendid perhaps than useful.'
The Gentleman's Magazine, December 1832

'What encouragement is there for any man of eminence to allow his productions to be choked in the midst of insufferable twaddle and mawkish absurdity? But, as the case stands, for every ten pages of readable matter, we have at least ninety of frothy nothingness, written by nobody knows who.'
Fraser's Magazine, December 1832

'However much we may desire to say of a lady only that which is pleasant, we are compelled to state that the change [of editorship] has not been advantageous to the work... The volume is made up of mere nothings. She has not succeeded in giving dignity to the class of work to which it belongs.' [Unlike Lady Blessington who, in the critics' opinion had produced in the 'Book of Beauty' the perfect annual, including a 'very sweetly written tale of sin and sorrow'.]
The New Monthly Magazine, on Mrs Caroline Norton's editorship of the 'Keepsake' for 1836

The Belle of a Season: 'This is one of Mr Charles Heath's illustrated works. Our readers

will readily believe that it is got up with taste upon every portion of it; and that, in especial, the business of the engraver has been well performed. No person better than Mr Charles Heath can 'superintend' the publication of a beautiful book; his success in this department of the publisher has been deservedly great but he like other men has his prejudices, and he will do well to conquer them. The Frenchified fripperies of Mr Chalon are going, or rather are gone, out of fashion... to have unmeaning faces of mere mawkish prettiness is no longer desired by our English ladies...'
The Art Union, December 1839

Europa: 'It is better for this type of print to be published by art societies as the public cannot appreciate its excellence. The print... is in all respects admirable; as an engraving indeed it bears evidence of being the work of many hands: but there are parts of it worthy of the first burin of the country [presumably Charles Heath is meant].'
The Art Union, March 1840

'Mr Charles Heath has this year produced five annuals. 'The Keepsake', the editorship of which has been transferred to the accomplished Countess of Blessington, the 'Book of Beauty' which of course remains in the Lady's hands: the 'Picturesque', descriptive of Belgium, the 'Children of the Nobility', and a novelty, good as well as new, 'Legends of Venice'... To Mr Charles Heath the public owe a large debt; he has now catered for their amusement and information for a long period; and has no doubt achieved that success to which he is undoubtedly entitled. In the whole range of London publishers there is no man of greater enterprise, no one who has so strenuously laboured to maintain the reputation he has acquired for good taste and matured judgment.'
The Art Union, November 1840, p.179

Cattermole's Historical Annual: 'We hope it will be pre-eminently successful; we cannot doubt that it will be appreciated by all persons of sound judgment; and that Mr Heath will be thus induced to render annual publications the medium of communicating matters that are not created to be forgotten – the sooner the better.'
The Art Union, January 1841

'The Picturesque Annual is certainly a graceful and elegant assemblage of literary trifles. Mr Heath is now as able as he has ever been to exercise upon his public the judgment, taste and liberality for which he has long been celebrated; but the public are not as ready with the necessary recompense and the adage holds good in this as in all other matters 'We must cut the coat according to the cloth'.
The Art Union, December 1841

The Picturesque Annual: On the 'American in Paris'... "in execution they [the

engravings] are worthy of the high and palmy state of the genus to which they belong; and confer great credit... to the universally acknowledged taste and judgment of Mr Charles Heath... Again we thank Mr Charles Heath for a valuable contribution to our imported Literature and Art."
The Art Union, December 1842

Such a catalogue of comment would not be complete without some reference to what the various literary figures of the day thought about the Annuals in general, and Charles Heath's role in producing contributions from some of them. The advent of the Annuals, with their editor's ability usually to pay a disproportionate price for some literary trifle or other so as to give their production *ton*, created quite a stir amongst the literary fraternity. The element of hypocrisy in their various reactions is all too evident.

'The literary department, make what exertions you will, must be as inferior in its effect upon the sale to the pictorial one, as it is in its cost. At the best... these Annuals are picture books for grown children. They are good things for the artists and engravers.'[17] [He contributed to six of them between 1825 and 1829.]

'I have not seen the 'Keepsake' yet, neither have I heard from its editor. He has o'erstept the modesty of puffing in his advertisements, and may very likely discover that he has paid young men of rank and fashion somewhat dearly for the use of their names.[18]
Southey (Poet Laureate) to Allan Cunningham, ca. 1829

'Watts says I go about depreciating other annuals out of regard for "The Keepsake". This is untrue, I only said "As the Keepsake paid poets best, it would be the best work." This is not depreciating.'[19]

'It would disgrace any name to appear in an Annual'[20] [He actually contributed to four of them.]
Wordsworth

'A yearly publication called the 'Keepsake' of which the plates are beyond comparison beautiful, but the letterpress indifferent enough'...[21] [contributions to eight Annuals between 1825 and 1853].
Sir Walter Scott

'Alfred is desirous of putting his wits to profit, and begins to think himself a fool for kindly complying with the daily requests of Annuals without getting anything in return' [contributions to three Annuals, 1831-51]
Tennyson (Poet Laureate) (Hallam)[22]

Coleridge has recently been here. He too is deep among the prophets, the year-servers

– the mob of gentlemen annuals. But they'll cheat him I know.'[23]

[Coleridge contributed many poems to no less than five Annuals.]
Charles Lamb to Bernard Barton, 11 October 1828.

J.G. Lockhart (Sir Walter Scott's biographer, and Editor of the Quarterly Review) called the Annuals 'painted bladders', and the Keepsake, 'this toyshop of literature', yet contributed to four of them between 1825 and 1829.[24]

'An intelligently edited annual is not only an anomaly but also a certain failure' [contributed to three Annuals, notably the 'Keepsake' and 'Book of Beauty'].[25]
John Ruskin

'My name would suffer' [he contributed to at least three of them].[26]
Thomas Moore

'I have stood off for a long time from these Annuals, which are ostentatious trumpery...'

'I shall hate myself in frippery, strutting along, and vying finery with beaux and belles, with "future Lord Byron's and sweet L.E.L's."' (Letter to Bernard Barton dated August 28, 1827, after being persuaded by Jameson and Coleridge to contribute to the 'Bijou').[27]

'It is my firm determination to have nothing to do with "ForgetmeNots"; pray excuse me as civilly as you can to Mr Hurst. I will take care to refuse any other applications'. (Letter to Moxon, March 18, 1828.)

'Yes, I am hooked into the 'Gem' but only for some lines written on a dead infant of the Editor's, which being as it were his property, I could not refuse their appearing; but I hate the paper, the type, the gloss, the dandy plates, the names of contributors poked up into your eyes in first page, and whistled through all the covers of magazines, the bare-faced sort of emulation, the immodest candidateship... the paper coarse; in short I detest to appear in an Annual.[27]

Wordsworth I see has a good many pieces announced in one of 'em [the 'Keepsake'], not our Gem. W. Scott has distributed himself like a bribe haunch. Don't think I set up for being proud on this point; I like a bit of flattery, tickling my vanity, as well as anyone. But these pompous masquerades without masks (naked names or faces) I hate. Besides they infallibly cheat you; I mean the booksellers...' (Letter to Bernard Barton, October 11, 1828.)

'For God's sake do not let me be pestered with Annuals. They are all rogues who edit them, and something else who write in them' [he wrote poems for four annuals, 1828-9].[28]
Charles Lamb

'I cannot disguise from you that I have strong objections to writing for an Annual' [he

contributed to five annuals between 1829 and 1855].[29]
Edward Bulwer (Letter to Lady Blessington)

'The binding of this book, by the way, is perfectly hideous – it looks like one of Lord Palmerston's cast-off waistcoats.'[30] 'The annuals tend to encourage bad taste in the public' [he wrote for three annuals, 1831-54].[31]
Thackeray on the 'The Keepsake' for 1838

'Mr Ned Plymdale... had brought the last 'Keepsake', the gorgeous watered-silk publication which marked modern progress at that time; and he considered himself very fortunate that he could be the first to look over it with her [Rosamond], dwelling on the ladies and gentlemen with shiny copper-plate cheeks and copper-plate smiles, and pointing to comic verses as capital, and sentimental stories as interesting. Rosamond was gracious, and Mr Ned was satisfied that he had the very best thing in art and literature as a medium for 'paying addresses' – the very think to please a nice girl. 'I think the Honourable Mrs S. is something like you' said Mr Ned. He kept the book open at the bewitching portrait, and looked at it rather languishingly. 'Her back is very large' she seems to have sat for that' said Rosamond... Mr Ned smiled nervously, while Lydgate, drawing the 'Keepsake' towards him and opening it, gave a short scornful laugh and tossed up his chin, as if in wonderment at human folly. 'What are you laughing at so profanely?' said Rosamond, with bland neutrality. 'I wonder which would turn out to be the silliest – the engravings or the writing here' said Lydgate...'
George Eliot: extract from her novel Middlemarch

'Truly the Annuals compose the most decorous body of secular literature ever published.'
B.A. Booth

Charles was well aware of the sneers of the literary world towards his Annuals, and especially as regards the use of aristocratic names as authors and poets whom no-one had ever heard of before, because of their snobbish appeal to the public. He was, as the proprietor of these Annuals, in a position to influence the literary contents, as well as acting as art editor with superintendence over his engravers. In general however he seems to have left the choice of literature very much to his editors, especially to the Countess of Blessington, who edited the 'Book of Beauty' almost from the start, and the 'Keepsake' from 1840 onwards as well.

There were numerous occasions however when, because a particular painting was commissioned by Charles for engraving, the editor had to find an author to write up a story around it; and this was no doubt one of the main reasons why, after the 1829 'Keepsake', to which so many literary figures contributed for high prices, most of the later editions contained little by any author of repute. The 'Picturesque Annual' occasionally had its own problems with its proprietor, notably when in the 1838 volume the editor announced that the next volume would be on the River Wye,[32] but in the event turned out to be on Versailles, as Charles was busy trying to cultivate the French market for his publications at the time, and enlisting the support of King Louis Philippe (to whom the 1839 volume was effusively dedicated) in the process.

The first volume of the 'Keepsake' for 1828, published for the Christmas season (as all the Annuals were) in 1827, proved a great success, with Charles claiming that 15,000 copies had been sold. He was clearly carried away by this, and the prefaces which he composed for subsequent editions give an idea of his state of mind in the following years, as the vogue for Annuals gradually subsided, try as he might to 'puff' his aims and his sincerity in cultivating public taste. In his preface to the 1828 edition he had said that his principal object was 'to render the union of literary merit with the beauty and elegance of art'... The list of embellishments... and of the artists leads us unhesitatingly to challenge a comparison with anything in this respect that has hitherto occurred' (a claim which his rival, Alaric Watts of the 'Literary Souvenir', dismissed as 'quackery').

In the 1829 edition, 'The universal approbation which the embellishments of the previous number excited, and its unprecedented sale have determined the Proprietor to make the most strenuous exertions to render the present as perfect as possible, both in literary matter, and in pictorial illustration... the enormous sum of 11,000 guineas has been expended... the Proprietor is induced to hope that his book will not be a mere floating production, to die with the season of its birth, but live, a reputed and standard work in every well selected library'. In 1830, 'The Proprietor has spared neither labour nor expenses to obtain the success he desires... the 'Keepsake' of last year has been found in every respectable bookdealers' shop in Europe, India and America'; and he goes on to hope that the book will have influence in promoting taste. In the 1831 volume, the year before Longmans took over as his publisher from Hurst Chance and Robert Jennings and Chaplin, 'The Proprietor asserts that his best exertions would ever be directed to render the 'Keepsake' worthy of the extensive and flattering patronage with which it had previously been honoured' and announced that some works would in future appear anonymously.

There were no more prefaces until 1838, when, clearly annoyed by criticism, he announced, 'The Proprietor having ascertained that a belief exists that articles for the 'Keepsake' have occasionally been selected less in relation to their intrinsic merits than to the names of their authors, has determined to escape the imputation by publishing the work anonymously [even the name of the editor was omitted]. If this mode obtain the public approbation it will be continued; but if otherwise he trusts that he will be considered justified in reverting to the original plan' [which he did in 1839].

This was the year in which the size of the edition and of the plates was much enlarged, and steel mezzotinting was introduced for the first time. It was also the year in which sales of all his Annuals entered into an irrevocable decline, which, together with his other publishing mishaps, notably the extraordinary but financially disastrous

'Tournament at Eglinton Castle', of which hardly any copies were sold, led to the appointment of unofficial trustees in bankruptcy in 1841 to handle his debts,[33] while continuing his projects as far as possible. One of these (or possibly their representative) was the redoubtable Joshua Bacon, manager of Perkins, Bacon and Petch, who was also a good friend. Longmans, while paying over Charles' earnings from all sources to his trustees, evidently carried many of his debts for him, thus allowing him to continue to appear as proprietor of such productions as were still viable (the 'Picturesque Annual' disappeared after 1845); and in 1843 and 1844 at least paid him a private allowance amounting to £400 a year, in recognition perhaps of all the profit he had made for them over the years.

He was not well, after all the strains and exertions of his many ventures, and his eyesight became poor; nevertheless, right up to his sudden death in 1848, he continued as the entrepreneur manager in a very real sense, to engrave himself when he could, and in his last two years the Longman accounts show that he was being paid modest sums for providing drawings of his own for others to engrave. Insolvent as he still was when he died with debts of over £2000, it would appear that many of these had been paid off by his trustees, mainly from the returns from Longmans of his half share in their various joint ventures together, some of which were still profitable.

In these lean years, Charles was not much inhibited in continuing to embark on some remarkable publications, not least his 'Heath's Beauties of the Opera and Ballet', dedicated to Queen Victoria (with her consent), which when it appeared in 1844 constituted the first work in the English language on ballet. Many of these works were inevitably reprints under different and often rather fanciful names, so as to use up the accumulation of unsold prints from earlier productions, but others, in which Charles appears as having superintended the engravers, were original, including translations from the French novelists of the day, with woodcuts.

Quite a flourishing business continued by selling off prints from past annuals to the public at all times of the year, reprinted from time to time depending on the demand; and to judge from the many deliveries of such prints to him, as well as to the print dealers, Charles Heath played an active part personally in selling these separate prints through his own contacts.[34] Much of the old stock was also auctioned off at his major sales in 1838/39 and in 1842 and 1848; Longmans' own remainder stock of 'Keepsakes' and 'Books of Beauty' were sold to the publisher E. Lacey in January 1847 for £400, while the copyright on the steel plates for most of the minor works which Charles had promoted in the previous decade were sold to another publisher, David Bogue, for £600, with Bogue taking over the publication of the 'Keepsake' and various reprints from 1848 onwards.

CHAPTER 4

Charles Heath and J.M.W. Turner, R.A. 1811-1838

THE WORKING RELATIONSHIP which Charles Heath maintained with J.M.W. Turner from 1811 until the ultimate failure of their great joint publishing venture together, the 'Picturesque Views in England and Wales', in 1838, though little noted was of considerable importance to both men, over a period when Turner was becoming increasingly recognised as an artist of genius.

Turner was well aware of the importance attached to gaining public recognition of his highly original style of painting by using such methods of reproduction as were available to him at the time. In consequence, as P.G. Hamerton described it in his 'Life of Turner' (1895):

'To all these various publications, which were spreading the name of Turner more and more amongst the public, may be added the plates published separately and at irregular intervals from the beginning of this century until the artist's death. Some of those were in mezzotint by Lupton, Charles Turner and others; but the majority were in that modern style of landscape engraving which is familiar to every reader, and which, with all its faults, unquestionably marks the highest point of perfection attained hitherto in the complete interpretation of landscape art on metal. It is not pure burin work, but a mixed style including a great deal of etching, much work with the point, and not a little ruling. But taken as a whole, in the hands of the marvellously skilled men who used it – such men as Miller, Cooke, Jeavons, Heath, Higham, Allen, Willmore and Wallis – it interprets landscape painting more completely than any other method. Mezzotint can render the tones of light and shade with unsurpassable accuracy but it is never so lucid and luminous as engraving, and consequently its effects of atmosphere can never be so pure... [Turner] educated a whole school of engravers and a very remarkable school it was...'[1]

In listing Turner's principal engravers, Hamerton omitted to say that, apart from Cooke, with whom he had an unhappy relationship on the financial aspect when working together up to 1826 on their 'Picturesque Views of the Southern Coast of England', Charles Heath was the only one with whom he was able to mount a publishing project: the others were only distinguished as engravers working for others on commission. The two men had originally met during the engraving in the Heath atelier in 1810/11 of Turner's painting 'Pope's Villa' which eventually appeared in John Britton's 'The Fine Arts of the English School'. On seeing a proof, Turner is said to have exclaimed: 'You can see the lights: had I known there was a man living could have done that I would have had it done before'.[2] Even though it was John Pye who is known to have done most of the work, with Charles engraving only the figures (which as the most delicate part was always his speciality), an impression had been made. About 1822, Charles Heath engraved two fine Turner drawings for the 'History of Richmondshire', both of which were topographical. Thus, when Charles, around 1825, decided to take on major projects involving not just his own labour but the management and supervision of teams of engravers, it was natural that he should find in Turner a painter after his own heart, and a subject matter which should cater for the vogue then current for landscape illustrations. As Finberg commented, 'Certainly Turner had no reason to regret the substitution of Charles Heath for Cooke as his impresario.'[3]

As intimated in Chapter 3, the initiative for the 'England and Wales' project – a work which has been described as 'the central document of Turner's art' – probably came from Charles, the entrepreneur, rather than from Turner. The first-hand evidence in the form of correspondence between Charles and his friend Dawson Turner, the Yarmouth banker and art patron, located by Dr John Gage at Trinity College Cambridge and edited by Eric Shanes (as reproduced at Annex D), shows Charles' initial enthusiasm and his subsequent difficulties due to lack of capital and declining public interest. Under the original arrangements, Turner was to provide 60 out of 120 water colours to Charles at 30 guineas each (or possibly 25 guineas together with 30 proofs of each engraving, if Alaric Watts' version is to be believed), which, after engraving, Charles was at liberty to dispose of to others at whatever profit he could get. Turner appears to have had no financial interest himself otherwise, while of the 95 engravings which eventually appeared by 1838, none bear Charles' name. While he may have engraved and touched the most delicate parts of each engraving himself (even after Turner himself had finished with them), his task was essentially to select the best and most suitable engravers for each subject, supervise their work, supply the publisher, Robert Jennings (who became Jennings and Chapman), and generally to promote the project as actively as he could.

Although the first three parts of the 'Picturesque Views' were published in 1827,[4] consisting of four engravings each, with descriptions, the work was long and tedious, and subscriptions were slow to materialise as the market had become somewhat surfeited with topographic prints. The lowest price for the four parts each of the 'Picturesque Views' was 14/-, or 1 1/2 guineas for each India paper proof.[5]

There was certainly no lack of energy on Charles' part in trying to promote sales of the prints as they appeared; and he also seems to have disposed of Turner's original paintings very quickly, in the same way as he was always supplying private print collectors with sets of proof copies of his productions. Only one of these watercolours is known to have been sold off at one of his many auction sales, and this, a painting of 'Havre', was used as an engraving for the 'Keepsake' of 1834, and not in the main project. In June 1829, Charles staged an exhibition of the water-colours in the Egyptian Hall, Piccadilly when 35 of them were on display, evoking highly favourable comment.[6] Just before the publication of Part 12 in May 1831, the Athenaeum Magazine reported that at an artist's 'Conversazione' Mr Charles Heath had a rich display of Turner's drawings with engravings from them intended for the forthcoming numbers of 'England and Wales' – we should say superior to any that have before appeared in the work'.[7] In mid-summer 1833, Moon, Boys and Graves exhibited no less than 66 of the original water-colours, most of them lent by their new owners, but only 100 subscriptions were recorded, many of which were not taken up. By 1835, with only two parts appearing each year, Longmans, who were doing well with publishing Charles' various annuals, took over their half financial share in the project 'by stock from Hodgson & Co'.[8] Unfortunately Longmans' records here were apparently destroyed in 1940 when Paternoster Row was bombed so that the rest of the story is unclear.

But, with Turner insisting on the use of copper exclusively for his 'Picturesque Views' (which probably suited some of the many engravers employed who had not yet mastered the new technique of steel engraving, but which could only produce short runs before re-engraving, involving yet further delays), the whole project became uneconomical. Charles himself was having to pay his engravers between 60 and 70 guineas for each plate, and the prints were not selling. Longmans decided to cut their losses and halt the project; and at the Southgate auction in June 1839,[9] the remainders, including many bound up volumes, were sold off; and Charles Heath had to dispose of his sets of proofs, the last for £41 in July 1842 at Sotheby's. It is tempting to speculate what might have happened had Charles been able to insist on turning over to steel rather than copper once the engraving had begun after 1826, providing an infinite number of copies which could have gone on selling for years, especially after 1843, when John Ruskin brought Turner's reputation with the public to a new peak as a landscape painter, with the publication of 'Modern Painters'; for, as it was, only 96 out of the 120 water colours had been engraved by 1838. Undoubtedly Charles suffered serious financial loss in the process, from which, together with other setbacks, he never recovered; even though Turner at the auction of the remainders went to the point of buying in the engraved plates himself for £3000, to avoid them, as he put it, 'being worn to shadows' by other publishers. He was also very understanding of Charles' difficulties, even though he had only a small stake in the project himself, and is recorded as having once returned bills to him amounting to £1000 advanced for work done for the 'Keepsake', expressing himself as 'willing to be paid or not at a future time, as the state of Mr Heath's affairs would decide'.[10]

Although Turner himself never mastered the line engraver's burin, he did learn mezzotint, and used this skill to retouch almost all the proofs submitted by the 19 or so engravers whom Charles engaged.[11] Unfortunately Turner had at first a dislike for steel engraving as the well-known anecdote of his meeting with Sir Thomas Lawrence illustrates. He called one day at a time when he [Lawrence] had just received a proof with which he was very much pleased. He showed it to Turner and said 'By the way, Turner, I wonder you don't have some of your drawings engraved on steel'. 'But why?' 'I don't like it; besides I don't choose to be a basket engraver.' 'A basket engraver, a basket engraver, Turner, what is that?' said the President. Turner looked at Lawrence with that malicious leer which, in his penetrating eyes, when not meaning mischief, conveyed more killing sarcasm than his words, and said 'When I got off the coach t'other day at Hastings, a woman came up with a basket of your Mrs Peel and wanted to sell me one for six pence'. Turner disliked the thought of his works being sold cheap.[12]

But after talking with Lawrence it seems more than likely that he changed his mind, assuming that what was good enough for Sir Thomas ought to do for him. For, in the self-same edition of the 'Keepsake' for 1829 in which 'Mrs Peel' (engraved by Charles Heath after Lawrence) appears as the Frontispiece, two engravings after Turner by Willmore, one of Charles' assistants, also appear (Lago Maggiore and Lago Albano). These two must have been engraved under Turner's habitual supervision, at about the same time as Sir Thomas was admiring his proof (perhaps the one of Mrs Peel); and they must have been engraved on steel to meet the long print run of 16,000, as noted by Allan Cunningham, so as to exceed the success of the 1828 first issue.

Shortly afterwards, Turner's designs for Rogers' Poems (published in 1830) and his 'Italy' (1834) were being engraved on steel in a project, with Moxon as publisher, which Samuel Rogers' himself directed, but which employed Charles Heath's best journeymen engravers, notably Goodall and Miller. From 1829 onwards Turner supplied the 'Keepsake' each year with an average of two drawings to be engraved on steel, which continued until the 'Keepsake' for 1838, with the exception of 1835; these were mostly views in France and Italy, and only two, the engravings of 'Virginia Water' painted in 1827, came from the 'Picturesque Views' series; these appeared in the 'Keepsake' for 1830.

Turner's fear that the multiplicity of steel-engraved copies would lessen the value of prints was well-founded enough but he must have realised that if his landscape paintings and drawings were to reach a much wider public (as he had already attempted to do with the mezzotints of his 'Liber Studiorum' between 1807-19) there was really no choice for him but to accept the new medium. While the engravings on copper for the 'Picturesque Views' were more illustrative and interpretive, and less 'original' and artistically inventive than for the 'Liber', when it came to using steel for Rogers' works, the same engravers whom Charles had commissioned, profiting no doubt from Turner's 'touches' and instruction, produced vignettes and prints which are generally recognised as being amongst the loveliest of the 19th century. For steel plates allowed etched strokes of hair-line delicacy to be laid very closely to each other, suggesting the most delicate mists of tone, the lightest parts of the design blending harmoniously with the white of the page. [13]

In its way, though a commercial failure, the 'Picturesque Views' was also a success, for bringing together a series of landscape engravings that have no equal, as well as a group of water colours which are unsurpassed in range and power.[14]

While the 'England and Wales' was still progressing, the Athenaeum magazine in 1831 published a rumour that 'Turner was about to engage with Mr Charles Heath in the publication of Views on the Loire'.[15] The Longman archive shows that this was indeed another of Charles Heath's publishing ventures; perhaps the first he undertook with Longmans in the long line of publications in which each had a financial share. A synopsis issued by Charles Heath on 1 June 1833 shows that the series was supposed to develop into the 'Rivers of Europe', to include the Meuse, Moselle, Danube and Rhine, presumably with Turner's concurrence, but this never materialised.[16]

While Charles' name does not appear anywhere in the 'Rivers of France' annuals which were published as 'Turner's Annual Tour', with letterpress by Leitch Ritchie (editor of 'Heath's Picturesque Annual' from its inception in 1832), there is no doubt that he was following the same pattern as for the 'Picturesque Views' with Turner, and commissioning engravers for him, but using the medium of an annual, which had then become so fashionable. When the series was discontinued after 1835, it would seem that it was not so much, as has been surmised, that the market had become saturated with prints of French scenery, but that sales from the outset in 1833 had been low (only 1617 copies), and continued to fall. Though priced at one guinea, its contemporary, Charles Heath's 'Keepsake', at the same price, was then selling over 6000 copies, and the 'Picturesque Annual' nearly 5000. Even with Turner's name, the effort was evidently not worth the return.

On the other hand, Charles can hardly have complained about any lack of interest in their main project as it progressed on Turner's part, and seems to have welcomed what others might have regarded as undue interference with the engravers he had commissioned, realising that as a great artist, Turner could actually teach his engravers the finer points of converting his colour into mere black and white, with all manner of shading. As Rawlinson commented: 'Probably no painter before him – unless possibly Rubens – ever so completely controlled the engraving of his own pictures, or ever set himself to educate the engravers who worked for him; certainly none ever bestowed the same infinite pains on every detail of every plate.'[17]

Both men were perfectionists so far as they could be, and it was probably this quality which each admired most in the other in their many dealings. As Shanes records: 'The engravers were much in awe of him and endeavoured to 'translate' the spirit of the original pictures to the more limited disciplines of a a purely etched line with a great deal of ingenuity. Edward Goodall, who engraved four plates for the 'Picturesque Views', once asked Turner how to translate a brilliant red in one of his pictures. Turner replied 'Sometimes translate it into black and at another time into white. If a bit of black gives the emphasis, so does red in my picture. In the case of translating it into white, he said, rather unhelpfully, after a brief reflection: 'put a grinning line into it that will make it attractive'.

Turner once asked Goodall to put two figures of his own invention into one of the engravings, and when the engraver demurred, his son Frederick had a very enjoyable time watching Turner paint them in himself on the original for subsequent transcription.[18]

From Charles Heath's correspondence with William Miller, the brilliant Quaker engraver who worked in Edinburgh (and would thus be out of Turner's reach), it is clear that he must have tried to get the best engravers to work on Turner's drawings. When Charles first approached him, Miller took the precaution of consulting George Cooke, the engraver to whom he had been apprenticed, who replied on 2 March 1827:

'You ask me about Charles Heath's application to you. His work will be a magnificent one, and I do really think you would be quite safe with him... Turner has behaved with such cruel unkindness to my brother and me that I am heartsick to find so great a man with such a debased and wretched heart. His demand to furnish the Drawings for the continuation of the 'Coast' was twenty-five guineas each – to make all !!!!! and to have prompt payment and twenty-five INDIA COPIES of the Work complete!!!!! This refused, he said 'Then I'll oppose you and commence a Work immedy' – which, in his fury he has, I believe, begun. I am troubled when I think of his ingratitude to my Brother, who was the first to introduce his splendid talents to distant realms. I am hurt and disgusted – it makes me loathe the man, whilst I adore his powers – but no more of him. Should you engage with him, let me advise you not to agree to some outrageous terms as to Proofs to be retained by the artist (instead of the engraver who builds his fame). You will have the friendship not to name the substance of this to anyone; but do not suffer him to rivet his Chains on your fine talent, be ready to engrave, but not enchained...'[19]

It would seem that Miller took this advice about proofs seriously, as Charles Heath wrote to him on 11 September 1830 to say: 'I shall send you Turner's Drawing and your Proofs etc., immediately.'[20] The later correspondence with Miller sets out the relationship. In a letter dated 6 August 1831 to him, Charles wrote:

My dear Sir,
I have received your beautiful plate from 'Turner', with which I am quite delighted. I enclose your bill for 60 guineas, which I hope will meet your wishes, but I have been obliged to make the Bill four Months instead of three – my publishers, Hurst & Co. having stopped payment, will rather inconvenience me. If this will not suit your purpose, I will forward you another and you can keep this on account of the 'Landscape Annual' Plates. Now, my dear Sir, get what assistance you please, but do not fail to let me have *both* plates by the 3rd of September. If you do I shall be seriously injured. Pray

exert yourself. I rely on your promise to deliver both mine before Mr Jennings, and I shall, of course, send you two or three for next year's Books. In a few days you will receive a most splendid Turner for the 'England'. In future I will, *provided you say not a word to any person* give you seventy Guins for 'The England'. Your Plates deserve much more, and should the work, when I have completed a volume, sell better, I hope to advance the price again to you. I shall send you a 'Turner' likewise for 'The Keepsake' next year, and *every year,* so that I hope you will do me as many plates as possible for all my works. I can give you more than you could possibly execute, at your *own price,* if you would confine yourself as much as possible to my works. Let me know what you think of this,

Yours, my dear Sir, most truly, Chas Heath.[21]

Again, writing from 6 Seymour Place on 15 August 1832 to Miller, Charles implies that he would have had one of his 'Turner' plates retouched and returned to him from London; and goes on to make it clear that, at long range, Turner was doing the retouching himself;

My dear Sir,
I have received your Plate for the 'Picturesque Annual' and like it very much. Stanfield is gone, and tho' he might perhaps have improved it, yet it is so beautiful that I am quite satisfied. The Turner you have just rec'd touched, I should feel particularly obliged if it were possible for me to receive by Monday next, as I find I cannot go till then to France, as I expected and I should *very* much wish to take a Proof with me, the subject is so good. The vignette I shall be obliged to you to make as exquisite as possible.

The price of your Plates I think perfectly just, excepting the two you charge forty five guineas, which I must make Fifty Guineas each. I shall therefore enclose a Bill for One Hundred Pounds in this Letter, as I have a stamp that will just cover that amount; the balance shall be added to the next Bill I have the pleasure of sending you. I shall forward, tomorrow or Friday, a Drawing by Turner for the 'England and Wales', and a Drawing by Turner for the next year's 'Keepsake', which if you could get done by next February, I shall feel very much obliged. I shall send one likewise for Mr Horsburgh. I shall feel particularly obliged if you will say how many 'Picturesque' and how many of the small Turners you can do for me by the end of next July. I will send you the Drawings before Christmas, and some in October and November, as both Stanfield and Turner are gone to make the Drawings, and I shall [sic] them directly they return. Mr Turner, I am afraid, will not be in London when your Vignette is done; therefore you must do as well as you can without his touches. I hope you will give me as much of your time as possible, and do me as many Plates. I have some idea of visiting Edinburgh; if I do, I shall certainly give you a call. Does Horsburgh work on steel, and would he like to do any Annuals?

Yours etc Chas Heath.[22]

Charles must have developed a considerable affection for Turner, despite his cantankerous reputation. Thornbury records that he once asked Turner the nature of some papers which were lying on the table, enquiring what he had got there. 'Oh' replied Turner, 'some old receipts and papers not wanted'. Mr Heath's attention had been attracted to a bill of exchange for £200, evidently unpaid, and due on the very day, of the existence of which Turner appeared to be wholly unconscious. Mr Heath was wont to declare that, in spite of his exactions, and the difficulty of bringing him to any reasonable terms, he had greater satisfaction in dealing with him that any other artist. When once he had pledged his word as to time and quality, he might be implicitly relied on.'[23]

Reviewing the exhibition at the Egyptian Gallery in June 1829, the Athenaeum referred to Turner's drawing of Stonehenge 'of which Mr Charles Heath relates a pleasant story. Mr Turner, he says, had a drawing of 'Stonehenge' and asked him if he would take it for one of the 'Views of England'. 'Stonehenge! such a subject! But you may as well see it... It would be of no use, the subject would never do.' Other drawings were proceeded with: on the back of one of these, Mr Heath happened one day to cast his eye on the Stonehenge: but he had not objected to the subject, bad as he had deemed it. He eagerly purchased the drawing; and few, we are assured, are they who will condemn this change of resolution. The subject all will own was an ungracious one; but this very defect has served to display the talent of Mr Turner'.[24]

The main problem which Charles must have had with Turner was his insatiable demands for large numbers of engravers' proofs, which meant that subscribers, who were expected to pay a high price of at least 10 guineas for the collection (or £48 per volume for India proofs before letters), were liable to receive prints which already showed some wear. Some 30,000 such proofs were found in his studio when Turner died in 1851, and he expected Charles to supply him personally; he had originally contracted to receive 30 proofs of each engraving from his watercolours, besides 25 guineas, and made sure he got them.

There is an interesting correspondence illustrating Turner's interest here, when, writing to the artist George Jones from Rome on October 13, 1828, he said: 'May I trouble you to drop a line into the twopenny post to Mr Charles Heath, 6 Seymour Place, New Pancras Church, or send my people to tell him that if he has anything to send me, to put it in a letter (it is the most sure way of its reaching me) directed to me 12 Piazza Mignanelli.'[25] The reference here was presumably to the despatch of engravers' proofs to him for advice and correction, or possibly Turner was expecting his supply of finished proofs to continue to be sent to him while he was away. In any case, his letter to Charles which followed is self-explantory:

12 Piazza Mignanelli, Rome 28 November 1828.
My dear Sir, I think of leaving here about the first of January and therefore supposing that early in returning I shall have the pleasure of seeing you again in Queen Anne [St].

So it will be not worth while to send any prints after you receive this without very urgent cause, or so that it can be in Rome by Xmas day or end of Decr. Wishing you the compliments of the season, Keepsakes, etc

Believe me yours most truly, J.M.W. Turner.'[26]

As for the 'Keepsakes etc' there is no other record of what Turner's views on them may have been. He was evidently ready to supply Charles Heath's annuals especially with a wide variety of subjects for illustration until 1838, as providing good steady publicity for him in the eyes of their subscribers, and would have been perfectly aware of the advantages both to himself and to Charles in doing so. There are 17 engravings after Turner in the 'Keepsake' alone. Turner preferred Charles Heath to be his promoter, not only because of his reputation as an engraver, but because he had access to, and the confidence of, the finest engravers in Britain to do justice to his work; as evidenced by the friendly cooperation between the two men over 27 years.

But there is another aspect of their relationship which is of some significance. As an engraver, Turner may well have chosen Charles Heath as a specialist in figure work (which is what he would have noticed about the engraving on 'Pope's Villa' in 1811, and 'flesh' was the most delicate of techniques). For, as Shanes has pointed out,[27] the 'Picturesque Views' were meant by Turner not so much as a series of landscapes, as about the people who invariably figure in them, a 'systematic exploration of human beings' in their attitudes of 'labour, sorrow and death'. While Charles is not known to have engraved any of the 'Picturesque Views' himself, it may be assumed that he provided the figure work to quite a few of them, to Turner's satisfaction, and no doubt motivated the engravers working for him on this aspect as well.

CHAPTER 5

Charles Heath's Artistic and Business Relationships

IN AN AGE IN WHICH the public were increasingly interested in illustrations to the works of living authors and artists, as distinct from classical subjects, it was inevitable that Charles should have been concerned with establishing contact with the leading authors of the day. Little is known about these contacts in the period up to 1825, but almost as soon as he had set himself up as a promoter of gift books, and Annuals in particular, it followed that he had to enlist the support of literary men and, because he was starting in competition with existing Annuals, he had to go one better if he was to succeed. With all the engravers' resources in the trade at his disposal, he may have felt confident that his prints would prove superior to his rivals, but he, as proprietor, still had to have competent editors and make an exceptional effort to ensure that 'the literary department' was given special attention.

The first issue of the 'Keepsake', in 1828, though it sold 15,000 copies at nearly twice the price of any of its competitors, was only able to sell as well as it did because, bound in red watered silk, it was a novelty (together with the 'Amulet' edited by S.C. Hall, which was bound in blue silk), and had some fine plates, many of them engraved by Charles' own hand. He must have realised that he would have to do rather better: and, armed with what for those days must have seemed like almost unlimited cash derived from the previous years profits, he duly set off on a tuft-hunting tour to capture the main literary lions; i.e. Sir Walter Scott, Wordsworth, Southey and Coleridge. He did not bother himself with authors such as Charles Lamb, as they were known to dislike contributing to Annuals; but knowing of Sir Walter Scott's financial plight, he even had hopes of enlisting him as his editor. In various visits which caused considerable alarm amongst his rivals, the first was thus to Sir Walter, whose graphic account speaks for itself:

30 January 1828: 'After Court hours I had a visit from Mr Charles Heath, the engraver, accompanied by a son of Reynolds, the dramatist. His object was to engage me to take charge as editor of a yearly publication called the 'Keepsake' of which the plates are beyond comparison beautiful, but the letterpress indifferent enough. He proposed £800 a year if I would become editor and £400 if I would contribute from 70 to 100 pages. I declined both but told him I might give him some trifling thing or other and asked the young men to breakfast the next day.'

31st January: 'I received the young gentlemen to breakfast and expressed my resolution which seemed to disappoint them, as perhaps they expected I should have been glad of such an offer. However I have since thought there are these rejected parts of the 'Chronicles' which Cadell and Ballantyne criticised so severely, which might well enough make up a trifle of this kind, and settle the few accounts which will I nill I have crept in the this New Year. So I have kept the treaty open. If I give them 100 pages, I should expect £500.'

1 February: 'I had my two youths again to breakfast but I did not say more about my determination save that I would help them if I could make it convenient. The Chief Commissioner has agreed to let Heath have his pretty picture of a study at Abbotsford by Edwin Landseer.'

28 February: 'I got a letter from the young man Reynolds accepting on Heath's part my terms for article to the 'Keepsake', namely £500. I to be at liberty to reprint the work after 3 years, Mr Heath to print it in the 'Keepsake' as long and as often as he pleases but not in any other form. I shall close with him.'

10 March: 'Received letters from the youth who is to conduct the 'Keepsake' with blarney on a £200 bank note. No blarney in that. I must set about doing something for these worthies.'

13 April 1828: 'Amused myself by converting 'The Tale of the Mysterious Mirror' into 'Aunt Margaret's Mirror' designed for Heath's what'd'ye call it. Cadell will not like it, but I cannot afford to have my goods thrown back upon my hands. The tale is a good one and is said actually to have happened to Lady Primrose, my great-grandmother, having attended her sister on the occasion.'[1]

Charles and Reynolds followed this up with a visit to the Lake District to see Wordsworth, where, although not recorded by the poet, they found a sympathetic hearing also; according to Alaric Watts (of the 'Literary Souvenir'), 'Wordsworth allowed himself to be carried away in this auriferous stream'.[2]

Southey, the Poet Laureate, came next. In a letter to his daughter in February 1828, he wrote 'Charles Heath, the engraver, who *is* the 'Keepsake' was here last week... He... has bespoke 4,000 yards of red silk at 3/- a yard, for binding the next volume. Writing to Allan Cunningham on 24 February, he added:

'Charles Heath proceeded expeditiously to business, presented me with a 'Keepsake' from his pocket, said that he had been into Scotland for the express purpose of securing Sir Walter [Scott]'s aid, that he had succeeded, that he now came to ask for mine, and should be happy to give me fifty guineas for anything with which I would supply him. Money, money, you know makes the mare go – and what after all is Pegasus, but a piece of horse flesh? I sold him at that price a pig in a poke; a roaster [*sic*: ?rooster] would have contented him: 'perhaps it might prove a porker' I said; improvident fellow as I was not to foresee that it would grow to the size of a bacon pig before it came into his hands! I sold him a ballad-poem entitled 'All for Love, or a Sinner well saved' of which one and twenty stanzas were then written. I have added fifty since and am only halfway through the story. It is a very striking one, and he means to have an engraving made from it. First come, first served is a necessary rule in life; but if I could have foreseen that you would come afterwards, the rule should have been set aside; he might have had something else and the bacon pig should have been yours. Heath said that Sharpe was about to start a similar work of the same size and upon the same scale of expense; this I take it for granted is yours [i.e.... the Anniversary].'[3]

Coleridge, whom Charles left his editor to tackle, was visited in the autumn of 1828, and Alaric Watts was told by the poet what had happened in a letter dated 14 September:

'Mr Frederic Reynolds called on me with a letter of introduction from Wordsworth in which Wordsworth informed me that he had been introduced [*sic*: ?induced], as likewise Southey and Sir Walter Scott, to furnish some poems to a work undertaken by Mr Heath, with Mr Reynolds as his editor; that the unusually handsome terms would scarcely have overcome his reluctance had he not entertained the hope that I might be persuaded to give my name; and that besides Sir W. Scott, Southey, Wordsworth and myself, Lord Normanby, as Mr Reynolds believed, and Mr Moore were to be the only, or all but only, contributors. In short, he hoped I would write. Mr Reynolds offered me £50, more by way than all my literary labours if I may except my salary from the Morning Post, and Courier had procured me' [the only condition was that Coleridge was not to write for any other annual except the Literary Souvenir].[4]

In total, the various financial inducements handed out in the course of this extraordinary promotion during 1828 amounted to some 1600 guineas (about £100,000 at current rates). Alaric Watts claimed the last word when he wrote: 'The immoderate and injudicious expenditure of these sums... was unsuccessful in securing in any commensurate degree the success of Mr Heath's speculation; and the work passed out of his hands into those, I believe, of his publishers. He however continued to superintend the engravings of this and other similar enterprises. Conducted with more prudence and moderation, the 'Keepsake' continued to maintain for many years an important position among the Annuals, and was, I believe, the last survivor of them.'[2]

The 1829 'Keepsake', packed as it was with contributions from so many literary heavyweights, did manage to maintain sales at at least the level of the previous year. But this sort of expenditure could obviously not be kept up, and from then onwards it was left almost entirely to the editors of Charles' Annuals to attract literary contributions, usually for no payment at all. During her periods of editorship up to 1848, the Countess of Blessington was by far the most successful in playing this role, with her salons almost every evening; and all sorts of literary men, from Edward Bulwer, Walter Savage Landor and Monckton Milnes to Dickens and Disraeli were pressed into service, together with a great many lesser or completely unknown fry. There is no evidence that Charles himself participated at these salons, even though it was usually open to anyone known to Lady Blessington to call in at Gore House to exchange the literary and political gossip of the day; at the same time he clearly enjoyed a cordial relationship with Lady Blessington herself, and encouraged and promoted her many literary efforts, as the following letter to him dated 14 May 1839, indicates:

Gore House
My dear Mr Heath,
I return the receipt signed and in two or three days Messr Longmans shall receive the article on cards, desired. The article on it, in the letter you sent me from Mr William Longman is so clever that no improvement can be made on it, and if not a law ought to be made one, as it is based on the true foundation on which all laws should be passed – good sense. I have not had a proof of the 'Belle of a Season' for three weeks. How is this? Do pray let me have the plates however unfinished, for the Book of Beauty and Gems –

Believe me, my dear Mr Heath
Very sincerely yours
M. Blessington

With regard to the title of the book, I think 'Desultory Thoughts' from the note book of...' seems the best – Maxims they are not, and the word looks pretentious [the book was published in the same year entitled 'Desultory Thoughts and Reflections']. The enclosed note from a Mr Mitchell will amuse you – Having an opportunity of sending a copy of the Idler in Italy to my Brother this day I sent to every library in the West End having previously tried Mr Colburn in vain – I then employed Mr Mitchell and the enclosed is his answer proof of Mr Colburn's delight.'[5]

Lady Blessington's constant companion, the remarkable dandy, Count d'Orsay, who was himself no mean draughtsman, also took a keen if somewhat patronising interest in Charles Heath's activities, as exemplified by his letter of 26 October 1833 to Charles addressed to him at his country home 'Norbiton House, Kingston':

Dear Sir,
Lady Blessington has told me, that you wish to have my opinion about the engraving

from her Portrait – I have examined it attentively and I am entirely of the opinion that you will very much improve the likeness by following my advice, which can be done very easily. You will reduce the Size of the Face in removing the Hair from the *Forehead*, as I have done in the Engraving which I return. I agree with you in thinking the chin a little too long – but the defect which most strikes me is, that the neck is to [*sic*] thin, which gives to the Face a heavy look – If you will attend to those observations you will add much to the beauty and *harmony* of the Portrait.

Will you have the kindness as soon as the corrections are made to let me have a proof.

If you compare this *scraped* engraving with another, you will be sensible of the improvement –

I am yours very sincerely
Ch d'Orsay[6]

This was not the famous portrait of Lady Blessington by Sir Thomas Lawrence, as a girl, but the portrait by Edward Parris which appeared as the frontispiece to the 'Book of Beauty' of 1834 (the year in which she took over as editress), engraved by Thomson, but being supervised by Charles.

Most of Lady Blessingtons' literary lions (including some very minor ones) must have been involved with Charles, especially as he had the difficult task of matching the engravings to the literary output in his Annuals, and vice versa on occasions. An example is Edward Bulwer's reply to Lady Blessington's appeal to him to save her from the drudgery of pot-boiling herself by contributing:

Knebworth
October 20, 1836
'I shall be most delighted to save you any trouble in looking over the proofs of the novel [probably 'The Victims of Society'] which will besides be a great luxury to me. If in any other book I could be of use in filling up in outline, or in any work for Heath, contributing any assistance by contributions, no matter how much or how little, believe me I should be most unfeignedly happy.'[7]

With the other well-known authors of the day, notably those whom he had approached during his tour in 1828, contacts do not seem to have continued, due in part no doubt to the fact that he was no longer prepared (or able) to pay them such extravagant sums. In February 1829, apparently in answer to a request from Sir Walter Scott that he should engrave for him, Charles replied:

'You are well aware that the whole of my time is so much occupied that I have not undertaken a Plate for any publisher the last three years – at the same time if possible I will exert myself to oblige you. There is however one condition which I trust you will not object to, namely that instead of money you pay me for any Plates I may engrave by writing as many pages per Plate as may be agreed on. Under these circumstances I would endeavour to meet your wishes. I trust it will not be long before we receive the promised Tale for the next volume of the 'Keepsake' as we are now going to press. I suffered such a severe loss by not being earlier last year that I am making double exertions to be out sooner next, it makes some thousands difference in the sale.

'I think the prospectus of your plan of republishing all your Novels and Tales with Plates is excellent, and certain of a great sale – but you must not be offended if I say that as they are not *new* works the *Plates* will be a great attraction, particularly now when the Arts are so appreciated – much of the extensiveness of the sale will depend on their *excellence* both as to design and Engraving. I saw at Mr Graves a Portrait of yourself by *Wilkie* – intended as a Frontispiece in the Work. If my advice is worth anything I should say do not engrave it – *there is no resemblance.* Mr Edwin Landseer has the finest likeness of you in the World.

I hope you will excuse my freedom and allow it to pass as it is meant,
With best respects I remain Dr Sir,
Your most sincerely obliged
Chas Heath
P.S. I hope for an answer that I may arrange accordingly.'[9]

In the event Charles does not seem to have got one, although Sir Walter did eventually contribute another though much shorter article to the 'Keepsake' for 1832.

As to the editors of his various productions in the 1830s and 40s, Charles seems to have dealt with, and appointed them in a very businesslike way. When 'L.E.L.' failed to produce a very appealing 'Book of Beauty' at the first attempt in 1833, he had no compunction about replacing her with the Countess of Blessington, who, with all her contacts and snob appeal, proved a great success; and Miss Landon was probably very willing to go, as she was already editing 'Fisher's Drawingroom Scrapbook' every year, and finding it increasingly hard, especially as she had to write so much of the work herself. When another social hostess and authoress, Mrs Caroline Norton (one of Sheridan's daughters) succeeded the young Frederick Mansel Reynolds as editress of the 'Keepsake' for 1836, her performance was judged so bad that she lost her job, and Lady Stuart Wortley who had no literary pretensions (but at least a title) was persuaded to take over for a few years, reasonably successfully.

Charles Heath's engravings found their way into the hands of many publishers, but after 1826, when he decided to be his own master in a rather more positive way than his father had aspired to be in the early 1800s, he worked principally with Jennings and Chaplin (on the 'Picturesque Views', and the 'Landscape Annual' for 1830/31), Hurst, Chance (as Hurst, Robinson had become), and from 1832 onwards almost exclusively with Longmans, with occasional cooperation with the new publisher David Bogue, and his predecessor Charles Tilt. While he might have aspired to becoming so, as John

Boydell had become in the 1780s, as Maberly commented in 1844 'it has become perfectly hopeless for an engraver to attempt to be his own publisher'.[9]

Instead he seems in his arrangements with his various publishers after 1826 to have followed the formula originally suggested in that year to John Murray. While he, as proprietor of any new publishing venture, would employ the editor, commission and pay the engravers chosen by means of three or four month bills of exchange, and generally supervise and promote the work, the publishers would arrange for all the printing, publishing and distribution requirements at their expense; in addition they would be expected to make advances to Charles to cover his overheads, to be repaid out of profits which would be equally divided.

In good times, this seems to have worked well, with the publisher getting the best of the bargain, and with Charles receiving at least £4000 per annum from his Annuals and other ventures. Out of this he would have had to pay his engravers at rates varying from 30 to 70 guineas for each print depending on size, together with each artist at between 10 and 20 guineas. Charles would also have been responsible for the design work, including the various forms of fancy binding adopted; and it is interesting to note that when the 'Keepsake' (and the 'Amulet' edited by S.C. Hall) for 1828 on its first appearance was bound up in watered silk by the binder Francis Westley, this was probably inspired by the well-publicised plight of the Spitalfields silk industry, which faced ruin from foreign competition.[10]

It would have been typical of Charles to have tried to help an ailing industry such as this, while introducing a luxury binding calculated to appeal to the sort of public who would buy his gift books. With one or two exceptions, such as in 1837/8 when plush velvet was used for binding the 'Picturesque Annual', the practice continued until 1847 for the 'Keepsake' at least. Such was the impression created, that these Annuals were regular Christmas presents for Queen Victoria to give away to her family and others: a taste no doubt originally created by the direct supply to her mother, the Duchess of Kent, of the 'Book of Beauty' for 1837 on 1 December in the preceding year, together with a large paper copy to her daughter, then Princess Victoria.[11]

Queen Victoria herself appreciated these Annuals as evidenced by the entry in her journal for December 5, 1838, at a time when Charles was planning the 'Picturesque Annual' for 1840, which was to be about Windsor Castle. 'Looked at some small prints of Versailles which Heath had brought down to Lord Conyngham; and he (H.) is anxious to make some sketches of Windsor for the next year's Annual, but we fear Sir Jeffrey may oppose, as he has to have leave to publish some. Lord M. [Melbourne] said Sir Jeffrey must be asked, and he will say: 'Won't hear of it etc.'[12] In the event permission was evidently given.

Charles was also very active in getting Longmans to introduce Annuals to several export markets, notably to France, where 'Le Keepsake Français' appeared in 1831, with English engravers linked to French authors. Charles had friends in France, possibly from his father's time, and made several visits there to make arrangements with various agents in Paris for distribution, and to set up in particular the subject matter for the three 'Picturesque Annuals' which between their 1841 and 1843 numbers featured Belgium and Paris in the Winter and Summer respectively, edited by Jules Janin. In 1837, a special French edition of 'Gems of Beauty' was sent to Messrs Delloy of Paris involving 600 copies, while in 1843, Longmans' distributors there, Messrs Aubert, sold over 350 copies of Charles Heath's main Annuals.

As Charles wrote to du Roveray on 6 June 1828: 'I sent you the bill the moment I received your letter which was not till Tuesday morning as I was out of London – as for risk that is out of the question as the partners are as respectable in Paris as 'Longmans' in London – they pay me large sums every year. I had the Bill made payable here for the convenience of discounting as I found it difficult to turn Bills in francs and payable in Paris but if you think there is risk you are quite right not to do it – for myself I never mean to run any if I know it'.[15]

Perhaps the highlight for him occurred in 1839, when he made a presentation of Turner's 'Picturesque Views', bound up, to King Louis Philippe, who presented him in return with a fine gold snuffbox with diamonds, on which the Art Union commented: 'This is not a little matter... when Kings give examples of generosity we may expect them to be followed'.[16] This was the period when British steel engraving had acquired a high reputation in Europe, and was regarded by many as superior to its French counterpart; while middle-class French taste was equally absorbed in the literary topics of the 'age of sentiment'. It was John Pye who made the point that 'The superiority of English engravings in the period 1810-35 was due to their "being free translations from pictures instead of being cold, rigid copies".' In his view engraving in England partook 'more of the character of a fine art than in any country.'

Considerable consignments of Heath's Annuals were also shipped to the United States at the time, where the fashion for American Annuals had also caught on, but with inferior engravings; Longmans' agents there were Appleton & Co. of New York, and Lea & Blanchard of Philadelphia. In Prussia, their agent was Asher in Berlin from 1834, and in Silesia and Saxony Messrs T.O. Weigel of Leipzig.[17]

The visits which Charles paid to France in 1839 served to create even more financial confusion for him, as during his absence several large bills fell due for which there was insufficient cover; the Perkins Bacon letterbooks contain several somewhat agonised letters to him from Joshua Bacon, who seems to have ended up by financing him largely out of his personal (or his firm's) pocket.[18] When in March 1841, trustees had to be appointed to manage Charles Heath's finances, Longmans opened new accounts paying them all profits which were still accruing from his ventures in order to pay off his debts, and at the same time paying the engravers direct and generally assuming responsibility for keeping these publications in being, while Charles continued to promote and administer them.[19] Because of this, it is known that in the 1840s, Lady Blessington received £250 per annum from each of the two Annuals she edited, reduced to £150 for the 'Keepsake' of 1846, and the same for the 'Book of Beauty' of

1847. Jerdan, in his Autobiography stated:

'As an author and editor of 'Heath's Annual' for some years, Lady Blessington received considerable sums. I have known her to enjoy from her pen an amount somewhere midway between £2000 and £3000 per annum'. Of Mis Power [Lady Blessington's niece who became editor of the Keepsake in 1850] 'I never heard her say the exact amount of her literary profits [i.e. Lady Blessington's] any particular year. I believe that for some years she made, on the average, somewhat about a thousand a year; some years a good deal above that sum.'

With only £500 per annum from the Annuals, it must have been the case that Lady Blessington had to rely increasingly on the profits of her 'silver fork' novels, which Charles also promoted for her, and on which her various publishers are believed to have paid her £400 down on each occasion, in order to maintain her life-style and her sumptuous salon at Gore House, besides financing many impoverished Irish relatives. She still had quite a considerable income from her late husband's estates in Ireland, but their rents fell away substantially in the hard times of the 1840s.

It was with the artists who drew or painted for the engravers, and with the engravers he employed, that Charles must have been most concerned. With his father's reputation behind him, and his own well established in the 1820s, the family firm seems to have had little difficulty about attracting the best illustrators in their field, especially as the fashion for book illustration had produced an over-supply of engravers, and many artists who specialised in this type of work. Charles of course had his own atelier, with apprentices and assistants on a fairly large scale for those days; but at the same time he would employ independent and journeymen engravers for particular projects, depending on their skills and availability. A typical example of his style was a letter he wrote to B.P. Gibbon in 1828: 'I have a picture by Mr Edwin Landseer of two dogs belonging to Sir Walter Scott, it was undertaken by Mr Westwood and is etch'd by Mr Webb and 'bitten in'; if you could take it up directly and get it me finished in time for my 'Keepsake' of this year, I shall esteem it a favour, as it is necessary we should not be idle for even a day...'[19]

Although Charles himself did very little engraving completely on his own account after 1826, except for some of the earlier plates in the 'Keepsake' series, he remained throughout a keen supervisor, who by his retouches and specialisation in engraving the human face and figure ensured that any plates appearing under his name or supervision should be of as high a quality as might be possible; the term 'highly finished plates' which was sneered at as yet another 'puff' by literary figures such as Lamb and Thackeray meant precisely what they were. Charles Heath was, after all, a master engraver, and like many another distinguished artist before him, came to regard his talents as better employed in guiding and instructing his fellows, rather than refusing to delegate as earlier engravers such as Sharp, John Landseer, and even Abraham Raimbach and John Pye had done. An interesting example of Charles Heath's supervisory style has survived in pencil in his own hand on a trial proof of a print by Robert Staines (assistant to Edward and William Finden) entitled 'The Green Room at the [Paris] Opera' engraved for the Picturesque Annual for 1843. He comments: 'The lamps are too light' and 'There wants some touches about this woman – her waist is too thick': but then a kindly touch: 'If you will go carefully over these figures and put them into effect which will take very little time and you will let me have the plate for one hour on Monday, I will go over the faces for you and it will then please the painter much better and save you a world of trouble'.[20]

Another interesting example is the steel engraving of Mrs Peel, which appeared in the Keepsake for 1829, and has been much praised since. It bears the signature of Charles Heath, but a very early proof copy is lettered in manuscript: 'Lane reduced, Goodyear etchd figure, Webb etchd fur and feathers, J.H. Watt drapery and hat, Rhodes worked up hat feathers, D. Smith background, and C. Heath flesh'. Another example is an engraver's proof of the 'Prophet of St Paul's' after Chalon, for the 1830 Keepsake, which shows the engraving in four different states after reduction, and the words 'No.2 state by J.H. Watt, Rhodes graved up white drapery, D. Smith remr [i.e. remainder], and C. Heath flesh'.[20] An even more intriguing example from Charles Heath's atelier are engravers' proofs in two states of preliminary work, plus the finished proof of the steel engraving of 'The Widowed Bride' after Sharpe by Edwards, which appeared in the Keepsake for 1834; here there is included the actual original of the graph paper used for the reduction in size from the original drawing.[21]

The method employed was to divide the space to be engraved upon into a series of squares on the graph paper, produced by horizontal and vertical lines cutting each other. The spaces are each numbered; with the figures in the margins at the top and at the side. The picture to be copied would have had the same number of lines stretched across it with cotton thread, so that the designer would be able to reduce the proportions of the original to the smaller surface to be engraved. The next stage would be to etch in the outline of the design on the plate itself, together with the leading parts, meaning in practice that almost everything except the white parts would be covered.

The second trial proof shows how the plate looked after the burin, or graver, had been used. Everything has been strengthened, lights have been heightened, and shadows have been deepened, and the rich texture of the costume has been introduced. The final plate shows the last stage, the print in proof, ready for its issue to the public. The flesh has been engraved, and rounded forms and life given to the chalky patches of the previous trial proof. It is in this stage that in every part of the plate touches have been added to give colour and add a sparkling reality to the engraving. The size is just 5 centimetres by 6, yet this does not affect the quality or the excellence of the workmanship, but rather enhances it.

With the increasing need to meet precise deadlines for finished prints in such productions as the Annuals it was inevitable that degrees of specialisation should develop in the atelier, and that collaboration between engravers engaged on a project should be managed. With the possible exception of the Finden brothers, who followed very closely the techniques of the Heath family engravers, but equally lacked resources and collapsed under the financial strain, no other ateliers existed to match the combined efforts which Charles was able to put into his enterprises. Yet he was not an autocrat, and seems to have been much respected by those who worked for him. Nor did he scorn the work of other engravers, but wanted his own atelier to learn from their example. John Burnet, writing in 1850, commented: 'I ought also to record the approbation of my brother artists [for Burnet's engraving of Wilkie's 'The Blind Fiddler']. Mr George Doo and Mr James Watt, two of our first historical engravers, told me that their master, the late Charles Heath, had bought a proof to be hung up in their studio for an example'.[22]

In addition to Turner, with whom perhaps he had the closest relations, a great many artists of the day at one time or another had their work engraved either by Charles himself or under his auspices. His father's old friend for instance, Thomas Stothard R.A., was a prime contributor of drawings and paintings for engraving almost until the year he died in 1834. There is evidence that Sir Thomas Lawrence, President of the Royal Academy (who was also an old friend of his father's), had close contacts with him at least as early as 1821.[23] Engravings after Sir Thomas appeared in the 'Keepsakes' for 1828-30 and again in 1835, and in Thomas Moore's works (published in 1840), all engraved by Charles. In the period up to 1825, perhaps the most regular contributors were Robert Smirke R.A., C.R. Leslie R.A. and Richard Westall R.A., in addition to Stothard; while thereafter a wide range of artists are to be found with their works engraved especially for the Annuals and giftbooks for which Charles acted as art director and promoter. The most notable of these were Henry and Edward Corbould (both related to the family by marriage), Thomas Uwins R.A., and J.M. Wright, together with A.E. Chalon R.A. and Edward Parris, especially for the illustration of Lady Blessington's works. Some of these, notably Richard Westall and Henry Corbould, came to specialise in commissioned drawings for engraved book illustration, in preference to exhibition paintings.

A typical case where Charles commissioned artists of his own accord is recorded by Farington in 1819-21, in which a somewhat reluctant Academician, Robert Smirke, was attracted into doing a set of Shakespeare designs for an edition which apparently turned out very profitably for the artist. On 26 November 1819, Farington related:

'Smirke came in the evening. He told me that Charles Heath, the Engraver, had proposed a commission to him, viz: to paint a Series of subjects from the whole of Shakespeare's plays, from which engravings should be made; and the prints sold without any letterpress. The calculation was that there would be 200 subjects for Smirke to paint upon a small scale. He said the thought of the undertaking disturbed his mind, so difficult he found it in designing to satisfy himself with what he had done and when he has completed a picture he feels as if it were a failure. I told him to proceed and told him nobody would think as he did.'[24]

The work duly progressed, and on 30 January 1821, Farington wrote: 'Smirke I called on. He was employed on his small pictures from which engravings are to be made... The original intention was to publish the whole without letterpress but it is now meant so to publish them or with the text free from notes at the option of the purchaser.'[24]

Charles in his entrepreneurial role after 1825 seems to have been much trusted by the artists involved; writing to his London contact from Naples in April 1828, for instance, Thomas Uwins said: 'The pictures... sent by the "Lady Keith" brig, which I hope will be delivered in about six weeks, are a "Confession" I intended for Charles Heath; and I want for it, frame and all just as it is, 25 guineas. If Charles Heath does not want to buy it, you will oblige me by not offering it to anybody else...' Uwins at that time had what he described as a 'diabolically malignant and powerful enemy' (probably Francis Shoberl, editor of the ForgetmeNot) who was thought to be blackening his name as an illustrator with the book dealer/publishers, so added 'Charles Heath and Ackermann are the only two persons I can depend upon not being acted on. They judge for themselves.'[25]

It was really no great wonder that when Charles died so suddenly in 1848, the Art Union, which had praised him as 'the first burin in England' (and in other respects), but had also criticised him during his lifetime, summed up his achievement in their obituary notice by concluding that 'he has probably created as much work for his professional brethren as any living man'. It seems a fair judgment even today.

CHAPTER 6

Frederick and Alfred Heath: the End of an Era

THESE TWO SONS OF CHARLES HEATH constituted the third generation of Heath family line engravers. They were both trained in the family atelier at a time when the skills developed for engraving on steel had reached their height in Britain, and they appear to have used no other medium, apart from steel mezzotinting. When Charles Heath died in 1848, they did what they could to continue, even though the family fortunes were still at a very low ebb. They were well supported by David Bogue, their publisher who had taken over Longmans' interest, and clearly determined to carry on the family tradition. A third, much younger son, Henry Charles (1829-98), seeing little future in line engraving, turned to miniature painting from which he seems to have made a good reputation and a fair living, becoming appointed miniature painter to Queen Victoria in 1893.

Frederick, who had worked closely with his father on a number of plates, took over the work of superintending engravings commissioned for the 'Keepsake', besides engraving for it himself; and his taste especially in steel mezzotints produced some fine but little appreciated work from engravers such as W.H. Mote and B. Eyles. It was probably due to the high standards he set, as much as to anything else, that the 'Keepsake' was still able to command a public until its final demise in 1858, long after the fashion for Annuals had faded away, and all the other Annuals had ceased production. On the other hand, even if the possibility to exercise it had still existed, it does not look as if either he or his brother Alfred had inherited their father's taste for entrepreneurship. From 1847 until his death in 1878, he contributed medium-sized steel engravings to the Art Union, published by Hodgson & Graves until 1849, when it was taken over by George Virtue and renamed the Art Journal. With a circulation of 25,000 copies by 1851, the Art Journal, appearing in monthly parts at two shillings and sixpence each, became recognised as the leading art magazine in Britain, bringing education in art to much wider levels of the population than the expensive Annual ever could.

Beginning with his prime responsibility for engraving the master roller die which was to produce the first postage stamps in 1840 (which has immortalised Frederick to philatelists), he seems also to have acted for many years as designer and engraver of many other postage stamps produced by Perkins Bacon & Co., until the firm lost the contract for engraving British and Colonial issues to Messrs de la Rue in the 1870s. It is known for instance that he was responsible for the engraving of the 5/- New South Wales stamp, issued in 1861 to the design of his brother-in-law Edward Corbould; and for the tiny halfpenny British stamp issued in 1870.[1]

During the 1840s, the Longmans archive show that he was being paid between 40 and 50 guineas, depending on size, for each of the small plates engraved for the 'Keepsake', which represented the standard rate. But when he died on 26 March 1878 at his home at 87 Sussex Road, Holloway,[2] his personal estate was 'under £100', so that the last years of his life must have been difficult for him, with few commissions to engrave. His brother was his executor, and his last plate, appearing in the Art Journal for 1879, was entitled 'The Queen of the Vineyard'. In the subjects he chose to engrave, he had moved away from landscape or personality prints to storybook compositions to meet the changing fashion of the time. But it was the form of engraving itself which had become obsolete, and this was no doubt a source of sadness to him, as a fine and meticulous craftsman who was only concerned with practicing his art in the ways he knew.

Very little is known about Alfred, whose career was intended to follow that of his elder brother, beginning with his first engraving for the 'Keepsake' in 1836, at the age of 24. He too was well-trained, and though not inspired in his style of engraving, he had a delicate quality which Frederick lacked. His output was not high however, and though he must have helped Frederick a great deal in the production of engravings during the last years of the 'Keepsake', commissions thereafter did not come easily, and he only engraved once for the 'Art Journal'; he seems to have preferred religious subjects, which were also in vogue at the time. His last years are believed to have been largely employed in teaching the arts of engraving, although it is not known who his pupils may have been. When he died on 30 January 1896 at his home at 8 Somerset St, Battersea,[2] he left estate valued at £105, only marginally more than his brother had done.

The lives of these two brothers, reduced to the sort of straitened circumstances in which most engravers seems to have lived in this period, due to their father's misfortunes, was well summed up by Raimbach in the 1840s: 'The retirement and independence of spirit is the main virtue of the engraver's profession... This is perhaps the only circumstance that can be named in its favour, in comparison with various other branches of the fine arts; the slowness of its process, and the difficulty of its acquirement, together with the very inadequate remuneration for unequalled toil and seclusion, without even a chance of a good prize in the lottery of professional life rendering the smallest possible return for the greatest personal sacrifices'.

Algernon Graves, from the vantage point of the print dealer and publisher painted a similar if slightly less gloomy picture: 'People in the 60s bought prints if they were well done and they liked the subject, not because of the engravers, though in the

70s Couzens and Lucas came into fashion. My impression has always been that successful painters lived on a far higher scale than engravers. Engravers earned their money by great manual toil, and very slowly, and consequently they knew the value of money and lived well within their means. I do not remember often meeting another engraver at the house of any that I visited, neither do I remember that any of them were given to entertaining, their whole souls were in their work, and many an evening when I have visited them have found them hard at work with their burin or scraper by gaslight. They mostly seemed to have two or more plates of different sizes on hand at once, and were invariably at work on the smaller ones at night. In my early days, my father was fond of giving small dinner parties and it was seldom that there were not one or two engravers present, and many a commission to engrave a picture was given during the evening; the painter of the picture was usually present'.[3]

John Ruskin, in his 1872 lectures, referred to the 'skill, the modesty, the patience of this entirely industrious race – copyists with their heart';[4] and as a regular contributor to Charles Heath's Annuals in the 1840s, he must have known Frederick and Alfred in his dealings there. He paid particular tribute to the skill of Miller and Goodall (amongst Charles Heath's principal engravers) and to the 'oldtime engravers who made lines and then drew alongside them'. But he then launched into a diatribe against the way in which they had destroyed their own art. In his 1865 lectures:

'Has the reader ever reflected on the patience and deliberate subtlety and unostentatious will involved in the ordinary process of steel engraving; the process of which engravers now with doleful voices deplore the decline and with sorrowful hearts expect the extinction after their own days? By the way – my friends of the field of steel – you need fear nothing of the kind. What is there mechanical in your work; of habitual and thoughtless, of vulgar or servile, for that indeed the time has come; the sun will burn it up for you very ruthlessly, but what there is of human liberty and of sanguine life, in finger and fancy, is kindred of the sun, and quite inextinguishable by him... a square inch of man's engraving is worth all the photography that were every dipped in acid... only it must be man's engraving, not machine's engraving... put more sunshine on your steel and less burr.'[6]

And seven years later, in 1872:

'Engravers complain that photography and cheap woodcutting have ended their finer craft. No complaint can be less grounded. They themselves destroyed their own craft by vulgarising it. Content in their beautiful mechanism, they ceased to learn and to feel, as artists; they put themselves under the orders of publishers and printsellers; they worked indiscriminately from whatever was put into their hands from Bartlett as willingly as from Turner, and from Mulready as carefully as from Raphael. They filled the windows of printsellers, the pages of gift books, with elaborate rubbish, and piteous abortions of delicate industry. They worked cheap, and cheaper – the got armies of assistants and surrounded themselves with schools of mechanical tricksters, learning their stale tricks with blundering avidity. They had fallen – before the days of photography, into providers of frontispieces for housekeeper pocket books. I do not know if photography itself, their redoubted enemy, has even now ousted them from that last refuge... Such the fault of the engraver – very pardonable; scarcely avoidable however fatal. Fault mainly of humility.'[5]

Though there was much truth in what Ruskin had to say, he was, as might be expected from academic criticism, insufficiently aware of the commercial considerations which the line engravers had to take into account. Such engravers as Charles, Frederick and Alfred were determined to maintain standards, but they had to charge accordingly for their quality, and could not maintain their custom in the face of cheaper though inferior competition. Ruskin's strictures seem not directly aimed against them, even though Charles and his atelier did increasingly resort to etching and the use of the ruling machine in turning out many of their prints to meet deadlines, with some loss of quality; but they could not have stayed in business as long as they did if they had not done so. The real debasement to the trade occurred due to a number of other reasons, some of which had originated in James Heath's time towards the end of the 18th century, when 'chalk' or stipple engraving of a certain type was introduced, cutting corners for the pure line engraver and, as Sir Robert Strange put it in 1791, 'from the nature of the operation, and the extreme facility with which it is executed, it has got into the hands of every boy of every printseller in town, and of every manufacturer of prints, however ignorant and unskilful'.[6]

John Landseer inveighed against these practices amongst many others,[7] while Raimbach (who did not practise it) claimed that 'to the introduction of steel engraving, by multiplying almost indefinitely the number of impressions each plate would produce, may in great degree be attributed the decline and debasement of the art, exercised on a small scale. The embellishment of books are no longer what they have been and the recent discovery and application of the electrotype [ca. 1840] bids fair to effect similar results as regards works of a large size. This most ingenious process has the power of reproducing, and at a comparatively small expense, any number of facsimiles... whereby an indefinite amount of prints, all equally good, may be taken from them, consequently greatly lessening the value of the aggregate and destroying... the long-established system of proofs and early impressions which contributed so much to the advantage and respectability of the profession, by holding out inducements to connoisseurs and lovers of rarity to form collections of choice examples'.[8]

The Art Union in 1839 provided a shrewder comment on the decline of the technique: 'The laborious style of line engraving, though sufficient to supply the demand for the portfolios of the curious, was inadequate to the purposes of framing and domestic decoration; a more expeditious method was called into action and hence arose that flood of dotted or stippled prints which overspread the country'.[9]

John Burnet, writing in 1850 as an engraver himself, provide perhaps the best analysis of the reasons for decline, against which Frederick and Alfred had to struggle so hard, and which led to the end of the family dynasty.[10] In the first place, he maintained, artists had begun to claim copyright when their works were to be engraved; thus Graves had to pay Landseer 3000 guineas for his 'Peace' and 'War' and for his 'Wellington'. This meant that for large prints, the engraver's fee had to be reduced by the publisher to offset the extra cost; and the market was dominated for this type of print in consequence by Wilkie, Morland and Landseer. Secondly, mezzotint on steel, being faster than steel engraving, had almost extinguished the line engraving of large works, even of landscapes. Thirdly, lithography had by then virtually extinguished stipple or dotted engraving, while machine ruling, which produced broad tints over loose etching, had also eliminated line engraving.

From the other end of the spectrum, the number of print publishers had increased to the point at which more and more variety was constantly in demand, as fashion changed; and the line engravers could not cope with these changes of pace. Even more important had been the flood of cheap prints coming in from abroad, especially from France, now that duty on imported lithographs had been reduced to one penny each. Though these were soon to be at a disadvantage also, Burnet maintained that for small works, steel engravings could still hold their own; for each engraving in Scott's Waverley novels for instance, the cost had been only a halfpenny per volume per engraving yet Cadell had been able to afford to pay engravers 80 guineas for each plate. Even in the 1860s and 70s, this might still be true of the long printing runs still to be expected from stalwart authors such as Sir Walter Scott, but this could not save the lesser works for the engravers, unless there were special circumstances.

By way of a valedictory to these oldtime engravers from a vanished age, Andrew Tuer's summary of their lives and qualities, written in 1882, still conveys a hint of their human condition:

'To translate with fine intelligence into black and white, and to print such translations mechanically, is the surest way yet approved as combining true art with multiplicity of production. An engraver must possess intellect: he must undergo thorough mechanical training, and combine artistic perception with a natural and intelligent deftness of hand and power of expression. He is no mere copyist; and yet a copyist cannot do his work well without qualities such as these… like the translator of a book he has to think in two languages – in colour and in black and white… (this) makes him an interpreter rather than an imitator… The performing musician has almost as great a glory as the composing musician; for he must assimilate his composer's music, and make it live by expression. To do this thoroughly and finely requires something like genius – receptive genius. To become a skilful line engraver requires keen artistic instincts, a love of the work, and years of devoted and persevering study. Unremitting patience, a microscopic eye and a steady hand are valuable and perhaps indispensable to those who follow the profession; but without higher qualifications than these, an engraver cannot hope to win undying laurels.'[11]

Author's Note

There are other Heath engravers in the period, but none appear to be related at all closely to the Heath family engravers noted above. Of the others, the best known is William Heath (1795-1840) who had a brother, or cousin, Henry Heath, who died about 1835. Both were distinguished as caricaturists in the style of Cruickshank, but William was also an etcher of military and naval subjects on a considerable scale.

There is also Percy Heath (fl. 1832-50), possibly the same as 'J.P. Heath' who engraved for Charles Heath's 'Picturesque Annual' for 1839 amongst others. He produced an improved engraver's ruling machine which was described in the Transactions of the Society of Arts journal for 1837.

References

Introduction

1. Public Record Office, London, Vol 2.515 RA 2604/52

Chapter 1

1. Man: 'Lithography in England 1801-10'
2. BMPR 190.b.1
3. T. Fisher in the Gentleman's Magazine, March 1808
4. Twyman, p.32
5. Farington, p.2535
6. Dictionary of National Biography: Charles Heath (by Lionel Cust)
7. Farington, p.4387
8. Quoted by Jupp
9. Sandby, p.278
10. Farington, p.4156
11. Pye, p.316
12. Farington, p.5107
13. Farington, p.5114
14. Farington, p.5127
15. Farington, p.5142
16. Levis
17. Farington, p.4995
18. Farington, p.4996
19. Farington, p.5003
20. National Library of Scotland. Ms 789
21. Longman archives I, 101, No.150
22. Bain: 'John Sharpe, Publisher and Bookseller'

Chapter 2

1. Mackenzie, Bathe, passim
2. Mackenzie, p.66
3. Dyer, p.29
4. Mackenzie, p.64, Heath records, p.103
5. Society of Arts Transactions, Vol 38, p.47
6. Mackenzie, p.77
7. Muir, Augustus, pp.1-3
8. Heath records, pp.103-4
9. Samuel, p.58
10. Perkins Bacon records
11. Samuel, pp.60-61
12. Lowe, pp.58-61
13. Heath, J.D., p.25. Charles and Frederick received 50 guineas for this pioneer work.
14. Longman archives I, 101, No.13B

Chapter 3

1. Adams: entry pp.356-7.147 '1825 Views in London'
2. John Murray archives
3. Britton, p.313
4. Ruskin: 'My First Editir' (1876). Works Vol 36, p.94
5. Knight Vol II, p.53
6 Vizetelly, p.143
7. Hall, p.307
8. Hogg, p.294
9. Watts Vol II, p.269
10. Watts Vol II, pp.157-8
11. Watts Vol II, p.153
12. Renier, p.12
13. Fraser's Magazine, December 1837.
14. Madden Vol I, pp.269-70
15. Madden Vol I, p.275, Vol II, p.196
16. Madden Vol III, p.43
17. Renier, p.12
18. Renier, p.14
19. Hogg, p.296
20. Boyle, p.2 (preface)
21. Sir Walter Scott's Journal

22. Renier, p.15
23. Renier, p.14
24. Griggs Vol II, p.416 and 420
25. Ruskin, Works Vol 35, pp.24-25
26. Lord John Russell Vol V, p.314
27. Renier, p.9
28. Ainger Vol II, p.274
29. Lytton Vol I, p.449
30. Fraser's Magazine, December 1837
31. Booth quoting the 'Oxford Thackeray, Art Criticisms' p.355
32. Leitch Ritchie's 'River Wye' was published separately (see 1839(3) in Charles Heath's catalogue) in an edition of 1000 copies of which only 409 were sold (Longman archives)
33. Longman archives
34. Perkins Bacon records

Chapter 4

1. Hamerton, p.210
2. Shanes, p.10
3. Finberg, p.301
4. Shanes, p.11
5. Finberg
6. Shanes, p.12
7. Shanes, p.13
8. Shanes, p.14, P. Muir pp.68-70
9. Shanes, p.15, The auction house was that of Southgate & Son, 22 Fleet St, not 'Southgate & Co'. Charles Heath auctioned some of his own effects the same month at Christies (Annex B(7)), but did not sell his two sets of 'Turner' proofs until April 1840 (Sothebys) and a final set in July 1842
10. Thornbury Vol II, p.129
11. Bell
12. Thornbury Vol II, pp.147-8
13. Godfrey
14. Shanes, p.15
15. Athenaeum for 1831, p.76
16. Finberg, p.302
17. Rawlinson Vol I, p.lxiv
18. Shanes, p.12
19. Miller, p.123
20. Miller, p.130

21. Miller, p.137
22. Miller, p.139
23. Thornbury Vol I, p.395
24. Quoted by Shanes, p.12
25. Finberg, p.308
26. Pierpont Morgan Library R-V Autographs.Misc. Artists
27. Shanes, p.18

Chapter 5

1. Sir Walter Scott's Journal
2. Watts Vol I, p.269
3. Southey, p.322
4. Watts Vol I, p.292
5. Longmans archives (Mss letters)
6. Pierpont Morgan Library R-V Autographs. Misc. Artists
7. Sadleir, p.204
8. National Library of Scotland, Ms 3908
9. Maberly, p.161
10. Chick, quoting R. Burnet 'A Word to the Members of the Mechanics Institute', 1826
11. Longmans archives
12. Queen Victoria's Journal
13. Getty Center, 'Archives for the History of Art'
14. Art Union, March 1839, p.24
15. Finberg, p.357
16. Longmans archives
17. Perkins Bacon letterbooks
18. Longmans archives: account books 'Trustees of Mr Charles Heath'
19. Free Library of Philadelphia
20. Heath Engravings (proofs property of the author)
21. Hayden: pp.208-10
22. Burnet, p.277
23. Windsor Castle Library RA Add W5/95
24. Farington pp.5432 and 5607
25. Uwins, p.101

Chapter 6

1. Lowe, p.164
2. Somerset House probate records

3. Graves, p.39
4. Ruskin, Works Vol 22, p.387
5. Ruskin, Works Vol 19, p.88 and Art Journal for April 1865 pp.101-2
6. Clulow: footnote
7. Landseer
8. Raimbach, p.139
9. Art Union, May 15, 1839, pp.57-58
10. Burnet, pp.275 et seq.
11. Tuer, p.78 and 81

Bibliography

Abbey, J.R. *Travels in Aquatint and Lithography*, 1770-1860 (Curwen Press, 1956)
Acland, Alice. *Caroline Norton* (Constable, 1948)
Adams, B. *London Illustrated 1604-1851* (Library Association 1983)
Ainger (Ed.). *Letters of Charles Lamb*, 1915
Alexander, D. and Godfrey, R.T. *The Reproductive Print from Hogarth to Wilkie* (Yale, 1980)
The Art Journal. (1849, 1866-70, 1872, 1874, 1877, 1879)
The Art Union. (March, May, July, October-December 1839, February-March and May 1840, 1841-2, 1848)

Bacon, E.D. *The Line-Engraved Postage Stamps of Great Britain* printed by Perkins, Bacon & Co. Two volumes (Chas. Nissen & Co. 1920)
Bain, Iain. *John Sharpe, Publisher and Bookseller* (Laverock Press, 1960)
Bain, Iain. *Thomas Ross & Son* (Journal of the Printing Historical Society No.2 (1966))
Bathe, G. and D. *Jacob Perkins, His Inventions, His Times, and His Contemporaries* (Historical Society of Pennsylvania, Philadelphia, 1943)
Bell, C.F. *Turner and His Engravers* (The Studio, 1903/4)
Benthall, G. *Works of J.H. Mortimer* (Victoria and Albert Museum, National Art Library, unpublished Mss 13466 (p.3)
Binyon, L. *Catalogue of Drawings by British Artists*, Vol II (British Library 1898-1907)
Booth, B.A. (Ed:) *A Cabinet of Gems*: short stories from the English Annuals (University of California, Berkeley, 1938)
Britton, John. *Autobiography*, Vol I (Privately printed, 1850)
Burnet, James. *Autobiography* (Art Journal, 1850)
Boyle, A. *An Index to the Annuals, 1820-50* (Andrew Boyle, Worcester, 1967)

Chick, Dr Arthur (Ed:). *The Book Historian No.1* (October 1989, for subscribers)
Connally, Willard. *Count d'Orsay* (Cassell, 1952)
Coxhead, A.C. *Thomas Stothard R.A.* (A.H. Bullen, 1906)
Coxhead, A.C. *The Life of Stothard* (London, 1919)
Cruse, Amy. *The Englishman and His Books in the early Nineteenth Century* (G.G. Harrap,

1930, and Benjamin Blom, New York, 1968)
Cunningham, Allan. *Lives of the Most Eminent British Painters, Sculptors, and Architects,* Vol IV (John Murray, 1830-37)
Clulow, G. *A Half Century of Line Engraving 1780-1830* (Journal of the Society of Arts Vol 45, May 1897)

Dafforne, J. *Pictures by William Mulready* (Virtue & Co., 1872)
Dafforne, J. *Modern Art* (Virtue & Co., 1877-86)
Dawson Turner, Mrs E. *One Hundred Etchings,* (privately printed, 1825)
Dictionary of National Biography (entry on Charles Heath by Lionel Henry Cust)
Dodd's History of English Engravers (British Museum Additional Mss 33401.f, ca.1820, unpublished)
Dyer, J.C. *Specimens and Descriptions of Perkins and Fairman's Patent Siderographic Plan to Prevent Forgery of Banknotes* (London 1819)
Dyson, Anthony. *Pictures to Print* (Farrand Press, 1984)

Eliot, George. *Middlemarch* (Blackwood, 1871)
Engen, Rodney. *A Dictionary of Victorian Engravers* (Chadwick-Healey, 1979)
Encyclopaedia Britannica (11th edition: Line engraving)

Fagan, L.A. *Handbook to the Department of Prints and Drawings in the British Museum* (G. Bell & Sons, 1876)
Fagan, L.A. *History of Engraving in England* (Sampson Low, 1893)
Farington, J.F. *Diary 1793-1821* (Yale, 1978)
Faxon, F.W. *Literary Annuals and Gift Books* (Boston, 1912 and Private Libraries Association, 1973)
Finberg, A.J. *Life of J.M.W. Turner* (Oxford University Press, 1939)
Fox, Celina. *The Engraver's Battle for Professional Recognition in Early Nineteenth Century London*
Fielding, T.H. *The Art of Engraving* (Nattali, 1844)
Fraser's Magazine for 1837 and 1842

Gage, J. *The Correspondence of J.M.W. Turner*
The Gentleman's Magazine (March 1808, December 1827, December 1831, December 1832, December 1843, 1849)
Godfrey, R.T. *Printmaking in Britain* (Phaidon Press, Oxford)
Goodall, Frederick. *Reminiscences* (Walter Scott Publishers, 1902)
Graves, Algernon. *Engravers I Have Known* (The Printseller, Vol I (1903) p.39)
Griffiths, A. *Prints and Printmaking* (British Museum, 1980)
Griggs, E.L. (Ed:) *The Unpublished Letters of S.T. Coleridge* (Constable, 1932)
Guise, Hilary. *Great Victorian Engravings* (Astragal Books, 1980)

Hall, S.C. *Retrospect of a Long Life* (Bentley, 1883)
Hamerton, P.G. *Etching and Etchers* (MacMillan, 1880)
Hamerton, P.G. *The Graphic Arts* (Seeley, Jackson and Halliday, 1882)
Hamerton, P.G. *The Life of J.M.W. Turner* (Seeley & Co., 1895)
Hayden, Arthur. *Chats on Old Prints* (T. Fisher Unwin, 1906)
Heath, George. *Records of the Heath Family 1744-1910* (Privately printed, 1913)
Heath, James Dunbar. *The Line-Engraved Postage Stamps of Great Britain* (Perkins, Bacon & Co., 1909)
Herman, Luke. *Turner Prints* (Phaidon, 1990)
Hind, A.M. *List of the Works of Foreign and Native Line Engravers in England*
Hind, A.M. *A Short History of Engraving and Etching* (Constable, 1908, revised 1923)
Hogg, D. *Allan Cunningham* (Hodder & Stoughton, 1875)
Holloway, M. *Steel Engraving in Nineteenth Century British Topographical Books* (Holland Press, 1977)
House, S. *Dictionary of British Book Illustrators and Caricaturists 1800-1914*
Hunnisett, Dr Basil. *Steel Engraved Book Illustration in England* (Scolar Press, 1980)
Hunnisett, Dr Basil. *An Illustrated Dictionary of British Steel Engravers* (Scolar Press, 2nd edition, 1989)

Jerdan, William. *Autobiography* (London, 1852)
Jupp, E.B. *Descriptive List of Original Drawings, Engravings, etc, Illustrating the Catalogue of the Free Society of Artists, 1760-91* (privately printed, 1871)

Knight, Charles. *Passages of a Working Life* (Bradbury and Evans, 1864)

Landseer, J. *Lectures on the Art of Engraving* (Royal Institute, 1807)
Lamb, Charles. *Letters* (Moxon, 1837, MacMillan 1888)
Levis, Howard C. *Bibliography in the English Language Relating to the Art and History of Engraving* (Ellis, 1912)
Lippmann. *Engraving and Etching* (Graves & Co., 1906)
Longman Archives. University of Reading (unpublished)
Lytton, Earl of. *Life of Edward Bulwer, 1st Lord Lytton* (Kegan Paul, 1883 and 1913)
Lowe, Robson. *The British Postage Stamp of the Nineteenth Century* (The National Postal Museum, 1968)
Lister, Raymond. *Prints and Printmaking* (Methuen, 1984)

Maberly, J. *The Print Collector* (London, 1844)
Mackenzie, A.G. *The Bank of England Note* (Cambridge University Press, 1953)
Mackenzie, I. *British Prints* (Antique Collectors Club, 1987)
Madden, R.R. (Ed.) *Literary Life and Correspondence of the Countess of Blessington* (Newby, 1855, 2nd edition)

McLean, Ruari. *Victorian Book Design and Colour Printing* (Faber and Faber, 1972)
Man, F.H. *Prints – History of an Art* (Skoura Press)
Man, F.H. *150 Years of Artists' Lithographs* (Heinemann, 1953)
Miller, W. *Memorials of Hope Park* (privately printed, 1886)
Muir, Percy. *Victorian Illustrated Books* (Batsford, 1985)
Muir, Augustus. *The History of Baker Perkins* (Heffer, 1968)

Pennell, Joseph and E. Robin. *Lithograph and Lithographers* (J. Fisher Unwin, 1915)
Perkins Bacon & Co. *Records and Daybooks* (Royal Philatelic Society, unpublished)
Poulter, G.C.B. *The Corbould Genealogy* (Harrisons, Ipswich, 1935)
Pye, John. *Patronage of British Art, A Historical Sketch* (Longmans, 1845)

Queen Victoria's Journal for December 5, 1838 (Windsor Castle Library)

Rawlinson, W.G. *The Engraved Work of J.M.W. Turner R.A.* Vol I (MacMillan, 1908 and 1931)
Raimbach, M.T.S. (Ed:) *Memoirs and Recollections of the Late Abraham Raimbach* (F. Shoberl, 1843)
Redgrave, R. and S. *A Century of British Painters* (Phaidon Press, Oxford (reprint), 1981)
Renier, Anne. *Friendship's Gift: An Essay on the Annuals and Gift Books of the Nineteenth Century* (Private Libraries Association, 1964)
Royal Academy Exhibition Records
Russell, Lord John (Ed:). *Memoirs, Journal and Correspondence of Thomas Moore* (London, 1853-6)
Ruskin, John. *My First Editor: an Autobiographical Reminiscence*
Ruskin, John. *Castus of Aglaia*
Ruskin, John. *Ariadne Fiorentina* (Works, edited by E.T. Cook and A. Wedderburn, London, 1906)

Sadleir, Michael. *Blessington d'Orsay: A Masquerade* (London, 1947) (Published in the U.S.A. as *The Strange Life of Lady Blessington,* by Farrar, Strauss, 1947)
Sandby, William. *History of the Royal Academy* (London, 1862, reprinted by Cornmarket Press, 1970)
Scott, Sir Walter. *Journal,* January-February 1828 (Oliver and Boyd, Edinburgh, 1941, and Oxford University Press, 1972)
Shain, Michael. *Book Illustration Line Engraving* (Antiquarian Book Monthly Review, February 1976)
Shanes, Eric. *Turner Studies* Vol.4 No.1 'New Light on the "England and Wales" Series' (Tate Gallery, 1984)
Shanes, Eric. *Turner's Picturesque Views in England and Wales* (Chatto and Windus, 1979)
Slater, J.H. *Engravings and their Value* (6th edition, 1906)

Smith, G.W. *James Heath, Engraver to Kings and Tutor to Many* (published by the Author, 1989)
Sotheby's Auction Catalogues, 1830, 1840 and 1842
Southey, C.C. *Life and Correspondence of T. Southey* (London, 1849)
Strahan, E. *The Art Gallery of the International Exhibition* (Boston, 1877)
Studio Magazine for 1923. 'British Book Illustration Yesterday and Today'.
Society of Arts, Transactions, Vol 38 (1821)
Samuel, Marcus. *Security Printing by Jacob Perkins before 1840* (The London Philatelist, 1982)

Thornbury, W. *Life of Turner* (Hurst and Blackett, 1862)
Tuer, Andrew. *Bartolozzi and his Works* (Hamilton Adams, 1882)
Twyman, Michael. *Lithography 1800-1850* (Oxford University Press, 1979)
Thackeray, W.M. 'A Word upon the Annuals' (*Fraser's Magazine*, December 1837)

Uwins, Mrs S. *Memoir of Thomas Uwins R.A.* (Longmans, 1858)

Vizetelly, Henry. *Glances Back Over 50 Years* (Colburn, 1893)

Wakeman, Geoffrey. *Victorian Book Illustration* (David and Charles, 1973)
Watts, A.A. *A Narrative of his Life* (Bentley, 1884)
Whitman and Salaman. *The Print Collector's Handbook* (Bell and Son, 1918)
Worman, E.C. *George Virtue and the British 'Numbers' Game* (A.B. Bookman's Weekly, 15 June, 1987)

Zigrosser, C.D. *Prints* (Peter Owen, 1963)

ANNEX A

Assistants and Pupils in Charles Heath's Atelier

A. Assistants

*** J.B. Baylis
*** W. Radclyffe
*** R. Rhodes (1816)
*** D. Smith
*, *** F. Stone
*, *** T. Wallis
*, **, *** J.T. Willmore

B. Pupils

*, **, *** J.H. Watt
*, *** R.J. Lane (1816-21)
*, **, *** E.J. Roberts (lived in, and became assistant)
*, *** T. Fairland
*** J.H. Hurdis
*** James Kirkwood
*** John Kirkwood
*, **, *** Joseph Goodyear (1822-25)
** J.B. Allen
, * J.H. Robinson (1814-16)
* W. Radclyffe

(Worked for)

W. Miller
** R. Wallis
*** J. Pye
B. Eyles
R. Staines

W.H. Mote
(and many others)

Key
* Engen ** Hunnisett *** Lister

ANNEX B

Auctions of Charles Heath's Prints, Books and Property

1. 9-13 May 1826 and 14-17 June Robins, Southgate, 22 Fleet St London (a) (By order of the assignees) [See overleaf for list]

2. 15 June 1826 Jones and Hearne (b)

3. 27 January 1832 Sothebys, London (c). 'Sale of the very choice and valuable Drawings and Cabinet Pictures by Eminent Modern Artists, the property of Mr Charles Heath esq, collected by him for his various publications.'
[111 lots, mostly drawings and paintings for Annuals, were sold for £1295.13.0.]

4. ?1833/4 Auction sales are mentioned in these years in Charles Heath's entry in the *Dictionary of National Biography*, probably in error for the 1832 sale.

5. 2-3 March 1837 Christies, London (d)

6. 7 June 1838 Christies, London (e)

7. 5 June 1839 Christies (f). Advertised in the Art Union for May 1839 (p.79)

8. 23-28 April 1840 Sotheby's, London (g). Sale of Charles Heath's proofs of Turner's 'Picturesque Views'.

9. 23-26 July 1842 Sotheby's, London (h). Sale of Charles Heath's proofs and books.
[the sale produced £675.11.6. from 655 lots, mainly unsold copies of Annuals]

10. 27 May 1848 Christies, London (i)
Gage (p.79A) comments: 'Charles Heath's sales between 1826 and 1848 included paintings and drawings by Bonington, Cox, Martin, Stothard, Linnell, Maclise, and Creswick, and lithographs by Gericault, and Delacroix, but only one Turner drawing (Havre), published in the Keepsake for 1834.

All the auctions mentioned above are listed by Lugt.
Catalogues are located as referenced above, as follows:

(a) Getty. The DNB entry incorrectly gives the auction date as 'March 1826'
BMPR. B2-1/8 BMPR. B2-1/10
(b) Bibliotheque Nationale, Paris
(c) Getty (Sotheby microfiche). National Art Library, Victoria & Albert Museum, London (Reference: 23.XX)
(d) Christies, London
(e) Getty. Frick Museum, New York. Courtauld Institute, London
(f) Frick Museum, New York
(g) Getty (Sotheby microfiche). BMPR. B2-31/11
(h) Getty (Sotheby microfiche). British Library. S-CS 239(6).
(i) Christies, London

Books and Prints sold by Charles Heath's Assignees in May and June 1826, of which no other record has been found

A. Books with engravings by Charles Heath

Item 54. *Common Prayer Book* ('after Corbould')
Item 55. *Parry's Voyages*
Item 362. *Views in Chester* (etchings after Pickering)

B. Separate Prints (by James or Charles Heath)

Item 11 & 406. Burke
Item 11 & 406. Sheridan
Item 116. Earl of Dartmouth, after Phillips
Item 167. Mary, Queen of Scots
Item 167. Sir John Moore
Item 168. Mr Sinclair
Item 168. Mr Bunn
Item 168. Mrs Crouch
Item 169. Dryden
Item 169. Paley
Item 169. Burns
Item 169. Dr Blair.
Item 169. The Pretender
Item 281. Lord Clarendon

Item 349. Lucien Bonaparte's Charlemagne (private plate)
Item 403. Lord Willoughby de Broke
Item 403. Mrs Chinnery
Item 404. Henry Salt
Item 405. Duke and Duchess of Kent
Item 406. Lord Bacon
Item 407. Duke of Bedford.
Item 407. Mrs Barbault
Item 408. Nicol (the printer)
Item 408. R. Jodrell

ANNEX C

Analysis of print-runs, sales and payments made to Charles Heath for his main Annuals and gift books (1832-47)

	THE KEEPSAKE					PICTURESQUE ANNUAL					BOOK OF BEAUTY					TURNER'S ANNUAL TOUR				GEMS OF BEAUTY
Year	Printed small	Printed large	Sold small	Sold large	Paid to CH	Printed small	Printed large	Sold small	Sold large	Paid to CH	Printed small	Printed large	Sold small	Sold large	Paid to CH	Printed small	Printed large	Sold small	Sold large	Printed
1832	7376	231	6918	159		7327	402	6780	201											
1833	6808	171	6498	112	£3000	5656	222	4942	128		2874	85	2329	45		1617	109			
1834	6111	122	5097	70	£2950	5123	142	3727	90	£1513	4271	87	2649	48	£1046	1417	175			
1835	3868	110	3277	41	£2980	3349	114	1971	38	£1362	2709	75	2362	30		1297	159	1293		
1836					£3000					£1850						Children of Nobility				
1837	5268	74	3531	45	£2920	4631	69	3108	42	£1650	4500	57	2754	34	£1250			1442	10	2000
1838		3696		2978	£1250		2996		1981	£1450	1837									2294
1839						49	3438	27	1817	£1500		3196		2799						
1840					£700		3451			£1425	49	3997	28	2482						
1841				2604			2174	23	1769	£1120	49	3025	24	2515		427				
1842	23	3102		2331	£1800*		2500		1624											
1843	23	3100	12	2128			2000		1420											
1844	23	2885	9	1934			1994		1311		25	3000								
1845									1155			3000		2017						
1846												2500		1880						
1847												2399		1555						

Note: Numbers sold, as recorded above, relate only to the current year of issue; there were some sales thereafter, with remainder sales in 1840, 1842 and 1848

Source: Longmans archives: extracts from accounts

* = paid to trustees

ANNEX D

Correspondence Relating to Turner's 'Picturesque Views in England and Wales, 1826-36'.

This correspondence between Charles Heath and Dawson Turner relates to J.M.W. Turner's 'Picturesque Views in England and Wales, 1826-36'.

Letter from Charles Heath to Dawson Turner dated 19 February 1825.

I have just begun a most splendid work from Turner the Academician. he is making me 120 Drawings of England and Wales – I have just got four and they are the finest things I ever saw they cost me 30 Gins each and I have been offered 50 Gins each by two or three different Gentlemen. The Drawings, what is very unusual they will yield a Profit as much as the Plates, they will be engraved the size of the coast work of Cookes, "any one who has seen them says it will be the best and most lucrative speculation ever executed of that description. I mean to have them engraved by all the first Artists. Messrs Hurst & Robinson are to have half the work on condition they find all the capital necessary – so that I have half the Drawings and half the Profits at no risk – I shall send you fine Proofs of course of the whole work. The Art of Engraving never flourished as it now does – there is so much doing that every Engraver is full...

Extract from letter from Charles Heath to Dawson Turner, 12 April 1825.

...I shall in my next parcel send you the first Plate for my grand work from Turner of England & Wales 120 Plates to be engraved by all the first rate artists.

Extract from letter from Charles Heath to Dawson Turner, 23 January 1826.

...the news of this morning is that Messrs Hurst & Robinson have commenced paying again – and from the quarters I have heard it from I think it true. but a blow has been struck that will be felt by every one the most distantly connected with them. nearly all the Booksellers have suffered and as for getting a farthing in the shape of money it is absolutely impossible and for Bills no one will look at them. the times are indeed aweful. For myself I know not what to do, I must candidly confess to you that I fear I shall one way and another be implicated beyond my means tho' I trust no one will eventually lose by me...

Extract from a letter to Dawson Turner from Charles Heath, after writing about the success of his first 'Keepsake' Annual.

14 December 1827: The return is beyond my most sanguine expectations – my Publishers cannot get them fast enough. The large paper are at a very large Premium selling for 5 guineas each. the small paper has sold already *ten thousand* and I must reprint... independent of the book I have sold by Mr Jennings nearly all the Proofs taken separately and sold at 2, 3 and 4 guineas a set...

Extract from a letter from Charles Heath to Dawson Turner, 27 February 1834.

...You are aware that Messrs Longman & Co. supply me with all the money I require for my four Annuals on the security of the works. Now my most beautiful & most splendid work, the "England & Wales" as you know proceeds but very slowly – the reason is want of Capital – could I get the number out 3 or four a year I should sell half as many more, get the work completed in three years when it would be a most valuable property. Now I propose for you to lend me on my own Bills payable with interest £1500 – or should it be required which I do not think it will, £2000... As your security I propose to make over to you the whole of the Plates & stock amounting in value if sold tomorrow to at least £4000...

Extract from a letter from Charles Heath to Dawson Turner, 11 July 1836.

When you were so kind and liberal as to lend me the £600 on my own Bills... to complete the England work from "turner" I fully expected to have accomplished it by about *this* time – but I fear it will now owing to the difficulties of getting all the Drawings from Mr Turner and other contingencies be after Xmas. The 21st number is just ready – 22nd will be in about 2 months – the other two at Xmas – which completes this most beautiful work, and I think I may safely aver that there will never be another like it...

Extract from a letter from Charles Heath to Dawson Turner, 24 April 1838.

I am happy to tell you that at last the "England & Wales" is completed and the last number will be published in a few days... P.S. As I shall not be able to dispose of the England & Wales as I mentioned till the next October sale of "Longmans" and as one of the 100 [pound] Bills comes due next Month which you so kindly cashed to enable me to complete it – perhaps you will oblige me by renewing it...

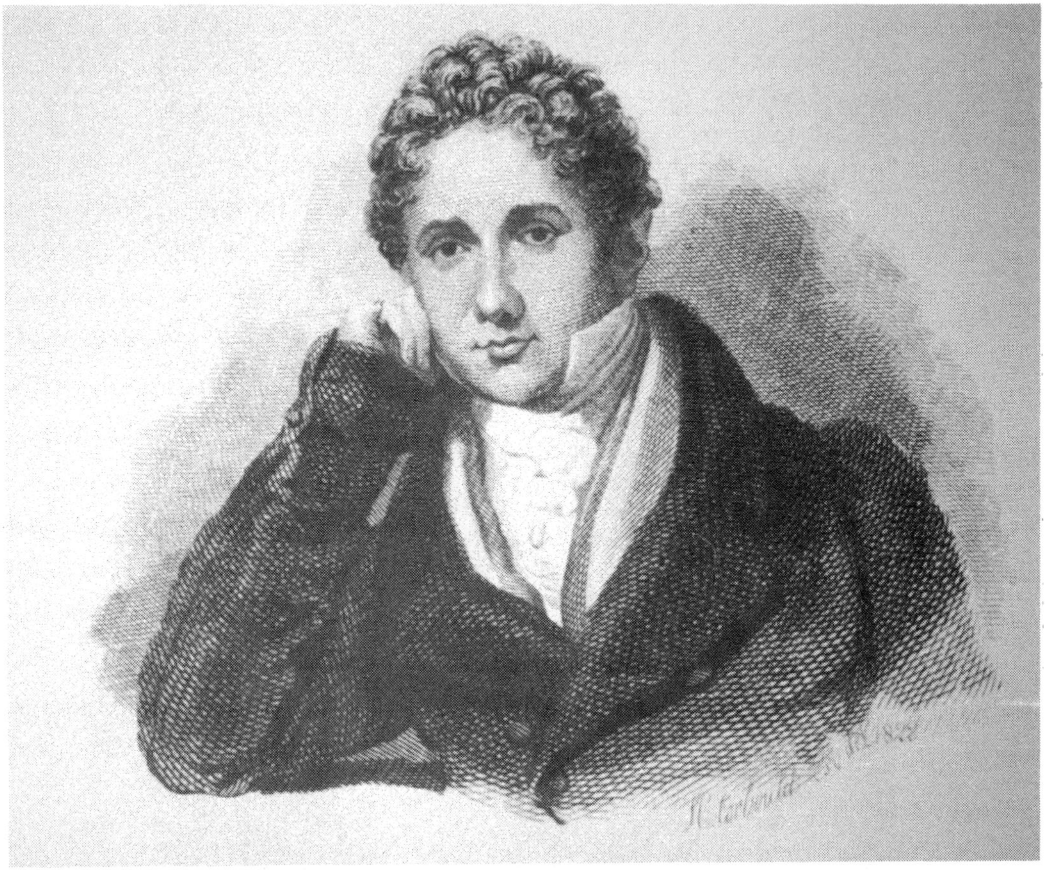

Charles Heath. Engraving by Mrs Elizabeth Dawson Turner, ca.1820.

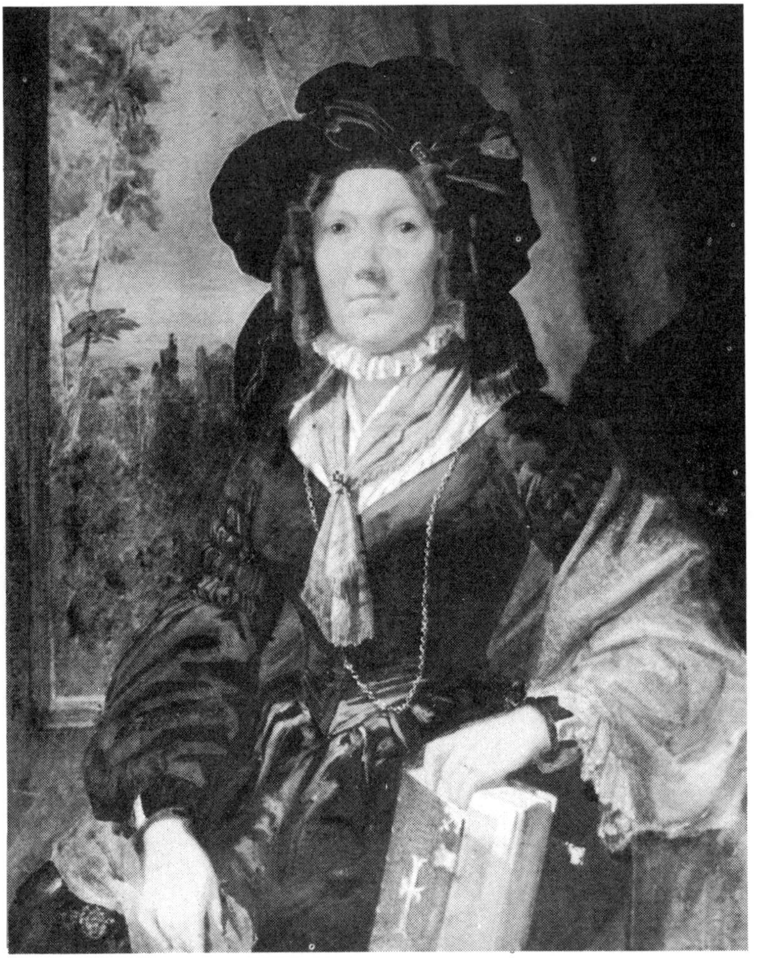

Mrs Elizabeth Heath, née Petch, after a painting by Edward Henry Corbould.

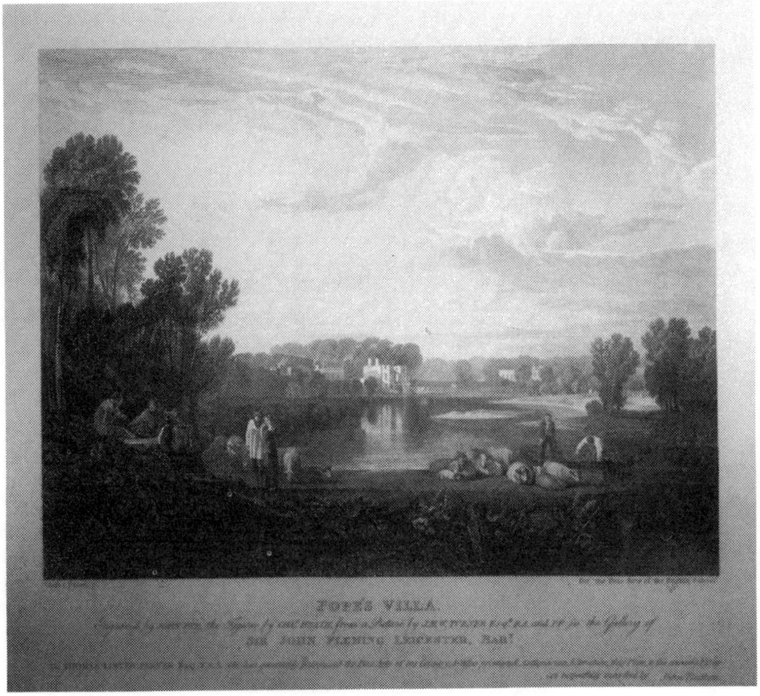

Line engraving: 'Pope's Villa' after J.M.W. Turner R.A., by John Pye and Charles Heath, 1811.

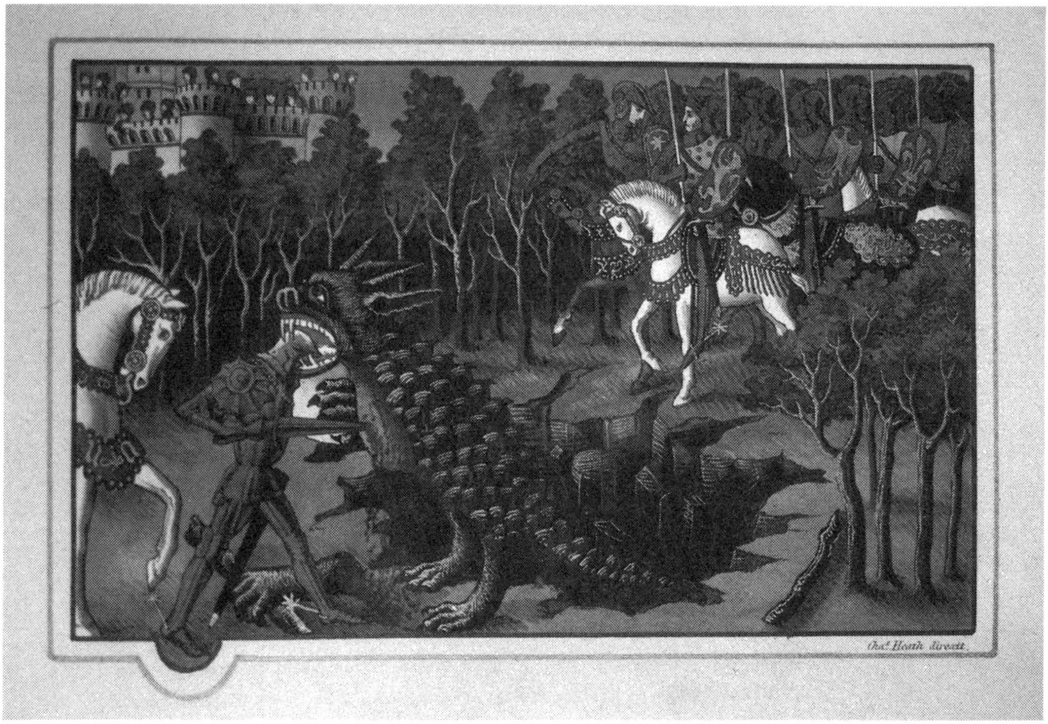

Coloured etching from 'The Valiant Knight Arthur'. Directed by Charles Heath. 1814.

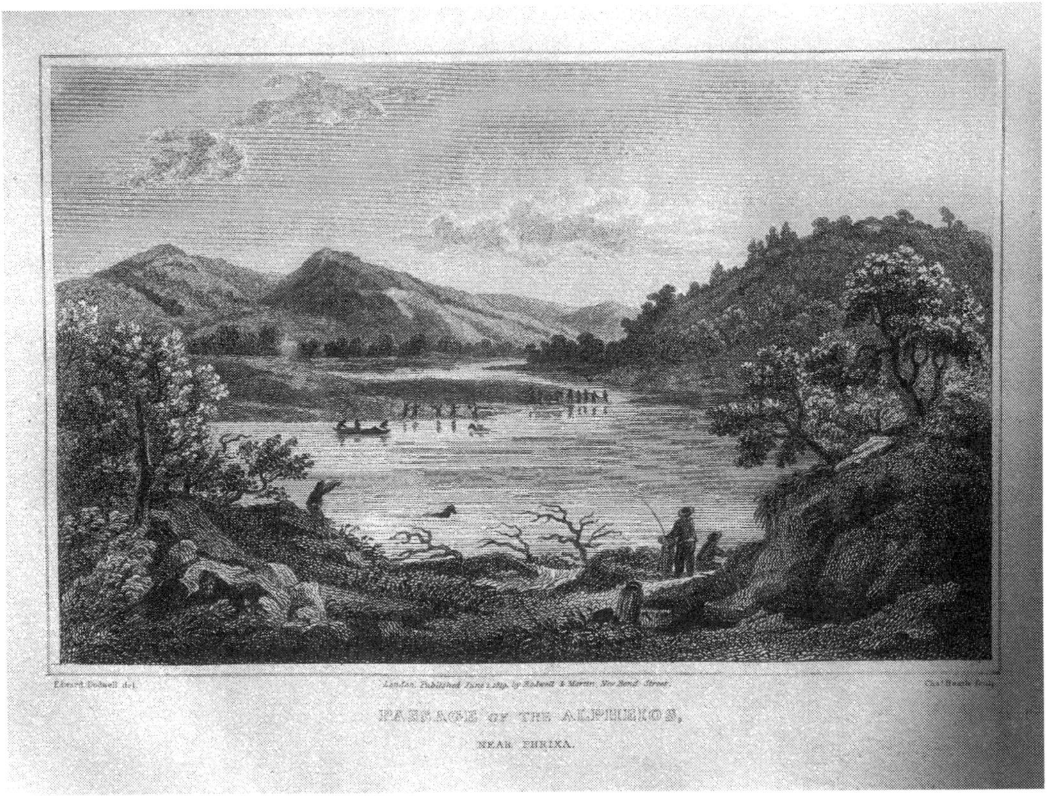

'Passage of the Alpheios' from Dodwell's Tour of Greece, *1819.*

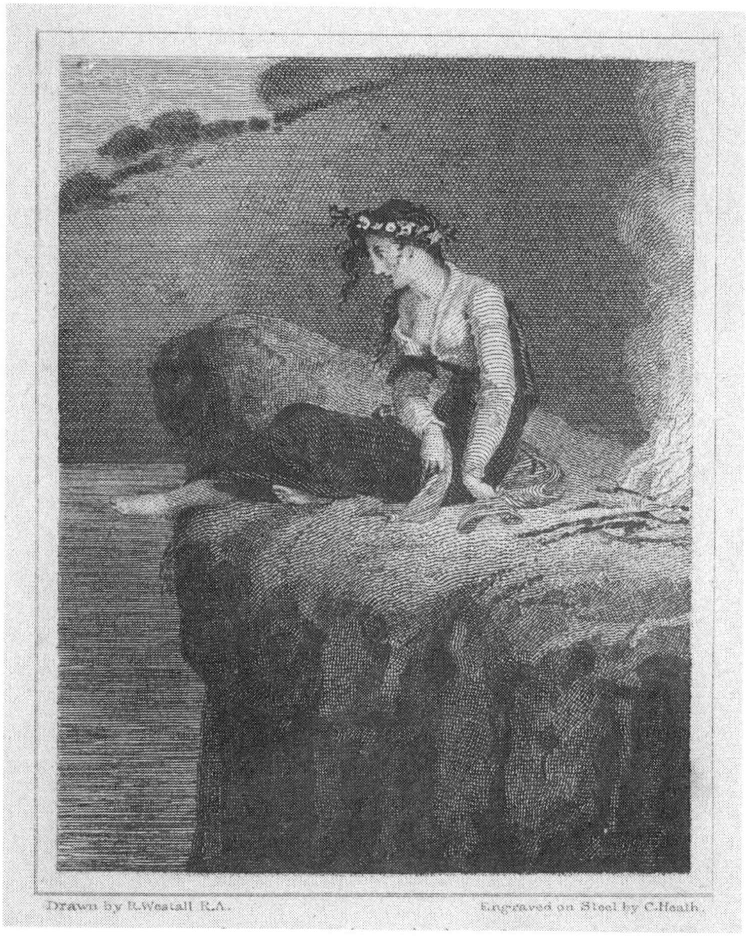

Campbell's Pleasures of Hope, *1820. A print from the first book with steel engraved illustrations.*

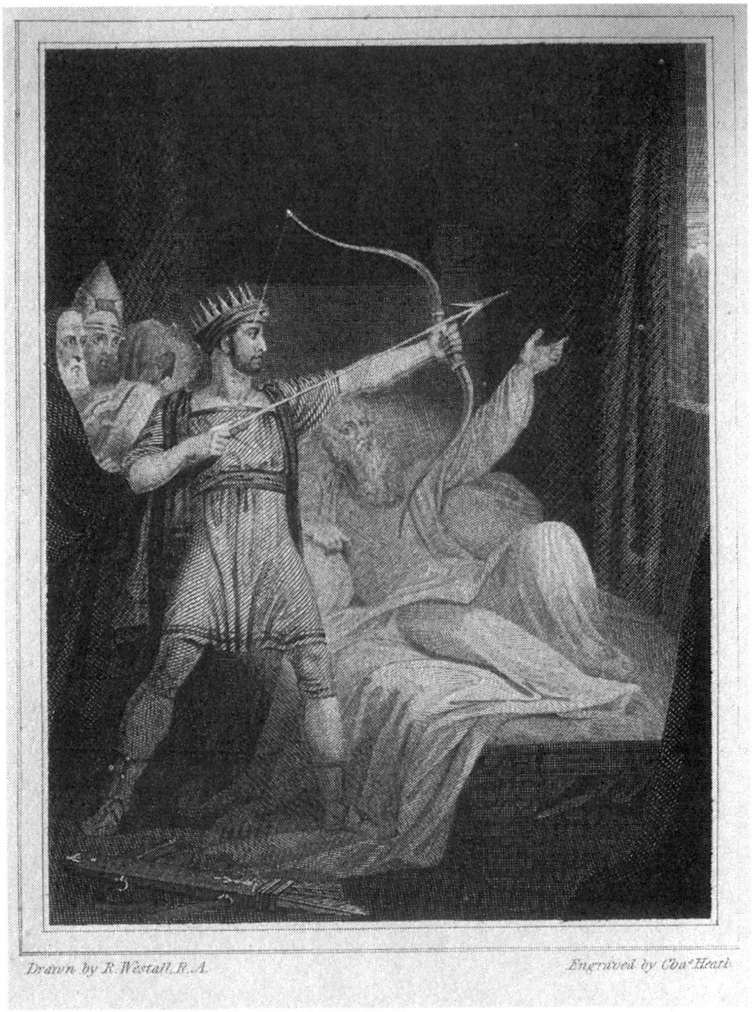

'Elisha on his Deathbed', engraving on copper, dated 1821, from the Holy Bible, *first published in 1815.*

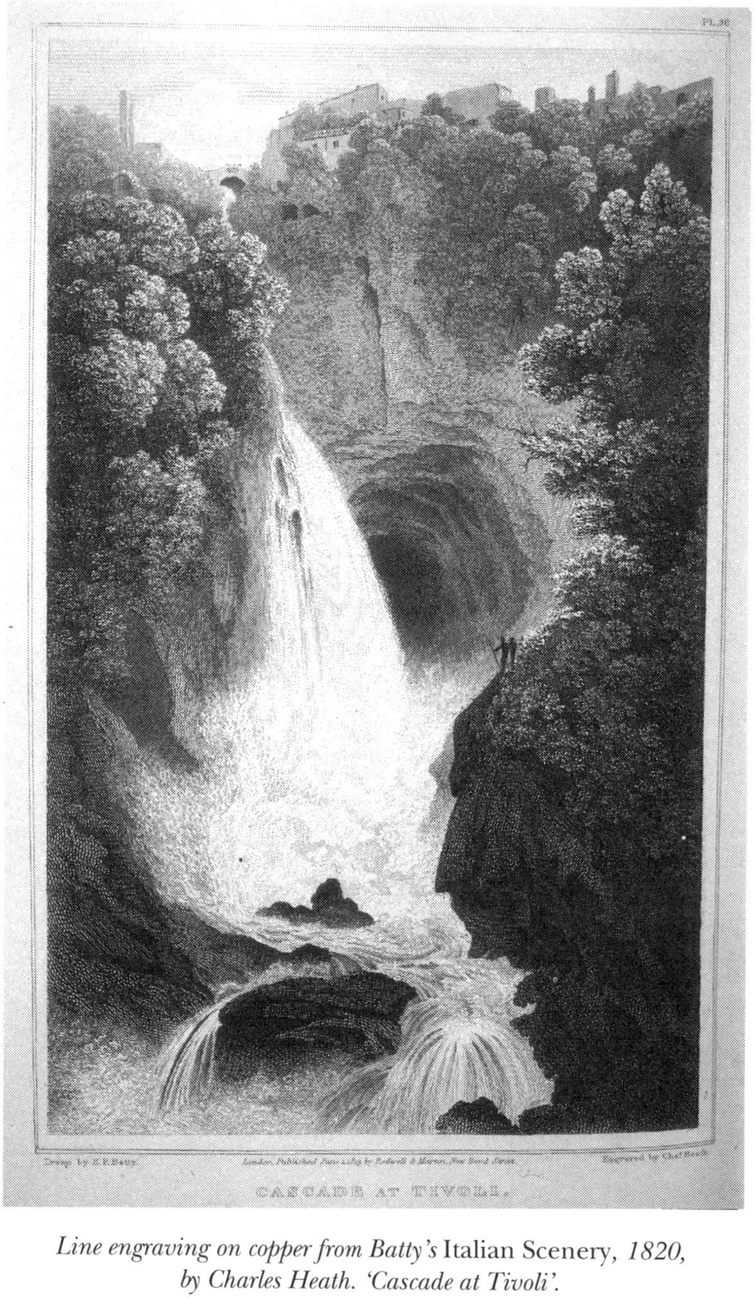

Line engraving on copper from Batty's Italian Scenery, *1820,*
by Charles Heath. 'Cascade at Tivoli'.

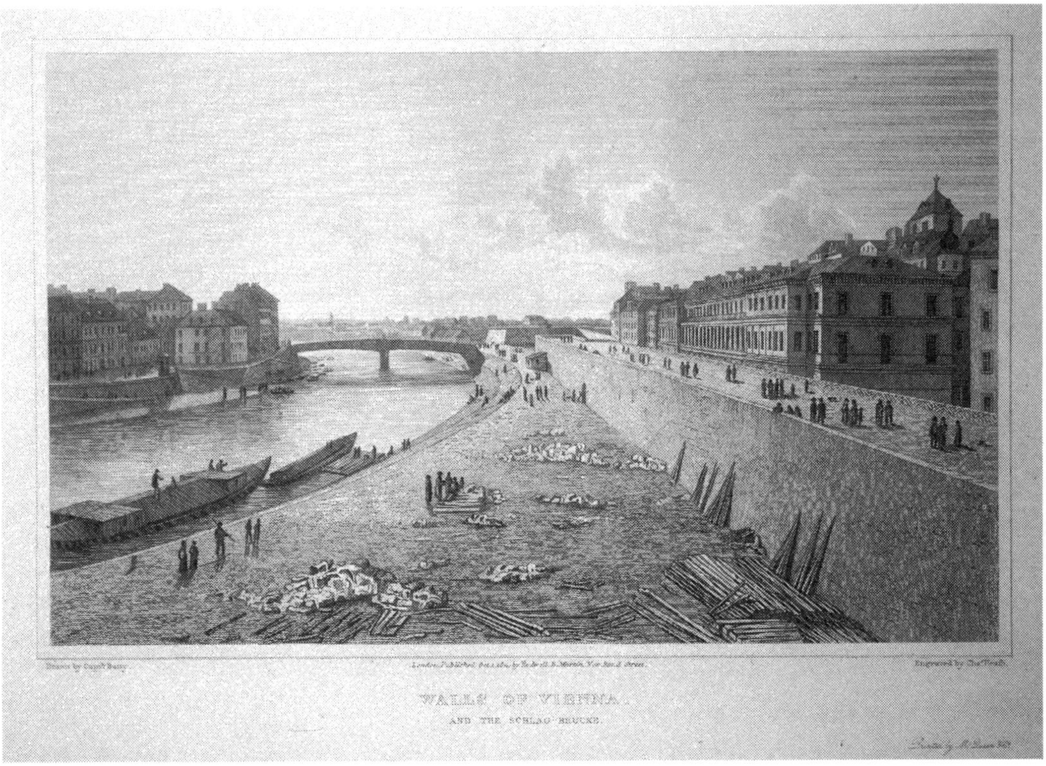

Line engraving on copper from Batty's German Scenery, *1823, by Charles Heath. 'Vienna'.*

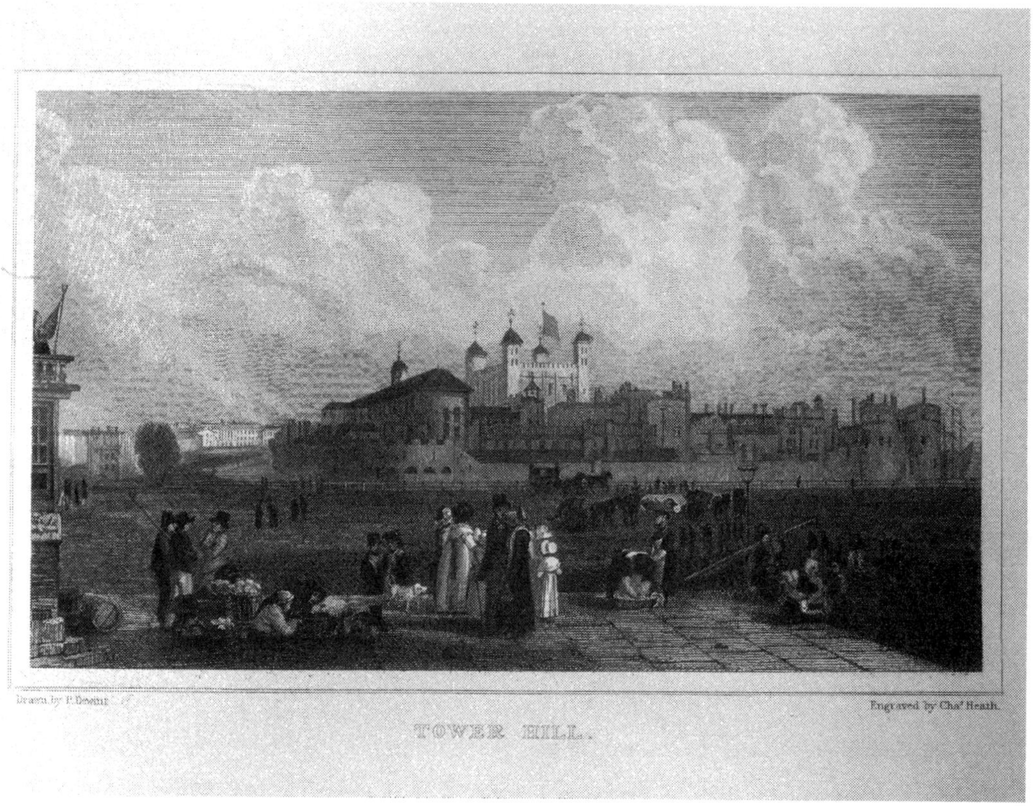

Steel engraving: 'Tower Hill', from Views in and about London, *1825.*

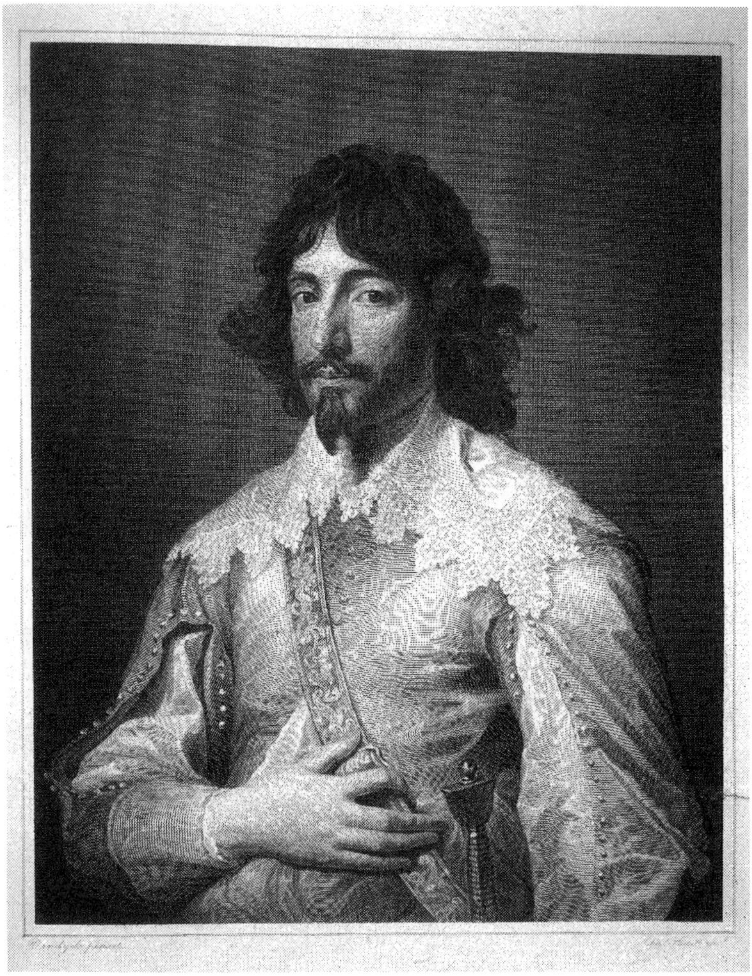

Charles Heath: Line engraving on copper, 1823. 'Gentleman of the Court of King Charles I.'

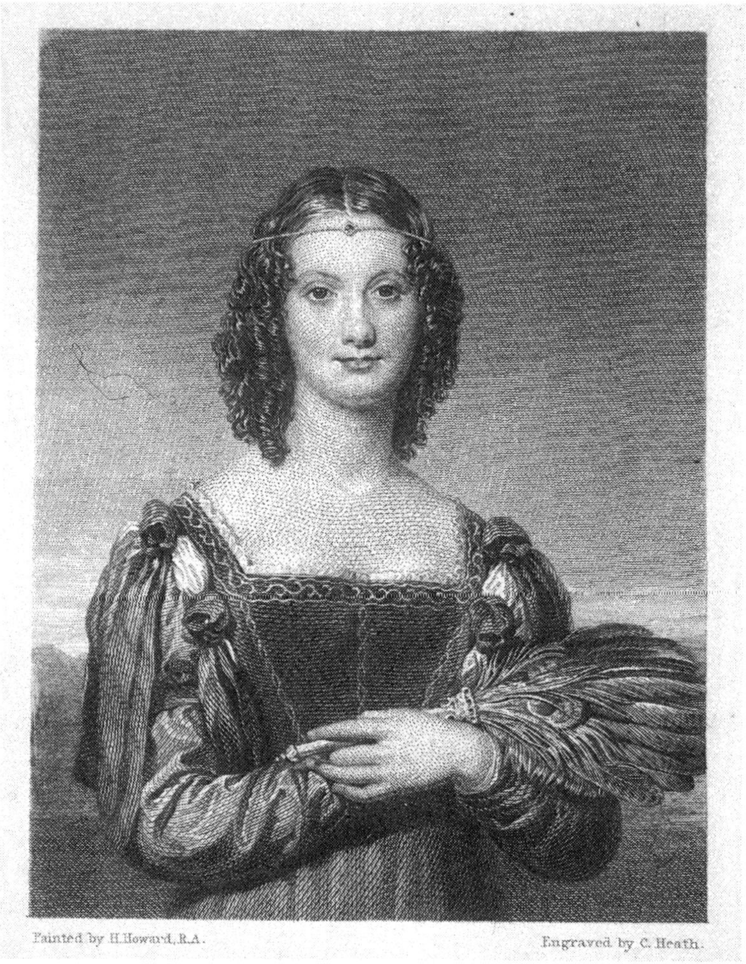

Steel engraving: 'Girl in a Florentine Costume',
from The Literary Souvenir, *1827.*

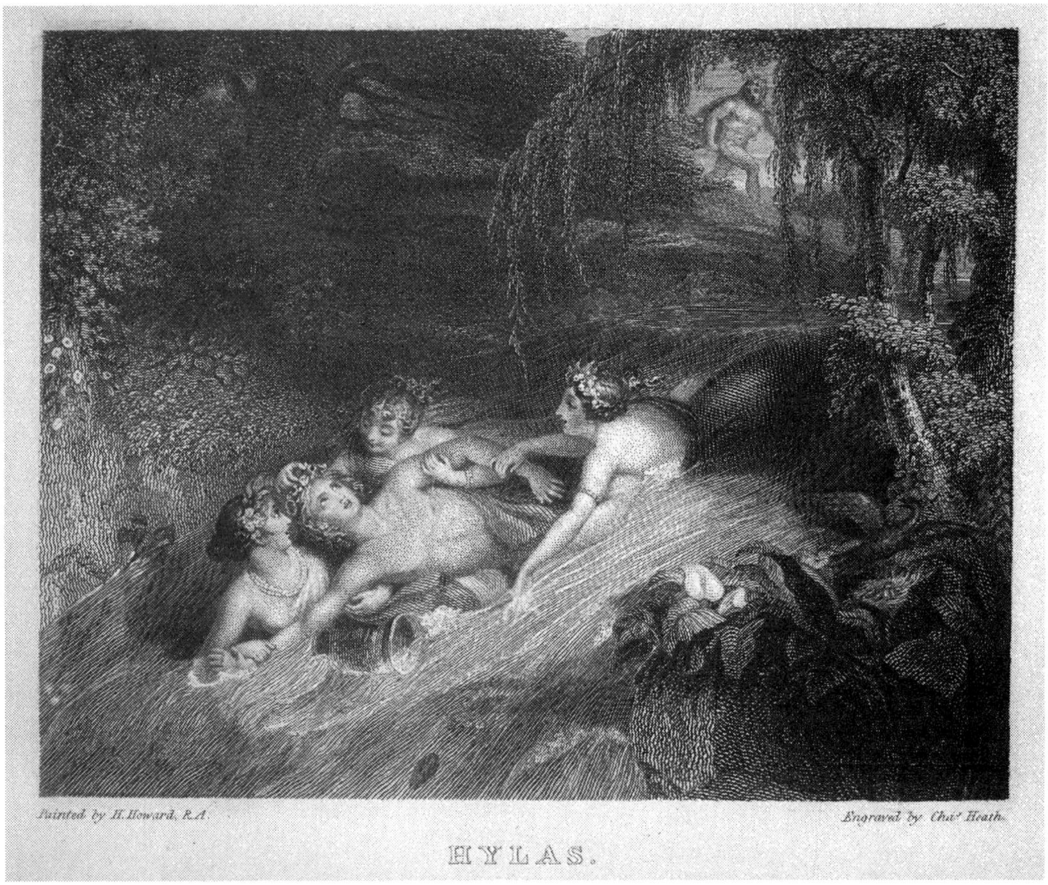

Steel engraving: 'Hylas' by Charles Heath, from The Keepsake, *1828.*

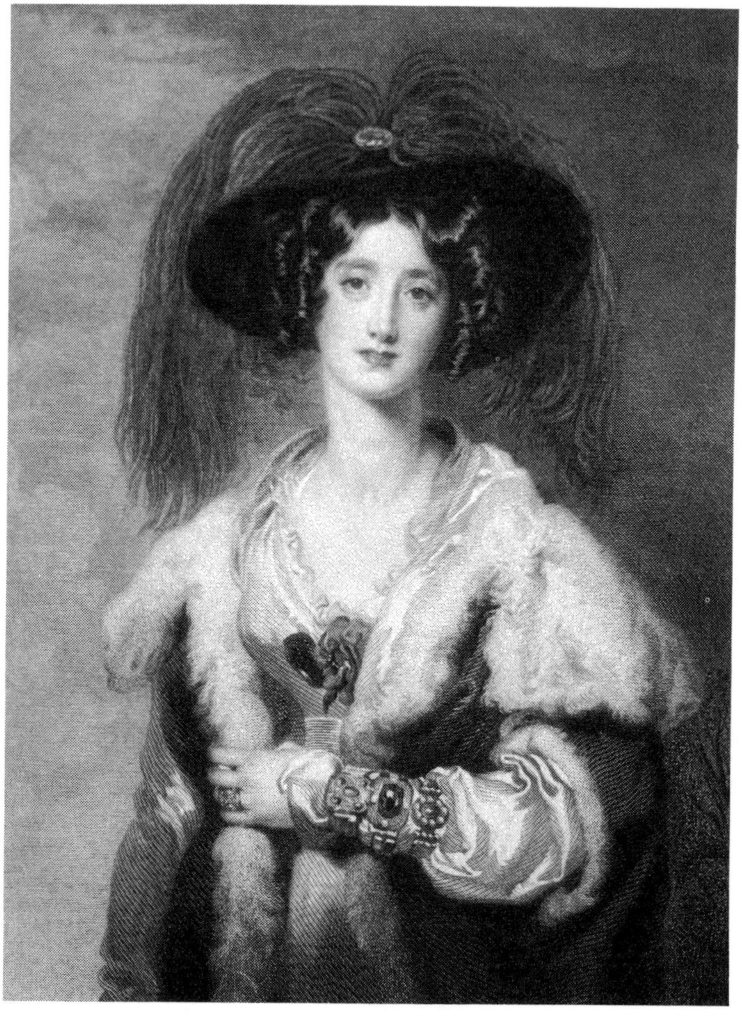

Steel engraving: 'Mrs Peel', from The Keepsake, *1829. 'Flesh' by Charles Heath.*

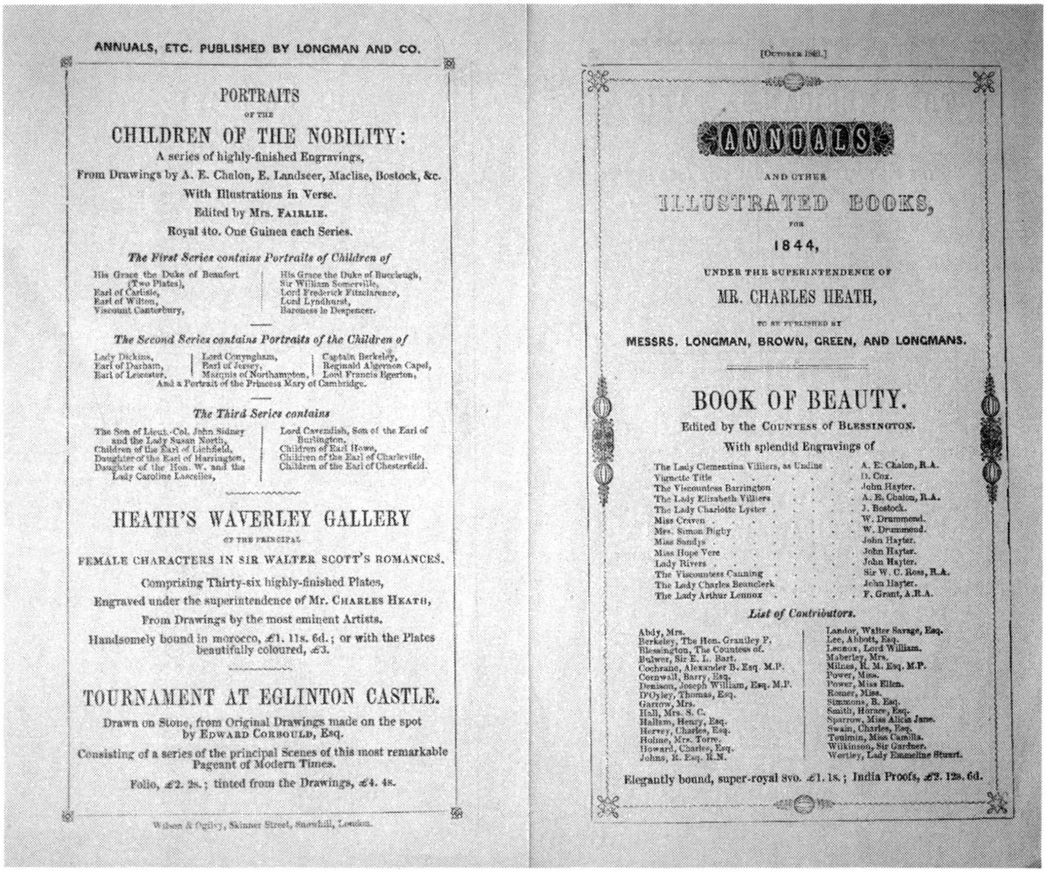
ANNUALS, ETC. PUBLISHED BY LONGMAN AND CO.

PORTRAITS
OF THE
CHILDREN OF THE NOBILITY:
A series of highly-finished Engravings,
From Drawings by A. E. Chalon, E. Landseer, Maclise, Bostock, &c.
With Illustrations in Verse.
Edited by Mrs. FAIRLIE.
Royal 4to. One Guinea each Series.

The First Series contains Portraits of Children of

His Grace the Duke of Beaufort (Two Plates),
Earl of Carlisle,
Earl of Wilton,
Viscount Canterbury,
His Grace the Duke of Buccleugh,
Sir William Somerville,
Lord Frederick Fitzclarence,
Lord Lyndhurst,
Baroness le Despencer.

The Second Series contains Portraits of the Children of

Lady Dickins,
Earl of Durham,
Earl of Leicester,
Lord Conyngham,
Earl of Jersey,
Marquis of Northampton,
Captain Berkeley,
Reginald Algernon Capel,
Lord Francis Egerton,
And a Portrait of the Princess Mary of Cambridge.

The Third Series contains

The Son of Lieut.-Col. John Sidney and the Lady Susan North,
Children of the Earl of Lichfield,
Daughter of the Earl of Harrington,
Daughter of the Hon. W. and the Lady Caroline Lascelles,
Lord Cavendish, Son of the Earl of Burlington,
Children of Earl Howe,
Children of the Earl of Charleville,
Children of the Earl of Chesterfield.

HEATH'S WAVERLEY GALLERY
OF THE PRINCIPAL
FEMALE CHARACTERS IN SIR WALTER SCOTT'S ROMANCES.
Comprising Thirty-six highly-finished Plates,
Engraved under the superintendence of Mr. CHARLES HEATH,
From Drawings by the most eminent Artists.
Handsomely bound in morocco, £1. 11s. 6d.; or with the Plates beautifully coloured, £3.

TOURNAMENT AT EGLINTON CASTLE.
Drawn on Stone, from Original Drawings made on the spot by EDWARD CORBOULD, Esq.
Consisting of a series of the principal Scenes of this most remarkable Pageant of Modern Times.
Folio, £2. 2s.; tinted from the Drawings, £4. 4s.

Wilson & Ogilvy, Skinner Street, Snowhill, London.

[OCTOBER 1843.]

ANNUALS
AND OTHER
ILLUSTRATED BOOKS,
FOR
1844,
UNDER THE SUPERINTENDENCE OF
MR. CHARLES HEATH,
TO BE PUBLISHED BY
MESSRS. LONGMAN, BROWN, GREEN, AND LONGMANS.

BOOK OF BEAUTY.
Edited by the COUNTESS OF BLESSINGTON.
With splendid Engravings of

The Lady Clementina Villiers, as Undine	A. E. Chalon, R.A.
Vignette Title	D. Cox.
The Viscountess Barrington	John Hayter.
The Lady Elizabeth Villiers	A. E. Chalon, R.A.
The Lady Charlotte Lyster	J. Bostock.
Miss Craven	W. Drummond.
Mrs. Simon Bigby	W. Drummond.
Miss Sandys	John Hayter.
Miss Hope Vere	John Hayter.
Lady Rivers	John Hayter.
The Viscountess Canning	Sir W. C. Ross, R.A.
The Lady Charles Beauclerk	John Hayter.
The Lady Arthur Lennox	F. Grant, A.R.A.

List of Contributors.

Abdy, Mrs.
Berkeley, The Hon. Grantley F.
Blessington, The Countess of.
Bulwer, Sir E. L. Bart.
Cochrane, Alexander B. Esq. M.P.
Cornwall, Barry, Esq.
Denison, Joseph William, Esq. M.P.
D'Oyley, Thomas, Esq.
Garrow, Mrs.
Hall, Mrs. S. C.
Hallam, Henry, Esq.
Hervey, Charles, Esq.
Holme, Mrs. Torre.
Howard, Charles, Esq.
Johns, R. Esq. R.N.
Landor, Walter Savage, Esq.
Lee, Abbott, Esq.
Lennox, Lord William.
Maberley, Mrs.
Milnes, R. M. Esq. M.P.
Power, Miss.
Power, Miss Ellen.
Romer, Miss.
Simmons, B. Esq.
Smith, Horace, Esq.
Sparrow, Miss Alicia Jane.
Swain, Charles, Esq.
Toulmin, Miss Camilla.
Wilkinson, Sir Gardner.
Wortley, Lady Emmeline Stuart.

Elegantly bound, super-royal 8vo. £1. 1s.; India Proofs, £2. 12s. 6d.

Longmans brochure of Charles Heath's publications, 1844.

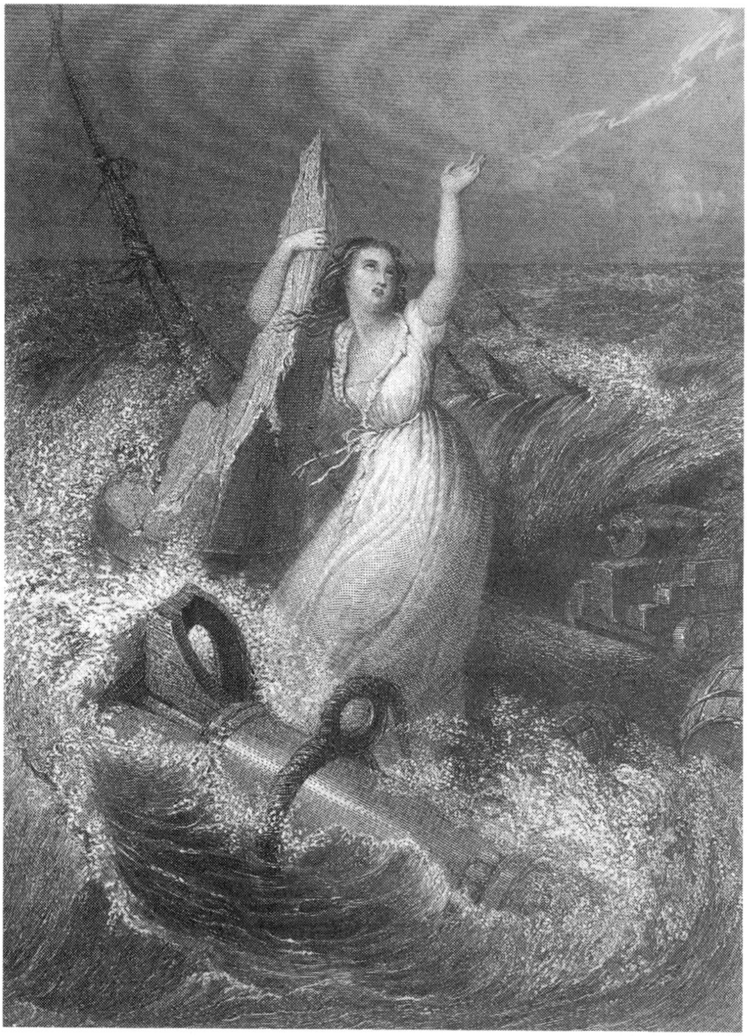

Etched steel engraving: 'The Last Moment' from
The Keepsake *for 1848.*

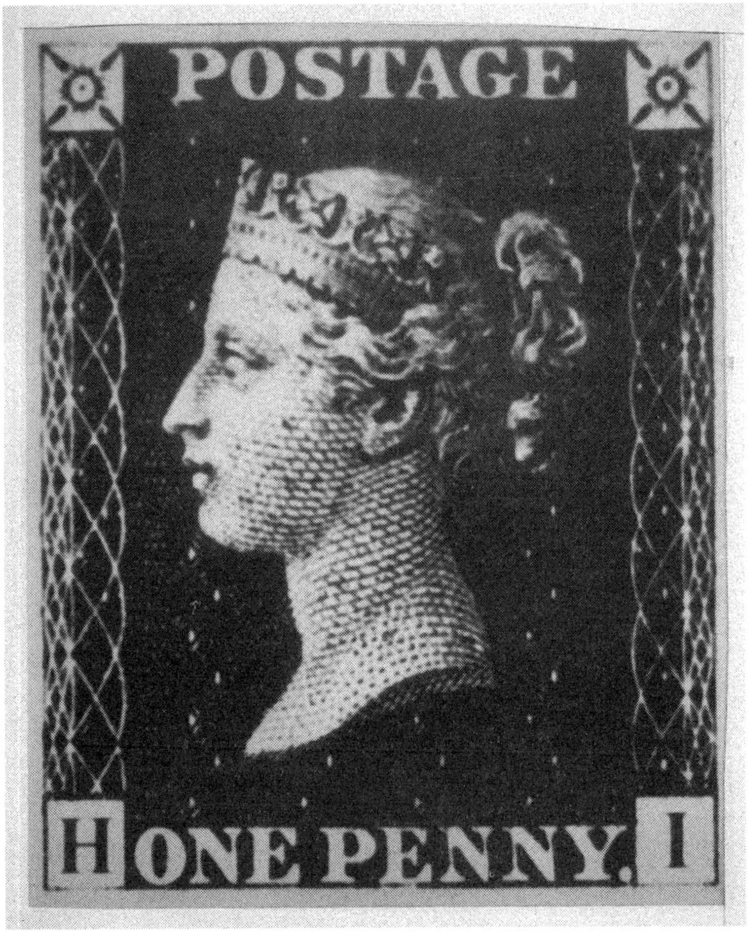

The line engraved first postage stamp, the 'Penny Black'.
Engraved by Frederick and Charles Heath, 1840.

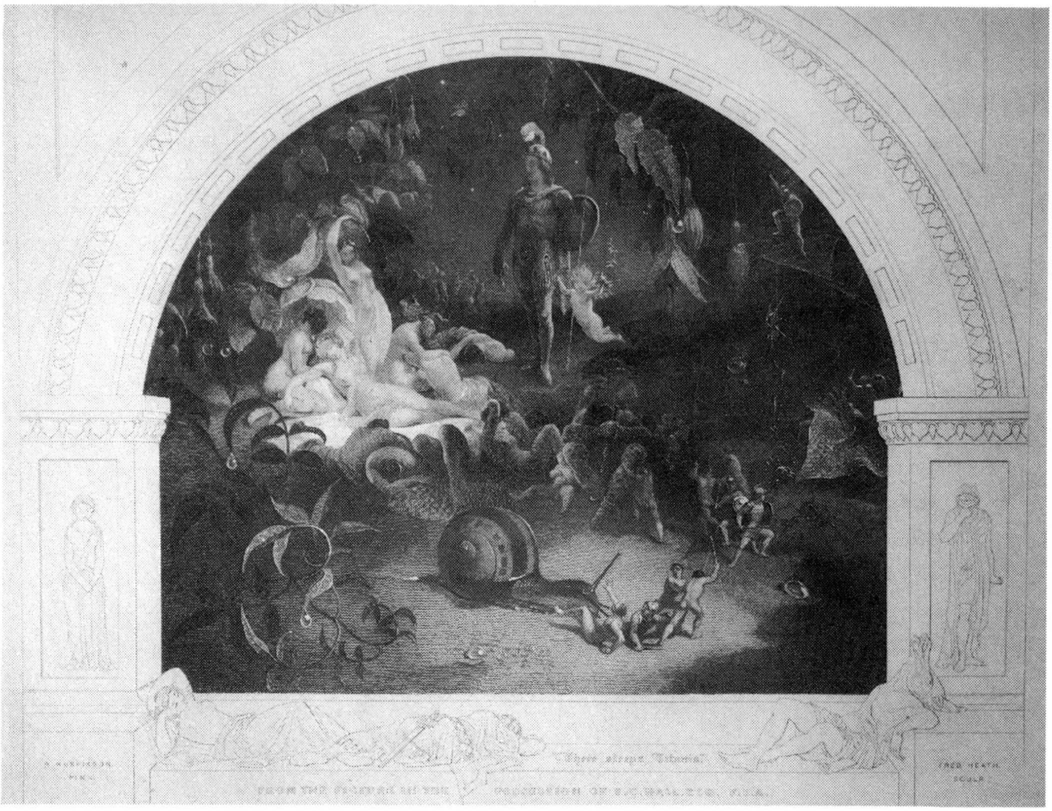

Frederick Heath: steel engraving, 'There sleeps Titania…' Art Union, 1848.

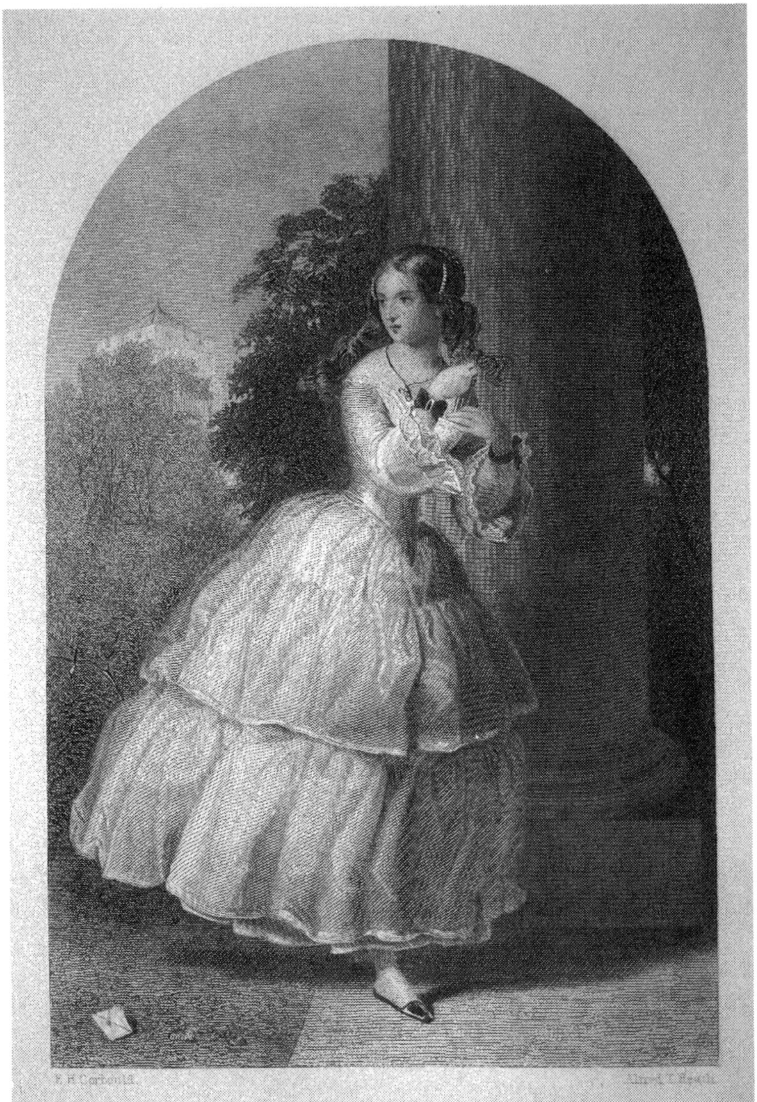

Alfred Heath, etched steel engraving: 'The Valentine'
from The Literary Gift Book, *ca.1856.*

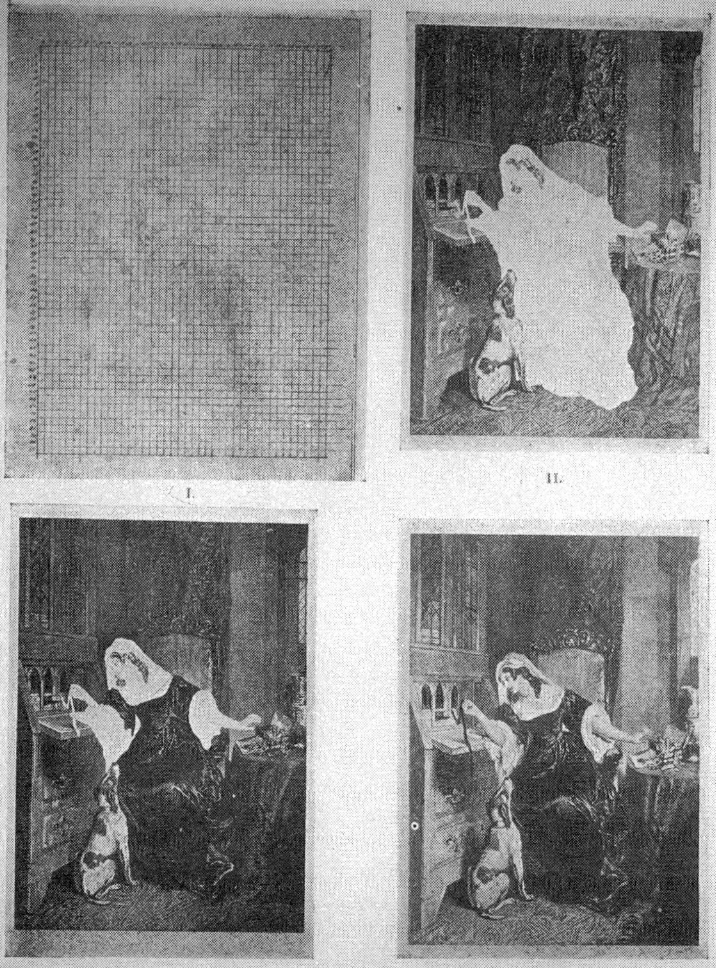

THE WIDOWED BRIDE.

Showing (I) The Reduction. (II & III) Engraver's Trial Proofs. (IV) Finished Proof.
From engraver's proofs, by Edwards.
(Size of original engravings, $3\frac{3}{8}$ in. by $4\frac{3}{8}$ in.)

[To face page 206.

The four stages in the making of a steel engraving.
1) The reduction.
2) and 3) The engraver's trial proofs.
4) The finished proof.

A Catalogue Raisonné of the Works of Charles Heath & His Sons

References

*	Author's collection
BMPR	British Museum Print Room
BL Mss	British Library Manuscript Department
BL	British Library
V&A	Victoria and Albert Print Library
NAL	National Art Library, Victoria and Albert Museum
RA	Royal Academy Library
NPG	National Portrait Gallery, London
Guildhall	Guildhall Library, London
Witt	Witt Collection, Courtauld Institute
Huntington	Huntington Library, Pasadena, California
NYPL	New York Public Library, New York
Houghton	Houghton Library, Harvard, Massachusetts
YCBA	Yale Center for British Art, Yale, Connecticut
Beinecke	Beinecke Rare Book and Manuscript Library, Yale University, New Haven
PFL	Philadelphia Free Library
Getty	Getty Museum Library, San Marino, California

Notes

a) Book references will be found in the bibliography.
b) Print sizes are given to the nearest centimetre.
c) Where a book engraving is dated, but the date of the publication of the book came later, the year entry and reference number (unless otherwise stated) relates to the earlier date. If there were several different dates for the book engravings, the book publication date is adhered to.

d) Where there is a reference to an earlier edition, which may have contained book illustrations by one or other of the Heath engravers, but has not yet been traced, the reference number relates to the later edition.

e) Where the date of publication of an illustrated book spans two or more years, the entry date in the catalogue is for the first years of the publication, unless the engravings can be separately identified by appearing in later volumes, or with specific dates of their own.

f) The place of publication is in London, unless otherwise stated.

g) Blank spaces under individual headings in the catalogue mean that no information has been found.

h) The 'size' of the plate, as shown in the catalogue, relates to the dimensions of the engraved design (vertical first, then horizontal), and does not include any caption there may be.

i) Engravings by Charles Heath can be distinguished from those of his father by the inscription 'Charles Heath', 'Charles Heath junr', 'Chas Heath', or 'C. Heath'. Prints engraved when the two men were working together (i.e. between 1807 and 1822) which carry the inscription 'Heath' (or 'James', 'Jas.', or 'I. Heath') are by James Heath.

Ref No.	Book Title (Separate Print: S.P.)	Engraved After	Nos.	Caption & Page Reference	Size (cms)	Other Engravers
1	**1791** S.P.		1	Head of a woman (? a housemaid)	8x5	
2	**1801** S.P.		1	Portrait of 'a gypsey'		
3	**1802** S.P.		1	'Apollo as a Warrior'	33x24	
4	S.P.		1	Hercules	21x13	
5	S.P.		1	Head of Christ	11x12	
6	S.P.		1	Head of a man	5x5	
7	S.P.		1	Infant with tambourine	14x9	
8	S.P.		1	Cupid with a horn ('Amor')	5x5	
9	S.P.		1	Three cherubs bathing	21x8	
10	S.P.		1	Boy playing a violin	20x10	

Publisher	Location & References	Notes
	BMPR.C.5*	Inscribed 'C. Heath sc Dec 24, 1791' Charles Heath's first etching at the age of 6 ¾
	Royal Academy (436)	Exhibited by 'Master C. Heath, 15 Russell Place' at the Royal Academy in 1801. Possibly his first work as an apprentice, in the form of a polyautograph.
	BMPR.190.b.1 BMPR.C.260 V&A.ES 102D (E1101-1899) Man 104	Included in 'Specimens of Polyautography' (Part IV) published in 1806 by G.J. Vollweiler, but with the date '1802'; it may have been intended for the first part originally published in 1803. This is probably the same print as that exhibited at the Royal Academy in 1802 entitled 'Satan arousing his troops (Milton)', inscribed 'C. Heath del' as No.459 'exhibited by Master C. Heath, 15 Russell Place'.
	Man 92	Pen signed 'C Heath'
	Man 95	Pencil signed 'C Heath del, trial proof'
	BMPR.C.260 Man 91	Polyautograph inscribed 'C. Heath 1802'
	Man 89 NYPL	Polyautograph 'C. Heath del'
	BMPR.C.260 Man 90	Polyautograph inscribed 'C. Heath May 27, 1802'
	BMPR.C.260 Man 87	Polyautograph inscribed 'C. Heath Feb 11, 1802'
	BMPR.C.260 Man 88	Polyautograph inscribed 'C. Heath Feb 15, 1802'

Ref No.	Book Title (Separate Print: S.P.)	Engraved After	Nos.	Caption & Page Reference	Size (cms)	Other Engravers
1	**1803** S.P.		1	Head of an Oriental wearing a turban	38x30	
2	S.P.		1	Scene from Paradise Lost		
3	S.P.	J. Britton	2	Two views of Stonehenge	22x12	
4	**1804** S.P.		1	Armida brought before Godfrey (Tasso's Jerusalem)		
5	S.P.		1	The contention of Achilles and Agammemnon (Homer's Iliad)		
6	S.P.		1	?Chronos	32x23	
7	**1805** S.P.		1	Entrance of Telemachus into the infernal regions		
8	**1806** S.P.		1	Miss F. Lewis		
9	S.P.		1	Master Betty		

Publisher	Location & References	Notes
	BMPR.C.260 Man 96	Polyautograph inscribed 'Mortimer invt, C. Heath del April 19, 1803'. Mentioned in Mackenzie's 'British Prints' (1987)
	Royal Academy (531)	Exhibited by 'Master Charles Heath'
J. Britton		Referred to in Britton's Autobiography Vol III No.5; it was said to have cost Britton £30.
	BMPR.190*.b.1 (72) Royal Academy (534)	Polyautograph inscribed 'C. Heath fecit. Exhibited at Somerset House, 1804'.
	Royal Academy (546)	Polyautograph inscribed 'C. Heath fecit. Exhibited at Somerset House, 1804'
	BMPR. Man 102	Pen signed 'C. Heath del'. This may be the same work as 'Father Time' (see U/D44)
	Royal Academy (662)	Polyautograph. Exhibited at Somerset House in 1805
	Royal Academy (363)	Exhibited at Somerset House in 1806.
	Royal Academy (364)	The Royal Academy record may be in error here, as the engraving of Master Betty, 'The Young Roscius', exhibited in 1806 was probably by James Heath, and not by Charles (unless he engraved a separate print of Master Betty of his own, which has not yet been traced). See Notes to 1807(8) in James Heath's catalogue, and pp.2537-8 and 2542 of Farington's Diary.

Ref No.	Book Title (Separate Print: S.P.)	Engraved After	Nos.	Caption & Page Reference	Size (cms)	Other Engravers
1	The British Gallery of Engravings (Rev'd E. Forster).	Sir Joshua Reynolds P.R.A.	2	1) The Infant Hercules 2) Ecce Homo	17x14 15x13	S. Middiman J. Heath A. Smith L. Schiavonetti J. Fittler A. Raimbach G. Noble I. Taylor W. Skelton J. Pye A. Cardon E. Smith W. Sharp J. Mitan J. Burnett Street Engleheart W. Bromley. N. Schiavonetti
2	The Poems of Ossian (translated by J. MacPherson).	W. White	2	Frontispiece: 'Fingal sat beneath a tree...' Title page: 'Who art thou? said Fingal...'	7x5 5x5	
3	Plays as performed at the Theatre Royal (Mrs Inchbald).	Singleton	1	Vol VIII Know Your own Mind 'Vastly well...'	8x7	J. Heath and others (see James Heath's Catalogue - 1800(3))
4	S.P.		1	Battle of the Angels (Milton). 'O friends, why not come on ?...'		
5	S.P.		4	Four designs from plays		

Publisher	Location & References	Notes
William Miller	* V&A.J.6,f* (1) only)	This volume contains five engravings by James Heath as well (see his catalogue for 1807(1). Although the work is dated '1807', the two prints here are inscribed as 'published in 1810'. They are nevertheless the first examples of large prints by Charles Heath.
J. Walker	*	An earlier edition had engravings by James Heath (see his catalogue for 1806(2)).
Longman, Hurst, Rees and Orme	*	This series was published between 1800 and 1807.
	Royal Academy (575)	? A polyautograph. Exhibited at Somerset House in 1807.
	Royal Academy (367)	Though not identified, these may have been intended for Mrs Inchbald's 'British Theatre' in one or other of its editions.

Ref No.	Book Title (Separate Print: S.P.)	Engraved After	Nos.	Caption & Page Reference	Size (cms)	Other Engravers
6	S.P.		1	Head of General Harington		
7	S.P.		1	Description of the Kymin pavilion		

Publisher	Location & References	Notes
T. Cadell and W. Davies	YCBA.B1978.43 342-522.p.45	The reference here is to a receipt dated October 1807 for £10.10.0 (ten guineas) paid by the publishers to Charles Heath. The print has not been traced.
	YCBA	The Kymin pavilion is near Monmouth on the River Wye.

Ref No.	Book Title (Separate Print: S.P.)	Engraved After	Nos.	Caption & Page Reference	Size (cms)	Other Engravers
1	The Stafford Gallery		24	Vol I		L. Schiavonetti
	(W. Ottley).	L.Bassano		1) The Last Judgement	27x20	W. Bromley
		N.Poussin		2) Penance	13x20	J. Fittler
		N.Poussin		3) The Extreme	12x19	P.W. Tompkins
		N.Poussin		Unction		J. H. Wright
				4) Ordination	13x20	J. Neagle
		N.Poussin		5) Marriage	13x19	G. Corbould
		N.Poussin		6) Moses striking the	11x16	E. Byrne
				Rock		W. Finden
				Vol II		J. Scott
		L.Caracci		7) St Francis with	7x6	J. Wright
				Angels		A. Smith
		A.Caracci		8) The Virgin Child	7x6	I.M. Delattre
				and St Francis		W. Finden
		A.Caracci		9) Christ on the Cross	9x7	J. Fittler
		A.Caracci		10) Danae	9x15	P. Tompkins
		A.Caracci		11) The Infant John	8x6	Worthington
				sleeping		F. Hay
		Guido		12) A Magdalen	6x5	Piccart
		Guercino		13) Landscape	7x10	C. Warren
		Guido		14) The Infant Christ	6x8	G. Corbould
		Domenchino		15) Vision of St Francis	8x7	T. Milton
		Domenchino		16) Landscape and	9x16	I. Taylor
				Figures		
		Domenchino		17) Christ bearing His	7x8	
				Cross		
		P.P.		Vol III		J. Romney
		Rubens		18) Peace and War	15x23	E. Finden
						J. Roffe
				Vol IV		J. Wright
		N.		19) Landscape, Cattle	8x10	J. Neagle
		Berghem		and Figures		P. Tompkins
		N.		20) Returning home in	8x10	I. Delattre
		Berghem		the evening		C. Warren
		N.		21) The Bridge	8x11	W. Finden
		Berghem				

Publisher	Location & References	Notes
Longman, Hurst, Rees and Orme	* V&A.DG 106 (Dyce 3127 and 3128) (1) and 18) only)	This work was published between 1808 and 1818, with most of Charles Heath's plates being dated 1816 or 1817. There are four volumes, Vols I-II and III-IV being usually found bound up together.

Ref No.	Book Title (Separate Print: S.P.)	Engraved After	Nos.	Caption & Page Reference	Size (cms)	Other Engravers
1	The Stafford Gallery (continued)	N. Berghem L. de Varges E. Bird R.A.		22) The Brink of the Ford 23) St John 24) The Death of Earl Douglas	8x10 13x9 13x21	T. Milton L. Byrne Dauthemare E. Byrne Fittler A. W. Warren R. Rhodes J. Landseer T.L. Busby S. Middiman J. Scott
2	The Adventures of Ulysses (Charles Lamb).	H. Corbould R. Corbould	2	Frontispiece: (p.34) Ulysses obliges Circe Title page (p.96) 'There came to him a young shepherd...'	8x5 5x6	
3	The Vicar of Wakefield (Oliver Goldsmith).	Thomas Stothard R.A.	2	Title page 1) No caption 2) The Wretched Delinquent	6x6 9x6	

Publisher	Location & References	Notes
T. Davison	*	First edition, 'For the Juvenile Library'.
W. Suttaby	BMPR.C.20 (Balmanno, Vol III)	These engravings are said to have been replaced by others by J. Romney in the 1813 edition.

Ref No.	Book Title (Separate Print: S.P.)	Engraved After	Nos.	Caption & Page Reference	Size (cms)	Other Engravers
1	The Lay of the Last Minstrel (Sir Walter Scott).	Richard Westall R.A.	6	1) p.20 'She raised her stately head…' 2) p.38 'An' dar'st thou warrior…' 3) p.80 'She thought some spirit of the sky…' 4) p.96 'Thus to the Ladye did Timlinn shew…' 5) p.148 'Yet not Lord Cranstoun…' 6) p.190 'The mitred abbot stretched his hand…'	11x9 12x9	J. Pye
2	The Life of Lord Nelson (Rev'd Clarke and J. M'Arthur).	Benjamin West P.R.A.	1	Frontispiece: 'The Immortality of Nelson'	23x19	J. Landseer A. Raimbach R. Golding A. Smith J. Neagle J. Fittler
3	Marmion (Sir Walter Scott).	Richard Westall R.A.	1	p.109 'Her look compos'd…'	12x9	J. Pye S. Noble J. Mitan Engleheart
4	Voyages and Travels to India, Ceylon, the Red Sea, Abyssinia and Egypt (1802-1806) (Voyages and Travels of Lord Valentia).	H. Salt	1	The Rumi Derwazah and the New Palace at Lucknow	16x22	Angus J. Greig J. Storer Cooper J. Mitan J. Landseer C. Warren Pollard J. Fittler

Publisher	Location & References	Notes
John Sharpe and Longman, Hurst, Rees, Orme and Brown	* V&A.93.D.217 (p.76,82) BL.3.K.5 NYPL.NCM	'Publ. 1.6.1809'. The 13th edition, published in 1812 contains the same engravings. The paginations given are those in the book itself, and not as shown on each print. The Longmans edition bears an 1808 date, and the plates appear respectively on pp.28,48,87,103,160 and 201. A '12th edition' was published in Baltimore by J. Cushing in 1812.
T. Cadell and W. Davies	* BMPR.C.13 Houghton *fEc75 N3337 W809c	Two volumes. The first life of Nelson to appear after his death.
John Sharpe and A. Constable, W. Miller and John Murray (7th edition 1811)	* BMPR.166.c.10 BL.c.70.E2	The engraving also appears in the 8th edition of 1811. The work includes an engraving by James Heath (see his catalogue for 1809(4)). See 1810(4) for a different edition with other engravings by Charles Heath.
W. Miller F.C. and J. Rivington	* BL.1602/15	'Published May 1, 1809'. Bound up in a four volume edition published by Rivingtons in 1811, with the illustrations in the fourth volume.

Ref No.	Book Title (Separate Print: S.P.)	Engraved After	Nos.	Caption & Page Reference	Size (cms)	Other Engravers
1	Cowper's Poems.	Richard Westall R.A.	2	*Vol I* p.328 1) The Lily and the Rose *Vol II* p.24 2) 'Kate is craz'd...'	10x7	J. Heath A. Smith Engleheart J. Romney R. Golding
2	Description of Ancient Terracottas in the British Museum.	W. Alexander	2	Plates VI and XXXII	5x19 6x7 and 6x9	G. Cooke H. Moses W. Bromley R. Rhodes A. Smith J. Neagle Skelton Fittler A. Cardon L. Schiavonetti Worthington
3	The Lady of the Lake (Sir Walter Scott).	Richard Westall R.A.	1	Frontispiece: 'In listening mood...'	11x9	A. Smith S. Noble R. Golding A. Raimbach Engleheart
4	Marmion (Sir Walter Scott).	Richard Westall R.A. Singleton	12	*Vol I* pp.52, 85, 110, 146, 164 *Vol II* pp.26, 49, 93, 110, 167, 170, 201	9x7	
5	Rasselas (Samuel Johnson).	Henry Corbould	1	'And spent day after day on the banks of rivulets...'	9x7	

Publisher	Location & References	Notes
John Sharpe	* V&A.J.6.f (1) only)	A two volume edition which also includes two engravings by James Heath (1810(3) in his catalogue). See also 1820 for another edition with different plates by Charles Heath, and an edition (U/D14) in the Dove's English Classics series ca. 1825. See also 1817(3) for another engraving for 'The Task', also published by Sharpe.
G. and W. Nicol	*	See also 'Description of Ancient Marbles in the British Museum' (1820(11)).
John Sharpe	* V&A.93.D.217 (p.27)	Dated '1.12.1810'.
A. Constable, Edinburgh	* V&A.J.6.b	A two volume sixth edition without captions, published in April 1810.
Longman, Hurst, Rees, Orme and Brown	V&A.I.113	Dated 'October 1, 1810'. For another edition with James Heath plates, see 1817(3) of his catalogue; see the 1827(10) edition in the Dove's English Classics series also.

Ref No.	Book Title (Separate Print: S.P.)	Engraved After	Nos.	Caption & Page Reference	Size (cms)	Other Engravers
6	Cook's British Classics.	Richard Cook	2	Vol II No.81 The Idler Vol XXIV p.107	12x8	
7	Elegant Extracts from the most eminent prose writers.	Richard Westall R.A. Henry Corbould	4	*Book I* 'Studio Fallante Laborem' *Book II* The vision of Mirza *Book IV* Demosthenes declaiming on the shore *Book IX* The disabled Soldier	4z6	J. Romney S. Noble J. Pye Davenport

Publisher	Location & References	Notes
W. Suttaby	BMPR.C.13	'Publ. April 30, 1810'.
John Sharpe J. Sharpe/W. Jennings (later editions)	* BMPR.167.c.21 (Book IV only) BMPR.C.20 (Book II only) BMPR.C.13 (Book I only)	Originally published in six volumes, described as 12 'books', this edition was reprinted ca. 1828. The first plate, of a beehive in Book I, closely resembles the frontispiece beehive engraved by James Heath (see 1808(3)1) in his catalogue).

Ref No.	Book Title (Separate Print: S.P.)	Engraved After	Nos.	Caption & Page Reference	Size (cms)	Other Engravers
1	The Fine Arts of the English School (John Britton).	J.M.W. Turner R.A.	1	p.19 Pope's Villa	17x23	Le Keux W. Bond J. Pye A. Cardon Scriven Godby J. Scott R. Roffe

Publisher	Location & References	Notes
Longman, Hurst, Rees, Orme and Brown	* Guildhall (Pr.V.TW1)	First published '1 April 1811' by 'Longman & Co and J. Taylor'. This engraving of one of his paintings so impressed Turner that in 1825 he formed a partnership with Charles Heath for the production of their 'Picturesque Views of England and Wales' based on Turner's watercolours (1838(3). In fact only the figures in the engraving were Heath's, the rest of the engraving being by John Pye, and, according to Pye's account, it was with him that Turner was particularly impressed.

Ref No.	Book Title (Separate Print: S.P.)	Engraved After	Nos.	Caption & Page Reference	Size (cms)	Other Engravers
1	Oriental Memoirs (James Forbes).	James Forbes	7	1) Pl.29 Scene of a melancholy event on the island of Salsette 2) Pl.63 A Gracia chieftain 3) Pl.21 Conclusion of a cheetah hunt 4) Pl.79 Temple of Alla Bhaug 5) Pl.5 Monkeys at Cubbee Burr 6) Pl.77 View of Bombay Green 7) Pl.12 Dancing girls and musicians	16x23 16x22 16x22 17x23 20x26 15x22 17x13	J. Shury J. Greig J. Storer T. Wageman W. Angus Bate
2	Pindar's Works (Peter Pindar, pseudonym for Rev'd John Walcot).	J.R. Smith	1	Frontispiece: 'Portrait of Peter Pindar esq.'	10x8	
3	The Vision of Don Roderick (Sir Walter Scott).	Thomas Stothard R.A.	1	'Lo, where the recreant spurs…'	13x10	
4	(?) Beattie's Poems.	Henry Corbould	1	pp.133-34. Young Beattie imploring a blessing on his father.	12x8	
5	Literary Anecdotes (John Nichols).	J. Jackson R.A.	1	*Vol III* Frontispiece: Portrait of John Nichols F.S.A. (1745-1826)	14x12	Basire Collyer
6	The Works of Miss Catherine Talbot (Rev'd M. Pennington).		1	Frontispiece: 'Catherine Talbot'	7x6	

Publisher	Location & References	Notes
White, Cochrane (1812) Bentley (1834)	*	The plates at 4) and 6) are dated '1812'. The others are dated '1834', when Bentley re-issued the work with additional illustrations.
J. Walker, G. Wilkie, J. and G. Robinson, G. Goulding	*	In five volumes, with no other illustrations.
White & Co	BMPR.C.20	'Published May 1, 1812'.
Longman, Hurst, Rees, Orme and Brown	V&A.I.113	'Published Aug 12, 1812. This may have been one of the engravings in a later edition than Rivingtons re-issue of Beattie's Poems in 1811 (see the notes in James Heath's catalogue at 1801(2).
J. Britton	V&A.GG.56	Published in 1812 in six volumes, the plate is dated 'July 1, 1811'. See Vol. III of John Britton's Autobiography (No.13) for further reference.
F.C. and J. Rivington	* (9th edition)	Dated '8 June 1812'; the ninth edition is dated 1819. The portrait of Miss Talbot is stated as 'being in the possession of the late Mrs Elizabeth Carter'.

Ref No.	Book Title (Separate Print: S.P.)	Engraved After	Nos.	Caption & Page Reference	Size (cms)	Other Engravers
7	Elegant Extracts from the most eminent British Poets.	Richard Westall R.A. Henry Corbould	5	1) Book I 'Sudden he starts…' 2) Book III 'In angry mood…' 3) Book IV 'Where sits the dame…' 4) Book V 'No sense have they…' 5) Book X (or VI) 'There in a lonely room…'	4x6	J. Romney J. Pye E. Finden W. Finden A. Smith
8	Campaign of the British Army in Portugal (H.L. Eveque).		1		39x54	
9	S.P.	J.M.W. Turner R.A.	1	High Street, Oxford	39x60	J. Middiman J. Pye
10	S.P.	Benjamin West P.R.A.	1	'Our Saviour Healing the Sick in the Temple'	56x76	
11	Description of the collection of Ancient Marbles in the British Museum (Part I).	Henry Corbould	2	1) Pl.XI Head of Hercules 2) Pl.XII Another head of Hercules	10x25	See 1820 (11)

Publisher	Location & References	Notes
John Sharpe J. Sharpe/W. Jennings (for later editions)	* BMPR.C.20 Vol III	See the companion volume of prose published by Sharpe at 1810(7). See also the 1790(3) and the 1791(2) entries in James Heath's catalogue. This edition was republished by Sharpe/Jennings ca. 1828 'in 12 books'.
	Mackenzie (British Prints, 1987)	
	Engen: J. Pye entry in his Dictionary of Victorian Engravers	Turner completed his painting in March 1810. Pye and Middiman did most of the engraving, with Charles Heath being responsible for only the figures. In 1818, a companion print, 'Oxford from the Abingdon Road', appeared (1818(5)).
G. and W. Nicol	BMPR.C.82 Sandby's History of the Royal Academy, Vol I p.278	Published '1 May 1812' as an 'Aquafortis by Chas Heath Junr'. In 1811 the directors of the British Institute bought Benjamin West's painting for £3000, with 60 members of the Institute subscribing 50 guineas each. Charles Heath, whose mother was related to West by marriage, was given the commission to engrave, and is said to have received 1800 guineas for his work, which took him 11 years to complete. 840 prints were subscribed for, at 5 guineas each, within a year, and according to Farington (p.4156) the Institute received upward of £9300 from sales of the picture and the engraving.
G. and W. Nicol	BMPR.242.a.12	See 1820(11) for details of Charles Heath's engravings in subsequent parts.

Ref No.	Book Title (Separate Print: S.P.)	Engraved After	Nos.	Caption & Page Reference	Size (cms)	Other Engravers
12	The Poems of Ossian	T. Uwins R.A.	2	1) Frontispiece. 'It is night, and I am alone...' 2) Title page. 'I will approach my love...'	9x6 7x6	

Publisher	Location & References	Notes
J. Walker and J. Harris		A pocket edition, seemingly a forerunner of the Dove's 'English Classics' series, or Thomas Tegg's pocket editions.

Ref No.	Book Title (Separate Print: S.P.)	Engraved After	Nos.	Caption & Page Reference	Size (cms)	Other Engravers
1	Rokeby (Sir Walter Scott).	Thomas Stothard R.A.	3	1) p.21 'What carest thou...' 2) p.117 'But far apart in dark divan...' 3) p.294 'Full levelled at the baron's head...'	12x9	J. Pye W. Finden Engleheart
2	Pennant's London.	M. Griffith	2	1) Sir Henry Lee 2) Sir Richard Clough	10x8	

Publisher	Location & References	Notes
J. Ballantyne, Edinburgh, and Longman, Hurst. Rees, Orme and Brown	* (13th edition)	
J. Faulder, White, Cochrane & others	Adams, p.160 Huntington 109976.I.137 and 109976.I.578	'C. Heath direxit'

Ref No.	Book Title (Separate Print: S.P.)	Engraved After	Nos.	Caption & Page Reference	Size (cms)	Other Engravers
1	A Voyage to Abyssinia (Henry Salt).	H. Salt	34	1) p.3 View of obelisk and church at Axum 2) p.20 Waterspouts in the Mozambique channel 3) p.28 View of government house on the island of Mozambique 4) p.28 View of government house at Mesurii 5) p.116 Castle of the Sultan of Aden and Lahadj 6) p.130 An Arabian child dressed in his holiday suit. 7) p.169 (1) Sketch of the rocky coast of the island of Amphila 8) p.169(2) Sketch of a building in Avergale 9) p.198(1) Ayto Debib 10) p.198(2) Guebra Muhedin 11) p.229 Sketch of a daro tree at the bottom of Taranto 12) p.239(1) Baharmagash Yasous 13) p.239(2) Bahara Subhart 14) p.239(3) Lasta soldier 15) p.249 View of the mountain of Derra Damo 16) p.251 Sketch of the mountains of Adowa 17) p.259 Sketch of the Sanga or Galla oxen	9x13 17x23	MacPherson

Publisher	Location & References	Notes
F.C. and J. Rivington	*	
	V&A.O.4.b (6) only	

Ref No.	Book Title (Separate Print: S.P.)	Engraved After	Nos.	Caption & Page Reference	Size (cms)	Other Engravers
1	A Voyage to Abyssinia (continued)			18) p.262 Sketch of Mr Pearce's house at Chelicut 19) p.282 An Abyssinian slave girl 20) p.302 Various sketches of church items 21) p.336 Dofter Esther, a learned Abyssinian 22) p.337 Berilla, an Edjow Galle 23) p.352 A view of the mountains of Samen and the river Tacazze 24) p.357 View on the banks of the Tacazze 25) p.358 View in the neighbourhood of the river Tacazze 26) p.394 Outline of an Abyssinian drawing 27) p.399 Sketch of a scene halfway down the pass at Atbara 28) p.401 Abyssinians reposing 29) p.408 Abyssinian household articles 30) p.411 Greek inscri-ptions found at Axum 31) p.440 A group of the Torah Shiho 32) p.506 Camels after a march 33) p.lxii (1) Erodia Amphilensis 34) p.lxii (2) Abyssinian locust		

Publisher	Location & References	Notes

Ref No.	Book Title (Separate Print: S.P.)	Engraved After	Nos.	Caption & Page Reference	Size (cms)	Other Engravers
2	The Bioscope, or Dial of Life.	Thomas Stothard R.A.	1	Title page	12x8	
3	The History of the Valiant Knight Arthur of Little Britain (edited by E.V. Utterson).		25	Hand coloured etchings without captions	5x13 to 9x7	
4	Thyrza, and The Bride of Abydos (Lord Byron).	Thomas Stothard R.A.	2	1) 'The voice that made these sounds...' 2) 'What, not receive my foolish flower?...'	10x8 9x8	
5	Miscellaneous Works (Edmund Gibbon) (edited by Lord Sheffield).	H. Walton	3	1) Vol I p.250 Pavilion and terrace at Lausanne 2) Vol I p.296 Sheffield Place, Sussex 3) Vol I p.428 Fletching Church, Sussex	10x15	J. Fittler
6	Topography and Natural History of Hampstead (John James Park).	W. Alexander Conde	3	1) p.222 The Old Church at Hampstead 2) p.286 The Poor House at Hampstead 3) p.320 Lady Erskine's Monument	12x19 15x21 14x10	S. Smith J. Quilley

Publisher	Location & References	Notes
John Murray	RA (Frost Vol XI)	'Publ. June 1814'.
White, Cochrane	*	Described as 'A New Edition', and sub-titled 'A Romance of Chivalry', this extraordinary work is represented as a reprint from Lord John Bourchier (Lord Berners) English translation of the second edition of a French romance of 1582. The designs by Charles Heath (his one and only essay into the Gothic style of the period) are in imitation of mediaeval illuminated illustration. 25 copies were printed on large paper, with hand coloured illustrations of the etchings on one side of the page, and the uncoloured etchings on the other; 175 copies were printed in addition, with only the etchings.
John Murray	V&A.J.6.f (1) only) * (2) only) BMPR.C.20 (2) only)	These two poems appear to have been published earlier than the collected edition of Byron's works illustrated by Charles Heath's engravings in 1819(2). 2) is dated 1814, and is found in an extra-illustrated 'Life of Thomas Stothard' by Mrs Bray (p.84).
John Murray	Houghton *EC75.G3525 796 nd V&A.Z.7.b BL.830K.26 (2) only)	Five volumes, 'Published Jany 1, 1815'. The engravings are inscribed 'C. Heath direxit'.
Nichols, Son and Bentley	* Guildhall V&A.A.12.b (3) only)	The engravings are dated '1 Jan 1814', although the publication date was apparently later; there was a second edition in 1818. 3) is engraved in oval.

Ref No.	Book Title (Separate Print: S.P.)	Engraved After	Nos.	Caption & Page Reference	Size (cms)	Other Engravers
7	S.P.	T. Phillips	1	George, Earl of Dartmouth, Lord Chamberlain of His Majesty's Household. A.D. 1810.	43x34	

Publisher	Location & References	Notes
J. Boydell and G. Colnaghi & Co.	*	Inscribed 'Chas Heath junr'.

Ref No.	Book Title (Separate Print: S.P.)	Engraved After	Nos.	Caption & Page Reference	Size (cms)	Other Engravers
1	The Holy Bible.	Richard Westall R.A.	31	*Vol I* 1) Frontispiece: Moses receiving the law 2) Hagar and Ishmael 3) Abraham offering Isaac 4) Isaac discovering he had blessed Jacob 5) Mother of Moses 6) Manoah's sacrifice 7) Samson betrayed 8) Ruth gleaning 9) Saul and the Witch of Endor 10) David and Bathsheba 11) The Prophet Ahijah 12) Elijah raising the Widow's son 13) Elisha on his deathbed *Vol II* 14) Esther before Ahasuerus 15) The Peaceable Kingdom 16) Jeremiah foretelling the siege of Jerusalem 17) Daniel in the Lions' Den 18) Jonah cast forth into the sea 19) The vision of the horses *Vol III* 20) Tobias and the Angel	12x9	

Publisher	Location & References	Notes
White, Cochrane	* BMPR.166.d.15 V&A.J.6.f (10),20) and 23) only)	Three volumes. 'Embellished with engravings by Charles Heath'. 'Ruth gleaning' (8) (Macklin's Bible, 1800), and 'Daniel in the Lions' Den' (17) (Josephus 1785) were both engraved by James Heath as well (see 1800(4) and 1785(1) of his catalogue). There was a U.S. edition of this Bible published by Kimber and Sharpless in 1823.

Ref No.	Book Title (Separate Print: S.P.)	Engraved After	Nos.	Caption & Page Reference	Size (cms)	Other Engravers
1	The Holy Bible (continued).			21) Judith and Holofernes 22) New Testament frontispiece 23) The Angel of the Lord warning Joseph 24) The Annunciation 25) Christ reasoning with the doctors 26) The Adoration of the Shepherds 27) Christ raising the widow's son 28) Christ's Agony 29) The Entombment of Christ 30) Christ instructing Nicodemus 31) Christ appearing to Mary Magdalen		
2	The Holy Bible (Macklin).	P.J. de Louther-bourg R.A.	2	Vol VII 1) I Maccabees ii v.23-25 Matthias punishing idolatry 2) I Maccabees vi v.43-46 Heroism of Eleazar	31x25	J. Landseer R. Golding W. Bromley
3	Encyclopaedia (Constable).		1	Frontispiece		

Publisher	Location & References	Notes
Thomas Macklin	Huntington 112962	See James Heath's catalogue 1800(4) for his plates in Vols I-VI of Macklin's Bible.
Archibald Constable, Edinburgh	National Library of Scotland MS.789	Two letters from Archibald Constable to Charles Heath in July 1814 and on 10 February 1815 record the receipt of 'plates', but no copy has been traced. Charles Heath apparently charged 50 guineas for the plate, which Constable thought was too much.

Ref No.	Book Title (Separate Print: S.P.)	Engraved After	Nos.	Caption & Page Reference	Size (cms)	Other Engravers
4	Laurel (The Poetical Works of Collins, Pomfret, Dr Johnson, Hammond etc).	R. Cook	4	1) Vignette title page 2) Avenging angel standing over kneeling man (Gay) 3) 'Sudden he starts...' 4) Boy reading to teacher (Shenstone)	4x5	J. Romney
5	The Lord of the Isles (Sir Walter Scott).	Richard Westall R.A.	4	1) p.35 'The younger knight...' 2) p.118 'Hark, hears he not...' 3) p.212 'He raised the page...' 4) p.269 'Then foremost...'	12x9	Engleheart J. Pye
6	The History of Persia (Sir John Malcolm).	W. Webbe W. Sundt	21	*Vol I* 1) p.254 Sculpture on the face of a mountain near the ruins of Shahpoor 2) p.255 Sculpture on the face of a mountain near the ruins of Shahpoor 3) p.257 Front view of the excavation called Tank-e-Bostan 4) p.258 Sculpture on the northern side of the interior of the cave of Tank-e-Bostan 5) p.258 Sculpture on the southern side of the interior of the cave of Tank-e-Bostan	16x22	

Publisher	Location & References	Notes
Suttaby, Evans and Fox	* BMPR.C.13	
Longman, Hurst, Rees, Orme and Brown	* V&A.93.D.217 (p.78) (1) only)	'Publ. April 1815'. Also contains an engraving by James Heath (1815/16(2) in his catalogue).
John Murray and Longman, Hurst, Rees, Orme and Brown	*	Two volumes. Engravings 1),2),3),4),6),7),16),17),18) and 21) are inscribed 'Chas Heath direxit' i.e. 'under the direction of'; all the other plates are inscribed 'sculpsit' i.e. engraved by Charles Heath. The drawings for engravings nos. 16-20 were by W. Sundt, and the others by W. Webbe.

Ref No.	Book Title (Separate Print: S.P.)	Engraved After	Nos.	Caption & Page Reference	Size (cms)	Other Engravers
6	The History of Persia (continued).			6) p.258 Sculpture on the southern side of the interior of the cave of Tank-e-Bostan (interior of arch)		
				7) p.258 Sculpture on face of the rock near Tank-e-Bostan		
				8) p.423 View of the city of Maragha		
				9) p.505 Shah Tamasp	13x10	
				10) p.525 Shah Abbas the Great		
				Vol II		
				11) p.44 Nadir Shah		
				12) p.115 Kurreen Khan		
				13) p.160 View of the town of Yezdikhaust	17x24	
				14) p.262 Aga Mohamed Khan		
				15) p.314 Futter Aly Shah	13x10	
				16) p.522 Front view of the palace at Isfahan	17x22	
				17) p.522 Private palace in the Char Bagh		
				18) p.524 Tomb of Esther and Mordecai. Tomb of Avicenna	15x10	
				19) p.525 View of mountain of Kaufelau-Kôh		
				20) p.596 Encampment of wandering tribe	16x22	
				21) p.602 Ghishkee tribe		

Publisher	Location & References	Notes

Ref No.	Book Title (Separate Print: S.P.)	Engraved After	Nos.	Caption & Page Reference	Size (cms)	Other Engravers
1	The British Theatre, or a Collection of Plays by Mrs Inchbald.	Singleton P.C. Poole J. Woodforde R.A. Henry Corbould	71	*Vol I* *Oroonoko* 1) 'This dagger will instruct…' *She Would, and she Would not* 2) 'Oh this malicious jade…' *Vol II* *A cure for the Heart Ache* 3) 'Why don't you finish…' *The Poor Gentleman* 4) 'Oh never speak to that…' *To marry or not to marry* 5) 'Dear master, raise.' *Barbarossa* 6) 'My virtuous son…' *The Suspicious Husband* 7) 'Your servant cousin…' *Vol IV* *Tancred and Sigismundo* 8) 'Perfidious woman, die…' *A New Way to Pay Old Debts* 9) 'How! Thunderstruck' *The Recruiting Officer* 10) 'Let me see: young and tender…' *Vol V* *Lionel and Clarissa* 11) 'She's gone, by the Lord…' *The Jealous Wife* 12) 'Help! Murder! Help!'	8x7 10x8 or 11x7	

Publisher	Location & References	Notes
Longman, Hurst, Rees, Orme and Brown Hurst, Robinson (1824)	* (less Vols X to XII) V&A.J.6.b (2) and 51) only) BMPR.C.13 (7),40) and 48) only) NYPL. +KZ32067 (18) only) NYPL. +KZ5981 (28) only) NYPL. +KZ231899 (30) only) NYPL. +KZ319611 (31) only) NYPL. +KZ32087 (36) only)	Originally published in 1806-8, the 'British Theatre' was re-issued in 'A New Edition' in 20 volumes in 1816, and again in 1824. Some plates of the 1816 edition are dated '1817'. 31) see 1807(3) for an earlier version, also after Singleton. 35) The original drawing (20x15) is by Charles Heath himself; it has been preserved in the Castle Museum, Nottingham (reference 1904-241) (perhaps because Charles Heath sent it to one of his relatives there); this drawing is also referred to in Benezit's Dictionary of Artists and Engravers, under Charles Heath. 70) See also Sandby Vol I, p.329. In engraving so extensively for this set, Charles Heath may well have been following his father's example in engraving for Bell's Theatre (see 1791(1) of James Heath's catalogue). Another version with the same artist and publisher includes 3) and 53), and in addition contains 'The Duenna' (R.B. Sheridan) with a frontispiece in the same style: ''Tis false you have more appetite than hair'.

Ref No.	Book Title (Separate Print: S.P.)	Engraved After	Nos.	Caption & Page Reference	Size (cms)	Other Engravers
1	The British Theatre (continued).			*King Lear* 13) 'His sleep is sound...' *The Merchant of Venice* 14) 'Beg that thou must...' *Vol IV* *She Stoops to Conquer* 15) 'Fly to your spark...' *The Stranger* 16) 'Dear Father! Dear Mother!...' *Vol VII* *Othello* 17) 'Here's my husband...' *The Point of Honour* 18) 'My Father! In such a moment...' *Douglas* 19) 'Do not despair...' *Vol VIII* *Macbeth* 20) 'I have done the deed...' *Cymbeline* 21) 'Good masters, harm me not...' *Rule a wife and have a wife* 22) 'And here's a chain...' *Vol IX* *The Gamester* 23) 'Can you forgive me?' *Isabella* 24) 'Ha! I am distracted too...'		

Publisher	Location & References	Notes

Ref No.	Book Title (Separate Print: S.P.)	Engraved After	Nos.	Caption & Page Reference	Size (cms)	Other Engravers
1	The British Theatre (continued).			*The Revenge* 25) 'Groan on, and with the sound...' *Vols X-XII* *The Belle's Stratagem* 26) 'Laetitia, he's my sweetheart...' *The Dramatist, or Stop Him who Can* 27) Vapid: 'Prologue or Epilogue...' *The Provok'd Husband* 28) Lady Townley: 'Support me...' *The Brothers* 29) Philip: 'I am strongly tempted...' *Zara* 30) Lusignon: 'My Son, my Daughter...' *Know Your Own Mind* 31) Millamour: 'Vastly well.' *Love Makes a Man* 32) (Cibber) *Louisa (Cumberland)* 33) Act IV *Vol X* *The Siege of Damascus* 34) Phocyas: 'Villain thou liest...' *Vol XI* *King Henry V* 35) 'Rather proclaim it, Westmoreland.' *Vol XII* *The Orphan* 36) Monimia: 'What? Speak!...'		

Publisher	Location & References	Notes

Ref No.	Book Title (Separate Print: S.P.)	Engraved After	Nos.	Caption & Page Reference	Size (cms)	Other Engravers
1	The British Theatre (continued).			*The Deserted Daughter* 37) Lady Anne: 'Forgive this rude tumult.' *Vol XIII* *The Distressed Mother* 38) 'Oh do not Sir divide...' *George Barnwell* 39) 'To gaze upon your beauty...' *King Richard III* 40) 'Awake, Richard, awake...' *The West Indian* 41) 'Unhand me, Sir...' *Vol XIV* *The Good Natured Man* 42) Come you dog, confess...' *The Way to Get Married* 43) 'My Julia! Oh give her...' *The Maid of the Mill* 44) 'No, no, follow your gentleman...' *The Wheel of Fortune* 45) 'With your leave, I want...' *The Wonder! A Woman Keeps a Secret* 46) 'Pray let me go, Madam...' *Vol XV* *A Bold Stroke for a Wife* 47) 'Very well, Mr Pillage...' *The Beaux' Stratagem* 48) 'Oh pray Sir, spare'		

Publisher	Location & References	Notes
	BL.1507.316 (7) (38) only	

Ref No.	Book Title (Separate Print: S.P.)	Engraved After	Nos.	Caption & Page Reference	Size (cms)	Other Engravers
1	The British Theatre (continued).			*The Castle of Andalusia* 49) 'Oh you most beautiful...' *Vol XVI* *The School of Reform* 50) 'Ah it is my son.' *The Honeymoon* 51) 'Why what the devil' *The Battle of Hexham* 52) 'Strike not on thy allegiance...' *John Bull* 53) 'There, 'tis fit it should...' *Vol XVII* *The Beggar's Opera* 54) 'Give her another glass...' *King Henry IV Part I* 55) 'Your money...' *King Henry V* 56) 'Do you like me, Kate...' *King Henry VIII* 57) 'Read o'er this...' *The Rival Queens* 58) 'My wrongs cry out' *Vol XVIII* *Wild Oats* 59) 'Ah thou sly and deceitful...' *Speed the Plough* 60) 'Dickens and Daisey, what a gentleman...' *The Surrender of Calais* 61) 'Here, take this trash...'		

Publisher	Location & References	Notes

Ref No.	Book Title (Separate Print: S.P.)	Engraved After	Nos.	Caption & Page Reference	Size (cms)	Other Engravers
1	The British Theatre (continued).			*The Man of the World* 62) 'What is the matter wi' yer…' *Vol XIX* *Everyman in his Humour* 63) 'Hold, hold under thy favour…' *The Rivals* 64) 'Well, now they are coming…' *The Conscious Lovers* 65) 'Rise, rise my child…' *Jane Shore* 66) 'Why should I wander?' *Vol XX* *Much Ado about Nothing* 67) 'But are you sure?' *The Heir at Law* 68) 'Respect him, for he's an Ll.D.' *Love in a Village* 69) 'Your honour, look out…' *Lady Jane Grey* 70) 'Softly, my Lord…' *The Mountaineers* 71) 'Alas, Octavian…'		
2	The Seasons (James Thomson).	Richard Westall R.A.	4	Frontispiece 1) 'The shepherd's lyre…' 2) Spring: 'Together let us spread… (p.2)' 3) p.46 Summer: 'She with the sylvan pen…' 4) p.116 Autumn: 'By strong necessity…'	6x5 6x7	W. Finden J. Pye

Publisher	Location & References	Notes
John Sharpe	* NYPL. +KZ11071 BMPR.166. c.11	Although NYPL also records a copy dated 1807 with Westall drawings and James Heath engravings, this edition was apparently first published in 1816; there were second and third editions in 1817 and 1818 (the plates in the third edition being curiously dated '1819'). Reissued also in 1822, with the same plates.

Ref No.	Book Title (Separate Print: S.P.)	Engraved After	Nos.	Caption & Page Reference	Size (cms)	Other Engravers
3	The Traveller and the Deserted Village and other Poems (Oliver Goldsmith).	Richard Westall R.A.	2	The Traveller p.31 'E'en now perhaps...' The Hermit p.78 'Turn, gentle Hermit...'	5x6 6x7	J. Mitan J. Pye W. Finden
4	Gray's Works (edited by Rev'd J. Mitford).	H. Corbould J. Rich-ardson Eccardt	1	*Vol II* Frontispiece: Thomas Gray	13x10	J. Hopwood
5	S.P.	J.H. Mortimer R.A.	1	'Reposo' (A man seated under a tree, resting his head on his hand)	15x9	
6	S.P.	Thomas Stothard R.A.	1	Hope an anchor of the Soul	10x7	
7	Poesias o Rimas Juveniles (Arriaza).		6	*Vol I.* Title page vignette p.1 'De amor escribe...' p.76 vignette *Vol II.* Title page: (same as *Vol I*) p.1 'La Amistad y el Amor...' p.151 'Tal vez juega el ingenio...'	5x5	

Publisher	Location & References	Notes
John Sharpe	* BMPR.166.c.11 V&A.J.5.c	Reprinted in 1819, and as 'The Deserted Village' in 1822 (3).
J. Mawman	Houghton +fEC75.G7948 C816m YCBA.B1977. 14 15079 (IR.93)	'Published May 25 1816'. Inscribed 'C. Heath and J. Holl' sculp'. The copy in the YCBA is dated 1814, and is presumably a proof.
Thomas Palser	V&A.J.4.B	A polyautograph, referred to in G. Benthall's 'Life and Works of John Mortimer' (1955, p.187 unpublished) under V&A reference L2252-61-1961 and 86W50-55. Inscribed 'Mortimer invt, C. Heath del.'
J. Power, Dublin	BMPR.C.20 (Balmanno Vol 3)	See also 'A Selection of Popular and National Airs' (1820(13)) of which this print may be a forerunner.
Imprenta Real, Madrid	*	Two volumes in one, published in Spanish. 'C. Heath direxit' inscribed on all plates.

Ref No.	Book Title (Separate Print: S.P.)	Engraved After	Nos.	Caption & Page Reference	Size (cms)	Other Engravers
1	Pompeiana (Sir William Gell and John P. Gandy).		44	1) p.114 View of the street of the tombs 2) p.117 Interior of tomb of Naeroleia 3) p.118 Tombs of Scaurus 4) p.120 Plans of an insulated tomb 5) p.120 Side view of the tomb of C. Quietus 6) p.120 View in the street of the tombs 7) p.120 Outside the gate of Herculaneum 8) p.120 Gate of Nola outside 9) p.136 Various ornaments 10) p.166 View of Villa Suburbana 11) p.166 Triangular room in villa 12) p.168 Meeting of the two streets 13) p.168 View in the house of the Vestals 14) p.168 Painting in the house called Vestals 15) p.170 Court of house of surgical instruments 16) p.170 Pictures and ornaments 17) p.175 House of Actaeon 18) p.176 House of Actaeon, side of room	10x15 9x14 10x15	H. Moses S. Porter G. Cooke W. Lizars C. Hollis R. Wallis F.C. Lewis

Publisher	Location & References	Notes
Rodwell and Martin	*	Published between 1817 and 1819. A second edition with the same plates appeared in 1821.

Ref No.	Book Title (Separate Print: S.P.)	Engraved After	Nos.	Caption & Page Reference	Size (cms)	Other Engravers
1	Pompeiana (continued).			19) p.176 Painting, tiles and ornaments in house of Actaeon		
				20) p.178 Ornaments, painting, etc.		
				21) p.186 Entrance to house of Pansa		
				22) p.187 Peristyle or inner court of house of Pansa		
				23) p.188 Restoration of atrium		
				24) p.189 Oven and mills	15x11	
				25) p.190 Tetrastyle careldium in house south of Basilica		
				26) p.190 Side of a room	11x12	
				27) p.192 Side of a room		
				28) p.194 Painting		
				29) p.218 View of the forum and Basilica		
				30) p.218 View in the forum		
				31) p.220 Ornaments from the Basilica		
				32) p.224 View of the temple at north end of forum		
				33) p.224 View of the temple of Bacchus		
				34) p.224 View of the temple of Bacchus looking towards Vesuvius	10x15	
				35) p.228 Paintings in the temple of Bacchus	4x15	

Publisher	Location & References	Notes

Ref No.	Book Title (Separate Print: S.P.)	Engraved After	Nos.	Caption & Page Reference	Size (cms)	Other Engravers
1	Pompeiana (continued).			36) p.229 Paintings in the temple of Bacchus 37) p.230 Paintings in the temple of Bacchus 38) p.230 Paintings 39) p.230 View of new temple, west of forum 40) p.230 Paintings 41) p.252 Entrance portico to Greek temple 42) p.253 Remains of Greek temple 43) p.253 View in the Great Temple 44) p.253 View of the school behind the Greek theatre	7x10 10x15	
2	Table Talk (William Cowper).	Richard Westall R.A.	1	Frontispiece: 'Yon cottager who weaves…'	5x4	
3	The Task (William Cowper).	Richard Westall R.A.	2	Frontispiece 1) 'Forth goes the woodman…' 2) 'Great skill have they…'	5x4	
4	Adventures of Telemachus (Charles Lamb).	Thomas Stothard R.A.	1	Shipwreck of Telemachu		
5	The Bibliographical Decameron (T.F. Dibdin).	G. Lewis	1	*Vol III* p.344 Thomas Percy D.D. Bishop of Dromore	12x9	Worthington Scriven

Publisher	Location & References	Notes
		42) was engraved with James Lewis. 44) was engraved with R. Wallis.
John Sharpe	V&A.J.4.d	A companion volume to (3) below.
John Sharpe	* BMPR.166+. a.20(2) only) V&A.J.6.f V&A.J.4.d (1) only)	Dated '1 Oct 1817'. See 1810(1) for another edition of Cowper's Poems published by Sharpe with another Charles Heath engraving for 'The Task'.
J. Coxhead		
T.F. Dibdin	BL.N.L.7.b YCBA	

Ref No.	Book Title (Separate Print: S.P.)	Engraved After	Nos.	Caption & Page Reference	Size (cms)	Other Engravers
6	Don Quixote (Cervantes).	Robert Smirke R.A.	2	*Vol IV* 1) p.88 Don Quixote giving advice to Governor Sancho 2) p.490 Death of Don Quixote	12x10	R. Golding J. Heath C. Armstrong Finden J. Fittler J. Scott A. Smith J. Mitan Engleheart A. Raimbach
7	Correspondence between a mother and her daughter at school.	W. Hilton A.R.A.	1	Frontispiece: Mother and daughter	11x7	
8	Elizabeth (Mme Cottin).	Richard Westall R.A.	1	Part II The Dying Missionary (p.114)	7x5	G. Corbould W. Finden J. Romney
9	Lalla Rookh (Thomas Moore).	Richard Westall R.A. Robert Smirke R.A.	6	1) Frontispiece 2) p.46 'He raised her veil…' 3) p.148 'She shook her sparkling wreath…' 4) p.198 'While the princess sat…' 5) p.234 'Strange and new…' 6) p.314 'The Enchantress'	10x7 11x9	W. Finden J. Romney (12th edn) C. Rolls H. Rolls J. Hollis J. Brown F. Bacon L. Stocks E. Scriven (19th edn)

Publisher	Location & References	Notes
T. Cadell and W. Davies	* BMPR.166.d.13 (proofs)	A four volume edition with many engravings from James and Charles Heath's atelier. See 1820 (6) for a later edition of Don Quixote with Charles Heath engravings. 1) is dated 12 August 1817. Charles Heath received 16 guineas each for three vignettes which he engraved in addition for this work.
Taylor and Hessey	*	
John Sharpe	* V&A.J.5.c	
Longman, Hurst, Rees, Orme, and Brown	* (3rd edn) BMPR.166.d.12	The 12th edition, published in 1824 has two additional engravings by Charles Heath, at p.184. 'The youth so fleet and bold...' and at p.316 'And now a spirit form'd...' The 19th edition published in 1838 has another at p.133 'One morn a peri...' by Charles Heath, though this edition has plates all 'engraved under the superintendence of Charles Heath' and the plate is inscribed by Scriven in later editions. See also Smirke's 'Lalla Rookh' (U/D 5) and 'The Lady's Magazine' for 1822(8).

Ref No.	Book Title (Separate Print: S.P.)	Engraved After	Nos.	Caption & Page Reference	Size (cms)	Other Engravers
10	Paradise Lost (John Milton).	Richard Westall R.A.	4	*Vol I Book I* 1) 'Then with expanded wings...' (p.8) *Book V* 2) 'Lowly they bowed...' (p.144) *Vol II Book VII* 3) 'He with his consort Eve...' (p.1) Book XI 4) 'Down from a hill...' (p.1)	7x7	J. Mitan W. Finden J. Pye A. Raimbach G. Corbould
11	Paradise Regained and Minor Poems (John Milton).	Richard Westall R.A.	3	Comus p.2 1) 'Sabrina fair...' L'Allegro p.13 2) 'The frolic wind...' Sonnets p.3 3) 'As that dishonest victory...'	7x7	E. Finden W. Finden J. Mitan Engleheart J. Romney R. Rhodes
12	Young's Night Thoughts, or The Complaint.	Richard Westall R.A.	1	Night VII p.153 'Is it that things terrestrial can't content?...'	7x7	Engleheart A. Smith E. Portbury
13	S.P.		1	Portrait of Milton		S. Noble E. Finden J. Robinson G. Corbould R. Rhodes

Publisher	Location & References	Notes
John Sharpe	* BMPR.166.c.11 V&A.93.D.217 (p.5.7.11) V&A.95.E.18 (2) only)	Two volumes, containing a plate by James Heath also (see 1817(2) of his catalogue). The BMPR copy of 2) is dated 1816. 2) was re-engraved by J.H. Robinson for a re-issued edition in 1822.
John Sharpe	* BMPR.166.c.11 V&A.93.D.217 (p.14) (2) only)	1) is dated '24 August 1816'. The first edition in 1817 was followed by a second in 1819.
John Sharpe	* BMPR.166.c.11 NYPL.ME ZHM (Grolier 201)	This edition was reprinted in 1823. See also 1824(2) for another edition with completely different engravings by C. Heath.

Ref No.	Book Title (Separate Print: S.P.)	Engraved After	Nos.	Caption & Page Reference	Size (cms)	Other Engravers
1	The History of St Paul's Cathedral in London (William Dugdale).	Henry Corbould	15	1) p.200 Four statues: (Sir W.Jones, J.Howard, Dr Johnson, Sir Joshua Reynolds) 2) p.202 Two sarchophagi (Capt. Hardinge, Capt. Burgess) 3) p.203 Two sarchophagi (Capt. Miller, Capt. Faulkner) 4) p.204 Lord Collingwood, Earl Howe 5) p.205 Sir John Moore, Sir Ralph Abercromby 6) p.206 Capt J.Cooke, Marquis Cornwallis 7) p.207 Generals Craufurd and MacKinnon. Capt. Westcott 8) p.208 Lord Rodney, Capts. Mosse and Rieu 9) p.469 (supplement) Capt. Duff, Viscount Nelson 10) p.470 Sir Isaac Brock, General Bowes 11) p.471 Lt. Col. Myers, General Hoghton 12) p.471 General Marchant, Sir Samuel Hood 13) p.472 Sir W. Ponsonby, Sir Thomas Picton	14x10 10x20 21x20 10x20 21x20 12x20 18x20 13x20 18x20 10x18 21x20 10x18 20x20 16x21 15x18 11x20 20x20 12x16 12x17 11x15 10x15 10x14 15x14 15x20 16x20	W. Finden J. Coney W. Byrne

Publisher	Location & References	Notes
Lackington and Longman	BL.749.f.2 YCBA	'Publ. June 1, 1818'. A set of etchings.

Ref No.	Book Title (Separate Print: S.P.)	Engraved After	Nos.	Caption & Page Reference	Size (cms)	Other Engravers
1	The History of St Paul's Cathedral in London (continued).			14) p.472 Generals Gore and Skerritt 15) p.472 General Hay, General Ross, Col. Cadogan	14x13 11x9 10x13 11x14	
2	Travels in Egypt, Nubia, the Holy Land, Mount Libanon and Cyprus in the year 1814 (Henry Light).	H. Light	11	1) Frontispiece: Jerusalem from the convent of the Latin monks 2) p.44 Ruin'd bridge near tombs at Sioul 3) p.51 View from the west side of Elephantina 4) p.58 North front of ruins at Garteas 5) p.60 South view of the Ruins at Tacefa 6) p.63 Entrance to cataracts of Galabshee 7) p.64 Propylaeon at Galabshee 8) p.68 Portico at Garsery 9) p.77 Excavation in rock at Deir 10) p.88 South view of ruins at Ouffeddoonee 11) p.242 Port of Larnaca, Cyprus	10x47 11x17 10x16 11x17 11x16 11x17 12x17	W. Smith Shepherd J. Watt
3	Hervey's Meditations and Contemplations.	Richard Westall R.A.	4	1) Frontispiece: 'Let their loins bless...' 2) p.9 'Her hands trembling...' 3) p.201 'He faints...' 4) p.273 'When I consider...'	9x7	

Publisher	Location & References	Notes
Rodwell and Martin	*	
E. Edwards F.C. and J. Rivington	* V&A.J.6.f	The plates are dated '20 March 1816'.

Ref No.	Book Title (Separate Print: S.P.)	Engraved After	Nos.	Caption & Page Reference	Size (cms)	Other Engravers
4	Thoughts in Prison (Dr William Dodd).	Richard Westall R.A.	1	Title page: Clergyman at a desk, with a girl kneeling	4x6	
5	S.P.	J.M.W. Turner R.A.	1	View of Oxford from the Abingdon Road	39x60	J. Pye
6	S.P.	W.J. Newton R.A.	1	Benjamin West, President of the Royal Academy	38x30	

Publisher	Location & References	Notes
Chiswick Press	* BMPR.C.13	Dr Dodd was executed for fraud.
	Engen's Dictionary of Victorian Engravers: J.Pye	Engraved with John Pye, with Charles Heath engraving only the figures; see also 1812(9).
W.J. White	YCBA.B. 1977 14.12722	'Published Jany 1, 1818'. See Farington's Diary p.4995-6 and 5003. There is a copy in the Castle Museum, Nottingham (reference 04-241).

Ref No.	Book Title (Separate Print: S.P.)	Engraved After	Nos.	Caption & Page Reference	Size (cms)	Other Engravers
1	A Classical and Topographical Tour through Greece (Edward Dodwell).	A. Pomardi	23	*Vol I* 1) p.37 Drawbridge at Corfu 2) p.219 Mosque near Libadea 3) p.239 Katabathea 4) p.256 Ruins of Thespeia 5) p.289 Monument of Lysicrates 6) p.339 Inside view of the Parthenon 7) p.346 Erectheion 8) p.356 West end of the Pandroseia 9) p.361 Athens 10) p.499 Pantelic Quarries 11) p.503 View from the Castle of Phylaeon 12) p.523 Colossal ion 13) p.536 Theatre at Thorikos 14) p.553 Cave near Bari in Attica *Vol II* 15) p.120 Pharsalia 16) p.143 Mount Parnassos 17) p.148 Thebes 18) p.188 Corinth 19) p.270 Ruins of Troezen 20) p.282 Ruins of Methana 21) p.340 Passage of the Alpheios 22) p.375 Theatre at Megalopolis 23) p.394 Ruins of Lykosaura	10x16	Radcliffe Smith Lizars E. Byrne T. Owen Reynolds Moses Hollis Hobson

Publisher	Location & References	Notes
Rodwell and Martin	* V&A.Z.12.a (4) only)	Published in two volumes.

Ref No.	Book Title (Separate Print: S.P.)	Engraved After	Nos.	Caption & Page Reference	Size (cms)	Other Engravers
2	Byron's Works.	Richard Westall R.A.	17	*Vol I* *Childe Harold* 1) p.50 'Her lover sinks...' *Vol II* 2) p.18 'But when I stood...' 3) p.162 'No drop of that clear stream...' *Vol III* *The Giaour* 4) p.43 'There will be pause...' 5) p.49 'There is blood upon...' *The Bride of Abydos* 6) p.127 'And that last thought...' 7) p.93 'His keen eye shone...' *The Corsair* 8) p.170 'The white sail set...' 9) p.193 'What is that form?...' 10) p.224 'He turned not...' *Vol IV* *Lara* 11) p.13 'But Lara's prostrate form...' 12) p.50 'Save that when struggling...' *The Prisoner of Chillon* 13) p.166 'I saw the expectant raven...' *Vol V* *Manfred* 15) p.68 'Back ye baffled fiends...'	10x8	C. Armstrong J. Romney Engleheart E. Finden W. Finden

Publisher	Location & References	Notes
John Murray	* V&A.93.D.217 (p.83) V&A.J.6.f (1), 4), 6), 15) and 17) only)	The plates are all dated 'Published Dec 1, 1819'. Vols II and V of the 5 volumes are dated 1823. There were several later versions of Byron's Poems using at least some of the original prints in this edition; an undated edition ca. 1850 for instance includes 11),14) and 15). A letter from Charles Heath preserved in the John Murray archives and dated '24 July 1818'; shows that he was working on these plates after a serious illness; in view of the delay, he suggested that some of the plates might be put in the hands of 'Mr Finden, Engleheart, Robinson, etc' to be engraved with their names (the idea does not seem to have been taken up by Murray). A letter from John Murray, dated '24 December, 1818' shows that he would pay £10 for the drawings ('or guineas') and the engravings were 'not to exceed £20' each' in the event Charles Heath (who had apparently talked Murray into letting him do the work in the first place) was asking £300 for the first six plates.

Ref No.	Book Title (Separate Print: S.P.)	Engraved After	Nos.	Caption & Page Reference	Size (cms)	Other Engravers
2	Byron's Works (continued).			*From the Turkish* 16) p.203 'These gifts...' *The Dream* 17) p.250 'And in the last...'		
3	The Arabian Nights.	Richard Westall R.A.	12	Vol I Frontispiece (p.211), p.45, p.79 Vol II Frontispiece (p.310), p.215, p.247 Vol III Frontispiece (p.98), p.38, p.161 Vol IV Frontispiece (p.11), p.21, p.337 No captions	7x9 8x6	
4	A Descriptive account of the mansion and garden seats of White Knights (T.C. Hofland).	Hofland	2	1) p.74 Cedar Seat 2) p.110 New Fishing Seat	22x28	L. Byrne T. Medland T.C. Lewis R. Peake Rawle T.C. Stadler
5	Description of the Western Islands of Scotland (John MacCulloch).	Mac Culloch	3	1) Frontispiece: Curved gneiss in Lewis 2) MacLeod's Maidens in Skey 3) Entrance to Fingal's cave on Staffa	13x19 13x18 14x21	H. F. Rose J. Stewart Byrne J. Archer J. Cross
6	Victories of the Duke of Wellington.	Richard Westall R.A.	1	Salamanca	21x26	T. Fielding
7	Musae Biblicae, or the Poetry of the Bible.	Paul Brill	1	Frontispiece: Abraham surveying the Ruins of Sodom	4x7	

Publisher	Location & References	Notes
Rodwell and Martin (Vols I, II, & IV) C. and J. Rivington, Rodwell and Martin, John Sharpe, and others (Vol III)	* BL.634.d.11-14 BMPR.C.13 (Vol II p.247 only)	Published in four volumes between 1819-25.
	YCBA.5425 Folio A V&A.J.8.a BL.192.f.16	An alternative title is '14 views of the mansion and garden seats of White Knights'. White Knights was the seat of the Duke of Marlborough, near Reading, and this work was presumably specially commissioned by him. The plates are described as 'Etch'd by C. Heath'.
A. Constable, Edinburgh and Hurst, Robinson	BL.579.i.12	Three volumes. These illustrations are rather weakly etched.
Rodwell and Martin	* NYPL.MEM F459.wv	'Published 1 Aug 1819'. A set of 12 aquatints, only one of which is inscribed as by Charles Heath; it is the only recorded example of his work in this medium.
Longman, Hurst, Rees, Orme, and Brown, and J. Hatchard	NYPL. + KZ3338	

Ref No.	Book Title (Separate Print: S.P.)	Engraved After	Nos.	Caption & Page Reference	Size (cms)	Other Engravers
8	The Sketchbook of Geoffrey Crayon (Washington Irving).	Richard Westall R.A.	?	?		
9	The Pleasures of Hope (Thomas Campbell).	Richard Westall R.A.	4	1) p.21 'Or lisps with holy look...' 2) p.25 'Piled on the steep...' 3) p.58 'But pauses oft...' 4) p.79 'Thrice from his trembling lips...'	7x5	

Publisher	Location & References	Notes
C.S. van Winkle, New York	NYPL	Two volumes. There was also 'A New Edition' with different plates (1821(7)).
Longman, Hurst, Rees, Orme and Brown	*	Described as 'A New Edition' with copper engraved plates dated 1818. Another 'New Edition' dated 1821 contains the same four plates, but this time inscribed 'Engraved on Steel by C. Heath', dated 1820, and printed by 'Perkins, Fairman and Heath'. The Longmans archive shows that two of these steel-engraved plates were commissioned by them in August 1820, thus becoming the first ever examples of steel engraving in book illustration, which was to revolutionise the industry. Another edition, with the same steel plates, appeared in 1822. See also 1806(3) in James Heath's catalogue for details of earlier illustrated editions of this popular work. An edition of Campbell's Poems published by Effingham Wilson in 1833 contains three out of the four prints from 1820, but dated 1830, and showing that as they were printed by Perkins, Bacon (the successors to Perkins Fairman & Heath), they had presumably had to be re-engraved. These prints are stated as being published also by Henry Colburn and Richard Bentley.

Ref No.	Book Title (Separate Print: S.P.)	Engraved After	Nos.	Caption & Page Reference	Size (cms)	Other Engravers
1	Italian Scenery	Miss	38	1) Vignette	13x10	G. Corbould
	(Captain Batty).	Batty		2) Aiguebelle	12x20	W.H. Smith
				3) Pass of Bramante		J. Lewis
				4) Lanslebourg		R. Wallis
				5) Turin	13x21	R. Rhodes
				6) Turin		C. Askey
				7) Genoa		Freebairn
				8) Rapallo		S. Mitan
				9) Castle of Larenza	20x13	E. Finden
				10) Pisa		
				11) Florence		
				12) Florence		
				13) Villa Borghese		
				14) S.E. view of Florence		
				15) Ponte del Palazzo		
				16) Terni		
				17) Rome from Palatini		
				18) Coliseum		
				19) Arch of Janus		
				20) Santa Croce		
				21) Temple of Minerva		
				22) St Peter's		
				23) Tomb of Plautino		
				24) Tivoli		
				25) Tivoli		
				26) Tivoli		
				27) Tivoli		
				28) La Riccia		
				29) Lake Albano		
				30) Virgil's Tomb		
				31) Ischia and Procida		
				32) Lago d'Agnano		
				33) Arco Felice		
				34) Naples (Capo di Chino)		
				35) Venice		
				36) Lago Maggiore		
				37) Bridge of Gondo		
				38) Ross Boden glacier		

Publisher	Location & References	Notes
Rodwell and Martin	* NYPL. +KZ3338 (30) only) V&A.J.4.d (2) and 3) only)	The first in Rodwell and Martin's 'European Scenery' series, with plates originally published on March 26, 1818. The engravings are on copper, not steel, as so often described in dealers' catalogues.

Ref No.	Book Title (Separate Print: S.P.)	Engraved After	Nos.	Caption & Page Reference	Size (cms)	Other Engravers
2	Self Cultivation Recommended (Isaac Taylor).	I. Taylor	1	Frontispiece: 'I must now think for myself...'	9x7	
3	Swiss Scenery (Major Cockburn).	Major Cockburn	26	1) Vignette: William Tell tower 2) Mont Blanc 3) Sallencer 4) Martigny tower 5) Great St Bernard 6) Felsenburgh 7) Rhone bridge 8) Chillon 9) Clarens 10) Vevay 11) Neuchatel 12) Fribourg 13) Interlachen 14) Lauterbrun 15) Grindelwald glacier 16) Wetterhorn 17) Engelberg 18) Lucern 19) Lake of Zug 20) Altorf 21) Devil's Bridge 22) Goschenen 23) Ariolo 24) Bellinzona 25) Lugano 26) Constance	11x10 12x20 13x20	E. Goodall C. Westwood J. Lewis C. Askey R. Wallis A. Freebairn H. Robson W.B. Smith G. Corbould E. Finden C. Pye W. Radclyffe
4	The Pilgrim's Progress (John Bunyan).	Richard Westall R.A.	6	1) Frontispiece: 'Do you see yonder?...' 2) p.44 'Now as he was sleeping...' 3) p.190 'Brother, I see...'	7x6	

Publisher	Location & References	Notes
Baldwin, Cradock and Joy	*	The portrait of the young man here resembles Charles Heath himself, as he appears in the Dawson Turner portrait of about the same period.
Rodwell and Martin	* V&A.Z.12.6 (4) only) V&A.J.4.d (21) – 23) only)	One of the 'European Scenery' series. Published on May 1, 1820, the work contains 60 engravings, plus two vignettes in all. The book was published in parts, the first of which was advertised in November 1818 as containing five engravings by Charles Heath.
Hurst, Robinson	*	'A New Edition'.

Ref No.	Book Title (Separate Print: S.P.)	Engraved After	Nos.	Caption & Page Reference	Size (cms)	Other Engravers
4	The Pilgrim's Progress (continued).			4) p.204 'Oh, said Christian...' 5) p.220 'Then he took her again...' 6) p.286 'The Lion came on...'		
5	Poetical Works of Mrs Elizabeth Rowe.	J. Thurston	1	Frontispiece: 'A bright ethereal youth...	8x6	F. Engleheart
6	Cowper's Poems (William Cowper).	Richard Westall R.A.	2	1) Frontispiece: 'I was a stricken deer...' 2) Title page: 'Descending now...'	6x5 5x4	
7	Don Quixote (Cervantes).	Richard Westall R.A.	22	*Vol I* Frontispiece +5 *Vol II* Frontispiece +4 *Vol III* Frontispiece +4 *Vol IV* Frontispiece +5 No captions	8x7 8x6	
8	Paul and Virginia (J.H.B. de Saint-Pierre).	Richard Westall R.A.	5	1) Frontispiece/Title page 2) p.36 'Don't be afraid...' 3) p.56 'Virginia loved to repose...' 4) p.104 'In that spot I found Paul...' 5) p.146 'It was 'Virginia'...'	6x5 7x5 6x7 7x6	

Publisher	Location & References	Notes
Suttaby, Evance and Fox	* BL.11661.a.12	
F.C. and J. Rivington and others	*	The plates, which are dated '1 May 1820', re-appeared in an early English Classics edition of 1825, published by Longmans. See also 1810(1) for earlier engravings of Cowper's Works by Charles Heath; and 1798(1) in James Heath's catalogue.
Hurst, Robinson	* V&A.J.6.f (3 prints only)	Described as 'A New Edition'. For an earlier version, see 1817(6). According to Farington (p.5325), this new edition was intended as a rival to the 1817 edition, with Westall's drawings substituted for Smirke's; on p.5611, Farington gives details of the payments made to Westall. There is perhaps a parallel here in James Heath's only partially successful attempt to rival Boydell's Shakspeare in 1802.
John Sharpe, and others	* V&A.J.5.c (1) only)	The plates are dated 1819 and 1820. A French version appeared in 1823, with designs by A.J. Desenne. See 1828(2) for a later edition with different engravings by Charles Heath.

Ref No.	Book Title (Separate Print: S.P.)	Engraved After	Nos.	Caption & Page Reference	Size (cms)	Other Engravers
9	Tales of the Genii (Sir Charles Morell).	Richard Westall R.A.	8	*Vol I* Frontispiece, p.56, p.134, p.197 *Vol II* Frontispiece, p.50, p.99, p.297 No captions	7x6	
10	Illustrations to Crabbe's Poems.	Richard Westall R.A.	31	No captions	9x8	
11	Description of the Collection of Ancient Marbles in the British Museum (Parts IV, VI, VII and VIII).	Henry Corbould	10	*Part IV* 1) Pl.VI Phigalian marbles: a female between two centaurs 2) Pl.XV Two Greeks fighting an Amazon 3) Pl.XXI Battle scene *Part VI* 4) Pl.XIII Ilissus: Headless male lying on one side 5) Pl.XIV Ilissus: Back of headless torso *Part VII* 6) Frontispiece: two headless bodies 7) Two horses 8) p.51 Metape VI Centaur fighting headless Greek 9) p.55 Metape VIII Centaur fighting Greek *Part VIII* 10) Pl. XIX Procession of horse riders	10x25 and various	G. Corbould Engleheart Cooke Burney Landseer Robinson E. Finden W. Finden Burnett Moses Freebairn Doo Bromley Newton J.H. Watt Greatbatch Warren Davenport

Publisher	Location & References	Notes
Rodwell and Martin	* V&A.J.6.f	Two volumes. See also 1805(5) in James Heath's catalogue for an earlier version.
Longman, Hurst, Rees, Orme and Brown	V&A.J.8.a	Charles Heath accepted this commission on January 19, 1820, promising to deliver by March 1821, at 40 guineas per engraving.
G. and W. Nicol	BMPR.242. a.12	Part IV was published in 1820 with 1) being dated 'May 1, 1819'. Part VI was published in 1830, with the etchings being dated '8 November 1828'. Part VII was published in 1835, with the etchings dated 'December 1826'. Part VIII was published in 'June 4, 1839'. See also 1810(2) to which this work may have been connected, and 1812(11) for Part I. See also 1856 for Part XI, in which both Alfred and Frederick Heath were involved (Frederick Heath's catalogue, 1856(24)).

Ref No.	Book Title (Separate Print: S.P.)	Engraved After	Nos.	Caption & Page Reference	Size (cms)	Other Engravers
12	Robinson Crusoe (Daniel Defoe).	Thomas Stothard R.A.	21	No captions	12x9	
13	A Selection of Popular National Airs (Henry Bishop).	Thomas Stothard R.A.	2	1) Hope and Love (Cupid in a boat, being despatched by ?one of the Graces 2) Commonsense and Genius	13x18 12x16	
14	The Poetical Works of Sir Walter Scott.	Sir Henry Raeburn R.A.	1	Frontispiece: Sir Walter Scott	9x7	
15	Boydell's Illustrations of Holy Writ.					
16	The Odyssey of Homer (A. Pope).	Richard Westall R.A.	1	Frontispiece	7x6	

Publisher	Location & References	Notes
T. Cadell and W. Davies	* V&A.J.5.c V&A.I.65 (E1381-1907 and 20569.12)	Two volumes, published 'Feby 1, 1820'. Although 21 in number, rather than the original 16 (including the title page), the plates appear to be otherwise almost identical with those engraved by T. Medland after Stothard in 1790 for the Stockdale edition. The 1790 edition was republished in 1804 with Medland's plates dark and worn. The five additional plates are: 1) Crusoe and Xury alarmed at the sight of a lion. 2) Crusoe terrified by the Goat. 3) Crusoe's men vowing vengeance for the death of their comrade. 4) A Chinese gentleman at dinner. 5) Crusoe travelling in Chinese Tartary. In 1), 3) and 5) the composition has been reversed.
J. Power, Dublin	* V&A.J.2.c BMPR.C.20 (Balmanno Vol 3)	Frontispiece dated '1 Jan 1820'. The words to this selection were by Thomas Moore, and the series is believed to date from 1818-26. See also 1816(6).
Archibald Constable, Edinburgh	NYPL. +KZ3813 YCBA	Published in twelve volumes, without other engravings.
C. Whittingham	*	An early volume in the English Classics series.

Ref No.	Book Title (Separate Print: S.P.)	Engraved After	Nos.	Caption & Page Reference	Size (cms)	Other Engravers
1	Scenery of the Rhine, Belgium and Holland (Captain Batty).	Captain Batty	2	1) No.23 Andernach 2) No.36 Ypres	12x21	
2	Craven's Tour through the Southern Provinces of the Kingdom of Naples (Richard Keppel Craven).	R.K. Craven	12	1) p.24 Benevento 2) p.44 Castle of Lucera 3) p.118 Polignano 4) p.142 Castle of Otranto 5) p.150 Castle of Brindisi 6) p.176 Taranto 7) p.212 Cassano 8) p.300 Entrance to Faro of Messina 9) p.330 Maida from Nicastro 10) p.354 Lauria 11) p.364 On the road near Silignano 12) p.378 Salerno	11x17	Hawkins J. Walker
3	Illustrations to Shakspeare.	Robert Smirke R.A.	4	1) Frontispiece: *The Tempest.* Caliban 2) *The Tempest.* On the island: Ferdinand and Miranda 3) Frontispiece: *Twelfth Night* 4) Title page: *Merry Wives of Windsor*	10x8 7x7	W. Finden J. Mitchell Engleheart

Publisher	Location & References	Notes
Rodwell and Martin	V&A.Z.8.b (1) only)	The third publication in the 'European Scenery' series (see 1820(1) and (3)). 1) re-appeared later in 'The English Keepsake' or 'Talisman' (U/D 36) though in a reduced form. It was also republished by Robert Jennings on 1 July, 1825.
Rodwell and Martin	* BMPR.174.a.7 V&A.J.6.f V&A.Z.12.a (3) only) NYPL.PC.1.2.1 SL (Walker 1825 edition)	These engravings were republished in 1825 by John Walker, described as 'Italian Scenes, A Series of Interesting Delineations of Remarkable Views', and bound up with 14 other views of Italy, mainly by Taylor.
Rodwell and Martin, Hurst, Robinson, R. Jennings	* (3) only) BMPR.165. b.22 BMPR.C.13 V&A.J.6.a (4) only)	88 plates were issued in this edition, after Smirke's drawings, between 1821 and 1834, and several publishers were involved, including publishers in the U.S.A. Hurst, Robinson, for instance, published re-issues in 1825 and 1829, which included 12 more engravings by Charles Heath (without captions) as follows: Romeo and Juliet Act I Sc.IV, Act II Sc.II, Act III Sc.V, Henry IV Part I Act II Sc.III, Act II Sc.IV (Falstaff), Title page, Act II ScIII, Act V Sc.IV, Twelfth Night Act IV ScIII, The Taming of the Shrew Act II ScI, and The Merry Wives of Windsor Act I Sc.I. and Act III Sc.III.

Ref No.	Book Title (Separate Print: S.P.)	Engraved After	Nos.	Caption & Page Reference	Size (cms)	Other Engravers
4	Travels in Georgia, Persia, Armenia, Ancient Babylonia etc, etc, during the years 1817-20 (Sir Robert Ker Porter).	Sir Robert Ker Porter	35 + 9	*Vol I* 1) Sketches of a bas-relief: (Chardin/ Niebuhr. Lebrun) 2) p.492. Pl.13 At Mourg Aub. 3) p.516. Pl.17 At Nakshi Roustan 4) p.522. Pl.19 A bas-relief at Nakshi Roustan 5) p.537. Pl.20 At Nakshi Roustan 6) p.540. Pl.21 At Nakshi Roustan 7) p.543. Pl.22 At Nakshi Roustan 8) p.548. Pl.23 At Nakshi Roustan 9) p.557. Pl.24 At Nakshi Roustan 10) p.571. Pl.27 At Nakshi Rajab 11) p.572. Pl.28 At Nakshi Rajab 12) p.585. Pl.31 At Persepolis 13) p.590. Pl.32 At Persepolis 14) p.591. Pl.33 At Persepolis 15) p.598. Pl.35 At Persepolis 16) p.601. Pl.36 At Persepolis 17) p.642. Pl.46 At Persepolis 18) p.652. Pl.47 At Persepolis	 30x19 (item 3) 16x22 (item 4) 16x23 (item 5) 25x18 (item 11)	J. Clark Hall

Publisher	Location & References	Notes
Longman, Hurst, Rees, Orme and Brown	* Abbey Travel Vol II Item 359 BMPR.C.195 (proof of 12) only)	Published 1821-2 in two volumes. Etchings/lithographs.

Ref No.	Book Title (Separate Print: S.P.)	Engraved After	Nos.	Caption & Page Reference	Size (cms)	Other Engravers
4	Travels in Georgia etc (continued).			19) p.656. Pl 48 At Persepolis		
				20) p.672. Pl.52 At Persepolis		
				21) p.673. Pl.53 At Persepolis		
				22) p.677. Pl.54 At Persepolis		
				23) p.706. Pl.57 At Shiraz	16x23	
				24) p.707. Pl.58 Sassanian coins	25x18	
				25) p.720. Pl.34 Ornamental stairs at Persepolis	4x48	
				26) [At end] Plates 37-43, 49-50	21x39	
				Vol II		
				27) p.828. Pl.60 At Besitoon	16x34	
				28) p.828 Pl.62 At Tackti Bostan	32x26	
				29) p.828. Pl.63 Tackti Bostan	25x40	
				30) p.828. Pl.64 Tackti Bostan		
				31) p.188. Pl.65 Tackti Bostan		
				32) p.191. Pl.66 Tackti Bostan	13x24	
				33) p.424. Pl.79 Found at Babylon, coins etc	17x25 24x16	
				34) p.425. Pl.80 Found at Babylon, cylinders etc		
				35) p.597. Pl.82 At Salmos	14x26	

Publisher	Location & References	Notes

Ref No.	Book Title (Separate Print: S.P.)	Engraved After	Nos.	Caption & Page Reference	Size (cms)	Other Engravers
5	Mavor's Spelling Book.	Thomas Stothard R.A.	1	Title page, with three oval vignettes	12x8	
6	Memoirs, Historical and Topographical of Bristol (Samuel Seyer).	Rev'd J. Eagles	1	*Vol I* p.59 View of Caer-Odor	11x21	F. Blore W. Lander S. Rawle J. Lambert
7	The Sketchbook (Washington Irving).	C.R. Leslie R.A.	2	*Vol I* p.131 1) 'A Royal Poet' 2) 'Philip of Pokanoket'	11x8	E. Scriven C. Rolls
8	Gertrude of Wyoming (Thomas Campbell).	Richard Westall R.A.	3	Frontispiece: 1) p.11 'And I the eagle of my tribe...' 2) p.21 'It was in this lone valley...' 3) p.34 'The chief, his old bewildered head...'	7x6	
9	The Monastery (Sir Walter Scott).	Richard Westall R.A.	8	Title page: 1) 'Landed' 2) The Lady of Avenel 3) First Invocation 4) The Spirit of Avenel 5) Warden reproving Julian Avenel 6) Mysie Happer's Visit	9x7	

Publisher	Location & References	Notes
Longman, Hurst, Rees, Orme and Brown	BMPR.C.20 (Balmanno, Vol III)	'Publ Sept. 10,1821' and inscribed 'Perkins & Heath Patent Hardened steel plate'; possibly the second book with Heath steel engravings (see Notes to 1819(9)). A letter from Longmans to Charles Heath dated '8 December 1824' states that the plate is 'worked out', and asks for another drawing.
J.M. Gutch, Bristol	BL.10350.i.1 YCBA	
John Murray	* BMPR.167.c.21 p.59	'A New Edition' (see 1819(8) for first edition). See also entries for Irving in 1825(11).
Longman, Hurst, Rees, Orme, and Brown Longman, Hurst, Rees, Orme, and Brown and John Murray	* * BMPR.165.a.18 V&A.J.6.f	There are at least three editions with the same plates: 1) An 1816 issue with the plates dated that year. 2) An 1821 issue described as the 'Eighth' edition with plates dated '1819'. 3) Described as the Ninth Edition, but with the same plates inscribed 'Engraved by C. Heath... Perkins & Heath Hardened Steel Plate 1822', and with a publication date '1825'. 2) appears to be the fourth (or fifth) book produced with steel engraved illustrations; (see Notes to 1819(9), 1821(5), Debrett's Peerage (1822) and Pinnock's Goldsmith Histories of Greece and Rome (1823)9)&10)). Re-engraved and re-published in 1833, with 1830 dates (see Notes to 1819(9).
Hurst, Robinson	V&A.93.D.217 YCBA.B1984. 21 143 (6) only) NYPL. +KZ (8) only)	

Ref No.	Book Title (Separate Print: S.P.)	Engraved After	Nos.	Caption & Page Reference	Size (cms)	Other Engravers
9	The Monastery (continued)			7) Catharine discovered 8) Halbert		
10	The Lady of the Lake (Sir Walter Scott).	Richard Cook	1	'Then safe though fluttered...'	11x9	
11	Kenilworth Illustrated: or the history of the castle priory.	C.R. Leslie R.A.				J. Scott Engleheart Rolls
12	Illustrations to the Works of Sir Walter Scott.	Richard Westall R.A. A. Chalon R.A. Henry Corbould	14	*Guy Mannering* 1) The dead body of Kennedy 2) The Meeting of Meg Merrilies, Brown and Linmont 3) Meg Merrilies attending upon a dying smuggler 4) 'At this moment the door opened...' 5) The death of Meg Merrilies 6) 'As he was about to turn his borse's head...' 7) The sudden appearance of Meg Merrilies on Gibbie's Knowe *The Abbot* 8) 'But it is over, and I am Mary Stuart once more...' 9) Roland Graeme offering his services to the Queen 10) Roland introduced to Sir Halbert Glendinning	10x8 9x7	

Publisher	Location & References	Notes
Longman, Hurst, Rees, Orme, and Brown	BMPR.C.13	'Publ. March 29, 1821'.
Hurst, Robinson	YCBA	
Hurst, Robinson & Co	1) NYPL. +KZ3846 2) NYPL. +KZ2881 3) NYPL. +KZ3691 4)-5) +KZ 6) NYPL. +KZ3844 7) NYPL. +KZ3928	1) to 8) are dated '1821'.
	8) NYPL. +KZ2443 9) NYPL. +KZ2450 10) NYPL. +KZ2379	8) See 'Pictorial Illustrations to the Waverley Novels (1829(3) where this print is dated 1831 (possible re-engraved). 9) and 10) are both dated '1824', so presumably belong to a later edition.

Ref No.	Book Title (Separate Print: S.P.)	Engraved After	Nos.	Caption & Page Reference	Size (cms)	Other Engravers
12	Illustrations to the Works of Sir Walter Scott (continued).	W. Allen		*The Legend of Montrose* 11) Captain Dalgetty consigning Gustavus		
		Liversage		*The Fair Maid of Perty* 12) Girl kneeling in front of a monk		
		Richard Westall R.A.		*Ivanhoe* 13) 'The Tournament'		
		Catter-mole		*Old Mortality* 14) Jenny Dennison, Edith and Halliday		

Publisher	Location & References	Notes
	11) NYPL. +KZ4762	11) is dated '1820'.
	12) NYPL. +KZ	12) may be the same as 'Juliet' at p.36 in 'The Keepsake' (see 1833(1)2)).
	13) V&A	
	14) NYPL. +KZ	14) probably belongs to a later edition.
	YCBA	

Ref No.	Book Title (Separate Print: S.P.)	Engraved After	Nos.	Caption & Page Reference	Size (cms)	Other Engravers
1	French Scenery (European Scenery France) (Captain Batty).	Captain Batty	28	1) Frontispiece 2) Dieppe 3) Dieppe 4) Rouen 5) St Germain-en-Laye 6) Banks of the Seine 7) Paris 8) Paris 9) Halle au blé 10) Porte St Denis 11) St Denis 12) Pere Lachaise 13) Hôtel de Ville 14) Pont Nôtre Dame 15) Isle du Palais 16) Nôtre Dame 17) Palais of the Luxembourg 18) Pantheon 19) Pont de Jena 20) The Louvre 21) The Louvre 22) St Cloud 23) Petit Trianon 24) Auxerre 25) Lyons 26) Strasbourg 27) Bordeaux 28) Boulogne (St Nicholas)	21x18 13x21 20x14	S. Porter J. Roffe R. Wallis E. Finden S. Mitan E. Roberts C. Askey G. Corbould J. C. Edwards H. Le Keux F. Blore
2	The Shipwreck (Falconer).	Richard Westall R.A.	1	Frontispiece: 'And O protect my wife…'	6x5	E. Portbury W. Finden E. Finden Engleheart
3	The Deserted Village (Oliver Goldsmith).	Richard Westall R.A.	1	Title page: 'Down where yon anchoring vessel…'	7x7	

Publisher	Location & References	Notes
Rodwell and Martin	* NYPL. +KZ3341 NYPL. +KZ6902	Published in the European Scenery series. Captain Batty is described as 'of the Grenadier Guards'. The NYPL copy also includes engravings of the 'Barrière de Neuilly' and the 'Barrière de Passy'.
John Sharpe	*	
John Sharpe	V&A.J.5.c	'Publ. Aug 1, 1822'. See 1816(3) for an earlier edition, with different engravings.

Ref No.	Book Title (Separate Print: S.P.)	Engraved After	Nos.	Caption & Page Reference	Size (cms)	Other Engravers
4	Tales of the Hall (Crabbe).	Richard Westall R.A.	11	1) 'And would the butler and the cook surprise…' 2) 'Who is there?' 3) 'It turn'd, and I beheld…' 4) 'At the bed's feet' 5) 'And while the admiring people…' 6) 'With what strong interest…' 7) 'The fair ones took me…' 8) 'While the rough husband…' 9) 'He went and he returned…' 10) 'My father's look…' 11) 'There she ope'd her door…'	9x8	
5	The Iliad of Homer (Pope's Iliad).		2	1) Frontispiece: 'The good old Priam…' 2) 'This past he slaughtered…'	7x5 8x5	
6	Debrett's Peerage and Baronetage.		1	Frontispiece: George IV in coronation robes	11x7	
7	Dangerous Errors.	Thomas Stothard R.A.	1	'Lord Tavernier, as he pressed the bending fragile form…'	8x7	

Publisher	Location & References	Notes
John Murray	BMPR.C.13	The prints are dated 'Jan 1822'. See 1820(10) for the companion volume of illustrations to Crabbe's Poems, although this was published by Longmans, and not Murray.
F.C. and J. Rivington	*	See 1827(7) for another edition, with different engravings.
F.C. and J. Rivington (and others)	*	An early example of steel engraving. The same engraving was used in the 1823 edition of Debrett's.
T. Relfe	BMPR.C.20 (Balmanno, Vol III) RA (Frost Vol IX)	

Ref No.	Book Title (Separate Print: S.P.)	Engraved After	Nos.	Caption & Page Reference	Size (cms)	Other Engravers
8	The Lady's Magazine, or Mirror of the Belles Lettres.	Robert Smirke R.A.	2	Lalla Rookh: The Fire Worshippers 1) p.512 'The youth so fleet and bold' The Light of the Harem 2) p.641 'And now a spirit form'd...'	10x8	J. Heath J. Robinson W. Finden J. Romney
9	Outline Engravings and Descriptions of the Woburn Abbey Marbles.	John Flaxman R.A.	2	1) Pl.V Apollo Musagetes, Minerva and the Muses 2) Pl.XXXVII Group in the Pediment of the Temple of Liberty	32x47	
10	S.P.	W.T. Fry and Henry Corbould	1	Five portraits with the ornamental part described as 'Engraved by C. Heath'		W. T. Fry
11	S.P.	T.C. Hofland	1	Richmond from Twickenham Park	24x37	

Publisher	Location & References	Notes
S. Robinson	BMPR.166.d.12	Described as 'A New Series', these plates appear to have been taken from the 12th edition of Lalla Rookh; see Notes to 1817(9).
	Houghton Plc8 F7855 A8226	
T. Boys	NYPL. +KZ3069 +KZ3089	'Publ. April 1 1822'. 'Patent hardened steel plate. Fairman and Heath'. These are engraved portraits of Lord Binning, Lord Maitland, and three others.
Hurst, Robinson	BL.:L. Fagan (History of British Engraving, Vol III) YCBA.B1977. 14.11741	'Publ. Oct 1, 1822'. Fagan maintains that this print was actually the work of two of Charles Heath's distinguished pupils, J.H. Watt and G. Doo. See also 1827(12).

Ref No.	Book Title (Separate Print: S.P.)	Engraved After	Nos.	Caption & Page Reference	Size (cms)	Other Engravers
3	The Novels of Sir Walter Scott.	C.R. Leslie R.A.	17	*Waverley Vol I* 1) Frontispiece: Flora of the Glen 2) Title page *Vol II* 3) Title page: Holyrood *Guy Mannering Vol III* 4) Title page: Ellangoran Castle *The Antiquary Vol IV* 5) Title page: Ruins of St Ruth *Rob Roy Vol V* 6) Title page: Ruins of Inversnaid Fort Vol VI 7) Frontispiece: Francis Osbaldeston and Diana *Old Mortality Vols VII and VIII* 8) Title page: Craignathan 9) Bothwell Brig *Heart of Midlothian Vol IX* 10) Title page: St Anthony's Chapel *Vol X* 11) Interview of Jeannie Deans 12) Tolbooth, Edinburgh *Vol XI The Bride of Lammermoor* 13) Crichton Castle 14) The Ominous Incident at the Mermaidens Fountain	9x7 5x6 10x7 5x6	J. Mitchell J. Romney E. Portbury C. Rolls A. Warren E. Finden R. Baker W. Lizars Horsburgh Johnstone

Publisher	Location & References	Notes
Archibald Constable, Edinburgh and Hurst, Robinson (later Cadell and Whitaker)	* BMPR.C.13 (7) & 12) only) 7) NYPL. +KZ 11) NYPL. +KZ4088 13) NYPL. +KZ3091 NYPL Print Room (Bohn's edition)	Published between 1823 and 1833 in 41 volumes. See also 1821(12) for another edition with engravings by Charles Heath. The plates were reprinted several times, notably by H.G. Bohn in 1848 and 1862 as 'The Book of Waverley Gems'. This also included two engravings from 'The Monastery' by James Heath (see 1820(1)12) and 13) in his catalogue). 17) is described as 'The Countess and the Earl', and there are two additional plates by Charles Heath, 'The Betrothed' and 'Lady Eveline'. See also 'The Waverley Album' (undated (9) ca. 1840) which contains all these plates. See also Jennings and Chaplin's edition (undated (2-3) ca.1831) for other engravings of Sir Walter Scott's Novels by Charles Heath.

Ref No.	Book Title (Separate Print: S.P.)	Engraved After	Nos.	Caption & Page Reference	Size (cms)	Other Engravers
3	The Novels of Walter Scott (continued).			*A Legend of Montrose Vol XII* 15) Title page: Old Inverary 16) Dalgetty and Ranald *Kenilworth Vol XVIII* 17) 'The Countess Admiring...'	 5x6 9x7	
4	The Loves of the Angels (Thomas Moore).	Richard Westall R.A.	3	1) Frontispiece: 'From a clear lamp...' 2) p.22 'While thus I spoke...' 3) p.110 'He saw upon the golden sand...'	8x7 10x8	E. Portbury
5	Sicilian Scenery (Major Light).	P. Dewitt Major Light	10	1) Palermo 2) Cefalu 3) Castel Buono 4) Alicate 5) Santa Rosalia 6) Capuchin Convent, Taormina 7) Catania 8) Temple of Concord 9) Capuchin Convent, Syracuse 10) Syracuse	11x23 13x20	R. Wallis Middiman C. Askey E. Finden G. Corbould W. Cooke Jr E. Goodall J. Byrne H. Hobson J. Middiman W. Miller C. Lacey C. Westwood J.C. Allen W. Radclyffe G. Hollis J.C. Edwards J. Pye

Publisher	Location & References	Notes
	15) NYPL. +KZ	
	17) NYPL. +KZ4596	Dated '1824'.
Longman, Hurst, Rees, Orme, and Brown	*	'Engraved on steel by C. Heath: Perkins and Heath Hardened Plate'. Another edition, also dated 1823, has the same plates differently inscribed 'Engraved by C. Heath from drawings by R. Westall' i.e. presumably on copper, not on steel (see also the Notes to 1819(9) where much the same procedure seems to have been followed with the 'Pleasures of Hope'). The Illustrations were evidently issued separately from the text, and only few copies are known bound up together.
Rodwell and Martin	* BMPR.C.13	In the 'European Scenery' series.

Ref No.	Book Title (Separate Print: S.P.)	Engraved After	Nos.	Caption & Page Reference	Size (cms)	Other Engravers
6	The History of Richmondshire (Whitaker).	J.M.W. Turner R.A.	2	1) Kirby Lonsdale Churchyard 2) Ingleborough, from Hornby Castle terrace	19x28	
7	German Scenery (Captain Batty).	Captain Batty	11	1) The Danube 2) Junction of the Iller and Danube 3) Wasserburg 4) The Untersberg near Salzburg 5) The Danube near Linz 6) Linz 7) Linz 8) The Walls of Vienna 9) Baaden 10) The Danube near Vienna 11) The Danube near Leopoldsburg	13x21 20x14	W. Miller J.A. Rolph E. Blore R. Acon H. Hobson C. Westwood W. Wallis R. Wallis J. Allen G. Hollis R. Woolnoth T. Barber C. Askey T. Owen E. Roberts S. Lacey Finden Cooke W. Radclyffe J. Redaway H. Winkles G. Corbould J. Henshall W. R. Smith W. Tombleson
8	The Minstrel (James Beattie).	Richard Westall R.A.	3	1) Frontispiece: 'The wild harp rang…' 2) p.6 'With merriment, song and timbrels clear…' 3) p.38 'Responsive to the sprightly pipe…'	6x5 6x6	J. Mitan J. Robinson

Publisher	Location & References	Notes
D. Appleton, New York	* YCBA. B1977.14 6818	This work was first published between 1818 and 1823. According to Rawlinson, these two prints appeared in 1822.
Rodwell and Martin	*	Published in 1823 in the 'European Scenery' series, with the plates dated 'June 1, 1821'.
John Sharpe	* V&A.J.5.c	Published '1 Jan 1823', but with the proof plates in the V&A collection dated 'April 27 1816'. See the Notes to 1801(2) in the James Heath catalogue for details of earlier editions of Beattie's Poems, including 'The Minstrel', with James Heath engravings.

Ref No.	Book Title (Separate Print: S.P.)	Engraved After	Nos.	Caption & Page Reference	Size (cms)	Other Engravers
9	Pinnock's Improved Edition of Dr Goldsmith's Abridgement of the History of Greece.		1	Frontispiece: Portrait of Dr Goldsmith	14x8	
10	Pinnock's Improved Edition of Dr Goldsmith's Abridgement of the History of Rome.		1	Frontispiece: Portrait of Dr Goldsmith	14x8	
11	The Social Day (Coxe).		1	p.258 The Carpet Dance	22x15	C. Warren J. Scott W. Bond J. Byrne T. Bragge E. Scriven Moses J. Burnett
12	S.P.	H. Billinge	1	Wrexham Church in the County of Denbigh: Mrs Mary Myddleton's Monument (d.1747) by Roubilliac	45x27	
13	S.P.	Richard Westall R.A.	1	'The Girl at the Well'	30x23	
14	S.P.	Sir A. van Dyck	1	'A Gentleman of the Court of King Charles the First'	26x21	

Publisher	Location & References	Notes
G. and W.B. Whittaker	Dr B. Hunnisett (Greece only) * (Rome only)	Inscribed 'Hardened Steel Plate... Perkins, Fairman and Heath 1821', but 'Perkins and Heath Patent Hardened Steel Plate 1823' on the title page. Evidently an early use of steel, but not necessarily by Charles Heath.
Carpenter and Ackermann	BL.L.R.408 c.14	Although inscribed by Thomson, this print was finished by Charles Heath, as a tribute to him by Coxe witnesses. The postscript to the book's advertisement mentions that through 'the kind offices of Mr Charles Heath, at the request of Mr Henry Corbould... he has been enabled to publish the work this spring, which he had utterly despaired of, without omitting the plate in question'. 'Published July 1, 1823'.
H. Billinge, Wrexham	V&A.R.8.a(ii) (28010)	
Hurst, Robinson	* NAL. Special Collection 86.cc.20 (Vol II Artists' Autographs)	
Hurst, Robinson	* V&A.J.6.f	'Published for the Select Work of Engravings by William Buchanan... 1st October 1823'.

Ref No.	Book Title (Separate Print: S.P.)	Engraved After	Nos.	Caption & Page Reference	Size (cms)	Other Engravers
15	S.P.	S. Drummond (from a drawing by W.H. Brooks)	1	[Sir] William Parry	16x10	
16	S.P.		1	'James I, King of Scotland'		
17	S.P.	T.C. Mofland	1	View of the Thames from Richmond Hill	44x61	

Publisher	Location & References	Notes
Cherwood & Co	Huntington 109851.II pt.1.160a	'Publ Nov. 2nd 1823'. Parry is depicted standing on top of a globe with a shipwreck in polar ice below. As Parry was not knighted until 1829, and was only a naval lieutenant in 1823 when this print was first published, this was presumably a later reissue.
	NYPL. +KZ10774	The title should presumably have been 'James I King of England, and James VI of Scotland'.
Hurst, Robinson	* Mackenzie (British Prints, 1987)	Possibly a companion engraving to 1822(11).

Ref No.	Book Title (Separate Print: S.P.)	Engraved After	Nos.	Caption & Page Reference	Size (cms)	Other Engravers
1	The Works of Benjamin Franklin.	G. Hughes	2	1) Frontispiece: 'When they were about to satisfy their hunger...' 2) Title page: 'But if when the Husband rises in the morning...'	8x6 6x6	
2	Young's Night Thoughts, or The Complaint.	Henry Corbould	2	1) Frontispiece: 'What numbers...' 2) 'Warning for less...'	8x6 6x6	
3	Roderick, the Last of the Goths (Robert Southey).	Richard Westall R.A.	6	1) 'Before the cross...' 2) 'Well it was...' 3) 'To Roderick then...' 4) 'His loose robe this day...' 5) 'Behold the man...' 6) 'With firm ese...'	9x7	
4	Illustrations to Irish Melodies (Thomas Moore).	Thomas Stothard R.A.	6	1) 'Come send round the wine...' 2) 'Come rest in this bosom...' 3) 'But while o'er the roses...' 4) 'Rich and rare...' 5) 'Oh the heart that has truly loved...' 6) 'Beauty lies...'	10x7	
5	Gems of Devotional Poetry.	Thomas Stothard R.A.	1	Title page	7x6	
6	Gems of Lyric Poetry.	Thomas Stothard R.A.	1	Title page	7x6	

Publisher	Location & References	Notes
W. Baynes and Son, and others	*	Published in Dove's English Classics series.
W. Baynes and Son, and others	*	Published in Dove's English Classics series, and reprinted in 1845 by Thomas Allman. See also 1817(12) for an earlier version with different engraving by Charles Heath.
Longman, Hurst, Rees, Orme, and Brown	V&A.93.D.217 p.57 V&A.J.4.d p.34	
Robert Jennings and S. Robinson Hurst, Robinson	BMPR.C.20 (Balmanno, Vol III)	The Balmanno copies are marked (in pencil) 'never published'.
	BMPR.C.20 (Balmanno, Vol III)	
Thomas Tegg	BMPR.C.20 (Balmanno, Vol III)	Dated 'Sept 1824'.
Thomas Tegg	BMPR.C.20 (Balmanno, Vol III)	Dated 'Sept 1824'.

Ref No.	Book Title (Separate Print: S.P.)	Engraved After	Nos.	Caption & Page Reference	Size (cms)	Other Engravers
7	Poetical Sketches (Alaric Watts).	Thomas Stothard R.A.	2	1) Frontispiece: 'Then they fling the snow-white veil aside…' 2) p.30 'Upon his brow the damps of death…'	9x7	E.L. Roberts
8	The Improvisatrice and other Poems (L.E.L.) (Laetitia Landon).	J.M. Wright	4	1) Frontispiece: 'He heard her prayer…' 2) p.45 [No caption] 3) p.128 Rosalie 4) p.170 [No caption]	9x7	J. Pye
9	Tales of a Traveller (Washington Irving).	Thomas Stothard R.A.	5	1) p.65 [No caption] 2) p.75 German Student 3) p.145 The Young Italian 4) Wolfart Webber, or Golden Dreams 5) The Bold Dragoon	10x8	J.H. Watt J.C. Edwards
10	Poems (Samuel Rogers).	Richard Westall R.A.	6	Vol I p.14 1) 'Oft as he turned…' 2) p.25 'Want with her babes…' 3) p.38 'So thro' the grove…' 4) 'Her sense had fled…' 5) 'If o'er the mead…' 6) 'Flies from her home…'	9x7	
11	A Critical enquiry into Ancient Armour (Samuel R. Meyrick).	H. Bridgens	3	1) Frontispiece 2) Vol II 3) Vol III	9x18	H. Bridgens C. Hunt Maddocks
12	S.P.		1	Shakespeare		

Publisher	Location & References	Notes
Hurst, Robinson	BL.11642.aaa.24 (3rd edition) BMPR.C.20 (Balmanno)	
Hurst, Robinson	* V&A.J.6.f	There was 'A New Edition' in 1831. 'L.E.L.' was editress of Heath's 'Book of Beauty' from 1833 until her death in 1838. Disraeli described Miss Landon rather unkindly as 'the snub-nosed Brompton Sappho'.
John Murray	BMPR.C.20 (Balmanno Vol III) Witt (3) only)	
Hurst, Robinson	V&A.J.6.f (4) and 5) only Huntington 22341.I p.7 (1) to 5) only)	Oval prints.
R. Jennings	NYPL. +KZ10893 BL.562+.f.3 YCBA NYPL. +KZ10893	In 3 volumes.

Ref No.	Book Title (Separate Print: S.P.)	Engraved After	Nos.	Caption & Page Reference	Size (cms)	Other Engravers
1	Views in and About London.	P. Dewint William Westall A.R.A. Mackenzie	45 [49]	1) London Bridge 2) Burlington Arcade 3) View from Richmond Hill 4) Custom House 5) View of Waterloo Bridge 6) The Quadrant 7) London from Greenwich Hill 8) The Tower from the River 9) The Auction Mart, Bank etc. 10) Westminster Hall 11) Hampton Court 12) Cornhill 13) Tower Hill 14) Pool of London 15) Regent's Park 16) Windsor Great Park 17) View from terrace, Somerset House 18) Opera House 19) Sussex Place 20) London Bridge (second view) 21) Cornwall Terrace 22) Westminster Bridge 23) Green Park 24) Entrance to London Docks 25) St Pancras New Church 26) The Penitentiary 27) Battersea Bridge 28) All Souls' Church 29) The Monument	12x9 to 21x10	

Publisher	Location & References	Notes
[Hurst, Robinson]	* Guildhall 1), 2), 4), 7), 8), 10), 15), 20), 22), 31), 33), 34), 36), 37), 41), 45) only BL. Addit. Mss 33401 (Dodd's English Engravers)	In January 1826, Hurst, Robinson went bankrupt so that this work was never published, although a few proof sets of the engravings have survived, usually bound up with a text commentary on each view. Priced at £6 for the 45 plates, when bound in cloth. The Guildhall Library also holds prints in the same series of 'Bartholomew Lane' and 'Finsbury City Road' engraved by Charles Heath. A prospectus for this work, a copy of which is in the British Library, stated that it would be issued in monthly parts on '10 January 1825' at 9/- Imperial 8vo, or 14/- Proofs Royal qto'. The prospectus added 'The first talent in the empire has been employed in its execution'. Twelve numbers, each containing five engravings, were to be published, with the 'Picturesque Views' to be drawn by Dewint, and the 'Architectural' by Mackenzie and Westall, and all the engravings to be done by Charles Heath. Of the 60 prints originally intended, only 45 actually appeared, but in addition to the two extra mentioned above in the Guildhall Library, there is, according to Adams (London Illustrated 1604-1851) another view of Waterloo Bridge (besides 5)). A view of Windsor Castle, drawn by Dewint and engraved by Charles Heath, appears in the Literary Souvenir for 1826(3); this would make a total of 49 known in the series. 26) is also known described as 'The Milebank' i.e. Millbank.

Ref No.	Book Title (Separate Print: S.P.)	Engraved After	Nos.	Caption & Page Reference	Size (cms)	Other Engravers
1	Views in and About London (continued).			30) Lambeth Palace 31) Waterloo Place 32) Greenwich Hospital 33) Regent's Canal 34) St Pauls 35) Richmond Hill (second view) 36) Haymarket 37) Southwark Bridge 38) Regent Street 39) Regent Street (second view) 40) Richmond Bridge 41) Bow Church 42) Elgin Gallery 43) Somerset House 44) New buildings, Regent's Park 45) View from Old Palace Yard [46) Bartholomew Lane 47) Finsbury City Road 48) Waterloo Bridge (second view)]		
2	Theron and Aspasia (James Hervey).	Henry Corbould	2	1) Frontispiece: 'Father, not my will' 2) Title page: Figure of Christ	7x5 6x5	
3	Walton's Lives (Isaac Walton).	Henry Corbould J.M. Wright	2	1) Frontispiece 2) p.24 The Vision	13x8 10x7	W. Finden C. Rolls A.W. Warren J. Mitchell

Publisher	Location & References	Notes
J.F. Dove	* BMPR.167.c.21 p.34 (1) only)	In Dove's English Classics series. Published 'for the Proprietors'.
John Major	*	

Ref No.	Book Title (Separate Print: S.P.)	Engraved After	Nos.	Caption & Page Reference	Size (cms)	Other Engravers
4	Atala (or The Death of Abel) (Chateaubriand).	Henry Corbould	2	1) Frontispiece: 'Speak, Adam...' 2) Title page: 'The other day...'	7x6 6x5	
5	The Castle of Otranto (Horace Walpole) and The Old English Baron (Clara Reeve).	Henry Corbould	2	1) Frontispiece: 'See, Margery...' 2) Title page: 'You must go down here...'	7x6 5x5	
6	The Forget-Me-Not (Frederic Shoberl, editor).	Richard Westall R.A. T. Uwins R.A.	5	1) Dedication page 2) Frontispiece: The Parting Charge 3) The Two Pilgrims in Grey 4) The Tournament 5) The Rational Lunatic	9x7	G. Corbould W.T. Fry
7	The Literary Souvenir (Alaric Watts, editor).	J.M. Wright C. Fielding	3	1) Frontispiece: 'The decision of the flower' 2) p.23 The Bay of Naples 3) Ishmael and Miriam	10x7 7x11 10x7	E. Finden R. Baker W. Humphrys Fenn
8	Locke and Bacon (On the Understanding).	Henry Corbould	2	1) Frontispiece: 'Groans and convulsions...' 2) Title page: 'Nor a fond mother...'	7x6 6x5	
9	The Works of Lady Mary Wortley Montagu.	Henry Corbould	2	1) Frontispiece: 'He had the permission of visiting me in the seraglio...' 2) Title page: 'The swimming lover and the nightly bride...'	7x6 6x5	

Publisher	Location & References	Notes
W. Baynes and Son, Edinburgh and others	* Houghton, *FC8C3906A Eg 825a	In Dove's English Classics series.
W. Baynes and Son, Edinburgh and others	*	In Dove's English Classics series.
R. Ackermann	* V&A.J.6.f (3) to 5) only)	Charles Heath's first contributions to an 'Annual': the Forget-Me-Not was the first of its kind, having originally appeared in 1823. All the plates are marked 'Steel'. 1) is not inscribed, so that the attribution to Charles Heath is not certain.
Hurst, Robinson	* V&A.J.6.f (3) only)	The Literary Souvenir appeared for 11 years as an 'Annual', between 1825 and 1835 inclusive.
W. Baynes and Son, Edinburgh and others	*	In the Dove's English Classics series. Republished in 1852. Another version replaces these engravings with a print of John Locke, also by Charles Heath.
J.F. Dove	*	In the English Classics series. 'Published for the Proprietors'.

Ref No.	Book Title (Separate Print: S.P.)	Engraved After	Nos.	Caption & Page Reference	Size (cms)	Other Engravers
10	A Tale of Paraguay (Robert Southey).	Richard Westall R.A.	2	1) Frontispiece: 'Then come the unsteady step...' 2) p.98 'Like one entranced...'	8x6	
11	The Works of Washington Irving.	Richard Westall R.A.	7	1) Title page 2) Stratford on Avon 3) Vol I p.35 The Widow and her son 4) Vol II p.252 Girl sitting under an arch 5) Vol II p.254 'Pride of the Village' 6) The Wife 7) Rip van Winkle	8x7 6x5 6x5	
12	Dodd's Beauties of Shakespeare (Rev'd William Dodd).	Henry Corbould	2	1) Frontispiece: 'But what is this?' 2) Title page: 'Ghost: Mark me...'	8x6 6x5	
13	S.P.	Chantrey	1	Bust of Sir Walter Scott		
14	Hervey's Meditations and Contemplations	H. Corbould	2	1) Frontispiece: 'In vain does the consenting fair...' 2) Title page: 'The heavens are the most emphatical...'	7x6 6x5	

Publisher	Location & References	Notes
Longman, Hurst, Rees, Orme, Brown and Green	*	Probably these engravings were on steel.
S. Robinson R. Jennings	3)Huntington 22971.II.139 NYPL. +KZ10746 4) BMPR. 167. C.21 NYPL. +KZ10917 5)Huntington 22971.IV.371 NYP:.+KZ1925 6) NYPL.+KZ 7)Huntington 386281.II.242 NYPL. +KZ10747	In two volumes. 1) and 2) may belong to the first edition (see 1819(8)), while 3) to 5) come from The Sketchbook.
J.F. Dove	*	In the Dove's English Classics series. Republished by H. Washbourne in 1857, in 'A New Edition' but with the same engravings. See also Notes to 1832(3), which relate to quite a different version.
Hurst, Robinson	NYPL. Stuart collection	The NYPL copy is bound up in Hurst, Robinson's copy of 'Illustrations to Shakespeare' (1821(3).
J.F. Dove	*	In the English Classics series

Ref No.	Book Title (Separate Print: S.P.)	Engraved After	Nos.	Caption & Page Reference	Size (cms)	Other Engravers
1	The Amulet (or Christian and Literary Remembrance) (S.C. Hall, editor).	Richard Westall R.A. Henry Corbould	3	1) Frontispiece: The Hebrew Mother 2) p.277 'Infatuation' 3) p.342 'The Murmurer instructed'	9x7	J. Mitchell J. Martin E. Finden
2	The Forget-Me-Not (Frederic Shoberl).	Richard Westall R.A. Singleton	3	1) p.1 The Child's Dream 2) p.79 The Regretted Ghost 3) p.156 Evening Prayer	9x7 7x9	G. Corbould H. Le Keux E. Finden H. Winkles
3	The Literary Souvenir (Alaric Watts).	G.S. Newton R.A. P. Dewint	3	1) p.159 The Forsaken 2) p.219 Windsor Castle 3) First Kiss of Love	8x7 7x12	W. Hunphrys E. Finden W. Finden E. Goodall C. Rolls J. Thomson
4	Burns' Poems and Songs (Robert Burns).	Henry Corbould	2	1) Frontispiece: 'The expectant wee things…' 2) Title page vignette: 'A waeful wanderer'	8x6 6x5	
5	The Adventures of Telemachus (translated by Dr Hawkesworth).	Henry Corbould	2	1) Frontispiece: 'And blushing…' 2) Title page: 'Sometimes she stood…'	7x5	

Publisher	Location & References	Notes
William Baynes, F. Westley, and A.H. Dvais	*	This 'Annual' was published for 11 years between 1826 and 1836, and revived for a year in 1838 under a new editor, Charles Cecil, when it was advertised as 'an elegant literary present'.
R. Ackermann	*	The three engravings here reappeared in Marshall's Annual 'The Pledge of Friendship' in 1829.
Hurst, Robinson	*	Presumably because of the publisher's bankruptcy when it was being prepared, there are two versions of this 'Annual' in 1826. One of the editions, including 3) 'First Kiss of Love', was apparently spirited away from the bailiffs and printed elsewhere before the other plates were ready, so as to earn some profit to pay off debts (source: Dr Hunnisett). 3) was subsequently re-used about 1860, with a new (and rather less evocative title) of 'The Cottage Girl: or the marriage day', and published by the London Printing and Publishing Co. bearing the caption: 'Miss Clifton, from this hour I am devoted to you utterly'. 2) is in the same series as 'Views in London' (1825(1)), and must have been omitted, for unknown reasons.
J.F. Dove	* V&A.J.4.d (1) only)	In the Dove's English Classics series. 1) re-appeared in 'Selections from the English Poets' (1836(4)12).
J.F. Dove, Thomas Johnson, Manchester	*	In the Dove's English Classics series. Re-published by Johnson in 1848.

Ref No.	Book Title (Separate Print: S.P.)	Engraved After	Nos.	Caption & Page Reference	Size (cms)	Other Engravers
6	The History of Sandford and Merton (Thomas Day).	Henry Corbould	2	1) Frontispiece: 'And exhorted them...' 2) Title page: 'There poor little Tommy tumbled about...'	7x6	
7	The Improvement of the Mind (Isaac Watts).	Henry Corbould	3	1) Frontispiece: 'The child you have brought forth...' 2) 'If you spend some hours...' 3) 'From being born...'	8x6 6x5	
8	Romaine's Life Walk and Triumph of Faith.	Henry Corbould	2	1) Frontispiece: 'That whomsoever believeth...' 2) Title page: 'This is the privilege...'	8x6 6x5	
9	New Historical Description of Cheltenham (S.Y. Griffith).	J.D. Harding	2	1) p.96 The South-West View of Charlton Park 2) p.97 The North-East View of East Court	9x14	W. Radclyffe J. & L. Byrne J. Pye C. Pye J. Landseer R.L. Wright J. Radford H. Hobson

Publisher	Location & References	Notes
J.F. Dove	*	In the Dove's English Classics series.
J.F. Dove	BMPR.167.c.21 p.35 and 59	In the Dove's English Classics series. See 1814(2) in James Heath's catalogue for an earlier version.
J.F. Dove	*	In the Dove's English Classics series.
Longman, Rees, Orme, Brown and Green	BL.1783.cc.18 Huntington 304985.IV.329 and 330a	Inscribed: 1) 'To George Bragge Prowse (Engraved at his expense).' 2) 'To Alexander Nicholson, His seat (Engraved at his expense)'.

Ref No.	Book Title (Separate Print: S.P.)	Engraved After	Nos.	Caption & Page Reference	Size (cms)	Other Engravers
1	The Amulet (or Christian Literary Remembrancer) (S.C. Hall).	Henry Corbould	1	p.101 'Mayday in the Village'	9x7	C. Rolls W. Finden J. Romney E. Finden Engleheart
2	The Forget-Me-Not (Frederic Shoberl).	Henry Corbould J. Porter	2	1) p.231 Sir Roger de Coverley 2) p.269 Love and Duty	9x6 9x7	E. Finden A.W. Warren W. Finden H. Le Keux R.W. Smart Freebairn
3	Friendship's Offering (T.K. Hervey).	J.M. Wright	2	1) Frontispiece: 'The Bower' 2) p.325 'Coquetry, Gravity and Gaiety'	9x7	J. Cooke
4	The Literary Souvenir (Alaric Watts).	H. Howard R.A.	1	Frontispiece: Girl in a Florentine costume of AD 1500	8x6	J. Romney E. Finden W. Humphrys Engleheart J. Robinson R. Wallis J. Mitchell
5	Essay on Truth (James Beattie).	Henry Corbould	2	1) Frontispiece: 'Sceptics may wrangle...' 2) Title page: Vignette of Truth	8x6 5x5	
6	Evenings at Home (Dr Aitken and Mrs Barbauld).	Henry Corbould	2	1) Frontispiece: 'And looking up...' 2) Title page: 'The solitary hastened...'	8x6 6x6	

Publisher	Location & References	Notes
William Baynes, F. Westley and A.H. Davis	*	
R. Ackermann	* V&A.J.6.f (1) only)	
Lupton Relfe	*	Published as an 'Annual' between 1824 and 1844 inclusive. Charles Heath only contributed plates to the 1827 edition.
Longman, Rees, Orme, Brown and Green	* V&A.J.4.b	
J.F. Dove	*	In the Dove's English Classics series.
J.F. Dove	*	In the Dove's English Classics series.

Ref No.	Book Title (Separate Print: S.P.)	Engraved After	Nos.	Caption & Page Reference	Size (cms)	Other Engravers
7	Homer's Iliad (Pope's translation).	Henry Corbould	1	Frontispiece: 'When like the morning mist...'	8x6	
8	Horace (translated by Philip Francis).	Henry Corbould	2	1) Frontispiece: 'Beneath the rising sun...' 2) Title page: 'But beneath the mantling vine...'	8x6 6x6	
9	Dramas and Poems (Hannah More).	Henry Corbould	2	1) Frontispiece: 'He flies to where...' 2) Title page: 'With what angel sweetness...'	8x6	
10	Rasselas, and Dinarbas (Samuel Johnson).	Henry Corbould	2	1) Frontispiece: 'Dinarbas, pierced with wounds...' 2) Title page: 'In the morning as I was sitting on the grass...'	7x6	
11	S.P.	Henry Corbould	1	'Love's Lesson'	12x10	
12	S.P.	Sir Joshua Reynolds P.R.A.	1	Puck	36x27	

Publisher	Location & References	Notes
G.B. Whittaker G. Routledge	*	See also 1822(5) for an earlier version. The engraving on the title page is not inscribed, but is probably by Charles Heath. Another edition was published in 1837, and another by Routledge in 1845, in which draperies have prudishly been put on the engraving of the naked girl.
J.F. Dove	*	In the Dove's English Classics series.
J.F. Dove	*	In the Dove's English Classics series.
J.F. Dove	* V&A.J.6.c	In the Dove's English Classics series. See 1810(5) for an earlier version of Rasselas.
James Robins	V&A.J.6.c	'Publ 1 Jan 1827'.
R. Jennings	* Mackenzie (British Prints, 1987) L. Fagan (History of Engraving in England Vol III)	Fagan maintains that this print was the work of two of Charles Heath's distinguished pupils, J.H. Watt and G. Doo. See also 1822(11). Published March 1827 for the Proprietor.

Ref No.	Book Title (Separate Print: S.P.)	Engraved After	Nos.	Caption & Page Reference	Size (cms)	Other Engravers
13	S.P.	G.S. Newton	1	'The Lover's Quarrel'	28x22	

Publisher	Location & References	Notes
Charles Heath, 6 Seymour Place, and Robert Jennings, Poultry	*	Described as 'From the Original Picture in the Possession of James Brown esq. of Hare Hills Grove near Leeds to whom this Plate is by permission respectfully dedicated by his obedient servant Charles Heath.'

Ref No.	Book Title (Separate Print: S.P.)	Engraved After	Nos.	Caption & Page Reference	Size (cms)	Other Engravers
1	The Keepsake (edited) (W.H. Ainsworth).	Sir Thomas Lawrence P.R.A., H. Howard R.A., C.R. Leslie R.A., Stephanoff, Thomas Stothard R.A., Henry Corbould, J.M.Wright, J. Cristall A.E., Chalon R.A.	10	1) Vignette 2) Frontispiece: Selina, Marchioness of Clanwilliam 3) p.53 Hylas and Nymphs 4) p.82 The Lady's Dream 5) p.107 Peasant Girl 6) p.216 Rebecca 7) p.246 The Inconstant 8) p.278 The Convent of Chaillot (or, Louis XIV and La Valliere) 9) p.284 The Enchanted Stream 10) p.301 Virginia	 9x7 8x10 10x8 8x10 11x8 12x8 11x8	C. Rolls F. Goodyear W. Finden E. Roberts E. Portbury E. Goodall
2	Paul and Virginia, Elizabeth and the Indian Cottage.	Henry Corbould	2	1) Frontispiece: 'The noise of water…' 2) 'Falling down on her knees…'	8x5 6x6	
3	Byron's Poems (Lord Byron).	Henry Corbould	2 [4]	Vol I Frontispiece: 1) 'And these two tended him…' Vol II Frontispiece: 2) 'You can't gaze a minute…' [3) 'And Julia sate with Juan…' 4) 'And o'er him bent his sire…' 5) Don Alfonso finding the shoes in Julia's bedroom 6) Hours of Idleness: Archer hitting a man on a horse]	8x6 7x5 9x7 7x7	

Publisher	Location & References	Notes
Hurst, Chance, R. Jennings	* BMPR.167.c.17 (proofs) BMPR.C.13 (2) and 4) - 10) only) V&A.J.6.f (3) and 9) only) V&A.J.5.c (1) only) V&A.J.2.g (2) and 4) - 10) only)	Prepared in 1827 for the Christmas gift season, the Keepsake, priced at one guinea instead of the 12/- charged for other 'Annuals' previously, was the first 'Annual' which Charles Heath actually promoted, while at the same time engraving some of the plates himself, or jointly with other engravers in his atelier. The Keepsake survived all its rivals, finally expiring with the 1857 edition when Charles Heath himself had been dead for ten years. An interesting aspect about the vignette 1) is that it originally appeared in an edition of Samual Rogers' Poems of 1806, in which all the other illustrations were by Luke Clennell. This particular vignette, however, although not so inscribed (and thus not appearing in James Heath's catalogue) is believed to have been etched by James Heath at the time after Stothard: and the charm of this wreath of roses was copied by other vignette engravers including Charles Heath in designing the first edition of the Keepsake.
J.F. Dove	*	In the Dove's English Classics series. See 1820(8) for an earlier version. Re-published in 1840 by Scott, Webster and Geary.
J.F. Dove	* (Vols I and II) BMPR.167.c.21 p.43 (3) only) BMPR.C.13 (5) only) BMPR.167.c.21 p.52 (6) only)	The two known volumes here would appear to have been supplemented by at least four undated prints by Charles Heath, after Henry Corbould, which are listed as 3) to 6). 5) is described as a 'private plate' so may not have been published. Vols I and II are in the Dove's English Classics series, so that 3), 4), 6) may belong to later volumes in the series.

Ref No.	Book Title (Separate Print: S.P.)	Engraved After	Nos.	Caption & Page Reference	Size (cms)	Other Engravers
1	The Keepsake (editor: Frederic Mansel Reynolds).	Sir Thomas Lawrence P.R.A. Richard Westall R.A. Edward Landseer A.R.A. A.Chalon R.A. Henry Corbould J.Holmes Stephanoff	10	1) Frontispiece: Mrs Peel 2) p.50 The Country Girl 3) p.65 Lucy on the Rock 4) p.121 The Duchess of Bedford 5) p.166 Love 6) p.177 Jealousy 7) p.191 The Laird's Jock 8) p.218 Adalinda 9) p.344 Clorinda 10) (Presentation plate)	10x8 9x12 10x8 9x12 11x9 10x8 11x8	E. Portbury R. Wallis C. Rolls J. Goodyear W. Finden W.R. Smith D. Smith Engleheart
2	The Juvenile Keepsake (editor: Thomas Roscoe).	Henry Corbould J.M. Wright	3	Title page: 1) Henry Vernon 2) p.124 'Zoe and Muriotti' 3) p.154 'The Young Tyrolese'	6x6 9x7	F. Bacon W. Chevalier W. Radclyffe J. Lewis
3	Pictorial Illustrations to the Waverley Novels.	Alfred Chalon R.A.	1	The Abbot 'But it is over, and I am Mary Stuart once more...'	10x7	J. Horsburgh, R. Graves, W. Raddon, C.Rolls, C.G. Cook, A. Duncan, J. Mitchell, J.C. Edwards, J. Romney, A. Warren, J. Phelps C. Fox, A. Fox, W.H. West, S. Sangster, H.C. Shenton, Davenport,Engleheart W. Ensom, (and others)

Publisher	Location & References	Notes
Hurst, Chance	* BMPR.167.c.21 p.94 (7) only) V&A.J.6.f (7) only)	Although 1) Mrs Peel, has been praised as something of a master work by Charles Heath, Sir Thomas Lawrence considered it a failure. An early proof copy is marked 'Lane reduced, Goodyear etch'd figure, Webb etch'd fur and feathers, J.H. Watt drapery and hat, Rhodes worked up hat feathers, D. Smith background, and C. Heath flesh!' This is the print which Turner described to Lawrence as a 'Basket' print, because he was offered it for 6d from a basket of steel engravings by a woman selling them at Hastings, and considered that the use of steel was debasing the price which such engravings should cost. 3) reappeared in the 'Book of the Sea', see U/D (6) published ca. 1856.
Hurst, Chance	*	There is also a coloured vignette in this 'Annual' after Stothard, which is similar to that in the Keepsake for 1828 (see Notes to 1828(1)1)).
Robert Cadell, and Moon, Boys and Graves	*	Published between 1829 and 1833, the plate here is dated 1831: it may thus be a re-engraving in proof of 1821(12)8), which is also after Chalon. This collection of 97 proof impressions from editions of the Waverley Novels employed many of the best engravers of the period.

Ref No.	Book Title (Separate Print: S.P.)	Engraved After	Nos.	Caption & Page Reference	Size (cms)	Other Engravers
1	The Keepsake (editor: Frederic Mansel Reynolds).	Sir Thomas Lawrence P.R.A. D. Wilkie R.A. Henry Corbould Richard Bonington A.E.Chalon R.A. C.R.Leslie R.A.	6	1) Frontispiece: Lady Agar Ellis 2) p.145 Princess Doria 3) p.164 Zella 4) p.265 Francis I, and his sister 5) p.322 The Prophet of St Pauls 6) p.196 The Bride	10x9 11x9 10x8 9x7	Engleheart S. Mitan J. Mitchell F. Bacon R. Wallis J. Goodyear Freebairn E. Portbury
2	The Landscape Annual (Thomas Roscoe).	S. Prout	2	1) p.173 Petrarch's house at Arqua 2) p.247 Bologna	13x10 14x10	J. Lewis J. Tingle W. Wallis R. Wallis W. Miller J. B. Allen R. Redaway J. Willmore J. H. Kernot T. Jeavons J. Henshall Westwood J. Horsburgh W. R. Smith
3	S.P.	Thomas Stothard R.A.	1	'Home'	9x6	

Publisher	Location & References	Notes
Hurst, Chance	* V&A.J.6.f (2) and 5) only) V&A.J.6.c (3) only) V&A.J.2.g (1) only)	1) Lady Agar Ellis was formerly Lady Dover: U/D (65) may thus be the same print.
Robert Jennings and W. Chaplin (for 1831)	* V&A.J.2.G	Published between 1830 and 1839 inclusive, this 'Annual' was for the first two years inscribed 'Engraved under the direction of Mr Charles Heath'. The two plates here, which are dated '29 October 1829' were re-engraved in 1837(1).
James Robins & Co.	* YCBA B.1977.14 20859	This print may belong to an antraced Annual.

Ref No.	Book Title (Separate Print: S.P.)	Engraved After	Nos.	Caption & Page Reference	Size (cms)	Other Engravers
1	The Keepsake (editor: Frederic Mansel Reynolds).	C.J. Eastlake R.A. Stephanoff H. Howard R.A. Cristall A.E. Chalon R.A. Henry Corbould	8	Frontispiece: 1) Haidee 2) p.16 The Gondola 3) p.54 Mina 4) p.122 The Swiss Peasant 5) p.174 The Knight, the Monk and the Lady 6) p.183 Adelaide 7) p.315 The Orphan Boy 8) (Presentation plate)	 9x7 9x12 12x8 11x8 7x7	Thomson J. Edwards C. Rolls Brandard W. Miller R. Wallis W. Wallis J. Willmore J. Mitchell F. Bacon
2	The Improvisatrice (Laetitia Landon).	J.M. Wright	1	Frontispiece, p.22: Two men on a rocky shore	9x7	
3	Views in Paris (Paris and its Environs) (A. Pugin and C. Heath).	A. Pugin	200		8x11 and various	Various

Publisher	Location & References	Notes
Hurst, Chance	* V&A.J.4.d	
Longman, Rees, Orme, Brown and Green	*	Described as a 'New Edition'. See 1824(8) for the first edition, which does not contain this plate.
Robert Jennings and William Chaplin	* NYPL. Stuart collection 7777	Two volumes, which are usually bound up in one. 'Engraved under the superintendence of C. Heath.' The historical and topographical descriptions are by L.T. Ventouillac, in English and French. There was a second edition in 1833.

Ref No.	Book Title (Separate Print: S.P.)	Engraved After	Nos.	Caption & Page Reference	Size (cms)	Other Engravers
1	The Keepsake (editor: Frederic Mansel Reynolds).	Rochard Thomas Stothard R.A. Henry Corbould Miss I. Sharpe	4	1) Vignette. Frontispiece: 2) Mrs Stanhope 3) p.24 Constance 4) p.239 Do you remember it?...'	 10x8 12x9 10x8	J. Mitan J. Willmore F. Bacon C. Rolls H. Le Keux J.C. Edwards W. Miller W. Wallis R. Wallis J. Mitchell
2	Heath's Picturesque Annual (editor: Leitch Ritchie).	Clarkson Stanfield	2	1) p.227 Innsbruck 2) p.180 Mazorbo	9x14 11x14	J.B. Allen J.Smith S. Fisher T. Jeavons R. Wallis R. Brandard W. Radclyffe J. Carter J. Willmore E. Goodall W. Miller H. Jordan W.R. Smith
3	Shakespeare's Works.	Robert Smirke R.A. J.M. Wright Henry Corbould Stephanoff Richard Westall R.A.	25	*Vol I* 1) p.29 'Come away servant...' 2) p.61 'I do detest...' 3) p.63 'Will't please your worship...' 4) p.94 'I extend my hand...' 5) p.122 'You rogue...' 6) p.129 'Against my will...' 7) p.150 'While I thy amiable cheeks...'	9x7	R. Graves F. Bacon C. Rolls W. Chevalier H. Rolls Greatbatch T. Engleheart E. Portbury

Publisher	Location & References	Notes
Hurst, Chance	* BMPR.C.20 (1) only) NYPL. +KZ11081 (1) only)	1) is inscribed jointly by 'S. Mitan and C. Heath'.
Longman, Rees, Orme, Brown, Green and Longmans	*	This 'Annual' appeared between 1832 and 1845 inclusive. Besides providing a few engravings for the 1832, 1833 and 1835 editions, Charles Heath was also its promoter.
J.F. Dove	*	This edition may be a re-issue of an earlier edition by another publisher. The engravings 1),2),6),10),12),15),19) and 20) to 23) and 25) re-appear in 'Dodd's Beauties of Shakespeare', published by Scott, Webster and Geary in 1842. Scott and Webster published 'The Poems and Plays of Shakespeare' in 8 volumes also in 1832, containing the same engravings.

Ref No.	Book Title (Separate Print: S.P.)	Engraved After	Nos.	Caption & Page Reference	Size (cms)	Other Engravers
3	Shakespeare's Works (continued)			8) p.178 'Where lies this grief?...'	7x9	
				9) p.218 'And then the lover...'	9x7	
				10) p.241 'This to my mother...'		
				11) p.254 'You will not pay...'		
				12) p.305 'Come, I will fasten...'		
				13) p.345 'O save me, Hubert...'	7x9	
				14) p.386 'This chair shall be...'		
				Vol II 15) p.429 'Pish for thee, Iceland dog...'	9x7	
				16) p.469 'O fairest beauty...'		
				17) p.487 'Give me thy hand...'		
				18) p.564 'There sits a judge...'		
				19) p.620 'And whilst this poor wealth lasts...'		
				20) p.644 'My name is Caius Marcius...'		
				21) p.716 'Oh no answer, then I'll...'		
				22) p.736 'Vengeance is in my heart...'		
				23) p.793 'I pray, weep not...'		
				24) p.808 'Jesu, what...'		
				25) p.846 'There on...'		

Publisher	Location & References	Notes

Ref No.	Book Title (Separate Print: S.P.)	Engraved After	Nos.	Caption & Page Reference	Size (cms)	Other Engravers
1	The Keepsake (editor: Frederic Mansel Reynolds).	A. Chalon R.A. Liversage E.T. Parris J.M. Wright Stanfield	5	Frontispiece: 1) The Adieu 2) p.34 Juliet 3) p.82 The Bridesmaid 4) p.187 Malvolio 5) p.241 Verrex in the Val d'Aosta	 12x9 12x8 10x13	S. Mitan S. Lacey J. Goodyear W. Wallis R. Wallis T. Engleheart C. Rolls J. Edwards J.B. Allen F. Bacon
2	Heath's Picturesque Annual (editor: Leitch Ritchie).	Clarkson Stanfield	2	1) p.158 The Drachenfels 2) p.163 Near Bonn	10x14 9x14	J. Smith R. Wallis W. Hill W. Floyd S. Lacey J. Cousins J.C. Varrall J.H. Kernot J. Lewis R. Brandard J. Carter S. Fisher J. Willmore
3	Heath's Book of Beauty (editress: 'L.E.L.' Laetitia Landon).	W. Russell Henry Corbould J.M. Wright and others				

Publisher	Location & References	Notes
Longman, Rees, Orme, Brown, Green and Longmans	* V&A.J.2.g (5) only)	2) 'Juliet' may be the same subject as that recorded in Alaric Watts' diary on 27 February 1828: 'Wanted to engrave Juliet by Thompson for the Literary Souvenir but Charles Heath had pre-empted it.'
Longman, Rees, Orme, Brown, Green and Longmans	*	
Longman, Rees, Orme, Brown, Green and Longmans	*	Published between 1833 and 1849, with the Countess of Blessington as editress after 1838, and Charles Heath lending his name to it as promoter, this 'Annual' was yet another designed to appeal to the taste of the period. Charles Heath did not engrave himself for this work, so that no other details are relevant to this catalogue. 'Heath's Book of Beauty' for 1848 and 1849 was however subsequently re-issued as 'The Queens of England' by Mary Howitt in 1856, published by H.G. Bohn with the same illustrations.

Ref No.	Book Title (Separate Print: S.P.)	Engraved After	Nos.	Caption & Page Reference	Size (cms)	Other Engravers
1	The Keepsake (editor: Frederic Mansel Reynolds).	W. Boxall G.S. Newton R.A. B.R. Faulkner E.T. Parris	5	Frontispiece (p.105): 1) Mary Esdaile 2) p.53 Lady Keswynche (Milicent) 3) p.98 Amelie de Boufflers 4) p.140 The Proposal 5) p.174 First Affections	11x8 12x8	S. Mitan F. Engleheart J. Goodyear F. Bacon R. Wallis H. Miller J.C. Edwards J. Cousen C. Rolls

Publisher	Location & References	Notes
Longman, Rees, Orme, Brown, Green and Longmans	* V&A.J.6.f and V&A.J.4.d (1), 3) and 5) only)	

Ref No.	Book Title (Separate Print: S.P.)	Engraved After	Nos.	Caption & Page Reference	Size (cms)	Other Engravers
1	The Keepsake (editor: Frederic Mansel Reynolds).	Sir Thomas Lawrence P.R.A. Jenkins W.Boxall C.H. Aubrey J.M. Wright A.E. Chalon R.A. Retzsch G.Cattermole	8	Frontispiece: 1) Viscountess Beresford 2) p.23 My Aunt Mansfield 3) p.27 The Lady and the Novel 4) p.42 The Sledge 5) p.84 The Letter 6) p.140 La Vallière 7) p.169 The German Lovers 8) p.184 Lady Blanche	10x8 9x13 9x11 10x8 9x11	H. Cooke W.H. Mote F.A. Heath J.C. Edwards F. Bacon W. Chevalier C. Rolls J. Goodyear
2	Heath's Picturesque Annual (editor: Leitch Ritchie).	G.Cattermole	4	Title page: 1) Gallery in Craignathan Castle 2) p.77 Neidpath Castle 3) p.111 Crichton Castle 4) p.222 Murder of the Regent Murray	10x8 9x13	J. Goodyear T. Higham J.W. Appleton J.C. Armytage R. Brandard R. Wallis W. Radclyffe J.T. Willmore

Publisher	Location & References	Notes
Longman, Rees, Orme, Brown, Green and Longmans	*	
Longman, Rees, Orme, Brown, Green and Longmans	*	In the same year, these plates were also included in a separate publication, with 21 plates in all, entitled 'Illustrations to the Poetical and Prose Works of Sir Walter Scott'. The plates were 'under the superintendence of J. McCormick', and priced at half a guinea. These plates were also re-published in 'Heath's Gallery of British Engravings' between 1836 and 1838.

Ref No.	Book Title (Separate Print: S.P.)	Engraved After	Nos.	Caption & Page Reference	Size (cms)	Other Engravers
1	The Keepsake (editor: Mrs Caroline Norton).	F.P. Stepha-noff	1	p.267 The Hindu Girl	10x9	J. Thomson E. Radclyffe J. Edwards H. Brandard L. Stocks C. Rolls W. Chevalier J.T. Willmore J. Goodyear J. Cousins H. Ryall Griffiths
2	The Amaranth.	J.M. Wright Thomas Stothard R.A.	3	Frontispiece: 1) The Interview on the Road 2) p.49 Merry Margaret 3) p.96 Rose of the River	10x8	F. Bacon W. Kelsall W.J. Cooke
3	Heath's Gallery of British Engravings.	Sir Thomas Lawrence P.R.A., C.R. Leslie R.A., H. Howard R.A., A.E. Chalon R.A., R.P. Bonington, F.P. Step-hanoff,E.T. Parris, W. Boxall, J. Holmes, C.Stanfield,	41		11x14 10x8 9x12 and others	As listed under 'The Keepsake' for 1828-36, 'Heath's Picturesque Annual' for 1832, 1833, and 1835, 'Landscape Annual' for 1830

Publisher	Location & References	Notes
Longman, Rees, Orme, Brown, Green and Longmans	*	
A. Renshaw	*	This 'Annual', though it bears no date, is recorded by Faxon as published in 1836. A reprint was produced by T. Holmes ('Successor to E. Lacey') in the 1870s. 3) appears to be a reprint of 'There was a small skiff' engraved by Charles Heath for an edition of Scott's 'Guy Mannering' ca. 1831. (2) undated): this print also re-appeared as 'Come o'er the Sea' in an 1864 edition of Thomas Moore's Poems. 1) and 2) also appear to be taken from themes from Sir Walter Scott.
Longman, Rees, Orme, Brown, Green and Longmans	* V&A.J.6.f V&A.J.6.c V&A.J.4.m (E310-1905) V&A.J.2.g (not complete)	In four volumes. All the prints, of which each has a write-up alongside, are taken from editions of 'The Keepsake' between 1828 and 1836, 'Heath's Picturesque Annual between 1832 and 1836, and 'The Landscape Annual' for 1830, together with prints from 'Heath's Book of Beauty' from 1833 to 1836. The work was published between 1836-8. About 1845, Ackermann re-published Vol III of the 'Gallery' under the title of 'The Royal Book of Gems'. See also 1846(2) for 'Heath's New Gallery of British Engravings', which contains later re-issues of Charles Heath's engravings from the 'Annuals'. Ackermann & Spooner published an undated re-issue of Vol II of the 'Gallery' also.

Ref No.	Book Title (Separate Print: S.P.)	Engraved After	Nos.	Caption & Page Reference	Size (cms)	Other Engravers
3	Heath's Gallery of British Engravings (continued)	H.Corbould, G.S.Newton R.A., J.M Wright				
4	Selections from the English Poets from Spenser to Beattie.	Henry Corbould	12	1) p.24 Magna Carta 2) p.34 Milton, The Fall 3) p.41 'Black he stood, as night...' 4) p.54 Hudibras 5) p.68 Dorinda 6) p.86 Tate: Hero to Leander 7) p.144 Gay: The spell 8) p.204 Pope: Sappho to Phaon 9) p.240 Shenstone: Nancy of the Valley 10) p.264 'What numbers...' 11) p.291 Shaw: 'My hand she pressed...' 12) p.367 Burns: 'The expectant wee things...'	8x5	W. Finden
5	The Wreath of Friendship (A Token of Regard).	J.M. Wright	2	1) p.52 The Gypsy's Benediction 2) p.207 The Encounter	11x8 10x8	C. Rolls F. Engleheart Davies
6	Heath's Shakespeare Gallery.					W.H. Mote H. Robinson H. Holl and others

Publisher	Location & References	Notes
Scott, Webster and Geary	* V&A.J.4.d (1), 3) 5) and 10) to 12) only)	See 1842 for a later version entitled 'Book of the Poets, Chaucer to Beattie', with different engravings by Charles Heath. 12) here is the same as 1826(4)1).
Renshaw & Co	*	Undated, but published as an 'Annual' in 1836, according to Faxon.
Charles Tilt	* BL.644.h.7	'Engraved under the direction and superintendence of Mr Charles Heath.' Undated but published in 1836/7 according to the British Library catalogue. Advertised at two guineas (in morocco) in the Art Union No.2 of 1839. See 1848(2) for a reissue with a new name.

Ref No.	Book Title (Separate Print: S.P.)	Engraved After	Nos.	Caption & Page Reference	Size (cms)	Other Engravers
7	The Pirate, and Three Cutters (Captain Marryat).	Clarkson Stanfield				J.T. Willmore R. Brandard H. Cook J.C. Edwards A. Wallis S. Fisher J. Cousen J. Goodyear H. Griffith J.B. Allen W. Chevalier C. Jeavons
8	The Confessions of an Elderly Gentleman (Countess of Blessington).	E. T. Parris	6			
9	Gems of Beauty (editress: Countess of Blessington).		11			H. Austin H. Robinson J. Hall H. Cook W.H. Mote W. Edwards J. Penstone J.H. Egleton E. Scriven J. Thomson

Publisher	Location & References	Notes
Longman, Rees, Orme, Brown, Green and Longmans	* Beinecke 1971-720	20 plates, and a portrait of the author were advertised by Longmans in the Art Union for December 1839(p.192) as 'engraved under the superintendence of Mr Chas Heath'; there is nothing however in the 1836 first edition to say so. The Beinecke edition is later, and published by A. Fullerton. The book, in 3 volumes, was priced at 1½ guineas.
Longman, Rees, Orme, Brown, Green and Longmans	Sadleir Appendix III BL.838.c.28	This was a gift book written by Lady Blessington which appears in the Longmans archive to the account of Charles Heath; presumably he supervised the engravers and paid them.
Longman, Rees, Orme, Brown, Green and Longmans Virtue & Co	Longmans archives * (no date, ca.1850) BL.LR.299. bb.1 BL.LR.299. bb.2 BL.LR.299. bb.4	This series of gift books was published between 1836 and 1840; it was referred to in the Art Union in December 1839. It was not strictly an Annual, but originally issued in 4 parts over 5 years. The plates were described as 'Engraved under the superintendence of Mr Charles Heath with fanciful illustrations in verse by the Countess of Blessington'. Of the 11 engravings, 8 re-appeared in Heath's Portfolio of Engravings' at 1846(3).

Ref No.	Book Title (Separate Print: S.P.)	Engraved After	Nos.	Caption & Page Reference	Size (cms)	Other Engravers
1	Views of Cities and Scenery in Italy, France and Switzerland.	S. Prout	2	Vol I p.61 1) Water towers in Bologna Vol II p.72 2) Petrarch's House at Arqua	23x15	

Publisher	Location & References	Notes
Fisher & Son	BMPR.174. a.32 BMPR.174. a.33	Both prints appear to be larger engravings of the two by Charles Heath in Jennings' 'Landscape Annual' for 1830 (1830(2)). The work was published in both French and English.

Ref No.	Book Title (Separate Print: S.P.)	Engraved After	Nos.	Caption & Page Reference	Size (cms)	Other Engravers
1	Beauty's Costume (Leitch Ritchie).	E.T. Parris J.J. Jenkins F.P. Stephanoff Miss F. Corvaux E. Corbould J.J. Penstone Dyce			17x13 and 12x10	H.B. Hall J. Knight E. Scriven J. Jackman J. Hopwood J. Stodart W. Holl H. Robinson J. Penstone H. Cook H. Austin W.H. Mote W. Hewitt
2	Leila, or the Siege of Granada (Sir Edward Bulwer Lytton).	F.P. Stephanoff			12x10	H. Cook R.A. Artlett L. Stocks C. Rolls J. Goodyear E. Portbury W. Wrankmore F. Bacon
3	Picturesque Views in England and Wales (H.E. Lloyd).	J.M.W. Turner R.A.			17x23	E. Goodall R. Wallis W.R. Smith J.C. Varrall R. Brandard W. Miller T. Jeavons W. Radclyffe C. Westwood W. Tombleson J.B. Allen J. Henshall T. Higham S. Fisher J.H. Kernot J. Horsbrough W.J. Cooke R. Redaway

Publisher	Location & References	Notes
Longman, Rees, Orme, Brown, Green and Longmans	* NYPL	Two volumes of coloured engravings published in 1838/9. Of the 12 engravings in each volume, all are described as 'Executed under the superintendence of Mr Charles Heath'. These engravings reappeared uncoloured in 'Heath's Portfolio of Engravings' (1846) (3).
Chapman and Hall	*	This work contained many woodcut engravings 'Illustrated under the superintendence of Mr Charles Heath'. The book was dedicated by Edward Bulwer to the Countess of Blessington, a personal friend, and editress of 'The Keepsake' which Charles Heath promoted.
Longman, Rees, Orme, Brown, Green and Longmans	* NYPL.3-MCV T94-L7	'Engraved under the superintendence of Mr Charles Heath', this two volume work was the result of a 13 year cooperation between Turner and Heath, in the course of which 96 plates were issued in instalments, engraved on copper. The original publishers were Jennings and Chaplin, who transferred their interest to Graves and Moon, who then, owing to the financial difficulties of the project, due mainly to delay and the limited number of copies which could be produced, passed it on to Longmans.

Ref No.	Book Title (Separate Print: S.P.)	Engraved After	Nos.	Caption & Page Reference	Size (cms)	Other Engravers
4	Confessions of an Elderly Lady (Countess of Blessington).	E.T. Parris	8			

Publisher	Location & References	Notes
Longman, Orme, Brown	Sadleir: Appendix III BL.1208.i.6	'Engraved under the superintendence of Mr Charles Heath.' The successor to 1836(8). (q.v.)

Ref No.	Book Title (Separate Print: S.P.)	Engraved After	Nos.	Caption & Page Reference	Size (cms)	Other Engravers
1	A Book of the Passions (G.P.R. James).	Edward Corbould F.P. Stephanoff K. Meadows J. Jenkins			12x10	W. Wrankmore W.H. Mote F. Bacon J. Portbury W.H. Egleton H.C. Shenton L. Stocks C. Rolls J. Hopwood W. Holl J. Goodyear
2	The Tournament at Eglinton Castle.	Edward Corbould				
3	The Wye, Its Scenery and Associations (Leitch Ritchie).	T. Creswick				
4	The Governess (Countess of Blessington).	E.T. Parris	1	Frontispiece		

Publisher	Location & References	Notes
Longman, Rees, Orme, Brown, Green and Longmans	*	'Illustrated with 16 splendid engravings... under the superintendence of Mr Charles Heath.'
Hodgson and Graves	* Lot 262 of C.Heath's library auction on 24 July 1842. (Sotheby's) BL.S-C 239(6)	Described as published on 'August 30, 1839' in a series of lithographic plates 'under the superintendence of Mr Charles Heath', Sotheby's catalogue states: 'Of this work, which may be almost considered unpublished, there are 150 copies in cloth boards, 77 in sheet and 7 in colours'. It was actually published in 1840. There are references to this work in the *Art Union* for November 1839 (pp.170 and 174) and for February 1840 (p.28). It was competing with a rival publication on the Eglinton Tournament being published by Colnaghi and Puckle at about the same time. Unusually enough, Charles Heath's name does not appear in the work.
Longman, Rees, Orme, Brown, Green and Longmans	* Art Union 1839	According to Longman's advertisement in the *Art Union* for October 1839 (p.159), this work was published with 12 plates 'under the supervision of Mr Chas Heath', and priced at 12/-. It was originally intended to have been 'Heath's Picturesque Annual' for 1839.
Longman, Rees, Orme, Brown, Green and Longmans	Art Union 1839 Sadleir: Appendix III	This book is said to contain a portrait of the author 'engraved under the superintendence of Mr Charles Heath'; there is an advertisement of it in the *Art Union* for December 1839 (p.192).

Ref No.	Book Title (Separate Print: S.P.)	Engraved After	Nos.	Caption & Page Reference	Size (cms)	Other Engravers
1	The Belle of a Season (Countess of Blessington).	A.E. Chalon R.A.			20x15	H. Austin W.H. Mote H. Robinson W. Egleton J. Thomson J. Penstone H. Cook
2	Legends of Venice.	J.R. Herbert				
3	Moore's Poetical Works (Thomas Moore).	Sir Thomas Lawrence P.R.A.	1	Vol I Portrait of Thomas Moore	9x8	
4	S.P.	William Hilton R.A.	1	Europa	30x40	

Publisher	Location & References	Notes
Longman, Rees, Orme, Brown, Green and Longmans	* BL.789.e.9	Described as 'Splendidly illustrated from drawings by A.E. Chalon under the superintendence of Mr Charles Heath', this work was heavily criticised in an *Art Union* review in December 1839 (p.186), especially the 'Frenchified fripperies of Mr Chalon'. The prints were re-issued in Heath's Portfolio of Engravings (1846(3)).
		The *Art Union* in November 1840 referred to this production as the third 'Annual' which Charles Heath had had published that year, 'engraved under his superintendence'. There were 11 engravings, of which eight subsequently reappeared in 'Heath's Portfolio of Engravings' in 1846(3).
Longman, Rees, Orme, Brown, Green and Longmans	*	All the plates in Vols I to V of this work are dated 1840. See 1804(7) of James Heath's catalogue for an earlier portrait of Thomas Moore.
Charles Heath	V&A.EM 51 Art Union	This was Charles Heath's last major print, which took him seven years to complete and was not a commercial success. There is a copy of the engraving on p.254 of the *Art Journal* for 1855. The print was reviewed in the *Art Union* for March 1840 (pp.43 and 179).

Ref No.	Book Title (Separate Print: S.P.)	Engraved After	Nos.	Caption & Page Reference	Size (cms)	Other Engravers
1	Cattermole's Historical Annual for 1841.	George Catter-mole			12x7	J. T. Willmore J. Brain C. Rolls S. Bull H. Rolls R. Wallis W. Simmonds J.C. Varrall T. Goodman W. Radclyffe R. Staines W. Topham E. Radclyffe
2	Portraits of Children of the Nobility (editress: Mrs Fairlie).	A.E. Chalon R.A. J. Hayter J. Lucas Zeigler			21x16	W.H. Mote J. Brown H. Austin E. Scriven W. Edwards
3	Heath's Waverley Gallery of the principal female characters in Sir Walter Scott's romances.				15x10	J. Cook H. Austin J. Penstone G. Stodart T. Knight W.F. Holl W.H. Egleton W. Hopwood W.H. Mote J. Brown H. Robinson F. Holl W. Edwards

Publisher	Location & References	Notes
Longman, Brown, Green and Longmans	*	'With 15 highly finished engravings under the superintendence of Mr Charles Heath'. This work forms Vol I of Cattermole's 'The Great Civil War' (see 1846(4)). It was reprinted in 1842 as 'Heath's Historical Annual'. Vol II of 'The Great Civil War' was originally entitled 'Heath's Picturesque Annual for 1845', or 'Cattermole's Historical Annual for 1845'.
Longman, Brown, Green and Longmans	* (Vols I and III only)	'Engravings executed under the superintendence of Mr Charles Heath'. Published in three volumes between 1841 and 1843, and priced at one guinea each. 17 of the plates reappear in 'Heath's Portfolio of Engravings' (1846(3)).
C. Tilt and D. Bogue	*	Although dated '1841', this work was actually published in May 1840, and reviewed in the same month by the Art Union (pp.82-3). The plates are described as engraved 'under the superintendence of Charles Heath'. The work was originally published in monthly parts, each with three engravings, and priced at 2/6d. It was re-published as 'The Waverley Gallery', undated but ca. 1855 by D. Kent (late D. Bogue), and again in New York in 1860.

Ref No.	Book Title (Separate Print: S.P.)	Engraved After	Nos.	Caption & Page Reference	Size (cms)	Other Engravers
1	The Book of the Poets – Chaucer to Beattie.	Henry Corbould	18	1) p.19 Female at confession 2) p.85 Ariadne Deserted 3) p.110 Adam tempted 4) p.119 The Lady and the Fawn 5) p.121 The Combat of Hudibras 6) p.130 Hudibras and Ralpho 7) p.151 The Affectionate Mother 8) p.165 A Learned Lady 9) p.175 Christ's Agony 10) p.192 Impersonation of Spring 11) p.205 Contemplation of the Firmament 12) p.215 The Messiah glorified 13) p.248 The rustic spell 14) p.275 Poet expressing dislike of statesmen 15) p.400 The City Politicians 16) p.422 The WIld Horse 17) p.439 The solemn cockscomb 18) p.447 The cottager's children	6x6	Davenport Archer Collier Graves C. Rolls Ranson W. Finden Shenton F. Bacon Duncan Cook J. Romney

Publisher	Location & References	Notes
Scott, Webster, and Geary J.J. Chidley (1844)	* Houghton WKR.9.3.15	The second edition of this work, published by Chidley in 1844, contained only 17 plates by Charles Heath, but included two additional ones (p.50 'The Soul Departing' , and at p.379 'The Starry Firmament'); and at p.422 'The Jockey Senator' was substituted for 'The Wild Horse'. 10), 13) and 18) were omitted. Yet a third version, undated but published later by Darton, also has a frontispiece entitled 'Annot' engraved by Alfred Heath (1849(16)2); the title of the book had become 'The Book of the Poets – Chaucer to Browning'. Although 1836(4) was also published by Scott Webster and Geary, the plates here bear no relation to the earlier work.

Ref No.	Book Title (Separate Print: S.P.)	Engraved After	Nos.	Caption & Page Reference	Size (cms)	Other Engravers
2	The Keepsake (editor: Countess of Blessington).	P.F. Poole Liversage	2	1) p.219 The Mountain Girl 2) p.237 The Serenade	13x10 14x10	H. Robinson J.T. Willmore F. Radclyffe C. Rolls J. Brain L. Stocks E. Roberts H. Austin A. Heath F. Heath

Publisher	Location & References	Notes
Longman, Brown, Green and Longmans	*	

Ref No.	Book Title (Separate Print: S.P.)	Engraved After	Nos.	Caption & Page Reference	Size (cms)	Other Engravers
1	The Keepsake (editor: Countess of Blessington).	Sir William Ross A.R.A. R. Redgrave R.A. Eugene Lami	3	Presentation plate: 1) Duchesse de Nemours 2) p.81 'Waking dreams' 3) 'Dressed for the Ball' ('Bal Costumé')	 16x13 11x14 10x16	E. Radclyffe W.H. Mote S. Bull C. Rolls H. Robinson L. Stocks J. Willmore
2	Heath's Picturesque Annual (editor: Jules Janin).	Eugene Lami	2	1) p.132 A Parisian Family 2) p.155 A French Marriage at St Roch	10x14	T. Jeavons J.C. Varrall C. Rolls L. Stocks C. Mottram F. Heath W. Wallis R. Staines E. Radclyffe
3	English Pearls (or, Portraits for the Boudoir).					W.H. Mote

Publisher	Location & References	Notes
Longman, Brown, Green and Longmans	*	3) appears to have been misplaced, as it should have belonged to 'Heath's Picturesque Annual' ((2) below), with its special subject matter of 'Paris in the Winter'. It may be that this print missed the printer's deadline for the 'Picturesque Annual', and so got bound up with 'The Keepsake' instead. In any event, 3) reappears along with all the prints in the 'Picturesque Annual' for 1843 and 1844, in the combined luxury edition of 'Winter and Summer in Paris' published by Peter Jackson in 1845.
Longman, Brown, Green and Longmans	*	See Note on (1) above.
C. Tilt and D. Bogue	BL.1267.i.13	'Engraved under the superintendence of Mr Charles Heath', and described as 'From drawings by eminent artists with poetical illustrations' this work consists of ten large engraved portraits of various ladies, including one of Queen Victoria herself.

Ref No.	Book Title (Separate Print: S.P.)	Engraved After	Nos.	Caption & Page Reference	Size (cms)	Other Engravers
1	The Keepsake (editor: Countess of Blessington).	Louis David R. Redgrave R.A. P.F. Poole Edward Corbould	5	1) p.24 The Anglers 2) p.47 The [Daily] Teacher 3) p.71 The Coquette 4) p.80 The Gleaner 5) p.168 The first meeting	10x14 11x14 13x10	H. Robinson E. Radclyffe J. Brain W.H. Egleton W.H. Mote H. Holl W. Radclyffe
2	Heath's Beauties of the Opera and Ballet.	A. Warren			16x11	S. Williams
3	The Wandering Jew (Eugene Sue).					Valentin and others

Publisher	Location & References	Notes
Longman, Brown, Green and Longmans	* V&A.J.8.b (2) only)	2) was called 'The Governess' in the original painting.
D. Bogue	* NYPL. Stuart collection 11571	'Illustrations under the superintendence of Mr Charles Heath'. The work includes 10 steel engravings and numerous wood engravings; each page carries in addition an elaborate cartouche frame, each one different and in colours. While the plates are dated 'April/June 1844', there is no publication date given. This was the first book on ballet to be published in England, and contains a most obsequious dedication to Queen Victoria, for which he must have obtained permission beforehand.
Chapman and Hall	* BL.1459.h.7 Beinecke 1977-381	Executed 'under Charles Heath's supervision' and illustrated by woodcuts 'drawn by the first artists in Paris and executed on wood by the most eminent English engravers'. The work was published in monthly parts, and eventually in four volumes, of which the fourth contained only the woodcuts.

Ref No.	Book Title (Separate Print: S.P.)	Engraved After	Nos.	Caption & Page Reference	Size (cms)	Other Engravers
1	The Keepsake (editor: Countess of Blessington).	Louis David Cottrall F.P. Stephanoff	3	1) p.56 The Fair Client 2) p.204 The Rendez-vous 3) p.237 The Last Farewell	14x10 12x16 14x11	W.H. Mote E. Radclyffe A. Heath J. Willmore J. Brain F. Heath C. Rolls W.H. Egleton
2	Heath's Picturesque Annual (Cattermole's Historical Annual for 1845).	George Catter-mole	1	Frontispiece: Queen Henrietta Maria interceding for King Charles I (Scene from Sir Walter Scott's 'Woodstock')	12x16	W. Radclyffe F. Holl R. Wallis E. Radclyffe J. Willmore C. Rolls S. Bull L. Stocks J.C. Varrall C. Mottram W. Wallis R. Staines
3	The Chaplet (First and Second series).	P.F. Poole	1	p.128 The two lambs	12x10	W.H. Mote E. Goodall R. Wallis C. Rolls F. Heath W.H. Egleton E. Challis H. Robinson J. Cousen J. Willmore Hall J. Redaway S. Fisher J.C. Varrall H. Adlard T. Jeavons J. Carter

Publisher	Location & References	Notes
Longman, Brown, Green and Longmans	*	
Longman, Brown, Green and Longmans	* BMPR.166.d.24	The engraving here is known inscribed as by Frederick and not by Charles Heath. It reappeared in 'Fisher's Drawing Room Scrap Book' for 1849 however as inscribed by Charles; it also appears as by him in 'The Great Civil War' (1846(4)).
J. Harwood	*	This 'Annual' though undated, is recorded by Faxon as having been published in 1845/6. Two volumes.

Ref No.	Book Title (Separate Print: S.P.)	Engraved After	Nos.	Caption & Page Reference	Size (cms)	Other Engravers
4	Paula Monti (or, The Hotel Lambert) (Eugene Sue).	Jules David				A.J. Maso S. Williams A. Wagner

Publisher	Location & References	Notes
Chapman and Hall	*	Illustrated by woodcuts '20 engravings under the superintendence of Mr Charles Heath'.

Ref No.	Book Title (Separate Print: S.P.)	Engraved After	Nos.	Caption & Page Reference	Size (cms)	Other Engravers
1	The Keepsake (editor: Countess of Blessington).	Augustus Egg	1	p.266 The Exchange	9x14	J. Thomson E. Radclyffe W.H. Mote R. Wallis R. Staines J. Brain J. Le Keux J.B. Allen
2	Heath's New Gallery of British Engravings.		5	1843(1)3), 1844(1)1) to 4)		As for 'The Keepsake' for 1840, 1843 and 1844
3	Heath's Portfolio of Engravings (or, The Book of Plates).					
4	The Great Civil War (G. Cattermole).	George Catter-mole	1	p.275 'Queen Henrietta Maria interceding for the King'	12x16	
5	The Count of Monte Cristo (Alexander Dumas).	Valentin				

Publisher	Location & References	Notes
Longman, Brown, Green and Longmans	* BMPR.C.13	The BMPR proof copy is market 'F. Heath reduced, and etch'd, Staines all except flesh for C. Heath'.
D. Bogue	*	Also called 'Gallery of Engraving'. Plates 'executed under the direction of Mr Charles Heath' are all reissues of plates from earlier 'Keepsakes' and 'Picturesque Annuals'. The practice used here of reissuing plates from previous publications under a new name was following the example set by 'Heath's Gallery of British Engravings' ten years previously (see 1836(3)).
A. Fullarton	*	A similar reissue of 45 plates from earlier publications under a new name. The plates here are selected from 'Portraits of Children of the Nobility' (1841(2)), 'Legends of Venice' (or 'Illustrations of Venetian and other tales') (1840(3)), 'Beauty's Costume' (or 'Female Costumes of Various Nations') (1838(1)), and 'The Belle of a Season' (1840(1)). All engravings published 'under the superintendence of Mr Charles Heath'.
Fisher & Son	*	A reissue of Cattermole's Historical Annual for 1841 (see 1841(1) Notes) and 'Heath's Picturesque Annual' for 1845, with the print (1845(2)), believed to have been principally engraved by Frederick Heath. This reappeared in 'Fisher's Drawing Scrap Book' for 1849. The book in one volume was reissued by H.G. Bohn in 1852.
Chapman and Hall	Houghton *FC 8 D8914 Eg 846c	'Executed by the most eminent English engravers under the superintendence of Mr Charles Heath'. Woodcuts throughout.

Ref No.	Book Title (Separate Print: S.P.)	Engraved After	Nos.	Caption & Page Reference	Size (cms)	Other Engravers
1	The Keepsake (editor: Countess of Blessington).	Edward Corbould	2	1) p.33 The Rose Gatherer 2) p.227 Rachel	10x13 13x9	W.H. Egleton E. Radclyffe R. Wallis R. Staines J. Le Keux A. Heath
2	A Summer in Baden Baden	T. Johannot Eugene Lami Francais et Jaquemot	5	1) p.14 Conversation House 2) p.78 La Favourite 3) p.178 Saloon of the Conversation House 4) p.182 Dining Room 5) p.186 The Flower Room	16x10	J. Outhwaite Louis Marvy

Publisher	Location & References	Notes
Longman, Brown, Green and Longmans	*	
J. Mitchell	*	Although undated, there is a French version, *L'été à Bade*, published by Furne et Cie of Paris in 1847, and it can be reasonably assumed that both were published at the same time. The latter's reference is NYPL.ENB.8–*1SGK and Beinecke Altschul, 60. The English version was actually printed in Paris, with the illustrations consisting of wood engravings, soft ground etchings, four coloured lithographs, and line engravings.

Ref No.	Book Title (Separate Print: S.P.)	Engraved After	Nos.	Caption & Page Reference	Size (cms)	Other Engravers
1	**1848** The Keepsake (editor: Countess of Blessington).	H. Warren	1	p.36 The Last Moment	13x10	F. Heath W.H. Mote C. Mottram A. Heath J.B. Allen
2	Heath's Heroines of Shakespeare.					W.H. Mote W.H. Egleton J. Brown F. Holl W. Holl J. Knight B. Eyles W.J. Edwards B. Holl H. Austin
3	**1849** The Holy Gospels.					

Publisher	Location & References	Notes
David Bogue	*	This was probably Charles Heath's last engraving before his sudden death. For the first time, engravings in this 'Keepsake' are described as 'under the superintendence of Mr Charles Heath'.
W. Kent ('late D. Bogue')	*	'Engraved under the direction of Mr Charles Heath'. A reissue of 1836(6).
Chapman and Hall	NYPL. Stuart collection	With an engraved title page, and three wood engravings. Described as 'with numerous illustrations on wood, engraved under the superintendence of Mr Charles Heath'. Published after Charles Heath's death.

Ref No.	Book Title (Separate Print: S.P.)	Engraved After	Nos.	Caption & Page Reference	Size (cms)	Other Engravers
1	Illustrations to the Works of Lord Byron.					A. Heath H. Robinson W.H. Mote L. Stocks Stodart Willmore Cook Radclyffe C. Rolls
2	Guy Mannering (Sir Walter Scott).	J.M Wright Henry Corbould	3	1) 'There was a small skiff...' 2) 'They are coming...' 3) 'Ride your ways...'	10x8	
3	Rob Roy (Sir Walter Scott).	H. Richter	1	'Taking out another glove...'	10x8	
4	The Waverley Keepsake.	J.M. Wright	3	*Rob Roy* 1) p.153 'Taking out another glove...' 2) p.199 'What! Shedding each other's bluid...' 3) p.262 'She pressed my hand...'	11x8	J. Goodyear C. Rolls F. Bacon
5	Illustrations to Moore's 'Lalla Rookh'.	Robert Smirke R.A.	1	Title page: An Indian girl look into the water ('The Fire Worshippers')	8x8	
6	A Book of the Sea ('A Nautical Repository').	Richard Westall R.A.	1	'Lucy on the Rock'	9x12	R. Brandard J. Cousen W. Miller R. Wallis W. Flloyd J.T. Willmore Griffiths S. Fisher

Publisher	Location & References	Notes
A. Fullarton	* BL.789.f.30	Published ca. 1846. Plates 'engraved under the superintendence of Mr Charles Heath' from 'drawings by the first artists'. This may have been a reissue of Fullarton, possibly originally published by Tilt, David Bogue or Fisher.
Robert Jennings and R.W. Chaplin	V&A.J.6.f V&A.J.6.c NYPL. +KZ3863	Published ca. 1831; see Notes to 1823(3). 1) here was used by 'The Amaranth' in 1836(2) as 'Rose of the River' and in U/D (38) 2) (Moore's Works).
Robert Jennings and R.W. Chaplin	NYPL. +KZ3892	
R.A. Charlton	*	Published ca. 1845, probably as a reissue of Jennings and Chaplin's edition of Sir Walter Scott's novels (see 2/3 above) but including prints 2) and 3) which have not been noted elsewhere.
R. Jennings	BMPR.C.13	See Notes to 1817(9). This print probably appeared in one of the many later editions of 'Lalla Rookh' ca.1830 with a new publisher, although Longmans continued to publish new editions of it, at least up until 1838.
	* NYPL. Spens collection	Published ca. 1856. The print of 'Lucy' originally appeared in 'The Keepsake' 1829(1)3).

Ref No.	Book Title (Separate Print: S.P.)	Engraved After	Nos.	Caption & Page Reference	Size (cms)	Other Engravers
7	Heath's Versailles.					
8	The Historical Souvenir.	A. E. Chalon R.A. Henry Corbould	2	1) La Vallière 2) Zella	12x8 11x8	H. Robinson J. Thomas J. Mitchell J. Goodyear L. Stocks F. Bacon C. Cook
9	The Waverley Album.	C.R. Leslie R.A.			9x7	
10	The Rainbow.	George Catter-mole	2	1) Murder of the Regent Murray 2) Jane Shore	9x13	
11	Cecilia (Fanny Burney).	Henry Corbould	4	*Vol I* Frontispiece: 1) 'Warrant Master, Harrel never heard...' Title page: 2) 'And without waiting...' *Vol II* Frontispiece: 3) 'She sat down...' Title page" 4) 'I did fire and unfortunately aimed better...'	 8x6 7x6 8x6 7x6	
12	Sir Charles Grandison (Samuel Richardson).	Thomas Stothard R.A.	1	Letter XXIV. Sir Charles disarms Olivia	5x4	

Publisher	Location & References	Notes
Longman, Brown, Green and Longmans	*	A reissue under a different name of Heath's Picturesque Annual for 1839 (with no engraving by Charles Heath). Published ca. 1848.
	*	Published ca. 1840, in what may have been a pirated edition, as there is no publisher's name. The work contains 26 plates from the 1835 and later 'Keepsakes'.
Edward Lacey	*	Published ca. 1840, 'for Charles Heath'. The plates are the same as those in 1823(3). Another edition of this work was published in 1858 entitled 'Selections from the novels of Sir Walter Scott', with the same plates.
	*	An 'Annual' which appeared ca. 1840, and survived only one issue. 1) is the same as 1835(2)4).
J.F. Dove	BL.012613 DE.25 BMPR.167.c.21 (p.93 and 46)	Two volumes in the Dove's English Classics series.
?J.F. Dove	RA (Frost Vol III)	Published ca. 1824. See also U/D (39) for other plates from Sir Charles Grandison.

Ref No.	Book Title (Separate Print: S.P.)	Engraved After	Nos.	Caption & Page Reference	Size (cms)	Other Engravers
13	Belisarius and Numa Pompilius.	Henry Corbould	2	Frontispiece: 1) 'Beg forgiveness of Minerva...' Title page: 2) Belisarius reduced to beggary	7x6 6x5	
14	Cowper's Poems.	Henry Corbould	2	Frontispiece: 1) 'True answered...' Title page: 2) 'How oft...'	7x6 7x5	
15	Dryden's Poems.	Henry Corbould	2	Frontispiece: 1) 'Now low on earth...' Title page: 2) 'Then turning short...'	8x6 5x5	
16	Henry Kirke White's Works.		2	Frontispiece: 1) 'Maiden, wrap thy mantle round thee...' Title page: 2) 'As here deep hidden...'	7x6 6x5	
17	Hudibras (Samuel Butler).	Henry Corbould	1	Frontispiece: 'She laid him flat upon his side...'	8x6	
18	Paley's Natural Theology (Archdeacon Paley).		1	Title page: 'Whether anyone who saw a child...'	6x6	
19	Works of George Lyttleton.	C.R. Leslie R.A.	1	?Advice to a Lady		

Publisher	Location & References	Notes
C. and J. Dove	*	In the Dove's English Classics series, ca. 1830.
J.F. Dove	* V&A.J.6.c	In the Dove's English Classics series, ca. 1825. See 1818(1), 1817(2)3) and 1820(6) for other engravings to Cowper by Charles Heath. The V&A copy shows the Dove's English Classics publication date as '1827', but with Thomas Tegg as its publisher in 1824.
Scott, Webster and Geary	* V&A.J.6.c (1) only)	Published in the English Classics series ca. 1830, after Scott, Webster had succeeded J.F. Dove.
Scott, Webster and Geary	*	In the English Classics series, ca. 1828. See also 'The Beauties of Kirke White' (undated (30)).
J.F. Dove	*	In the Dove's English Classics series, ca. 1827.
Milner and Sowerby, Halifax	* NYPL. +KZ11	'Engraved for the English Classics'. Described as 'A New Edition', this is a reissue ca. 1850 of an earlier edition in the English Classics series.

Ref No.	Book Title (Separate Print: S.P.)	Engraved After	Nos.	Caption & Page Reference	Size (cms)	Other Engravers
20	The Adventures of Baron Munchausen.	Henry Corbould	2	1) 'They had drop't the portcullis...' 2) 'And blew up the bear...'	5x6 6x5	
21	The Lives of the Poets (Dr Johnson Lives Vols I and II).	Henry Corbould	2	*Vol I* Frontispiece: 1) 'To whom he laid open...' (Rochester) Title page: 2) 'Hard enough to qualify him...' (Waller)	7x5	
22	Theodosius and Constantina.	Henry Corbould	1	'The father could not forbear weeping...'	7x7	
23	Transmigrations of Indur.	Henry Corbould	1	'And looking up, he beheld...'	12x10	
24	The History of Tom Jones (Henry Fielding).	T. Uwins R.A.	4	*Vol I* Frontispiece: 1) 'It goes against me...' Title page: 2) 'I agree, answered Thwackum...' *Vol II* Frontispiece: 3) 'Mrs Miller actually understood this...' Title page: 4) 'She was standing with her back...'	5x8	
25	Mason on Self Knowledge.	T. Uwins R.A.	1	'For our sakes be became poor...'	8x5	

Publisher	Location & References	Notes
J.F. Dove	BMPR.167.c.21 (p.39 and 56)	In the English Classics series.
Scott, Webster	*	'Engraved for the English Classics.'
J.F. Dove	BMPR.167.c.21 (p.58) V&A.J.6.c	In the Dove's English Classics series.
J.F. Dove	* V&A.J.8.b	Two volumes ca. 1824. 'Published for the Proprietors of the English Classics'.
J.F. Dove	V&A.J.8.b	English Classics series.

Ref No.	Book Title (Separate Print: S.P.)	Engraved After	Nos.	Caption & Page Reference	Size (cms)	Other Engravers
26	Milton's Paradise Lost (John Milton).	Henry Corbould	3	1) Adam and Eve 2) Two hounds chasing a hare 3) Eve tempting Adam	15x10 7x6	
27	Rogers' Poems (Samuel Rogers).	Henry Corbould	1	p.48		
28	The Beauties of Chesterfield (Alfred Howard).		1	Frontispiece: Lord Chesterfield	10x7	
29	The Beauties of Cowper (Alfred Howard).		1	Frontispiece: Cowper	10x7	
30	The Beauties of Kirke White (Alfred Howard).		1	Frontispiece: Kirke White	10x7	
31	The Beauties of Sheridan (Alfred Howard).		1	Frontispiece: Sheridan	10x7	
32	The Beauties of Byron.		1	Frontispiece: Byron	10x7	
33	The Beauties of Fenelon.		1	Frontispiece: Fenelon	10x7	
34	The Beauties of Thomson.		1	Frontispiece: Thomson	10x7	
35	The Beauties of Pope.		1	Frontispiece: Pope	10x7	

Publisher	Location & References	Notes
J.F. Dove	V&A.95.E.18	In the Dove's English Classics series.
?J.F. Dove	NYPL. +KZ11143	?In the Dove's English Classics series.
T. Tegg	*	Similar in format to the English Classics. Published ca. 1833.
T. Tegg	*	Similar in format to the English Classics. Published ca. 1833.
T. Tegg	* NYPL. +KZ11	Similar in format to the English Classics. Published ca. 1833.
T. Tegg	*	Similar in format to the English Classics. Published ca. 1833.
T. Tegg	*	Similar in format to the English Classics. Published ca. 1833.
T. Tegg	*	Similar in format to the English Classics. Published ca. 1833.
T. Tegg	*	Similar in format to the English Classics. Published ca. 1833.
T. Tegg	NYPL. +KZ7481	

Ref No.	Book Title (Separate Print: S.P.)	Engraved After	Nos.	Caption & Page Reference	Size (cms)	Other Engravers
36	The Talisman, or English Keepsake.	S. Prout	1	Entrance to Andernach	8x12	W.J. Cooke W. Finden J. C. Edwards S. Lacey J. Henshall H. Warren E. Portbury
37	Elegant Extracts from the Best Authors.	J.M. Wright	1	Title page: A Turk with a fainted girl by a waterfall	9x7	J. Carter H. Rolls W. Ensom Chevalier C. Rolls E. Goodall Thomson
38	Moore's Poetical Works (Thomas Moore).	W. Boxall J.M. Wright	2	1) 'Mary' [Esdaile] 2) 'Come o'er the sea…'	11x8	
39	'Claudina and Camilla.'	Thomas Stothard R.A.	2	1) Father Mariscotti listening to Sir Charles 2) Sir Charles discusses Olivia	9x6	
40	Illustrations to Don Quixote (Cervantes).	Henry Corbould	4	1) Vol I p.17 2) Vol III p.182 and 3) p.312 4) People chasing a donkey. No captions		

Publisher	Location & References	Notes
Edward Lacey	*	Captain Batty's drawing of Andernach (see 1821(1)1)) seems to have been redrawn by Prout, and re-engraved in a reduced form.
	*	This work is not related either to 1810(7) or 1812(7).
Darton & Co	*	This is a reissue in the 'Standard Series of the Poets' edition. 1) is taken from 'The Keepsake' (see 1834(1)1)). 2) is taken from 'Guy Mannering' (see undated 2)). It reappears with the same title in Vol III of Moore's Poetical Works (1840(2) as engraved by Alfred and not Charles Heath. In the meantime it had also served as 'Rose of the River' in 'The Amaranth' (see 1836(2)3)).
W. Suttaby	BMPR.C.20 (Balmanno Vol III)	?From an edition of Sir Charles Grandison. See (12) undated.
	NYPL. +KZ2703 NYPL. +KZ3746	These plates appear to be later than the 1820(7) edition, with Westall designs.

Ref No.	Book Title (Separate Print: S.P.)	Engraved After	Nos.	Caption & Page Reference	Size (cms)	Other Engravers
41	S.P.	R.L. West	1	Hercules slaying the hydra	24x15	
42	S.P.		1	St George and the Dragon	45x15	
43	S.P.	Sir Robert Ker Porter	1	Cavalry charging	30x38	
44	S.P.		1	Father Time holding up a lithographic stone	31x22	
45	S.P.		1	Pomona (Flora) or Venus, surrounded by four cupids	30x35	
46	S.P.		1	Trees by a lake	15x10	
47	S.P.		1	Trees by a lake with figures	15x10	
48	S.P.		1	Cart horses in a wood	15x20	
49	S.P.		1	Shepherd with his flock	15x10	
50	S.P.		1	Francis I, King of France		

Publisher	Location & References	Notes
	Mackenzie (British Prints, 1987) Man 93	[Note: Items 41-49 and 51-56 are all polyautographs (lithographs) and would have been executed by Charles Heath mainly between 1801 and 1808.] A 'Polyautograph'. This term was changed to 'Lithograph' only a few years after the process was developed by Senefelder in Germany in 1798. See 1802-1807 for other examples.
	BMPR.C.260	
	Man 97	
	BMPR.190+. b.1. (p.73) Beinecke B1979.2.1 Man 103	'C. Heath del'. T. Fisher, in a letter on Polyautography on p.193 of the *Gentlemen's Magazine* for March 1808 refers to this work by Charles Heath. This may be the same work as 'Chronos' (see 1804(6).
	BMPR.190+. b.1 (p.72) Man 100	
	Man 99	
	NYPL. +KZ5582	

Ref No.	Book Title (Separate Print: S.P.)	Engraved After	Nos.	Caption & Page Reference	Size (cms)	Other Engravers
51	S.P.		1	Laura	15x5	
52	S.P.	?G. Walker	1	Valley with a cottage	20x30	
53	S.P.		1	Trees by a bridge	20x30	
54	S.P.		1	Landscape with a country house	20x25	
55	S.P.		1	Man with wheat in his hair.	32x20	
56	S.P.		1	A hunter aiming over a gate	6x7	
57	S.P.		1	An old man leaning against a wall	6x5	
58	S.P.	Henry Corbould	1	'Charitas' (A saint with cross and staff)	22x17	
59	The Beauties of Clarendon		1	Frontispiece: Clarendon	10x7	
60	S.P.	Henry Corbould	1	Figure of Justice (A girl on a podium)	5x6	
61	S.P.		1	Henry I	10x8	
62	S.P.	Henry Corbould	1	Homer		

Publisher	Location & References	Notes
	BMPR.C.260	
	Man 101	'C. Heath del.'
	BMPR.190+.b.1 p.78 Man 103	Inscribed 'C. Heath'.
	BMPR.167.c.21 (p.1)	
Thomas Tegg	*	ca.1824. See also u/d 28-34 for similar editions.
	BMPR.167.c.21 (p.97)	
	Huntington 110038I pt2.266	An oval print.
	YCBA.B1974. 12.102 NYPL. +KZ9559	

Ref No.	Book Title (Separate Print: S.P.)	Engraved After	Nos.	Caption & Page Reference	Size (cms)	Other Engravers
63	S.P.	G. Kugelgen	1	Alexander I, Emperor of Russia	15x10	
64	S.P.	Sir Thomas Lawrence P.R.A.	1	Lady Dover	20x15	
65	S.P.	Richard Westall R.A.	1	'Disobedience'	9x7	
66	S.P.		1	'The Boy in the Churchyard'		
67	S.P.	G. Pickering	1	View of a bridge at Farndon, Cheshire	18x28	
68	S.P.	Sully	1	David Hosack M.D., F.R.S.		
69	S.P.		1	Caroline Greeley		
70	S.P.	J. Bondon	1	Mr Laruset as Oberon in 'Ill met by moonlight' (*Midsummer Night's Dream*)		
71	S.P.		1	Cervantes		

Publisher	Location & References	Notes
	V&A.G.1.a (E2691-1888)	An early work, possibly for 'The Lady's Magazine', with 'ss' spelled with the old-fashioned 'ff'.
	V&A.J.6.f	A sketch etching/engraving which looks as if it was meant for an 'Annual', although it does not seem to have been published as such. Lady Dover however, according to Thornbury (Vol II p.70), became Lady Agar Ellis, so that this print may be one and the same as that which appeared in the Keepsake (1830(1)1)).
	V&A.J.6.f	
	Item 272 at Sotheby's auction on 4 May 1830	
	Huntington 304000 XVII49	This print may belong to John Britton's 'Antiquities of Cheshire'.
Joseph Delaplaine, Philadelphia	NYPL. +KZ4841 NYPL. +KZ14	
	NYPL. +KZ4672	
	NYPL. +KZ4807	
	NYPL. +KZ5463	Possibly a portrait engraving in the 'Beauties' series (see 28) to 35) undated).

Ref No.	Book Title (Separate Print: S.P.)	Engraved After	Nos.	Caption & Page Reference	Size (cms)	Other Engravers
72	S.P.	M.W. Sharp	1	Sunday Morning 'You dirty boy'	29x23	
73	S.P.		1	Scene at Abbotsford	9x12	
74	S.P.	Thomas Stothard R.A.	1	'The Poet'		

Publisher	Location & References	Notes
	Spreadeagle Inn, Stourhead, Wiltshire (National Trust)	
	BMPR.C.18	This may be the print referred to in Sir Walter Scott's Diary for 1 February 1828 relating to a loan by him to Charles Heath of a painting at Abbotsford to be engraved.
	G. Clulow (p.608, Society of Arts Journal, May 21, 1897)	Described as 'the figure and drapery are all done by the graver, while the background and accessories are etched, crossed with fine graver lines; for so small a subject there is wonderful, strength all through…'

Ref No.	Book Title (Separate Print: S.P.)	Engraved After	Nos.	Caption & Page Reference	Size (cms)	Other Engravers

Publisher	Location & References	Notes
		At the sale of Charles Heath's prints at Southgate, 9th to 13th May 1826, 'by order of the assignees' the following were listed as by Charles Heath, which have not otherwise been traced. Those marked * are probably by James Heath, in view of the subject. Lot 11 and 406 Burke* and Sheridan* Lot 54 Common Prayer Book, after Courbould Lot 167 Mary, Queen of Scots, and Sir John Moore* Lot 168 Mr Sinclair*, Mr Bunn*, Mrs Crouch* Lot 169 Dryden, Paley, Burns Lot 170 The Pretender Lot 281 Lord Clarendon* Lot 349 Lucien Bonaparte's Charlemagne (private print) Lot 362 Views in Chester, after Pickering (etchings) Lot 403 Lord Willoughby de Broke, Mrs Chinnery* Lot 404 Henry Salt Lot 405 Duke of Kent and wife Lot 406 Lord Bacon Lot 407 Duke of Bedford, Mrs Barbauld Lot 408 Nicol (printer)*, R. Jodrell

Ref No.	Book Title (Separate Print: S.P.)	Engraved After	Nos.	Caption & Page Reference	Size (cms)	Other Engravers
	Unidentified Prints, not indexed					
	a)	T. Uwins R.A.	1	Man with a chained lion.	10x8	
	b)	T. Uwins R.A.	1	'Teach me by this stupendous scaffold...'	10x8	
	c)	T. Uwins R.A.	1	Couple with two children in a valley	8x5	
	d)	Henry Corbould	1	Old man with two children	8x7	
	e)	Henry Corbould	1	Girl comforting a man on a sea-shore		
	f)	Henry Corbould	1	Couple looking at the moon		
	g)	Henry Corbould	1	Woman with three children sitting under an icy roof		
	h)	Henry Corbould	1	Man in a top hat with two children		
	i)	Henry Corbould	1	Man calling for help with two children and a fainting girl		
	j)	?	1	A mother beside a baby		
	k)	?	1	A white robed man with a lantern		
	l)	?	1	'Here he may many times have sat...'		

Publisher	Location & References	Notes
	V&A.J.8.b	
	V&A.J.8.b	
	V&A.J.8.b	
	BMPR.167.c21. p.44	
	BMPR.167.c21. p.44	
	BMPR.167.c21. p.44	
	BMPR.167.c21. p.44	
	BMPR.167.c21. p.45	
	BMPR.167.c21. p.45	
	V&A.J.4.d	
	V&A.J.4.d	
	YCBA.B1976. 1.147	

Ref No.	Book Title (Separate Print: S.P.)	Engraved After	Nos.	Caption & Page Reference	Size (cms)	Other Engravers
	m)	?	1	Woman by a pool in the mountains with a sleeping boy	12x9	
	n)	?	1	Girl slain by a man standing in a chariot	7x6	
	o)	?	1	Man walking with a stick by a church at midnight	4x6	
	p)	?	1	Man begging for mercy from another		
	q)	?	1	Woman on her death-bed with a man kneeling		
	r)	Thomas Stothard R.A.	1	Youth with a lyre looking at the moon with a cupid at his shoulder	10x8	
	s)	T. Uwins R.A.	1	Couple with a baby (?Adam and Eve)	15x12	
	t)	Richard Westall R.A.	1	'This is my wife, said Edward…'		
	u)	Casal	1	Boy with a spade and basket		
	v)	T. Uwins R.A.	1	Three men with a dog sitting at a table with wine	5x6	

Publisher	Location & References	Notes
	BMPR.C.13	
	BMPR.C.13	
	BMPR.C.13	
	BMPR.C.13	
	BMPR.C.13	
	RA. (Frost Vol VI)	
	BMPR.167.c.21 (p.34)	
	YCBA.B1977 14.20861	
	V&A.J.4.b	
	V&A.J.6.f	

Ref No.	Book Title (Separate Print: S.P.)	Engraved After	Nos.	Caption & Page Reference	Size (cms)	Other Engravers
	w)	F.C. Catel	1	Man embracing a girl	9x7	
	x)	T. Uwins R.A.	1	'Think what an equipage…' (Lady with floral background) 'Shenton, improved by Heath'	5x4	
	y)	T. Uwins R.A.	1	Dead man and woman with a burning and collapsing city in the background (?The Fall of Jerusalem)	16x10	

Publisher	Location & References	Notes
	V&A.J.6.f	
	V&A.J.8.b 28316C.35	
	V&A.J.8.b	

Ref No.	Book Title (Separate Print: S.P.)	Engraved After	Nos.	Caption & Page Reference	Size (cms)	Other Engravers
1	**1835** The Keepsake (editor: Frederic Mansel Reynolds).	Eliza Sharpe	1	p.60 'The Love Quarrel'	11x8	H. Cooke W.H. Mote C. Heath J.C. Edwards F. Bacon W. Chevalier C. Rolls J. Goodyear
2	**1840** Heath's Picturesque Annual.	Edward Corbould	1	Frontispiece: Queen Victoria on her favourite charger Theron riding in Windsor Park	17x12	E. Radclyffe J.B. Allen W.R. Smith Prior Le Keux W.Wallis Mottram J.T. Willmore J.C. Varrall W. Watkins
3	Moore's Poetical Works (Thomas Moore).	G. Jones R.A. Daniel Maclise R.A.	2	*Vol II* Frontispiece: 1) 'And aloft I sprang…' *Vol III* 2) 'Then if some bard…'	 7x7 7x11	A. Heath

Publisher	Location & References	Notes
Longman, Rees, Orme, Brown, Green and Longman	* NYPL. +KZ3139 V&A.J.6.f (1838 copy)	Frederick Heath's first published plate, aged 25. It was republished in 1838 in Vol IV of 'Heath's Gallery of British Engravings', as a 'Scene from 'The Bride of Lammermoor' (Chapter 23)'.
Longman, Orme, Brown, Green and Longman	* V&A.PR61 (E4380-1914)	
Longman, Brown, Green and Longmans	*	Published originally in nine volumes, but then republished in 10 by Longmans. Reprinted by Darton & Co. ca. 1864, but with only two plates, both taken from earlier works by Charles Heath; one of these 'Come o'er the Sea' was originally 'There was a small skiff' from 'Guy Mannering' ca.1831 (see Notes to 1836(2) in Charles Heath's catalogue).

Ref No.	Book Title (Separate Print: S.P.)	Engraved After	Nos.	Caption & Page Reference	Size (cms)	Other Engravers
3	**1841** Moore's Poetical Works (Thomas Moore).	Daniel Maclise R.A.	6	*Vol VI* Frontispiece: 3) 'Countless eyes...' Title page: 4) 'Upon a galliott's deck...' *Vol VIII* Frontispiece: 5) 'Sudden her brow...' Title page: 6) 'Twas first at twilight...' *Vol X* Frontispiece: 7) 'And the young maiden...' 8) Title page	 7x7 9x7 7x7 9x7 7x7	A. Heath
4	**1842** The Keepsake (editor: Countess of Blessington).	F. Stone P.F. Poole	2	1) p.77 Lady Jemima Heathfield 2) p.244 Teresina	13x10	H. Robinson J.T. Willmore C. Rolls J. Brain L. Stocks E. Radclyffe E. Roberts H. Austin A. Heath C. Heath
5	**1843** Heath's Picturesque Annual (Jules Janin).	Eugene Lami	1	p.169 'Leaving the Opera' (Sortie de l'Opéra)	10x16	T. Jeavons J.C. Varrall C. Mottram C. Rolls L. Stocks E. Radclyffe R. Staines W. Wallis C. Heath

Publisher	Location & References	Notes
Longman, Brown, Green and Longmans	*	
Longman, Brown, Green and Longmans	*	This plate was republished by Peter Jackson (successors to Fisher & Son) in 1845 in 'A Summer and Winter in Paris'. See the Notes to 1843(1) in Charles Heath's catalogue.

Ref No.	Book Title (Separate Print: S.P.)	Engraved After	Nos.	Caption & Page Reference	Size (cms)	Other Engravers
6	**1844** Heath's Picturesque Annual (Jules Janin).	Eugene Lami	1	Peasants' Ball (Bal de Paysans)	11x18	D. Roberts C. Mottram R. Wallis C. Rolls J. Allen J.T. Willmore H. Robinson W. Wallis R. Staines J.C. Varrall J. Mottram
7	The Keepsake (editor: Countess of Blessington).	F.P. Stepha-noff	1	The Surprise	9x14	C. Heath H. Robinson E. Radclyffe J. Brain W.H. Egleton W.H. Mote H. Holl W. Radclyffe
8	The Lady of the Lake (Sir Walter Scott).	Edward Corbould	2	Frontispiece: 1) 'But stumbling in the rugged dell...' 2) p.159 'She sate beneath the birchen tree...'	13x10	C. Rolls Bentley Fisher H. Robinson
9	**1845** The Chaplet	P.F. Poole	1	p.79 The Hindu Girl	12x10	See 1845(3) in Charles Heath's catalogue
10	Heath's Picturesque Annual.	George Catter-mole	1	p.152 'The King on his journey to the Scots'	11x16	See 1845(2) in Charles Heath's catalogue

Publisher	Location & References	Notes
Longman, Brown, Green and Longmans	* V&A.93.A.84	This plate was republished by Peter Jackson (successors to Fisher & Son) in 1845 in 'A Summer and Winter in Paris'. See the Notes to 1843(1) in Charles Heath's catalogue.
Longman, Brown, Green and Longmans	*	'The Surprise' here is an entirely different version from Corbould's in the 1842 'Keepsake'; see 6) in Alfred Heath's catalogue.
Carey and Hart, Philadelphia	*	An American edition, which presumably has a British equivalent.
J. Harwood	*	Although undated, this 'Annual' was published in 1845/6 according to Faxon. Charles Heath engraved a different version of the 'Hindu Girl' in 'The Keepsake' for 1836, (1836(1)) in his catalogue.
Longman, Brown, Green and Longmans	*	This is the same as Cattermole's Historical Annual for 1845. This print also appears in Cattermole's 'The Great Civil War', published by Fisher & Son in 1846. See the Notes to 1845(1) in Charles Heath's catalogue for the possibility of a second print in this series being engraved by Frederick, and not Charles Heath.

Ref No.	Book Title (Separate Print: S.P.)	Engraved After	Nos.	Caption & Page Reference	Size (cms)	Other Engravers
11	The Keepsake (editor: Countess of Blessington).	Cottrall	1	p.158 The Gondola	11x15	See 1845(1) in Charles Heath's catalogue
12	**1846** The Chaplet (Second Series).	F. Stone	1	p.140 Sad Thoughts	13x10	See 1845(3) in Charles Heath's catalogue
13	Hood's Poems (Thomas Hood).	E. Davis	1	*Vol I* Frontispiece: Bust of Hood	10x9	
14	**1847** S.P.	T. Uwins R.A.	1	A Neapolitan Wedding		
15	**1848** The Keepsake (editor: Countess of Blessington).	J. Nash Edward Corbould	2	1) p.63 The Crevice in the Tower 2) p.99 The Diamond	12x9	C. Heath W.H. Mote C. Mottram A. Heath J.B. Allen
16	S.P.	R. Huskis-son	1	'There sleeps Titania...' (p.306 Vol X of The Art Union for 1848)	16x19	
17	**1850** The Keepsake (editor: 'the late Countess of Blessington').	J.B. Smith Edward Corbould M.Wood	3	1) May Cumming 2) The Farewell 3) The Quarrel	15x11	W.H. Mote A. Heath B. Eyles J.B. Allen
18	**1851** The Keepsake (editor: Miss Marguerite Power).	W. Lee J.Jenkins C.Weigall Edward Corbould	5	1) The Fisherman Home 2) Lucy Penrose 3) The Introduction 4) The branding of Elgira 5) The Promise Fulfilled	10x13 14x11 10x14 14x11 11x13	W.H. Mote B. Eyles A.T. Heath

Publisher	Location & References	Notes
Longman, Brown, Green and Longmans	*	
J. Harwood	*	
E. Moxon	* (second edition)	
'Art Union of 1847, London'	V&A.J.8.b 28316A/3	This print took about three years to engrave. It does not figure in the Art Union's annual for 1847, so was presumably published separately.
David Bogue	*	
Chapman and Hall Knight & Co, New York	* Art Union NYPL.	The plate was re-used in an 1872 'Imperial' edition of Shakespeare, published by Knight & Co; another print by Frederick Heath was also used in this edition, according to the NYPL catalogue (in Vol I p.173 and 657).
David Bogue	*	'Engraved under the superintendence of Mr Frederick A. Heath.'
David Bogue	*	'Engraved under the superintendence of Mr Frederick A. Heath.'

Ref No.	Book Title (Separate Print: S.P.)	Engraved After	Nos.	Caption & Page Reference	Size (cms)	Other Engravers
19	**1852** The Keepsake (editor: Miss Marguerite Power).	M.Wood C.Weigall R. Buckner Edward Corbould	4	1) Lady Teazle 2) The Farewell 3) The Orphan 4) The Reverie	14x11 11x14 14x11 14x10	W.H. Mote B. Eyles A.T. Heath J.T. Willmore G.A. Periam
20	**1853** The Keepsake (editor: Miss Marguerite Power).	W. Lee C. Duke Lord Bury Edward Corbould	4	1) Jacqueline returning from market 2) The Imprisonment 3) A Belle's Strategem 4) Hotspur and Lady Percy	15x11 16x11 14x11 15x10	W.H. Mote B. Eyles A.T. Heath G.A. Periam
21	**1854** The Keepsake (editor: Miss Marguerite Power).	Edward Corbould C. Dukes C. Weigall	3	1) The Lovers 2) The Gleaner 3) The Snuff Box	14x11 15x11 11x14	A.T. Heath B. Eyles W.H. Mote
22	**1855** The Keepsake (editor: Miss Marguerite Power).	C.W. Cope R.A.	1	The Page	14x11	W.H. Mote B. Eyles W. Holl A.T. Heath
23	**1856** The Keepsake (editor: Miss Marguerite Power).	Edward Corbould M. Gillies	3	1) The Warning 2) Je Travaillais 3) Blanche and Ellen	14x11	W.H. Mote B. Eyles A. Heath
24	**1856** Description of the Collection of Ancient Marbles in the British Museum (Part XI).	Henry Corbould	4	1) Pl.XIX Bust of an Old Man 2) Pl.XXXV Statue of Venus 3) Pl.XLI A Satyr 4) Pl.XLVI Ceres	10x25 and various	See 1820(11) Alfred T. Heath
25	**1857** The Keepsake (editor: Miss Marguerite Power).	C. Dukes J.G. Naish	2	1) Agnes at the Spring 2) Too Late	14x10 14x11	W.H. Mote B. Eyles A.T. Heath

Publisher	Location & References	Notes
David Bogue	*	'Engraved under the superintendence of Mr Frederick A. Heath.'
David Bogue	*	'Engraved under the superintendence of Mr Frederick A. Heath.'
David Bogue	*	'Engraved under the superintendence of Mr Frederick A. Heath.'
David Bogue	*	'Engraved under the superintendence of Mr Frederick A. Heath.'
David Bogue	*	'Engraved under the superintendence of Mr Frederick A. Heath.'
Longman, Orme	BMPR.242. a.12	Although this part is dated '1856', the plates are dated '1851'. See 1820(11) of Charles Heath's Catalogue for other details of this long drawn out series. 1) and 4) here were engraved by Alfred Heath.
David Bogue	*	'Engraved under the superintendence of Mr Frederick A. Heath.'

Ref No.	Book Title (Separate Print: S.P.)	Engraved After	Nos.	Caption & Page Reference	Size (cms)	Other Engravers
26	**1864** The months (Samuel Manning).	Humphreys J. Gilbert		Wood engravings	22x22	Butterworth
27	**1866** S.P.	E.M. Ward R.A.	1	Alice Lisle	19x24	
28	**1867** S.P.	E.M. Ward R.A.	1	p.38 'James II at the landing of the Prince of Orange'	17x25	
29	S.P.	F.H. Calderon	1	p.164 'After the Battle'	19x24	
30	**1868** S.P.	T. Fald R.A.	1	'Going Home'	19x25	
31	**1869** S.P.	William Mulready R.A.	1	p.4 'Choosing the Wedding Gown'	23x19	
32	**1870** S.P.	H.S. Marks	1	'My Lady's Page in Disgrace'	18x25	
33	**1872** S.P.	F. Stone A.R.A.	1	'The First Voyage'	19x23	
34	S.P.	Edward Corbould	1	'The Lesson of the Passover'	19x23	
35	S.P.	J. Pettie A.R.A.	1	'What d'ye lack, Madam?'	26x17	
36	**1874** S.P.	W. Hunt	1	'The Attack'	19x21	
37	S.P.	J. Pettie A.R.A.	1	'The Rival Roses'	17x25	

Publisher	Location & References	Notes
Religious Tract Society	NYPL.NC.1	
Virtue & Co.	*	[Note that Items 27 to 39 hereunder all appeared in the year given in the 'Art Journal' published by George Virtue, to which the page numbers given also refer.]
Virtue & Co.	*	
Virtue & Co.	*	Republished in the 'International Gallery' (Plate 15. Vol VII), Boston, 1886.
Virtue & Co.	*	
Virtue & Co.	* YCBA	Reproduced in J. Dafforne's 'Pictures by William Mulready', 1873.
Virtue & Co.	*	
Virtue & Co.	*	Reproduced in J. Dafforne's 'Modern Art', 1877.
Virtue & Co.	* NYPL	Reproduced in J. Dafforne's 'Modern Art', 1877.
Virtue & Co.	* NYPL	
Virtue & Co.	*	
Virtue & Co.	* YCBA	

Ref No.	Book Title (Separate Print: S.P.)	Engraved After	Nos.	Caption & Page Reference	Size (cms)	Other Engravers
38	**1877** S.P.	G.D. Leslie R.A.	1	p.164 'News from the War'	24x18	
39	**1879** S.P.	P. Seignac	1	'The Queen of the Vineyard'	19x23	

Publisher	Location & References	Notes
Virtue & Co.	*	Mainly etched.
Virtue & Co.	*	

Ref No.	Book Title (Separate Print: S.P.)	Engraved After	Nos.	Caption & Page Reference	Size (cms)	Other Engravers
1	**1837** The Keepsake (editor: Lady Elizabeth Stuart Wortley).	J. M. Wright	1	The Orphan of Palestine	9x11	H. Robinson E. Radclyffe L. Stocks W. Chevalier Knight J.T. Willmore H. Cooke J. Goodyear R. Brandard E. Portbury C. Rolls Grundy
2	**1840** Moore's Poetical Works (Thomas Moore).	G. Jones R.A. Daniel Maclise R.A.	7	*Vol I* Title page: 1) 'A Hebe of celestial shape…' *Vol II* Title page: 2) 'Twas thus by the shade…' *Vol III* Title page: 3) 'Come o'er the sea…' *Vol IV* Frontispiece: 4) 'For on thy deck…' Title page: 5) 'For when the last April sun…' *Vol V* Frontispiece: 6) 'Now by those stars' 7) 'Like rosy huntresses…'	 9x7 6x6 6x6 7x11 9x7	F.A. Heath

Publisher	Location & References	Notes
Longman, Rees, Orme, Brown, Green and Longmans	*	
Longman, Orme, Brown, Green and Longmans	*	

Ref No.	Book Title (Separate Print: S.P.)	Engraved After	Nos.	Caption & Page Reference	Size (cms)	Other Engravers
3	**1841** Moore's Poetical Works (Thomas Moore) (continued)	G. Jones R.A.	4	*Vol VII* Frontispiece: 8) 'The Mask is off…' Title page: 9) 'No sooner was…' *Vol IX* Frontispiece: 10) 'And then at night…' Title page: 11) 'Alas! That poverty'	 10x7 8x7 10x8 8x7	
4	The Keepsake (editor: Countess of Blessington).	Edward Corbould	1	The Elopement	15x12	W. Edwards E. Radclyffe L. Stocks W. Staines C. Rolls J. Willmore W.F. Holl F. Holl
5	Montgomery's Poetical Works (James Montgomery).	George Jones R.A.	7	*Vol I* Title page: 1) 'Yet suspending thy griefs…' *Vol II* Frontispiece: 2) 'Our mother first beheld him…' Title page: 3) 'Thus on his dulcet pipe…' *Vol III* Frontispiece: 4) 'Incognita…' Title page: 5) 'Twas but a dream'	 8x6 10x7	

Publisher	Location & References	Notes
Longman, Brown, Green and Longmans	*	
Longman, Brown, Green and Longmans	*	An edition of 1854 also has a frontispiece of Montgomery by Alfred Heath.

Ref No.	Book Title (Separate Print: S.P.)	Engraved After	Nos.	Caption & Page Reference	Size (cms)	Other Engravers
5	Montgomery's Poetical Works (continued)			*Vol IV* Frontispiece: 6) 'Tears of light slid down his cheek...' Title page: 7) 'On the rough waves...'		
6	**1842** The Keepsake (editor: Countess of Blessington).	Edward Corbould	1	p.67 The Surprise	13x10	H. Robinson J.T. Willmore E. Radclyffe C. Rolls L. Stocks E. Roberts H. Austin J. Brain C. Heath F.A. Heath
7	**1843** The Keepsake (editor: Countess of Blessington).	Edward Corbould	1	'Sir Eglantine's Ladye Love'	12x10	E. Radclyffe W.H. Mote S. Bull C. Rolls H. Robinson L. Stocks J. Willmore
8	**1844** The Forget-Me-Not (Frederic Shoberl, editor).	Edward Corbould	1	p.327 The Flight into Egypt	10x8	J.H. Kermot W.H. Mote W. Mossman J. Cochran H.T. Ryall C.W. Wass

Publisher	Location & References	Notes
Longman, Rees, Orme, Brown, Green and Longmans	*	
Longman, Rees, Orme, Brown, Green and Longmans	*	
Ackermann & Co.	*	

Ref No.	Book Title (Separate Print: S.P.)	Engraved After	Nos.	Caption & Page Reference	Size (cms)	Other Engravers
9	Heath's Picturesque Annual.	Eugene Lami	1	p.223 'The Family Concert'	11x16	D. Roberts C. Mottram R. Wallis C. Rolls J.T. Willmore H. Robinson W. Wallis J.B. Allen Staines Varrall J. Mottram
10	**1845** The Keepsake (editor: Countess of Blessington).	Edward Corbould	1	p.27 The Island Bride	13x10	W.H. Mote E. Radclyffe C. Heath J.T. Willmore J. Brain F.A. Heath C. Rolls W.H. Egleton
11	The Gallery of Scripture Engravings (John Kitto).	Antoine Zucchi	1	*Vol I* p.93 'They sold Joseph to the Ishmaelites'	16x11	W. Holl E. Benjamin W.H. Egleton W. Hill W. Mote G. Presbury R. Brandard H. Robinson H. Adlard H.B. Hall J. Tingle W. Watkins S. Freeman S. Bradshaw F. Holl W. Floyd J. Sands H. Rolls W. Radclyffe

Publisher	Location & References	Notes
Longman, Rees, Orme, Brown, Green and Longmans	*	See the Notes to 1843(1) and (2) in Charles Heath's catalogue. This plate was republished by Peter Jackson in 1845 in 'A Summer and Winter in Paris', and also by David Bogue in 'Heath's New Gallery of British Engravings' (see 1846(2) in Charles Heath's catalogue).
Longman, Brown, Green and Longmans	*	
Peter Jackson (late Fisher)	* NYPL. +KZ239 Hunnisett. p.46	In three volumes. The work was originally entitled 'Historic Illustrations of the Bible' and published by Fisher & Son between 1840 and 1843. Some of the prints were then reissued in 'The Sacred Gift (2nd series) by Rev'd Charles Tayler, and published by Fisher & Son in 1845. This much expanded edition contains what may well be the widest range of fine steel engravings ever published together in one work.

Ref No.	Book Title (Separate Print: S.P.)	Engraved After	Nos.	Caption & Page Reference	Size (cms)	Other Engravers
11	The Gallery of Scripture Engravings (continued).					S. Fisher E. Radclyffe J. Jenkins J. Outrim R. Staines W. Wallis J. Carter J.C. Bentley J. Thomson T. Barber J.W. Lowry G.W. Adcock W.H. Capone W. Chevalier
12	**1846** The Keepsake (editor: Countess of Blessington).	Edward Corbould	2	1) p.159 Ianthe 2) p.202 The Bell	14x10	J. Thomson E. Radclyffe W.H. Mote R. Wallis R. Staines J. Brain J. Le Keux J.B. Allen
13	Gems of European Art (S.C. Hall).	Corregio	1	*Vol II* p.35 (Second Series) The marriage of St Catherine	21x16	Various
14	**1847** The Keepsake (editor: Countess of Blessington).	Edward Corbould	2	1) p.143 The Heiress 2) p.258 The Jew's Daughter	14x10 13x10	W.H. Egleton E. Radclyffe R. Wallis R. Staines J. Le Keux C. Heath
15	The Keepsake (editor: Countess of Blessington).	E.H. Weigall	1	p.193 Phoebe	12x9	F.A. Heath C. Heath W.H. Mote C. Mottram J.B. Allen

Publisher	Location & References	Notes
Longman, Brown, Green and Longmans	*	
G. Virtue	* NYPL. NAL Hunnisett. p.46	
Longman, Brown, Green and Longmans	*	
Longman, Brown, Green and Longmans	*	

Ref No.	Book Title (Separate Print: S.P.)	Engraved After	Nos.	Caption & Page Reference	Size (cms)	Other Engravers
16	**1849** The Keepsake (editor: Countess of Blessington).	Edward Corbould A.Bouvier W.Fisher	3	1) Bereavement 2) Annot 3) Lilias	14x10 13x10	W.H. Mote J. Allen Varrall W.H. Egleton
17	**1850** The Keepsake (editor: Miss Marguerite Power).	Edward Corbould T.F. Marshall	2	1) The Exile's Wife 2) The Fatal Error	14x11	W.H. Mote B. Eyles F.A. Heath J.B. Allen
18	**1851** The Keepsake (editor: Miss Marguerite Power).	Edward Corbould T.F. Marshall	2	1) Kathleen 2) The Closing Scene	14x11	W.H. Mote F.A. Heath B. Eyles
19	**1852** The Keepsake (editor: Miss Marguerite Power).	Edward Corbould	2	1) Pontius Pilate's Daughter 2) Mabel	14x10	W.H. Mote B. Eyles J. Willmore F.A. Heath G.A. Periam
20	**1853** The Keepsake (editor: Miss Marguerite Power).	Edward Corbould Margaret Gillies	2	1) The Sanctuary 2) Young Jamie	15x10 14x10	F. Heath W. Mote B. Eyles G.A. Periam
21	S.P.	Sir A.W. Calcott R.A.	1	The Weary Wayfarer	15x12	
22	**1854** The Keepsake (editor: Miss Marguerite Power).	Edward Corbould A. Solomon	3	1) Sisters of Seville 2) La Toilette 3) Ora May	14x11 15x11	W.H. Mote F.A. Heath B. Eyles
23	**1855** The Keepsake (editor: Miss Marguerite Power).	Edward Corbould W.J. Grant	2	1) Juliet and Friar 2) The Broken Snare	14x11	W.H. Mote B. Eyles W. Holl F.A. Heath

Publisher	Location & References	Notes
David Bogue	*	
David Bogue	*	'Engraved under the supervision of Mr Frederick A. Heath.'
David Bogue	*	'Engraved under the supervision of Mr Frederick A. Heath.'
David Bogue	*	'Engraved under the supervision of Mr Frederick A. Heath.'
Virtue & Co.	*	'Engraved under the supervision of Mr Frederick A. Heath.'
Virtue & Co.	Art Union	'Engraved under the supervision of Mr Frederick A. Heath.'
Virtue & Co.	*	'Engraved under the supervision of Mr Frederick A. Heath.'
Virtue & Co.	*	'Engraved under the supervision of Mr Frederick A. Heath.'

Ref No.	Book Title (Separate Print: S.P.)	Engraved After	Nos.	Caption & Page Reference	Size (cms)	Other Engravers
24	**1856** The Keepsake (editor: Miss Marguerite Power).	W.J. Grant Miss R. Solomon A.J. Simmons	3	1) The Glee Maiden 2) The Governess 3) The Reconciliation	15x11 11x14 15x11	F.A. Heath B. Eyles W.H. Mote
25	**1857** The Keepsake (editor: Miss Marguerite Power).	A. Solomon M. Gillies	2	1) The Lady Violet 2) The Bride	15x10 15x12	F.A. Heath W.H. Mote B. Eyles

Publisher	**Location & References**	**Notes**
Virtue & Co.	*	'Engraved under the supervision of Mr Frederick A. Heath.'
Virtue & Co.	*	'Engraved under the supervision of Mr Frederick A. Heath.'

Ref No.	Book Title (Separate Print: S.P.)	Engraved After	Nos.	Caption & Page Reference	Size (cms)	Other Engravers
1	Illustrations to the Works of Lord Byron.	Edward Corbould	1	Haidee entering the cave	13x10	W.H. Mote E. Radclyffe H. Cook T. Stodart J.T. Willmore H. Robinson L. Stocks J. Thompson C. Rolls W. Radclyffe
2	The Literary Gift Book, for fireside, seaside and garden.	Edward Corbould	2	1) p.51 The Valentine 2) p.80 The Sisters	15x10 (rounded top)	B. Eyles W.H. Mote
3	S.P.		1	George IV	10x9	
4	S.P.	Edward Corbould	1	Miss McRea taken by the Indians	12x18	

Publisher	Location & References	Notes
A. Fullarton	*	See 1) undated in Charles Heath's catalogue, which is the same work ca. 1846. An altogether different 'Haidee' appeared in 'The Keepsake' for 1831 (1831(1)1) in Charles Heath's catalogue, engraved by him.
James Blackwood	* Huntington 109979.I.47 Huntington Pr Box 520/ 58:2	Although undated, this book has a preface by 'G.F.P(ardon)' dated October 1856. The binding is identical with that of 'The Keepsake' for 1856, but otherwise there is no duplication.

Index

I. CHARLES HEATH: ILLUSTRATED BOOKS

Debrett's Peerage and Baronetcy	1822(6)
Dodd's Beauties of Shakespeare	1825(12)
Dodd's Thoughts in Prison	1818(4)
Dodwell's Classical and Topographical Tour through Greece	1819(1)
Don Quixote	1817(6)
Don Quixote	1820(7)
Don Quixote	u/d(4))
Elegant Extracts from the Best Authors	u/d(37)
Elegant Extracts from the most eminent British poets	1812(7)
Elegant Extracts from the most eminent prose writers	1810(7)
Elizabeth	1817(8)
Encyclopaedia (Constable)	1815(3)
English Pearls	1843(3)
English Poets, Selections from the	1836(4)
English School, The Fine Arts of	1811(1)
Evenings at Home	1827(6)
Falconer's The Shipwreck	1822(2)
Fenelon, The Beauties of	u/d(33)
Forget-Me-Not, The	1825(6)
Forget-Me-Not, The	1826(2)
Forget-Me-Not, The	1827(2)
Franklin, Works of Benjamin	1824(1)
Friendship's Offering	1827(3)
Gems of Beauty	1836(9)
Gems of Devotional Poetry	1824(5)
Gems of Lyric Poetry	1824(6)
Gertrude of Wyoming	1821(8)
Gibbon's Miscellaneous Works	1814(5)
Goldsmith's Poems: The Traveller etc	1816(3)
Goldsmith's The Deserted Village	1822(3)
Goldsmith's Vicar of Wakefield	1808(3)
Governess, The	1839(4)
Grandison, Sir Charles	u/d(12)
Gray's Works	1816(4)
Great Civil War, The	1846(3)
Hampstead, Topography and Natural History of	1814(6)
Heath's Beauties of the Opera and Ballet	1844(2)
Heath's Book of Beauty	1833(8)
Heath's Gallery of British Engravings	1836(3)
Heath's Heroines of Shakespeare	1848(2)
Heath's New Gallery of British Engravings	1846(2)
Heath's Picturesque Annual	1832(2)
Heath's Picturesque Annual	1833(2)
Heath's Picturesque Annual	1835(2)
Heath's Picturesque Annual	1843(2)
Heath's Picturesque Annual	1845(2)
Heath's Portfolio of Engravings (The Book of Plates)	1846(3)
Heath's Shakespeare Gallery	1836(6)
Heath's Versailles	u/d(19)
Heath's Waverley Gallery	1841(3)
Hervey's Meditations and Contemplations	1818(3)/1825(14)
Historical Souvenir, The	u/d(8)
Holy Bible (Macklin), The	1815(2)
Holy Bible, The	1815(1)
Holy Gospels, The	1849(3)
Horace	1827(8)
Hudibras	u/d(17)
The Improvement of the Mind	1826(7)
The Improvisatrice	1824(8)
The Improvisatrice	1831(2)
Johnson's Lives of the Poets	u/d(21)
Jones, The History of Tom	u/d(24)
Juvenile Keepsake, The	1829(2)
Keepsake, The	1828(1)
Keepsake, The	1829(1)
Keepsake, The	1830(1)
Keepsake, The	1831(1)
Keepsake, The	1832(1)
Keepsake, The	1833(1)
Keepsake, The	1834(1)
Keepsake, The	1835(1)
Keepsake, The	1836(1)
Keepsake, The	1842(2)
Keepsake, The	1843(1)
Keepsake, The	1844(1)
Keepsake, The	1845(1)
Keepsake, The	1846(1)
Keepsake, The	1847(1)
Keepsake, The	1848(1)
Kenilworth Illustrated	1821(11)
Kirke White, The Beauties of	u/d(30)
Kirke White, Works of	u/d(16)
Lady of the Lake, The	1810(3)
Lady of the Lake, The	1821(10)
Lady's Magazine, The	1822(8)

Tale of Paraguay, A	1825(10)
Tales of a Traveller	1824(9)
Tales of the Genii	1820(9)
Talisman, or English Keepsake, The	u/d(36)
Theatre Royal, Plays as performed at	1807(3)
Theodosius and Constantina	u/d(22)
Theron and Aspasia	1825(2)
Thomson, The Beauties of	u/d(34)
Thomson's Seasons	1816(2)
Tournament at Eglinton Castle, The	1839(2)
Transmigrations of Indur	u/d(23)
Travels in Egypt, Nubia, Holy Land, Lebanon and Cyprus	1818(2)
Travels in Georgia, Persia, Armenia, Ancient Babylonia etc	1821(4)
Valiant Knight Arthur, History of, The	1814(3)
Victories of the Duke of Wellington	1819(6)
Views in and About London	1825(1)
Views in Paris	1831(3)
Views of Cities and Scenery in Italy, France and Switzerland	1837(1)
Voyages and Travels of Lord Valentia	1809(4)
Voyage to Abyssinia (Henry Salt)	1814(1)
Walton's Lives	1825(3)
Wandering Jew, The	1844(3)
Washington Irving, Works of	1825(11)
Watts' Poetical Sketches	1824(7)
Waverley Album, The	u/d(9)
Waverley Keepsake, The	u/d(4)
Waverley Novels, Pictorial Illustrations to, The	1829(3)
Western Islands of Scotland, Description of	1819(5)
White Knights, A Descriptive Account of	1819(4)
Woburn Abbey Marbles, Description of	1822(9)
Wortley Montague, Works of Lady Mary	1825(9)
Wreath of Friendship, The	1836(5)
Wye, its Scenery and Association, The	1839(3)
Young's Night Thoughts	1817(12)
Young's Night Thoughts	1824(2)

II. CHARLES HEATH: SEPARATE PRINTS

Abbotsford, Scene at	u/d(73)
Alexander I of Russia	u/d(63)
Apollo as a Warrior	1802(3)
Armida brought before Godfrey	1804(4)
Battle of the Angels	1807(4)
Binning, Lord, and four others	1822(10)
Boy in the Churchyard, The	u/d(66)
Boy playing a violin	1802(10)
Carthorses in a wood	u/d(48)
Cavalry charging	u/d(43)
Cervantes	u/d(71)
Charitas	u/d(58)
Cherubs bathing	1802(9)
Christ, Head of	1802(5)
Chronos (?)	1804(16)
Clough, Sir Richard	[see 1813(2)]
Contention of Achilles and Agamemnon	1804(15)
Cupid with a Horn	1802(8)
Dartmouth, Earl of	u/d(75)
Designs from plays	1807(5)
Disobedience	u/d(65)
Dover, Lady	u/d(64)
Europa	1840(4)
Farndon, Cheshire, Bridge at	u/d(67)
Father Time	u/d(44)
Francis I	u/d(50)
Gentleman of the Court of King Charles I, A	1823(14)
George, Earl of Dartmouth	1814(7)
Gips(e)y, A	1801(2)
Girl at the Well, The	1823(13)
Greeley, Caroline	u/d(69)
Harington, General	1807(6)
Head of a Man	1802(6)
Head of an Oriental wearing a turban	1803(1)
Head of a Woman	1791(1)
Henry I	u/d(61)
Hercules	1802(4)

Index

I. FREDERICK HEATH: ILLUSTRATED BOOKS

II FREDERICK HEATH: SEPARATE PRINTS

III. ALFRED HEATH: ILLUSTRATED BOOKS

IV. ALFRED HEATH: SEPARATE PRINTS

GEMS IN A GRANITE SETTING.

GEMS IN A GRANITE SETTING:

BEAUTIES OF
THE LONE LAND
OF DARTMOOR

BY

WILLIAM CROSSING
Author of "A Hundred Years on Dartmoor," etc.

DEVON BOOKS

First published 1986 by Devon Books
Reprinted 1987

ISBN 0-86114-787-1

British Library Cataloguing in Publication Data

Crossing, William
Gems in a granite setting: beauties of
the lone land of Dartmoor.
1. Dartmoor (England) —— Description and
travel
I. Title
914.23'5304823   DA670.D2

DEVON BOOKS

Publishers to the Devon County Council

Devon Books is a division of A. Wheaton & Co. Ltd who represents:

Design, Editorial & Publicity
Production & Manufacturing
A. Wheaton & Co. Ltd, Hennock Road, Exeter EX2 8RP
Tel: 0392-74121   Telex: 42749 (WHEATN G)

Sales & Distribution
Town & Country Books, P.O. Box 31, Newton Abbot TQ12 5XH
Tel: 080 47 2541

A. Wheaton & Co. Ltd is a member
of the Pergamon Group of Companies

Printed and bound in Great Britain
by A. Wheaton & Co. Ltd, Exeter

CONTENTS.

Glimpses of valley and upland,
Of places of old renown,
Of jewels that bountiful Nature
Has set in Devonia's crown.

INTRODUCTION TO THE 1986 FACSIMILE EDITION

To lovers of Dartmoor there can be no name better known and more respected than that of William Crossing. It is almost sixty years since this man, a native of Plymouth, died, but the abiding popularity of his books remains as a fitting tribute to his life's work.

His dedication and love of Dartmoor is evidenced by the fact that, after a somewhat uncertain start in life, from his middle twenties onwards he devoted himself to the exploration and study of the great wilderness, to the exclusion of almost every other interest. To Crossing, Dartmoor became a passion. So much was this the case that he was accepted as the leading authority on the moor during his own lifetime, this despite being a contemporary of many of the most prominent Dartmoor writers, among them Robert Burnard, Sabine Baring-Gould, and Richard Hansford Worth.

Crossing's first book about Dartmoor, *The Ancient Crosses of Dartmoor*, was published in 1884, and was followed by numerous other books, the last of which was a slim volume of verse entitled *Cranmere: The Legendary Story of Binjie Gear and Other Poems.* Along with his books, Crossing was engaged in the writing of articles for local newspapers and periodicals, and it was from these that two books were later published: *A Hundred Years on Dartmoor* (1901), and *Gems in a Granite Setting* (1905). Another series of articles, published under the title *Present Day Life on Dartmoor*, was published in book form in 1966 as *Crossing's Dartmoor Worker*, with an introduction by Brian Le Messurier, who also provided an introduction for the 1965 reprint of *Crossing's Guide to Dartmoor.*

Leaving aside this last work, the Guide, which is indispensable and unique, I consider *Gems in a Granite Setting* the best of all Crossing's books. It deals with many of the most attractive and fascinating aspects of Dartmoor with a sensitivity and perception found in the works of no other author.

It gives me great pleasure to know that this splendid work, so long out of print and practically unobtainable, is now to be made available to a wider readership. I count it as a great compliment that I should be asked to write this introduction.

HAYTOR VALE
MARCH 1986

HARRY STARKEY

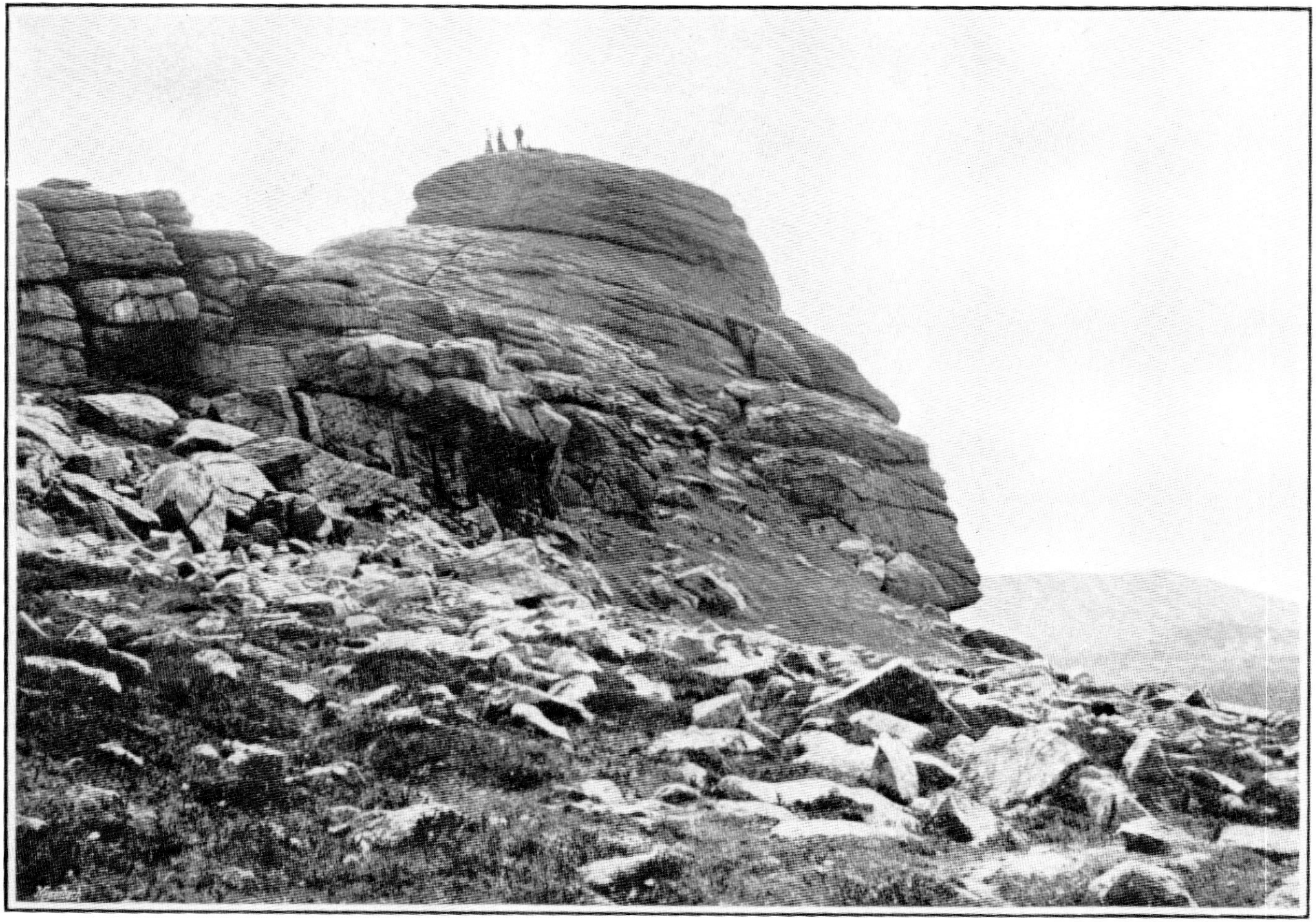

SEE PAGE 11.

Heytor with Saddle Tor and Ripon Tor in the distance.

PHOTO BY ERNEST CROFT.

"The jutting crag and rocky pinnacles rising from the clatter."

INTRODUCTION:

DARTMOOR SCENERY.

Solitude of the Moor——Its Influence on the Imagination——Groupings of the Tors——The Clatters——Distant Views——The Moorland Streams——Border Valleys——Gardens of the Moor——Wild Flowers——Old Farmhouses——Ancient Paths——Dartmoor not the Home of Trees——Lights and Shadows——A Gathering Storm——The Garb of Winter——Veils of Mist——A Summer Day——Scenery intended for Man's Delight——The Iron Crown of Lombardy——The Granite Diadem of Devon.

Haunts of wild beauty, where the glowing mind
Drinks deep the fulness of some heavenly sense.
—Sophie Dixon.

THE testimony of writers not natives of the county, who have recorded their appreciation of the varied scenery of Devon, is particularly valuable, in that it was not called forth by "the power of local sympathy," but was prompted solely by that which met the eye, and which could not fail to appeal to the soul of a lover of Nature ; and the praises of old Danmonia's beauty, sounded through the years, and which poets have loved to sing, find an echo to-day. Those who look upon the wild grandeur of its coasts, its peaceful valleys where streams hide themselves in summer beneath spreading boughs, or run prattling in the sunlight by orchard and meadow ; or who seek the quiet of its upland combes, where the breeze brushes only the rowan and the thorn, join in its eulogy. Devon has something to offer to all. Tree-clothed hills descending to the sea ; red cliffs that rise from restless surges ; meads where the scent of wild flowers floats upon balmy air ; towns renowned in ancient story ; villages that wear their old-time look ; and in its midst, rising in "haughty solitude," the granite-capped heights of Dartmoor.

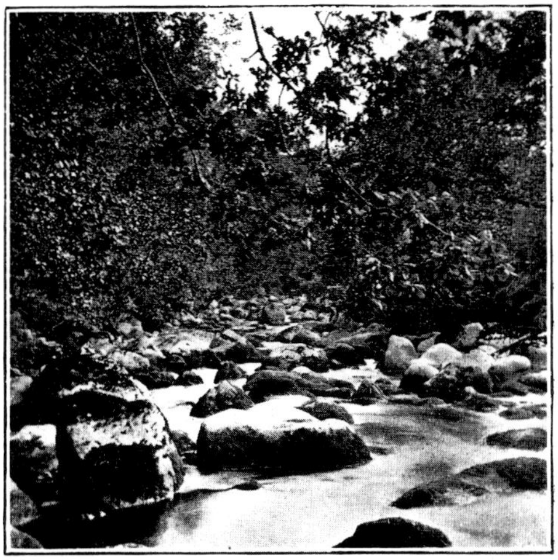

Photo by] [Ernest Croft.

The Plym near Shaugh Bridge.

"Where streams hide themselves in summer beneath spreading boughs."

There are few greater contrasts than that exhibited by the desolate Moor and the fruitful valleys by which it is encircled. And this at once strikes the beholder, who finds his way to one of its frontier hills. On one side he sees fertility; on the other barrenness. On this hand farms and villages that speak of the labours of man; on that a wide waste which shows few signs of his intrusion. Yet it is the latter which the more forcibly attracts him, though he cannot explain why this is so. He feels an irresistible desire to penetrate into its remote parts, and when he lets his footsteps lead him thither is impressed by its vastness and its solitude. On its border heights he had but to turn his face and a smiling scene presented itself; he stood on the huge barrier of this silent land, and saw that it was placed in the midst of a garden. But now he looks only upon the grim Moor; there is no longer the village nestling in the sheltered vale; the homestall with the fruits of a bounteous harvest in its yards; the orchard and the grove. Nothing but great undulating sweeps of heathy land, and granite tors of fantastic shape. Yet he is impelled onward, possessed with a feeling that this lone region hides within itself much that will delight him. Already in imagination he lives in a long past day, for there is nothing to remind him of the present. The ruins of dwellings and mouldered sepulchres, scattered on the slopes, serve only to show that centuries have flown since man here found an abiding place. It is the solitude of Dartmoor that fascinates. That sense of loneliness which oppresses the wanderer who seeks its recesses, bidding him hasten to where he may find companionship, is not without a certain charm; indescribable it may be, but none the less powerful. In the very dreariness of the waste there is an attraction; it acts upon the imagination, and the influence it exerts is a lasting one. Those who have once set foot upon Dartmoor, who have climbed its giant tors, have listened to the plaintive music of its streams, or have passed into its solitary places, where the cry of the curlew alone is heard, will, if they be true lovers of Nature, ever feel a longing to revisit it.

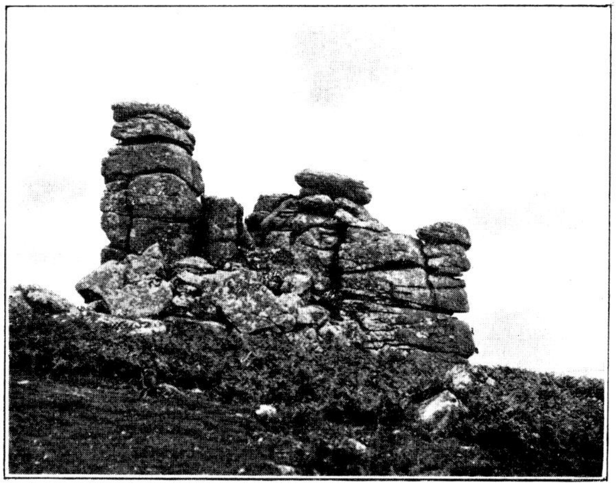

Photo by] [Mrs. Ernest Croft.

Hound Tor.

"Granite tors of fantastic shape."

The more the explorer learns of Dartmoor the greater appears the difficulty of gaining a complete knowledge of it. Every hill and valley, every river and brook, each tiny combe yield him something, whether he be in search of the picturesque or of the memorials of the past. He perceives it to be a field practically inexhaustible, but if he be enthusiastic he will not tire in his quest. During a life-long acquaintance with the Moor I have visited every part of it, and have had opportunities of observing it in all its moods. It would be too much to lay claim to knowing "every inch," but I think I can say that throughout the length and breadth of the Moor there are few acres with which I am unacquainted. I have passed over it alone, by day and by night, in all seasons of the year, and in all weathers. I speak therefore with no degree of uncertainty when I say that the rambler on Dartmoor will find it to be an ever-widening field, and will also meet with an ever-increasing reward.

It is to its tors that Dartmoor owes so much of the grandeur of its scenery. In places where these are wanting, such as in the south quarter of the Forest and on the great fen that occupies so much of the north quarter, the wanderer is impressed solely by the remoteness and loneliness of the region; there is little for him to really admire. He walks in a wilderness, the strange aspect of which is sufficient to attract him though he looks upon nothing but stretches of boggy land. But how different are the feelings inspired by those scenes in which a group of tors form the chief feature. The jutting crag and the rocky pinnacles rising from the clatter powerfully arrest the attention and awaken thoughts of the sublime. It is still wild Nature on which the observer looks; still a silent land in which he wanders; but unlike the vast sea of dead peat, these strange forms tell him of the mighty forces that have been in operation through the ages. Though Nature's work has gone forward unceasingly upon the fen, it was not so apparent; here he is reminded of it forcibly.

In some parts of the Moor the effects presented by the groupings of the tors are particularly fine. Let the rambler find his way to Hound Tor Combe, near the source of the Becky Brook, and he will see something of this. Or let him stand upon Langstone Moor, and look upon Staple Tor rising immediately behind Roose Tor; or at the bend above the falls on the Doe Tor Brook, where rock-piles rise on each side of the combe; or by Cramber Tor, whence he will see the stony hills above the valley of the Mew; or on Black Down, and gaze upon the tors of Tavy Cleave. The tors always add to the impressiveness of the scene, but there are localities in which Nature has placed them in such a way as to be more than ordinarily striking.

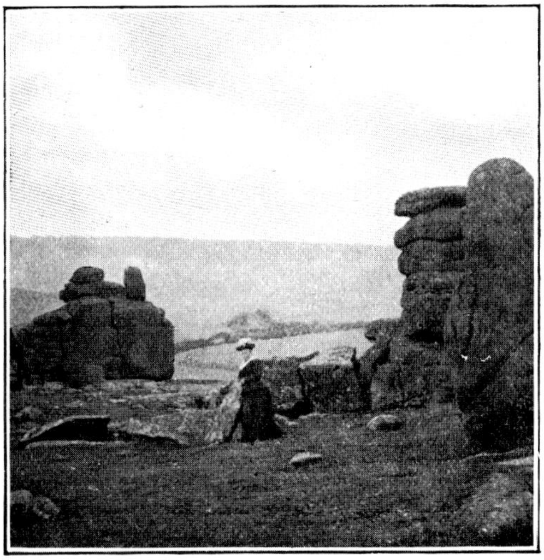

Photo by] [Ernest Croft.

Hound Tor Combe from Hound Tor.

"Let the rambler find his way to Hound Tor Combe."

Good effects are produced in places where an opening between two tor-crested hills discloses a more distant height crowned in the same manner; or where two tors are seen as one, an illusion only dispelled when the beholder's position is changed. Sometimes a tor looks as though it stood upon a hill comparatively near, whilst in reality it is placed upon another far distant.

The change in the appearance of these rock masses when viewed from different standpoints is not a little striking. On one side we trace, perhaps, a resemblance to a ruined castle; on another we see the gigantic form of some animal, or a rude likeness to the human figure. Here a lonely watch-tower, that might well have been the work of Titans, appears to rise from some lofty ridge, but when our footsteps have led us to the valley beyond it, we look back only upon shapeless rocks. Aided by certain atmospheric effects the forms these rugged piles wear are sometimes weird in the extreme, and these appearances, it is not improbable, gave birth to some of the superstitious fancies of a former day.

To what may be termed the accompaniments of a tor the Moor is indebted for much of its ruggedness. These are the clatters and scattered masses of rock so often seen on the sides of the hills on the summits of which the tors are placed, and which once formed part of the latter. Time was when the tors must have risen to a great height above the turf, and have presented far more fantastic forms than those they exhibit at the present day. But no streams of boulders would then be seen on the slopes, and what the scenery of the Moor gained in the increased height of its tors, it lost in the bareness of its hillsides. These streams of rocks and stone-dotted commons do very much towards giving the Moor its distinctive character, and we can therefore value the ruins of the tors almost as much as the tors themselves.

The views these rocky summits afford are, with scarcely an exception, extensive, and as most of the tors are situated on the borders of the Moor, the prospects are also varied. But though varied there is no discordant element. The beholder may look into wild solitudes on one hand, and on the other upon an undulating country, where cornfields and woods, and pasture lands and orchards beautifully alternate, but there is nothing startling in the contrast. It is one, and a very marked one, but being Nature's handiwork no violence is done. Nearly the whole of Devonshire can be seen from Dartmoor. In the southern part one looks upon the cliffs beyond Exmouth, and upon the Channel stretching far away down the Cornish coast; from the northern frontier the view is bounded by the Bristol Channel off Bideford Bay and the hills of Exmoor; eastward a part of Somerset is visible, and in the west the granite hills of Cornwall. And being a point of vantage whence so much of the Garden of the West can be viewed, it is itself also a feature in the picture presented from any elevated part of the county. Its outline is bold and distinct, and though not truly mountainous, it yet rises high above the surrounding country.

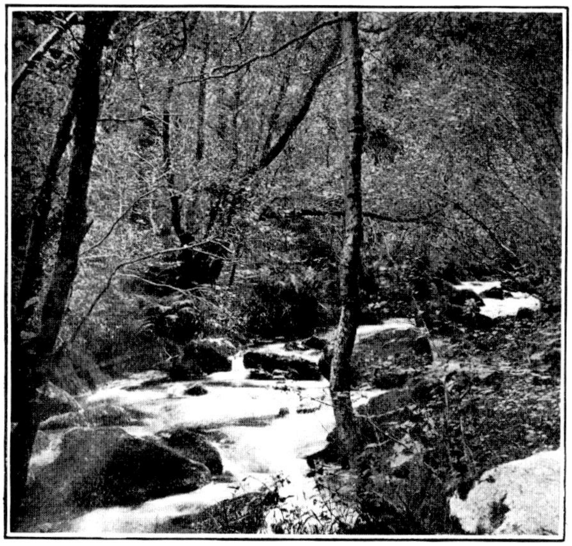

Photo by] [Ernest Croft.

Near Liswell Meet.

"It is the streams that give to it its beauty."

But if the tors impart to Dartmoor much of its grandeur, it is the streams that give to it its beauty. Rising for the most part in its silent places, where the melic grass grows luxuriantly in the peaty soil, and rushes border swamps that hide beneath a treacherous covering of moss, their course is at first slow. Can it be that the dull and sluggish stream oozing from the bog will ever become the thing of life and purity that cheers the valleys with its music? If we follow it we shall see that ere it has gone far on its journey to the insatiable ocean it awakens from its torpor; the sunbeams call forth a responsive smile; its baby voice is heard; it breaks into song. From the hollows of the hills tiny streamlets roll down to lose themselves in its flood. By-and-bye larger brooks, seeking its companionship, come hastening from the combes, and the mingled waters flow in a wider channel. Rocks rise up, but offer no bar to its everlasting progress. It leaps aside, and falls into foam that the morning light faintly gilds and the glowing sunset tinges with a warmer hue. Broom and gorse and heather line its banks, and the mountain ash waves over its rippling surface. Its mission has begun. It has brought life to the valley and rendered fair the scene. The waters of the dreary fen have called forth flowers.

Clearness and swiftness of current, numberless small cascades and deep pools, characterise all the Dartmoor rivers. A reach of placid water, except in a few instances, is a thing unknown. When we have mentioned the Taw immediately above Birchy Lake, the North Teign near the Walla Brook, the West Dart below Two Bridges, the Swincombe above the ford, and the Plym by Trowlesworthy, we shall have exhausted the list of streams on which such is to be seen.

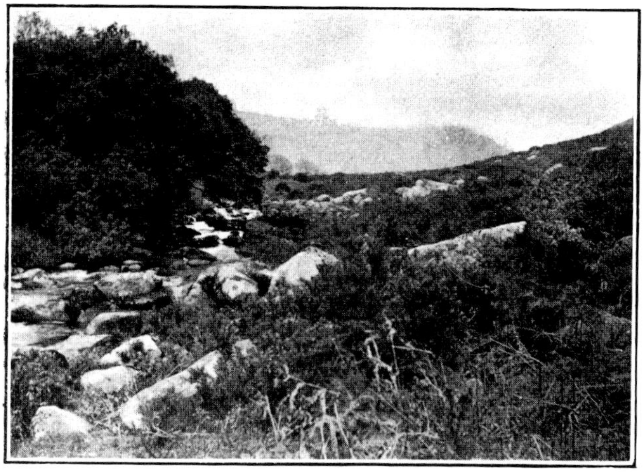

Photo by] [Ernest Croft.

East Dart and Seven Sisters.

"Where the Moor has planted his foot."

It is where the rivers leave the Moor that the finest scenery is found. There the valleys are deep and narrow, their sides being often wooded, though along with this sylvan adornment some of the wildness of the waste is not infrequently observable. In places the valleys still show more of the heather and grey boulders than they do of the oak and the birch, and even where the trees are thickest grand and imposing rock masses rise above them. Where the Moor has planted his foot, and has forbidden the woods to encroach further upon his domain, Nature has woven the wild and the beautiful, and thus has formed the romantic. Having brought the heathery hills and the waving woods together, she has blessed the union, and has dressed the place of their meeting in her choicest garb.

The rambler who makes his way into the Moor through one of these gorges cannot but be impressed by this gradual yielding to its power. As he advances the trees become fewer, and the undergrowth that at first impeded his progress is less dense, until at length bare steeps alone are seen. Then high above the narrow vale grey tors appear, their rugged forms clearly defined against the sky. Here is the clatter, the wilderness of rocks, reaching from the foot of the grim piles almost to the river's brink. Here are the stony places in which the seeds borne upon the wind and scattered find no depth of earth. But for the ripple and the music of the running water there would be no sign of life—no sound to break the silence. When the hills fall back, and something of the barrenness beyond is revealed, the stream becomes more than ever a companion. It is the one thing that cheers the indescribable loneliness of the waste.

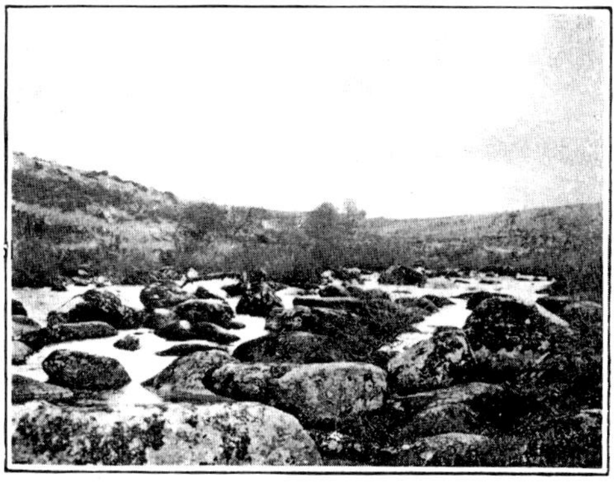

Photo by] [Mrs. Ernest Croft.

The Dart at Huccaby.

"But for the ripple and the music of the running water."

But although the interior of the Moor is the home of Nature in her wilder form, she has even there in places relaxed her sternness. Little nooks that hide themselves so effectually that their existence is unsuspected by the casual rambler may be found in some of the river valleys, and afford protection to bushes and plants that would not thrive in a less hospitable situation. There is one on the Red Brook, a tributary of the Avon; another on the Erme, above Piles Wood; one in the little valley through which the Shavercombe Brook runs down to the Plym; one also on the Upper Mew below Black Tor, and on the Rattle Brook, a stream falling into the Tavy. There are, indeed, few of the Dartmoor rivers that do not boast of at least one such "beauty spot." But while it is true that these tiny gardens are found in solitary places they are not so often seen in the recesses of the Moor, though I do know of some even on the fen. Near the springs of one of the arms of the Tavy, the branch rising to the southward of Cut Hill, and which, indeed, is regarded by the Moormen as being the true stream, is a little dell that might attract attention anywhere, but which in that dreary region becomes positively beautiful. The winds that sweep across the bog pass over it, and ferns have found a home there, and struggle with the heather to peep at the sun. Further down the stream, and while yet its course is through the peat, I have seen foxgloves on its banks. Away on the borders they are met with wherever we go, and so are often passed by unheeded; but here, in the desolate fen, how different it is. These purple flowers growing by the peat-stained waters of the infant stream, delight in a manner such as the rarest hothouse blooms could never do.

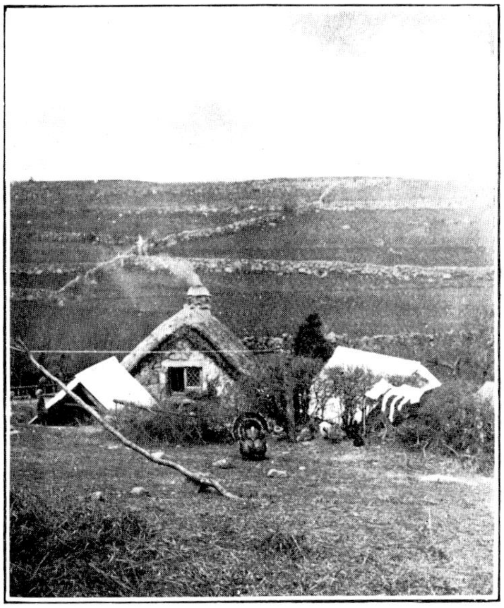

Photo by] [Mrs. Ernest Croft.
"The dwellings of the hill farmers and warreners."

The dwellings of the hill farmers and warreners are a feature in a Dartmoor view, especially when they stand in remote places, as at Teign Head, Huntingdon, Trowlesworthy, Reddaford, and Doe Tor. Many of them still preserve their primitive look, and around all are seen the rough granite walls of enclosures often of ancient date. Olden associations cling to some, particularly such as are found in those parts of the Forest settled in early times, and this, of course, gives them an interest apart from their picturesque appearance. Though, speaking generally, trees seem out of place on Dartmoor, the sycamores so frequently seen sheltering these hill farms are never so. The reason is that the dwellings have been placed in situations where the winter winds cannot smite them, and that is exactly where Nature would have placed the trees.

In certain places even a rough moor track can add an interest to the scene. Not in the remote and wilder parts of the Forest, for there they would tend to destroy its primeval aspect, but in spots nearer the haunts of men and yet unfrequented, they serve to awaken thoughts that their surroundings alone would fail to arouse. A stream comes tumbling down a narrow glen, foaming and fretting where the boulders obstruct its course, a stranger yet to anything but what Nature has made. By-and-bye its murmurs cease, and it spreads itself over a wide, pebbly bed, which it covers only to the depth of a few inches. On either side the bank is worn away, and the prints of hoofs are seen in the soil. It is a fording-place, where the moorman and the hunter cross, and to which the half wild ponies and cattle come to quench their thirst. Perhaps it has been in use for hundreds of years, and those who looked upon it in some far away time saw it exactly as we see it to-day. With thoughts such as these the ravine becomes something more to us than it would did the ford not exist. The picture now possesses a feature that compels us to look upon it.

There is one part of Dartmoor which, though abounding in beauties, is out of harmony with its surroundings. It is that beheld from the summit of Dartmeet Hill, where the plantations and enclosures of Brimpts give to the scene an aspect altogether foreign to the Moor. In the valley the effect is not the same, but seen from the hill one cannot help feeling that trees and fields do not belong to Dartmoor. In the lowlands, or on the borders of the Moor, it is the trees that create the beauties, but in Devon's hill-country extensive groves do not find a proper place. It cannot be denied that there is much to admire in the flourishing trees of Brimpts and Bair Down, and we do not wonder that the natives are proud of the Cowsic Horse-shoe, as the fine belt near Two Bridges is termed, but at the same time one does not go to Dartmoor to see trees. It is rather to look upon a land from which they are absent that the rambler makes his way thither. An ancient oak wood, such as that of Wistman, or the copses below Black Tor and on the Erme, we will love; and delight, too, in finding an ash or a few sycamores here and there, but we desire no more. With these, and withies and thorns, the heather and the ling, furze and broom, ferns and a few wild flowering plants, the adornments of the Moor are complete.

Nowhere, perhaps, are the effects of light and shadow so striking as on Dartmoor. At times a distant hill is seen bathed in sunshine, while others in the foreground lie sombre beneath the clouds. Or we walk in the full glow of the sun below some lofty height which thrusts itself up into gloom, looking frowningly on the golden world below. One side of a valley will smile in the brightness of a summer day; the other is grey and chill. A stream catches the rays shot from an unclouded sky, and the ripples on its surface break them into a thousand pieces; it glides towards a ledge of rocks, and falls into a deep hollow which is ever in shade, and becomes dark and sullen. A tor rises in the noonday beams like a friendly beacon, but while we yet look the cloud shadows give it the semblance of a frowning stronghold.

Beautiful as Dartmoor is beneath a clear sky, and however inviting to the rambler it may then be, it is on a dull day that its wild grandeur becomes most impressive. We all love to look upon the sea of heather with the blue alone above it, but if we would know what the old Forest truly is we must seek it when clouds obscure the sun and its radiant mask is laid aside. Then, when no genial influences abound, its hills appear dark and forbidding and its crags more bold. But it is a picture on which we would not always look. Having seen the desert wear its grimmest aspect, we turn away and wait with pleasurable anticipations the time when it shall put on a smile.

It is when a storm is gathering that Dartmoor is most sublime. To watch, in those spots from which "man is far away," the oncoming of the tempest inspires one with awe. At first there is a deep silence and a gloom settles over the waste. The cattle, heeding the warning, seek the sheltered valleys, and the birds disappear. But Nature is hushed only for a time. From the great cloud sailing across the darkened sky a few raindrops fall and a low rumbling is heard. Then a vivid flash lights up the Moor, followed by a peal of thunder, the rain descends in torrents, and the storm rages among the ancient hills.

When Dartmoor wears the white garb of winter its beauties are not all hidden. It has put on a dress that has altogether changed its appearance, it is true, but it is nevertheless one that well becomes it. Take your stand where you can look upon the tors, rising black on the snow-covered ridges, or go into the valleys where the banks of the streams are decked with icicles, and you will admit that it is not alone in sunny hours that Dartmoor can charm.

The effects produced by the mists that at times envelop the Moor are not a little strange. Well-known places can scarcely be recognised, and a bush or a rock, or other similar object, will often present the most weird form. From elevated points the tors will sometimes be seen rising above a dense white cloud, like islands in a sea. At others mist wreaths float about their crests, now hiding, now revealing the towering rocks, as though an enchanter called them into being, or rendered them invisible at will.

But while the old Moor should be seen at all seasons by those who would know it well, it is in the summer that the rambler seeks it for enjoyment. From early morn till the night shadows fall he may wander among its hills, nor find one hour hang wearily during the long day. What more inspiring time than when the matin of the lark is heard and the dews drip from briar and sedge? Below in the curving valley a silvery veil obscures the stream, but when the sun peeps over the hill it floats upward in light, fleecy clouds, and vanishes. Nature smiles in the unbroken light, and when a few hours have passed a warm glow rests upon the Moor. Noon is at hand, and though the wide expanse offers no shelter from the rays of the sun the wanderer is not oppressed, for a gentle breeze fans his brow. The time speeds away; the hum of insects is no longer heard; the sun begins to decline. Lower and lower it sinks, and in the hollows formed by the folding hills the purple hue of the heather deepens; but the valley yonder, open to the west, is full of crimson light. Darker grow the tints of evening; the sun slowly sinks, and by-and-bye his glory is gone. The light lingers in the sky, and ere objects have become indistinct the moon comes forth to walk through the summer night.

The Iron Crown of Lombardy consists of a broad circlet of gold studded with precious stones cut by cunning artificers, and so dazzling are the rays shot from their facets that the iron rim to which the diadem owes its name is forgotten by the beholder. In the Granite Crown of Devon are also gems of rare beauty, yet as one looks upon them they do not render him oblivious to the roughness of their setting. That is recognised, but it is also seen that harmony prevails. One is a clever work of art, where brilliancy is made to conceal the less precious metal, lest its too prominent intrusion should mar it; the other, the work of Nature, where the whole picture is revealed, and in which there could not be an incongruous feature. In the one, though the skill of man has accomplished much, the ideal is not, and never could be, reached; in the other there is perfection.

The more beautiful of the gems in Devon's rocky crown are those set in its circlet, as it were—those found on the fringe of the granite region. On the arches and the mound, if we may metaphorically regard the swelling hills and the lofty tors as such, they are not only fewer in number but for the most part must be likened to uncut stones—to rough diamonds. Of outward show there is little, but that does not lessen their value. The lonely tarn, with its broken bank on the wind-swept height, may not be a thing of beauty, but if it yields something of interest in the examination of it, it cannot be without its worth. The investigator will become the lapidary that shall bring its latent qualities to light.

And now, like some fair lady searching for the prettiest among her jewels, admiring now an emerald, now a ruby or a pearl, let us look upon the crown placed on the brow of the land of fruit and flowers and find for ourselves the gems that bedeck it.

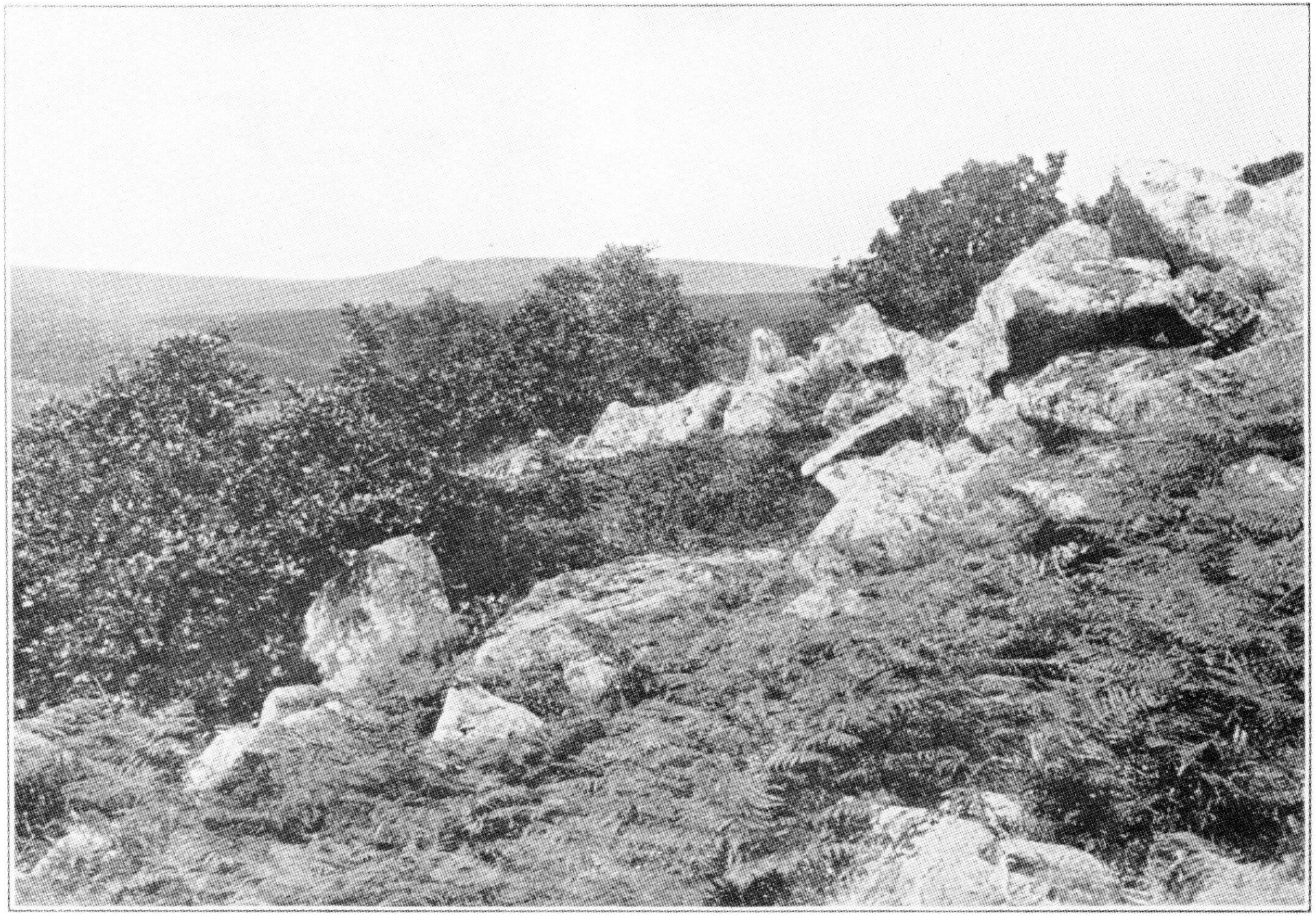

SEE PAGE 21.

Wistman's Wood.

PHOTO BY C. R. ROWE.

"Groves of dwarf oaks, growing from the midst of a clatter."

GGS-B

I.

WISTMAN'S WOOD.

TREES FELLED BY THE TINNERS——WISTMAN'S WOOD ONE OF DARTMOOR'S "THREE REMARKABLE THINGS"——CARRINGTON'S DESCRIPTION OF THE WOOD——A STONY SHELTER——PROBABLE AGE OF THE TREES——THE WOOD ON FIRE——DERIVATION OF ITS NAME——THE WEALAS.

Of this grove—
This pigmy grove, not one has climb'd the air
So emulously that its loftiest branch
May brush the traveller's brow. The twisted roots
Have clasp'd, in search of nourishment, the rocks,
And straggled wide, and pierced the stony soil :—
In vain, denied maternal succour, here
A dwarfish race has risen.

—CARRINGTON.

THOUGH it is certain that trees never formed part of the covering of Dartmoor to any considerable extent, it is equally so that they formerly grew in some numbers in a few of the more sheltered spots of the great uplands. It is not, indeed, probable that many giants of the woods flourished there, but that the sides of some of the river valleys were in places clothed with thickets of birch and dwarf oaks, and that alder grew near the banks of the streams, there is not wanting evidence to show. Trunks of trees have often been found below the surface by peat cutters and others, or have been exposed by the falling away of portions of the bog. An instance of the latter came under our notice a few years since, when some large pieces of oak were found partly uncovered in the vicinity of Cranmere Pool. In the early spring of 1901 we saw two very fine pieces at Cholwich Town, that had been dug up not long before at a spot known as Whithill Yeo,* where the Torry takes its rise. The oak was very dark in colour and extremely hard, and when shaved with a sharp knife showed a beautiful polish. We also remember a number of trees being found under the surface on the slope below Saddlesborough, in the parish of Shaugh, in 1885, the trunk of one of which measured nearly four feet in circumference. A moorland dweller named John Bishop, who for many years was a familiar figure in the Dart valleys, once told us that he had frequently dug up roots and trunks of alder near his cottage at Swincombe, and that the wood was very hard.

It would be easy to multiply instances were such necessary, and to show that in a former day the valleys of the Moor were in many cases different in appearance from what they are at present, though certainly not to such an extent as to materially alter the aspect of the Moor. But there is no need that we should go below the surface for this proof. In many a spot which the hillside shelters from the wind specimens of the mountain ash are seen, or one or two thorns, or perhaps an oak, the sole relics of some

* This name is pronounced with the first "i" long; it is a corruption of White Hill Yeo.

ancient grove ; and that these are not more numerous is not entirely due to decay. The tinner has probably robbed Dartmoor of many of its sylvan honours. He was allowed to supply his blowing-houses with "carbonem," that is, peat-coal, a writ of Henry III. directing the Bailiffs of Lydford to permit them to do this being still extant* ; and in a Charter of Edward I. the right is confirmed to the tinners to procure brushwood for smelting the tin, according to ancient custom. But it is probable that they did not stop at peat or brushwood, but in spite of the Forest law that no green oak was to be touched, laid their axes to the root of many a good tree. Gradually the scanty covering of the valleys would disappear, and thus to-day, with the exception of the oaks at Brimpts, the only ancient groves on the Moor are those of Black Tor Copse in the north, Wistman's Wood in the centre, and Piles Wood in the south, all three of which, curiously enough, lie nearly in a straight line. Of these Wistman's Wood alone is within the Forest, the other two being in its purlieus.

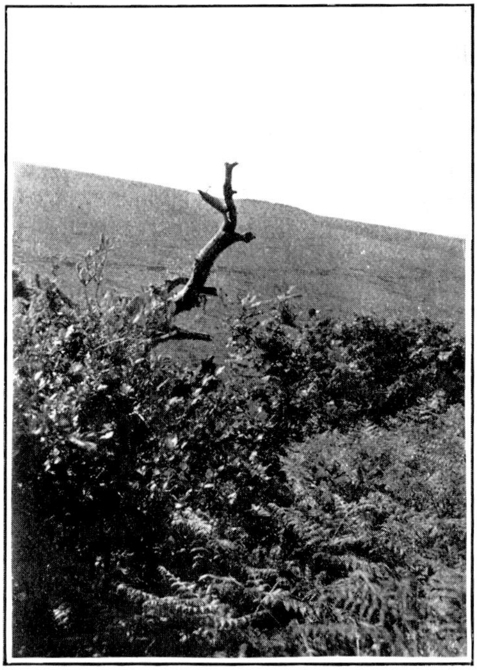

Photo by] [C. R. Rowe.

The edge of the wood.

"The scanty covering of the valleys."

Three hundred years ago Wistman's Wood was, as at the present day, deemed worthy of note. We have this on the authority of Tristram Risdon, of Winscot, in the North of Devon, who between the years 1605 and 1630 travelled through every part of the county, collecting materials for a complete description of it, "for the love of his country and countrymen," and which interesting account he left behind him in manuscript. In his mention of Dartmoor, which is only a brief one, he speaks of the Forest as containing three remarkable things, one being Crockern Tor, another the Tomb of Childe the Hunter, and the third "some acres of wood and trees, that are a fathom about, and yet no taller than a man may touch to top with his hand, which is called Wistman's Wood." This appears to be the earliest mention of the wood, the statement in Mrs. Bray's *Tamar and Tavy* that it was described in a perambulation of the Moor made soon after the Norman Conquest, and preserved in the Duchy of Cornwall Office, being incorrect. There is no reference to the wood in any survey or perambulation of the Forest, nor is there any record of one being made prior to 1240.†

About two centuries after Risdon described Wistman's Wood it was noticed by Carrington, who tells us that so dwarfed were its trees that the topmost branch of none of them raised itself sufficiently high to "brush the traveller's brow." But Carrington was a poet, and we cannot expect a wooer of the muse to trouble himself about such a

* Rex baillivis de Ledefard salutem. Precipimus vobis quod permittatis stagnarios nestros Devonie capere et habere carbonem in mora nostra de Dertemore ad stagnariam nostram sicut habere consueverint tempore domini Johannis patris nostri et nostro, nec eis inde faciatis vel fieri permittatis molestiam vel impedimentum. Teste apud Turrim London. 18 die Julii. (1222. 6th Henry III.)

† Mrs. Bray made this statement on the authority of Archdeacon Froude, but it is apparently a mistake, no evidence in support of it being forthcoming.

prosaic matter as the precise measurements of an object, or such-like trifling details. If any traveller ever passed through the wood—which we should be disposed to doubt—whose head was higher than the trees, it must have been in the days when there were giants in the land. A popular description of the wood is that it consists of five hundred trees five hundred feet high, meaning that each one is only a foot in height, a statement which, if it cannot claim a poetical licence like the former, is at least entitled to that latitude usually accorded to humour.

Wistman's Wood is situated on the left bank of the West Dart, one mile and a half above Two Bridges. It consists of three separate groves of dwarf oaks, growing from the midst of a clatter, and extending for rather less than half a mile along the eastern side of a narrow valley, formed by the hill known as Bair Down on the west, and the ridge on which is placed the conical Longaford Tor on the east, and being closed in at the upper end. Trees and rocks are mixed in inextricable confusion, and over the latter the explorer will find it necessary to climb. To penetrate far into the wood means a continuous scramble, with every chance of slipping now and again into some deep hole between the boulders, which the thick covering of moss frequently hides from view. But it is only by forcing one's way into the midst of the wood that a true idea of it can be obtained. And it is worth the trouble, for certainly no other such wood as this exists.

The trunks of these ancient oaks are clothed with moss like the boulders, which perhaps makes them appear to be, as Risdon says, "a fathom about," though in reality they are not nearly so much in circumference. The trees thrust themselves from between the rocks composing the clatter, but only to spread their boughs over their hoary faces, and in many cases they rest upon the stones. One may very comfortably sit on the bough of an aged oak with his feet touching the ground, as it were, an achievement certainly not possible in most woods.

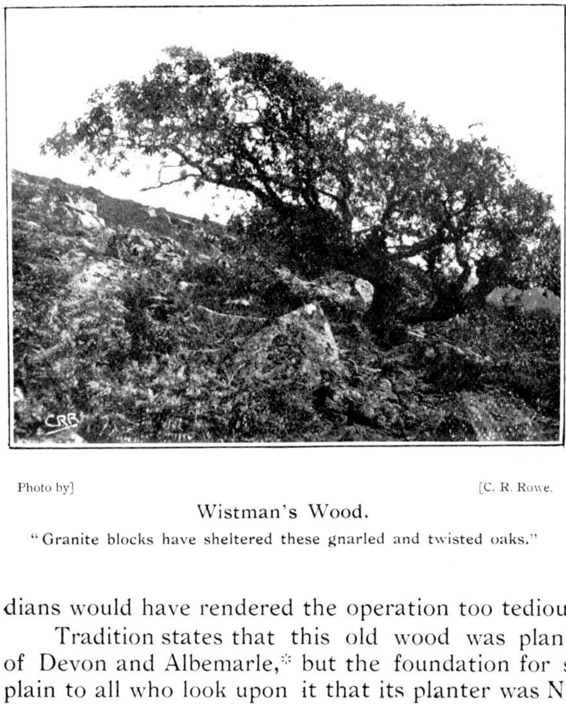

Photo by] [C. R. Rowe.

Wistman's Wood.

"Granite blocks have sheltered these gnarled and twisted oaks."

The clatter, which at first appears so ill-suited for the growth of trees, has in reality been the defender of the wood. The granite blocks have sheltered these gnarled and twisted oaks from the rude blasts that sweep across the Moor, and shall continue to shield them. The cattle which roam at will over the slopes of the old Forest cannot approach the oaks of Wistman to browse upon their tender leaves, for the rocky barrier bids them defiance. Even the tinner was deterred from felling them, for their granite guardians would have rendered the operation too tedious.

Tradition states that this old wood was planted by Isabella de Fortibus, Countess of Devon and Albemarle,* but the foundation for such a story is indeed shadowy. It is plain to all who look upon it that its planter was Nature, and she has shown us here that

* There is no reason for supposing that the Forest, within which, as stated above, the wood is situated, was ever in the hands of Isabella de Fortibus. Her mother, the Countess Amicia, was the holder of Walkhampton Common, which land formed part of her gift to Buckland Abbey when it was founded by her, and which grant was confirmed in 1291 by the Lady Isabella, but she never held any part of the Forest.

even in the most unpropitious circumstances she can cause the plant to spring up and grow into a tree, and put forth leaf and acorn in due season.

On a large stone in the clatter is an inscription setting forth how one of the Wistman oaks was sacrificed to curiosity, for certainly its destruction served no useful purpose. It enabled the number of its concentric layers to be counted, and its age, or approximate age, to be ascertained; but it does not appear that any other object was gained. The inscription runs thus: "By permission of H.R.H. the Prince of Wales, Wentworth Buller, on September 16th, 1866, cut down a tree near this spot; it measured nine inches in diameter, and appeared to be about one hundred and sixty-eight years old." A portion of the trunk of this tree seems to have been sent to the Albert Memorial Museum at Exeter, a section of wood there being labelled as follows: "Section of the trunk of a Dwarf Oak (Quercus robur, var. pedunculata) from the ancient grove at Wistman's Wood, Dartmoor. Deposited by order of H.R.H. the Prince of Wales." Mr. F. R. Rowley, the curator, informed me that, according to the record books of the museum, both vertical and transverse sections of the trunk were sent, and appears to have come from Mr. Wentworth W. Buller, in January, 1871.

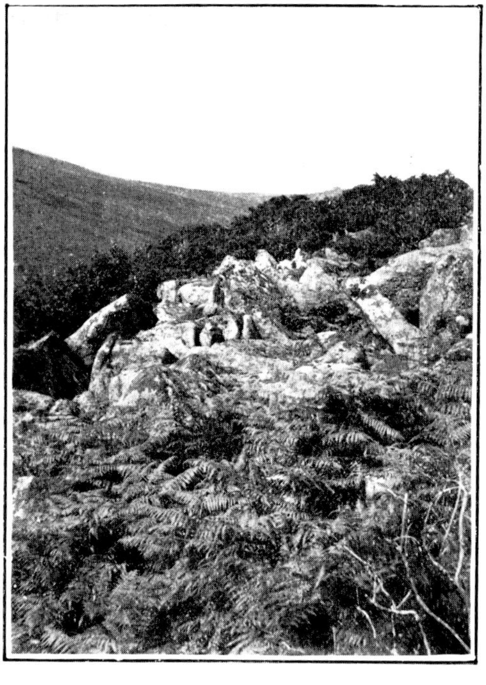

Photo by] [C. R. Rowe.

Wistman's Wood from the Valley.

"Stunted oaks in the rocky valley."—*(See Page 23.)*

According to a writer in the *Gardener's Chronicle*, some of the oaks of Wistman's Wood are of an age far greater than that which the specimen cut down by Mr. Buller was supposed to have attained. He considered it possible that there were trees growing in the wood that were in their prime in the days of William the Norman. One of these tough and twisted dwarfs that he observed was not less than fifteen feet high, but it probably did not rise to more than two-thirds of that height above the clatter. At all events, the average height of the trees is not more than about ten feet. Many of the trunks are entirely hidden, while the boughs often spread nearly a dozen feet in every direction.

In the summer of 1886 the centre grove of Wistman's Wood was set on fire, but whether by accident or design was never ascertained. Fortunately the damage done was not so great but that the old wood in a few years regained its former appearance.

It has been suggested that the name of this relic of a time when the valleys of the Moor were less bare than at present is a corruption of *usig maen coed*, literally *water stone wood*, meaning the stony wood by the water. Such a derivation is not an unlikely one, though there is another that offers itself as being equally probable. The Britons of the West, who had settlements on Dartmoor, were known to the Saxon invaders as Wealas, meaning foreigners, or such as were not of their race, a word synonymous with *Welsh*.*

* The word is thus of Teutonic origin, and may probably be traced to the German verb "Walschen," to "jabber," and hence was applied to those who spoke an unknown tongue. It has been pointed out by Mr. Thomas Stephens in his book, *Welshmen*, that "wherever the Teutons settled they called the surrounding peoples Welsh." The name is found in various forms in different parts of Europe.

In the will of King Alfred the people of the Westcountry are called *Weal-cynne*, that is *Welsh kind*. It is significant that the older among the Moor people often call the ancient grove Welshman's Wood, and that this name was in use a hundred years ago is on record. It is by no means improbable that *Wistman* is simply a corruption of *Welshman*, the change taking place prior to Risdon's time (that is if the rendering in his MS. really is Wistman), but not being adopted by all. The idea that the name is derived from the Druids, or *wise men*, is merely a fanciful one, for which there is not the slightest foundation.

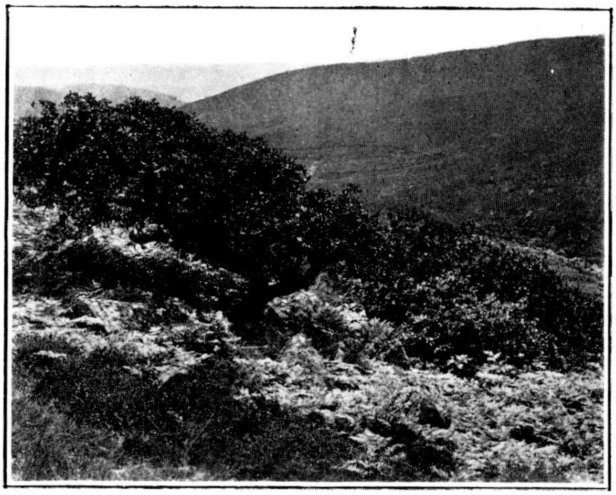

Photo by] [C. R. Rowe.

Wistman's Wood.

"The trees thrust themselves from between the rocks."—*(See Page 21.)*

Perhaps at no time are the dwarf oaks of Wistman more impressive than when seen towards the close of a dull autumn day; when the long arms peep through their scanty covering brown and sere, clasping the dark-coated rocks, and the topmost branches are bare; when the wind sweeping down the valley moans as it passes over them, as though lamenting that their beauty has gone; when the air is chill and the Moor is drear, and the coming shadows render indistinct the tor upon the hill. At such a time the old Forest can show no picture more weird than the stunted oaks in the rocky valley of the Dart—the solitary grove which men call the Wood of Wistman.

But it is in the long summer days, when the far-off fields of the lowlands are golden with ripening grain, and the trees in the orchards are laden with fruit, that the visitor bends his steps to Wistman's Wood. He sees it in its garb of green, when the leaves conceal the gnarled boughs and quiver in the gentle breeze, when their sheen brightens all the valley, when it is a thing of beauty—an emerald adorning Devonia's crown.

II.

FUR TOR.

A LONELY HILL——A WILDERNESS OF PEAT BOG——OLD PATHS TO LYDFORD AND OKEHAMPTON——AN ELEVATED LAND——ROCK MASSES——EVIDENCES OF DECAY——AN OLD-TIME PASTURAGE GROUND——CUT COMBE——AN IMPORTANT PASS——SUGGESTED DERIVATION OF THE NAME——AN OASIS IN THE DESERT.

And here enthroned in silence,
The tors majestic stand,
Like sentinels gigantic
Above that dreary land.
—F. B. DOVETON.

OF all the tors of Dartmoor none is more impressive than the fine pile of Fur Tor, which, standing in lonely grandeur in a secluded part of the Forest, possesses a charm such as belongs to no other. Seen from a point not far below Little Kneeset, on the bank of an arm of the Tavy, usually spoken of by the Moor people as the Amicombe, the appearance of the great hill covered with masses of granite from base to summit, and crowned with huge rocks, is wonderfully striking. It is neighboured by no others of a similar character, but by lofty ridges whose surfaces of peat are clothed with the cotton and melic grass, or wear a scanty garb of heather. On the confines of the Moor, where the tors mostly abound, this granite-strewn height would take its place among those worthy of special notice, but here, far away in the wilds and remote from all others, it becomes an object of particular interest.

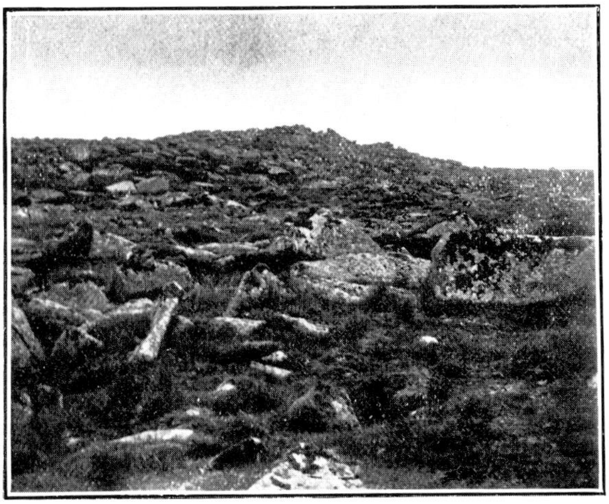

Photo by] [C. R. Rowe.

Fur Tor.

"The great hill covered with masses of granite."

The situation of Fur Tor in a part of the Forest not easily accessible except from a few points, unless it be to those who know the district well, has caused it to be comparatively little visited. While most Dartmoor ramblers have scaled the bosses of Hey Tor, or climbed to the summit of Yes Tor and Great Mis Tor, or such better-known heights, the lonely hill that rears its rugged crest in the wilderness of peat bog they have been content to view from a distance. But,

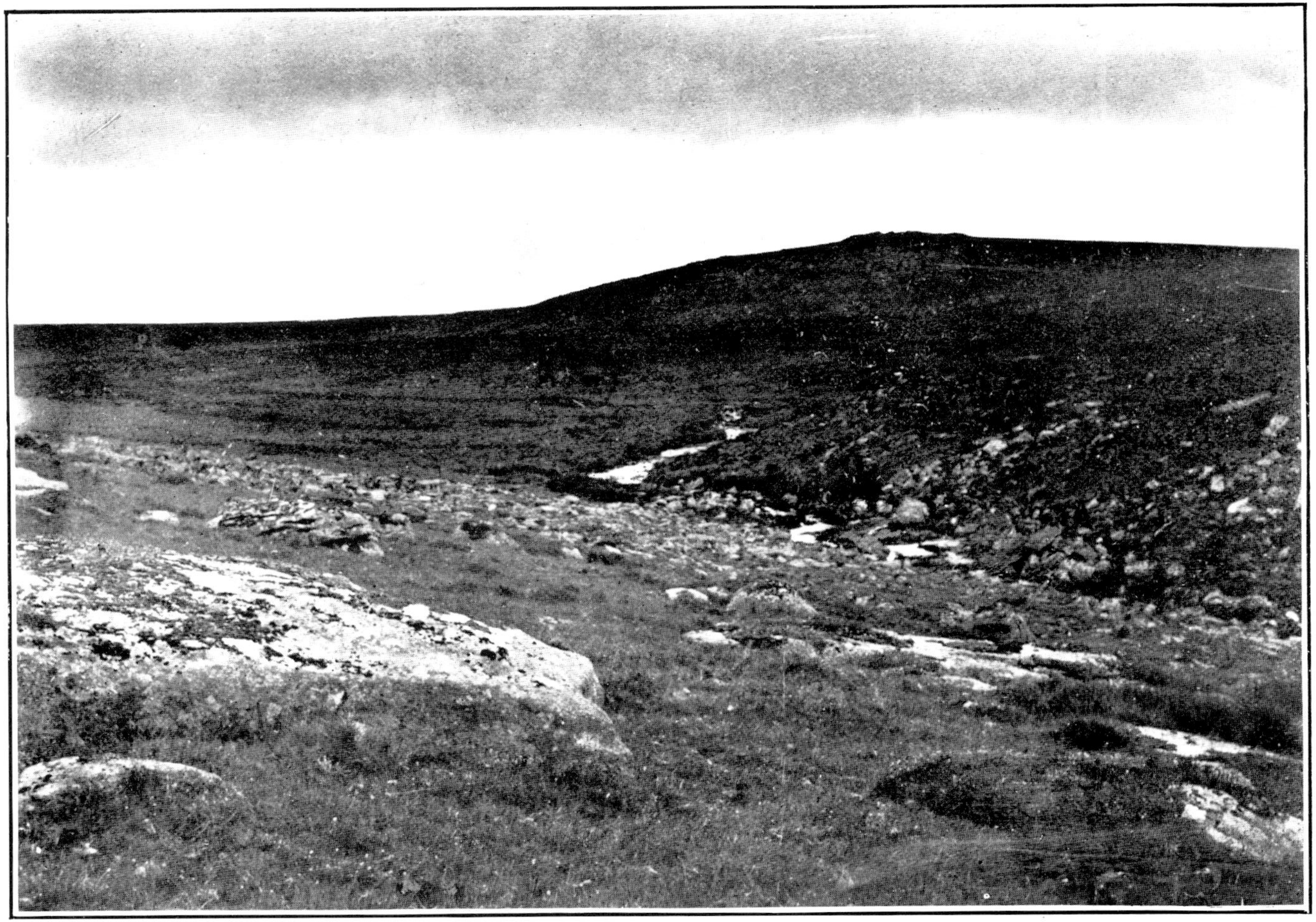

SEE PAGE 24.

Fur Tor from Watern Oke.

PHOTO BY C. R. ROWE.

"The lonely hill that rears its rugged crest in the wilderness."

notwithstanding its isolation now, there was a time when the grey rocks of Fur Tor looked down upon others than Moormen visiting their pasturage grounds. Around the base of the hill there sweeps an ancient track, over which passed the men of Chagford and North Bovey, and others living on the eastern side of the Moor, when on their way to Lydford, where, as that was the place at which for centuries the Chase Courts of Dartmoor were held, business must occasionally have taken them; and it also served as a means of communication between Okehampton and certain parts of the Forest. That it was used at an early period by the settlers in the East Dart and Wallabrook valleys, existing documentary evidence indirectly proves; but it was probably a cattle track long prior to their time.

Fur Tor occupies a commanding situation at the extremity of a bold headland, projecting in a north-westerly direction from the long, boggy range extending from the head of the Cowsic and the West Dart to Okement Hill, a distance of several miles. On this range is Cut Hill, which rises to a height of 1,981 feet, and is visible from nearly every eminence on the Moor. From its flank springs the headland, Fur Tor being about a mile north-west by west of the summit of the hill, which is marked by a small artificial mound of peat. On the east side of this headland is Cut Combe, down which flows a feeder of the Tavy, bending westward to join the stream referred to as being often called the Amicombe. The united waters run by the edge of a plain extending from the foot of the tor-crowned hill, part of it being good pasturage ground, and part of it broken and boggy. South-westward of the headland, where the ground slopes from the tor much less steeply than on the east and north, is the stream usually regarded as the Tavy proper, and which meets the Amicombe at the western end of the plain. It has its source in a well-defined depression, the sides of which are thickly covered with heather, in the midst of the great bog on the southern slope of Cut Hill, and about half a mile from its summit.

Fur Tor consists of a number of piles of rock, which are divided into two groups, about one hundred yards apart. The eastern group is the chief, and consists of four distinct piles, one of them, however, being much smaller than the others. The easternmost of these piles, though not of great height, at once arrests the attention from the peculiarity of its stratification. The granite is seen in thin horizontal layers, giving the whole mass quite a different appearance from that presented by the other piles. The ground slopes very steeply to the north-east, the whole of the hillside being covered with masses of rock, not so much in the manner of a clatter, which is a multitude of boulders lying closely together, as resembling a number of small tors, many of very fantastic shape, with lumps of granite strewn between them. These masses cover a vast area, extending round to the north and north-west slopes of the hill.

Less than fifty yards distant from the eastern pile is another congeries of rocks, which, however, presents nothing remarkable; but a little further away the largest and highest of the piles composing Fur Tor rises from the turf. This consists of a number of huge rocks placed one upon the other, its greatest height being at the north-western end, where the elevation attained is probably over forty feet. On the surface of the highest rock the wind and rain and frost have left their mark. Three hollows may there be seen which it has taken ages to form, and the work, though we cannot perceive it, is still progressing. It has gone on deepening and enlarging the basins, and will continue to do so until the rock shall be worn through; the power that created shall destroy. In one, near the edge of the granite mass, the water has already pierced for itself a way through the stone, and the worn perforation is visible from the ground.*

This great pile stands on a level plateau, and its ruin is proceeding more slowly than that of the smaller ones placed on the brow of the hill. But it is advancing nevertheless; silently and imperceptibly, it is true, but none the less surely. No one can look closely upon a Dartmoor tor without being struck by the work of destruction that is in

* These basins were first noticed by the Rev. E. A. Bray, on visiting the tor in the year 1802. In *A Few Remarks on Dartmoor*, the Rev. E. Spencer has sketched in a very interesting manner the process by which the tors are slowly going to ruin.

the whole of the ground between an old way called the Lich Path, near the head of the Cowsic, and Okement Hill, being of such a character as to be impassable by beasts. But as though Nature designed to provide a means of crossing over this boggy range she has narrowed it very considerably near its centre, and the ground is there hard almost to the top. Here on one side is Cut Combe, and on the other the valley of the East Dart. On the summit of the ridge there was only a narrow piece of bog to be crossed, and here the peat has been removed, and a hard surface, over which the grass has grown for centuries, has been formed. Two large slabs of granite set upon mounds, one on each side of the way, mark the path at this point. From this cutting through the peat bog the hill, on the shoulder of which it is formed, and the combe below it, have derived their names.

On the side of Cut Combe the track is marked by stones raised on low cairns, and by means of these the traveller is conducted from the opening, or pass, between the foot of Fur Tor and Little Kneeset, to the cut on the hill. This pass, which leads from the Amicombe, or Upper Tavy valley, to the combe, was a very important one, and Fur Tor served to mark its situation. Now the meaning of the Celtic word referred to is a *pass*, or *opening*, and it is similar in sound to the name borne by the tor. This word is *Ffor*, and it appears to me to be not unlikely that the tor obtained its name through its contiguity with the pass, which must have been in use in very early times. In the minds of the Moor people the two are always connected, for although the track is often spoken of as Cut Lane, it is more generally called Fur Tor Cut, particularly by those living on the northern and north-western edge of the Moor. Mr. Spence Bate was of opinion that *fur* was a corruption of the Celtic word *fawr*, meaning *great;* thus *twr fawr* (the noun coming before the adjective) would be the *great tor*. But *fawr* would be pronounced more like *vour* than like *fur*, *f* having the sound of *v* in Celtic, *a* having a broad sound, and *w* being equivalent to *oo*. It is also well to point out that one of the early forms of the name of the tor is Forter, the first part of which has precisely the same sound as *Ffor*, *ff* being equivalent to our letter *f*.

The rambler who essays to make his way from the foot of Amicombe Hill to the Dart valley will see as he approaches the pass, to which the tor will direct him, the two stones marking the cut across the lofty hill above the combe. He will see, too, the lonely tor from the point that we have indicated as being the one from which its appearance is particularly striking. Its summit is lost to view as he nears it, but the huge hill, covered with the ruins of the piles on its crest, grows more impressive. It stands out boldly from the boggy heights that stretch away on either side of it, and in wonderful contrast to their desolate look. They are dark and always wear a frown; the hill of Fur Tor is covered with grass, and smiles in the sunshine. It is an oasis in the desert, where grey rocks take the place of trees; a bright jewel in a sombre mantle.

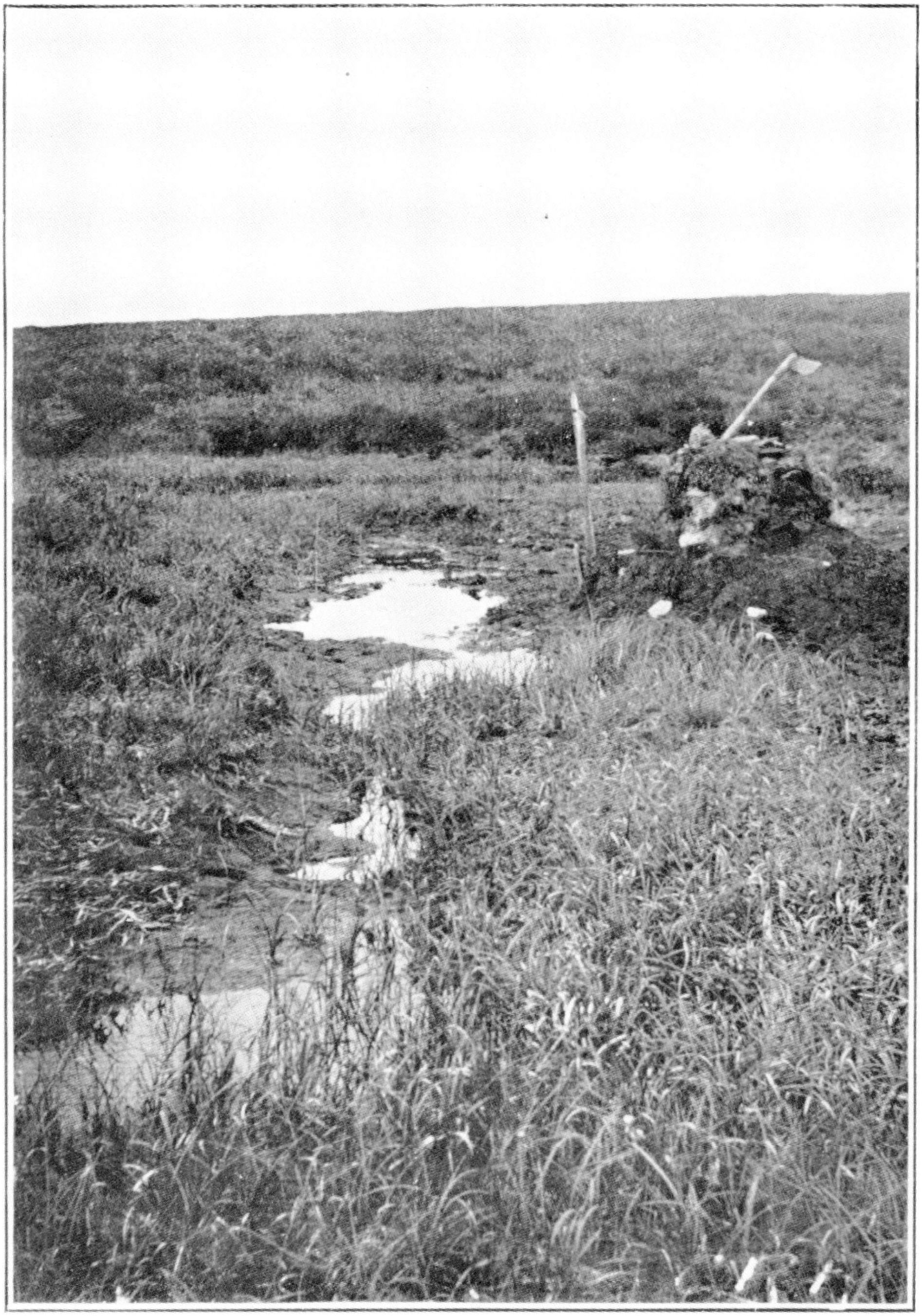

SEE PAGE 35.

Cranmere Pool.

PHOTO BY C. R. ROWE.

"Cranmere Pool is irregular in shape."

III.

CRANMERE.

THE DARTMOOR EXPLORER——CRANMERE AN OBJECTIVE——ITS SITUATION——A FOUNTAIN OF RIVERS——EARLY MENTION OF CRANMERE——THE LAKE OF CRANES——A NOVEL POST-OFFICE——HOW THE BANK WAS BROKEN——DARTMOOR LEGENDS.

Where once was a tarn on the lonely Moor,
  The springs of Ockment near,
A darksome hollow now is seen
  On the hill-top bleak and drear,
And the gossips still the story tell
  How Binjie drained Cranmere.
—THE LEGEND OF BINJIE GEAR.

AS the Alpine climber's ambition is to make the ascent of Mont Blanc, so the great aim of the Dartmoor explorer is to visit Cranmere. And when he has accomplished his object he finds it to be nothing more than a hollow in the peat bog, and wonders, perhaps, how it is he has always heard it referred to as a pool. But notwithstanding this, he does not return from it disappointed, unless, indeed, he had expected to find nothing less than a lake. And the reason of this is that, however unattractive Cranmere may be in itself, the ramble thither has taken him through some of the most solitary parts of Dartmoor, and has enabled him to look upon primeval Nature—to see her in her rudest garb. It is not the pool he thinks of when he has penetrated into the recesses of the Moor and stands beside its broken bank, but of the wilderness in which it is placed. With that he cannot fail to be impressed. Cranmere must be regarded as an objective to be gained not so much for what itself has to show as for what the journey to it will reveal. It is in this that the explorer really meets his reward.

Time was when this black, peaty hollow was filled with water, upon the surface of which, when ruffled by the mountain breeze, the reflected rays of the sun sparkled like myriads of diamonds, and brightened the face of the grim old desert. Then was Cranmere worthy to be counted as one of the gems of the Moor; and because it has lost its lustre, because it has been robbed of its beauty, shall it be refused a place among them now?

A good deal has been written about the difficulty of finding Cranmere, and "travellers' tales" have been told of the ignorance of the Moormen concerning it. But there is nothing surprising in the fact that strangers should fail to discover it, particularly when it is remembered that it cannot be seen until one is within a few yards of its brink. There are numbers of objects on Dartmoor that could not be found any more readily by those unacquainted with the locality. But it has been the fashion to attach something of the mysterious to Cranmere, and to speak of it as concealing itself from the explorer. The latest Ordnance Survey Map has, of course, done much to remove the difficulty of the search, but it is always best for the stranger to take a guide with him. And this not only that he may be conducted to the spot he desires to reach, but, what is also of importance, that he may learn something of the objects of interest passed on the way. Besides, it is one thing to steer by the map, and thereby possibly flounder into a mire, and quite another to gain your objective in a comfortable manner. On Dartmoor, notwithstanding its openness, it is often true that "the longest way round is the shortest way home."

With regard to the Moormen's knowledge of Cranmere, it is only those connected with the north quarter of the Forest who would be likely to be acquainted with it. Speaking generally, it is in the pasturage alone that the Moorman feels much interest, and such a place as Cranmere, which, situated in the midst of the fen—or *vain* as he terms it—is not approached by cattle, would not claim much notice from him. I remember taking a Moorman to the so-called pool many years ago, who, although he had long pastured cattle in the east quarter of the Forest, and had frequently been within half a mile of it, was ignorant of its exact situation. And I am acquainted with men at the present time, natives of the Moor, who have spent all their days on it, and yet have never set foot on that part of it lying around Cranmere. Still, there are those whose duties take them there, for sheep range over the fen, and are sometimes seen at the pool. I once knew a farmer who for years was a Moorman of the north quarter, and who was at one time in the habit of visiting the pool, or passing close to it, every day. It was not possible to ride over the fen, so his pony was left at some distance off, tethered to a ring-bolt fixed into a rock for that purpose.

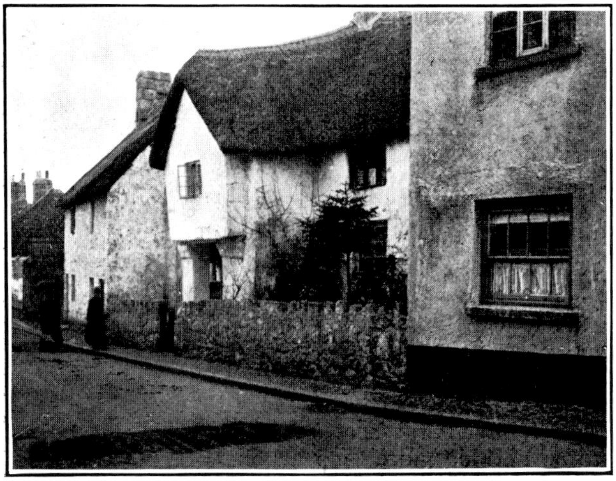

Photo by] [Mrs Ernest Croft.

Chagford.

"About six miles to the east."

Cranmere Pool, to give it the name by which it is usually called, is situated on the northern edge of a boggy plateau, about six miles from Chagford, Okehampton, and the village of Lydford, which places lie approximately to the east, north, and west respectively; Two Bridges is about seven miles south. The tourist who essays to reach it from either of these points must, of course, expect to find the distances rather greater, unless he can contrive to follow the example of the proverbial crow. Around the plateau the most important of the Dartmoor streams take their rise. On one side of it, and less than half a mile east by north of the pool, is the fountain-head of the Taw; on another side, somewhat further removed, and in a south-easterly direction, are the springs of the East Dart; westward of the plateau are two feeders of the Tavy, one rising not quite half a mile southward of the pool; and on the north side of this elevated stretch of fen is the head of the West Ockment. So near to Cranmere is the latter that the stream has been said to flow from it. But this is not so; the springs of the Ockment are in a little hollow many feet below it, though in the days when the pool really was such it poured its overflow into that river, and this probably gave rise to a belief that in it it had its source.

There is no spring in the bed of the mere; the water that at one time filled it was the drainage from the great bog.

But the belief has at all events the respectability of antiquity. As early as the fifteenth century it existed, for William of Worcester, in his Itinerary, speaks of the river flowing below Okehampton Castle, which river, he says, had its source at "Cremere in Thertmore." This is the earliest mention of the lonely tarn, and the form of the name would almost seem to suggest that its present appellation is a corruption of an older one, and that it is not derived, as generally supposed, from the crane. But what is more probable is that the pool did bear the name of Cranmere or Cranemere in the fifteenth century, but that it was pronounced as the ancient chronicler has spelt it, as it sometimes is by the Dartmoor man at the present day.

It has been thought that the name is traceable not to the birds which are supposed to have resorted to the pool, but to the Celtic word *aun*, meaning *water*. But however this may be, the popular idea is that Cranmere means the mere, or lake, of cranes, in which connection it is worthy of note that in the south quarter of the Forest there is also a large tract of fen, where, near an eminence known as Crane Hill, is a hollow that it is plain to see was once a pool. It goes by the name of Ducks' Pool, and was in all probability emptied of its water by the tinners, there being some very extensive workings quite close to it.

Dartmoor men usually refer to the heron as a crane, and in the opinion of ornithologists the true crane once frequented the Moor. But for sixty years previous to 1830, according to Dr. Moore, only four specimens had been procured in Devon. The most recent of these, he says, was a fine male, shot in the parish of Buckland Monachorum, in September, 1826.

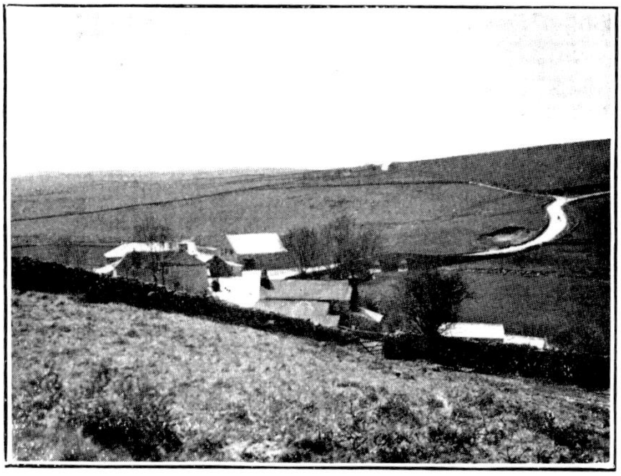

Photo by] [Mrs. Ernest Croft.

Two Bridges.

"Is about seven miles south."—*(See Page 34.)*

Cranmere Pool is irregular in shape, and its size cannot accurately be given, owing to the encroachments of the heather on the west side, where the ground slopes down to the black, peaty bed. But from measurements which I took in 1881, placing the tape on what I considered was the true margin of the pool, I found it to be one hundred and ninety-two yards in circumference. Its deepest part was at the eastern end, where the bank is about ten feet high. Where the heather has not covered the bottom of the hollow, there the peat is seen, wet and spongy in the winter, dry and dusty in the summer. Near the centre is a tiny cairn, erected by the late Mr. James Perrott, of Chagford. Mr. Perrott made no note of the date, only remembering that the work was done during the time of the Crimean War, and that this was so is proved by a communication to the press, made some years ago by Mr. W. L. Munday, of Horrabridge, in which he states that the cairn was formed in 1854. A tin, or other small receptacle, was placed in the cairn by Mr. Perrott for the reception of the cards of visitors to the pool, and a small book was also provided in which they might enter their names. Later on, when postcards were introduced, a custom sprang into existence among visitors to Cranmere of leaving addressed cards there, with the request that the next comer would post them at the nearest office they might happen to reach. As the regularity of the postal system depends very largely on the season and the climatic conditions, it may perhaps be only right to state that occasionally letters are not dealt with quite so expeditiously as is generally considered desirable, but the novelty of receiving a letter posted in the middle of a Dartmoor bog, probably amply compensates for any trifling delay in delivery the recipient may experience.

Quite recently it occurred to two Dartmoor ramblers that the jar with the leaden cover, which for some time had done duty as a receptacle for cards, and as a post-box at the pool, might well be replaced by something better, particularly if the entries made by visitors were to be preserved. The sanction of the Duchy was obtained, and a zinc box and a specially prepared book having been provided they were deposited at the pool. The box is fitted with a deep cover, and is thus well protected from the rain should it penetrate into the little hollow in the cairn. It bears the inscription :—" Authorised by the Duchy. Cranmere Pool. Box containing visitors' book. —H. P. Hearder, Plymouth, 1905." The book is furnished with a waterproof cover, and has the words " Dartmoor," " Cranmere," and the date, " 1905," burnt into its edges. On the first page it is set forth that it is placed at the pool with the sanction of the Duchy, by two lovers of the Moor. A hope is expressed that visitors will record their names and impressions. This is signed by Mr. H. P. Hearder and Mr. H. Scott-Tucker, the donors. It is pleasant to think that in these prosaic days there are those who take such an interest in the curiosities of Dartmoor. It is frequently a race to get to the pool, and the odds are that many who try never do get there. Those who succeed and reach the winning-post, as it were, will not improbably grumble at the roughness of the course. But one thing is certain : though they may never become attached to such Dartmoor racing, they will, if they leave their signatures at Cranmere, help to make a book.

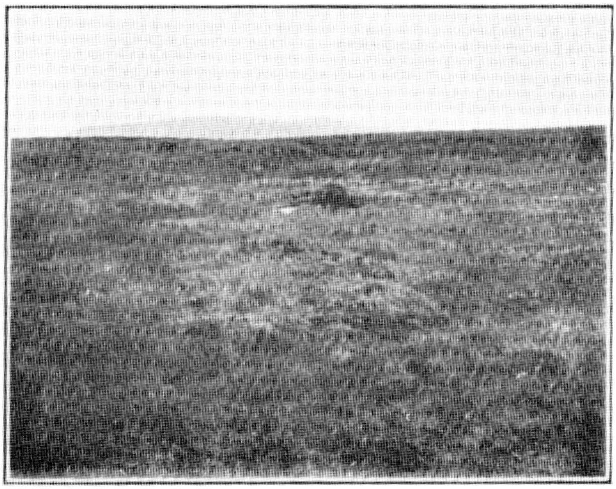

Photo by] Cranmere Pool. [C. R. Rowe.

"The silent waste."—*(See Page 37.)*

The " Urn of Cranmere," as Carrington calls it, is broken, and can no longer hold the " liberal mountain flood." How this came about is not quite known, though more than one story is told in explanation of it. The rift, which is in the northern bank, is many feet in width, and extends down to the bed of the pool, and that this was intentionally made seems certain. One version of the circumstance is that the bank was dug through in a dry season by a miller of Okehampton, in order that the water might run into the Ockment, which stream turned his mill-wheel. Another is that it was the work of Moormen who, having had sheep drowned in the pool, decided to rid themselves of a source of danger to their flocks. And a third relates how a fox having gone to earth there, an endeavour was made to dig him out, which operation undermining the bank, it gave way beneath the pressure of the water.

But stories more weird in their character attach to this dried-up tarn. Cranmere was once haunted by a misshapen dwarf, the spirit of one who in his "days of nature" had been Okehampton's Mayor. The tradition tells us that one Benjamin Gayer, who in the seventeenth century filled the civic chair, was condemned after death to labour at the impossible task of baling the water of the mere with an oat sieve. By its margin the unquiet spirit laboured year after year, wearing the form of an ugly dwarf. But every dog has his day, and even Binjie, as he was called, was able to free himself, and to be revenged. Finding a sheepskin on the Moor he covered his sieve with it, and rapidly emptied the pool of its waters. The Ockment rose, and rushed in a mighty flood down the valley, sweeping everything before it, and reaching the town of Okehampton, submerged it, and drowned all the inhabitants. It is probable that the tradition is much older than the seventeenth century, and that it has merely been fastened on to Benjamin Gayer. It is also not unlikely, if there is any truth in the story of the miller, that the latter part of the legend is a modern addition suggested by his action.

Cranmere is also said to be haunted by a black colt, and this, too, it seems, is the restless spirit of Gayer. After his death he reappeared in Okehampton, and caused such annoyance that a number of clergymen were convened to "read him down." But although they brought all their learning to bear and addressed him in various languages, there was no result until one spoke to him in Arabic. That was more than the spirit could stand, and he intimated the fact to the speaker. Being vanquished, Gayer was promptly turned into a black colt, a halter was put upon him, and a man set upon his back with instructions to ride him to Cranmere. The orders were carried out, and on the edge of the great morass that girds the lonely pool, the colt was left, and there, according to the gossips' story, he may be seen to this day.

The rambler over the silent waste on-reaching Cranmere finds himself within a hundred and fifty feet of the highest point of the Moor. But though on so elevated a spot, the lowlands are hidden from his sight except in one place. There the receding hills above the valley of the West Ockment afford him a narrow view of far-away pastures. But for that he looks only upon a wilderness, and sees nothing but what Nature has formed.

IV.

THE ISLAND OF ROCKS.

Course of the West Ockment——Meldon Gorge——Shelf Stone——Branscombe's Loaf——A Rocky Ravine——The Slipper Stones——An Ancient Grove——Survey of the Forest——Sir Thomas Wise——Black Tor Copse in the Seventeenth Century.

Broad slopes of green before us lie,
Where fern and foxglove wave in glory;
And rounded tops, which kiss the sky,
With granite blocks are piled on high,
Like castles in enchanted story.
—T. Vernon Wollaston.

NEAR where the Red-a-ven comes down from under Yes Tor to swell the waters of the West Ockment, the latter stream issues from the romantic Meldon Gorge, on its way to the cultivated country below the Park of Okehampton. From its rise near the broken bank of Cranmere to the point where it leaves the Moorlands its course is through a succession of scenes of an impressive character. As it comes forth from its forbidding-looking birthplace, its flood stained with the peaty soil, the little stream moves slowly and knows only a desolate region; but by-and-bye, increasing in volume, its current becomes more rapid, as though it were impatient to exchange the frowns of Nature for her smiles. Under Great Kneeset it runs to meet the Brim Brook, and flowing below Lints Tor, passes an ancient crossing-place known as Sandy Ford, one of the points marking the boundary of the Forest. Below this the valley narrows and the hills on either side rise higher. On one hand is the giant flank of Willes, and on the other the steep slope below Stinka Tor and the Slipper Stones. Two miles further down the stream makes a bend, the hills still rising precipitously, and enters Meldon Gorge. At the lower end of this, and near its confluence with the Red-a-ven, about two miles from Okehampton, we meet it, and shall make our way by its bank to the long valley below the ancient ford, that we may look upon the beauties it has to show.

Crossing the tributary that comes tumbling down from the foot of Yes Tor, and following a cart track on the right bank of the river, we skirt Longstone Hill, the name of which probably points to the former existence upon it of a menhir. The gorge is narrow, and the hills on either side rise to a height of two hundred and fifty feet above the stream, those on the left, or eastern side, sloping still further upward for another thousand feet or more. Above the steep scarp across the stream is Meldon Down, on one part of which, when the night wind was howling over the Moor and the rain descended in torrents, the Royalists and Parliamentarians met in battle at the time the Cromwellian Major, James Chudleigh, held Okehampton.

We cross a little feeder of the Ockment, and passing the ruins of a mine building in a hollow, reach the foot of Homerton Hill, which, in one place, is so steep that it would only be possible to ascend it by climbing. It is like a huge dome, and is covered

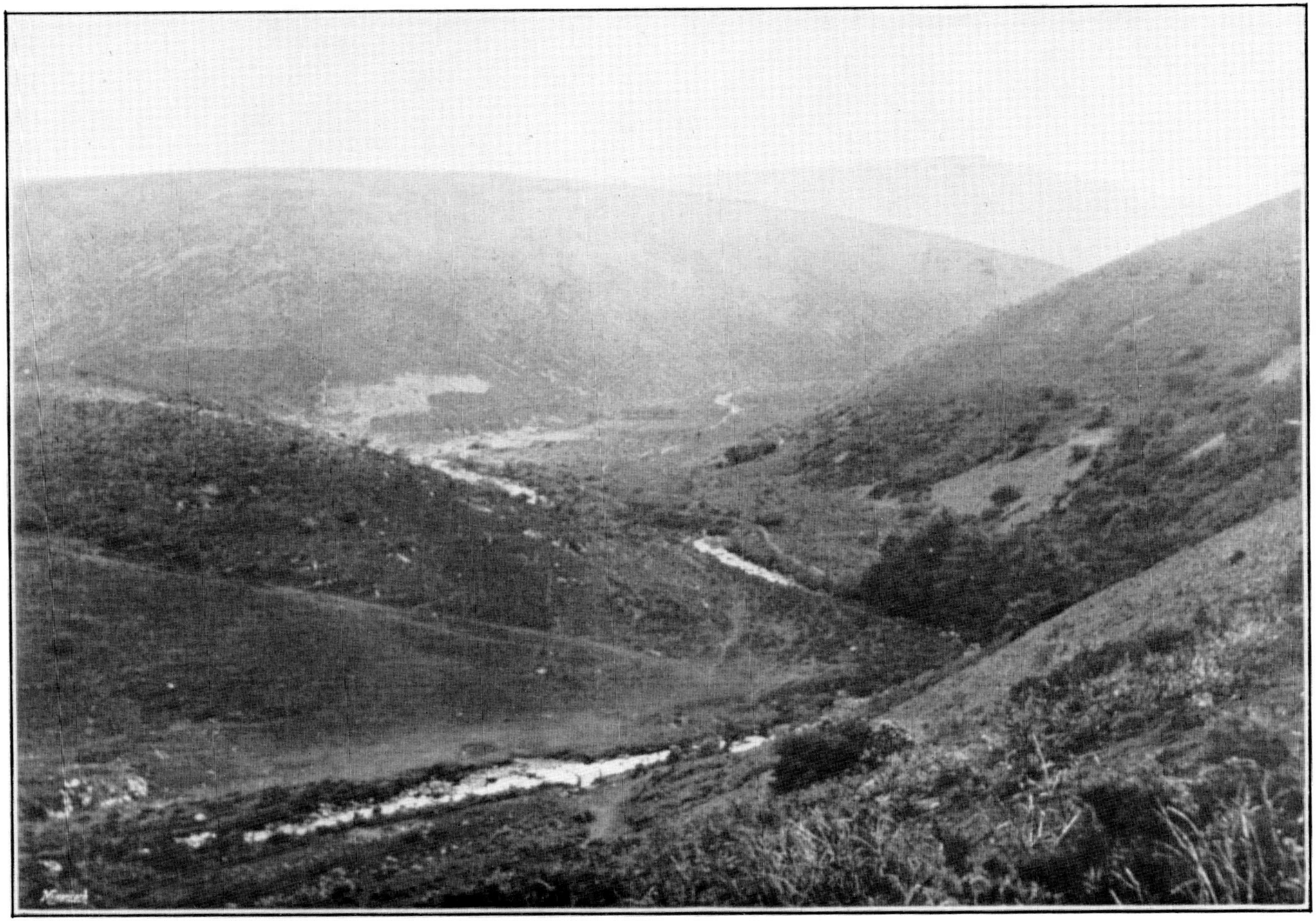

SEE PAGE 32.

PHOTO BY ERNEST CROFT.

Meldon Gorge.

"Following a cart track on the right bank of the river we skirt Longstone Hill."

with short grass, in this respect presenting a decided contrast to the hill we see rising from the further bank of the stream, which is clothed with heather. As we near the bend, which is known as Vellake Corner, we shall notice that the valley widens and that its bottom is perfectly flat. The stream does not flow through the centre of this, but at the very foot of the hill on the western side, a grassy plateau extending from its brink to the hill on the east. Over this we pass, and following the contour of Homerton, leave the gorge and enter the long valley.

Through a cleft in the hills on the further side of the stream the little Vellake feeder comes down. One branch of this, though in the summer it scarcely deserves the name, being then often dry, rises in Corn Hole, a hollow below the highest part of Corn Ridge, the eminence rising on the right as we advance. On its flank, and not far from the river, we notice Shilstone Tor, which, like Longstone Hill, will suggest to us the former existence here of an ancient monument. The name, it is not unlikely, is a corruption of "shelf stone"—the first word appearing in the Devon vernacular as "shil" — and would well describe the dolmen, or cromlech, in which the quoit, usually a flattish stone, may be likened to a shelf. But there are no vestiges of any megalithic monument to be seen in the immediate vicinity of the pile, and it is quite probable that the "shelf stone" was nothing more than one of the rocks of the tor itself, which, overhanging those on which it rested, presented a resemblance to the object in question.

Ere we have proceeded many steps on our way up the valley we become aware that it is totally unlike the gorge through which we have just passed. During our progress up the latter we saw only hills covered with grass and heather, with one or two enclosures on the western slopes, and there was nothing to cause us to imagine that aught but the bare Moor lay before us. But now trees appear on the eastern bank, and, further on, also on the opposite side of the stream, and we begin to realise that this rocky valley conceals a picture of sylvan beauty. It is a wild beauty, and on that account the more powerfully appeals to us.

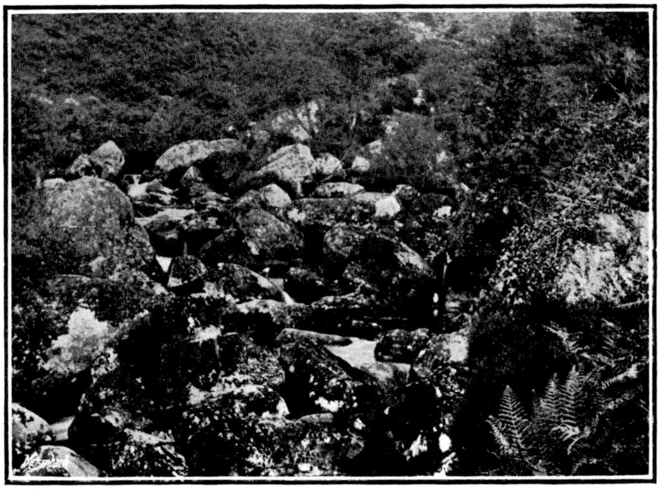

Photo by] [Ernest Croft.

Below the Island of Rocks.

"This rocky valley conceals a picture of sylvan beauty."

A sullen roar strikes on the ear, and the Ockment, hitherto our joyous companion through the defile, comes rushing impetuously towards us in a fretful mood, as though its course had been rudely disturbed. The roar becomes louder as we advance, and suddenly the gleaming foam of a cascade comes into view. When we near the fall we see that immediately above it two streams, or what appear to be such, unite. But the narrowing of the valley a little further on tells us that we look upon the Ockment alone, which has scooped out two courses for itself up yonder, but only that the waters may mingle again. And to the charming spot which these arms encircle men have given the name of the Island of Rocks. But the rocks are not naked like those of the grim tor thrusting its piles above the clatter; they wear a mantle of green, amid the folds of which the summer breezes play.

The Island of Rocks is about one hundred and twenty yards in length and about twenty-five yards in breadth. It is placed at the lower end of a narrow, rugged defile, through which the Ockment runs, descending nearly two hundred feet in a distance of between three and four hundred yards. The island is entirely covered with trees and undergrowth, as also is the eastern bank of the stream. There are only a few boulders near its lower end left unconcealed, and these are heaped in the manner of a tiny tor. It is a spot such as might well serve as a hold for the elves who were once said to haunt the glen, though it provides no velvet sward for their moonlight revels. But on the banks this is found, and the river would be no barrier to the pixies. But they are gone, and the glen is haunted now only by the seeker after the wildly beautiful and romantic. And he finds it here without blemish, for all is Nature's work.

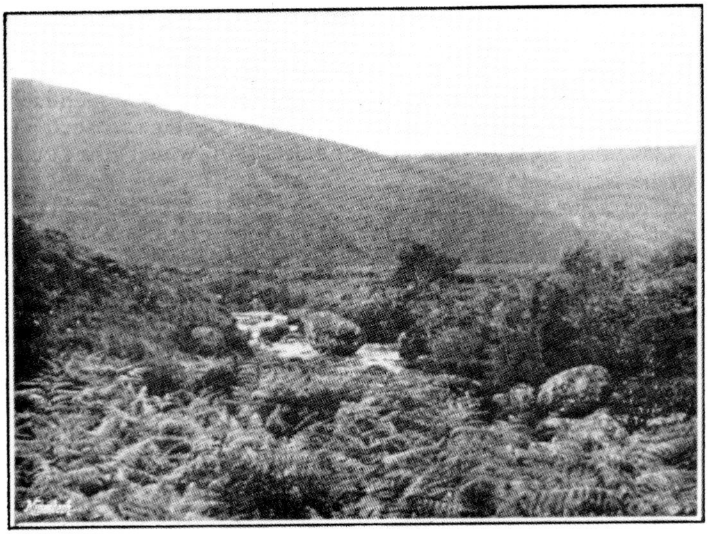

Photo by] [Ernest Croft.

The West Ockment.

"In the bed of the river is an immense boulder."

But it is not the island, beautiful as it is, that is the most impressive feature of this valley; that is to be found in the wild ravine above it, to which the name of the former has often been attached, though certainly most inappropriately. If it be sought to know why, the reply that it is so—one somewhat analogous to that of Wordsworth's little cottage girl—will probably scarcely be deemed satisfactory. It has been sought to improve upon this by giving the glen the name of the Highland Rocks, which, however, only creates confusion. The island, it may be mentioned, is often spoken of by the Moormen as the Isle of Dogs, but for no other reason than that they have chosen to give it that name. But what matters it how it is called? Nature has here planted a garden in the wilderness, and its true name is beauty.

Looking down the stream, which the bend below Homerton does not permit us to trace far, we find the view closed in by the slope of South Down. Along this a disused watercourse forms a convenient path by which this part of the common may be reached from the Moor gate near Meldon. In the bed of the river is an immense boulder, which we shall not fail to notice, the absence of other rocks near it rendering it very conspicuous.

And now let us resume our way up the valley, finding for ourselves a path above the side of the ravine. At every step the scene becomes more impressive, and the beautiful and the romantic unite in a manner that cannot fail to cause the most supreme delight. It is a mingling of oak tree and fern; of mountain-ash and bushes of the wild raspberry; of sturdy thorns and withies that bend to the breeze; of briar, and ivy, and heather, and whortleberry, half-shrouding grey masses of granite; of rushing river and gleaming foam, and deep pools; of rugged tor and hills that shut out the world. And the sound of falling waters alone strikes upon the ear; now rising like a deep sigh, and anon filling the air with its thunder.

And so we gain the top of the glen, and, drawing nearer to the brink of the stream, look down and throughout its length. The glimpses we have been able to obtain of it through the tangled foliage, though sufficient to show that it is very steep, were not such as to enable us to estimate this correctly. But from its upper end its whole course is revealed to us, and we see that it can be likened only to one long cataract.

At this point Black Tor, which was in sight from near the island, is now seen to consist of three piles, rising one above the other. It is placed on a spur of the elevated land crowned by Yes Tor and Willes, and though considerably less in height than those points, yet towers high above the vale. As we make our way along the bank of the stream, where in the tiny bays the ripples dance over red and yellow pebbles, we find that although we are penetrating deeper into the wilds, we are yet to meet with more trees. Below the tor, and very near to the river, along which it extends for nearly half a mile, is the grove of ancient oaks known as Black Tor Copse, and which, like Wistman's Wood, forms one of the curiosities of Dartmoor. Before reaching it we pass another island in the stream, smaller than the one below the ravine, and altogether different in character, being covered only with a smooth sward and patches of heather. Just above it the western bank recedes considerably, and there is a great hollow in the hill, which here rises some five hundred feet above the stream. At the head of the valley is a rounded hill, not of great elevation, but seen from the point we have now reached, the rock on its crest, which resembles a small tower, stands up boldly against the sky. This is Lints Tor, and beyond it rise the hills in the more solitary parts of the Forest.

Except that the trees of Black Tor Copse are not so large, and that they do not grow from the clatter quite in a similar manner to those at Wistman's Wood, the two groves are not very much unlike. The boulders that have proved the defence of one have also preserved the other, but the poverty of the soil has not permitted the trees in either to become other than dwarfs. It is a good example of the woods that once clothed many of the upland valleys.

Three hundred years ago Black Tor Copse was of much greater extent than it is at present. Its higher end is now a good half-mile outside the Forest, the boundary line crossing the West Ockment at Sandy Ford, whereas at the time referred to the wood was crossed by that line. This is proved by a return to a perambulation, or survey, of the Forest made in 1609, in which the jurors, after naming Sandy Ford as a bound, state that Blacktorrebeare, as the wood was then called, was partly in the Forest and partly on the Venville Common. Its mention occurs in a presentment which the jurors made concerning one William Chastie, who in the month of July, 1609, killed a stag in the Forest near the wood, and which, it appears, he took to Sir Thomas Wise, of Sydenham. Sir Thomas, who was knighted at the Coronation of James I., was the builder of that mansion, and also of the house at Mount Wise, which, it is said, was until about the end of the seventeenth century the only one to be seen in what was until lately the borough of Devonport.

Other evidence in the same direction is afforded by a document without date, but which appears to belong to the earlier years of the seventeenth century. And it not only proves that a part of the copse was then within the Forest, but also explains its disappearance. The wood was felled, for the entry relates to its sale. It reads thus: "40s. from 8a. underwood growing within the Forest of Dartmoor in a certain place there called Black Tores beare."

Trees were also felled at an earlier date in that part of the copse situated outside the Forest, as is shown by an entry in the Lydford Court Rolls of the 29th of Elizabeth, where William Bowdon is named as having cut down certain oaks in Blacketers Beare "infra Forestam." It may be mentioned that a farm on the borders of the Moor in the neighbourhood of the wood is called Bowden.

When our ramble has brought us to the end of this valley we may make our way back to Meldon by the hillside above the oak wood. By so doing we shall look down upon the romantic scene through which our wandering steps have led us. But from whatever point we view it, we shall have nothing for it but words of praise. Wooded glens and foaming rivers, and oaks that grow on rocky slopes, are met with in many places on the Dartmoor borders; but how often are they seen upon the Moor itself? Nature has only brought them together in one place there, and that is at the Island of Rocks.

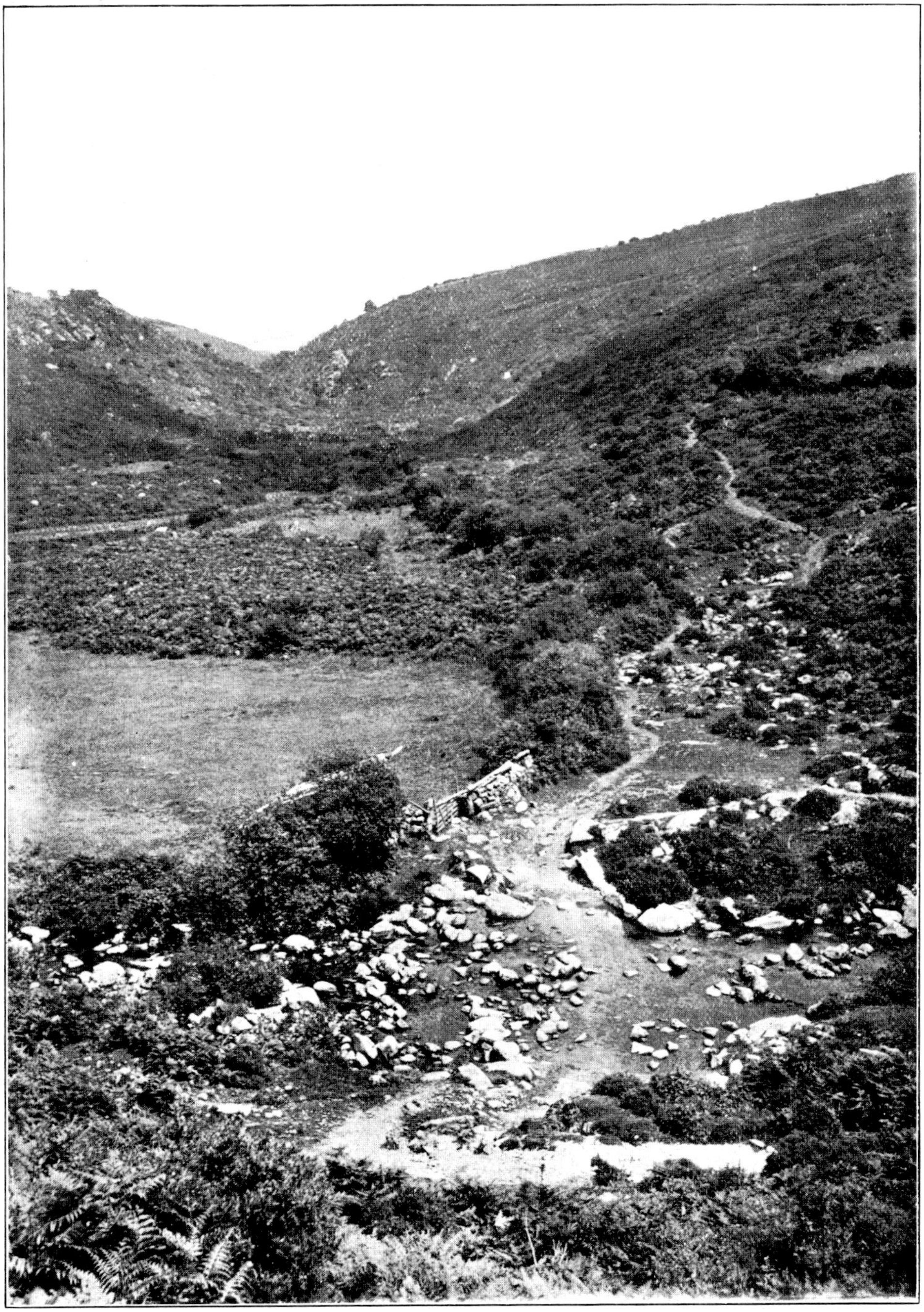

SEE PAGE 49. **Belstone Cleave.** PHOTO BY C. R. ROWE.

"The ford on the stream, and the path climbing the side of the hill."

V.

THE BELSTONE CLEAVES.

Border Settlements——A Thirteenth Century Parson——Early Memorial Stones——Cosdon——Belstone in Domesday——Venville Rent——Cavaliers and Roundheads——A Foraging Party——Cleave Tor——Moorland Music.

Happy valleys of sunshine and pleasures,
Where streams sparkle gold, and the wood-pigeons coo.
—Eden Phillpotts.

WHEN the rambler on Dartmoor is leaving its slopes for the lowlands he finds that, except in a few localities, it does not suddenly lose its wildness; the rugged hills are left behind, but smiling pastures do not at once appear. Before reaching these he passes through a borderland of brakes and little crofts, in which rocks are often almost as plentiful as grass; there is a gradual softening down of the ruder features before the fields with their tall hedgerows and trees surround him. It is seldom the change from Devonia's desert to the champaign country is a violent one; still there are not wanting spots in which this is found. And so of the Moorland villages. Shaugh and Sheepstor, for instance, are typical border settlements; everything about them speaks of the Moor. Others, from which the rock-strewn hill is not seen, possess little but their granite-built cottages to remind the visitor that he is close to the waste; while others, again, though from them the tor, or the heather-clad height, be in view, have through a process of modernising lost much, if not all, of their original appearance. Among the latter we may mention the village of Belstone, or, as the name sometimes appears, Belston, in the north-eastern corner of Dartmoor, which though possessing traces of its old-time character, is quite unlike what it was even a quarter of a century ago. The humble inn has disappeared, and a modern hotel has taken its place; well-built residences and trim cottages are seen where once lowly thatched dwellings stood; the village no longer wears a primitive, rustic air, but one which speaks plainly of the summer visitor. The grandsires of the present generation of Belstone men would, if they could look upon it, fail to recognise it.

But though very much of the old has given place to the new in this Dartmoor village, and things are not as of yore, its surroundings, in which its charm is found, are still much as ever they were. The grand hill of Cosdon across the valley of the Taw wears the same appearance now, except at the foot of its northern slopes, as it did on that July day in the year 1240, when twelve knights of the shire met there to commence their perambulation of the Forest, by command of Richard, Earl of Cornwall; the "cry" of the river still rises from the western valley, on the side of which the great rock looks down upon the meeting of the waters, as when in the first Edward's time the dependents of Lord Hugh Courtenay, Baron of Okehampton, drove to the chase above it the cattle they had seized from the monks at Westford; the range of tors southward of the village is now as it was when in 1296 "the parson of Beleston" was fined for turning oxen on the Forest without having previously entered them on the books of the clerk, save that man has despoiled the ridge of some of its scattered granite. The village may wear a newer aspect, but on the Moor that neighbours it time has wrought little change.

More than one locality on the borders of Dartmoor is famed for its cleave; Belstone has in its vicinity three of which it can boast. The word signifies a deep, narrow valley —a cleft through the hill, as it were—but, as in most instances rock masses rise precipitously from their sides, the Moormen often regard the principal of these as forming the cleave, the word thus being with them synonymous with cliff.* The parish of Belstone lies between the Taw, on the east, a stream rising in the Cranmere morasses, and the East Ockment, on the west—the village occupying an elevated position above the former. The valley by which the Taw leaves the Moor forms one of the cleaves that add so greatly to the attractions of the place, and this bears the same name as the parish. The East Ockment, after receiving the Black-a-ven, runs past the enclosures of an old hill farm to seek the shade of Halstock Woods, and quits the Moorlands through the Belstone West Cleave, flowing thence to Okehampton to meet its sister stream from Meldon Gorge. But just before it bids adieu to the uplands it receives the Moor Brook, which comes down from the commons through a beautifully wooded valley known as Halstock Cleave. This, though entirely in the parish of Okehampton, is yet sufficiently near to Belstone to be accounted one of its attractions.

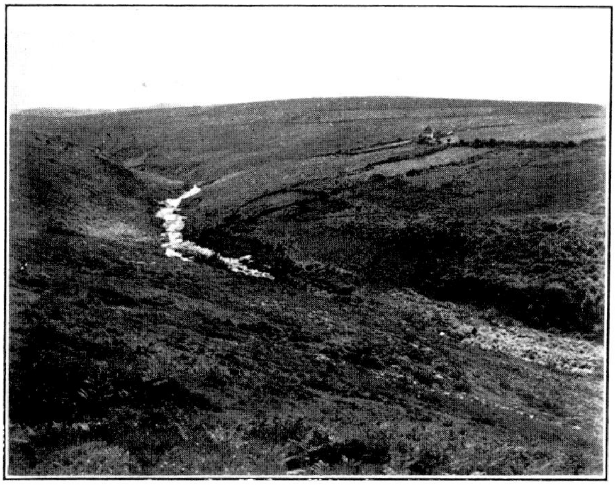

Photo by] [C. R. Rowe.

The East Ockment.

"Runs past the enclosures of an old hill farm."

Three miles and a half from Okehampton, on the Exeter highway, is the village of Sticklepath, whence an upland road leads to Belstone Cleave. At the point where this diverges, and on the very edge of the common, is an upright stone bearing several rude markings, and a Latin cross in relief, and which, together with others in this neighbourhood, I have elsewhere noticed.† The locality is rich in memorials of Early Christian times, there being no less than six crosses near the foot of Cosdon. Following the road the rambler will soon find himself in the cleave with the Taw on his left, and on the further side of this the hill, which terminates only at the summit of Cosdon, rises precipitously. The common on the right is also steep, but the road runs for some little distance at its foot, being carried near the river. When it commences to climb the slope we leave it, and follow the latter as it comes fretting and chafing down from Taw Marsh. But we halt at this point to look upon the great hill beyond the stream, which, although we gain no idea as yet of its true size, reveals itself sufficiently to convince us that this is considerable.

We see that the hill for some distance above the entrance to the cleave is clothed with trees; then these give place to a steep slope that comes down nearly to the stream, where firs and various shrubs are growing, but which yet wears an air of semi-wildness.

* Some remarks on this subject will be found in the chapters on Lustleigh Cleave and Tavy Cleave.

† *Ancient Stone Crosses of Dartmoor and its Borderland.* Chap. XI.

This is Ska, or Skaigh, Warren, an enclosure stretching up to another wood that clothes the shoulder of the hill towards South Zeal. We notice the zigzag paths that are carried up its side, and the rustic bridge thrown over the river by which access to them is gained. At the head of the valley are the enclosures of Birchy Lake, a farm near the river, but to the left is the open Moor, where there are no more trees or shrubs, but only the heather and the whortleberry. But if it be the season of the year when the former is in bloom, what a glorious picture does old Cosdon present. Little wonder that the river dances in the sunlight, and the skylark's song is heard in the blue. It is for joy that the ancient hill, clad in his robe of beauty, smiles upon the valleys for which for so many months he had nothing but a frown. We pass onward, noticing Ivy Tor across the stream, and the rock masses above us on the right (the true Belstone Cleave if the name in this instance be derived from *cliff: vide supra*), and following the Taw shall only leave it when it bends to the left. Then we ascend the slope in front, as by so doing we shall see to great advantage the valley up which we have made our way.

Viewed from this point, which is not far from Belstone Church, the cleave forms a pleasing picture, though not so characteristic of the Dartmoor borderland as formerly. Still there is much that bears the genuine Moorland stamp. Here are seen little enclosures, doubtless formed with much toil, standing in the midst of a wilderness of gorse; here is the ford on the stream, and the path climbing the side of the hill; further down grey crags—the nearer mass being The Cliff and the one beyond it, Ivy Tor—while in the distance we obtain a glimpse of the cultivated country.

Not far from this spot is Birchy Lake, and to trace the Taw upward from that place to Steeperton Tor, where it comes down through a narrow defile, and to return by way of the southern ridge, already mentioned, will prove to be a ramble full of interest. On this ridge are Ock Tor, Winter Tor, Higher Tor, and Belstone Tor, the latter two, below which the granite is strewn in great confusion, being not very far from the village to which our walk has nearly brought us.

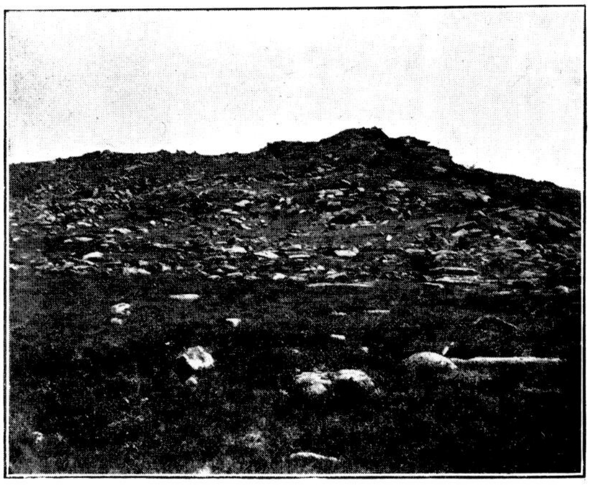

Photo by] [C. R. Rowe.

The Southern Ridge.

"The granite is strewn in great confusion."

The earliest mention of this place is in Domesday, where the name appears as Bellestham. About two hundred years later its form had changed somewhat, for we find it referred to as Beleston. But there is not a great difference in the meaning of these two names. The first is the *ham*, or the pasture lands, of Bel, or Belles, and the second is the *ton* or town of the same—the word *town* signifying simply a farmhouse, as it does in many places on the Dartmoor borders at the present day. We can readily suppose that Belles, or someone who inherited his land, would build a house upon it, and thus the change in the name would be accounted for. There is no necessity for imagining one to be a corruption of the other. The form in use at the present time differs only from that of the thirteenth century in the elision of the fourth letter, and the addition of a final *e*.

In the time of Henry II. the place belonged to Baldwin de Belston, who held three knights' fees under the barony of Okehampton. Most of the family, Risdon states, were called by that name after Baldwin de Brionys, the first lord of Okehampton, to whom, and to whose house, they were devoted.

Belstone is one of the ancient vills, that is a parish, or part of a parish, possessing certain rights on Dartmoor. In 1502 we find the venville rent of Belstone to be 3s.; in 1624 it was 4s. 4d. The Forester of the north quarter, who makes the return in the last-named year, adopts a phonetic style of spelling; that is, if the sound of the letter *t* in the name of the place was dropped at that time, as it is by the Dartmoor man at present, for he sets down the amount as having been received by him "for the venvell Rente of Bellsoun."

During the Civil Wars there is no doubt that Belstone—out-of-the-way place though it was—had its share of the excitement. The farmer at East Lake, in the parish, once received a visit from one of the contending parties that was not at all to his liking, but whether from Cavalier or Roundhead does not transpire. The commissariat department presumably not being in a flourishing condition, the good farmer's house was entered, and a number of cheeses and loaves of bread were taken away in a cart. As may naturally be supposed, when the troopers departed the farmer thought he had seen the last of his food supply. But this was not so. On the top of the hill leading to Belstone he afterwards found the cheeses and the loaves scattered over the road. It was supposed that the men who had taken them had been pursued by the enemy, and had hurriedly unloaded the cart in order to make good their escape.

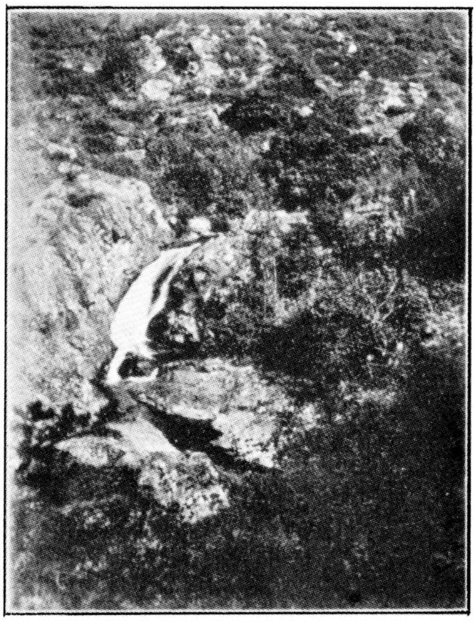

Photo by] [C. R. Rowe.

In the West Cleave.

"We linger by the waterfall where the moss drinks up the spray."

From the village a lane leads past the entrance to the old vicarage to the commons on the west side of the parish, and following this we shall, on entering upon them, find ourselves near a tor placed on the brow of a hill. This is Cleave Tor, or to give it the name by which it is generally referred to in the neighbourhood, Cleave Rocks, and it is unlike any other on Dartmoor. Instead of rising from the turf, as most tors do, or jutting abruptly from the hillside, Cleave Tor runs straight out from the surface of the ground, and only attains height in consequence of the hill sinking very rapidly from that point. But Cleave Tor is not of granite; hence this dissimilarity to the other tors of the Moor.

But when we stand beside it we shall be rewarded with a sight such as is not often seen, even on the borders of Dartmoor. We look down upon the Belstone West Cleave, of which the common sloping steeply before us forms one side, and the Halstock Woods the other. Immediately opposite to us is a narrow valley through which the Moor Brook hastens to meet the East Ockment, though the streams are hidden from our view. This is the Cleave of Halstock, and above it, nearly reached by the coppice that climbs its side, is the beautiful Ashbury Tor, which the heather and the whortleberry are striving to conceal.

We descend the slope to the river, in whose depths white clouds intermingle with pebbles of amber. We look into the old wood, where softly whispering zephyrs coquette with green leaves, then heedlessly pass on their way. We linger by the waterfall, where the moss drinks up the spray, and then, like an overloaded sponge, suffers it to escape in crystal drops to the dark pool beneath. Slowly we follow the stream down the valley, where the ferns and the foxgloves grow, the waving woods on one hand and the bare Moor on the other. Here perchance De Brionys, or Ranulph Avenel, or Fitzroy, or Robert Courtenay, roused the lordly stag, and galloped to the hills of the open Moor. Then the twanging horn and the baying of the hounds broke the silence of the cleave, and made music for the hunters. The music that falls upon our ears is that of rustling leaves and hurrying waters. A less inspiriting tune, it may be, but one whose effects shall be more lasting. Often in the turmoil of life will our souls be refreshed when our thoughts turn to that lovely valley, and the sweet song of joy and peace that came up from its depths.

VI.

GIDLEIGH CHASE.

A Notable Stream——Trees and Heather——A Harbour for Deer——Gidleigh Castle——Rights of Gidleigh's Ancient Lords——A Change of Ownership——A Massive Wall——Feather Bed Lane——Gidleigh Tor——A Wonderful View.

Through thy glens
Once rang the hart's bell free,
The mountain wolf led forth her cubs
Beneath the dark pine tree ;
And where the broom and the birchen sprays
Hang o'er the sparkling rills,
The giant deer with branching horns
Passed upward to the hills.
—Richard John King.

NO river of Devon has more romantic associations than the Teign, for not only does it pass through some of the grandest scenery of the West, but for a distance of many miles its banks are lined with objects of antiquarian and historical interest. Both on its northern and southern branches are numerous remains that take us back to pre-historic days. Examples of the stone circle are found ; of the stone row, the menhir, and the pound ; and of the ruined huts of a people now forgotten. It is true that in its solitary course through the Moorlands the natural accompaniments of the Teign (or, at all events, of its northern branch) are surpassed by those of other streams that have their birthplace there, for it is not until the confines of the Moor are reached, and the river is about to leave the hills whence it has sprung, that it becomes impressive. When the Moor is left behind the North and South Teign unite, and their place of meeting, a sequestered spot, where trees fling their leafy arms over the waters, will be well known to visitors to Chagford. To trace the southern branch to this confluence, immediately above which it is spanned by Leigh Bridge, would well reward the explorer, but it is the North Teign that is to be our companion now. This, the more important stream, when it leaves the waste enters Gidleigh Chase, and only quits it shortly before reaching the place where the waters meet.

Gidleigh Chase extends from the common near Scorhill Tor to the confluence of the Blackaton Brook and the Teign, a distance of about a mile and a half, but its breadth is not so great.* It covers the sides of a deep valley, wooded for the most part, though in places are green glades, and heather-clad slopes dotted with masses of granite. The channel of the Teign is choked with boulders, between which the stream forces its way, and occasional glimpses of it gained through the foliage reveal dark rocks and gleaming foam. Wildness is happily blended with sylvan beauty. Nature has not been tamed ; only some of her sterner features are absent. This tract of wooded

* We refer to the area over which the chase once evidently extended. This is now divided into two properties, as will be seen further on.

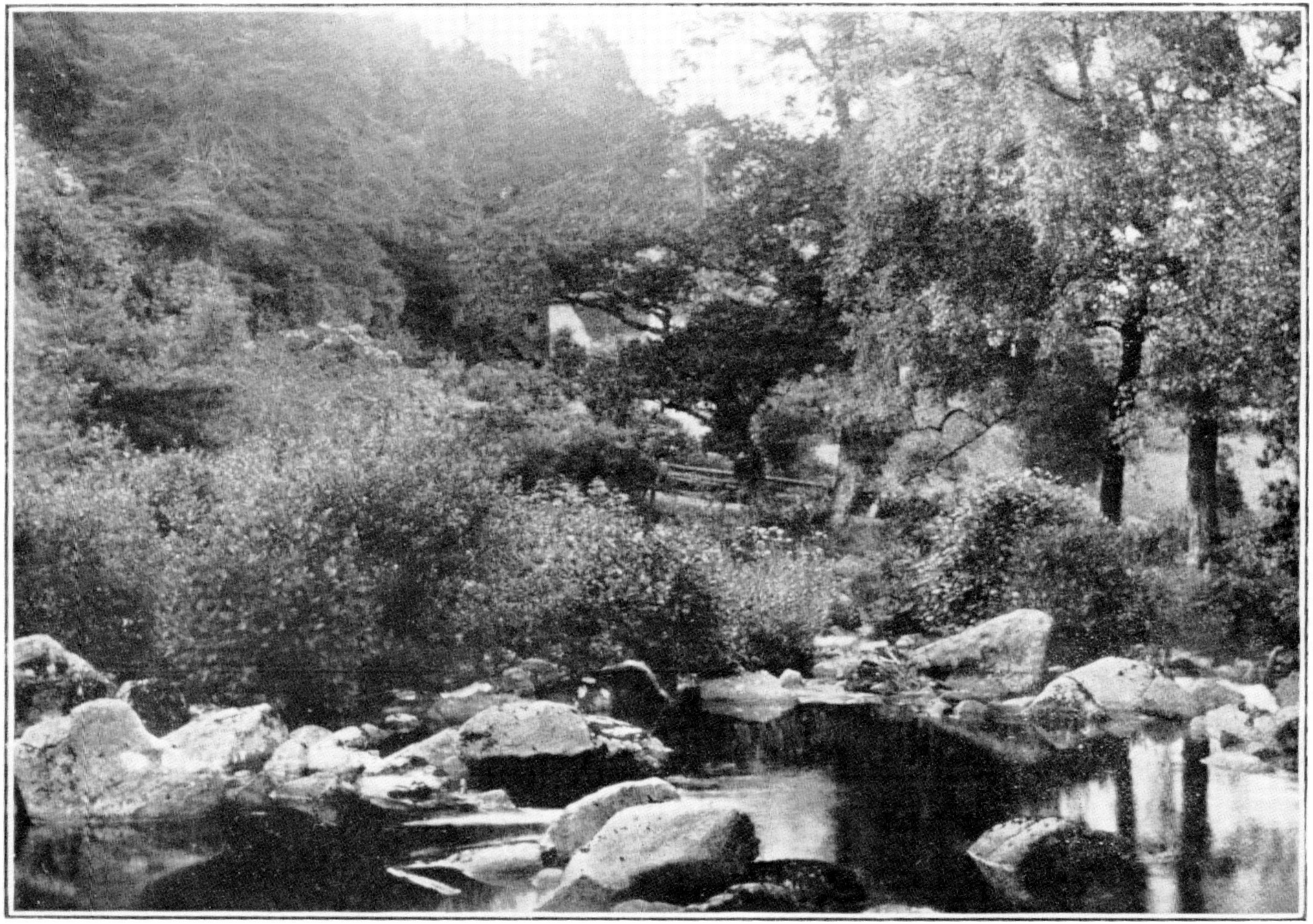

SEE PAGE 52

The North Teign below Gidleigh Park.

PHOTO BY C. R. ROWE.

"No river of Devon has more romantic associations than the Teign."

steeps is generally referred to as a park, and, inasmuch as it is enclosed, is one. But only in one part can it be said to possess features of the kind usually associated with such; it partakes far more of the character of a chase than of a deer park. There can be little doubt that such a harbour for deer lay open to the Moor during its possession by Gidleigh's earliest lords; then, as their hunting ground, it would be a chase, for, like a forest, such was unenclosed.* The wall at present surrounding it is ancient, but does not go back to those old times. The castle of this lordship is rather more than a quarter of a mile outside the boundary, and this would point to the enclosure of the chase having been effected at some period subsequent to its erection. When the castle was built the limits of the hunting ground were probably defined by bond marks alone, and only when more of the land within the manor was brought under cultivation would an enclosing wall, to prevent the deer from ranging, become necessary.

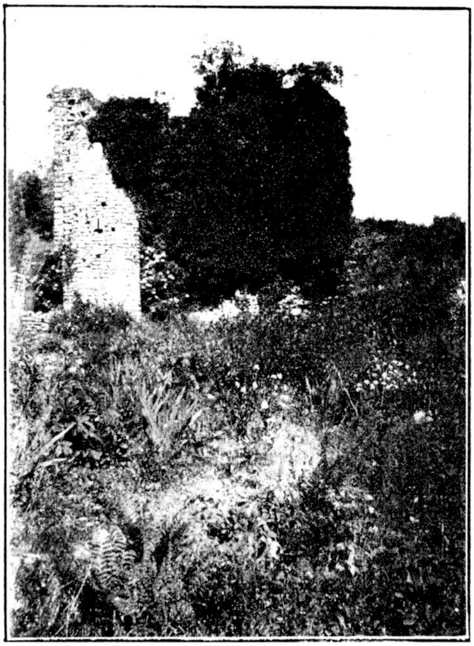

Photo by] [C. R. Rowe.

Gidleigh Castle.

"A square tower, apparently of the fourteenth century."

All that remains of the home of Gidleigh's ancient lords is a square tower, apparently of the fourteenth century, and it is not probable that the castle was ever very large. At the same time the ruins represent only a part of it. Mr. A. Guy Whipham, the owner of the manor, informs me that the foundations of walls in the immediate vicinity of the tower are to be seen, and that he has found a quantity of freestone in old buildings in the locality, which seemed to have been used for mullions, and this, there cannot be a doubt, came from the castle. If the freestone was useful for building purposes, so, of course, was the granite that we may be sure was largely used in the structure, and hence the disappearance of the walls. Mr. Whipham has carefully preserved the stone, for which he will earn the thanks of all who find an interest in the memorials of the past.

In the tower is a lower chamber, and steps leading to an apartment over it. Picturesque though the ruin be there is little in it to interest the casual visitor, though it certainly gives a character to the hamlet that distinguishes it from all others on the Dartmoor borders. But it possesses an attraction for the student of Dartmoor history, as being one of the four castles connected with the Moor. The others were Lydford, Okehampton, and Plympton, each of far greater importance than Gidleigh, which has hidden itself away in this corner of the borderland, and has lost whatever history it may once have had.

Close by the ruin is the manor house, the church, a couple of cottages, a modern residence, and the manor pound; this is the whole of Gidleigh. The lords of Gidleigh as

* "There be three for venery or venatical pleasure, viz., a forrest, chase, and park; they all agree in one thing, which is that they are habitations for wild beasts. The two first lye open, the last inclosed. The forrest is the most noble of all, for it is a franchise of so princely a tenure, that, according to our laws, none but the King can have a forrest. If he chance to pass one over to a subject, 'tis no more forrest, but frank chase."—*Howell's Familiar Letters*. But Coke states that "if the King doth grant a Forest to a subject, and granteth further that upon request made in Chancery he and his heirs shall have Justices of the Forest, then the subject hath a Forest in law."

owners, not only of that manor, but at one period of the adjoining manor of Throwleigh also, possessed rights over that part of Dartmoor stretching from the south-eastern foot of Cosdon to the down southward of the Teign, and being for some distance conterminous with the Forest. The first lords, it is generally supposed, were the Prouzes, or Prouses, though it is also stated that the manor was previously held by the Gidleys. However this may have been, it is certain that in the thirteenth century it was in the possession of the family of Prouz, and later in that of the Gidleys. The last of this family who lived in the parish sold the property towards the latter part of the eighteenth century. After passing through other hands, the manor and estate of Gidleigh, with the advowson, were purchased in 1819 under a decree of Chancery by the Rev. Dr. Whipham, grandfather of the present owner.

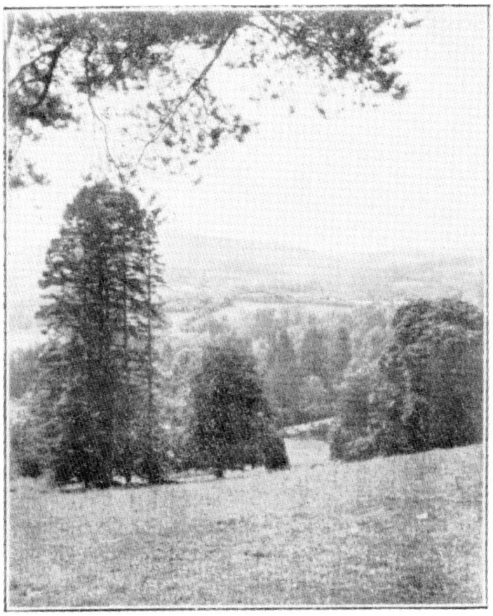

Photo by] [C. R. Rowe.

Gidleigh Park.

"From which one looks upon border country."

The estate comprises among other lands the greater portion of the wild tract within the wall, the only part of it not included being at the upper end, on the left bank of the Teign, and which forms the grounds of Scorhill House, now the property of the Rev. E. B. Layard. Gidleigh Park House, the residence of Mr. Whipham, is at the lower end, on the same side of the stream, and here the grounds, from which one looks upon border country and far off farm lands, are laid out in the manner indicated by the name. There is an entrance to the park not very far from the church, and another between Highbury Bridge and Murchington, and one also on the Chagford side where the Teign is crossed at Gidleigh Park Bridge. According to tradition a subterranean passage leads from the castle to the river near this bridge. There are three openings there, but they appear to be nothing more than mine adits.

Being private property Gidleigh Chase is one of those gems in the granite crown of Devon that the Dartmoor rambler must be content to view from a distance. He may look upon it as he does the regalia in the Tower, from all sides, but may not examine it too closely. But there are many points from which he can obtain a view of it, and it is not less beautiful because a little removed.

The upper end of the ancient chase is not far below the confluence of the Walla Brook and the North Teign, near which is the well-known Holed Stone.* Scorhill Tor, or Scorhill Rocks, as the pile is more often called in the neighbourhood, is on the down just above this object, and if the visitor proceeds past it he will soon reach the wall of the chase, and will not fail to be struck with the great difference between it and the ordinary newtake wall. Not only are the stones composing it very massive, but it is much higher and furnished with a rude coping. This wall runs from the river below towards the *stroll* conducting to Creaber Pound and the road to Berry Down, then turning eastward is carried for a considerable distance, and forms the northern boundary of the chase. The

* This stone the antiquaries of a former day, who peopled the Moor with Druids, spoke of as a tolmen, and associated it with imaginary religious ceremonies.

Teign has at first the wooded slopes only on its left bank, on the right bank being an open common, named Brimstone Down. But a quarter of a mile further down trees appear there also, and soon it is seen that on this side the woods are thickest. Here, too, there is an enclosing wall.

Along the upper part of Brimstone Down a road runs from Teigncombe to Batworthy, passing the Round Pound and the groups of hut circles so well known to antiquaries. A view of the upper end of the chase is here obtained, and from other points on the common glimpses of the stream below. The contrast afforded by the tree-clad sides of the valley and the sweep of dusky moor that is seen stretching away to the left is very striking. Under Batworthy a clam is thrown across the Teign, there being a path leading from that farm through the Scorhill portion of the chase to Gidleigh Church.

The walk from Brimstone Down past Teigncombe, and down what in playful irony is called Featherbed Lane, to Leigh Bridge and the Puckie Stone,* is one that will enable us to get some good views of the ancient hunting ground. One great hill rising from amid the trees on the further side of the valley, with fine rock masses on its summit, will particularly arrest the attention at whatever season of the year it may be seen; but if it be when the heather is in bloom the picture it presents will not readily be forgotten. The eminence, which towers boldly above the tangled woods, is clothed with short grass, on which are patches of ferns and heather. On its crest is a tor, not of great height above the turf, but consisting of several fantastically shaped piles of rock. This is Gidleigh Tor, though it is seldom that it is spoken of as such, the name by which it is almost invariably called being Prinsep's Folly. It forms the highest part of the chase except where the latter abuts upon Gidleigh Common.

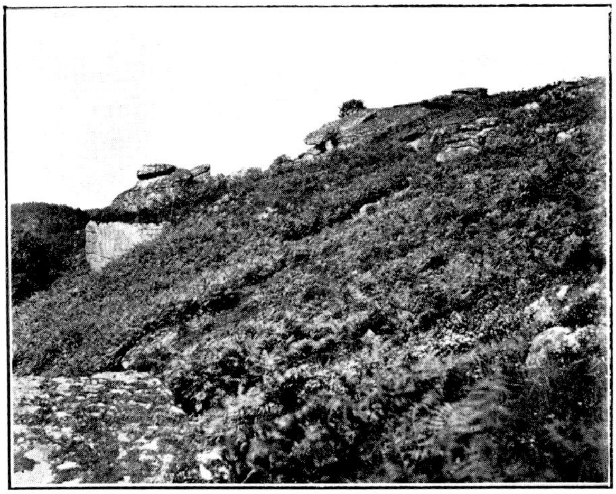

Photo by] [C. R. Rowe.

Gidleigh Tor.

"Several fantastically shaped piles of rock."

More than fifty years ago a house was built on this tor, and some ruined walls still mark its site. It is usually reported in the neighbourhood that it was never completed, but I have learnt from Mr. Whipham that this is incorrect. It was not only finished, but was occupied for a time by a caretaker. In 1846 Mr. Whipham's father, the late Rev. Arthur Whipham, rector of Gidleigh and owner of the estate, granted a lease for ninety-nine years of two-and-a-half acres of land immediately adjoining Gidleigh Tor to his friend Mr. Thomas Levett Prinsep. The rock cluster was chosen as a site for a dwelling—though one which it is probable would not commend itself to many—and there a house was built, but before Mr. Prinsep could occupy it he died suddenly in his boat at Teignmouth. His widow surrendered the lease in 1851, but previous to this the house was pulled down and the fittings and material sold by auction. Surely no house was ever built in such a situation before. Mr. Prinsep's idea—it cannot be called a plan—appears to have been to incorporate his dwelling with the

* In all probability a corruption of *pixy*.

rocks of the tor, but with what object it is not easy to see. Quite close to the portions of wall that remain is an open sward, unencumbered with rocks, on which a house might very well have been erected, though the situation would certainly be an exposed one. But though Mr. Prinsep's choice of a site for his house may not commend itself to us, we can scarcely regard its local name of Prinsep's Folly as a fitting one. The folly does not appear to have been in building the house so much as in pulling it down, and that was a work for which he was, of course, not responsible.

A short distance from the site of the dismantled house, and within a few feet of the summit of the hill, is a small octagonal tower. It is roofless, but the walls, round which there is a plinth about four feet high, are intact. There is a good doorway with a pointed arch, and a small window, each being enriched with mouldings. One side of the little building is covered with ivy, the stem of the plant being several inches in diameter.

But it must be confessed that a house on Gidleigh Tor would possess one advantage. Nowhere could a more magnificent view be found than that on which the beholder looks from the crest of this hill. It is most extensive, and embraces many of the chief places of interest on the eastern borders of the Moor. Away to the north-east a wide expanse of country is seen, where fields and trees fade away in the blue distance. Yonder across the valley is the little town of Chagford, and further away the romantic gorge of Fingle, and above it the ancient hill camp of Cranbrook Castle. East Down, at the foot of which North Bovey hides itself, is seen to the south-east, and beyond, the great masses of Hey Tor, and the huge ridge of Hameldon. Up the valley, and very near to us, is Kes Tor, and turning northward we see the giant Cosdon, at the base of which are fields and farmhouses, and then as our eye travels back it lights upon the tower of the little church of Gidleigh, just seen above the trees.

But we have not yet mentioned the chief object in the view. We have named mostly those that are distant, and have not turned our gaze upon the scene of grandeur that lies immediately below us. There we look upon the wild chase, and shall mark the windings of the river, though we see it not, for it is hidden far down in the depths of the wooded valley. There are the recesses to which the deer retreated at the coming of the dawn, and where was heard the horn of the old-time hunter. Now, the deer are gone, and the horn hangs in the hall, but the memories of those days this wild valley shall never lose.

We leave the tor and pass down the hill carpeted with sward dotted with patches of heather, the bright tints of purple and green causing the dark woods below to look darker still. We make our way through the ferns that clothe the slope, and we reach the trees, and listen to the "cry" of the river. It is too far down for the sounds to strike other than faintly on the ear, but we know something of what it could tell us. How that when it left the Moor and found that its course was to lie through Gidleigh's ancient chase, it leapt laughingly forward to lose itself amid the beauties that awaited it.

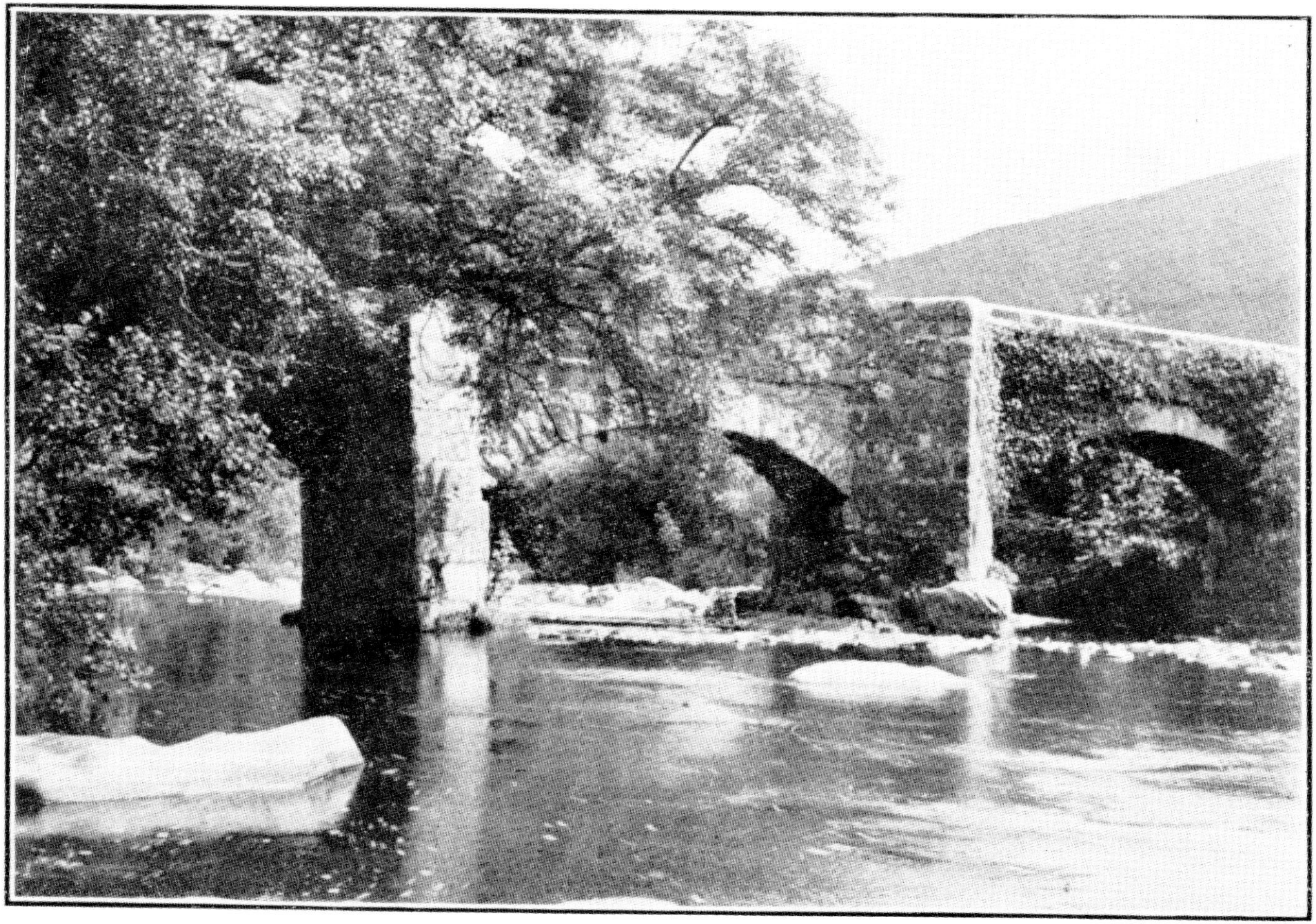

SEE PAGE 64.

Fingle Bridge.

PHOTO BY C. R. ROWE.

"An old bridge in the depths of a valley."

VII.

FINGLE BRIDGE.

A Romantic Valley——Nature's Gift——Ancient Hill Forts——An Old Bridge ——Packhorse Tracks——Prestonbury——Cranbrook Castle.

Nature, clad in Beauty's garb,
Fair and wonderful to see,
Speaks with no uncertain sound
Of its Maker's majesty.
—Richard Burrow.

A DEEP valley, one side covered with copse alternating with stretches of heather, the other a bare scarp with jutting crags. Further down, trees on either side, and then more heather clothing a hill rising precipitously for several hundred feet. Running through the valley a clear stream, spanned near the foot of the bold hill by a grey old structure of three arches, bearing a name that will sound familiar to the readers of Ossian, though far removed from the scenes his heroes knew. This is Fingle Bridge, happily placed in the midst of some of the most romantic scenery in Devon, and the river is the Teign, which on leaving the steeps of Gidleigh and, as Risdon would say, saluting Chagford, enters this valley to add another to its many charms. Somewhat removed from Dartmoor is the valley, much enclosed land lying between it and the commons bordering upon the Forest. But geologically it belongs to the great waste, being on the edge of the granite region, and therefore forms part of the diadem that Devon so proudly wears.

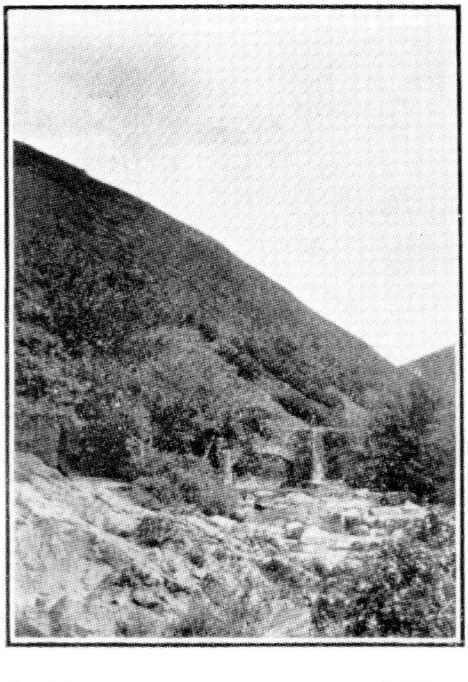

Photo by] [C. R. Rowe.

Prestonbury.

"Towering high above us, its foot almost planted in the stream."—*(See Page 62.)*

Nowhere in the Westcountry has Nature been more lavish in her gifts than in this part of the Teign valley, for the rambler who takes the river for his guide and makes his way downward from the little market town of Chagford, will find that even when several miles separate him from his starting point he is still surrounded by the beautiful, and has not once lost it from the time of his setting forth. The gorge of the Teign extends from Whiddon

Park to Clifford Bridge, a distance of about four miles, and throughout there is that which cannot fail to charm the wanderer.

Between the folding hills the course of the river is an ever-curving one, and at each bend new scenes of loveliness present themselves. And in the green depths of this great rift that the Teign has made the sounds fittingly accord with the sights, for the ear is charmed with the songs of birds, the music of the running waters, and the soft whisperings of the wind among the trees. It is impossible to look upon scenes like this without a feeling of deep gratitude to the Creator for having placed us in so beautiful a world.

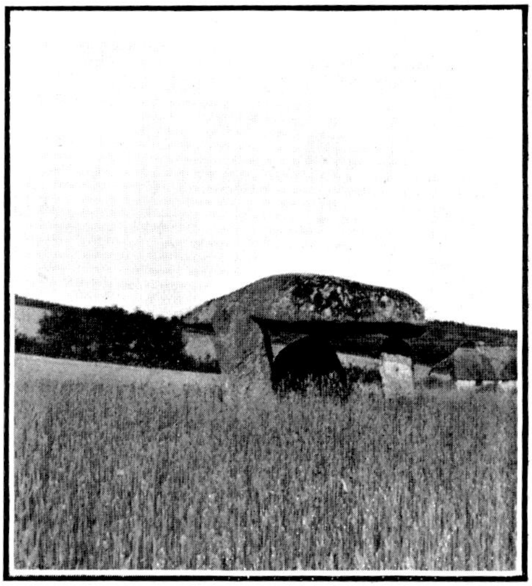

Photo by] [C. R. Rowe.

Drewsteignton Dolmen.

"A good example of these megalithic structures."

(See Page 63.)

It has been thought that this long, deep valley, which forms a pass into the hill country, was perhaps the scene of the final conflicts between the Britons and the Romans who were seeking to penetrate into the West. However this may be, it is certain that at some distant period men found good reason for fortifying it, for the remains of their entrenchments may still be seen. One of these ancient camps crowns the precipitous hill to which we have alluded. Its name is Prestonbury, and if we stand on Fingle Bridge we see it towering high above us, its foot almost planted in the stream. Another, further down the river, and on the southern side of the valley, is known as Wooston Castle; and a third, also on that side, is on the down towards which the road leads, through the wood, from the bridge. This is Cranbrook Castle, and after we have lingered awhile by the stream we will climb the hill and mount its mossy rampart.

The first time I ever looked upon Fingle Gorge was on a warm summer morning, when the whole valley was bathed in golden light. Since then I have seen it under other skies, but never did it lack beauty. The seasons may change, and the trees cast off in succession their bright green garb and their mellow-tinted autumn dress, but the gorge of Fingle has yet its charm. The ferns may be crisp and sere, and the heather have lost its purple, but the scene is not less impressive. The hand of winter takes nothing from the great masses of rock that rise in majesty from the steep sides of the valley, and the happy river does not cease its song because clouds obscure the sky.

The road that crosses the Teign at Fingle Bridge forms a means of communication between the northern part of the parish of Moretonhampstead and Drewsteignton. Made in the days of packhorses, the approach to the river from the south is hardly adapted for wheels, but on the Drewsteignton side the bridge may be conveniently reached. That there was very early a passage on the Teign at this point is certain. One of the old tracks leading towards it runs near Lynscott, a farm about a mile and a half distant, and here an object that may well be supposed to have marked its direction was discovered a few years ago. This was a mutilated granite cross, which with thoughtful care has been erected on a suitable spot near where it was found. A stone bearing an incised cross is also to be seen on the side of the hill westward of the bridge.

Clarendon has given it as his opinion that but for the death of Sydney Godolphin having taken place there Chagford would never have received a mention. But Clarendon was unacquainted with what Chagford had to offer, while we who know this do not wonder that the name of the little town is not only often heard, but is linked in the memory of those who have visited it with some of the most beautiful scenes in Devon. If it had been said of the neighbouring village of Drewsteignton that but for the existence in its vicinity of the dolmen, or cromlech, known as the Spinsters' Rock, the place would probably never have gained its present celebrity, there might have been some truth in the remark. Not that the village is without its attractions. Indeed, the contrary is the case; but that it is chiefly visited by those desirous of seeing the fine stone monument in the parish there is little doubt. This village may be reached from Fingle Bridge by ascending the hill northward with Prestonbury on the right, and turning to the left where the road branches. The Spinsters' Rock stands on Shilstone Farm, about two miles west of the village. It consists of three supporters, and a quoit, and though striking in appearance, is rendered less so than would have been the case were its surroundings of a different character. From an antiquarian point of view, however, it is well worthy a visit, as it is certainly a good example of these megalithic structures. Some years ago it fell, but fortunately there were those in the neighbourhood with sufficient reverence for antiquities to effect its speedy restoration.

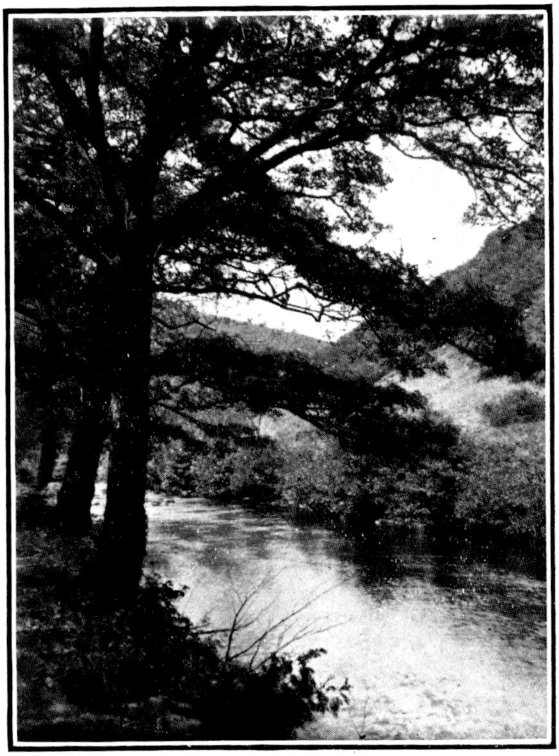

Photo by] [C. R. Rowe.

The path by the river.

"A placid reach over which trees fling their long arms."

It is above Fingle Bridge that the valley exhibits its wildest aspect; below it the scenery is of a softer character. The hills become more thickly wooded, and as the rambler makes his way down there is less to remind him of the Moor. A path on the right bank of the Teign will enable him to descend the gorge from Fingle Bridge with ease, and at each step he will meet with that which will delight and interest him. Sometimes the river is hidden from sight, the narrow way passing through thick undergrowth; at others the path is carried along its brink; here its voice is heard, as though it were chiding the boulders that rise up in its way; further on it is silent, and the rambler looks upon a placid reach over which trees fling their long arms, and where the bushes that bend to kiss it are reflected in its depths. By-and-bye the wanderer through these tranquil shades will reach Clifford Bridge, and if Moretonhampstead has been his starting-point he may return thither by the road running over Mardon Down, from which elevated piece of common he will obtain extensive views of the Dartmoor borderland.

And now we will leave the depths of the valley and pass up the steep acclivity, clothed with trees, to Cranbrook Castle. Our road climbs it by a series of zigzags, and at the angles glimpses of the gorge are obtained. From one of these we are rewarded by something more than this, for a truly beautiful view there unfolds itself. It is a picture of wooded steeps, with crags beyond, and still further away smiling pasture lands, with the hill of Cosdon rising against the sky. Ere we reach the top of the ascent we turn once more, for the bold hill of Prestonbury, up whose precipitous slope we looked from the bridge, is now below us. Its adaptability to the purpose to which it was put is here very apparent, for it is seen to entirely command the deep pass. The entrenchments on its summit are said to cover an area of about twenty-five acres, and consist of a large rectangular enclosure and numerous outworks. Though always imposing, when the heather with which its sides are covered is in bloom Prestonbury is a glorious sight.

Passing upward, we leave the copse and find ourselves on Uppacott Down, on the highest part of which, at an elevation of eleven hundred feet, is Cranbrook Castle. This hill-fort covers a space of about seven acres in extent. It is defended by a rampart having a double ditch on the south and a single one on the west side, and may be regarded as an excellent example of early castrametation. Conspicuous in the extensive view commanded from this ancient fort is the great mass of Dartmoor, the whole of its eastern frontier from Cosdon to Hey Tor being in sight. There we note more than one tor or hill near to which we know some scene of loveliness is hidden, and when we find ourselves in their midst we shall in like manner be able to look across to Cranbrook, and it will serve to remind us of an old bridge in the depths of a valley through which flows a beautiful river ever singing its song.

GGS-E

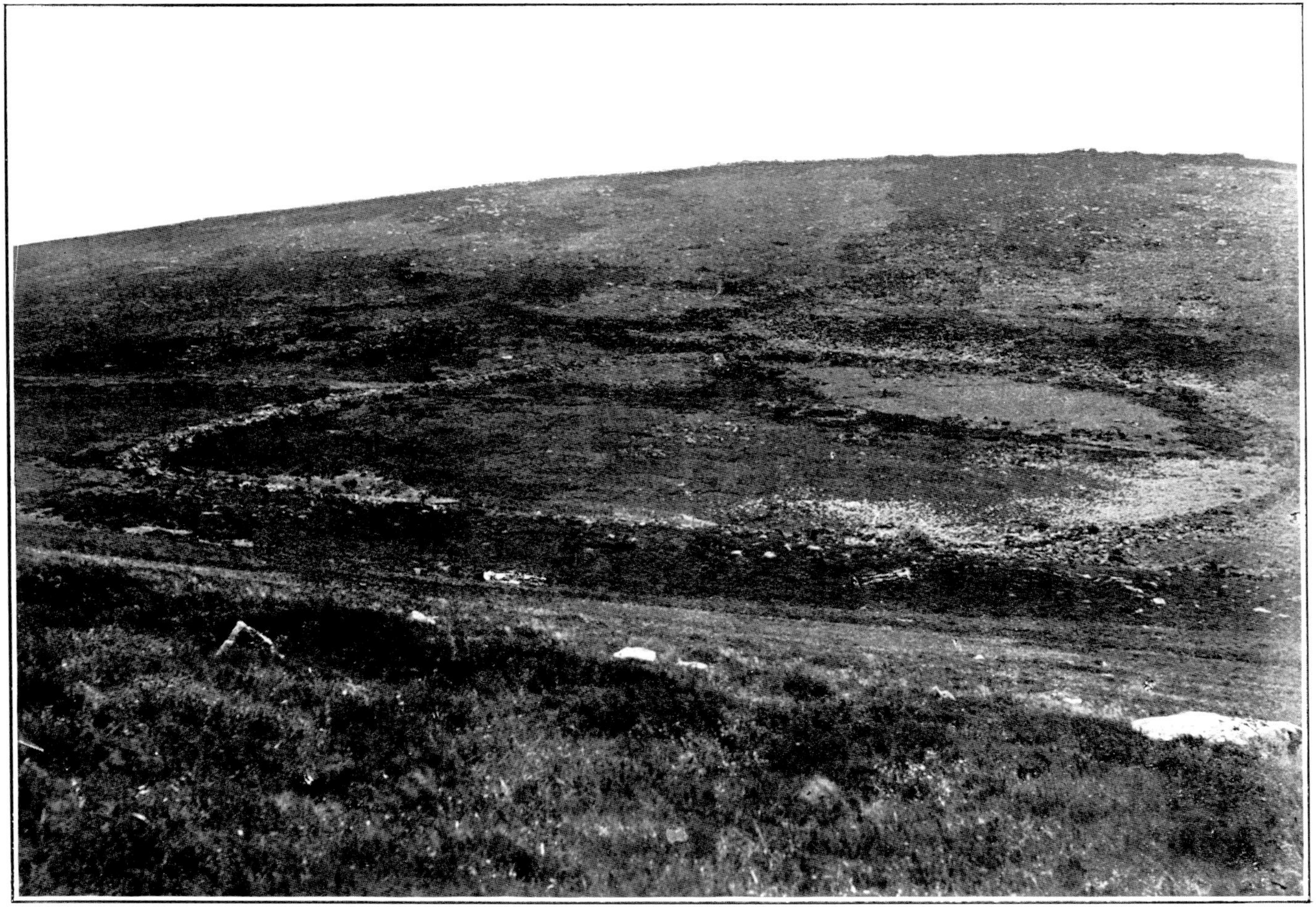

SEE PAGE 68.

Grim's Pound.

PHOTO BY C. R. ROWE.

"A ruin belonging to a long past age."

VIII.

GRIM'S POUND.

Hameldon——Theories Concerning Grim's Pound——A Massive Wall——Entrance to the Pound——Ruined Huts——Their Internal Arrangement——Grim, the Viking——Grim's Pound in Ancient Days.

> Hallowed by that instinct which reveres
> Things fraught with characters of elder years.
>
> —Felicia Hemans.

On the eastern side of Dartmoor is a lofty tract of land, over four miles long and a mile or more wide, and running north and south. It extends from Dunstone Down on the south to Shapley Common on the north, the central, and greater, portion of it being known as Hameldon. From most parts of the Moorland district it forms a conspicuous feature in the view, and from around Princetown is seen throughout its whole length, rising as a huge ridge on the further side of the Forest. About one mile from its northern extremity the forces of Nature have rent open the western side of this great hill, and formed a wide combe, or hollow, above which rocks have thrust themselves, the pile to the south being named Hameldon Tor and that to the north Hookney Tor. In this hollow, in a fairly sheltered position on a gentle slope, is the ruined wall of an ancient enclosure, similar to those found in many parts of the Moor, and which is known by the name of Grim's Pound.

We remember seeing in the summer of 1874 several men engaged in cutting a road on Shapley Common, and on inquiring learnt that it was being made to connect the Princetown highway with the road in the valley below Challacombe, and thus provide a more direct means of communication than then existed between Grendon and Cator and other places in their neighbourhood and the town of Moretonhampstead. This road was carried across the lower end of the wide combe in the huge hill to which we have referred, and within a quarter of a mile of the ancient enclosure. For the greater part of the year it is used only for local traffic, which, of course, is very trifling, but in the summer excursion coaches and other conveyances of a like character pass over it. It is probable that during the comparatively few years this road has been opened more persons have seen Grim's Pound than ever looked upon it throughout the previous centuries of its existence.

There is probably no single object of antiquarian interest on Dartmoor concerning which so many theories have been advanced as about this ruined enclosure between Hameldon and Hookney Tors. According to the various views of archæologists it has been a temple of the sun; a seat of judicature: a gigantic tin store; a cattle fold; a place of retreat from an enemy; and the fortified settlement of men of the Neolithic age. That it was ever a temple, or a place where laws were framed or justice dispensed, could only have been imagined at a time when all stone remains were associated with dark and mysterious rites, or with curious ceremonies. But that it has served as the shelter of the tin-seeker, as the herdsman's protection from beasts of prey, and as a stronghold there can be little doubt. As to its belonging to the Neolithic age, we shall be quite safe in believing not only that Grim's Pound was erected at such a period, but all the other hut settlements on Dartmoor also, if we do not make the mistake of imagining that by that term a definite age in the world's history is meant, and forget that it is simply a stage in the history of a race or tribe. There is no necessity for thinking that flint knives could only have been used at a period exceedingly remote.

But it is no part of our present plan to discuss the various theories respecting the use or age of this ancient enclosure. There is nothing to lead us to suppose that the purpose it served differed from that of other walled hut clusters on the Moor, and which it is not difficult to see. The rampart would act not only as a protection to the men, but also to their cattle from wolves or other wild animals at night. We call these enclosures pounds, and such in a measure they were, though we can readily understand that when building their wall the settlers had in view the possibility of an attack by an enemy. Forays were not known only in the Middle Ages or the days of Rob Roy.

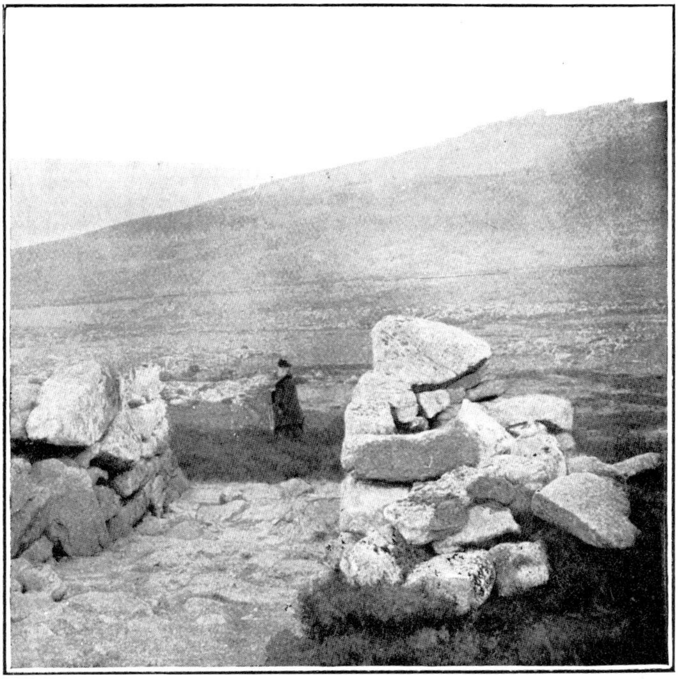

Photo by] [Mrs. Ernest Croft.

Entrance to the Pound.

"The wall at this point is composed of enormous blocks of stone."—*(See Page 69.)*

The earlier antiquaries knew of no other enclosures on the Moor similar to Grim's Pound, and so they held it up as a wonder. Had they taken the trouble to explore the great waste they would have found a good many "temples," and, if so disposed, might have assigned one to each of the heathen deities. In the valleys of the Dart, the Avon, the Erme, or the Yealm excellent examples of these circular enclosures would have been met with. But we do not intend to follow in the footsteps either of the antiquaries of a hundred years ago, or of those of more recent times. We are viewing Grim's Pound as a ruin belonging to a long past age, and as such it cannot fail to possess an interest. It is precious as an old-time relic, and the softening influence of the centuries that have passed since the day the first breach was made in its wall have lent it, if not a beauty that appeals to the eye, one that does not speak in vain to the imagination. And thus it may well be reckoned among the gems that add a value to the Moor. As such we shall look upon it, without permitting ourselves to enter into antiquarian speculations, a course which will be quite as useful as endeavouring to persuade ourselves that we can read its true history.

Grim's Pound, like most of the ancient enclosures on the Moor, is roughly circular in shape, and covers an area of about four acres. It has been said to be the largest of its kind to be seen there; but this is a mistake, though it is certainly the finest example of a protected hut settlement that Dartmoor can boast, the remains of its wall showing that this was of greater width than is usual in these erections, while the stones that composed it are more massive. The latter, however, is probably as much the result of accident as design; the chosen site being plentifully strewn with large blocks, they were, of course, made use of. The wall of this enclosure, which measures over five hundred yards in circumference, is now nothing more than a huge ring of stones, which at first sight appear as though they had been thrown confusedly together. But on a closer inspection it will be seen that they were originally laid in courses, a plan that was probably adopted by the builders of the other pounds on the Moor, but of which traces only remain in those where the stones are of large size. There can be no doubt that the wall in most of these enclosures was double, the space between having been filled with earth; they were, in fact, like immense hedges, eight to ten feet in width, and faced with stone. In some cases the walls of the small circular huts found in every part of the Moor are formed in a manner precisely similar.

When mining was in such a flourishing condition in the neighbourhood as to warrant a house of entertainment being established within half a mile of Grim's Pound, there was much passing over a path that led through the wide combe to Heytree Down, whence roads branch to North Bovey and Manaton. When this first came into use the ancient enclosure was found to block the way, and as there were people in those days who possessed no more veneration for the stone remains of a bygone age than, unfortunately, many do at present, breaches were made in the wall, and the path was taken straight through it. These breaches, especially that on the lower, or western, side of the enclosure, have been supposed by some to be the original entrances. But there was apparently only one, and that was situated on the south-east side. It is shown to be on that side on a plan by Mr. A. C. Shillibeer, who made a survey of Grim's Pound, in 1829, under the superintendence of the Rev. J. H. Mason, at that time vicar of Widecombe. The entrance was then blocked by the stones that had fallen from time to time from the wall on either side, and in that state it remained until a few years ago, when it was cleared. It is only right, however, that the visitor should be informed that this opening has been restored. Were this omitted he might be led to wonder how any antiquary could possibly have placed the entrance anywhere else than where it is now seen.

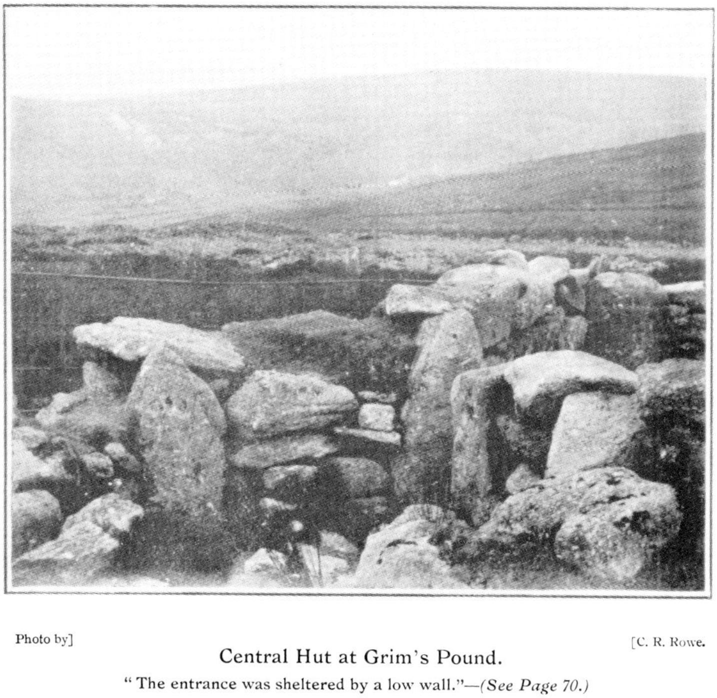

Photo by] [C. R. Rowe.

Central Hut at Grim's Pound.

" The entrance was sheltered by a low wall."—*(See Page 70.)*

The wall at this point is composed of enormous blocks of stone, and though not so throughout, is here over ten feet thick. The entrance is seven feet wide, and there are three steps to descend into the Pound, the ground here being higher without than within. Though now not exceeding four or five feet at its highest part, the wall when in a complete state was probably more than twice that height. With regard to its thickness, a condition of things the reverse of this exists. The fallen blocks have scattered themselves over a much wider space than was originally occupied by the wall, as can be seen where the lower courses remain. Many of these blocks are four and five feet long, and some are as much as eight and nine feet.

There are the ruins of twenty-four huts in Grim's Pound, of the usual circular shape, and investigations conducted here a few years ago showed the internal arrangement of these. When the earth was cleared from them some were found to have a portion of the floor raised in the manner of a dais, which was probably the couch or bed-place. Cooking-holes and cooking-stones were also found in them, as well as a flat stone level with the floor, which might have been used for splitting bones upon. These valuable investigations have been continued in different parts of the Moor, and have resulted in the discovery of many other huts exhibiting the same arrangement. The wall of one of these huts has been restored, and the height of the door jambs show that to enter it would be necessary, not exactly to creep, but to stoop very low. The entrance was sheltered by a low wall forming a kind of passage, a contrivance seen in other examples of these primitive dwellings. The hut is now enclosed within iron hurdles in order that it may not suffer damage from cattle.

A little stream bearing the name of Grim's Lake rises above the enclosure towards the north-east, and, passing under the wall, runs for a short distance just within it. The brook, however, sometimes dries up in the summer, and it is probable that the branch of the Webburn in the valley below was the source upon which the people who dwelt in this settlement depended for their water supply.

The speculations of the earlier antiquaries as to the use of Grim's Pound were made without an acquaintance with the other walled hut clusters on Dartmoor. When these are examined it will be seen that Grim's Pound differs from them chiefly in having a more massive wall, though even in that particular there are pounds that approach it very closely, notably one on the Avon and another on the Erme. The arrangements internally are for the most part the same, though there are some in which no hut circles exist. These walled clusters, which may be counted by the dozen, as well as others not enclosed, are not only found in close proximity to ancient tin stream works, but, what is more important, comprise a greater number of huts where the workings are extensive. This to my mind points to a connection between them, and I have seen nothing in recent discoveries to cause me to alter my opinion formed many years ago. There is no necessity for supposing that because a people had found that a certain ore they were able to obtain was in requisition by others, and therefore of value to themselves as an article they could barter, that they understood its preparation and use. And besides, old customs survive in the midst of progress; one tribe uses an iron hatchet, while another is content with one of flint.

In many of these walled hut settlements the ruins of the circular dwellings are found not only within the enclosure, but also outside it, in some instances being quite close to the stone rampart. This is not the case at Grim's Pound, but there are at the same time a number of hut circles in its vicinity without any protecting wall. It is necessary that this should not be lost sight of by the antiquarian visitor who may seek to draw conclusions as to the purpose of the pound. And in addition to ruined dwellings other remains exist near by. Close to the tor on Hookney Down there is a barrow, and another will be found at King Tor, not far off; this latter on being opened some years ago was found to contain a kistvaen. Further north, on Shapley Common, are a number of hut circles, some of them being built of massive blocks of granite and forming excellent examples. Numerous barrows are to be seen on the lofty Hameldon, and rather over three-quarters of a mile distant, in a south-easterly direction, is a circular enclosure known as Berry Pound. This lies on the further side of the hill, and though its rampart is low and altogether different in character from that of its more celebrated neighbour, it is not without interest. These remains, which are all within a radius of about a mile of Grim's Pound, may be reached without difficulty.

But what will probably excite the curiosity of the visitor more than the barrows and hut circles is the stone row on Challacombe Down, a part of which is visible from the combe. There the stones are seen standing up sharply against the sky on the top of the ridge to the west. This row, which consists of three well-defined lines, was first noticed by Mr. John Prideaux, in 1828. Recent investigations have led to the belief that this monument originally consisted of eight parallel rows, but the remains of the supposed five are so scanty as to render this doubtful. The length of the row is about one hundred and seventy yards, its direction being approximately north and south. The visitor will probably consider that it has lost its most attractive feature when he learns that the stones comprising this row were until a few years ago lying prone upon the heath. But it is none the less a matter for congratulation that the monument has been re-erected. While it is certain that we cannot look upon it with that degree of interest usually awakened by the contemplation of an object which has come down to us untouched from early times, we still feel that we would rather see these old grey stones erect than that they should lie upon the turf, where the encroaching vegetation might in time obliterate them.

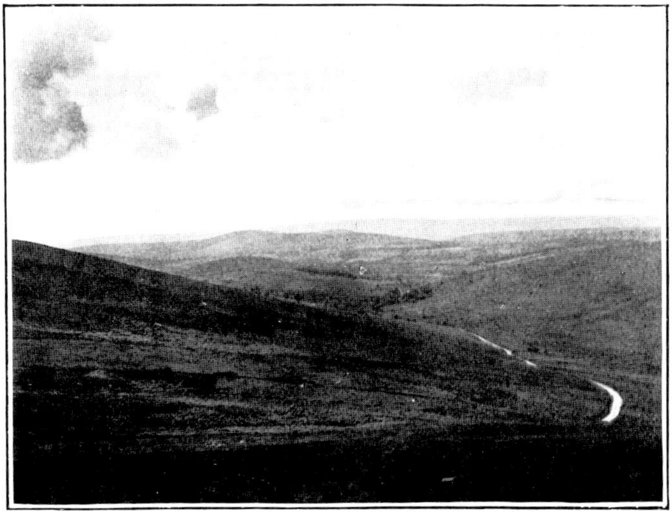

Photo by] [C. R. Rowe.

View from the hillside near Grim's Pound.

"The valley through which the road runs towards Challacombe."

Concerning the derivation of the name of the interesting enclosure we have been noticing we offer no remarks here. Several suggestions have been made, but there seems to be only one that is worth remembering. And that not on account of its probability, but because it is interesting and fanciful. The late Mr. C. Spence Bate contended for a Scandinavian occupation of the Dart valleys, and supposed the founder of this settlement to be a viking named Grim. In the southern part of the Forest is an object which in the year 1240 bore the name of Grymsgrove, which Mr. Bate considered he could identify with a kistvaen near the head-waters of a feeder of the Plym. This he regarded as the grave of Grim; and suggested that it might be the burial-place of the warrior who built the fortified settlement below Hameldon Tor.

A good general view of the Pound is to be obtained either from the slope below Hookney Tor, or from the brow of the hill on the Hameldon side. From the former the visitor may also look down the valley through which the road runs towards Challacombe, upon that part of the Moor in which the cultivator seems to have wrestled with the waste with more than ordinary success. Bare hills surround his enclosures, and beyond these is the high land of Southern Dartmoor.

And now let us, in imagination, look upon Grim's Pound as it was in the days when there were dwellers in its huts, and ruin had not laid its hand upon its rampart. It is evening, and the autumn sun has gone down behind the hill across the narrow valley, but a soft light yet lingers in the sky. The great wall, the lower part of stone and the upper of turf, encircles a cluster of low, round cabins, the sides of which rise only a few feet above the ground. The roofs are of rushes laid upon poles, the ends of which are seen at the point where they converge, and where an opening takes the place of a chimney. Through the open doorway of more than one is seen a dull, red glow, that speaks of the preparation of the evening meal within. The ground in the enclosure is muddy, and in places the trampling of cattle has converted it into a quagmire. Into some of the huts, set apart for the purpose, cows which have just yielded their milk are sheltering, and maidens are bearing away their well-filled earthen jars. Near the entrance to the enclosure two or three young men, rudely dressed in the skins of beasts, are leaning idly against the wall, watching a group of children gambolling with a young hound.

Presently the sound of voices is heard without. It is Alcan and his comrades returning from the stream, and bearing with them a basket of openwork covered with hide, and partly filled with tin ore. As they enter the enclosure Blaenor comes from the further side, where the cows have been secured. The men stop and show him what they have brought, but he scarcely heeds them, and they bear it to a hut where the fruit of their labour is stored. Blaenor, as he turns from them, gazes anxiously towards the southern hill.

The shadows deepen, and the roseate tinge in the western sky grows fainter, and gradually gives place to a dull grey. The wind comes moaning up the valley, and the partly-withered ferns amid the rocks shake their brown fronds with a rustling sound as it passes. Still Blaenor stands by the entrance looking towards the rocky steep.

Dinerth, a white-bearded patriarch, comes from his hut, and, like Blaenor, bends his gaze towards the south. Where are the beasts that have been pastured all day upon the hill? It is long past the hour at which they should have been brought back to the fold. Where is Bugail, the herdsman? Can any ill have befallen him or the beasts? Suddenly a trampling is heard, and scarcely have Blaenor and the youths moved from the entrance when a herd of cattle rush through the opening, and spread themselves over the enclosure. A few moments after Bugail follows with two immense dogs.

Why has he stayed so late upon the heath? He points to the flanks of one of the beasts, which is torn and bleeding, and he shows, too, the blood upon the fangs of his dogs. A wolf has been disappointed in his meal, that is all, and the dogs have had their revenge for his attack upon the animal it was their duty to guard.

The entrance is secured, and a little later the men are all within their dwellings. The Moor is dark, but when the night wind now and again blows aside one of the curtains of deer skin that hang across the entrance of the huts a bright gleam shoots forth and reveals the red cattle lying around them. In an instant all is again in darkness, and but for the distant howl of a wolf no sound breaks the silence of the night.

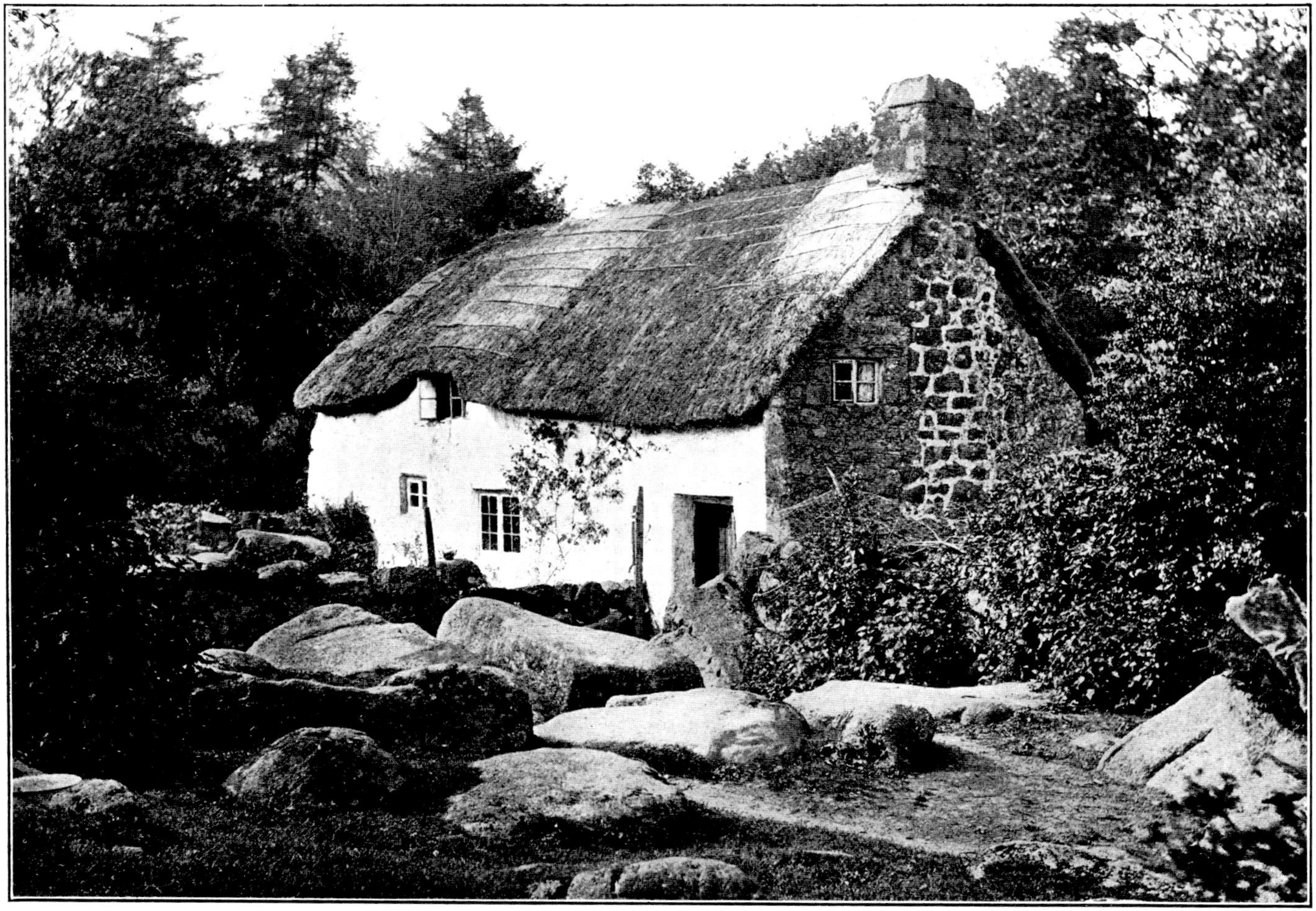

SEE PAGE 78.

Little Silver.

PHOTO BY ERNEST CROFT.

"Close by is the thatched cottage called Little Silver."

IX.

LUSTLEIGH CLEAVE.

A Border Parish——Lustleigh Church——The Parson's Loaf——Boveycombe Cliff——A Range of Crags——An Ancient Camp——Little Silver——Manaton——The Bovey River.

In haste, rapture-smitten,
  I climb the steep tor
Where the camp of the Briton
  Looks over the Moor.
Like the sea in its trouble
  The granite hills rave,
Each hillock a bubble,
  Each mountain a wave.
—A. H. A. Hamilton.

THE River Bovey, which rises near the eastern boundary line of Dartmoor Forest, not far from the Warren House Inn, on the Princetown and Moretonhampstead road, is described by Risdon as "a pretty brook," and he also tells us in his quaint way that it "intermixeth its waters with Teign, and in its course communicateth its name to some townlets." The first of these "townlets" by which it flows is North Bovey, as picturesque a village as one would desire to see, with its grove of oaks ornamenting the spacious green, its ancient cross, and primitive air. Another is Bovey Tracey, some half-dozen miles further down the stream, which the visitor will doubtless consider more deserving of Risdon's epithet. Between these two places the river runs for some distance through a deep valley, in which, and in its surroundings, there is so much that is romantic, so much that is beautiful, that he who seeks its recesses, or climbs its steep sides, cannot but feel that its praises have been all too faintly sung. This is Lustleigh Cleave, fair home of the fern, of the hawthorn, the foxglove, and the oak, where the stream foams among lichen-stained boulders, and grey crags rise from grassy slopes.

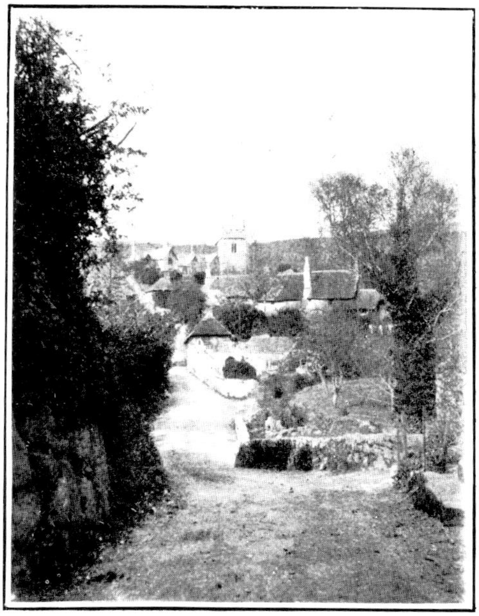

Photo by] Lustleigh. [A. Edmund Spender.
"The village is situated in the Valley of the Wray."—(See Page 76.)

Lustleigh, though forming one of the Dartmoor parishes, and being well within the boundary of the granite region, is yet at a considerable distance from the Forest. Between it and that ancient hunting-ground are parts of other parishes, so that within its limits are no great stretches of heath, no solitary tracts where signs of man's presence are wanting. Lustleigh is, indeed, on the outer fringe of the borderland, and the work of the husbandman is abundantly evident. But it has not spread itself everywhere, and there is much that remains unsubdued. The wildness inseparable from the scenery of a granite district is charmingly mingled with the efforts of the cultivator. Wooded slopes are in pleasing contrast with bare hills; the rugged goes hand in hand with that which is softer, but neither seem out of place. And it is this blending of rock and heath, of wood and field, that gives to the borders of the Moor their great attraction. For desolation the morasses of the interior must be sought; for sternness, the rocky valleys nearer the confines; but beauty, except in a few favoured spots, must be looked for only in the broad circlet where man has wrestled with Nature.

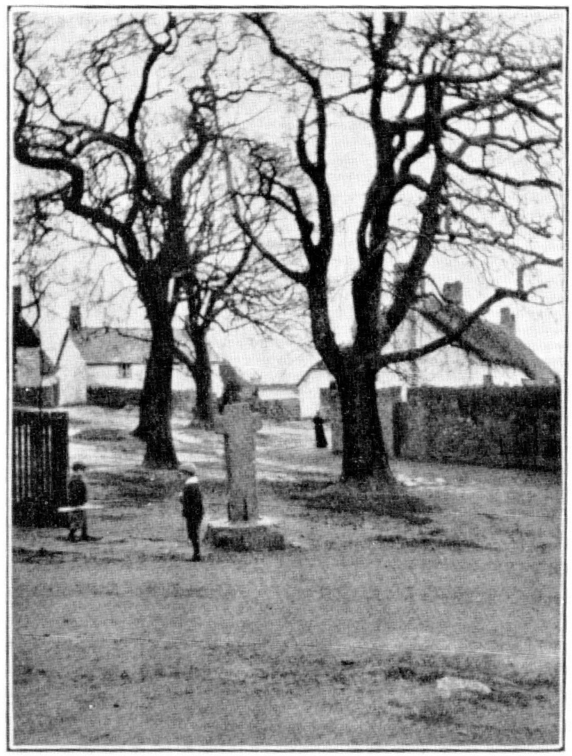

Photo by] [A. Edmund Spender.

North Bovey.

"As picturesque a village as one would desire to see."—*(See Page 75.)*

The village of Lustleigh is situated in the valley of the Wray, a small tributary of the Bovey, which rises not far from Moretonhampstead. It is through this valley that the branch railway from Newton Abbot to the latter place runs, entering it shortly before Lustleigh Station is reached. While it is of course in its surroundings that the charm of Lustleigh lies, there is much in the village that is pleasing. One or two objects are of special interest. Not far from the station is the Bishop's Stone, in all probability the base of a cross, and said to bear the arms of Bishop Grandisson. Some traces of carving may be observed on one of its sides. In the south porch of the church is an ancient inscribed stone, and this, or the former, has been thought to be the object referred to in a document setting forth some early boundaries as the Writelan Stone.* The visitor interested in ecclesiastical architecture will find in Lustleigh Church specimens of four different orders, there being a Norman font, some Early English work in the chancel, a Decorated transept, and a Perpendicular nave. A tomb on which are the effigies of a knight and a lady was supposed early in the seventeenth century to be that of the Dinham family, and there is also an effigy of Sir William Prouz, who at one time possessed the manor. Another monument, but one which Nature erected, is also to be seen not afar from this secluded village. This is the Map Stone, or Parson's Brown Loaf, situated, appropriately enough, near the rectory. How it came to bear an appellation

* *Ancient Stone Crosses of Dartmoor and its Borderland*, Chap. XV.

so suggestive of the giving of a stone in the place of bread we are unable to say. Perhaps it might have been regarded as typical of the kind of loaves supplied to the parsons of Lustleigh in the good old times. If so, they had nothing to complain of as far as their size was concerned, though they might certainly have grumbled at their hardness.

Lustleigh Cleave is less than a mile distant from the village, and may be conveniently reached by a path that leads to the top of the ridge forming its eastern side. As the visitor makes his way up the steep track the crags occasionally show themselves, and when, by-and-bye, they come into full view, he has gained the crest of the hill, and an extensive prospect, bounded by the sombre heights of the Moor, lies before him. Having reached this elevated spot, he will have no difficulty in finding some point of vantage from which to look down upon the cleave and view its principal features.

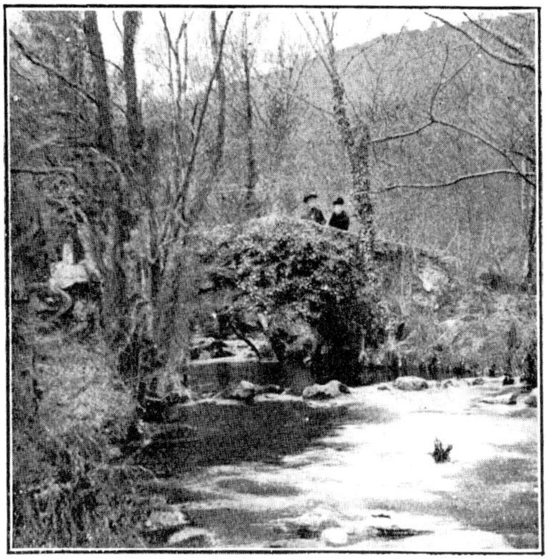

Photo by] [Ernest Croft.

The Bovey.

"Screened by the leafy woods."—*(See Page 78.)*

What is now usually regarded as Lustleigh Cleave is a narrow valley, rather less than two miles in length, through which the Bovey flows in a south-easterly direction. On the side nearest the village is a hill clothed with grass and ferns, on its summit being a range of crags, while others, in places, spring from midway up its slope. It forms a bold ridge, rising over four hundred feet above the stream, and is seen from any prominent position on the eastern escarpment of the Moor. It boasts no sylvan adornment like the opposite side of the valley, which is all luxuriance; its covering is a humbler one, yet since this is decorated with the graceful fern, it lacks not beauty.

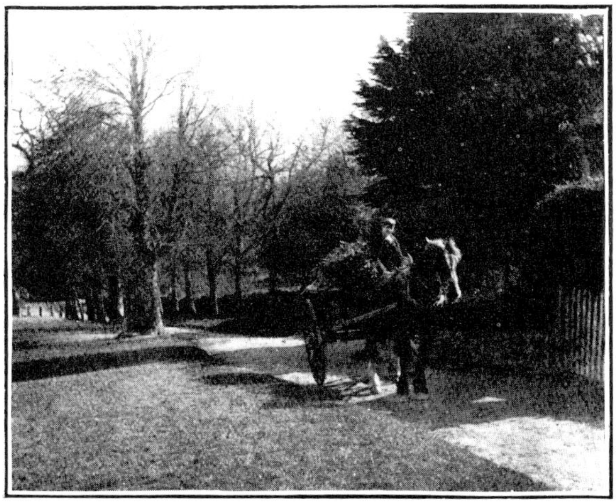

Photo by] [A. Edmund Spender.

Manaton Green.

"There is no village on the Dartmoor borders that has a more pleasing appearance."—*(See Page 79.)*

With reference to the word cleave, though often applied to a valley it would seem in the present instance to be a corruption of cliff, and not of cleft, for in title deeds in the possession of Mr. A. R. Hunt, of Torquay, this craggy hill is described as Boveycombe Cliff and Bortor Down.* The older name of the valley thus appears to have been Bovey Combe, but as such is seldom or never heard at present, we have adhered to the one by which it is popularly known.

* Cleave; cliff or cleft? *Vide* Chaps. V., XXIV.

Among the rock-piles on this ridge three are regarded as tors, and are named as such. The one nearest its south-eastern end is Sharp Tor—of course, changed in the Devon vernacular to Sharpiter—close to which is a logan known as the Nutcrackers; that near its centre, and within a short distance of Foxworthy, is called Ravens' Tor; and the one at the northern end of the hill is Hunters' Tor. Other piles have also fanciful names attached to them, one being known as Harton Chest, and another as The Foxes' Yard. A rock near the river, and not far from Foxworthy Mill, bears a name which should render it a fit companion to the Parson's Loaf. It is the Round of Beef, the very sound of which is calculated to arouse anticipations of the most pleasing kind in the mind of the visitor who has been wandering all day on the Moor.

The view from this hill is more extensive than that commanded from across the valley, but we are not inclined to think it quite so fine. But the picture is, nevertheless, one such as is seldom met with, and cannot fail to impress. There is a wealth of green field and wood, of beetling crags and dusky hills; a pleasing combination upon which the eye delights to look.

The remains of an ancient camp on this ridge may possibly point to the same period as do those overlooking the gorge of the Teign, and form one in the great chain of forts considered to have been thrown up by the men of the West to check the advance of the invading Roman. It is situated near the northern end of the hill, and not far from Hunters' Tor, and within it a clump of fir trees is now growing. In those turbulent times the quiet valley below may have been rudely disturbed, and the sounds that now delight the ear have perhaps been drowned by the din of battle. But we shall probably prefer to remember it as it now is, rather than let imagination paint a picture of those dim old years, in which strife should take the place of the peace that is now reigning there.

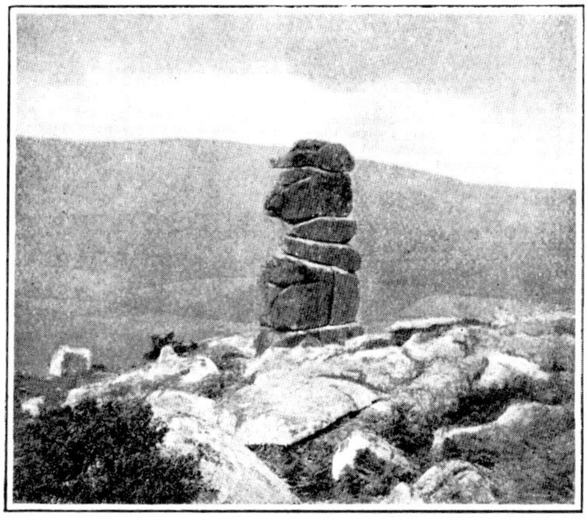

Photo by] [Ernest Croft.

Hayne Down.

"Is the curious rock known as Bowerman's Nose."— (*See Page 79.*)

Looking across the valley the tower of Manaton Church is seen, and towards this we shall make our way by a green path that trends along the side of the hill and gradually descends to its foot. Here the bracken is tall, reaching in places almost to our waist, and stretches away to the left like a gently ruffled sea. The further bank of the river is clothed with trees, and these extending up the valley seem at its higher end to block the way.

We reach the woods through which our path will lead us by Foxworthy Farm to an old clapper thrown over the stream, whence a steep path climbs the hill to Manaton. Close by is the thatched cottage called Little Silver, picturesquely placed in what will be readily agreed, by those whose topographical knowledge will enable them to judge, to be one of the most delightful nooks in Devon. The Bovey, screened by the leafy woods, flows by with a soft murmuring sound that falls upon the ear like a soothing lullaby, its sparkling waters kissed by the ferns that bend over its bank. The charming effect of the varying light and shade, when summer clouds float like veils of gauze across the sky, the glimpses of the thickly-wooded steep on the Manaton side of the vale, the little cottage round which the trees lovingly press and where the rocks have scattered themselves as though to protect, and the pleasing accompaniment of the singing of birds which find a home in this secluded spot, will not soon be forgotten. It is a dream of sunshine and sweet music.

The wooded side of the valley of Lustleigh Cleave is in the parish of Manaton, which may thus claim to share in the renown it has brought to this part of Devon. The village of Manaton, like that of North Bovey, possesses its green, but, unlike the latter, it can boast no ancient grove upon it. But there is no village on the Dartmoor borders that has a more pleasing appearance than Manaton. The green, which is of considerable extent, is level and carefully kept. Close to the church is the ancient church-house, and on the opposite side is the entrance to the vicarage. One feature that North Bovey possesses is absent from Manaton. It has no village cross. A former vicar removed it in order to prevent the continuance of superstitious practices. We can commend him for his determination to suppress these, but it is unfortunate that he was unable to do so without destroying an interesting object of antiquity.

Manaton Tor is close to the village; and on Hayne Down, which is also not far distant, is the curious rock known as Bowerman's Nose. Hey Tor and Hameldon, and a number of other noteworthy hills, are also within easy reach; in fact, the explorer of the eastern borderland of Dartmoor could not have a better centre than this romantically-situated village.

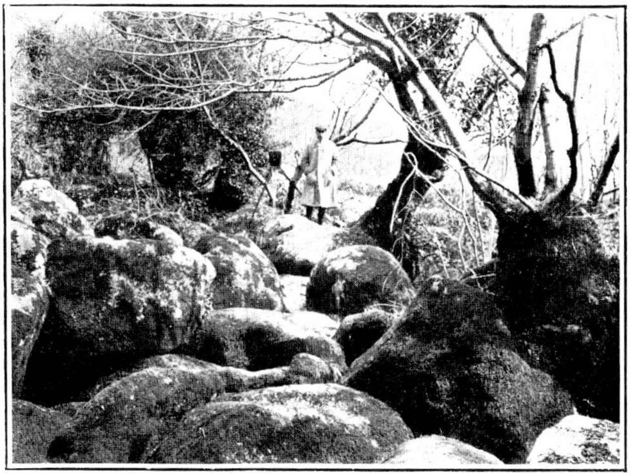

Photo by] [Mrs. Ernest Croft.

Horsham Steps.

"Boulders . . . entirely hide the stream."

Bidding adieu to Little Silver, we retrace our steps through the wood and once more find ourselves upon the down. But now we follow the course of the stream, which pursues its way over a bed of pebbles, or between boulders from whose coats of moss the spray from the tiny cataracts is hanging like drops of dew. On our left is now the craggy hill, and as we gaze towards its crest we may in imagination trace the outline of some rude temple. But Nature was its architect, and she has formed her pillars of the enduring granite untouched by the tool, and draped them in living green. On the other side of the stream is a tangled wood, where oak boughs half veil grey rocks. If we cross and force our way through the undergrowth to some point where an opening will enable us to look upon the scene below, we shall gain the most romantic view of the cleave.

At one place the river may be passed over easily, unless it chance to be in flood. This is at Horsham Steps, where its channel is filled in such a manner with boulders as to entirely hide the stream. It can be heard as it forces its way below these masses of granite, but is not seen until it has passed the curious impediment, and falls into Horsham Bay. Lower down are footbridges, and by the higher one the visitor may reach Water Rock, where is a magnificent view of the valley and its surroundings.

When the Bovey has left the cleave it receives the waters of the Becky Brook, and shortly afterwards those of the Wray, the united streams flowing past Bovey Tracey to fall into the Teign.

X.

HOUND TOR COMBE.

A Beautiful Brook——Summer and Winter Scenes——Carved Rock on Rippon Tor——Hey Tor——The Lady's Leap——Rock Clusters——Hound Tor——Becky Fall.

There, mountain-spires uplift their stony crests
And pierce the clouds recumbent on their breasts;
There, silvery aspens bend in light arcades,
And sycamores wave cool and darksome shades:
And there the ashen trees with beeches blend,
And clustering oaks a greener roof extend.
—Samuel Wills.

NO stream on Dartmoor with so short a course as the Becky Brook will compare with it in beauty. From its source, a little to the northward of Hemsworthy Gate, to the point where it joins the Bovey, the distance is not much over four miles, and yet within this it flows by some remarkably fine tors, passes through a beautifully-wooded valley, and at one point tumbles over a wilderness of boulders, and forms the well-known Becky Fall. This little stream rises at the head of Hound Tor Combe,* which is situated partly in the parish of Ilsington and partly in that of Manaton. Above it, to the south, towers the frontier height of Rippon Tor; on its eastern side rise Saddle Tor, the twin granite masses of Hey Tor, Holwell Tor, Smallacombe Rocks,† and

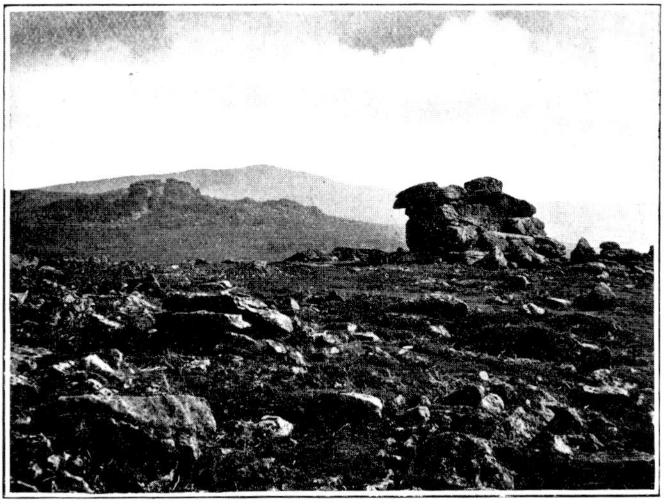

Photo by] [Mrs. Ernest Croft.

Rock Pile above Holwell Farm.

"A good view of the further side of the combe is gained."—*(See Page 83.)*

* Cymric-Celtic, Cwm, a hollow, a dingle: A.S., Coombe, a low valley. On Dartmoor the word is usually applied to small valleys closed in at the upper end.

† This pile has sometimes been called Grea Tor, but we believe wrongly so. Grea Tor is situated on the other side of the valley, but being often spoken of as Grea Tor Rocks the existence of a second pile bearing the name has been supposed. Hence the mistake. See *post*.

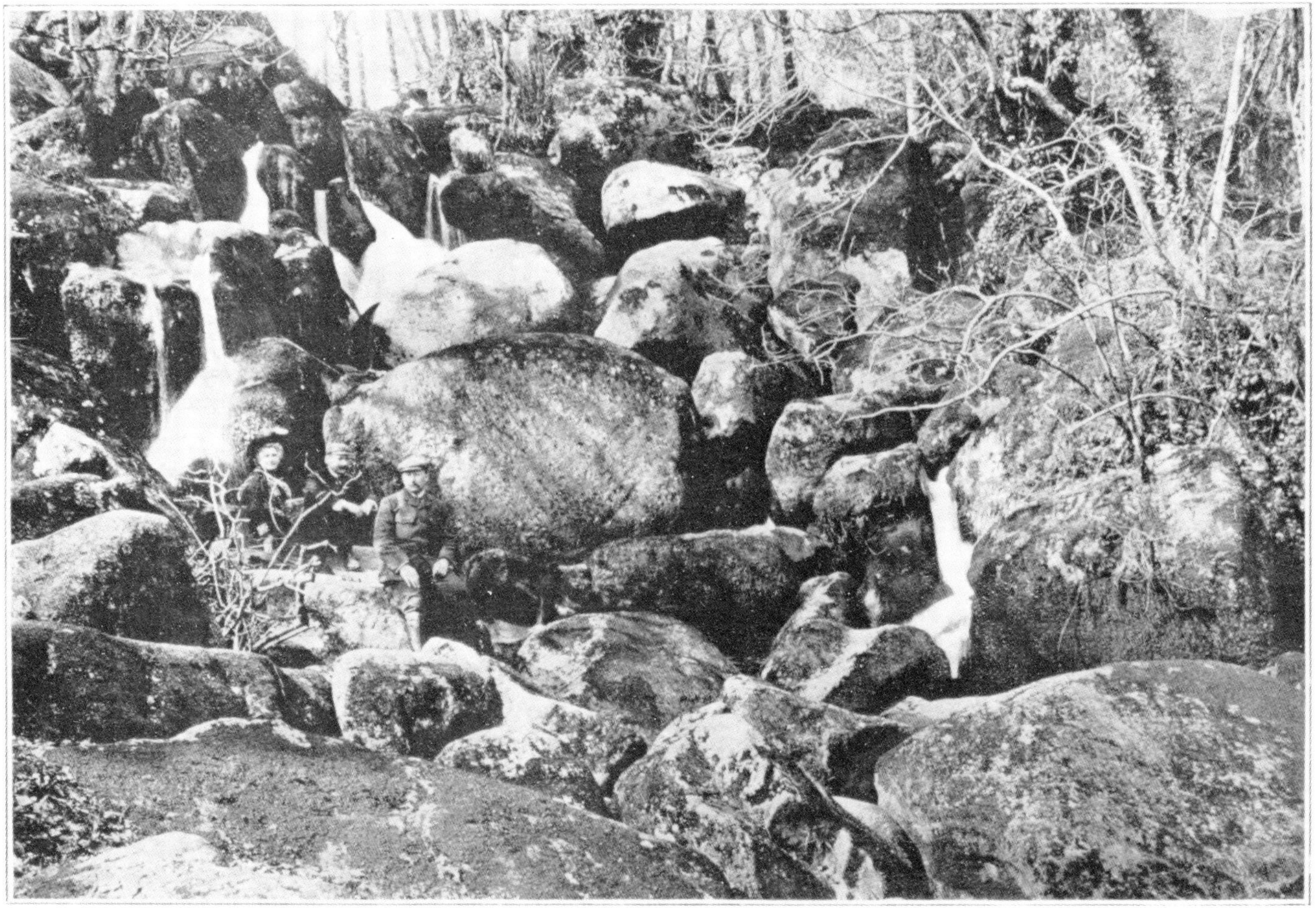

SEE PAGE 80.

PHOTO BY MRS. ERNEST CROFT.

Becky Fall.

"Tumbles over a wilderness of boulders."

Leighon Tor; to the west is a tor above Holwell Farm, sometimes known as Holwell Rocks, from which a good view of the further side of the combe is gained, the beautiful Grea Tor, in whose clefts the mountain ash finds a home, and Hound Tor, the latter ranking among the finest on the Moor.

Ever since when in our younger days we gathered crab-apples in Hound Tor Combe, or rambled by its brook and climbed the tors upon its sides, we have felt an affection for it, and this is as great as ever it was. Whether seen from the banks of the little stream or looked upon from the heights which form part of the picture, it cannot fail to impress. We have seen it at the close of a summer day, when the rays of the setting sun have given to the great bosses of Hey Tor a roseate hue, leaving the lower rocks cold and grey. We have seen it in the early morning, when everything, from the chattering brook to the sun-tipped pinnacles of Hound Tor, wore a smile. We have looked upon it when mist-wreaths have partially hidden its tors, and when the happy little valley has seemed to lose its true semblance, and to become a weird thing. And we have stood upon its sides when it has been covered with a mantle of snow, when the charms we had been accustomed to behold were hidden. But it was decked in fresh ones, the garb of Old Winter never wanting beauty.

Rippon Tor, with Saddle Tor and Hey Tor, are very prominent objects from many parts of South Devon. There are several tors on the Moor that far exceed them in height, but the downs which they crown rise immediately from the lowlands, and this causes them to appear to rival several tors, the altitude of which is much greater. There is no rock-pile on the actual summit of the hill which is known as Rippon Tor, though there is one very near to it. But the Dartmoor rambler should by all means ascend this eminence for the sake of the extensive view commanded from its crest. There is much seen towards the south-west that its slopes hide from the observer on Hey Tor, besides which it has the advantage in height. On the top is a cairn, near to which, many years ago, I found a kistvaen, but so covered with turf as to be almost indiscernible. It is unusual to see one of these ancient graves in so lofty a situation, though there are not wanting instances of such on the Moor. Two other objects may be seen here, which I also discovered about the same time, but to them much less interest attaches. They are unfinished millstones, and the remark as to the situation of the kistvaen will also apply to them, for those engaged in cutting such stones did not generally go to the summit of a tor to do so, as is evidenced by the examples found in different parts of the Moor.

But what will more probably attract the visitor's attention is an object that will also be found near to the cairn, and one which I have described in another place.* It is a large cross cut in relief on a block of granite, and is the only example of the kind in the Moorland region.

On the pile of rocks alluded to as being near the summit of this hill is a fine logan, though its rocking power is not so great as formerly. It is plainly to be seen from the Ashburton road southward of Hemsworthy Gate.

Saddle Tor immediately overlooks the upper end of the combe. Near it there is a very fine view looking down the valley, which from this point seems to be bounded by the ridge of Lustleigh Cleave. The tor is close to the road leading from Hemsworthy Gate towards Ilsington and Bovey Tracey. Hey Tor is about a half-mile distant, and so fine is the turf here, that the walk from one to the other across the common is much more like passing over a smoothly-shaven lawn than over a bit of Dartmoor.

No tor on the Moor is so often visited as Hey Tor, for while none presents a more striking appearance, few are so easy of access. Consisting of two large masses of rock set on a lofty ridge, and rising to a considerable height above the turf, it forms a conspicuous object in the view from any elevated point for many miles around, and also from the low land in the neighbourhood of Newton Abbot. Steps have been cut in the

* *Ancient Stone Crosses of Dartmoor and its Borderland.* Ch. XVI.

rock by means of which the visitor may easily ascend to the summit of one of the piles; the top of the other can only be reached by climbing. The view is magnificent. On one side a beautifully diversified country, bounded by the Channel; on the other, the hills above the valley of the Teign, and the wide Moor. But wonderful as the prospect is, it does not impress in the same manner as do the scenes beheld from the tors that rise in lonely places. There is more beauty, but the stern grandeur of the heart of the Moor is wanting.

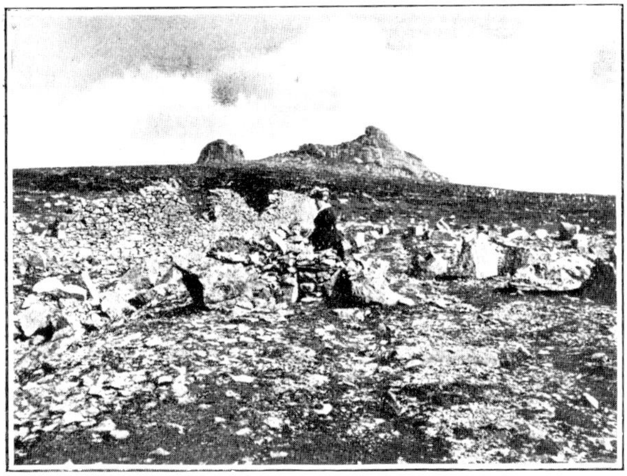

Photo by] [Mrs. Ernest Croft.

Hey Tor.

"Two large masses of rock set on a lofty ridge."—*(See Page 83.)*

It is rather amusing to read that the steps cut in the rock were those "by which the Druidical priests ascended to the rock basin on the summit, and where they performed their ceremonies, while the superstitious multitude were assembled below."* It is not stated that the Druids cut the steps, but we presume that this is what is intended to be conveyed, and if so, it forms the only instance among the thousand and one things they were once credited with having done on the Moor, of their accomplishing anything useful.

Hey Tor has its legend, though it is one which seems to have escaped notice; but a quarter of a century ago the story of the Lady's Leap was related in the neighbourhood. It seems that a certain ancient squire of Ilsington had a beautiful daughter, of whom he was exceedingly proud. There were many suitors for her hand, but it was the old story —the one she favoured the squire would not hear of. He had his own plans for his daughter's future, and when the proper time, as he considered, had arrived, he made them known to her. She would, of course, be aware, the squire told her, that he had only her interest at heart. But he had lived many years in the world, he said, and he had learnt what, very likely, she was as yet ignorant of. And that was the desirability of possessing the means to make life comfortable. Not that he set too great a store upon money; he particularly wished her to understand that; but he could assure her it was a very necessary thing. She might suppose him to be wealthy, but none knew his circumstances better than he did himself. In choosing for her a partner in life he had felt it to be incumbent upon him to see that this important point should not be neglected. After much consideration he had come to the conclusion that a certain wealthy squire whom he named was the fit and proper person upon whom to bestow his child. She might be quite sure that he had thought solely of her welfare, and she would, of course, feel it to be her duty to act in accordance with his desires.

But, strange to say, the squire's fair daughter felt nothing of the kind. On the contrary, she was determined that she would never bestow her hand on the man her father had chosen for her. He might be as rich as Crœsus, she argued, but if so he was also old enough to be her grandfather, and she perferred youth and poverty to old age and riches. So she went to the favoured suitor, who possessed both the former qualifications, and told him what had occurred. He was entirely of her opinion. What was filthy lucre

* Notes to Cottle's poem of *Dartmoor*, 1823.

compared to his love? And as for the means of living, why trouble themselves about a matter so trivial? There was no poetry in it, and consequently no attraction for them. Let them be married first, and then if any necessity for giving attention to such a thing did arise they would have ample time to do so.

But the squire of Ilsington had taken his measures, and from that time his daughter was kept under surveillance, though he foolishly neglected to watch her waiting-maid. He had determined to wed her to the man of his choice, and tears and entreaties were of no avail. The wedding-day arrived, and the old bridegroom was beside himself with joy. He had settled I do not know how many manors upon his bride, and vowed he would do anything for her. She had taken him at his word, and had insisted that he should give a breakfast on the down under the rocks of Hey Tor, and also that it should be partaken of before the wedding ceremony took place. The old fellow, with one foot in the grave and the other in a gouty shoe, was only too delighted to humour the beautiful girl he was expecting to lead to the altar, and he had readily acceded to her wishes.

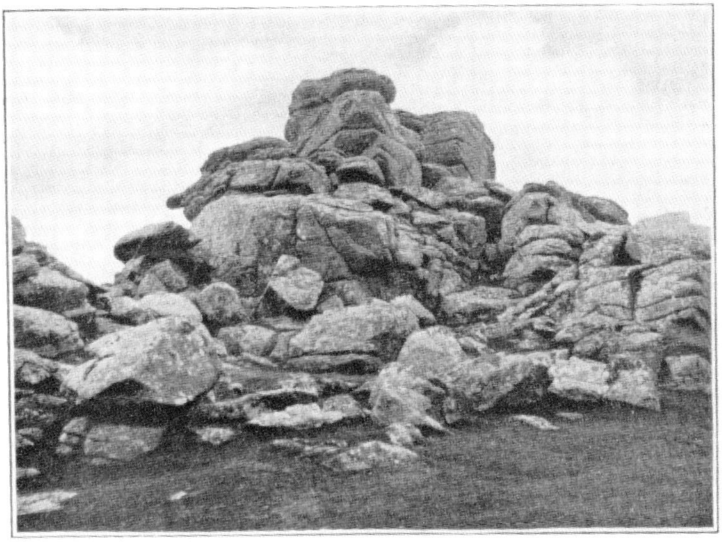

Photo by] [Mrs. Ernest Croft.

Hound Tor.

"Whose hoary piles rise to an immense height above the ground."—*(See Page 87.)*

When the party reached the rocks they found a splendid repast set out upon the turf, to which, with appetites sharpened by the Dartmoor air, they were soon doing ample justice. When the squire of Ilsington and the old beau were hobnobbing together the bride expressed a wish to be alone for a short time. Her father at first demurred to this, but she entreated him not to deny her request, urging that she did not ask him to allow her to withdraw to a distance, but merely to the summit of the tor, where she would not be out of his sight. That was a different matter, so the squire raised no further objection.

The beautiful girl walked slowly away, and having ascended to the top of the lofty rock, waved her handkerchief to those below (for a needlessly long time they thought) and then sat down as though in meditation. After a few minutes she arose, and those of the guests who had been watching her (it must be confessed they were not many, the attention of the majority being devoted to the good things spread on the turf) imagined she was about to return. But to their horror she suddenly flung up her arms, and leaping out into space disappeared behind the rocks. Instantly all was commotion. Chickens and turkeys were forgotten, and the jellies and custards no longer possessed an attraction. Everybody jumped up, except the antiquated lover, whose gouty toe utterly prevented him from joining in the scramble, and rushed to the tor, expecting to find the bride lying dead on the ground. But when they reached it they only saw her and her lover, mounted on swift steeds, speeding away across the head of Hound Tor Combe in the direction of Widecombe. The old beau was furious. The squire sent to Ilsington for horses, and they galloped after the fugitives. But it was too late. When they reached Widecombe the nuptial knot had been tied. Some fathers would have been in a terrible rage, but the squire of Ilsington was not at all displeased. In fact he rather enjoyed the situation. His daughter had not only got the man of her choice, but the old beau's manors into the bargain.

Below Hey Tor, and about a quarter of a mile from the Becky Brook, is Holwell Tor. Westward of the combe is Holwell Down, and it is rather strange that this name should appear on each side of the brook. The same thing is found in another name occurring here—Grea Tor—which, although that pile is on the west side, is, as we have already observed, sometimes applied to Smallacombe Rocks, which are on the east. This, which has led to some confusion, may possibly point to the bestowal of comparatively modern names on some of the tors, that had perhaps lost their more ancient ones.

From Holwell Tor, near to which is a group of hut circles, the rambler may make his way along the side of the hill to Smallacombe Rocks, where there are similar remains, and to Leighon Tor, both piles being worth a visit. Or he may cross the valley to Grea Tor, whose lofty rocks rise from a bed of turf and whortleberries, and give shelter to the mountain ash.

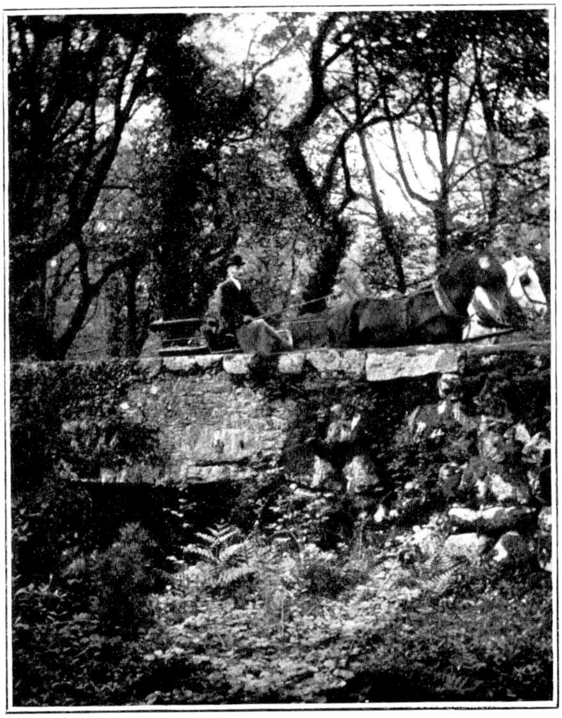

Photo by] [Ernest Croft.

Bridge over the Becky Brook below Leighon.

"A clapper of one opening."—*(See Page 87.)*

But the finest tor overhanging this combe is undoubtedly that which gives name to it, and very near to which the rambler who has climbed from the Becky Brook to the summit of Grea Tor will find himself. Hound Tor is usually approached from Swallerton Gate on the other side of the common, but is not then seen to the best advantage. Viewed from any other point, however, it is a most impressive pile, but perhaps shows itself best from the lane leading from Hound Tor Farm to the down. The rocks are there seen cresting a lofty hill almost mountainous in its outline, and piled in such a manner as to convey the impression that very little force would cause them to topple over. Seen, too, from the valley just above Leighon, it is exceedingly fine. And however much the tor may impress the beholder when viewed from a distance, it will certainly not prove less striking on a closer examination. In its partly fallen piles the imagination may trace the ruins of some mighty stronghold, and one can well believe that in the days when tors were thought to have been used as rock temples by the Druids, the followers of Stukely and Borlase regarded Hound Tor, which covers a very large area, and whose hoary piles rise to an immense height above the ground, as having been one of more than ordinary importance.

Having looked upon the combe, with its brook, and its rocks, its stunted trees, and small enclosures, we shall now make our way to the Becky below Leighon, in order that we may claim a closer acquaintance with it. If our path lies from the fine tor just noticed, we descend the lane towards the farm of Great Hound Tor, situated at the foot of the hill, where, according to Lysons, Hugh of Hound Tor had a manor house in the time of Richard I. On reaching the stream, over which the road to Leighon is carried by a clapper of one opening, we turn left down the valley, which grows more wooded as we proceed, and after a pleasant walk of less than a mile shall reach Becky Fall.

Here is a delightful picture of a tree-hidden dell, through which a little stream rushes down a steep and rocky channel, turning and twisting among mossy boulders, and forming numberless cascades. A charming retreat, where the heat of the summer day is exchanged for a delicious coolness. A spot always beautiful, whether it be when the sun has in part sealed up the springs of the stream, or whether it comes rushing down in flood. A fitting place in which so sweet a little brook as the Becky should speak its farewell to the combe that gave it birth.

XI.

BAG TOR MILL.

Ilsington—Road to Halshanger—A Quiet Nook—Birthplace of John Ford, the Dramatist—Bag Tor House—John Dunning, First Lord Ashburton—A Clever Lawyer.

A limpid, clear, and lovely brook
Flowed swiftly through this quiet nook;
And when the sun was hot and high,
And not a breath was in the vale,
Its murmured freshness rushing by
Supplied the place of fanning gale.
—Samuel Carter.

IT would be impossible to name a single parish among those that go to make up Dartmoor in which natural beauty is not allied with old and interesting associations. That which delights the eye goes hand and hand with that which will pleasingly occupy the mind. And this is particularly true of Ilsington, within the bounds of which, as we have already seen, among so much else that is attractive, and the castle-like rocks of Hey Tor, the lofty Rippon Tor, and the charming Hound Tor Combe. The village, which bears the same name as the parish, is situated at some distance from the verge of the commons, and is not particularly suggestive of the Moor, but it none the less possesses features that invite the attention of the visitor. The church, dedicated to St. Michael, is chiefly Perpendicular, though some parts are older, and has an embattled tower with a projecting stair-turret on the southern side. In the graveyard are several curious tombstones, among them being one of more than ordinary interest. It marks the burial place of Thomas Ford, of Sigford, the date of his death being expressed in a chronogram. There are lych-gates at the east end and also at the west end of the yard. Near the church formerly stood the manor house built by Sir H. Ford in the seventeenth century.

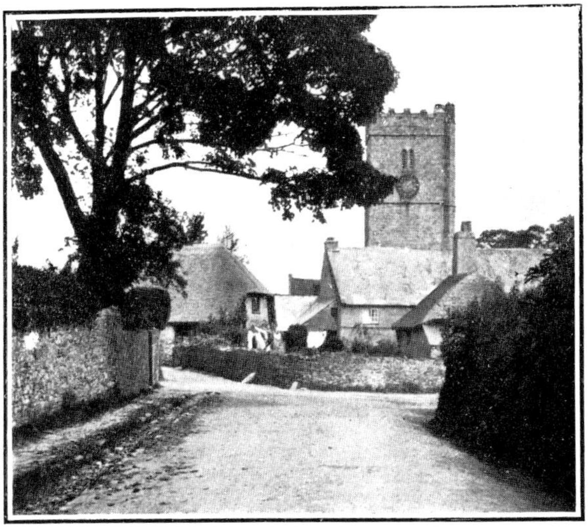

Photo by] [Mrs. Ernest Croft.

Ilsington Church.

"An embattled tower with a projecting stair-turret."

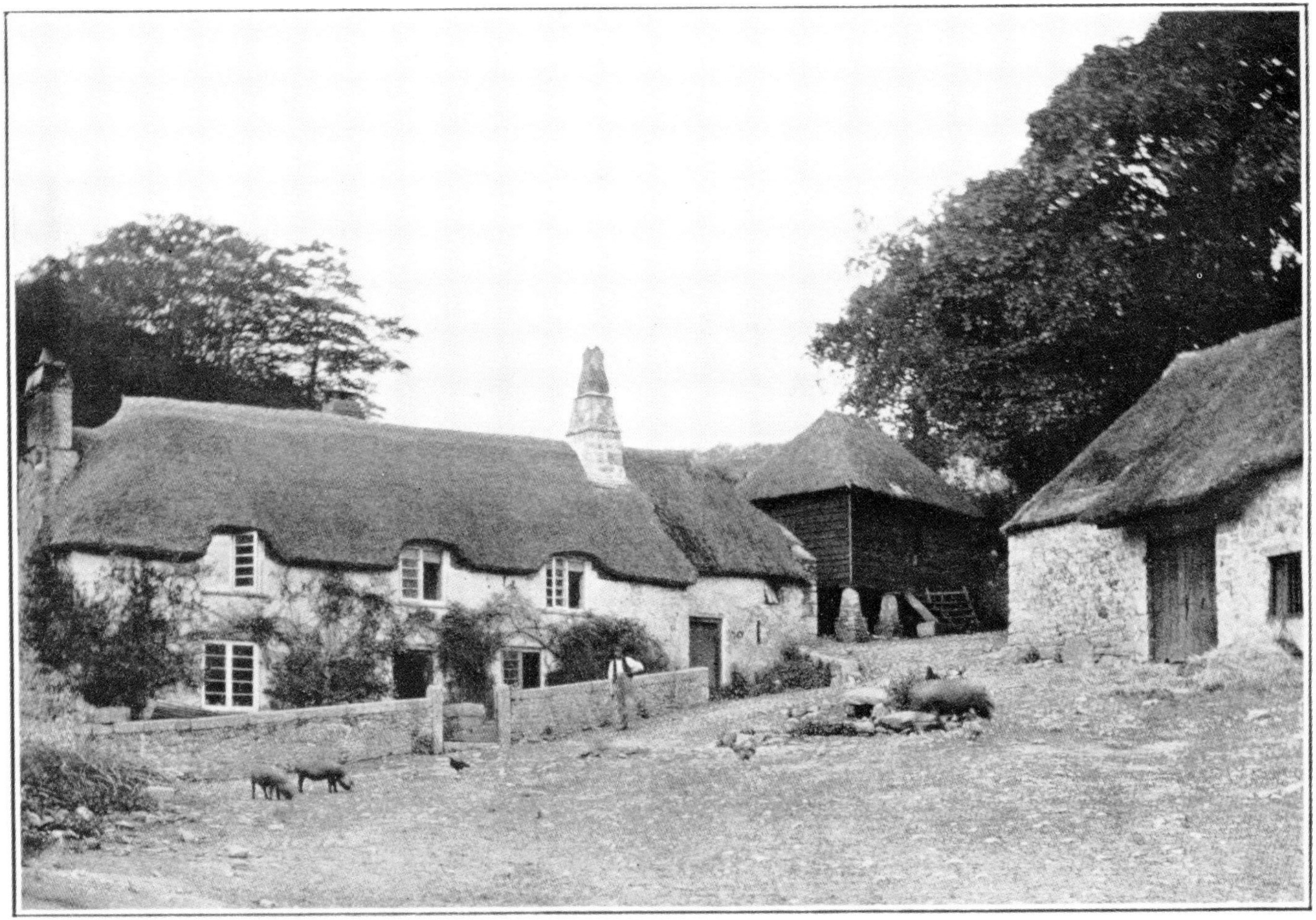

SEE PAGE 91.

A Border Farmhouse.

PHOTO BY ERNEST CROFT.

"Its walls hung with creepers, its roof of thatch."

Rather more than a mile from the village the road to Halshanger makes a sweep round the upper part of a narrow valley, and crosses a tiny stream that issues from a thicket growing on the verge of the Moor. Below the little bridge is an old mill standing beneath stately trees, and everywhere are ferns and moss and undergrowth. When the summer sun is high, and the downs that rise up to the rock-crested heights become a thirsty land, here is delicious coolness, for the fierce rays beat only on the leafy screen that hangs above. In the filtered light, soft and subdued, the wild plants preserve their freshness. Here and there a stray beam, shooting through some opening between the interlacing boughs, lights upon a broad hart's-tongue, or the fronds of the sweet-scented lastrea, but only to mingle gold with the living green. Nature speaks to the wanderer, and bids him stay awhile, and look upon her work in this fair dingle, where quietude runs through all the dreamy hours of the day. It is a picture breathing of repose, for the murmurs of the brook tend only to lull the senses. Nothing of the Moor is visible but a part of one high, round hill, rising above the thicket whence the stream comes, and which the natives speak of as Punchaford Ball. Near this hill is Bag Tor, a low pile that may be seen from the road under Saddle Tor, and which has given name to several objects in the locality, the old mill being one of them. This it shares with the charming spot in which it is placed, for by no other name than Bag Tor Mill is the latter known.

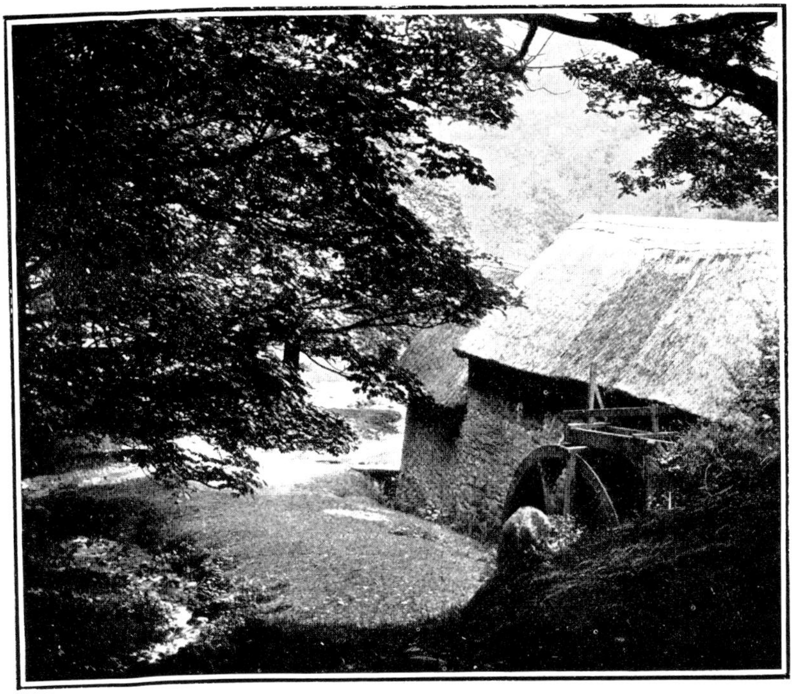

Photo by] [Ernest Croft.

Bag Tor Mill.

"An old mill standing beneath stately trees."

Other pleasing rural sights surround this combe, though hidden from view by the trees. Above are enclosures creeping up to the common; below, a fertile valley, where the fields show a marked contrast to those that hug the waste. Near at hand is a farm-house, which, with its walls hung with creepers, its roof of thatch, and out-buildings similarly covered, forms an attractive picture.

That Bag Tor Mill was a familiar scene to one of England's dramatists in his childhood is certain, for the baptismal register of Ilsington shows that John Ford, the friend of Shakespeare, was born in this parish in 1586, and probably at Bag Tor House.

XII.

THE DART AT HOLNE CHASE.

Course of the Dart——The Ruddycleave Water——The Buckland Woods——The Lovers' Leap——The Raven Rock——Hazel Tor——Buckland-in-the Moor——Holne——Distant Views of the Dart Valley.

Bold is the rush of the kingly Rhine,
Bright is his coronet, bright is his wine.
Soft, in the shade of his mountain zone,
Laughs the blue glance of the bounding Rhone.
Proudly the yellow-haired Tiber may flow,
Singing his dirge to the dead below.
Which of the river gods, which may it be,
Beautiful Dart, to be mated with thee?
—Rev. H. J. Whitfield.

Few will be inclined to believe with Risdon that the Dart took its name from Dartmoor, but will rather be disposed to look upon the river as having itself given name to the Moor. We shall, however, quite agree with him when he states that it passes "through the Moor by a long, solitary course," for though nearly three hundred years have flown since he wrote these words the upper branches of the stream water a district which is the same now as ever it was—a stronghold of Nature, a silent land into which man seldom intrudes. This child of the wilderness, as the Dart has been called, and the title is appropriate to all the streams of the Moor, leaves its upland home below Leigh Tor, a ridge of rocks near the hamlet of Pound's Gate, at the southern end of the parish of Widecombe. Shortly before reaching the foot of this tor it sweeps by the hill on which is placed the village of Holne,

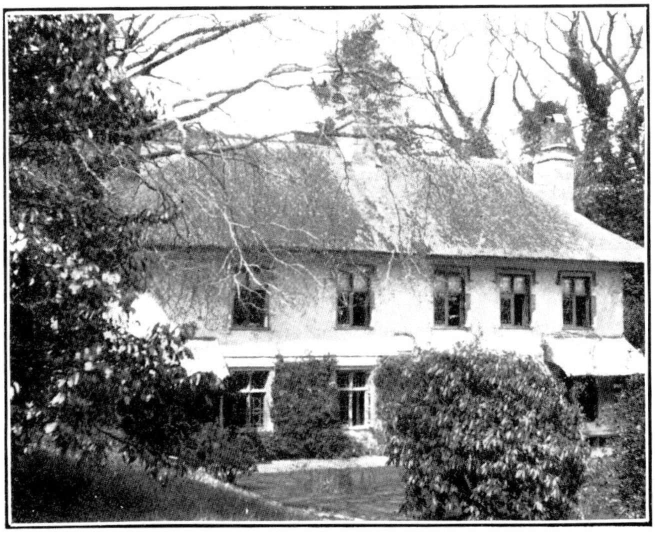

Photo by] [C. R. Rowe.

Holne Vicarage.

"Overlooks the valley through which the Dart hastens to cheer by its music the ancient chase."—(See Page 98.)

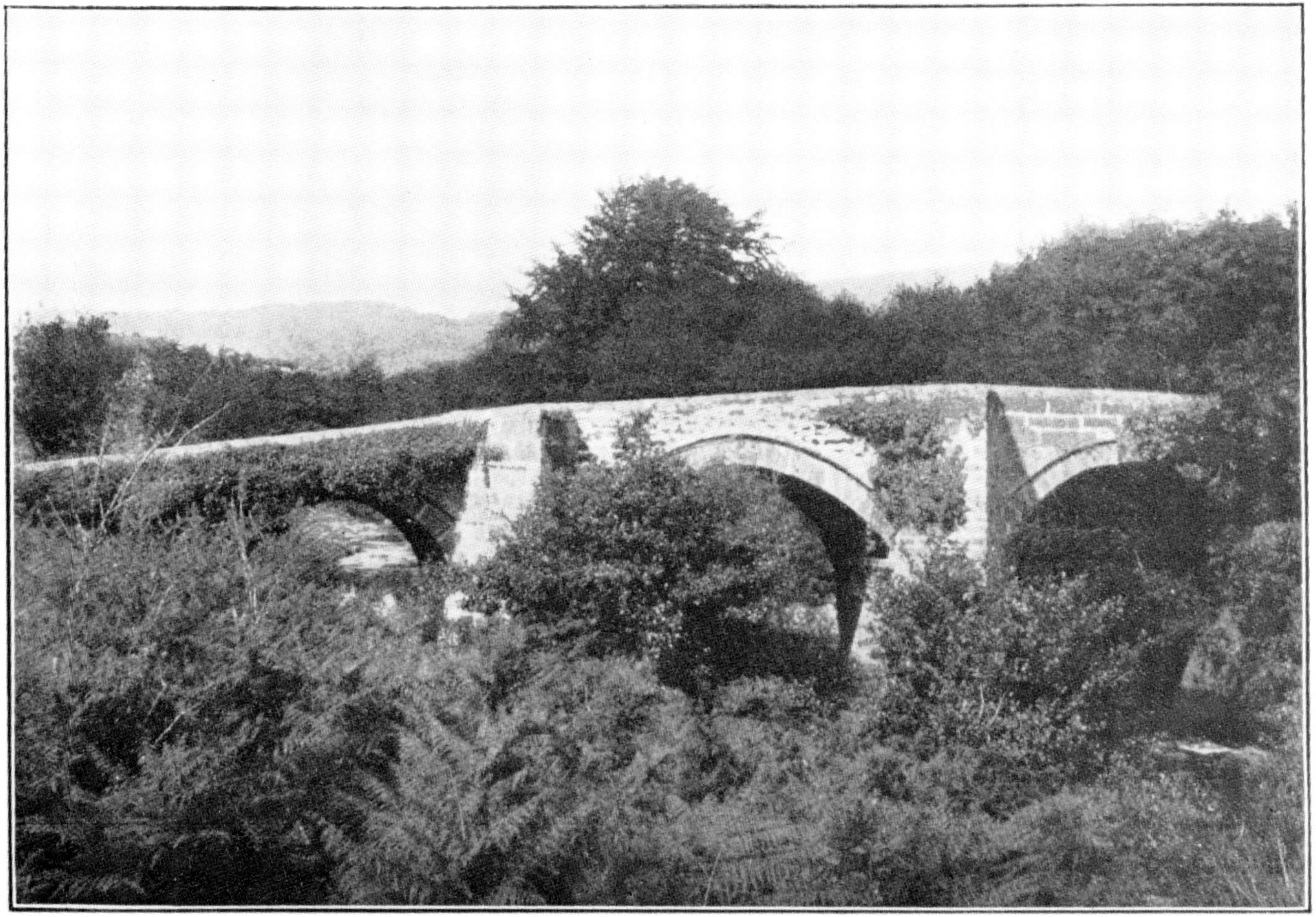

SEE PAGE 97.

New Bridge.

PHOTO BY C. R. ROWE.

"Close to the bridge is one of the entrances to that romantic tract of rock and wood called Holne Chase."

though it is not in sight. Fields and woods clothe this side of the stream, the other being a bare common rising to a considerable height. The river here makes a sharp bend to the left, soon afterwards passing under New Bridge, which carries the Ashburton road, and is distant between three and four miles from that town. Close to the bridge is one of the entrances to that romantic tract of rock and wood called Holne Chase, of which the Dart forms the boundary on three sides, the river here making a great sweep northward and then turning and flowing due south.

If the Dart has up to this point been the child of the wilderness, it is now to spend its youth in the green wood. Not long after it reaches the chase the common on its left bank is exchanged for the groves of Spitchwick and Buckland, and then for nearly three miles tall forest trees and tangled undergrowth clothe the sides of the vale through which it runs. Still further down the woods below Hembury listen to the music of its waters, and it is not until it nears Buckfast that the scene again changes, and the sylvan accompaniments of the noble stream give place to pasture fields and orchards.

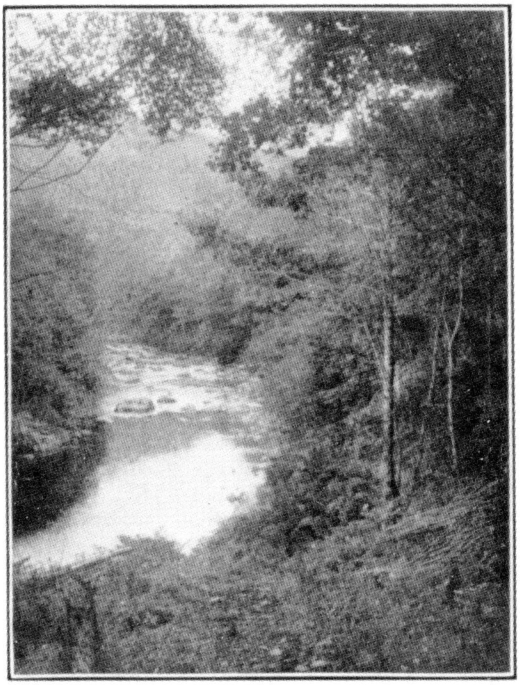

Photo by] [C. R. Rowe.

In Holne Chase.

"The beautiful river, which Risdon terms Dartmoor's 'first begotten.'"

Less than a mile below New Bridge, and where the grounds of Spitchwick approach the Buckland Woods, the Dart receives the Webburn, which little river is noticed in our remarks on Lizwell Meet. Ere they have long been companions they are joined by the Ruddycleave Water, a stream rising on Blackslade Down, about half a mile west of Rippon Tor. Not far from its source this tributary is crossed by the road leading from Halshanger to Scobetor and Widecombe, and again by the Ashburton road near the Church of Buckland-in-the-Moor. Here it may be seen pursuing its noisy way through the wood as though impatient to join the greater stream in the valley below.

And now the beautiful river, which Risdon terms Dartmoor's "first begotten," increased in volume by the liberal offerings of the brooks, speeds on by the wild chase where the oaks and the hollies grow, and where the mossy crag springs from a carpet of heather. By-and-by a shattered cliff, which the ivy clasps as though to protect it from further decay, thrusts itself from the dark foliage, and beyond it are more oaks and hollies, and mountain ash and ferns. Across the stream, on the Buckland side, the woods rise steeply from its edge, a waving mass of green. The river runs slower now, for the water is deep, and here, where it bends, a great rock lifts itself from the flood. It bears the name of the Lovers' Leap, and tradition has it that from its summit two lovers flung themselves into the dark waters that lave its foot. But for what reason we know not, for the story is silent on the point. As it is one that is related of similarly situated rocks, not only in this country, but in various parts of Europe, we shall probably not be inclined to place much faith in it. When a tradition attaches to an object the latter, of course, becomes more interesting, but we need not feel much regret that so little of ancient story is related of this romantic rock in the Buckland Woods. So beautiful is it in itself that it needs no legend to attract us.

It has been considered by many that the Dart at the Lovers' Leap is seen at its finest. Those who love it best, where it forces its way through some rock-strewn vale, its murmuring heard only by the curlew, may not be prepared to endorse this view, but they will, at all events, be ready to acknowledge that nowhere throughout its course is the picture, of which it forms the principal feature, more enchanting than that presented at the spot where it kisses the foot of the rock with the forgotten story in the valley below Buckland.

Further down the stream is another mass known as the Raven Rock, and far above it the pile of Ausewell Rock, or, to give it the name it bears in the locality, Hazel Tor. This pile is not far from the road leading from Ashburton to Buckland-in-the-Moor, and which skirts the beautiful woods for some distance.

The parish of Buckland is now not quite correctly described by the adjunct to its name. Though part of it still lies in the Moor, the hand of industry has long since assailed the hill above the woods, and where once were commons on which the heather and the whortleberry alone grew, there are now fields in which cattle graze, or where the husbandman reaps his crops. Buckland does not boast of a village. There is a church and a few cottages, that is all; yet the little place is by no means wanting in interest. At the churchyard gate the road branches. Northward the way leads to Widecombe; in the other direction it runs down through the woods to the river we are noticing, which it reaches near the point where it receives the Webburn.

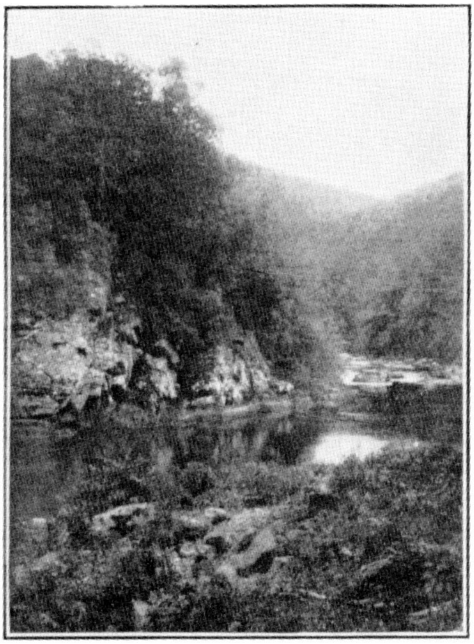

Photo by] [C. R. Rowe.

The Lovers' Leap.

"The rock with the forgotten story in the valley below Buckland."

When the Dart leaves the Raven Rock behind the end of the chase soon comes in sight. Here, at some distant period, the river scooped out for itself a fresh channel, the bed of gravel over which it once flowed being now some eighty feet above it. A little further down, and it runs beneath Holne Bridge, its farewell murmurings to the scenes through which it has of late been meandering mingling with the song with which it welcomes new ones as it speeds onward to the vale below Hembury.

From Holne Bridge, so happily placed at the gate of the wild vale, the road to the Moor climbs a rather long hill, near the summit of which a branch leads to the village from which the bridge derives its name. Holne will always possess an interest, apart from that with which its natural attractions, and its connection with the Moor, endow it, as being the place in which Charles Kingsley first saw the light. The house in which he was born stood on the site of the present vicarage, which is situated at a little distance from the village, and overlooks the valley through which the Dart hastens to cheer by its music the ancient chase. Beyond are the hills that tower over the vale of Widecombe—and wood and field, heathery down and rugged tor, fill the other parts of the delightful picture.

But of all the views that the hills round Holne present none exceed that obtained from the road near the Moor-gate at Stock.* Indeed, we believe it would be difficult to find a finer throughout the Moorland borders, if indeed in Devon. The beautiful Dart is not in sight, but its course can be traced by the foldings of the hills. The bold common above New Bridge is seen, and the vale where the Webburn sings its song of joy at meeting the great river from the silent land. The trees of the chase and the Buckland Woods crowd the deep valley in which the river loses itself. Above are breezy downs, with here and there a bold rock silhouetted against the sky.

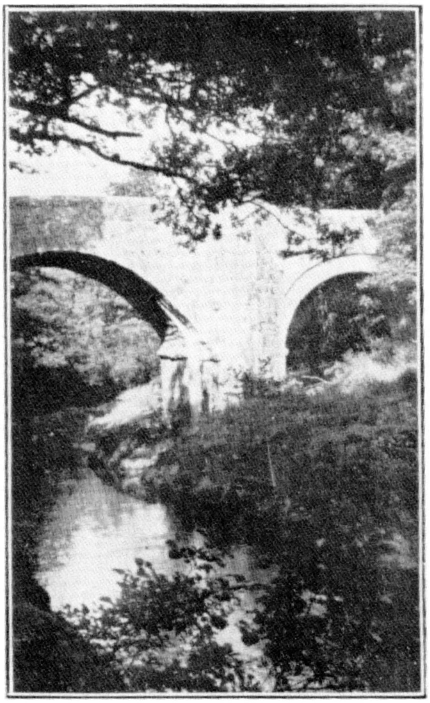

Photo by] Holne Bridge. [C. R. Rowe.

"Happily placed at the gate of the wild vale."

(See Page 98.)

One of these rock masses we particularly notice, and if we were to take our stand upon it we should see the Dart where it bids farewell to the Moor. This is Buckland Beacon, and though the view gained from it must yield the palm to that obtained from the road near Stock, it is nevertheless beautiful. From that point of vantage we should look down upon the windings of the noble stream, though we should be unable to trace its course very far. Nor should we see the gorge through which it issues from the uplands, nor the spot whence it seeks the recesses of the woods, for the trees that grow upon the steep hillside obscure the view. But glimpses of it would not be denied us; and if the skies should be clear and the sunbeams dance upon its bosom, we should see through the breaks in the foliage the flash of myriads of gems amid the rocks that its never-ceasing flow has bared.

* This is the gate opening upon Holne Moor, on the road from Ashburton and Buckfastleigh to Hexworthy and Princetown.

XIII.

LIZWELL MEET.

THE TWO WEBBURNS—MEETING OF THE STREAMS—BLACKADON TOR—THE CAVALIER—A WOODED VALLEY—MANOR OF SPITCHWICK—PONSWORTHY.

Through boughs in yon forest recesses
  The sun shyly kisses the ground,
Where the blushing hung head of the foxglove,
  And the bracken uncurled, may be found.
      —FLORENCE GERTRUDE ATTENBOROUGH.

NOT the least important of the streams that go to swell the waters of the Dart is the Webburn, which, as we have already seen,* joins that river where its course between the Buckland Woods and Holne Chase commences. There are two branches, known respectively as the East and the West Webburn, and these flow through a part of Dartmoor more than ordinarily interesting. They unite in a lovely valley, not far from the little church of Leusden, the confluence bearing the name of Lizwell Meet.

The East Webburn, which appears to have been anciently known as the Niprell, has its source at the head of the long vale of Widecombe, the giant tors of Honeybag and

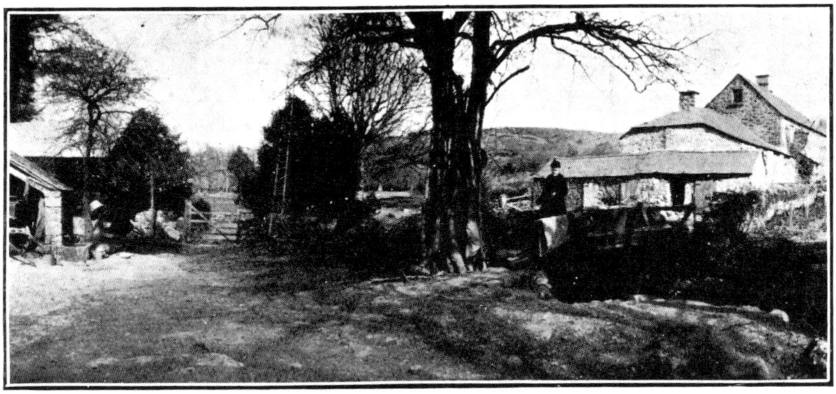

Photo by] Cockingford Mill. [Mrs. Ernest Croft.

"On the road from Halshanger to the Forest."—*(See Page 103.)*

Chinkwell looking down upon the infant stream from one side, and the huge Hameldon from the other. Near the village in which for seven centuries, and probably during a much longer period, the Forest-dwellers have married or been given in marriage, and where they have found their last resting-place, the little river runs, almost in the shadow of the tower of the Cathedral of the Moor. Then its course is by the hamlet of Dunstone

* *Vide* Chap. XII. *ante.*

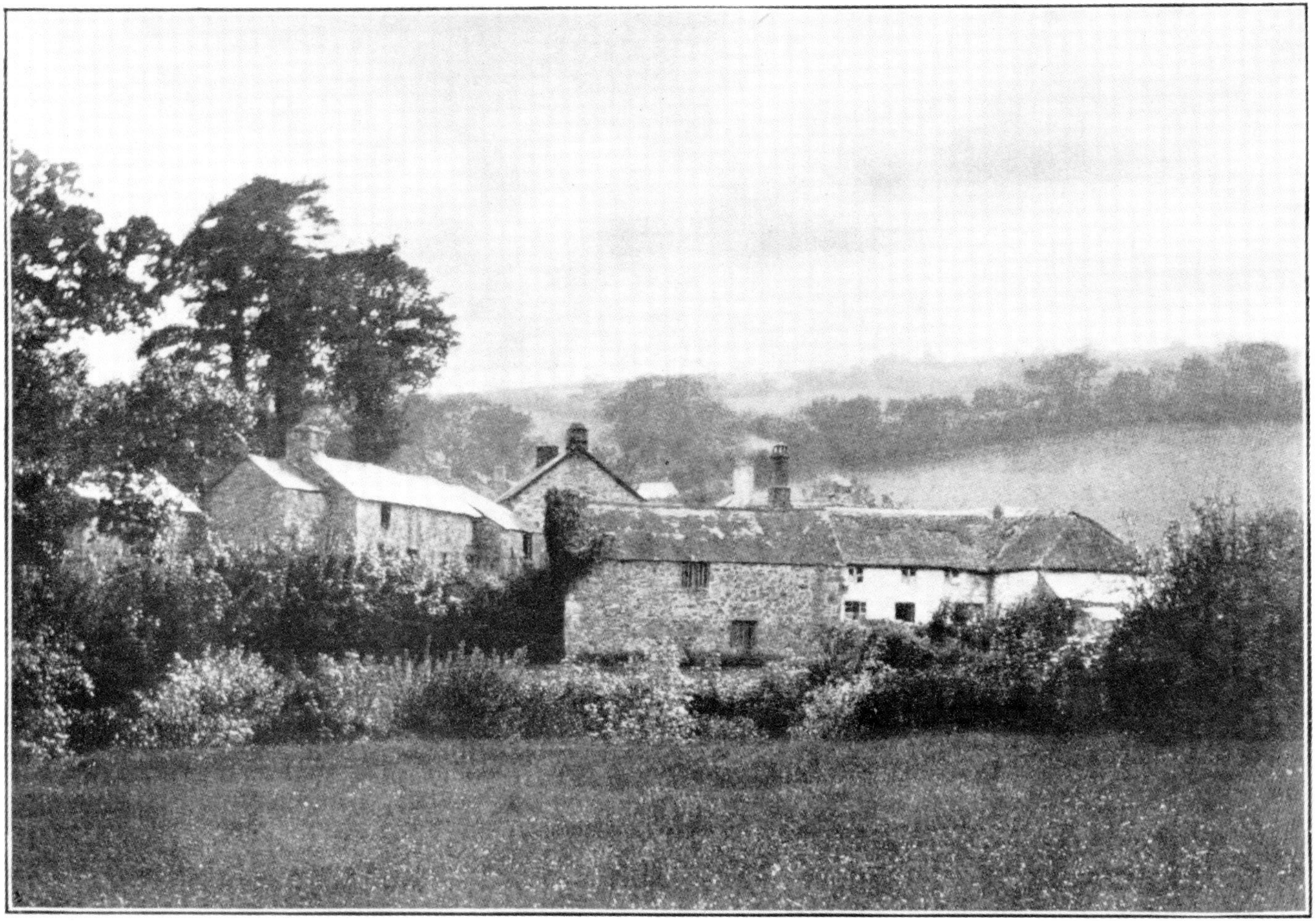

SEE PAGE 106.

PHOTO BY ERNEST CROFT.

Ponsworthy.

"The hamlet through which the West Webburn flows."

to the mill at Cockingford, on the road from Halshanger to the Forest, and so down to the woods, where it finds the companion with which it hurries onward to lose itself in the Dart.

The West Webburn comes down from under Challacombe Common, which is situated to the west of Hameldon, and flowing near Grendon and Cator, afterwards passes Shallowford and Jordon Mill. Thence it runs to the hamlet of Ponsworthy, a pleasant little border settlement, seated deep in a valley, below which it reaches the woods, and the place where the one-time Niprell comes singing from the long vale. From its source to Shallowford, though outside the boundary of the Forest, it is yet quite near that part of the Royal hunting ground where the early farm settlers dwelt. And it is a district around which interest must always cling, since it is the only part throughout the whole of the Moor that we have any early account of. It is but a meagre one, but it lets in some light upon the old Dartmoor story.

The meeting place of these two rivers of Widecombe is in one of those charming nooks that contrive to hide themselves from the gaze of the passer-by, and give scarcely a hint of their existence. A wealth of foliage is seen, it is true, but not only at this particular spot, and but for the rocks of Blackadon Tor there would be nothing to draw attention to it. The grey pile is, however, a striking feature in the scene, and should that be approached the beauties which the valley has so modestly concealed begin to reveal themselves, and thus unexpectedly discovered give greater delight. Nature has here been bountiful, yet, in the bestowal of her gifts, heedless whether the rock and the stream, the shading tree, and the plants that carpet the earth, should form a paradise only for the birds of the air or meet the eye of man.

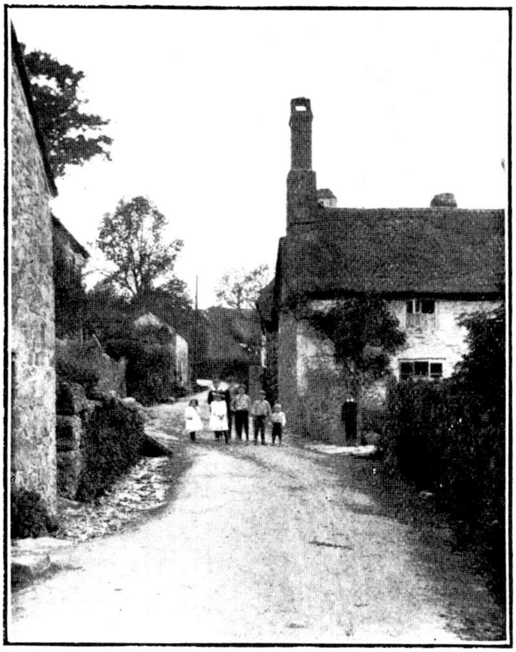

Photo by] [Ernest Croft.

Ponsworthy.

"A pleasant little border settlement."

Blackadon Tor is close to Leusden Church, which little modern sanctuary is situated about three-quarters of a mile from the hamlet of Ponsworthy, and near the road running from Pound's Gate through that place to Widecombe. Around the tor cluster memories of one who in his day was a keen sportsman, and known to all who hunted the fox, or fished the streams, in this part of Dartmoor. Those who knew old Tom French are growing very few, but his name will nevertheless long be heard in the Widecombe valley, for many are the stories related of him. But tales of an older day than that which knew Tom French are told of Blackadon Tor. From one we learn how it became the hiding-place of a cavalier, or, as the natives have it, of "a vine genelman, back in the time o' the wars." His lady love used herself to bring him food, but notwithstanding this attention, she lost her hold upon his affections. Cupid delights to play poor mortals pranks, and so he brought upon the scene a beautiful peasant girl. The cavalier saw her one day when he had left his place of concealment for a brief space, and speedily discovered that the heart he had hitherto believed to be in the keeping of the lady to whom he was betrothed was now in the possession of the rosy-cheeked Dartmoor damsel. He could not, however, summon sufficient courage to tell the lady that he no longer loved her, but he determined that he would at all events not be so base as to accept food from her now that he had transferred his affections to another. Accordingly he cast into the Webburn the provisions that she brought to him, not, however, allowing her to see what he did, as he wished to avoid an explanation. But a man cannot live upon love, and so the cavalier soon discovered. The peasant damsel never brought him anything but kisses, and the consequence was that he began to pine away. One day when the lady came to the rocks and gave the signal, she received no answer. She approached his hiding-place, and found him lying dead upon a bed of leaves. She mourned him as a faithful lover, and so did the peasant girl, for she knew nothing of the lady's existence. They both cherished his memory, though one would certainly not have done so had he chanced to have told the other that he wanted something to eat. A dinner would have spoiled the romance.

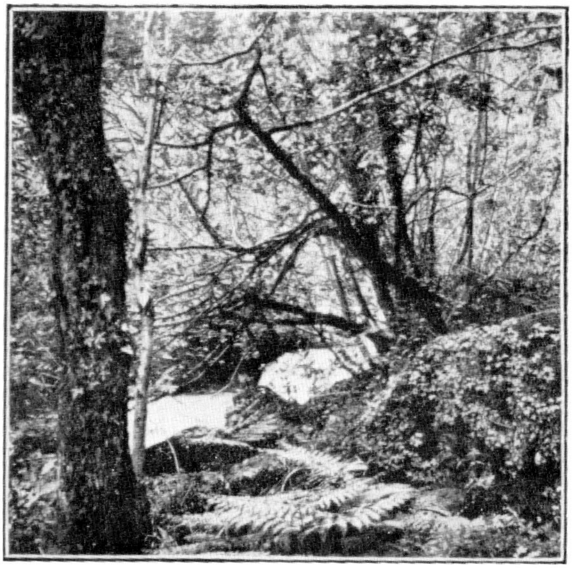

Photo by] The Woods at Lizwell Meet. [Ernest Croft.

"One of those charming nooks that contrive to hide themselves."— (*See Page 103.*)

From Blackadon Tor the rambler looks upon the valleys through which the Webburns come down; upon hanging woods, and steep banks, and sees that the meeting-place of the little streams is full of the romantic. Nor when he plunges into the leafy depths and stands beside the waters that the lofty Hameldon no longer separates, will the rambler be less impressed with his surroundings. Through the openings in the foliage, when a summer sun is in the sky, the rays dart upon the rippling stream, singing a plaintive air to the wild flowers that begem its banks, and patches of golden light are scattered upon the mossy ground. Though deep the solitude it is not oppressive, for companionship is not altogether lacking. In the pool is the wary trout, motionless save for an almost imperceptible movement of the tail; over the surface of the stream the gaudy dragon fly is flitting;

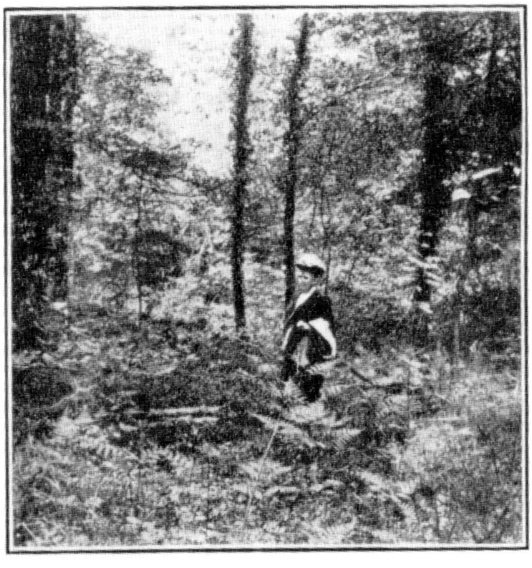

Photo by] Near Lizwell Meet. [Ernest Croft.

"The leafy depths."

and on the bough is the bird pouring forth her sweet notes in friendly rivalry with the tiny cascades. Yet amid this fair scene the waters must not linger; they go to meet the Dart which has been calling to them for ages. But no murmurs betokening sadness rise from the little river as it hastens on its way. It still sings merrily, and we cease to marvel at this when we look upon the beauties awaiting it. On one side are the wooded grounds of Spitchwick, and on the other the tree-clad heights of Buckland-in-the-Moor. Just before reaching the Dart it flows beneath the bridge over which passes the road to the Buckland Woods, and to the retired church upon the hill. From this crossing-place the visitor looks upon the scene which Keble has commemorated in his lines on the meeting of the little Webburn with the chief river of the Moor.

The manor of Spitchwick, which occupies the southern part of the parish of Widecombe has already been mentioned as being one of those left at his death by the first Lord Ashburton.* Under a decree of Chancery he purchased a long lease in the manor, but this expired many years ago, and the property has since changed hands several times. Lord Ashburton built a house there, and it became his favourite residence. It is situated on the slope of the hill above the Webburn valley, and not far from the present Leusden

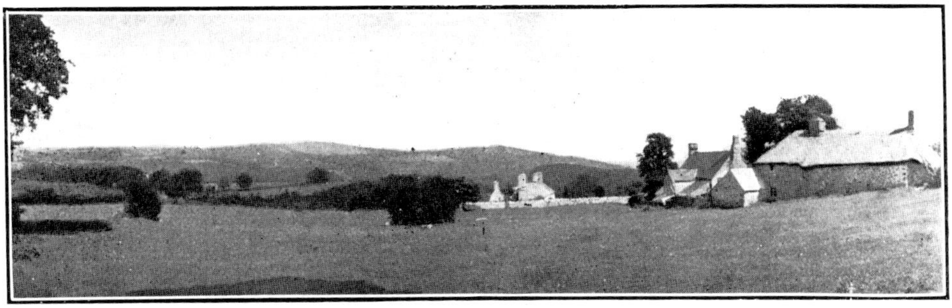

Photo by] [Mrs. Ernest Croft.

Pound's Gate.

"The distant common rising above the woods."

Church. The manor includes a considerable portion of the Moor, and is bounded for some distance by the Dart. The name is said to be derived from the Saxon word *spic*, meaning bacon, and to denote the early existence here of swine pastures.

Not far from the grounds of Spitchwick is the hamlet of Pound's Gate, from which place a fine view of the Buckland side of the Dart valley, with the distant common rising above the woods, is obtained. The hamlet is situated on the Ashburton road above Leigh Tor, the rocks below which the Dart bids farewell to the Moor,† and about a mile from New Bridge.

According to tradition Dartmoor is haunted by a Black Dog, and the animal has been seen more than once in this neighbourhood. It usually makes its appearance in lonely places when darkness covers the heath. I have gathered several stories of people having encountered it; indeed, I have known those who firmly believed that they had seen it. Some might perhaps be frightened at meeting such an animal, but not so Joey Brown. Joey was returning from the Forest Inn at Hexworthy, where he had been spending the evening, when on reaching the head of the steep lane leading from Sherberton Common to Ponsworthy, where was his home, he suddenly fell over some object in the road. Scrambling to his knees, which, however, he was only able to do with difficulty, his legs

* *Vide* Chap. XI. *ante*.

† *Vide* Chap. XII. *ante*.

being very unsteady—perhaps rendered so by his walk—he saw, dimly outlined against the star-lit sky, the dark form of some animal. Joey had often heard of the Black Dog of the Moor, and felt sure that he had met it at last. But he was not afraid of it; in fact, he said, when relating the circumstance, that he had never felt bolder in his life. He determined to risk whatever danger there might be, and set a mark upon the dog, so that when it appeared again a proof that he had really encountered it would be forthcoming. He therefore took off his scarf and tied it securely round the animal's neck, and staggering to his feet, went on his way, and at length reached home. In the morning Joey became the hero of Ponsworthy. Everybody was talking of his courage in daring to set a mark upon the Black Dog. But alas, his fame was not enduring. A simple thing caused him to fall from his lofty pedestal. It was the appearance in the hamlet of Farmer Smerdon's old black sow wearing a neckcloth.

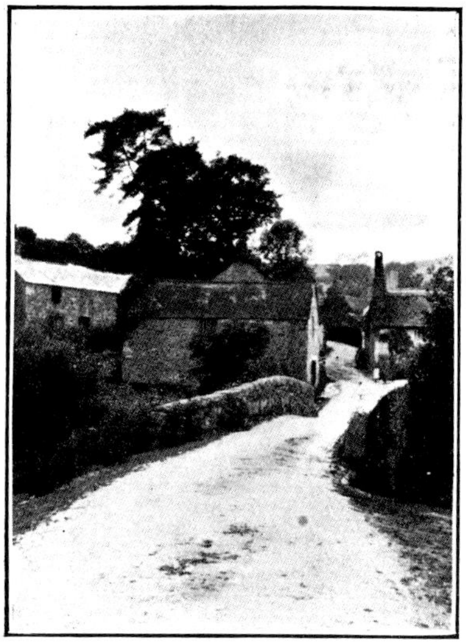

Photo by] [Mrs. Ernest Croft.

Ponsworthy Bridge.

"A small, one-arched structure."

Ponsworthy, the hamlet through which the West Webburn flows immediately before it enters the woods that extend up the valley from Lizwell Meet, bears a name the first part of which is probably derived from the principal object in it. This is the bridge, and if we really do see in the name the Celtic *pont*, it would point to the existence of such a structure at this spot, probably a clapper, in very early times. The latter part of the name is, of course, the Saxon *worthig*, a settlement, and the *bridge settlement* would exactly describe the place. Mr. William Burt in his preface to Carrington's *Dartmoor* cites the name of Ponsworthy as evidence of a Roman connection with Devon, considering the first part of it to be the Latin *pons*. Such it may possibly be, but I certainly incline to a Celtic derivation of the name.

Ponsworthy Bridge is a small, one-arched structure, and bears the date 1666, cut on a stone at the eastern end of the northern parapet. But the year which marked a great calamity in London probably saw no untoward event in this secluded place, though one that occurred in the parish twenty-eight years previously was no doubt then often the theme of conversation by the peat fire of a winter evening. In 1638 it was that the great thunderstorm occurred which did so much damage to Widecombe Church, and Ponsworthy was not without some memories of it. It is not recorded that the ravages of the storm extended to this hamlet, but its people, so the story goes, witnessed the dread appearance of the one who caused the tempest. Satan after having been supplied with drink at the inn at Pound's Gate,* galloped off to Widecombe town to destroy the church, and was seen as he passed through Ponsworthy. He was mounted on a coal-black horse, and the animal, so says the story, " struck vire wi' he's hoofs, an' didn' mun make a clatter whain he waint auver the bridge."

* *Tales of the Dartmoor Pixies* Chap. II.

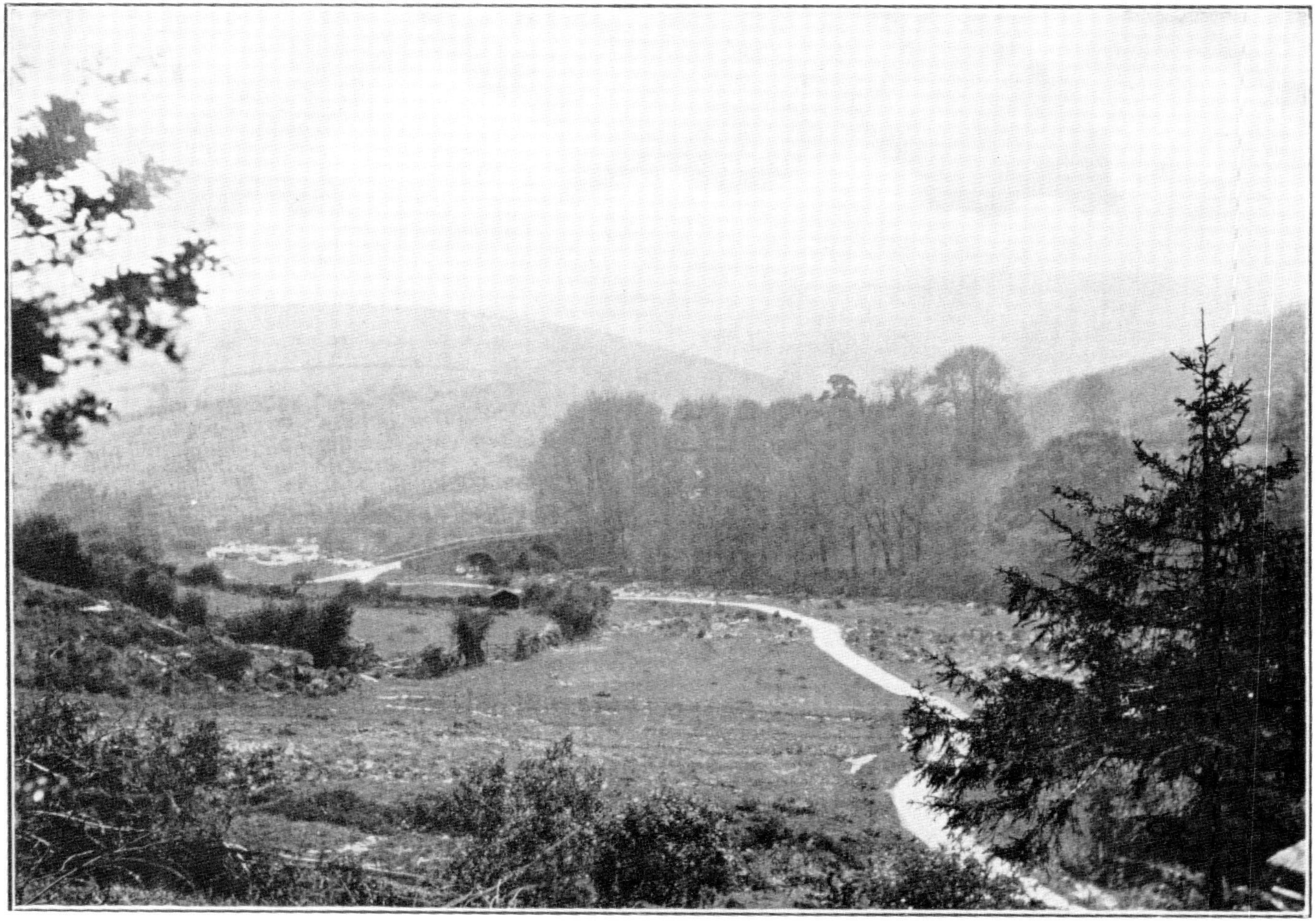

SEE PAGE 110.

Dartmeet.

PHOTO BY ERNEST CROFT.

"Nature has not been left in undisputed sway."

XIV.

DARTMEET.

EARLY REFERENCES TO THE DART——THE FOREST BOUNDARY LINE——AN ANCIENT FARM——OLD OAKS——SCENE BELOW YAR TOR HILL——HEXWORTHY——HUCCABY CLEAVE——ANTIQUITIES——AN IMPORTANT TRACK OF EARLY DAYS.

It was here they met one wintry morn,
Never again were their lives forlorn;
No priest was required to make them one,
For their wedding-day was known to none;
The stream of their lives right merrily sped,
Together they roamed where Nature led;
Their will was one, their purpose alone
In the Sea of Love to lose their own.
—J. C. (In the Visitors' Book at French's Cottage.)

THE two branches of Dartmoor's chief river, called respectively the East and the West Dart, have each a long course through the Forest, but do not mingle their waters within its confines. When they meet they bid it adieu, though the united stream has yet some miles to run before it leaves the Moor. These branches are referred to in the return to the Forest Perambulation of 1240, where the boundary line is traced to the point where the Walla Brook falls into the East Dart, "et sic per Dertam usque ad aliam Dertam." In a return of the Forest bounds made in 1609 the branches are also mentioned, the line being said to run "by the said Easter Dart to another Dart called Wester Dart." But there is no name given to the confluence of these two important streams in either of the returns, though it is probable that at the date of the latter the spot bore a similar one to that by which it is called at present. At all events, we find it mentioned in 1689 as Dartamet, or Dartameet. It was

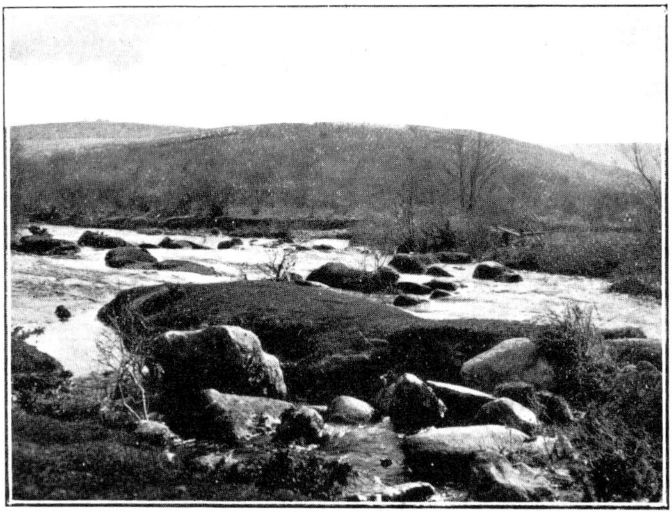

Photo by] [Mrs. Ernest Croft.

The Confluence of the Darts.

"Mentioned in 1689 as Dartamet, or Dartameet."

so referred to by Christopher Pearce in a deposition respecting the eastern boundary of the Forest. Though at that time residing in Exeter, Pearce was a native of Dartmoor, and until he was twenty-four years of age had lived at a place there called Sherwell, which is not much over a mile distant from the confluence. In alluding to the latter his words are: "Which place where the rivers meet is called Dartamet," and we may reasonably suppose it had always borne that name within his recollection. We do not know his age at the time the deposition was made, but the date of his birth would probably take us back to the middle of the seventeenth century, and perhaps much earlier. Towards the end of the following one the name again appears in the setting forth of the Forest limits. This is in the presentment of a jury at a Court of Survey held at Lydford Castle in 1786, where they state that in one part of its circuit the boundary line runs "down East Dart till it joins West Dart at a place called Dartsmeet."

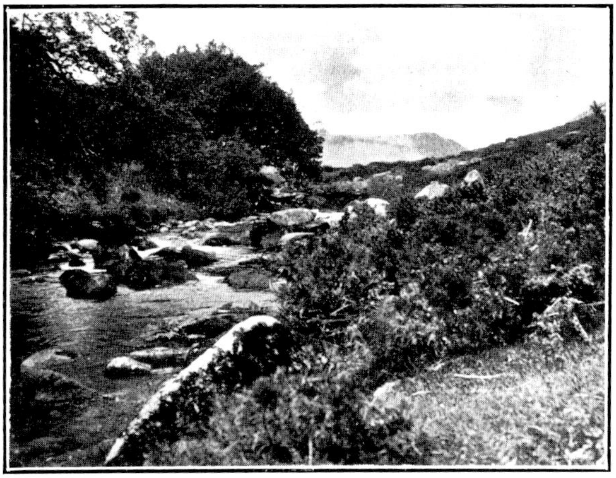

Photo by] [Mrs Ernest Croft.

On the East Dart.

"Above the bridge the Dart bends towards the west."—*(See Page 111.)*

There are grander scenes in the Dartmoor region than that presented by the valley at the point where its two principal streams unite. Nature has not been left in undisputed sway, and man's handiwork has banished much of the romantic. But the valley has, nevertheless, many beauties; there is nothing within the Forest, nor upon any part of its boundary line, of a similar kind. With the exception of a few places, such as where the latter crosses the roads near Princetown and at Newhouse, or where it runs by the farms of the settlers in the valley of the Walla Brook, this line is drawn through wild and desolate scenes. Throughout its entire length of nearly fifty miles it passes only a few solitary trees till it comes to the head of the valley in which the Dart's branches meet. Then immediately within the great tract, the limits of which it defines, the plantations of Brimpts clothe the hillside, and a prospect such as it has hitherto unknown comes into view. And it is one that it would be difficult to rival, even in the Dartmoor borderland. Certainly the valley is a finer sight here than when seen from the place where the waters meet, as the visitor will own if he but take his stand near the Walla Brook where it comes down from Babeny, and look in the direction of the river's flow.

The valley in which the East Dart and the West Dart become one stream is formed by Yar Tor Down and Dartmeet Hill, both within the bounds of the commons of Widecombe, on the east side, and the hill of Brimpts, which is part of the Forest, and a portion of Holne Moor, on the west. Standing on the bridge thrown over the East Dart, only a few yards above the confluence, and looking up stream, we see the trees of Brimpts on the left hand and the great bare hill surmounted with the rocks of Yar Tor on the right. Brimpts was probably a farm long before the history of Dartmoor commences, though there is little doubt it has been much added to since we first hear of it. This is in 1307, when it is mentioned in an account of the custodian of the Forest, made up to the 6th August in that year, on which date Edward II. granted the "free Chase of Dartmoor with appurtenances" to Piers Gaveston. When the favourite lost his head, the

Chase, or Forest as it still continues to be called, reverted to the Crown, there being then no Earl of Cornwall. But Brimpts did not belong to the earldom although within the limits of that tract of land which was an appanage of it. The farm was one of the ancient tenements of the Forest, and the entry in the custodian's account is merely that of the fine which one Gregory paid on succeeding to his father's holding there.

Though plantations form the chief wooded adornments of Brimpts other trees are not wanting—the remnants of a grove that probably once covered much of the sheltered slope. Many of these were felled at a time when rumours of invasion were in the air, and oak timber was required for the fashioning of England's wooden walls. About the same time a number of stately trees were cut down at Mount Edgcumbe to be used for a similar purpose. Whether they found their way to the shipyards we do not know; those which fell before the axe at Brimpts did not.

No contrast could well be greater than that afforded by the tree-covered hillside above this bank of the stream, and the bare common rising steeply from the other. On this hand pastures and thriving plantations; on that heather, and gorse, and rock. And yet there is nothing inharmonious in it; it is only when one ascends the hill up which the road leads towards Widecombe, and looks down upon the vale, that Brimpts seems out of its place, appearing, as it does, like a bit of the "in-country" dropped in the midst of the Moorlands.

Rather less than half a mile above the bridge the Dart bends towards the west, turning eastward higher up. Here a most charming view is presented looking up stream. At the foot of Yar Tor Hill, which descends with a bold sweep, is a small plain, extending to the river, and on this are patches of heather and scattered rocks. The opposite hill is clothed in great part with trees, and, having the same contour as the river, forms a huge amphitheatre. Near its highest part, and seen against the northern sky, is a clump of fir trees to which the name of the Seven Sisters has been given.

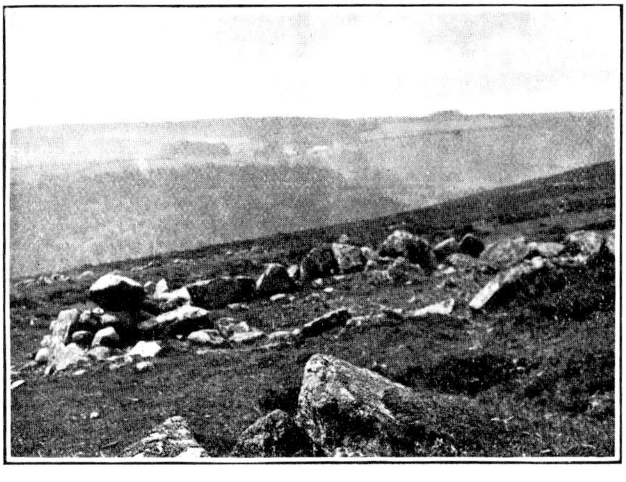

Photo by] [Mrs. Ernest Croft.

Ancient Enclosure on Yar Tor Hill.

"A small enclosure having at its eastern end a hut circle."—*(See Page 113.)*

Yar Tor is not seen to the best advantage from the bridge. A far better view of it is obtained from the top of the hill on the Brimpts side, near where the road passes one of the entrances to the grounds. But even this is not so good as that which one gets of it from the door of the Forest Inn at Hexworthy, where it is seen rising behind a nearer hill. And it is worth while going there, not only to see Yar Tor, but the whole picture commanded from that hostelry. It is far and away the finest view within the Forest of Dartmoor, though by no means what it was when I knew it first. Then there was nothing in the shape of habitations but a few ancient thatched dwellings to be seen. Now most of these have been swept away, and modern houses erected in their stead; and besides the abomination, in a rural scene, of corrugated iron, an incongruous feature in the shape of red brick has been introduced where only granite ought to be. I remember riding over

Holne Moor many years ago (my notes show me it was on the 20th August, 1875) in a cart returning from Hexworthy Bridge, in which a load of those red bricks had been taken to the site of the house. Had I known they were to be used to disfigure the landscape I should not have been so pleased to avail myself of the driver's friendly offer of a "lift." But Time, which changes everything, is toning down the vivid colour of the clay, and the patch of vermilion is year by year growing less offensive to the eye.

From the southern parapet of the bridge the other branch of the river is seen. A valley opens on the right, and through this the West Dart comes to meet its sister stream, its course here lying between the Forest and the enclosures of Cumston, or more correctly Combestone, a farm in the parish of Holne, which takes its name from a tor near by. The higher part of this valley, which is known as Huccaby Cleave, forms a romantic glen, where is a charming mingling of rock and wood and gleaming cascade. The waters fall into deep pools, overhung with dwarf oaks and fringed with ferns, the haunts of the otter, and where unsuspecting salmon lurk and hungry trout leap into the sunlight. Near the head of the cleave a few sycamores mark a former home, according to the old tales of the peasants, of the "little people" who once made their presence felt upon the Moor. It is a cave known to the dwellers in the neighbourhood as the Piskies' Holt, and which I have elsewhere described.* Its charming surroundings would render it a fitting abode for the frolicsome elves who live in Westcountry tradition, and we cannot wonder that the peasantry should once have regarded it as their haunt.

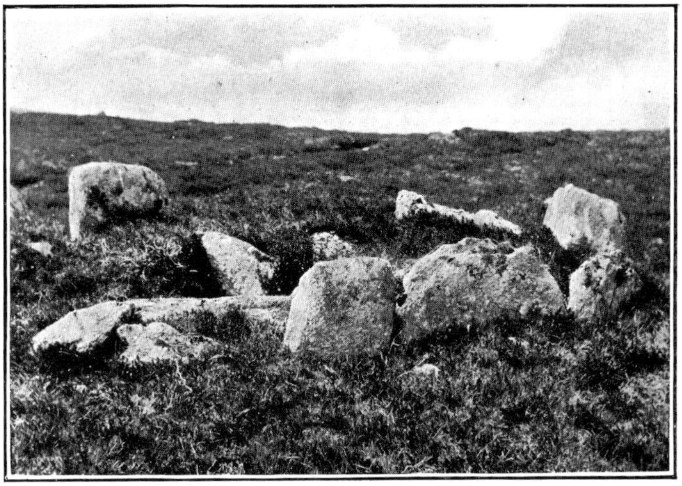

Photo by] [Ernest Croft.

Kistvaen near Yar Tor.

"Known in the neighbourhood as Money Pit."—*(See Page 113.)*

In a work published over fifty years ago it was casually mentioned that at Dartmeet was the junction of three parishes, and it is amusing to note that most of the guide-books duly record this fact, as though it were rare on Dartmoor, and ought not to be omitted. Had the writers of these possessed any real knowledge of the district they would have been aware that more than a score of instances of three parishes meeting are found on the Moor, eighteen of them being on the Forest boundary line.

Half a mile below the bridge the Dart makes a sharp bend and enters a deep gorge, but this forms no part of the Dartmeet valley. Readers of Eden Phillpotts' story, *The River*, will remember it as the scene of Sorrow Scobhull's meeting with Timothy Oldreive, when the latter learns from him that Nicholas Edgecombe has gone to meet his wife at the Piskies' Holt. Towering high above it are the rocks of Sharp Tor and Mil Tor on one side, and on the other the granite masses of Bench Tor, which name, by a series of gradations, has become in the Moorland vernacular—Binjie Tor. This gorge takes rank

* *Tales of the Dartmoor Pixies.* Chap. I.

among the finest on Dartmoor, and viewed from the lane between Holne Chase Hill and Holne village presents a particularly striking appearance.

The hill rising on the left as we look down the stream from Dartmeet Bridge, bears the same name as the confluence, but presents nothing remarkable. Were we to ascend it we should find upon it a number of low banks—reaves as they are usually called—crossing each other, and forming what are apparently small enclosures. It is, however, doubtful whether these are of very great antiquity, although they are similar to others found in different parts of the Moor which are considered to be of early date. Many years ago I was informed in the vicinity that a warren at one time existed on this hill, and the banks were said to have been formed in connection with that. There is no doubt that objects of comparatively recent erection on the Moor have been mistaken for genuine antiquities. I know of more than one instance where such has been the case.

But there are, nevertheless, some remains on this hill about the antiquity of which there can be no doubt, while on the slope of Yar Tor, north of the road, they are exceedingly numerous. If the visitor interested in archæology desires to examine these he will make his way up the road, and at the first bend will notice on the left a congeries of stones standing on the common. On approaching them he will find that they form the wall of a small enclosure, having at its eastern end a hut circle, the latter being a good example. Then, if he make his way upward, still keeping on the common, he will find other remains of a similar character; and will also meet with them on the slope under Sharp Tor, which pile he will see across the combe when he reaches the summit of the hill.

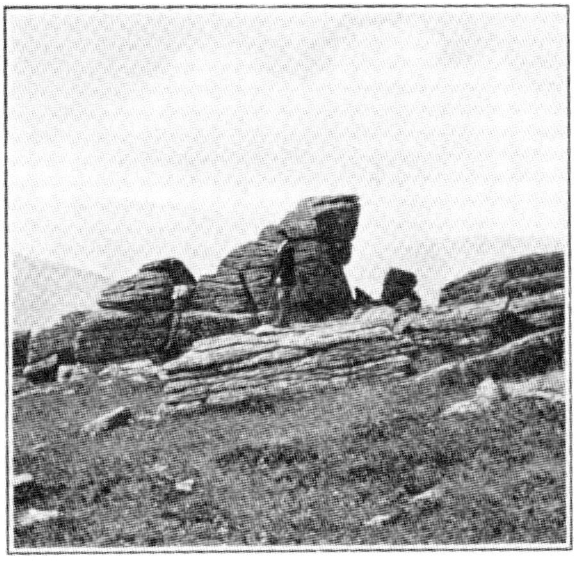

Photo by] [Ernest Croft.

Yar Tor.

"Consists of several fine masses of granite."—*(See Page 114.)*

Eastward of Yar Tor, and near the road that leads to Sherwell, is a kistvaen, surrounded by a circle of stones. It is usually known in the neighbourhood as Money Pit, a name which points to the belief formerly existing that these ancient graves were places in which treasure had been hidden. What the despoilers of this kist discovered we can, of course, only guess, but we may be quite sure it was something very different from that which the story says was found there. According to this a farmer of Pound's Gate dreamt that a considerable sum of money was concealed under the stone in the middle of the little circle in the dip between Yar Tor and Corndon Tor. He said nothing about it to anyone, but at nightfall made his way thither, determined to see what the stone might hide. With great exertion he threw it on one side, and was much disappointed at finding that the kist contained only a piece of flint, rudely carved in the shape of a heart. This he brought away with him, and placed it in a cupboard in his kitchen. From that time forth he was a changed man. Hitherto he had been a kind husband and father, and a stanch friend, but now his family were neglected, and he made many enemies by his churlish disposition. This state of matters continued for about twelve months, and then he suddenly became the good and warm-hearted man that he was formerly. He was at a loss to explain this even to himself, until one day going to his cupboard he found that the flinty heart was no longer there. A few days previously his little son had taken it for a plaything, and had lost it upon the Moor. Then he knew that it was the possession of the heart of stone that had altered his nature.

On Corn Down, north-eastward of the kist, are some fine cairns, as well as good examples of hut circles. The whole neighbourhood teems with the remains of a bygone day, and affords a good field for the study, not only of pre-historic monuments, but also of those belonging to later times.

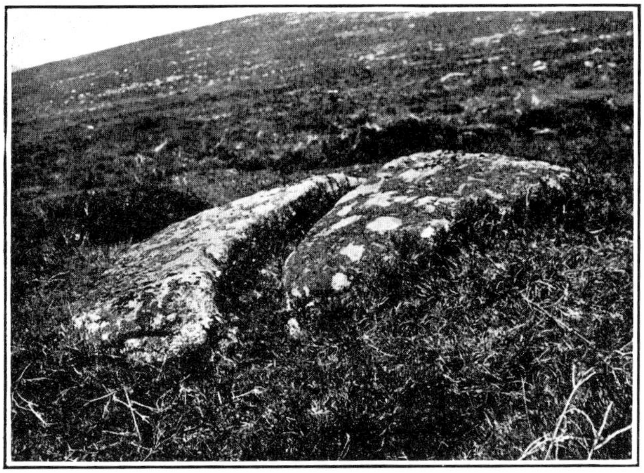

Photo by] [Ernest Croft.

The Coffin Stone.

"At which funerals passing from the Forest to Widecombe Churchyard invariably make a halt."—*(See Page 115.)*

Yar Tor is readily reached either by passing up over the down a short distance from the bridge, or by following the road to the top of the hill, and then striking left over the common. It consists of several fine masses of granite, and is worth a visit both on account of these, and for the extensive views obtained from it of those parts of the Forest lying near the East Dart and the Walla Brook. Below the northern side of the hill the road is seen descending towards Sherwell, which is situated quite close to the border line of the Forest, though not within it. It was here that Old Martha Whitchalse dwelt, the woman with the evil eye. To be overlooked, or ill-wished, as it is oftener termed on the Moor, by Martha was a fate to be feared, and nobody that knew her would have dared to incur her displeasure. The old woman lived alone. Her husband died not long after she had been wedded to him, leaving her with a little baby boy. When he grew to be a youth he got into trouble, having stolen some sheep on the Moor, and left the neighbourhood. The years went on, but Martha could never learn anything of him. But she cherished the idea that she should see him again ; and morose and sour as she was, seemed to have one warm place in her heart for her absent son. Age crept upon the dame, and her limbs became feeble, but she still retained her power over her neighbours, who stood in great fear of her. One day a stranger came down the hill, and asked her for a drink of water. Martha rudely threw a bucket towards him, telling him to fill it from the brook, for it was not for an old woman like her to fetch water for a strong man. The stranger filled the bucket, and after having drank, turned to the old dame and showing her a gold coin, told her that had she treated him civilly he should have given it to her, but as she had not done so he would keep the money for one more deserving of it. Martha turned her evil eye upon him, and shaking her bony finger in his face, warned him that his time was near. Before three days, she said, he would feel the effect of her power. The stranger laughed, and went on his way, but it fell out as the old woman had said. On the third day fearful pains seized him, and he gradually pined away. He was staying with a farmer near Post Bridge, and one evening he called him into his room, and told him who he was. His mother, he said, was named Martha Whitchalse, and had once lived in that neighbourhood. Then he spoke no more, and before the dawn arrived had passed away. They bore the news to the old dame, who heard them in silence, but a look of horror spread over her face when she learned that she had turned her evil eye upon her own son. From that hour she refused sustenance, and one morning they found her dead on her cold hearth-stone.

Another object of interest on Dartmeet Hill is the Coffin Stone, at which funerals passing from the Forest to Widecombe Churchyard invariably make a halt. This is beside a green path that leaves the road at the bend above the bridge.

On the site of the residence close to the bridge was formerly a cottage, where for many years dwelt George Caunter—Uncle George, as he was always termed. The old man could look back over many years of nineteenth century Dartmoor history, and was able to relate numerous stories of old times, among them being not a few in which, as he had "heerd tell," the pixies—or pisgies, as he preferred to call them—were concerned. Two others whose memories went far back also lived very near. These were the brothers Daniel and Joey Leaman. Their cottages stood by the river not far above the bridge. But alterations and "improvements" have taken place since the old men passed away, and you trace little of the former appearance of their dwellings now.

A stone in the bridge at Dartmeet bears the date 1792, before which time the river was crossed by a ford and a clapper, portions of the latter yet existing. On the eastern bank a sort of raised causeway is seen, which formed the approach to the rude bridge on that side, and on the western a buttress still remains in a state of good preservation. But the bridge was destroyed during a flood in the year 1826, and though "restored" some sixty-two years later, probably presents an appearance altogether unlike that of the original structure.

The ancient track which crossed the river at this place was of considerable importance, one branch of it forming the principal means of communication between the south-western part of Dartmoor and the extensive parish of Widecombe. This may be seen running through the enclosures near the little chapel at Huccaby to the West Dart, which it crosses at Week Ford. It is carried up the right bank of the Wobrook to Horse Ford, and may be traced from that point to the commons on the western side of the Forest.

The absence of any signs of a clapper on this part of the West Dart would almost lead to the supposition that the early settlers in Hexworthy were obliged to ford the stream. But this could hardly have been the case, for during a flood they would have found it impossible to do so, and without a bridge would, at such a time, be cut off from Widecombe and the eastern part of the Moor. There can be little doubt that a clapper did once exist on this part of the river. Unless it occupied the site of the present Hexworthy Bridge, its disappearance is probably to be attributed to a flood. Of one thing we may be certain. If such an event did happen it was in the days before "restorers" came upon the scene, which with the example of modern clapper building at Dartmeet before our eyes, we shall probably not deplore.

XV.

THE VALLEY OF DEAN BURN.

An Enchanting Scene——A Haunt of Herrick——A Romantic Vale——The Hound's Pool——Legend of Knowles, the Weaver——A Rocky Stream——Forest Paths——Lambs' Down Farm——Early Morning on the Moor.

Adown a dim ravine,
As a young child runs homeward through the dusk,
Just pausing here and there when first it starts
To pluck a flower, and singing as it goes,
A brook came bounding on from pool to pool.
—George Frederick Jackson.

So impressive is the scenery of the romantic glen of Dean Burn that Polwhele, who wrote more than a century ago, remarks of it that to enter it has the effect of enchantment. And he is right, though not quite in the sense he intended. The belief in Druidism so largely held by antiquaries of his time he fully shared, and it is therefore only to be expected that he would see in the narrow vale, where crags and oak woods rise above a brawling stream, a spot such as the Druids would have chosen for the performance of certain of their rites. But while nothing that presented itself to the mind of Polwhele may be seen by the wanderer who to-day makes his way into the recesses of the vale, he will none the less feel the effect of enchantment. It will not, however, be caused by a mystic priesthood, but by a priestess who stands as a visible link between man and his God. Her handiwork is seen everywhere, and her name is Nature.

The stream known as the Dean Burn rises on the borders of the Moor, in the parish of Buckfastleigh. Not far from its source is an ancient fording-place, close to which several tracks in use in a former day cross each other, and immediately below this it enters the deep and narrow valley mentioned by Polwhele. This, though not so well known as others on the fringe of Dartmoor, is as fully deserving of notice, and sheds upon that lonely land a lustre that does not pale before the richest of its gems. Except a small portion at its upper end, it is within the parish of Dean Prior, and extends for about two and a half miles in a south-easterly direction. Its sides are covered with oak coppice, and in places with larger trees, from the midst of which arise grey crags, festooned with ivy and other trailing plants. Above these wooded acclivities, for some distance below the head of the vale, are commons; throughout the lower part the trees climb from the little river to the fields, for cultivation has here wrestled successfully with the Moor.

The characteristics of this glen are truly expressed in its name. Here is the *dene*, the leafy wood; the *burn*, the rippling stream. And each comes lovingly to the other. The brook hastens down from the bare heights to hide itself beneath the trees; the trees press forward to welcome it, and fling their veils of green over its silent pools and broken waters.

When the Burn reaches the end of this vale, wherein so much that is beautiful is hidden, it flows under Warn Bridge, near to which is the sequestered hamlet of Dean Combe, situated about three and a half miles from Brent and one and a half from Buckfastleigh.

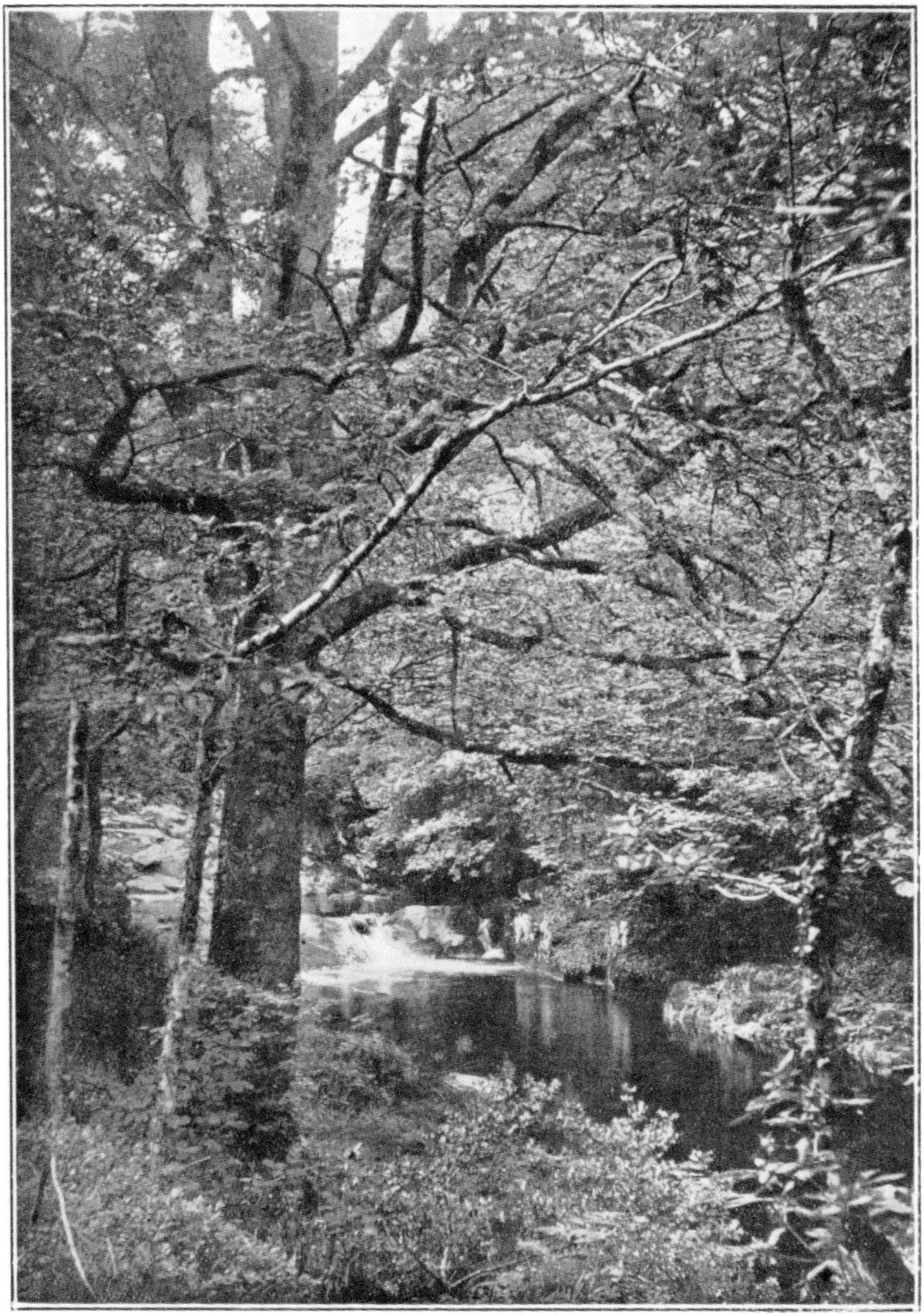

SEE PAGE 116.

In the Valley of Dean Burn.

PHOTO BY C. R. ROWE.

"The dene, the leafy wood; the burn, the rippling stream."

We shall enter the valley at a gateway close to the bridge, whence a cart track runs through the wood, and this for some distance will be our guide. Apart from the natural attractions of the spot, every step is fraught with interest, for we cannot but imagine that here the poet Herrick, who for so long made Dean Prior his home, often wandered. True, he does not sing its praises, and in taking his farewell of it tells us in effect that he leaves it without regret; but he could not have dwelt for years near to the valley without often passing this way. And who shall say, notwithstanding his seeming dislike of it, what inspiration he may not have derived from its brawling stream and its trees and rocks. The recollections of town life, which appears to have been attractive to him, may have sometimes rendered him impatient of his sojourn in this corner of Devon; but there must have been times when he found pleasure in it, or he would scarcely have remained so long in the parish as he did, nor have returned to it after the lapse of years. It was in 1629 that he first became its vicar, and he remained there until 1647, when he was ejected from the living. He retired to London, leaving Dean, as he thought, for ever. He would go back to it, he said, when the rocks turned to rivers, and the rivers to men. His delight at being released from what he termed his "long and dreary banishment" was unbounded; and yet he was again to become a voluntary exile in this obscure Devonshire parish which he had said he should never look upon with contentment, even were its streams silver and its rocks gold. But fifteen years work mighty changes, and though they did not effect such a transformation as Herrick had spoken of, yet at the expiration of that period he found that he could bring himself to live once more among a people whom he had described as being almost as rude as savages. In 1662, the Act of Uniformity having cleared the way, he returned to pass the remaining years of his life in his old home. It is strange that one who seems to have found a country life irksome should have been able to sing so sweetly of rural customs. But we forget his changeable nature and his inconsistencies in the charm of his poetry; we are content to remember him only as one who has left us beautiful thoughts clothed in beautiful language. He died in 1674, and Dean will always possess an interest, even were it still as he has described it, as having for so long a period been his home. The poet vicar rests in the graveyard of Dean Prior, and in the church is a tablet to his memory.

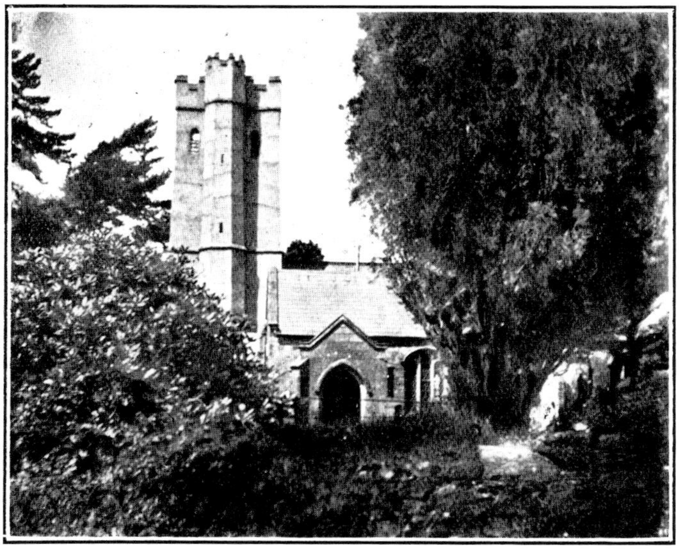

Photo by] [C. R. Rowe.

Dean Prior Church.

"The poet vicar rests in the graveyard."

Ere we have proceeded far into the recesses of the vale (our path runs on the left bank of the stream, and very near to it) we shall observe, just where the sides begin to grow higher, a lateral combe to the southward. Above the western slope of this is Skerraton Farm, the manor of which name, anciently written Sciredun, was formerly held by the service of finding arrows when the King should hunt in his Forest of Dartmoor. A track runs down this combe to a fording-place on the stream, close to which is a small clam, or wooden footbridge.

High above us, on the northern side of the valley, are the crags known as Dean Clatters, which we shall notice exhibit bolder features as we advance. Presently the sound of falling waters strikes upon the ear. At every step it grows louder, and on passing a large stone to the left of the path we come in sight of a fall, where the stream slides rapidly down a kind of narrow trough formed in the rock, into a deep basin, which the dwellers in the locality will tell us bears the name of the Hound's Pool.

To this a strange legend attaches; the pool is said to be haunted by a black dog, which may be seen at noon and at midnight engaged in the hopeless task of emptying it of its waters. Mr. Richard John King, whose knowledge of Devonshire folk-lore was very extensive, was the first to give us the story. It tells how a weaver of Dean Combe named Knowles was seen on the day after his burial working busily at his loom. His son at once acquainted the parson with the circumstance, and the good man lost no time in visiting the weaver's house. He commanded Knowles to come down from the upper chamber in which his loom was standing, and after some parleying the weaver obeyed. The parson then threw a handful of earth from the churchyard into his face and immediately the restless spirit of the weaver was transformed into a black dog. The clerical ghost-layer, ordering the animal to follow him, led the way to the Valley of Dean Burn, when a mighty rushing wind arose, before which the trees of the glen bent low. Then the parson took the hound to the pool below the waterfall, and, giving the animal a nut shell with a hole in it, bade it dip out the waters, on the completion of which task, but not before, it would find rest. And so the spectral hound still works wearily on, but is only visible when the hands of the clock mark the hour of twelve.

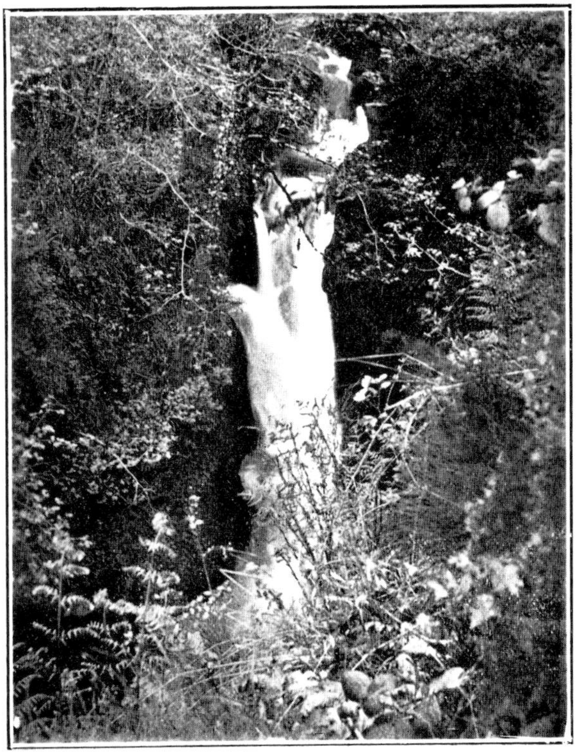

Photo by] [C. R. Rowe.

Cascade at the Hound's Pool.

"The sound of falling waters strikes upon the ear."

The waterfall at the Hound's Pool is not the only one we shall see—there is another, hidden by thick growth, just above it—for the bottom of the glen, as Herrick truly observes, is rocky, and tears the streams, "and makes them frantic." The scene at this spot is one which will detain us long in its contemplation; there is a blending of sublimity and soft beauty that cannot fail to deeply impress. The hoary rocks uplifting themselves from the side of the steep slope, the dwarf oaks, and the tangled undergrowth that fills the depths of the valley, go to make up a picture that will not soon fade from the memory.

By-and-by the path narrows, and becomes fainter, until it is lost in a forest of briars, and then we leave the stream and pass up the northern side of the vale to Wallaford Down.

Making our way along the verge of this fine, open common, whence the eye ranges over a wide and varied view, we proceed to Cross Furzes, where are the roads to which allusion has been made as intersecting each other near the upper end of the valley. These are formed on the lines of ancient tracks, some of which I have traced for a considerable distance.* One of them is the old Abbots' Way, which crosses the southern part of the Forest, and formed a means of communication between Buckfast Abbey and the Cistercian foundation at Buckland, and the Benedictine house at Tavistock. Another is a track which led along the southern verge of the Moor to Plympton, passing through Harford and Cornwood. These both crossed the Burn at a ford near by, to which we shall descend, and passing over the brook by means of a single stone clapper, shall find on reaching the shoulder of the hill confronting us that we are at the head of the valley. Here we have an exceedingly fine view of it throughout almost its whole length. We shall notice another lateral combe just below where we stand, and shall also not fail to observe the fine cliffs on the further bank of the stream. A nearer examination of these will well repay the visitor, and he will find that he may best reach them by following the tributary rivulet that trickles through the little side valley at his feet.

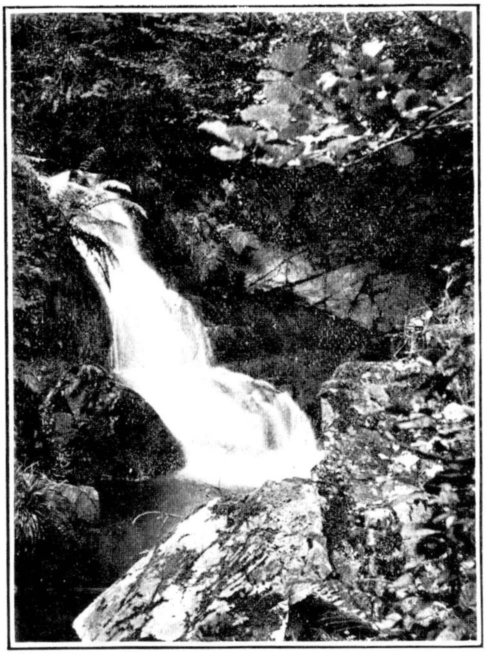

Photo by] [C. R. Rowe.

Cascade on the Burn.

"Hidden by thick growth."—*(See Page 120.)*

Near by is a ruined farmhouse, called after the common on which it stands, Lambs' Down, or, to give it its local appellation, Lemson. Though presenting in itself nothing of interest, it forms a pleasing feature in the view of the valley from a point near Skerraton Farm, where, its true nature not being discoverable, it wears the appearance of a mouldering castle of ancient days.

This ruin is haunted by the ghost of one Jan Meddler—that is if any credence is to be placed in the story. Jan, who lived here all alone after the building had gone partly to decay, was very penurious, and denied himself many of the necessaries of life. It was quite a mystery to his few neighbours why the old man should be so miserly, for he had no relatives for whom he could be saving his money. One day a mendicant happened to pass that way, and seeing Jan at his door, asked alms. Wonderful to relate, Jan was so moved by his tale of woe that he took a coin from his pocket and gave it to him. He supposed it to be a farthing, and the beggar thought the same. Disappointed at the smallness of the gift the man flung it from him, and cursing the old miser, went on his

* *Ancient Stone Crosses of Dartmoor and its Borderland*, Chap. XVI.

way. He had not gone long before Jan going to his hoard discovered that the coin he had offered the man was a guinea, and not a farthing as he had imagined. His fingers were covered with mud, and as he had held the coin for some time in his hand before he could finally make up his mind to part with it, he had so bedaubed it as to render it unrecognisable. With feverish haste he set about searching for it, but the piece of money having fallen on a heap of rubbish he was unable to find it. Day after day, and month after month, old Jan Meddler looked for it; he never wearied in his search, and it was while he was engaged in it that he died. Then his ghost continued the task; but it would seem without any satisfactory result, for though years have passed away since the miser's death the search is not yet ended. When the moon shines bright upon the Moor the old man's shade is still to be seen groping among the ruins—that is, by those who visit the place at the right time.

We cannot now trace the Abbots' Way with certainty from the ford below Lambs' Down Farmhouse, but we know the direction in which it ran, as it is plainly to be seen further out upon the commons. As we stand on the down near this ancient crossing-place on the Burn we may let our fancy stray back to the time when the brothers of Buckfast passed this way. We see the abbot on his palfrey, followed by a train of monks mounted on mules, ascending from the stream. They are abroad betimes, for their destination is the Abbey of Buckland, and the way across the Forest is long. The sun is but now beginning his daily journey, and the cold, grey light of the early morning yet lingers in the hollows of the hills. But under the rosy flush of the eastern sky villages and farmsteads, cornfields and woodlands, are revealing themselves, giving promise to the Moor of a speedy banishment of the shadows of the night. Down in the Valley of Dean Burn there is gloom and stillness, for the faint beams have not penetrated to its depths, and the morning breeze is so light that as it sweeps across it its leafy covering is undisturbed. But the voice of the Burn is heard coming up from beneath its canopy of green, and when the sun shall penetrate the living lattice its murmuring shall be changed to a joyous prattle. Moorward the heights wear a semi-transparent mask of mist, through which dark objects are dimly seen. Then, as the day opens wider its portals, and it rolls away, the shapeless forms gradually resolve themselves into rocks cresting the lofty heights. Soon they are no longer dark, for the sun has gilded their hoary faces and lighted up the clatter streaming from their sides. The abbot and his train, with minds not insensible to all these beauties, pass on to the Moor, and the lark upspringing pours forth her song to welcome them.

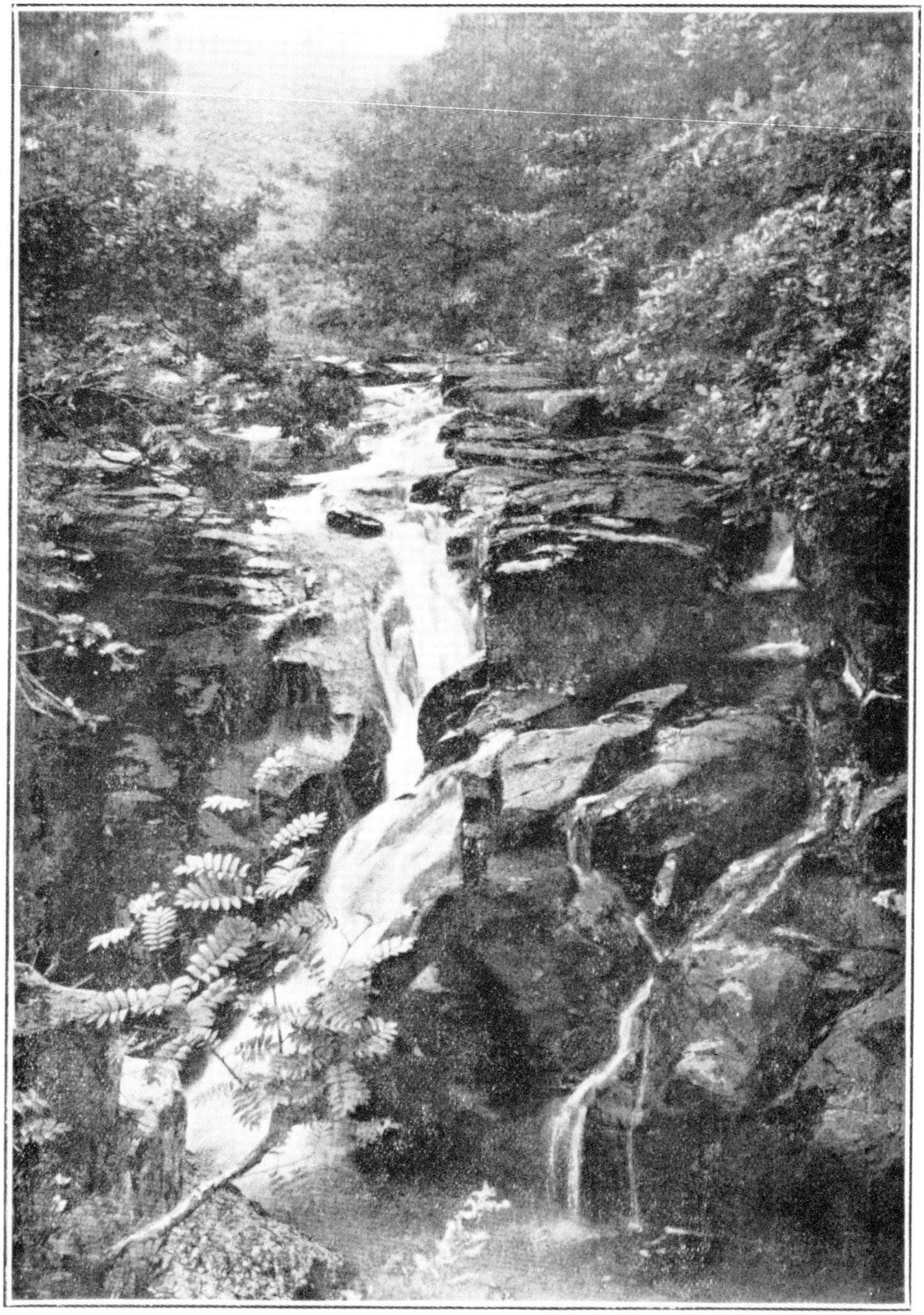

SEE PAGE 127.

Waterfall above Shipley Bridge.

PHOTO BY C. R. ROWE.

"The Avon here forces its way over a bed of rock, and suddenly tumbles into a deep pool."

XVI.

SHIPLEY.

North and South Dartmoor——Antiquities numerous in the South——The Avon——David of Sciredun——Didworthy Bridge——Zeal Pool and Cascades——Shipley Bridge——Henchertraw——The Story of Melys.

Forth from the mountain's riven side,
  The torrent bears its headlong force;
It bends the oak-bough to its tide,
  And shiver'd fragments mark its course;
The wanderer hears the thundering sound,
  And dread and awe his breast o'erflow,
He sees the impetuous waters bound,
  Yet where they tend he may not know.
—Anne Gibbons.

SOUTH Dartmoor, while its general characteristics are precisely similar to those of the northern part of the waste, differs from the latter in some points. The hills do not attain such an altitude as in the north, the fen district is not so extensive, the tors are fewer, and for the most part small. It is in fact less wild, though that aspect is sufficiently marked in places. Seas of waving bog-grass such as are seen in the north quarter are wanting, but there is yet a considerable tract of fen, extending from the springs of the Plym to the upper waters of the Avon.* No hillsides rent open by the rain are here, for the depth of peat is not nearly so great as in the neighbourhood of Cut Hill and around the sources of the Dart and Tavy; but there are nevertheless stretches of ground which the rambler would be inclined to describe as execrable, should he attempt to cross them, while below Fox Tor, and at Aune Head, are extensive mires, the latter being perhaps the worst on the Moor. The wildness of Cranmere has not here its counterpart, but desolate scenes meet the eye where the streams are young. Valleys quite like those of the West Ockment and the Tavy there are none, though it will be readily admitted by those who know the district that the gorge below Dartmeet presents features not one whit less striking; while no one who has looked upon the narrow pass through which the Erme flows when leaving the solitudes it has helped to cheer, can have failed to be impressed with the fine appearance of that cyclopean portal of turf and granite.

In its border scenery South Dartmoor is particularly happy. There is not a valley through which a stream quits the uplands from Holne Chase to Merivale that cannot boast of manifold beauties, and from each frontier height in that district the views, which embrace a wide extent of South Devon with glimpses of the Channel, are delightful. From an antiquarian standpoint the southern part of Dartmoor is of considerably greater interest than the northern. The evidences of early occupancy are here more abundant, and the examples of pre-historic monuments are finer. On the Tavy or the Ockments, the Taw or upper Teign, no such enclosed hut settlements as those on

* The Avon retains its Celtic appellation on the Moor, being there invariably called the Aune, and its source Aune Head.

the Avon, Erme, Yealm, or Plym are to be found, nor such groups of sepulchral remains as are to be seen on two of those rivers. Tin streaming seems to have been carried on to a much greater extent in southern Dartmoor than in its northern part, and this probably accounts for the more numerous vestiges of an ancient population.

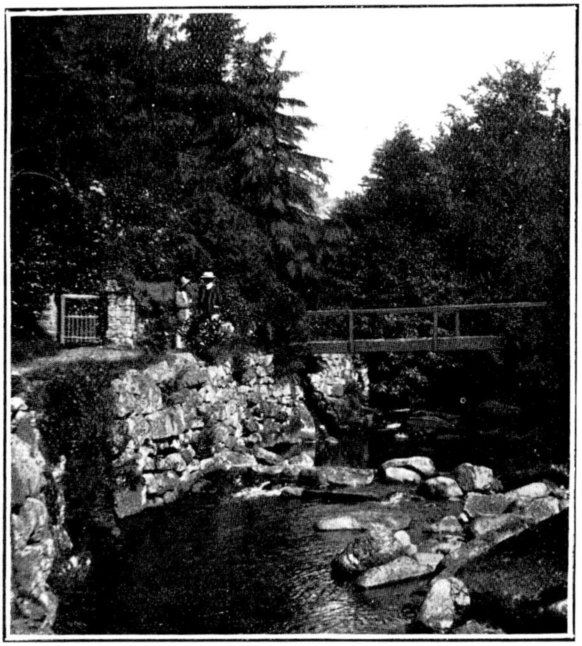

Photo by] [A. Edmund Spender.

The Avon at Brent Moor House.

"Trees line its banks and a clam connects them."

The southern part of Dartmoor is richer, too, in mediæval antiquities than the northern. On its verge were the four great religious houses of Tavistock, Buckland, Plympton and Buckfast, and the green paths leading from one to the other, marked here and there by an old granite cross, may still be traced upon the Moor, and lend an additional interest to a ramble over its breezy hills. Examples of every object of antiquity to be found in the Dartmoor district may here be met with, not excepting the dolmen, or cromlech, though the single specimen of the latter now remaining is in ruins.

One of the principal streams of South Dartmoor is the Avon, which rises on the high ground southward of Hexworthy, and in the neighbourhood of Ryder's Hill on the one hand and Cater's Beam* on the other. After a southerly course of nearly three miles it leaves the Forest, and then forms the boundary between Dean and Brent Moors to a point where it receives a feeder called Small Brook, when it enters Brent Moor, and runs through a part of it to the enclosed country. Half a mile below this confluence the valley narrows, and the river bending first to the left and then to the right, flows between Black Tor on the west and Shipley Tor on the east. Here it passes the grounds of Brent Moor House, enclosed over half a century ago, where trees line its banks and a clam connects them. Further down it is spanned by a grey moorstone bridge bearing the same name as the last mentioned tor, and this is also attached to the locality. An early form of it occurs in a land tenure deed of the time of Henry III., where it appears as Sappesleg, or, more probably, Sappesley. David of Sciredun (Skerraton, the farm on the side of the valley of Dean Burn, noticed in the previous chapter) held land at that place, and also at Sappesleg.

Shipley is about two miles and a half from the little town of South Brent, and may be reached by the road passing through the hamlet of Aish, or by the bridle-path running from Lutton to Didworthy, and thence to the Moor. In either case the way will take the visitor very near to Didworthy Bridge, by the low parapet of which we shall now imagine ourselves to be standing. A gate near the eastern end of the bridge opens upon a path running through a wood. For some distance it bears the river company, leading the

* The hill so called is wrongly placed on the Ordnance Map. It is there shown as being situated between Fox Tor and the upper Plym. Its true situation is between the Avon and Fish Lake, about two miles to the east.

rambler by the deep Zeal Pool, and the cascades above it, than which there are none more beautiful in the borderland of Dartmoor. At first the trees hide the river from view, but ere we have penetrated far into the wood we obtain a fine glimpse of it through the interlacing boughs, and also of another stream that has come down from the Moor to pour its waters into it. This is Red Brook, and it joins the Avon in a manner quite different from that in which most tributaries unite with a main river. The level of its bed is a few feet higher than that of the Avon, and a waterfall is consequently formed. This circumstance contributes in no slight degree to the beauty of the picture:—a picture of dancing waters and foam partly revealed; of moss and ferns and undergrowth; of creeping plants striving to wrap brown bark in a coat of green; of skies seen through the openings in a thick canopy of leaves.

When we pass on our way the Avon is again lost to view, but we are nevertheless speedily reminded that it is near to us. Though unseen it becomes audible. At first a low rumbling sound falls upon the ear, but rapidly grows louder as we proceed, and ere long we discover that the river we saw dancing so merrily over the pebbles a short distance below is here angry and impetuous. We have reached the deep Zeal Pool, and guided by the roar of the torrent we make our way over the carpet of moss and whortleberry plants that extends to its brink. Suddenly a narrow chasm opens before us, and the thunder of the waters becomes deafening. We look down and see that the Avon falls into this miniature canyon from a considerable height, to flow sullenly and in gloom, between rocky walls. It is almost with a feeling of relief that we turn away from the deep, dark pool, and regain the path. A few steps, and a brighter picture reveals itself.

Quite close to us is the stream, coming down beneath the arching boughs of an oak. On each side is a rock, that on the right being furnished with a low ledge, which Nature has fashioned in such a way as to give to it the appearance of a seat formed by art. Above the rocks, and extending as far up as the curving river will permit us to see, are a series of beautiful cascades, reaching from one bank to the other. The rocks are not seen, only the gleaming foam, but so regularly are they disposed as to be comparable with nothing else than a long flight of wide steps. Bushes fringe the banks, and meet in places overhead, but never entirely shut out the sunlight. Below is the yawning chasm where the Avon for a time is dark and forbidding, but we do not think of that when we look upon it here.

At the head of the wood we pass through a gate, and, still following the path, shall soon reach the road leading from the farms of Yolland and Downstow and the district beyond them, to this part of Brent Moor. Turning left a short walk brings us to Shipley Bridge, a picturesque old structure that shows little besides its parapets except when winter robs it of its leafy tent.

In the immediate neighbourhood of the bridge there is much that is interesting. Not far above it, and quite close to the road, though partly concealed by dwarf trees, is a fine waterfall. The Avon here forces its way over a bed of rock, and suddenly tumbles into a deep pool, where it encounters a huge mass of granite, and turns sullenly aside, but only to fall again. On the eastern bank of the stream are brakes, enclosed within rough stone walls, and stretching nearly up to Shipley Tor, where is a fine view of the narrow pass from which the river issues. Seen from that point the valley is almost Swiss-like in character, the fir trees in the grounds of Brent Moor House contributing greatly to this effect. Northward of the tor the lone Moor, untenanted save by cattle or half-wild ponies, stretches away to the horizon. In this direction are a number of hut circles, and other remains will be found on Dockwell Ridge near by. On Zeal Hill, above the western bank of the river, there are also some antiquities. These consist of two pounds, with hut circles, situated between the ruined buildings originally erected in connection with the peat works at Red Lake and Black Tor, the pile of rocks on the hill immediately above Brent Moor House. Remains of a similar character exist on Ryder's Plain, further to the north, and also in the valleys of the Red Brook and Bala Brook, where ancient tin workings abound.

But Zeal Hill should be ascended not only on account of the interesting vestiges of the dwellings of an early people that are scattered over its brow, but also for the reason that the best view of Shipley is to be obtained from it. From the bridge the path that climbs the hill from the Moor gate opening on the lane leading by Badworthy to Aish should be followed. By ascending this for a short distance, with the Zeal Farm enclosures on the left, and then striking across the common to the right, the visitor will be led to that part of the hill from which the view is commanded. The tors placed above the narrow pass, the river flowing over its granite bed, the slopes of heather, furze, and bracken on either side of it, the cottage and the border farm, and the wood that hides the deep pool and the waterfall, are all in sight, and together make up as pleasing a picture as any that the fringe of the Moor can show.

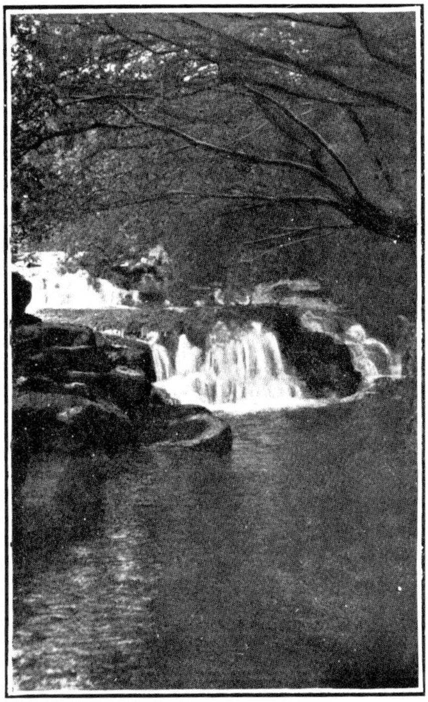

Photo by] [C. R. Rowe.

On the Avon below Shipley Bridge.

"A series of beautiful cascades."—*(See Page 127.)*

Among the out-of-the-way nooks on Dartmoor there is probably none more charming than Henchertraw, on the Red Brook, the tributary of the Avon which we noticed falling into that river as we made our way upward through the wood from Didworthy Bridge. This spot may be readily reached from Shipley either by way of the steep path already mentioned, or by means of another running through some fields. If we choose the former route we pass upward from the Moor gate by the Zeal Hill path, keeping near to the wall until we reach the end of it. We then make our way to the stream below, which we must cross, as our objective is situated on its western branch. Should we decide to take the other path we follow the lane from the Moor gate past Zeal Farm, not failing to notice the fine sycamores near the house, and crossing a bridge thrown over the brook whose bank we are seeking, shall enter a field at a gate on the right. Passing over this and another we reach a hunting gate and gain the common. The little river now becomes our guide and will presently lead us to the object of our quest.

Henchertraw is really Hencher Trough, the latter word being occasionally applied on the Moor to those miniature canyons formed by the narrowing of a stream, where the banks are unusually high. Sometimes the trough is a rock fissure; at others its sides are composed of soil and boulders, and it is through one of this kind that the Red Brook runs. A stranger wandering near it might be attracted by the tops of the mountain ash trees that bend over it, but he would otherwise not suspect the existence of its hidden beauties. It is only when he stands on the brink, and looks down upon the tiny stream that these are revealed to him. Then he sees innumerable little waterfalls, ferns, and moss-coated rocks, with, perchance, a gleam of sunshine darting through some opening and turning the crystal drops that hang upon the foxglove or the heather sprays into beads of gold. But the Red Brook is hastening on its way to the lower valley where another stream is flowing down to meet it and become its companion to the Avon. In that it is less happy than are we who may linger if we list by this delightful oasis, where the low murmuring of the waters and the humming of insects alone break the quiet of the Moor. Let us do so while I tell you its story.

The lark was heralding the new-born day with her sweet song when Garth, the tinner of the Red Brook, passed from his dwelling below Henchertraw to the stream works up the valley. It was earlier than he was accustomed to commence the duties of the day, though he was always astir betimes, but the morning being so inviting he had chosen to set out as soon as he had eaten his breakfast rather than wait for his companions, as was his wont. As he neared the scene of his labours, however, he saw something which led him to suppose that, early as it was, one of his fellow-workers was abroad before him. Amid the great heaps of stones thrown up by the tinners he caught sight of a figure, and though only a glimpse of it was afforded him, he did not doubt but that it was one of his comrades. He was, however, quickly undeceived, for as he drew near to the stone heaps the cry of a child fell upon his ear. He stopped for an instant to assure himself that this was what he heard, and then hastened towards the spot whence the sounds proceeded.

Between two of the heaps Garth came upon a little girl, scarcely more than an infant, crying bitterly. Her dress, though soiled and torn, was of rich material, and the tinner perceived at once that the child belonged to someone of high station. As soon as the little thing saw him she ceased crying and suffered him to lift her in his arms and to bear her from the stony ground to the soft turf that environed it. Then Garth, finding for her a soft cushion of heather, set her down gently, and, kneeling, asked her to tell him her name. The child looked up into his face, and, reading there only kindness, stretched out her tiny arms and patted his cheeks.

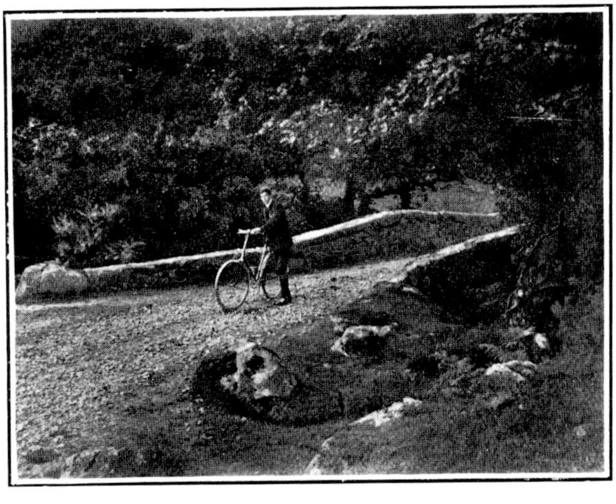

Photo by] [C. R. Rowe.

Shipley Bridge.

"Shows little besides its parapets except when winter robs it of its leafy tent."—*(See Page 127.)*

"Me Melys," she whispered.

Garth could learn no more. Who she was, or how she came there he was unable to discover. Searching among the stone heaps, he came upon the spot where it was evident that she had lain during some part of the night. A mantle was spread beside a boulder that rested on a small strip of turf, and it bore the impress of her little figure. But with alarm Garth saw that upon it was also the print of a man's hand in blood, and that the stones near by were smeared with the same crimson stain. He continued his search, and when his comrades came they aided him in it, but nothing more was found. Then Garth, carrying the little child and the blood-stained mantle, climbed to the highest points of the hills round about, and looked far over the waste. But the morning sun showed him only the cattle browsing on the slopes; no other moving thing was there. The soft wind whispering through the heather was all he heard. There was no voice to tell him what he wished to know. Garth turned away, and went down to his hut in the valley.

The tinner brought the child up as his own, and she shared his love with his little son, Hael, who had been motherless almost from his birth. The children loved each other, and as they grew in years their affection became stronger, and when Garth looked upon them he thought of the days when he and the wife who had been taken from him rambled by the streams as they did now, and often wondered how their companionship would end. And the years flew by, and Hael became a strong youth, and Melys a beauteous maiden. Still they wandered by the streams, and loved them, but none better than Red Brook, where it hid itself between the banks of Henchertraw. Thus it came about that one lovely summer evening found them standing side by side on the heathery brink, looking down upon the waters and listening to their plaintive music. The silent Moor was bathed in the golden glow of the setting sun, and Melys thought that she had never before seen it look so beautiful. For some time they stood in silence, and then Hael asked her whether she knew what the stream had been singing. She sought an explanation by a look, and he told her that its song was one of delight that it was about to find a companion that would never leave it, but would flow on and on with it to the end. He told her that he, too, wished for such a companion, and that his happiness would never be complete until he was linked to the one he loved. The sun went down, but still they stood by the brink of Henchertraw, and when the rosy mantle of the Moor was replaced by one of a sombre shade they were yet lingering by the stream. When the stars looked down upon the waste they saw the youth and maiden passing slowly through the valley. They reached the tinner's hut, and then they paused a moment. Hael drew Melys to him, and pressed her brow with his lips.

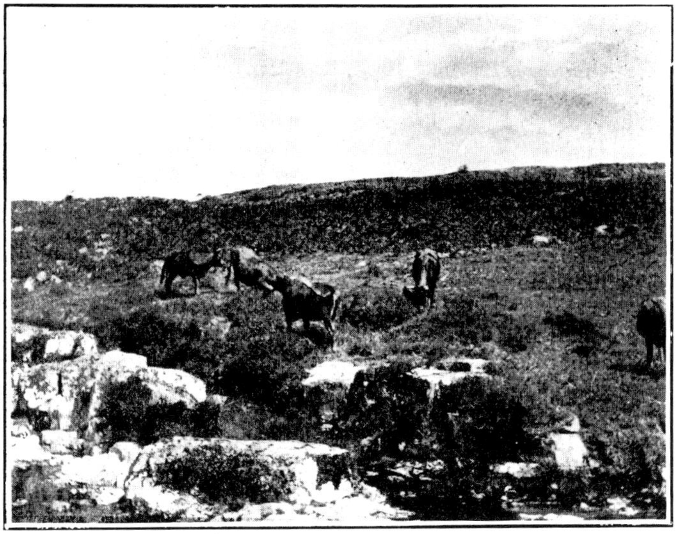

Photo by] [A. Edmund Spender.

Near Shipley Tor.

"The lone Moor, untenanted save by cattle."—*(See Page 127.)*

"Sweet one," he said; "my happiness is complete now."

The summer was numbered with the bright things that had flown, and the Frost King again reigned, when one afternoon, Garth, who was preparing to leave the stream work, was surprised at seeing two strangers approaching him. They were both mounted, and the foremost one appeared, from his bearing and costume, to be a person of rank, while his companion, who rode behind him, was apparently a servitor. They came towards the tinner, and reined up their horses.

"Hast laboured long here, friend?" demanded the one of noble mien.

"I have worked here, and in the valleys of the Avon and the Erme, all my life," answered Garth.

"Then you were in the neighbourhood when I last visited it," returned the stranger.

"It must be so; though I know not when that was."

"Fourteen years have passed since I saw this spot," answered the stranger, "and though I only looked upon it for a brief space, how well I remember it. Come, I will show you where I passed the night."

And he led the way among the stone heaps to the spot where Garth had so long before found the mantle.

"It is a sad story," said the stranger, "but I am here in the hope that it may yet have a bright ending. Fourteen years ago, tinner, I was journeying over the Moor to take ship at Dartmouth, whence I was to sail for Spain, to place my little daughter in charge of a relative of my dead wife. With me were three or four comrades, soldiers of fortune, who were to sail in the same ship in the hope of finding some work for their swords in the country to which I was bound. In passing over the Moor we got separated in a dense mist, and for several hours I rode on, but without any idea of the direction in which I was going. I had taken my child from my attendant just before I had lost sight of him, and for that I felt glad, for it would have maddened me to think she was exposed to danger on the Moor. When the mist lifted I found myself in this stream work, and my heart was full of thankfulness when I saw the cultivated lands below me, and knew that I was nearing the verge of the waste. But my joy did not last, for, my horse stumbling on the loose stones, I was violently thrown, and fell upon my head. I was rendered unconscious, and how long I remained in that state I know not. When I came to myself my first thought was of my child. I was unable to rise, but I contrived to spread my mantle on the ground, and, wrapping her in its folds, I watched her till she slept. Then I again relapsed into unconsciousness, and I have never seen her since. A few hours later my comrades discovered me, but the child was gone. Awakening, she had probably strayed among the stone heaps, but my comrades were unable to find her. Anxious to reach the ship in time, they speedily resumed their journey, taking me with them, though, as they afterwards told me, with little hope that I should live. I knew nothing of what had happened until I awoke from the delirium that followed upon my accident, and then we were on the sea. But we did not reach the coast of Spain; our vessel was captured by Moorish rovers, and we were taken prisoners to that country. From that time till some two months since I have been in captivity. A week ago I arrived in England, and resolved to set out at once to endeavour to gain tidings of my lost child. See, tinner, it was here I placed her. Shall I ever see her again?"

"You shall," returned Garth; "for it was here I found her."

The tinner told his story, and then, desiring the horsemen to follow him, passed from the stone heaps to the valley below.

When he drew near his hut he called his son to him and directed him to take the strangers' horses. The young man obeyed, and then Garth, bidding his guests enter, went in search of Melys. But she was not in sight, and once more he called to Hael, asking whither she had gone.

"I will find her, father," he replied, as he came up from the pasture croft. "But tell me; who are the strangers you have brought to our abode?"

"One is a noble, my son," returned Garth, "and though you may now wonder why he has sought a dwelling so lowly as mine, you will no longer do so when you learn who he is. Hael, I have found the father of Melys."

"Found her father!" cried Hael. "What do you mean?"

"It is as I say," answered Garth. "I have learnt from him by what chance she was left on the Moor."

"And does he know that Melys is here?" asked Hael.

His voice shook, and his cheek grew pale.

"Assuredly, my son; I have told him so. And I share the joy he feels at finding his child."

"Oh, father, father, what have you done!" cried Hael. "Melys loves me, and you have robbed me of her."

"Robbed you of her?"

"Aye, she is for ever lost to me."

"No, no, my son; you wrong Melys."

"Ah, father," said the young man bitterly, "the choice of a husband will not rest with Melys now. Think you the rich noble would consent that she should wed the son of a tinner? Father, she can never be mine; my heart is broken."

"But she shall not leave us. The noble shall not have her, Hael. Hasten, my son; conceal her, and let the noble go his way."

"I will, I will. Yet stay; that were to wrong Melys. No; though it will darken my life, she shall be restored to her father."

That night there was gloom in the hut of the tinner. Two men sat by the smouldering peat; the elder bemoaning the absence of one he loved, and stricken with grief to witness the anguish of his son; in the heart of the younger, the blackness of despair. But their sorrow was not deeper than that of the maiden who had been borne from a home dearer to her than the proudest castle in the land could ever be.

Snow covered the Moor; from the banks of Henchertraw great icicles depended, and the little stream below no longer sang its song of joy. At times the moonbeams were faintly reflected in the half-frozen pools, and then the drifting clouds would obscure them, and the sullen waters were lost in darkness.

Garth went to the door of his hut.

"Hael, my son; where art thou?" he cried.

But no answering voice broke the silence of the night. The old man called again and again upon his son, but only the echoes of the valley answered him. Then he strode from his door, and passed up by the bank of the Red Brook to Henchertraw.

There he found him, lying dead upon the snow. On the spot where he had so often wandered in happy hours with the maiden he loved, he had lain down to die. She had filled his life, and when they took her from him they took that also.

On the morrow came Melys. Her father, concerned to behold the grief which the separation from Hael occasioned her, had agreed that she should become his bride. Garth met her at the door, and it needed no words to tell her the fatal news. She never left the Moor again. She would remain, she said, where Hael had lived and loved her. Each day she walked over the hill to the spot where they had laid him amid the heather, and then she would return and linger until sundown by the brink of Henchertraw.

Still sings the little river, and the heather blossoms on its banks as of old. And still the ferns nod as the spray from the cascades lights upon them, and the quickbeam quivers in the summer breeze. Henchertraw is now as it was when Hael and Melys knew and loved it. I have wandered by it often, and it is not strange to me that they should have loved it. Nor will it be to you when your footsteps lead you there.

If when we linger by the stream
  Its tale it could but tell,
What light upon the past would gleam,
On that of which we now but dream,
  On what of old befell.

Of hunters we might learn, who chased
  The fierce wolf to his lair,
Who, all undaunted, danger faced,
In upland glen and dreary waste,
  And oft a grave found there.

Of noble dame and valiant knight,
  Of many a doughty deed,
Of gleaming spears and armour bright,
Of minstrel and of falcon flight,
  Of hound and prancing steed.

Of gentle youth and maiden fair,
  Who when the sun was low,
Stood on the marge and whispered there
Love tales that, knowing naught of care,
  Were radiant as its glow.

But when we linger by the stream
  Its tale of times long flown
It tells us not: we only seem
To see the past—'tis but a dream;
  To-day is ours alone.

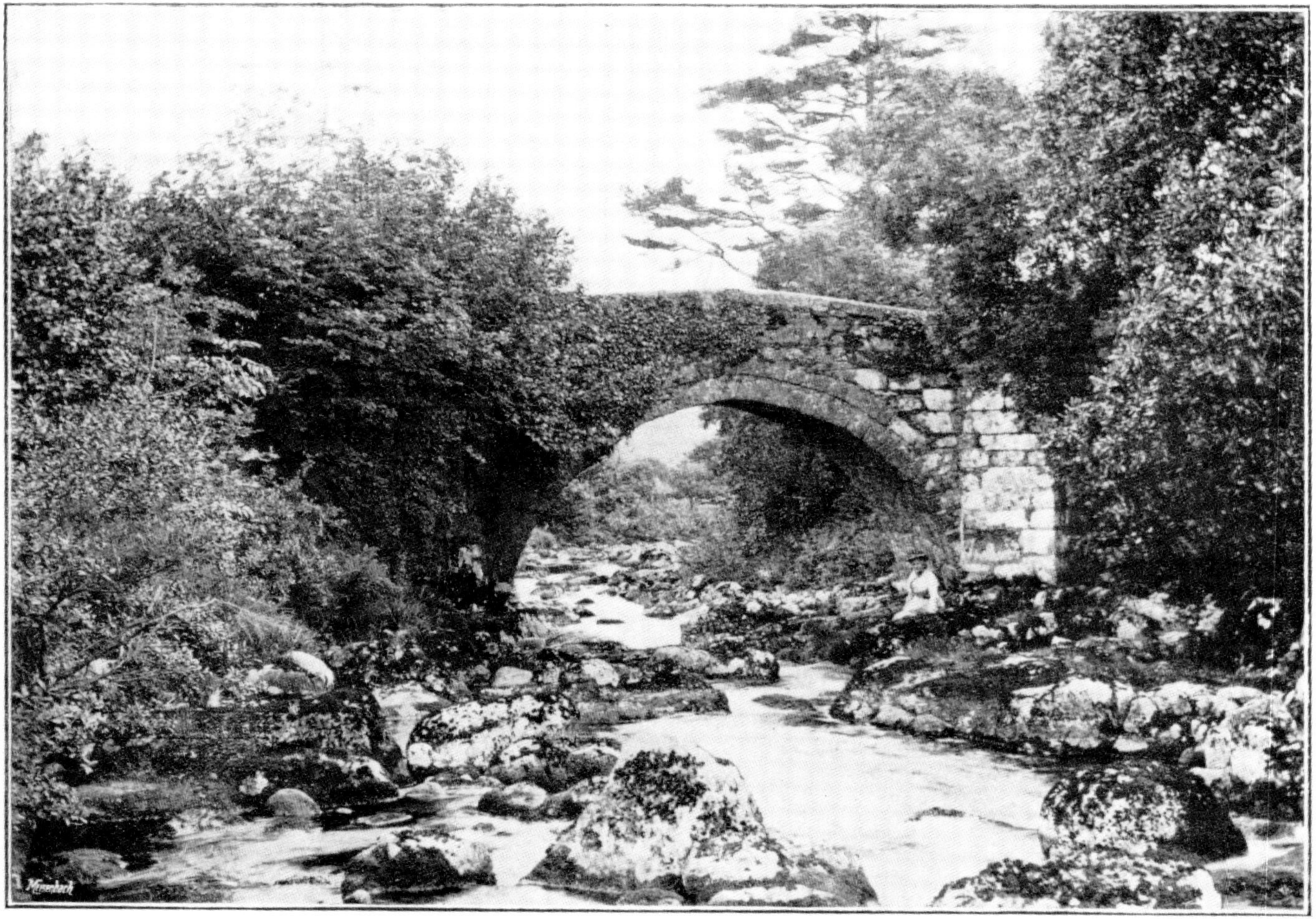

SEE PAGE 139.

Harford Bridge.

PHOTO BY ERNEST CROFT.

"Where the Erme bids farewell to the Moorlands,"

XVII.

HARFORD.

Stowford Cleave——A Border Scene——Harford Bridge——A Moorland Sanctuary——Speaker Williams——Bishop Prideaux——Tor Rocks——Piles Wood——Banks of the Erme.

> Its charms are like those little flow'rs
> Which scent the valley's zephyr breeze;
> Where innocence to charm embow'rs
> And sheds unconscious scents to please.
> —John Parminter.

WE are standing on the right bank of the Erme above Stowford Cleave, having made our way hither from Ivybridge by the riverside path that the hanging woods conceal. For companion we have had the beautiful stream, one of the most interesting rising on the Moor, which, though intervening foliage has at times screened it from our view, has ever been audible, now raising its voice to a roar where, pent between dark rocks, it rushed angrily to the pool below, and now chattering merrily as it spread itself over some broad shallow, where half-exposed amber pebbles were kissed by the sunbeams. In places we have found our path, carried at the foot of a steeply shelving slope, to be a rugged one, and we have seen that it has not only become worn by passing footsteps, but that, when swollen by summer freshets or by melting winter snows, the river has lapped its gravel and laid bare its stones. In others it has led us over a sward where the grass struggled for existence with

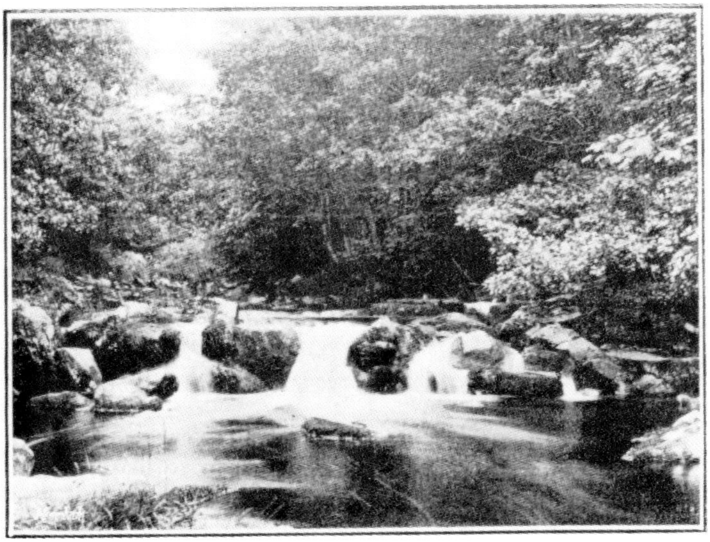

Photo by] [Ernest Croft.

The Erme above Ivybridge.

"For companion we have had the beautiful stream."

the moss, and a thick and yielding carpet was formed. On the little plateau near the bend of the river its devious way brought us through tall bracken, and when we had nearly lost it the sides of the cleave fell back, and there we stayed our steps. Hitherto the valley has been narrow, affording room in its depths only for the river and the track leading to the uplands; besides these we have seen nothing but the thick woods and the sky. Now we look upon another picture.

Close at hand are green pastures, but we know they do not extend far up the stream, for though we cannot yet see where they meet the waste, the sight of its hills assures us that the limits of the husbandman's operations will speedily be reached. The great steeps rising on either side of the Erme, one of which is surmounted with a cairn known as Stalldon Barrow, the other being crowned with three similar huge heaps of stones, and bearing in consequence the name of Three Barrows, bound the view as we look up the valley, and from them the Moor rolls away on each hand until we lose it behind nearer objects. To the right, embosomed in trees, is the tower of a church, which, when we

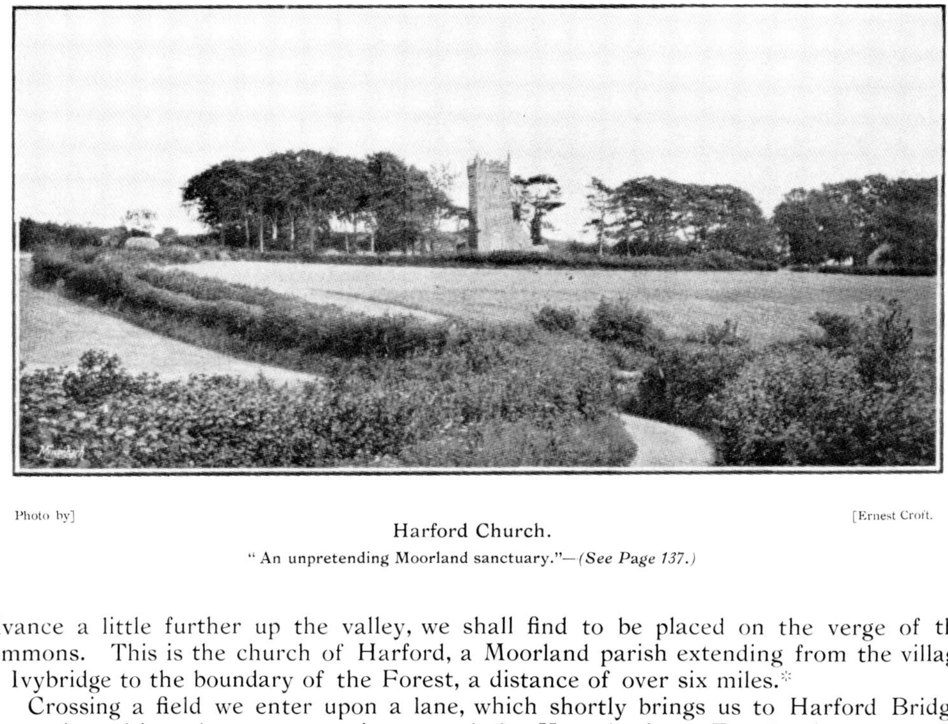

Photo by] [Ernest Croft.

Harford Church.

"An unpretending Moorland sanctuary."—*(See Page 137.)*

advance a little further up the valley, we shall find to be placed on the verge of the commons. This is the church of Harford, a Moorland parish extending from the village of Ivybridge to the boundary of the Forest, a distance of over six miles.*

Crossing a field we enter upon a lane, which shortly brings us to Harford Bridge, where the cultivated country terminates and the Moor begins. Few border scenes are more pleasing than that which here meets the eye, and when it is stated that within a radius of two miles are to be found a number of objects of antiquarian and historic interest—some fine rock-piles, several lofty hills from which are commanded views extending far into the northern part of the Moor, and embracing the whole of the South Hams with a wide expanse of distant Channel, the oak wood of Piles, the third of the ancient, solitary groves of the great waste—and that through the midst of these attractions runs a charming river, it will be acknowledged that Harford is not the least resplendent gem

* Harford Moor, as that part of the parish extending from the cultivated country to the bounds of the Forest is called, lies between the common lands of Cornwood on the west, and Ugborough Moor on the east.

in the diadem of old Danmonia. Having paused by the parapet of the grey moorstone bridge to look awhile upon the beauties that Nature in her bounty has here brought together to delight the eye of man, we pass up towards the little church.

This we shall find to be an unpretending Moorland sanctuary, having for neighbours only two or three houses, for Harford can scarcely be called a village. It possesses no features of particular interest in themselves, though there are two objects whose associations endow them with such. These are memorials of Thomas Williams, Speaker of the House of Commons in the reign of Queen Elizabeth, and of John and Agnes Prideaux, parents of John Prideaux, who was made Bishop of Worcester by Charles I. The former was of the family long resident at Stowford, two miles down the valley, a possession purchased of the Crown by John Williams in the time of Henry VIII. Those who were responsible for the lines on one of the brasses on his tomb were apparently not content that he had reigned, as it were, in the Commons House of Parliament, for they tell us that he now reigns in heaven "with myghtie Jove"; but we suppose that a poetic licence must be granted even to the writer of an epitaph.

John Prideaux's father, being a man of small means, and having twelve children, was unable to give him more than a very rudimentary education; but a lady, the mother of Sir Edward Fowell, noticing that he had an inclination for study, placed him at a school, and he made good use of his advantages. He had already failed to obtain a local appointment for which he had been a competitor—that of parish clerk of Ugborough—so when his school days were over he determined to seek his fortune afield. He set out on foot for Oxford, and on his arrival found employment in the kitchen of Exeter College. But he was ambitious to be something better than a scullion, and in his spare time applied himself diligently to his books. This attracted attention, and he was eventually admitted to the literary privileges of the college, and three years afterwards, in 1599, he took the degree of Bachelor of Arts. Step by step he advanced, and soon became distinguished for his great learning not only in England, but throughout the Continent. John Prideaux was never ashamed of his origin. When he first came to Oxford he wore a pair of leather breeches; these he always carefully preserved, and when raised to the See of Worcester they were kept with his Bishop's robes. Referring to his defeat in his candidature, when the test was that of "tuning the Psalm" in the church of the Devonshire village, he used to say: "If I could have been parish clerk of Ugborough I had never been Bishop of Worcester." His absence of false pride we can admire equally with his indomitable perseverance, and it is unfortunate that with such qualities he showed a spirit of intolerance. But he suffered for this, for having gone so far as to pronounce a sentence of excommunication on all within his diocese who took up arms on the side of the Parliament, he was afterwards deprived of his dignity, and became greatly reduced in circumstances.

In front of the lichgate is an open space, at the head of which a lane leads to the Moor. Here a green path runs eastward to Spurrell's Cross, whence it is continued to Owley Gate. But it also ran to a ford higher up the valley of the Glaze, from which point it may be traced for a considerable distance. This path is to be seen at Diamond Lane, not far from Badworthy on the Avon, and at the head of the Dean Burn valley. It is the track over which the monks of Buckfast Abbey passed when they journeyed to the house of the Augustine Canons at Plympton.* Roads of a more modern day have in places been formed upon it, and in others the ling and the furze have obliterated it; but this old-time path may yet be followed across more than one hill, and its direction can well be seen as it skirts the waste between Lambs' Down and the little church at Harford.

Almost close to this path, and at no great distance from Harford Gate, a small stream rises, and passes on its way to the Erme about a quarter of a mile south of the church. This is the Butter Brook, and where it leaves the common it flows at the foot of a fine

* Mention has already been made of this ancient way in the chapter on the Valley of Dean Burn (XV.).

pile known as Tor Rocks. This does not lift itself high above the surrounding waste as do most of the Dartmoor tors, and is therefore not seen until closely approached. But though its summit offers no extended view, it is not on that account less worthy of a visit. Its occurrence here is a happy one, for it imparts a feature to the little settlement below which, were it absent, would lack one of the true characteristics of a border hamlet. Interest is added by the presence of hut circles near it, some of them being rather good examples. The brook here enters upon the enclosed lands, and lower down, where a path crosses some fields, is spanned by a single stone clapper. The road to Ivybridge also crosses it by a bridge formed in a similar manner, but consisting of several stones, and being, of course, much wider.

From the Moor Gate near Tor Rocks we shall proceed northward along the verge of the common, keeping close to the wall of the enclosures on our left. When we reach the end of these we see that further out upon the Moor is yet another enclosure, the open space between stretching down the hill towards the river. This enclosure is known as Piles Newtake, and is of considerable interest both to the antiquary and to the hunting man, for within it are some very curious remains, while it also forms a harbour for foxes. We make our way to the corner of this, where is a gateway, and just without it, and a little up the slope, is an object that will not fail to interest us. This is a kistvaen, enclosed within a small circle of seven upright stones, though it is evident that originally there were more than this number. The kist, which is about three feet deep, is without a cover stone, this having in all probability been removed by the builders of the wall near by.

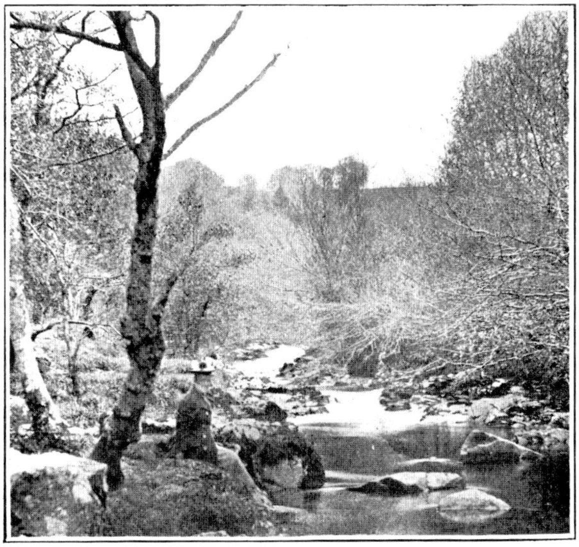

Photo by] [Ernest Croft.

The Erme below Harford.

"Its course is still to be amid scenes of loveliness."—*(See Page 139.)*

But of more interest than the antiquarian remains is the old oak wood by the river, which is also enclosed within the wall of the newtake. We may make our way to it by scrambling over the rocks that encumber this part of the enclosure, or, better still, pass down by its wall to the Erme. Following that stream upward we shall soon reach the wood, which we shall find extends for some distance along its left bank, where the river passes through a deep valley. It is similar in character to Wistman's Wood and Black Tor Copse on the Ockment, the trees being stunted and having a very aged appearance. Like those the oaks of Piles also grow on a rocky slope. Mosses and lichens cover the contorted boughs, and ferns and the whortleberry fill the crevices of the rocks from amid which the hoary trunks thrust themselves. Piles Wood is named on an old map of Dartmoor, now in the Albert Memorial Museum at Exeter, and which appears to be of fifteenth, or perhaps sixteenth, century date.

On the right bank of the Erme a path runs down to Harford Bridge, and if we can here find for ourselves a crossing-place over the river we may take it as our guide. Where the track on that side passes the foot of the steep and lofty hill which Stalldon

Barrow crowns, the old oak grove is seen to the best advantage. The Erme comes down from the upper valleys of the Moor with a song of joy, as though in delight at looking for the first time upon the fresh green of the oak leaves, and lovingly laves the bank that drops from the fringe of the venerable wood. Behind it rises the steep hill, strewn with granite, amid which a greater mass is seen, marking the Dungeon of Piles, where the fox so often strives to elude his pursuers. Higher still is Sharp Tor, and on the bulky height above it, a triple crown set upon its crest in old times to mark the resting-places of the dead.

Following the track we pass down the valley, and gradually the great sweep of Stalldon shuts from our view the gorge in which the lonely wood finds a shelter. We mark upon the down near us the pile of Tristis Rock, often called Hall Tor, the name borne by the ancient farm close at hand.* And we see, too, the little church tower amid the trees that we first looked upon from the head of the cleave. By-and-bye we again stand on the bridge where the Erme bids farewell to the Moorlands. She is leaving much that is beautiful behind her, but we do not sorrow for the impetuous river, for we know that its course is still to be amid scenes of loveliness.

* Hall was once in the possession of Colonel Chudleigh, the father of Elizabeth, Duchess of Kingston.

XVIII.

HAWNS AND DENDLES.

The Yealm——A Beautiful Border Valley——The Rogers Family——A Smithfield Martyr——Wood and Stream——Old Hannah, the Witch——A Romantic Glen——Blowing-Houses of the Tinners——A Hut Enclosure——A Ruined Kistvaen.

A little rivulet whose source
Was some lone mountain glen,
'Mongst much of yellow broom and gorse
Descended, and pursued its course
Among the homes of men.
—Luke Daniel.

The peeping skies, so bright among the trees
That part to show an azured field of light,
Topping the rounded lacework of the leaves
So clear behind the heron's heavy flight,
So warm before the creeping shades of night,
But not too full of gold to be imbedded,
And with the purple mountain ridges wedded.
—Joseph Cartwright.

Of all the Dartmoor streams that are not tributaries, the Yealm* alone has its source outside the bounds of the Forest. It rises on the extensive commons belonging to the parish of Cornwood, and flows for some distance between Stall Moor, on the east, and Pen Moor, on the west. About a mile and a half from its source it enters a wooded valley, and bids adieu to the uplands. This valley, like all those through which the rivers of the Moor come down from the wild fastnesses to the fertile pasture lands, possesses many beauties, though, from the absence of rock-masses, it is not so characteristic of Dartmoor border scenery as some others similarly situated. The name by which it is generally known is Hawns and Dendles.

There have been several conjectures as to the meaning of this rather curious appellation. The first part of it has been thought, and not improbably, to represent the Celtic word *aun, water;* it is sometimes spelt without the aspirate, though that this has belonged to it for more than a century there is ample proof. In the latter part of the name a corruption of the word *dingles* has been seen. But Hawns and Dendles would seem to be the names of persons; one known to us only in tradition, the existence of the other having the support of documentary evidence. According to local report a Madame Hawns once dwelt in this secluded spot, her possessions being presumably on the west side of the Yealm, since we there find a hill, peninsulated by that stream and Broadall Lake, bearing this name. The wood clothing the sides of the valley below, and extending to the enclosures abutting on the common eastward, is known as Dendles Wood, the latter, as certain title deeds prove, being a corruption of Daniel's. If there is

* Pronounced *Yam.*

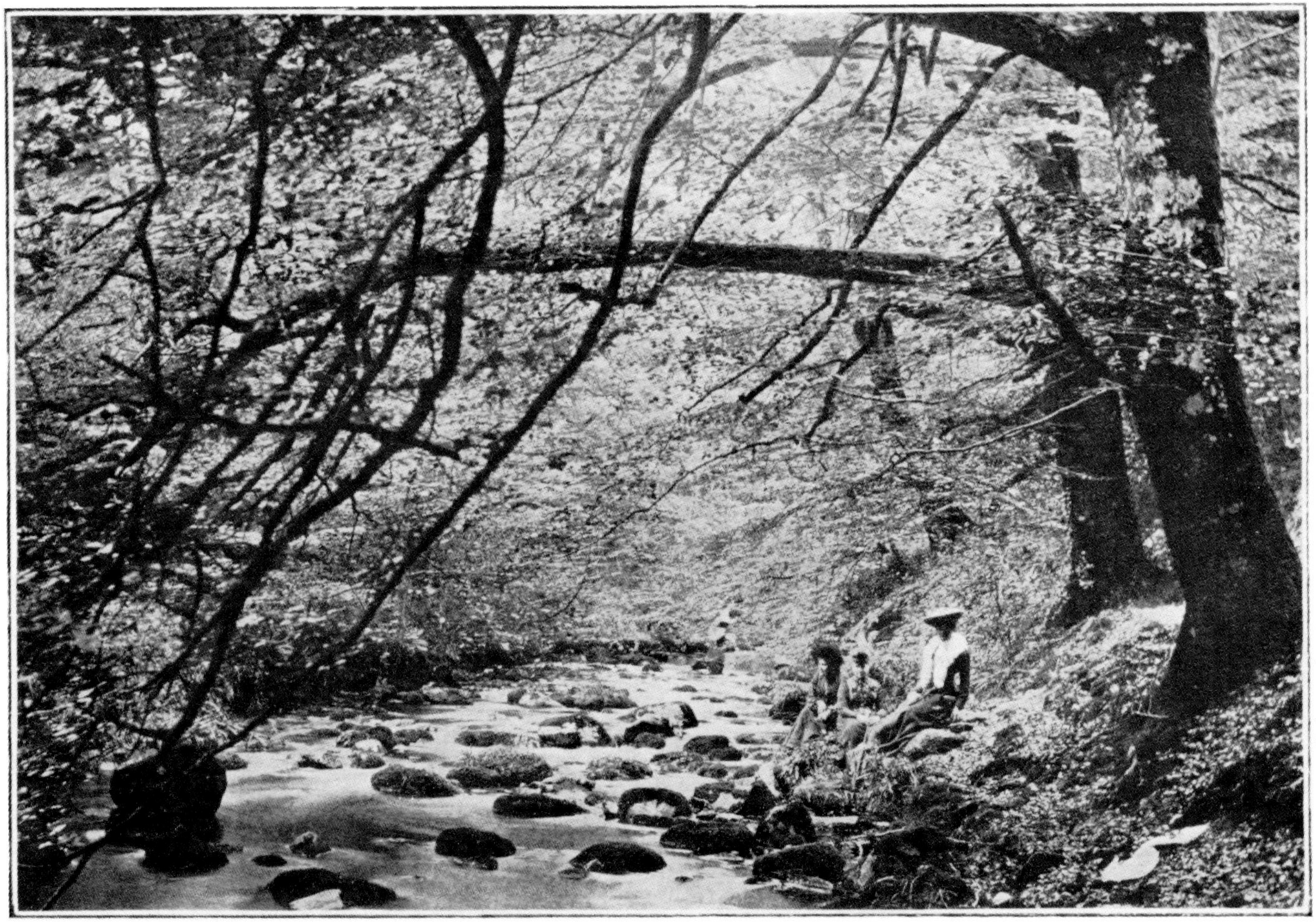

SEE PAGE 145.

PHOTO BY ERNEST CROFT.

By the Yealm in Hawns and Dendles.

"Wood and water are happily blended."

any truth in the story of Madame Hawns, this charming valley bears its present name in consequence of once having formed part of the lands of Hawns and Daniel.*

Situated about a mile and a half from Cornwood, or as it is sometimes called Cross, Hawns and Dendles is approached by pleasant lanes. The visitor leaves the village by the way leading to Harford, which he follows as far as the bridge over the Yealm, having on the right the beautiful domain of Blachford, now the property of the Misses Deare. An ancestor of the late Lord Blachford, John Rogers, was the first of the martyrs burnt at Smithfield during the reign of Mary. He was educated at Cambridge, and on leaving the University went to Antwerp as chaplain to the Merchants Adventurers. Here he met Coverdale and Tindal, and his intercourse with them led to his renouncing Popery. After residing abroad for some time he returned to England, and for preaching a sermon at Paul's Cross against the errors of the Roman Catholic religion was cited before the Council. He defended himself with such ability that he was dismissed, but was again summoned before them after the Queen's proclamation of the 18th August, 1553. He was confined as a prisoner in his own house, whence he was removed to Newgate, and was burnt at Smithfield on the 4th February, 1555. He was not allowed to say farewell to his wife, but wrote her an affectionate letter on the eve of his execution. He left eleven children. Several members of the family were Recorders of Plymouth during the eighteenth century, and Sir F. L. Rogers, who died in 1797, represented that borough in Parliament. In 1773 a school for the education and maintenance of poor girls of Devon and Cornwall was founded at Plymouth, pursuant to the will of Lady Rogers, who left £10,000 for the purpose. The school was removed to Ivybridge some years since. The fine Latin cross in memory of the late Lord Blachford, and of Georgiana his wife, standing in the village of Cornwood, was erected in 1901.

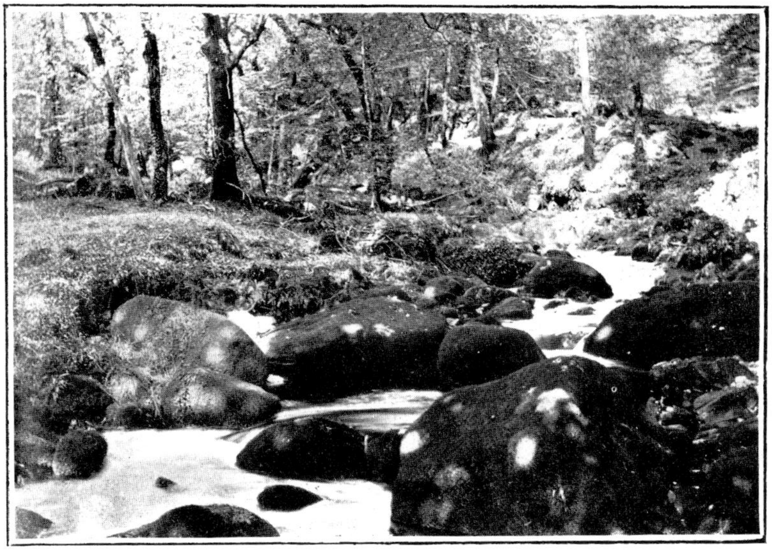

Photo by] [Ernest Croft.

In Dendles Wood.

"The beauties of the vale begin to reveal themselves."

Crossing the bridge over the Yealm, quite near to which is the vicarage, the visitor will turn left and, following the path by the river, shortly reach Wisdome Mill. Here he leaves the stream for a brief space, and passing up the hill soon enters the wood, where the beauties of the vale begin to reveal themselves. On either side of the path is low undergrowth, springing from a carpet of moss, dotted with clumps of ferns and other

* *Ancient Stone Crosses of Dartmoor and its Borderland.* Chap. IV.

plants, splashed with gold when the sunlight streams through the openings in the arch of leaves overhead. Down below, struggling to force its way past moss-covered boulders, is the river, whose rippling surface flecked with foam, the trees only partially hide. Another stream comes down to join it. It is the Broadall Lake, which like the Yealm has its source where no trees stretch their boughs affectionately over it as here; where the winds of the waste whisper by its cradle; where nothing is interposed between its baby bosom and the sky.

With this meeting-place of the little rivers a story of witchery is connected. In a hovel on the open Moor, not far from the edge of Dendles Wood, an old woman once dwelt with her only son. She was said to possess much skill in magic, and was greatly feared by all in the neighbourhood. To incur her displeasure was regarded as very unfortunate, and she was consequently shunned by farmer and peasant alike. How they lived was a mystery, for the son was never known to do any work, not even so much as till their garden, and yet they always appeared as though they had abundance of food. But the secret was at length discovered. A farmer who lived near by met with a succession of losses. First a valuable horse died, then a cow, then a number of sheep, and lastly the man fell sick. Then it was remembered that some time previously the farmer had expressed the opinion that a robbery committed at his place, when a number of hens were stolen, was the work of old Hannah's son, and everybody agreed that his misfortunes were to be attributed to her. She had "ill-wished" him, they said, and nothing could do him any good unless the spell could be broken. But how to do this nobody could tell. After much talk, however, the neighbours agreed to go in a body to Dendles Wood, where they could keep well out of sight, and there await events. This did not promise very much, but, they argued, it would at all events be moving in the matter, and it would be some sort of satisfaction to feel that they had done that, even if nothing came of it. Accordingly they mustered one day, and proceeded to the wood. Taking up a position on its edge they watched old Hannah's cottage, but could see no sign of her or her son. Nobody cared to venture out into the open, so they could do nothing but wait. After a time their patience was rewarded by the appearance of the old woman's son, who came from the cottage accompanied by a lurcher. The dog speedily set to work turning out rabbits, and each one it caught it threw back over its shoulder to the youth, who picked them up and put them into a bag which he carried. The secret of the old woman's food supply was explained. Nobody had thought about rabbits, for the dog had never before been seen. The farmers were incensed to see the youth helping himself to what they

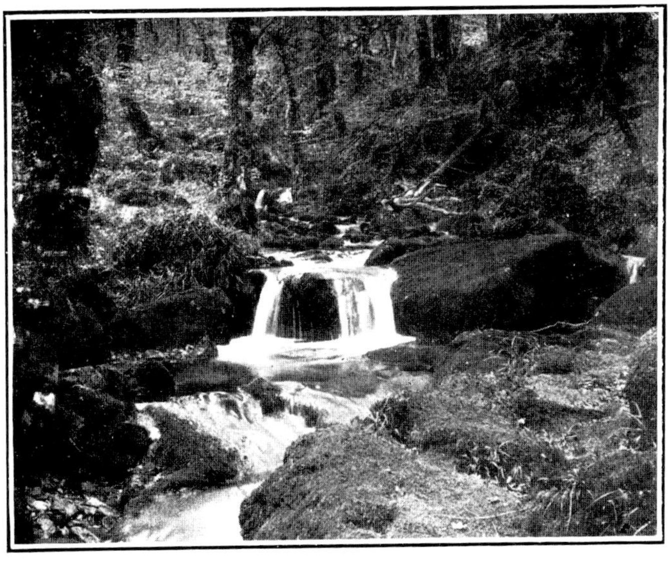

Photo by] [Ernest Croft.

The Yealm.

"Whence comes dreamy music to mingle with the sighs of the Moorland breeze."

(See Page 145.)

considered ought to be theirs, and forgetting all about old Hannah, rushed out to put a stop to his work. Immediately the dog set off down the hill at a furious pace, followed by the youth. Some of the farmers were mounted, and were soon at their heels, while the others made the best of their way on foot. The dog darted into the wood, but the pursuers kept up the chase, and when the animal reached the place where the Broadall Lake joins the Yealm they had nearly come up with it. The dog was about to cross the tributary stream, when some men appearing on the opposite bank, it turned and pointed up the Yealm. At this moment the old woman's son was heard shouting, "Rin, mawther, rin!" and the lurcher at once leapt on to a rock in the river in an attempt to reach the other side. But the rock was smooth and slippery, and it lost its foothold, and in another instant old Hannah was seen struggling in the stream. The witch's power was not proof against running water, and this had broken the spell by which she had assumed the form of a dog. From that time the farmer's health improved, but the witch gradually pined away, till at length it was reported that she was dead. The son having disappeared, the neighbours went one day to the old woman's cottage to satisfy themselves of the truth. And there they found her corpse, "a bunch o' bezom (broom) in wan hand, an' the skin ov a black cat in th' other."

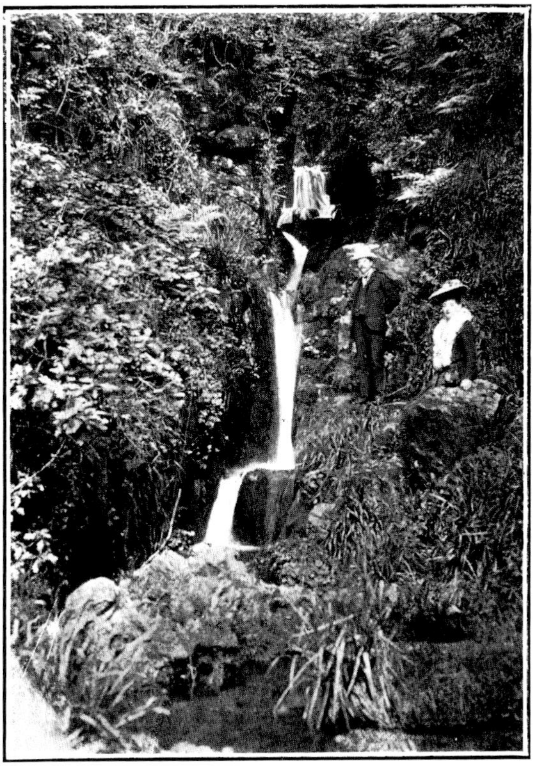

Photo by] Mrs. Ernest Croft.

Cascade in Hawns and Dendles.

"Pouring over the rocks the Yealm comes down from the Moor."

Above the confluence the bare hill of Hawns rises from the thick foliage that clothes the steep, and speaks of the proximity of the Moor. But little of its wildness is seen, nor does the rambler give much thought to it, for his immediate surroundings, in which wood and water are happily blended, have so much that is charming, that his attention is drawn entirely to them. From the main path narrower ones run down to the river, whence comes dreamy music to mingle with the sighs of the Moorland breeze that float through the dim wood. Footbridges cross it, and lead to a path on the further bank, where the trees run up to Dendles Waste, adjoining the piece of common to which its name is linked.

By-and-bye the melody of the river gives place to a louder sound, and when the descending path brings the rambler to its bank he sees in front of him a gleaming cascade. Here, pouring over the rocks, the Yealm comes down from the Moor, pressing impetuously forward as though eager to look upon the beauties of the valley. It goes on its way rejoicing, cheering by its presence the tree-clad steeps and the pleasant meads, even as it cheered the wilderness from which it sprung.

Although the Yealm has only a short course on the Moor, there are several objects on its banks there worthy of notice, and the rambler who, after having explored the valley, cares to trace it upwards, will meet with much that is interesting. Not far from its source is a romantic glen, into which the stream falls from a considerable height over a number of ledges of rock. It is one of those spots met with on the Moor that at once surprise and delight the stranger. When bare heath and broken hill are alone seen neighbouring the stream he may be following, he comes suddenly upon some waterfall, or beautiful pool, or hollow scooped out in the high bank and starred with tufts of purple. It is like finding a diamond on a beach of rare-coloured pebbles; all are good to look upon, but pale beside the one precious gem.

The old tinners who laboured by the upper waters of the Yealm were probably little influenced by the charms of this secluded glen when they erected their blowing-houses here; it was doubtless the shelter it afforded that attracted them. The remains of one of their buildings stands on the left bank of the stream just below the falls, and another on the right bank some distance above them. In both these little houses are stones with moulds, into which the smelted tin was poured. All the way down the valley the evidences of the former industry of the tinners are abundant.

But close to this glen are the remains of other houses of far greater age than those erected for the smelting of tin. On the slope above the eastern bank of the stream are numerous hut circles, many standing within an enclosure, the wall of which, like that of the other pounds on the Moor, is in ruins. It is only about three feet in height, but is spread over a width of about thirteen feet; the stones composing it are small. The hut circles, both within and without the enclosure, are in a fine state of preservation. The walls of many of them are of a different character from those usually seen in the hut circles of the Moor, being formed of stone and turf, whereas walls of stone only are generally found. They are also of greater width than any others on Dartmoor, one example having a wall ten feet thick. Further down, and quite near to the woods, is another group of these roofless huts, and clusters of them also exist on Broadall Lake and in other places in the vicinity.

Quite near to the large enclosure is a kistvaen in a ruinous condition, within a small circle of stones, deeply sunk in the turf. Though we can know nothing of the occupant of this despoiled grave, or of those who laid him here to rest, we can at least feel as we stand by the rude coffin of stone and look upon the scene around us, that, having something that they also possessed, something that has existed from their time to our own, there is a link connecting us. The beauty of the valley was theirs; to-day it is ours. They saw the mist roll upward at the dawn, and the hills throw off their darkness; they saw the wide-stretching heath at noonday, and the heated kine gathering at the waters; they saw the lofty crest of Pen Moor, clothed in a mantle of deepening purple, as it stood up against the crimson glow that suffused the sky when the summer sun was sinking. And we see these things now. They heard the river make music in lonely places. Listen! Standing beside the grave we may hear it, too. The young Yealm sings to us as it sang to them, and as it shall sing in the years to come when we, like the son of the desert who lies sleeping here, are forgotten.

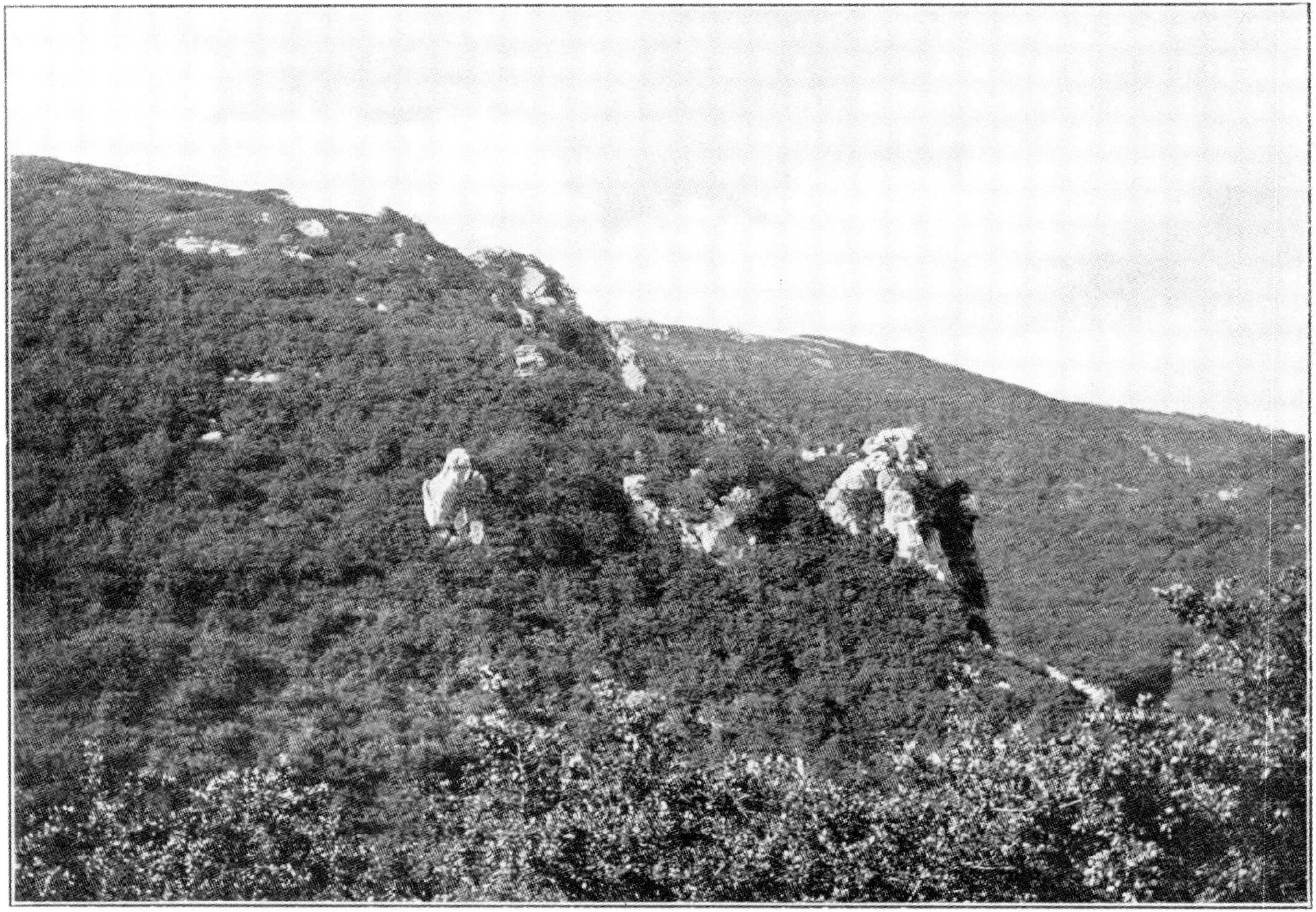

SEE PAGE 150.

The Dewer Stone.

PHOTO BY ERNEST CROFT.

"Its foot is planted amid the boulders with which the river bed is strewn, and bushes cover the slopes on either side of it."

XIX.

THE DEWER STONE.

THE PLYM——COURSE OF THE MEW——A WEATHER-BEATEN CRAG——THE WISH HUNTSMAN——MYSTERIOUS FOOTPRINTS——THE POET OF DARTMOOR——WIGFORD DOWN——CADAFORD BRIDGE——A WILD VALLEY——SHAUGH BRIDGE.

Streams
Bright-bursting headlong from the dusky cliffs!
Whilst opening on the skies, the mighty roar
Of rough cascades deafens the listening ear,
And swells the grandeur of the rugged scene!
Immensely rising from the cataract-foam
How frowns yon craggy mass! where shrieking birds
Plant their bleak aeries in its shrubby clefts;
High sails the hawk, and harsh the heron screams.
—NATHANIEL HOWARD.

FAR away among the hills of southern Dartmoor, and on the edge of a boggy plateau, a tiny stream trickles between black walls of peat. Slowly it sets out upon its journey to the unknown depths beyond the distant pasture-lands that the rift in the heathy ridges discloses. Anon it comes out into the light, and the peat is exchanged for banks covered with verdure, where the moss and the tall foxglove crowd to look upon the new-born thing, soon to become part of the life of the old Moor. It awakens to ecstacy and quickens its flow; it cheers the valley with its music, and the ancient hills that look down upon it; it runs by scattered heaps of stone which grey lichens have covered, and where long years ago it saw the tin-streamer at work; it passes the shallow where the old-time traveller was wont to ford it on his journey through that silent land; it flows where opening combes send down their silvery tributes, and upon whose sides, in days of which men can only dream, it witnessed the uprearing of monuments to mark the spot where the children of the desert slept; it winds between the hills where in a later time the warrener threw up harbours for the coney; it reflects the moorstone bridge, and speeds to the grateful shade of the trees

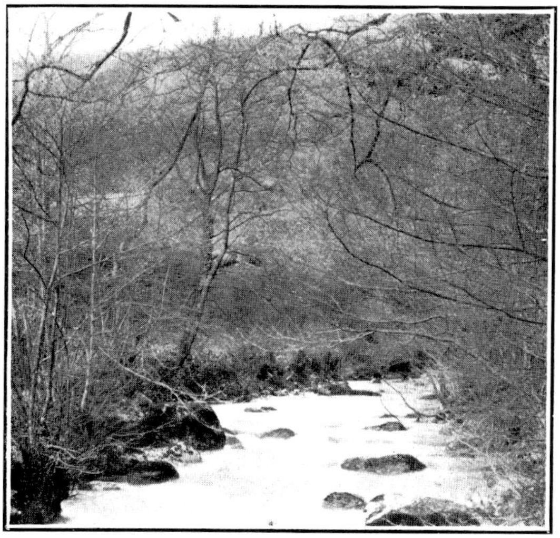

Photo by] [Ernest Croft.

The Mew near Shaugh Bridge.

"The stream, now hidden by trees, flows onward to meet the Plym."—(See Page 150.)

that find scant nourishment in a stony vale, below which the groves of the lowlands wait to welcome it. Men have given to this stream the name of Plym, and in turn it has bestowed it upon the town seated where it loses itself in the surges that rush to meet it from the western sea.

In a hollow near the flourishing little settlement founded in the midst of the waste a hundred years ago another stream rises. This is the Mew, and, like the Plym, it also has been a witness to much that man has done upon the Moor. It has scooped out for itself a channel through the valley where early settlers battled with the wilds, and formed their crofts and built their homestalls on the rugged slopes. Other streamlets come to join it, and it falls into the great basin which art has made above the gorge at Burrator, near the village at the foot of the giant tor. By peaceful Meavy, where the aged oak spreads its enfeebled boughs over the green by the lich gate, it goes merrily on its way. Fields and woodland happily mingling clothe the sides of the vale; then, further down, these approach more closely, and the stream, now hidden by trees, flows onward to meet the Plym. Then, in close companionship, they roll to the sea, where their secrets were carried ages ago.

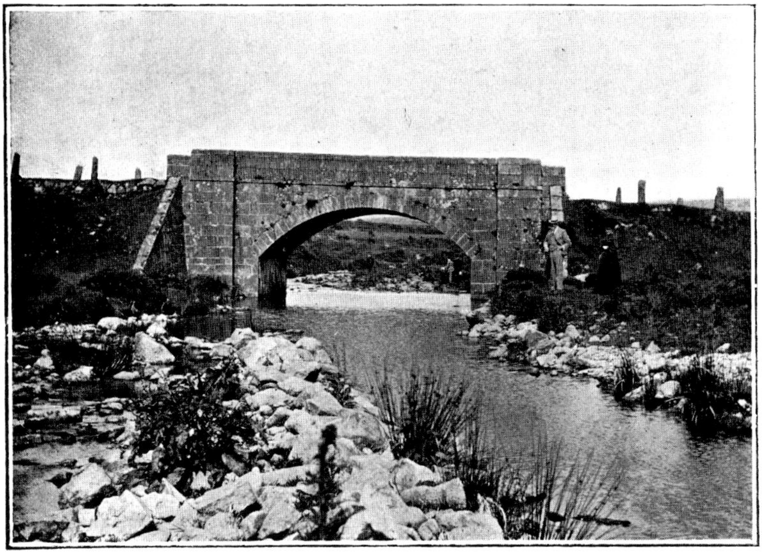

Photo by] [Ernest Croft.

Cadaford Bridge.

"The comparatively modern representative of an ancient structure."—*(See Page 152.)*

The hill peninsulated by these two Dartmoor rivers forms the southern extremity of a common, the main portion of which is known as Wigford Down. Its steep sides are covered in great part with oak coppice, the dwarf trees growing amid the masses of granite with which the ground is encumbered. Where the Plym swirls down from the stony valley below Cadaford Bridge, and not far above the confluence, a huge rock rises from the stream. Its foot is planted amid the boulders with which the river bed is strewn, and bushes cover the slopes on either side of it. Tufts of heather grow in its crevices, and ivy clings to its base; but the covering is scant, and its face is scarred by the storms that have swept over it. This grey mass, so often washed by the river when in flood, is well named the Water Stone, for such is the meaning of the appellation it bears.*

With the Dewer Stone is associated much that is mysterious. The swarthy huntsman that Forest tradition tells us haunts the Moor used here to be heard urging forward his wish hounds when the midnight storm was raging. From the rock-strewn valley came the sounds of pattering hoofs, and the roar of the river failed to drown the music of the

* Celtic *dwr* (w sounded as oo), *water*.

pack. In earlier days it was said he was wont to be seen, on his coal-black steed, bearing a long, slender pole, and shouting to his spectral hounds. As they dashed over the Moor fire shot from their eyes, and its light showed their great red tongues thrust from between their gleaming fangs. But that was long ago, and the peasant at length confessed that the wish huntsman no longer showed himself, but rode through the storm invisible. Now he would not like to say that the unearthly sounds he hears are other than those of the tempest.

And it was not only of the dark huntsman that they used to speak, but of one who was deemed far more terrible. Once when the snow lay deep upon the ground some peasants crossed the Plym, bent on tracking rabbits on the Dewer Stone Hill. They looked eagerly for traces, but in place of the tiny marks they had hoped to see were astounded at beholding the print of a naked foot, and beside it that of a cloven hoof. Though these were at first looked upon with fear and trembling, the peasants mustered sufficient courage to trace them through the snow. Up the steep path they were led, until at the summit of the hill the footprints ceased. That the Evil One had here led a human victim to destruction they did not doubt, and stayed not to ask themselves why he should have taken the trouble to ascend to the summit of a lofty height, when his path was a downward one. They were filled with horror at what they imagined had happened, and hastily made their way from the spot.

But another association clings to the Dewer Stone which rests not on tradition, but on the firmer rock of fact. The romantic vale below it was a favourite haunt of that wearied schoolmaster of Devonport, who yearned in vain to exchange his surroundings for the meadow and the woods—the poet Carrington. Compelled by an unkind fate to labour in the schoolroom, he could but rarely visit the scenes he loved. But when occasion offered he left the town behind him, and sought the place of the singing birds. The woods of Saltram claimed him then, or Mount Edgcumbe's stately groves, the winding Tamar, or the hills of Dartmoor. He tells us how that he often lingered near Shaugh Bridge, at the foot of the hill from which rises the Water Stone, until noon "unnoticed faded into eve," and how that to the Plym he owed "the few bright sunbreaks" that had cheered his life.

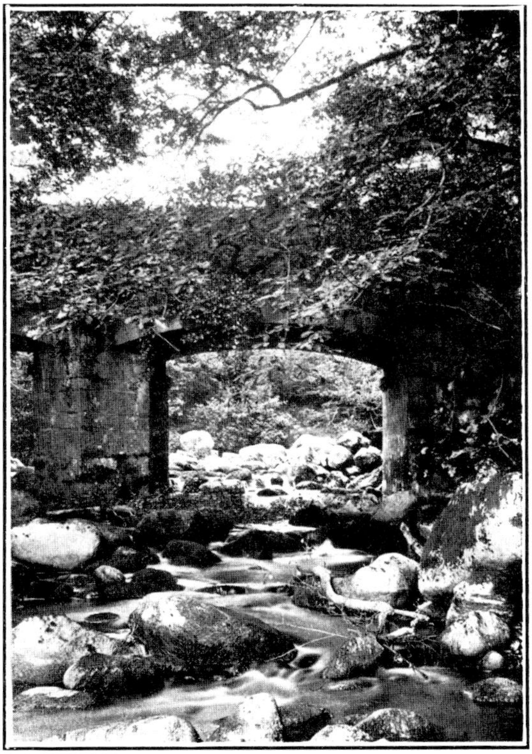

Photo by] [Ernest Croft.

Shaugh Bridge.

"The waters peacefully mingle . . . flowing in their young companionship beneath the arches."—*(See Page 152.)*

It was proposed to erect a monument to the memory of Carrington on the summit of the Dewer Stone, and a design was furnished by Mr. George Wightwick, the noted architect, but the scheme was never carried out. There is, however, a memorial to the poet on this hill, though it is one in which there is no display of the sculptor's art. It is a rock near the great cliff, on which is the following inscription:—"Carrington—Obiit Septembris, MDCCCXXX." But had the most elaborate monument been erected it could not have perpetuated the memory of this Westcountry bard so well as that which he himself set up. The thoughts he has transmitted to us with the pen will long outlast any work of the chisel.

At some distant time men, perceiving perhaps a strategic value in the Dewer Stone Hill, raised walls across its northern part, which, at a period when the sling was probably the only long-distance weapon, rendered it impregnable. If the rambler passes beyond these he will find himself on Wigford Down, from the highest point of which an extensive and varied view is presented. Several interesting relics exist on this common. More than one kistvaen standing within its circle of stones may be seen, and on the slope of the hill, near Cadaford Bridge, the upper part of an old cross.

Cadaford Bridge is the comparatively modern representative of an ancient structure. That there was a bridge here in the thirteenth century is proved by a charter of Isabella de Fortibus of the date 1291, in which it is mentioned. The name there appears as Cadaworth, and that it derived this from a dwelling or little settlement near by, now represented by Cadworthy Farm, there is no doubt.

But the attractions of the haunt of the poet of Dartmoor are by no means confined to the great rock by the water, or to the hill from the side of which it springs. The deep valley extending upward to Cadaford Bridge presents a scene of wildness that is most impressive, whether beheld from the heights above or from the bank of the stream. But he who essays to follow the latter must not expect to find the path an easy one; boulders cover the hillsides, and tangled undergrowth in places impedes the progress. Nevertheless the rambler who loves the rugged in Nature will, after he has threaded the maze of this stony vale, deem himself well rewarded for his trouble. The Plym rushes fretting through the defile, and seeks in a thousand ways to pass the obstacles that everywhere confront it. Here it dashes between dark rocks; there it rolls over a heap of boulders in a mass of foam. At one place—in North Wood—it falls from a high ledge into a deep pool, forming a fine cascade, which alone is worth a pilgrimage to see.

Few spots around our Devonshire uplands are more beautiful than the confluence of the Plym and the Mew. There the waters peacefully mingle between tree-shaded banks, flowing in their young companionship beneath the arches of Shaugh Bridge, which, though not possessing interest as an ancient structure, has yet been rendered by the seventy odd years of its existence sufficiently picturesque to harmoniously accord with its surroundings. The scene upon a summer morning, when the sunbeams pierce the arch of leaves and dance upon the surface of the stream, when the only sounds are those of the music which it makes and the songs of happy birds, speaks to us of peace. But there are times when all this is changed; when the rivers do not meet with a kiss, but mingle their floods with an angry roar. On the 27th of January, 1823, when the Moor was covered with snow, a sudden thaw took place, and, heavy rain falling, the river rose to an extraordinary height. Sweeping through the wild vale, the Plym rushed with tremendous force against the bridge, and carried away the causeway that led from it to the mill near by. The bridge appears to have been greatly damaged, for Carrington's son, writing in 1828, states that a few years previously to that date it was found necessary to demolish it.

But the Plym does not long continue in a wrathful mood, and the rambler mostly sees it when its bosom mirrors a sunny sky and the beauties on its banks.

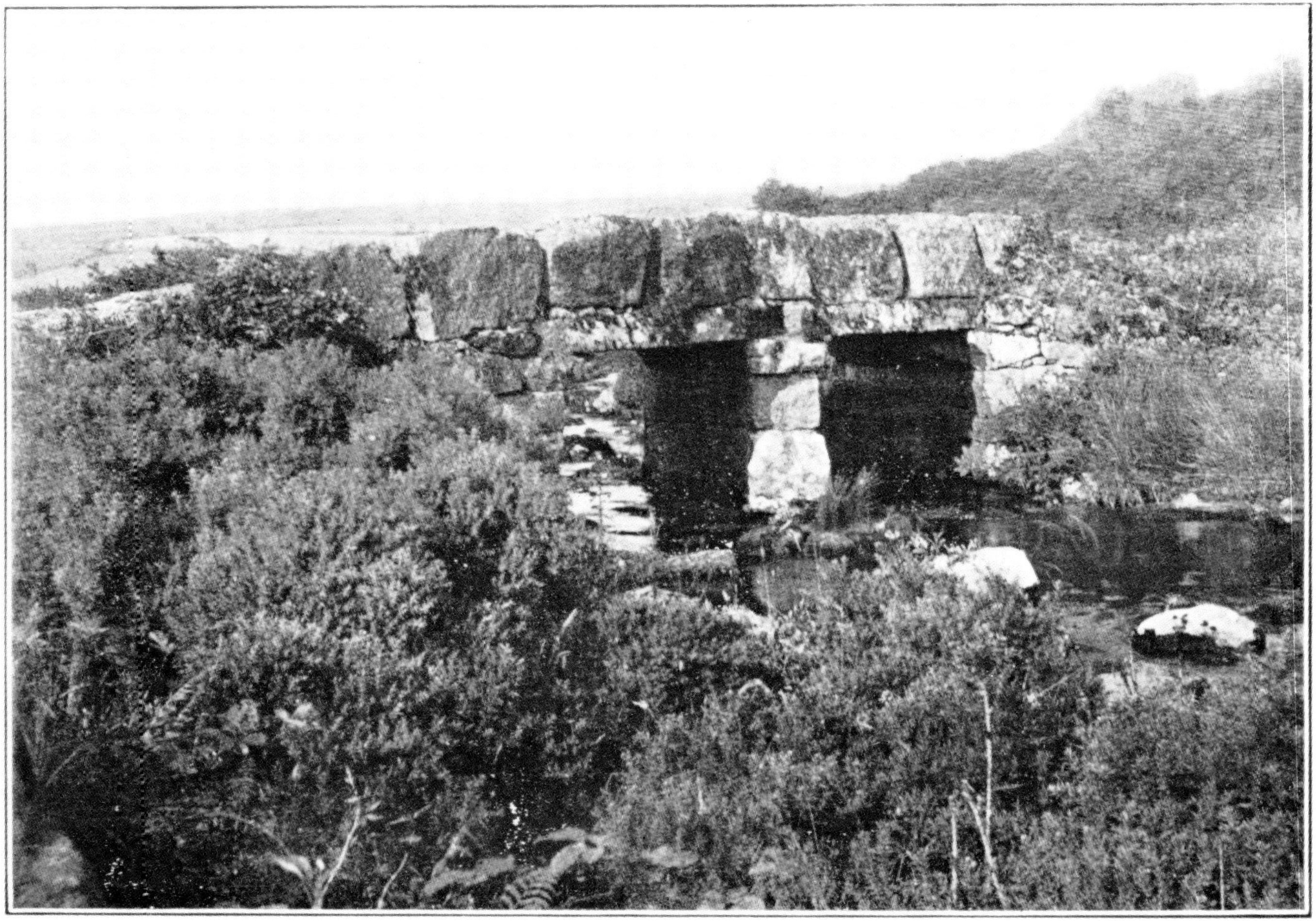

SEE PAGE 155.

Lether Tor Bridge.

PHOTO BY C. R. ROWE.

A clapper that perhaps replaces a much older one."

XX.

DEAN COMBE.

GRANITE-STREWN HILLS——BRACKEN AND FURZE BRAKES——NOSWORTHY BRIDGE——A BORDER VIEW——TORS AND ROCK MASSES——EVIDENCES OF THE TINNERS' FORMER PRESENCE——EYLESBARROW——SUBTERRANEAN CHAMBERS——A PIXY STORY——EARLY MENTION OF THE COMBE.

But wildest the mixture of shrub, bush and bramble,
And sweetest the scent which the wild flowers breathe,
Where the birchen-banks mark the stream's devious ramble,
And the ear drinks its musical murmurs beneath.
—REV. JOHN MARRIOTT.

NOWHERE perhaps are the characteristic features of Dartmoor border scenery more pleasingly presented than in the valleys running up into the commons above the Burrator Lake. Here are rude enclosures climbing part way up the sides of hills strewn with granite masses and crested with tors; farmhouses nestling in sheltered spots, and receiving additional protection from a few aged trees; narrow roadways winding through a wilderness of bracken; furze brakes dotted with sturdy hawthorns; and clear streams hastening from the commons to look upon new scenes. It is a blending of cultivation with the wildness of the Moor, in which the latter predominates. Not far above the head of the lake is Nosworthy Bridge, placed near the junction of three valleys, one being that through which the Mew comes down from its source at Devil's Bridge, another being watered by the Newleycombe Lake, and the third by the Narrator Brook. The latter stream was formerly called the Dean (or Dene) Brook, as is proved by the charter of Isabella de Fortibus, of the year 1291, referred to in the previous chapter, in which it is mentioned as bounding one of her manors. This ancient name is still preserved in that of the valley through which it runs, the same being known as Dean Combe.

To this retired spot, hidden behind the great mass of Sheeps Tor, let us now make our way, first directing our steps to Nosworthy Bridge. This may be readily reached from Dousland, from which it is distant about two-and-a-half miles, by the road passing Lowery, and skirting the northern shore of the Burrator Lake. It is formed on the line of an ancient track, and crosses the Mew at Lether Tor Bridge, a clapper that perhaps replaces a much older one, but our way will not lead us thither. Beyond Lowery a cottage is passed on the left, and a little further on, at Cross Gate, a road turns off to the right. This we follow, noticing Venny Lake Farmhouse as we descend the hill, and shall presently arrive at the bridge.

Nosworthy Bridge is a small structure of a single arch, spanning the Mew a few yards above the point where it receives the Newleycombe Lake. Here the stream, partly screened by foliage, comes down by the side of the common, above which Lether Tor lifts its lofty crest. Close to it a road, now entirely grass-grown, diverges from the one we are about to follow, and formerly led to Nosworthy Farmhouse, the ruins of which may be seen near by. This farm is one of four that are now included in the holding of Kingsett, the others being Newleycombe, Crazy Well, and

Roundy. The dwelling-houses belonging to them are, like Nosworthy, gone to decay, but parts of the walls yet remain to show where the early settlers in this valley had their homes. Ere we have proceeded many steps on our way we cross the Newleycombe Lake, but by a bridge altogether different in construction from that thrown over the Mew. This is in the style of the old clappers, and is formed of slabs of granite laid across the stream. Just beyond it our road passes between the enclosures belonging to Middleworth Farm, which here cover one side of the combe, on the other being a great rounded hill, shielded by the loftier Sheeps Tor from the south-westerly winds, and covered to its summit with dark fir trees.

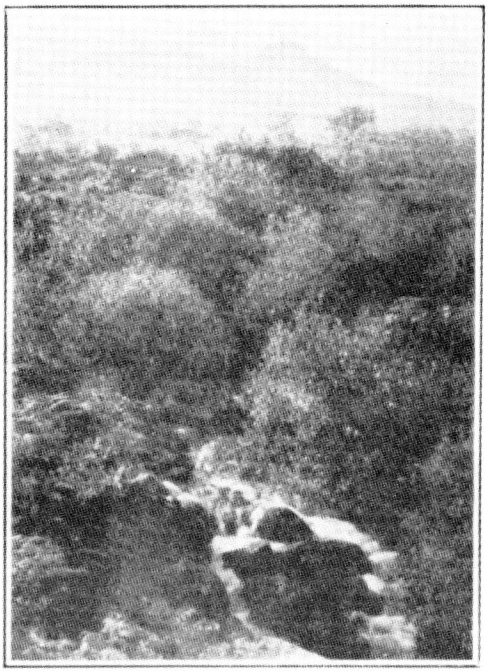

Photo by] [C. R. Rowe.

Near Nosworthy Bridge.

"The stream, partly screened by foliage, comes down by the side of the common, above which Lether Tor lifts its lofty crest."—*(See Page 155.)*

As we near the farm we notice very close to us on the left a pile of rocks, the blocks composing which are of large size. This though sometimes regarded as an outer pile of Down Tor, being placed on the flank of the hill on which the latter rises, is yet rightly given in the locality a distinctive name. It is there known as Snappers Tor, and while not of great height is certainly striking in appearance. Down Tor itself is about five hundred feet above the Burrator Lake, and forms a prominent object in this part of the Moor.

Passing Middleworth we reach a fine grove of beech trees, beyond which we find ourselves upon the open common. At a point where the road commences to descend we shall pause to look back upon the scene through which we have passed, for although its chief features are in view all the way up the combe, we shall hardly see them to better advantage than from here. At the foot of the hill, where the fir trees grow, and above which rises the bold brow of Sheeps Tor, the upper part of the Burrator Lake is seen. Beyond it there is a glimpse of Yennadon, with the plantation on its verge. To the right of this are fields, and then the great sweep of Peak Hill, with the farms of Lowery and Venny Lake on its lower slopes, and above the first-named homestead the tor of the same name. But the conspicuous feature in the view is the grand peak of Lether Tor, rising from a boulder-strewn height, and clearly defined against the sky. Its name signifies the steep tor, the present form as heard on the Moor having the true sound of its Celtic appellation, though not being orthographically correct.* The tor is seen above the beeches at Middleworth, which stand in the foreground of the picture, and from this point appear as two distinct groves. Snappers Tor, surrounded by scattered granite, which covers the hillside to the right, is again in view. The bit of the lake seen under the fir trees, the sharpness of Lether Tor, and the general wildness of the scene combine to give it almost a Highland character.

* The name is pronounced like the English word *leather*. The Celtic *dd*, or heavy *th*, appears in the name (that is, if we may be sure the tor is referred to) in a bailiff's account of the year 1476. It is there given as Leddertor, and the return of 1d. is made from John Northway for one acre of land there. In the Cymric-Celtic *llethr* signifies a *slope*, a *declivity*.

As we pass up the combe we shall notice that its sides exhibit a contrast to each other. On the southern, besides the fir-covered hill at the lower end, there is another clothed in a similar manner further up, and the common between these, and above the latter, is free from rocky protuberances. But the northern side, on which Down Tor rises, is rugged, and altogether more striking, being covered with granite from near the lower end of the combe to its head, where another tor, well named from its position Combeshead Tor, is seen. On the slope of this hill a huge block rises prominently from the surrounding granite masses. This is the Cuckoo Rock, which we shall see to better advantage when we reach that part of the valley opposite to it.

On nearing the entrance to Dean Combe Farm* the road turns down towards the little stream which we shall reach at a fording-place, the approach to it being roughly paved. Below it a single stone clapper spans the brook, which, however, is usually crossed by means of stepping-stones. Passing over these our ascending path brings us to a small grove of oak trees, where we have another exceedingly fine view. The objects beheld from our standpoint lower down still form the principal features, but in addition we now see the combe throughout, and shall find it to be covered near the stream with a thick growth of furze, withies, and thorns, with ancient oaks, sycamores, and beeches rising here and there above them, while ferns and wild flowers everywhere abound.

Proceeding on our way, the music of the little stream being no less pleasing to the ear than the fair scene we look upon is gratifying to the eye, we presently come in sight of Combeshead Farm, at the foot of the tor of that name. Near it we shall observe evidences of the former presence of the tin-seeker, in the form of immense deep cuttings, the sides of which the grass and heather have long since covered. To the right of the farm, and blocking, as it were, the head of the combe, is a hill on which grey granite is scattered, and above this rises the open common. On the sky line is an object that might at first be taken for a tor. But what look like rocks are really ruined walls, for on this windy height, which from a cairn on its summit bears the name of Eylesbarrow,† a house once stood. While it might cause surprise to learn that a dwelling should ever have been built on a spot so elevated and remote, it will, perhaps, occasion more when it is known that there was a time when near that lonely habitation an amusement such as we should be more likely to connect with the Burrator Lake was indulged in. In a pond formed close to it Mr. Deacon, the owner, used to keep a boat, and was able to treat his friends to a water trip on the top of a Dartmoor hill.

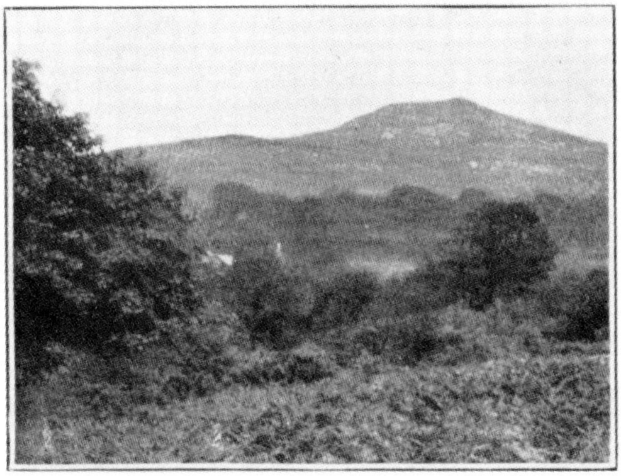

Photo by] [C. R. Rowe.

Down Tor.

"About five hundred feet above the Burrator Lake."—*(See Page 156.)*

Presently a path diverges to the right, but we follow the branch nearer the stream, and shall soon find ourselves abreast of the Cuckoo Rock, at the point where it is best seen. Passing another rock close to the brook, the top of which is covered with a

* Called in the neighbourhood Dennicombe.

† Pronounced Yelsboro.

luxuriant growth of ivy, we pause a moment to look back upon Lether Tor, which is here beheld to great advantage. Besides Sharp Tor, now seen rising behind it, few fresh objects are in sight, but the view from this point will nevertheless disclose features not hitherto observed.

Resuming our walk we cross another little ford, and speedily find ourselves among the old workings of the tinners close to Combeshead Farm.

These are very extensive, and are worth examination by those for whom such remains possess an interest. To all students of Dartmoor history such must appeal, for from the very earliest times the tin-seeker has laboured in its valleys, and for a considerable period the mining industry was so important that all who were engaged in it possessed privileges granted by the King. Among the heaps of debris are several curious excavations, one or two of which certainly appear to be the work of those who laboured here in the search for ore. The most striking consists of a dome-shaped chamber, nearly ten feet in height, and about eight or nine feet in diameter. It is hollowed out of the gravel, and is approached by a low, narrow passage. Others besides these are found in the locality, where they are usually regarded as having been formed for the purpose of storing potatoes in, a use to which they are still put, and this may indeed have been the original intention of some. It is also hinted that they were at one time found very convenient as store-places for illicit spirits. Be that as it may, that these curious excavations once held spirits of another kind the following story seems to show.

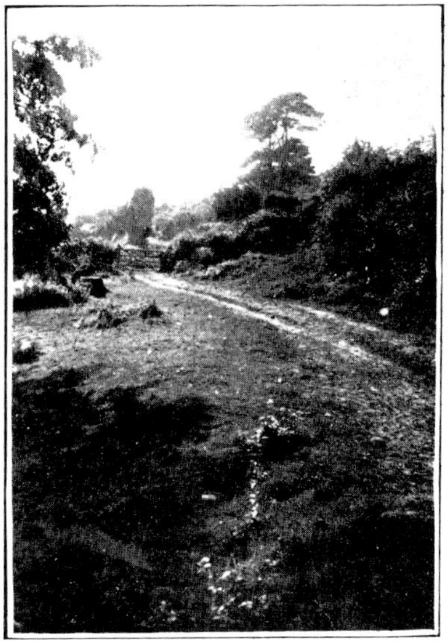

Photo by] [C. R. Rowe.

Gate at Dean Combe Farm.

"The road turns down towards the little stream." —(*See Page 157.*)

Late one evening, when the moon was flooding the Moor with her silvery light, a labourer was making his way down the side of Eylesbarrow, when he was startled at hearing the sound of voices, although no one was in sight. Moving cautiously forward he reached the edge of a gully, and peering into it beheld a scene that filled him with astonishment. An immense number of pixies were there hard at work, some with pick or shovel, while others were employed in carrying away gravel in little wheelbarrows.

Suddenly one of them shouldered his pick, and shouted, "Time for supper."

"Ees, I should zay 'twas," cried the countryman, "that's if you'm zo hungered as I be. But what be diggin' vur?"

"Tin," answered the pixy who had before spoken.

"Aw, helpin' ov the miners, be 'e? But why daun't 'e dig vur goold? I'd stap an' vill my puckets thain."

"After supper," said the pixy. "No supper, no gold."

"Then I'll hev zum zupper long wi' 'e, an' pick up the goold arterwards."

In an instant he felt himself impelled down the hill, the little people crowding round him in shoals. Almost before he was aware of it he was pushed into what he afterwards described as "a gert hall like wan o' they up nigh Combeshaid Tar." Preparations for supper were instantly commenced, though the countryman looked rather doubtfully at the kind of viands that were produced. Honey on plates no larger than a sixpence, and tiny berries, were not much to his taste, but he consoled himself with the hope that a pasty, or a piece of bacon, would surely be forthcoming later on. And there would certainly be "a dish o' tay," for he could see the kettle already steaming on the fire, notwithstanding that the pixies were constantly crowding round it, and almost hiding it from view.

"Bant mun b'ilin' eet?" he asked, going towards the fire. "He's a mortal long time, I zim."

"Take care, take care," cried a pixy; "don't knock over the brandis."

But unfortunately that is just what the peasant did. The corner of this triangular utensil on which kettles are set on the hearth, standing out further than he imagined, he struck it with his toe, and the kettle turning over, the fire was at once extinguished.

"No supper, no gold," shouted the pixies in chorus.

Instantly the peasant felt himself being borne rapidly through the air, and then all was blank. When he came to his senses he was lying on the Moor, near the gully in which he had first beheld the little people.

"No zupper, no goold," he said, as he rose to his feet. "There bant n'ither vur me, that's a zartin thing. Drat the little toads; I'd a vurgived mun the loss ov the zupper if they'd aunly laived me hev the goold vust."

Both Combeshead Tor and Down Tor are well worth a visit, and the rambler may easily return by way of these. The former is reached by following up the little stream where it bends eastward for a short distance, and then mounting the slope to the left. On leaving the pile he will strike across the common to Down Tor, which is in sight, and thence descend to the road near Middleworth. By adopting this plan he will not only obtain several good views of the Moor, but will also be afforded an opportunity of examining the fine group of stone remains situated between the two tors, and a little to his right as he proceeds.

Dean Combe is referred to by name in documents connected with the Forest, although it is not within its boundaries. Among the Court Rolls of the Duchy preserved at the Public Record Office are numerous presentments, one of which of the twenty-second of Henry VI. is to the effect that John Simon and John Holway committed damage to the extent of 100s. by burning the pasture of the King in the Forest of Dartmoor. The part of the Forest said to have been burnt by them is described as lying "between Foxtorre Combe and Den Combe, and between Newelcombe and Elysburgh." Of these Fox Tor Combe and Eylesbarrow only are within the Forest, and much of the swaling therefore appears to have taken place on the adjoining common of Walkhampton. This presentment would consequently prove that the Duchy possessed ancient rights over the purlieus of the Forest as well as within its bounds.

Another early mention of Dean Combe is in the return of the Forester of the west quarter, in 1506. The amounts received by him as fines of the vills, or what we now term venville rent, are set down, and among them is the sum of 18d. from the vill of "Dencombe in parochia de Walcanton." Here we not only have mention of the name, but we also learn that the farms in this retired valley formed one of the ancient vills, and consequently possessed extensive rights on the Forest.

XXI.

THE WALKHAM BELOW MERIVALE.

An Untamed Region——The Walla Cwm——Pu Tor——Rock Basins——Vixen Tor——A Wooded Valley——Sampford Spiney——Ward Bridge——Woodtown——Hucken Tor——Long Ash.

Through glen and gorge, thou lov'st to leap
O'er barriers tempest-strown;
To mingle with the hoary deep,
Gushes thy torrent down.
—Rev. Francis Phillott.

FROM no point on the line followed by the old perambulators of the Forest bounds does the ancient hunting ground present a wilder aspect than from the ridge on which is placed the cairn known as Limsboro. The wanderer from the valley of the Tavy who, after passing Wapsworthy or Bagga Tor, climbs the slope of Green Hill or Lynch Down, on reaching the summit suddenly sees before him a veritable desert, which, if beheld on a dull day, is almost repellent in its sternness. It is of the Moor moory; look where he may, save for the rocks of Fur Tor, and the piles above the valley of the Cowsic, nothing but brown hills meet the eye. No part of the wilderness within his ken has ever been tamed. Nature is here as of old; it is her home, and none have sought to drive her from it. That man has found his way hither the evidences of turf-cutting operations plainly indicate, but his work has gone no further. Dreary though the scene be, it yet fascinates; the beholder is almost impelled to seek the summit of the next ridge that he may discover what lies beyond it. The solitude, the wildness, is in a measure forbidding, yet he is held by that power of attraction the Moorlands possess, whether seen in sunshine or in shadow, in summer or in winter, at early morn or when night covers the hills with her mantle.

It is dawn upon the Moorlands, and the shadows of the night
Through the deep and silent valleys steal before the morning light;
Over yonder hill-top rises like a burning shield the sun,
Slowly wakes the grim old desert, and a new day has begun. .
All unseen a soaring songster pours her sweet and happy lay,
Making music with the streamlet that goes singing on its way,
Singing joyously, and laughing, when the sunbeams chase the mist
That has veiled it from the morning, and too long its bosom kissed.

It is noontide on the Moorlands, but upon no thirsty land
Shines the sun from skies unclouded; by the gentle breezes fanned
Ancient hills invite the wand'rer, and a thousand brooklets flow
Down their sides, in haste to render tribute to the streams below.
Silent all, save when the rushes whisper as the winds pass by,
Answered by the murm'ring waters, and the lonely curlew's cry;
Yet another voice we list to, but it speaks without a sound,
From within it comes, and tell us freedom breathes in all around.

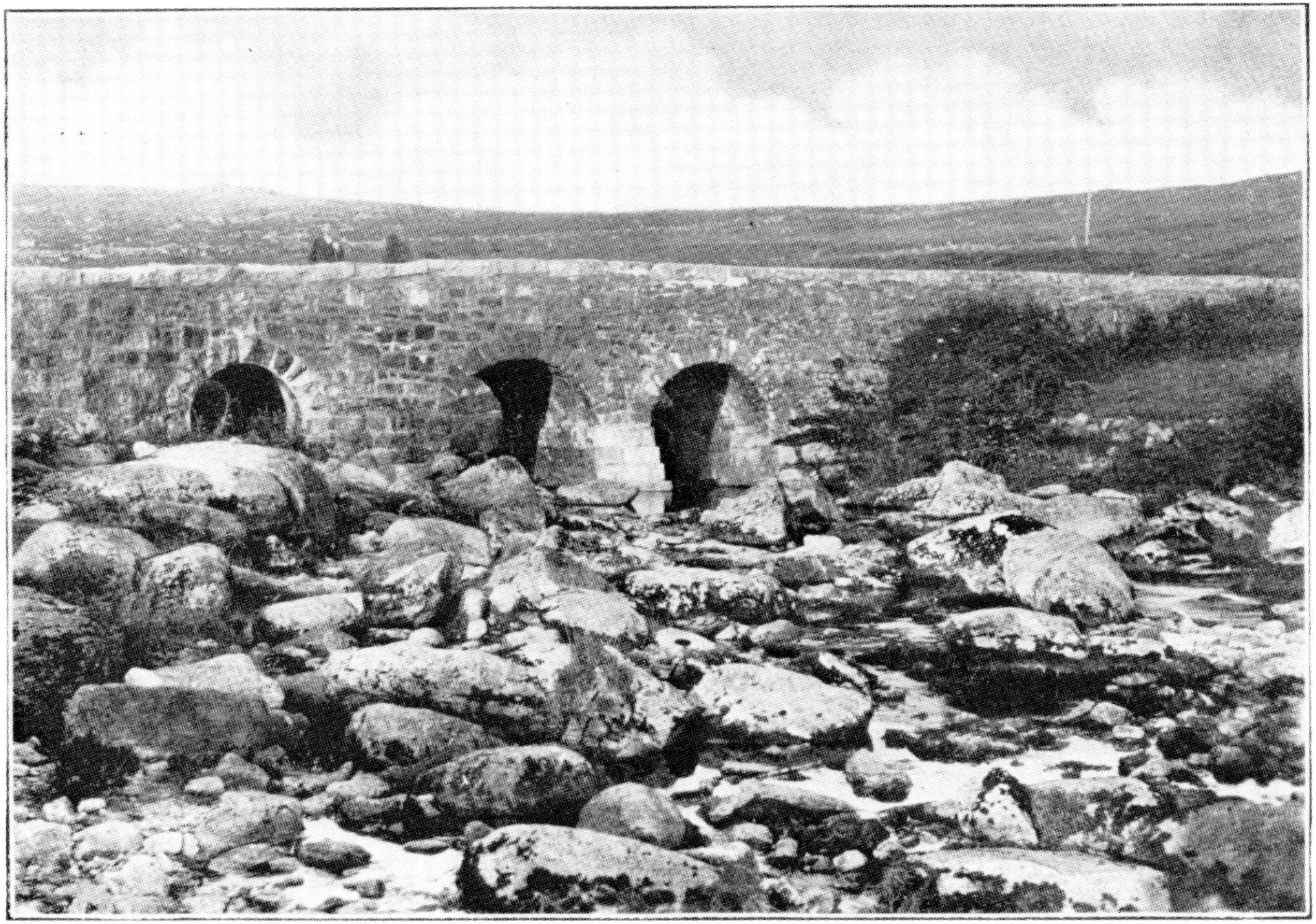

SEE PAGE 163.

Merivale Bridge.

PHOTO BY C. R. ROWE.

"On the road from Tavistock to Princetown."

It is evening on the Moorlands, and the deep'ning shadows creep
Through the lonely combes, and slowly climb the heather-covered steep,
In the west a dying radiance marks the pathway of the sun,
Speaks of its departed glory, tells us that the day is done.
Ended now the streams' sweet singing—e'er their songs at evening die—
Ceased the whisp'ring of the rushes as they list the night wind's sigh,
Heard no more the desert music, every bird has sought its nest,
O'er the fells a holy calmness waits upon the hour of rest.

It is night upon the Moorlands ; rising in the starry dome
Is the Lesser Light and Ruler that shall guide the wand'rer home ;
Not alone her lamp is lighted in the sky, for see a gleam
Midst the shadows of the valley quivers on the rippling stream.
Lo, the darkness falls not on us, and the pure and brilliant light
Speaks to us of that far country where there never shall be night ;
Resting over all the Spirit, by the angels ever sung,
That upon the waste of waters brooded when the world was young.

In this district, and about half a mile from Limsboro, but hidden from the western sky by the hill on which that cairn stands, a river rises that appears to have formerly borne the name of the Store (at least in one part of its course), but which we now call the Walkham. At all events Risdon nearly three hundred years ago referred to it as the Store, though there cannot be a doubt that it was then also known by the name it bears to-day; the same, or nearly the same, by which it was called long prior to Risdon's time. In the thirteenth century it is mentioned in a charter as the Walkamp, and at a period anterior to that was probably one of the numerous Wallas on the Moor.* The present form of the name of this stream is neither more nor less than a corruption of *Walla cwm*, or combe, the valley of the Walla, the latter probably being the beautiful gorge we are about to notice. The evidence in favour of such a supposition, and it appears to us sufficiently strong, is afforded by the situation of the village of Walkhampton, the *ton*, or town, near the Walla combe.

A little over a mile from its source the stream is crossed by the ancient Lich Path, a track still of considerable service to the Moorman and the hunter. Further down the river bends to the right under Greena Ball, and after leaving the Forest again turns, and flowing southward between the rock-strewn flank of Great Mis Tor and Langstone Moor, runs at the foot of the ridge crowned with the fantastically shaped piles of Staple Tor, and reaches Merivale Bridge, on the road from Tavistock to Princetown. Below this it enters the valley that has become so justly celebrated for the beauty of its scenery, and where tree-clad steeps are overlooked by granite-dotted commons, from which rise rugged tors. This runs approximately north and south, and rough tracks are carried along the sides, from many points on which exceedingly fine views are obtained. One of the piles placed above it is Pu Tor, and from this we may well commence our investigations.

Pu Tor is conveniently reached from Tavistock or Horrabridge. From the former town the way lies over Whitchurch Down and through Quarry Lane; from the latter the road leading by the entrance to Grimstone is followed to Plaster Down, the north-eastern corner of which abuts on the common above Sampford Spiney, and from this the tor rises. From whichever of these places it is approached it comes into view some time before it is reached, and though it does not compare in size nor height with many of the tors in this part of the Moor, at once attracts attention by the prominence of its situation and the boldness of its outline. When antiquaries believed the rock-piles on the Moor to have been appropriated by the Druids to some mysterious purposes connected with

* Risdon says: "Now let us hasten to Horrowbridge, where the river Store streameth along, after it hath watered Sampford Spine." *Survey of Devon:* written prior to 1640. In the charter of Isabella de Fortibus confirming the grant of certain lands to Buckland Abbey, the bounds of the manor of Walkhampton, are drawn "per medium cursum aquœ de Tavie et de Walkamp." The date of this charter is 1291.

their worship, Pu Tor was regarded by them as having been one of the temples of that priesthood. Its peculiar form, and the existence of rock-basins upon it, led to this belief, which, to say the truth, we almost envy them for being able to entertain. The tors of Dartmoor as the older antiquaries knew them were invested with an interest they can never possess for us. The light of the torch held up by the geologist and the archæologist enables us to read, if not the whole truth, at least very much of it, but this may not be all gain. The romance that once clung to these hoary rock-masses has been ruthlessly torn away, and we can no longer associate them with bards and venerable seers. It is now known that the rain drop, and the frost, and the wind, have scooped out the basins on the tors, and not the hand of man. The Druids have vanished before research like the morning mist that the rising sun dispels, and Nature has taken their place.

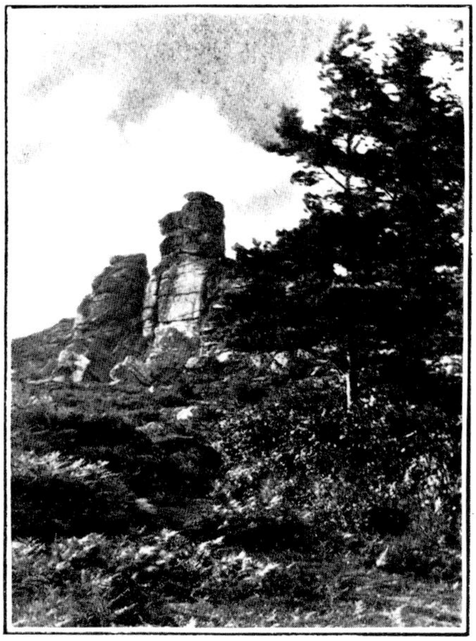

Photo by] [C. R. Rowe.

Vixen Tor.

"Seen from any point is a very striking pile."—
(See Page 165.)

But notwithstanding that Pu Tor has been stripped of much that was once thought to belong to it, it is yet by no means devoid of interest. Its higher part consists of four piles of rock, each nearly facing a cardinal point. The space between the northern and western piles is occupied by a natural barrier of rocks, but between the other piles the spaces are clear, except in one place, where, however, the rocky wall is low and does not obstruct the view. From the centre of this rude enclosure we look upon three distinct pictures, framed by the grey granite masses. To the north-east we see Great Mis Tor and Staple Tor, with the summit of Vixen Tor peeping over the common in the foreground. South-eastward the tors on the further side of the Walkham Valley fill the view; and towards the south-west we look across smiling farm lands to Roborough Down, with the confluence of the Tamar and the Tavy beyond, and further away the Cornish hills and Mount Edgcumbe, and a streak of silver where the Channel seems to neighbour the sky. We stand in Nature's picture gallery, and when we look upon what she has displayed we begin to feel that the absence of the Druids is not so much to be lamented after all.

The rock-basins are, with one exception, on the northern pile. The most perfect of these is about ten inches deep, and its longest diameter two feet ten inches; it is furnished with a sort of lip. On the west side of the tor are a number of rocks heaped in great confusion, and forming a clatter. Between two large stones on its northern side, a small oak tree is growing. But it spreads its tiny branches over their surfaces, the wintry blast forbidding it to lift them towards the sky.

Leaving this cluster of rocks, from which we have obtained so wide a view, we make our way down the slope in an easterly direction, with the enclosure belonging to Pu Tor Cottage on our right. At the distance of about a quarter of a mile we shall strike a Moor track, and following it towards the north shall obtain occasional glimpses of the wooded valley below, and a constant view of hill and tor. On passing Heckwood Tor, a pile quite close to the path, the lower end of Beckamoor Combe presents itself, with Vixen Tor rising grandly from the brow of the hill on its further side. We may if we choose pass down into the combe, and crossing the little stream that flows through it, climb the opposite steep to the tor, or we may reach it by way of the farm bearing its name. If we decide upon the latter we pass through a gate on the right, and keeping a little to the left as we cross the newtake, shall find a narrow path, which will lead us down by the side of a granite quarry to the road by which the farm is approached. Here we shall pause to look upon the tor, for it is nowhere seen to greater advantage than from this spot. On the further side of the combe is the farmhouse, though from some points hidden from view by trees and bushes, for we have here reached the wooded part of the valley, and on the hill behind it rises the tor. Viewed from the common beyond, it exhibits a resemblance to the Egyptian Sphinx, and seen from any point is a very striking pile. But above this romantic glen its rocks tower so majestically, and impart such a wildness to the scene, as to deeply impress the rambler whose steps have brought him hither.

It was Mr. E. A. Bray, afterwards vicar of Tavistock, who first noted the resemblance borne by Vixen Tor to the Sphinx, there being an entry to this effect in his journal of 1801. A few years later Dr. Berger, who made a geological report on the Moor, also speaks of it. Accompanied by his friend, Mr. Necker, he was journeying from Two Bridges to Tavistock, and on passing over that part of the Moor near the tor, they were both struck at once with its likeness to the famed Egyptian rock. From another point this resemblance is lost, and the pile assumes quite a different form. Here the fancy may see the figure of a man with a cocked hat, with a tall and corpulent lady behind him, as though they were seated on horseback in the mode formerly known as "riding double." Mr. Bray also noticed this, and recorded it in his journal. On October 3rd in the same year his entry was made, Mr. Bray ascended Vixen Tor in company with a friend. He found three basins on the summit, one being eight inches in depth, another nine, and the third fourteen inches. Before descending he left a twopenny piece in one of them. In the autumn of 1831 Mr. Bray took a young friend to the tor. The latter climbed to the top, but saw nothing of the twopenny piece, indeed, he could distinguish but few traces of the basins, for the surface of the tor was covered with mould, grass and moss. The thirty years that had elapsed since Mr. Bray made the first ascent had wrought a change, and as he remarks, there is here some data as to the period of the formation of vegetable mould in the hollows of rocks.

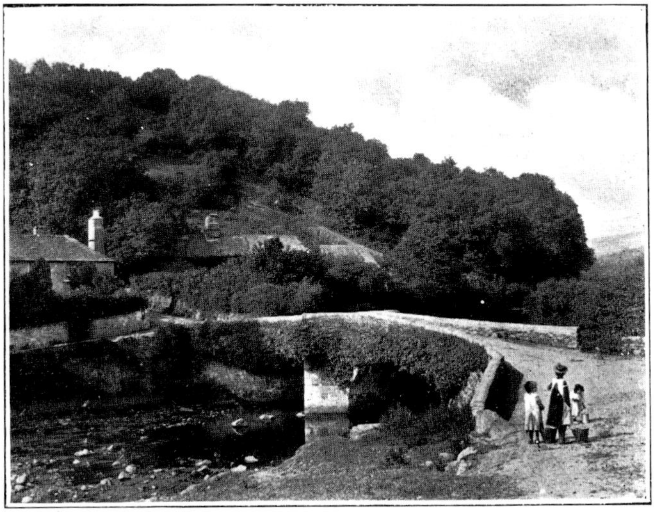

Photo by] [C. R. Rowe.

Huckworthy Bridge.

"On the direct road from Tavistock to Cornwood."—*(See Page 167.)*

The road down the valley, which, after having examined the tor, we shall follow, leads from the farm to Sampford Spiney, and runs roughly parallel to the track by which we reached Heckwood Tor, but at a considerably less elevation. Ere we have proceeded far we shall notice close to the wayside, by the wall of a plantation, a large carefully worked granite stone, hexagonal in shape. It was cut many years ago for some work in connection with the Plymouth Breakwater, but owing to a flaw was thrown aside as useless. Near by, on the opposite side of the road, is a tor, which though its size may not render it striking, is nevertheless so well placed as to add in no small degree to the picturesqueness of the spot. It was here that one Roody, who was in league with a band of smugglers, decapitated a sheep with a billhook, when leaping from the rocks to escape from his pursuers. At this point we have a view of the gorge, though the Walkham itself is not visible, the banks being thickly fringed with trees. A little further on the road ascends to the gate at Hecklake, and as we make our way towards it more of the beautiful valley reveals itself. The contrast afforded by its tree-covered sides and the heights that overtook them, where is only turf and heather and rock, is very striking. Below, a mass of waving green, whence rise the songs of birds; above, silence, and the sternness of the granite waste.

Passing through the gate we find ourselves on the common below Pu Tor Cottage, and still following the road shall speedily reach the little moorland settlement of Sampford Spiney.

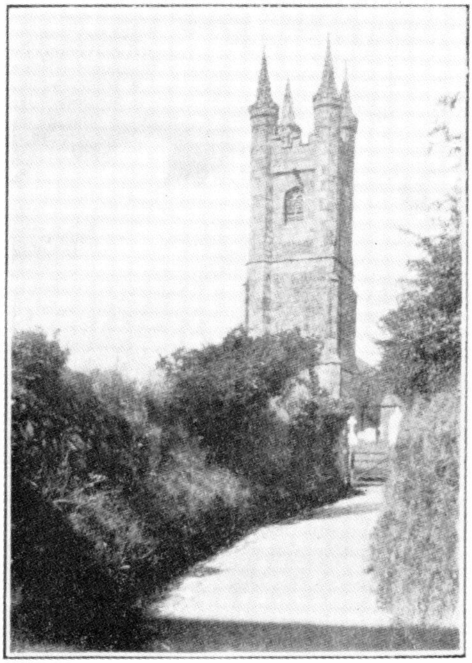

Photo by] [C. R. Rowe.

Walkhampton Church.

"A prominent landmark in this part of the Dartmoor borderland."—*(See Page 167.)*

This sequestered hamlet consists of a church and school, an ancient manor house, now a farmhouse, and a cottage or two, grouped round a green, on which is a widely-spreading tree, and an old cross, with a few other dwellings not far off. The church formerly belonged to Plympton Priory, the arms of which religious house are carved on a stone in the south face of the tower. The road from this place to Plympton, over which the monks passed, was formerly marked by a number of stone crosses, some of which, and the remains of others, are still to be seen.* The church possesses a chalice and cover of the middle of the eighteenth century, and a paten, presented by John Ridout, Esq., of Moortown, in 1811.

The second name of this parish is derived from its ancient lords, the Spinets, which family held the manor in the time of Henry II. It has since been in the families of Drake, Bidgood, and Hall, and is now owned by Captain Hall-Parlby, of Manadon. Nothing has disturbed the quiet of the hamlet; removed from high roads and railways, it wears its old restful air.

Bidding adieu to this delightful rural scene, we leave the green by the road southward of the church, and keeping to the left, and down hill, shall at the distance of three-parts of a mile reach Ward Bridge, round which the sweetest charms of the valley cluster. It is true that the present structure is far less picturesque than the one it replaces, which was swept away in the great flood of July, 1890, after standing for some three hundred years, but its modern appearance does not detract from the beauty of the scene. And we do not think of its age when we look upon its surroundings. These are all unchanged.

* I have described this old monks' path in my *Ancient Stone Crosses of Dartmoor and its Borderland.* Chaps. V., VIII.

The storm destroyed only the work of man; a brief season, and that which Nature claimed as hers wore the same face as before. The trees at the foot of the steeps on either side fling their boughs over the waters, and so narrow is the valley here that these almost interlace. In the river bed are immense boulders of granite, brought down from the stony hillsides about Great Mis Tor during winter storms or summer floods. It is a picture of a white-flashing stream, and green leaves quivering in the sunlight, and patches of blue sky. The voice of the waters is borne upon the soft wind, and the sweet notes of unseen warblers blend harmoniously with their chant.

On the left bank of the river below Ward Bridge is the estate of Eggworthy, and on the right bank is Woodtown, the residence of Mrs. Collier, widow of the late Mr. W. F. Collier, who was an enthusiastic admirer of the Moor, and a brother of Mr. A. B. Collier, the well-known Dartmoor artist. From that part of Walkhampton Common in the vicinity of Inga Tor the house is in full view, and its delightful situation at once arrests the attention of the rambler. Embosomed in trees, which in this sheltered valley grow most luxuriantly, it fully justifies its name.

Further down the river is Huckworthy Bridge, a picturesque structure on the direct road from Tavistock to Cornwood and the southern borders of the Moor. Half a mile distant the village of Walkhampton, in local parlance Wackinton, nestles under the hill on which its church, a prominent landmark in this part of the Dartmoor borderland, is placed. Below Huckworthy the Walkham flows amid fresh beauties, knowing no other accompaniment throughout its course to the Tavy.

Leaving Ward Bridge we pass up the hill to the east, and presently arrive at a point where our road, which runs up to the common near by, is crossed by another coming up the valley from Walkhampton. Here we turn to the left, and crossing a small stream by a comparatively modern clapper of two openings near Withill Farm, shall pass Davy Town Farm and make our way along the narrow lane to Hucken Tor, or as it is usually called in the locality, Okel Tor. The scene presented as it comes into view is truly characteristic of the Dartmoor borders. The rude walls of small enclosures, encumbered with scattered granite, are seen on the hillside to the right; to the left is the valley, and beyond rise rocky peaks. There is a slight ascent towards the tor, through which the road may be said to pass. The approach to the cluster is between two immense rocks, one of which overhangs in such a manner as to form a rude canopy. When we pass through the opening we find ourselves amid a number of granite masses of fantastic shape, not of great height, but none the less striking. Many of these being draped with ivy, and all rising from a wilderness of dwarf oaks and heather and whortleberry plants, render Hucken Tor one of the most beautiful on the Moor. Across the valley Vixen Tor and Pu Tor are prominent objects, and towards the north the huge hill crowned with the rocks of Mis Tor is seen rising boldly from a wide sweep of common. Altogether nearly a score of tors are in sight, the beholder being almost surrounded by them. Through the break in this circle of granite pinnacles he looks over cultivated country and sees far away the great wall on the heights above Bovisand, on the east side of Plymouth Sound, and the trees that clothe the steeps of Mount Edgcumbe.

From the tor we pass on to the Long Ash Brook, which we cross by a clapper ruder in construction than the one near Withill Farm. Situated in a spot little frequented it is not so well known as some on the Moor, but it may be regarded as an excellent example of these bridges. It is best seen from below and from the left bank of the stream.

Passing Long Ash Farm, we soon reach the common in the vicinity of the well-known stone rows. Here we again meet the Walkham as it comes down from the solitude. So far it has looked only upon dreary bog-land, rugged tor, and heather slopes. We see it flow beneath the bridge at Merivale, and mark its course to the fir trees that stand at the entrance to the gorge. Then we know that it is about to become familiar with the fern and the waving tree—with the beauties of the vale that have given such delight to us.

XXII.

PETER TAVY COMBE.

A Sequestered Village——Peter Tavy Mill——A Moorland Path——The Monk's Adventure——Cascades and Crystal Pools——Stevens' Grave——Langstone Moor——Smearn Down——Cudlipp Town——The Valley of the Tavy.

> Where every morn a quire of Silvans sung,
> And leaves to chatt'ring windes serv'd as a tongue,
> By whom the water runs in many a ring,
> As if it fain would stay to heare them sing,
> And on the top a thousand young birds flye
> To be instructed in their harmony.
>
> —Browne.

TWO miles from Tavistock a road leaves the Okehampton highway, and, crossing the Tavy at Harford Bridge, runs up the valley above the left bank of that river to the commons at Bagga Tor, whence a peat track leads to the Forest. About a mile above the bridge the road passes through the village of Peter Tavy, one of those sequestered little places that add so much to the interest of the Dartmoor borderland. Here a small stream, usually called the Peter Tavy Brook, but which at one time bore the name of White Lake, or Wed Lake, comes down from the Moor through a narrow combe to fall into the Tavy just below. This combe does not exhibit features of wild grandeur like some of the valleys on the fringe of the waste, but it has charms of another sort. It possesses a simple beauty which, though it may not impress like that of the deep vales where the crag thrusts itself from the oak woods, nevertheless appeals to the eye. Above the northern side of the combe is Smearn Down, and on the southern are the commons from which rises the conspicuous Cocks Tor Hill. At its upper end—towards the east—is the dusky ridge whence Roose Tor and the Staple Tors look down upon the valley of the Walkham.

In approaching the combe from the village, to which it is quite near, the way lies by the mill. Though not presenting the same appearance now as it did in the days when Mrs. Bray wrote, this is yet a picturesque building, and merits the attention of the artist. Mrs. Bray states that it had been sketched a number of times, and that pictures of it hung at Somerset House and the Water-colour Exhibition had never failed to find purchasers. Immediately in front is a bridge, which we cross, and, following a path on the bank of a stream, shall shortly enter upon the down.

We are here at the lower end of the combe, the sides of which, clothed only with grass and lumps of trap rock (for the valley is outside the line of the granite), slope directly to the brook, the southern one being the steeper. Overlooking this is Great Combe Tor, which is approached by a continuation of the path we have followed. A footbridge carries it over the stream, and it may be seen climbing the hill towards the pile. This path forms the most direct route between Peter Tavy and Merivale Bridge. It runs at the northern foot of Cocks Tor Hill, and across the shallow valley between that eminence and the ridge on which the Staple Tors are placed, passing at this point

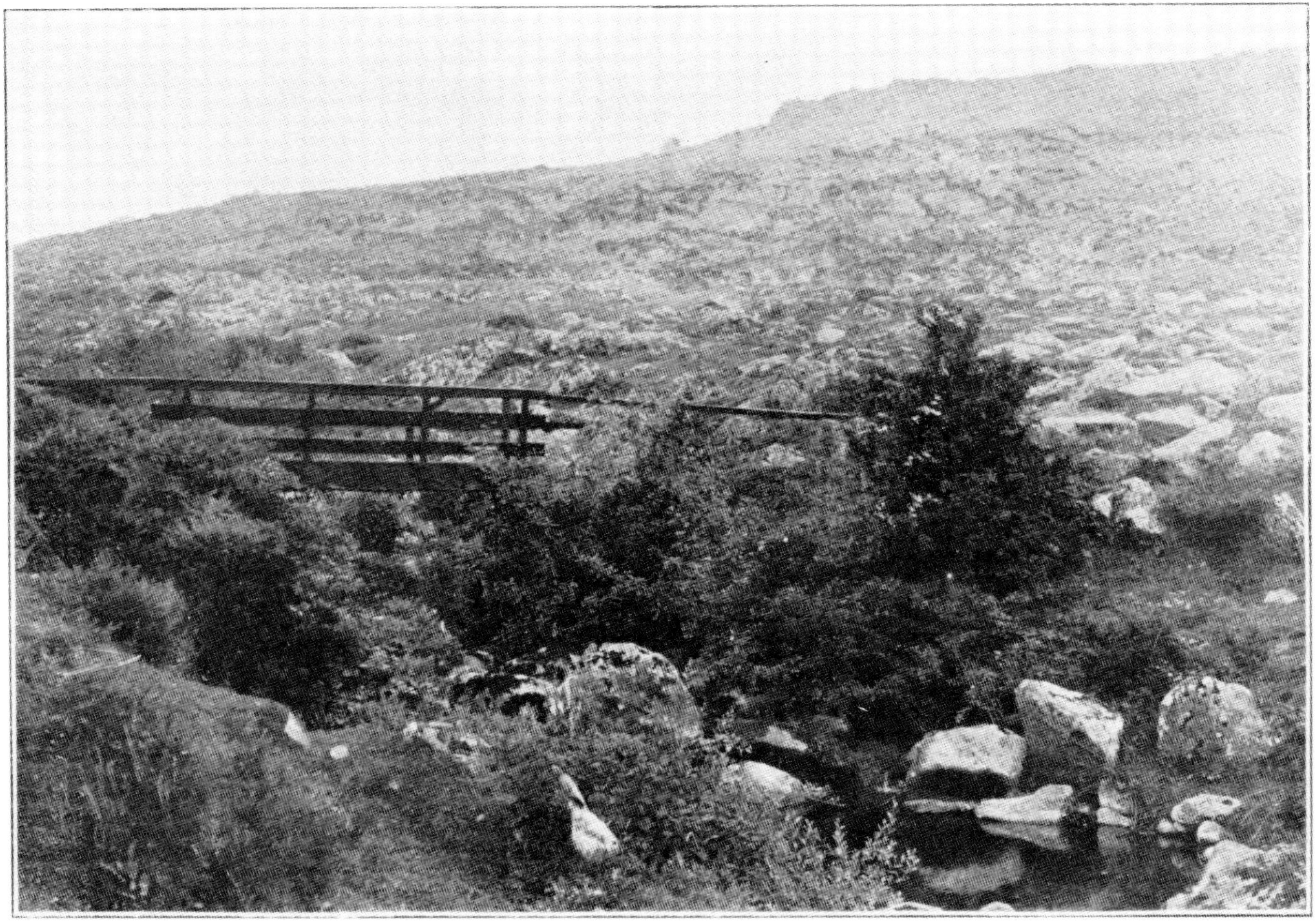

SEE PAGE 168.

PHOTO BY C. R. ROWE

Peter Tavy Combe.

"The sides . . . . clothed only with grass and lumps of trap rock . . . . slope directly to the brook."

the head of Beckamoor Combe. Here it loses its character of a green path, and is rudely paved with flat granite stones to the top of the ridge, over which it passes a few yards to the south of Great Staple Tor. The stones were laid down by labourers who passed this way daily to the quarries, not so much for the purpose of forming a good path, as to serve as a guide when darkness, or the state of the weather, rendered such necessary. And this they certainly do most admirably. I have passed over the path alone on the darkest night, when, in addition, the Moor has been enveloped in a thick mist, and have not gone a foot out of my way.

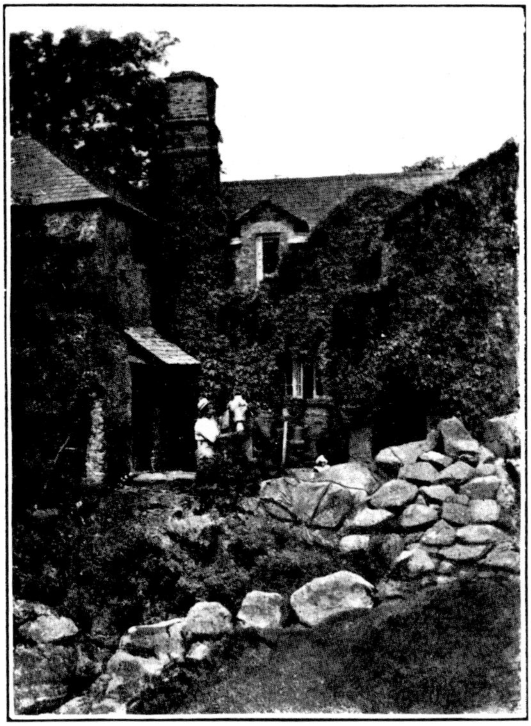

Photo by] [C. R. Rowe.

Peter Tavy Mill.

"In approaching the combe . . . the way lies by the mill."— (*See Page 168.*)

From the brow of the hill in front of Great Combe Tor there is a good view of the combe itself, besides one of the surrounding country. This, however, is not nearly so extensive as some obtained in the vicinity, for many hills near at hand greatly exceed the tor in elevation. But a number of objects are seen to advantage, among them being Brent Tor, which from no point presents a finer appearance.

It was at Great Combe Tor that one of the brothers of Plympton Priory once met with an adventure. Let us ascend it, and while you feast your eyes upon the delightful prospect it commands you shall hear the story.

The light was fading in the winter sky when two monks rode out of the little settlement of Sampford Spiney, their nags' heads being turned towards Tavistock Abbey. They were the bearers of letters to the abbot, from the prior of Plympton, to whose house they belonged, and had started on their journey early in the forenoon. Ere this they should have reached their destination, but certain halts by the way—necessary, they considered, both for man and beast—had delayed them longer than they had bargained for. But the good host at the inn at Meavy was so loud in the praises of his ale—which it could not be denied was particularly good—that they had felt almost compelled to drink a double portion lest he should be offended; and the parson of Sampford had been so pressing with his metheglin, that it would have been nothing short of a breach of good manners had they not suffered him to fill their cups each time he expressed a wish to do so. The hours sped so pleasantly that the day was gone before they knew it, and thus it came about that they found themselves some four miles from their destination when darkness was settling over the Moor.

Although the hour at which they should have arrived at the Abbey on the Tavy had long gone by, they proceeded at a very sober pace. Not for the reason that such befitted holy men, for that consideration would not then have weighed with them, but for one very different. Though neither was an accomplished horseman they were not altogether unused to the saddle, but now they kept their seats only with the greatest difficulty, and dared not break into a trot.

"We are bewitched," cried the hindmost one, grasping his horse's mane to save himself from falling; "it is the work of Satan."

His companion crossed himself, and endeavoured to reply, but found that the power of the Evil One had so affected him as to render his speech incoherent. He gave vent to a few guttural sounds, finishing with a loud "Whoop," as though to show that he had not altogether lost the use of his vocal organs. The exclamation so startled his nag, the animal being unaccustomed to hear his rider shout in such an unseemly manner, that he set off at once into a brisk canter, and in less than a minute had disappeared in the darkness. His companion called upon him to stop, but he might as well have spoken to the lumps of granite that encumbered the common. He endeavoured to follow him, but was unable to determine in which direction he had gone. He looked about for the path, but could see none, and then he realised that he had lost his way.

Several hours passed, and still the monk urged his tired horse over the Moor, in the vain hope of finding a road or shelter. The wind had risen, and came sweeping across the heath, bringing with it the rain-laden cloud. The big drops pattered on the monk's head, and presently his cowl clung like a wet rag to his shaven crown. Cold and hungry he pursued his weary way, but knew not whither it would lead him.

At length, to his great joy, he espied a light, and attempted to urge his steed towards it. But the animal would not move, and the monk therefore hastily dismounted and went forward on foot. He had not taken half a dozen steps, however, before he learnt the reason why his horse had refused to stir. A mire lay before him, and the unlucky brother of Plympton Priory, stepping upon its treacherous surface, instantly sank into it up to his knees. It was some minutes before he could extricate himself, and then he only did so by chance. No sooner did he feel firm ground under his feet than he looked about for his horse. But the animal, having no notion of standing on the edge of a mire, had sought some more secure spot, and was nowhere to be found. Then the monk looked once more for the light, and rejoiced to see that he was now very near to it. Again he went towards it, but to his mortification it retreated, and try as he might, he could never overtake it. He was puzzled to understand who could be out on the Moor on such a night, and at length he began to imagine that some magical influence was at work.

"I will follow it no longer," he cried; "the Evil One is seeking to lead me astray."

But it was not the Evil One; it was only Will-o'-the-Wisp.

Another hour passed away, during which the monk had tramped some distance over the Moor, until he was nearly ready to drop from exhauston. Suddenly he ran against a rock, bruising his shins and biting his tongue. The pain was so great that he was unable to refrain from uttering an exclamation of a kind not usually allowed by holy men to fall from their lips.

"I trust that has relieved you; it is good to give free expression to one's feelings sometimes."

The monk started, for the voice sounded close to his elbow.

"Who is there?" he asked.

"One who like yourself seeks shelter from the storm. Come nearer; you will find this rock a capital protection from the rain."

"Where are we?" asked the monk.

"On Dartmoor," was the reply.

"I am painfully aware of the fact," returned the monk. "But in what particular part of it may we be?"

"We are at Great Combe Tor," answered the stranger, stepping forward.

"I am as wise as ever," said the monk, looking narrowly at him.

It was very dark, and the stranger's form and features were scarcely to be distinguished, but the monk managed to see that he wore a curled moustache and a peaked beard, and also that on his head was a peculiarly shaped cap with a tall feather.

"Yes," continued the stranger, "we are at Great Combe Tor, and down in the valley yonder is the village of Tavy St. Peter. I'll warrant now that while you are here drenched to the skin, filled with water as it were, there are many in the alehouse there full of a much more potent liquor."

"Miserable sinners," ejaculated the monk.

"Nay, pardon me; sinners they are, I grant you; indeed I have reason to be sure of it, but they are not miserable. You do not drink strong waters?"

"Heaven forbid!" cried the monk.

"I regret to hear it, because in your present wet condition I feel sure such would do you good, and I was about to offer you some."

"That is, I do not habitually drink them, but on an occasion like the present ——"

"Exactly," interrupted the stranger, producing a flask and handing it to him, "Drink; you will find it good, I assure you."

The monk took a long draught, and smacked his lips as he gave back the flask. The liquor was a little fiery, he thought, but certainly seemed to be of excellent quality.

Then the stranger took from his wallet a venison pasty, and begged his companion to help himself to some of it, saying that he knew he must be famished after wandering so long upon the Moor. Finding a sheltered place among the rocks they made themselves as comfortable as the circumstances would allow.

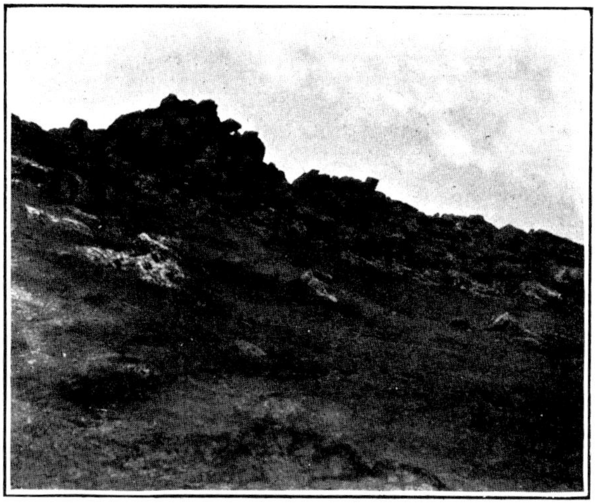

Photo by] [C. R. Rowe.

Great Combe Tor.

"'Where are we?' asked the monk. . . .
'We are at Great Combe Tor,' answered the stranger."—*(See Page 172.)*

"You are a jolly good fellish," said the monk, drinking from the flask (which appeared to contain an inexhaustible supply of liquor) for the twentieth time; "shake handsh. Wheresh do you live?"

"I usually roam about," replied the stranger, evasively.

"I see, a travellersh. But wheresh can I come and see you."

"Oh, you shall come and see me by-and-bye. Lots of people do."

"That's because you're such a good fellish. I shall look—look forward to meeting you."

"You shall have a warm welcome, I give you my word," said the stranger.

"I'm sure of thatsh. But look heresh: I want to go to Tavishtock—to the Abbey. Can't shtay here all nightsh."

"Then follow me," said the stranger, rising. "I know the way about pretty well."

How the monk got across the common he never knew, but presently he found himself by the side of the road in which his horse was quietly standing. The stranger helped him into the saddle.

"Farewell," he said, "and remember we shall meet again."

"Good nightsh. Which waysh Tavishtock?"

"Your horse's head is pointing towards it," answered the stranger.

"That'sh well. But, I forgot, you haven't told me your namesh."

"Nicholas, at your service."

"Not Old Nicholas, I suppose," said the monk, laughing.

"Yes, indeed," replied the stranger; "Old Nicholas."

"The devil!" cried the monk.

"You have hit it exactly," said the stranger, with a bow.

The good brother of Plympton Priory urged his horse forward, but the animal, suddenly turning, galloped off with him in the opposite direction, and never slackened his speed until he reached the gate of Tavistock Abbey.

"Wheresh should we have got to," asked the monk, patting his horse's neck, "had we gone the waysh the devil wanted us to go?"

It was nearly midnight when he crept into bed, and so fatigued was he with his night's adventure that he was soon fast asleep. In the morning his fellow traveller whom he had lost sight of after leaving Sampford Spiney, was brought into the Abbey in an almost dying condition, having lain upon the open Moor all night.

"Ah," said the monk, as he looked upon him, "he has had a sorry time. Better by far to receive help from the devil than to spend a stormy winter night on Dartmoor."

Retracing our steps we descend the path to the little footbridge, and crossing it shall make our way up the combe by the right bank of the stream, which comes tumbling down in a succession of miniature cascades. It is not long our companion, however, for on approaching some enclosures we shall leave it, and mount the stone-strewn slope to the left to Little Combe Tor. This presents nothing remarkable, being merely a small cluster of rocks, none of which rise very high above the ground, but the view of the combe obtained from it is good, and renders it worthy of a visit. In the pleasing scene beheld from it the imagination may delight to picture a former haunt of the water nymphs, and by giving it further rein, and clothing the banks of the little stream with trees, a trysting-place of the Forest fairies. Here are crystal pools in which the nymphs might well have disported themselves, singing the while in chorus with the cascades. We do not hear their tuneful voices now, but the brook is not silent. Nor does it sing alone; for though the naiads are gone, the happy birds that have made their home in this charming valley pour forth their melodies in unison with it. Whether it be the song of the nymphs they sing we cannot tell; but we feel that it is one not less sweet.

Bidding adieu to the attractive spot that has given rise to these reflections, we bend our steps towards the bottom of the combe, where we shall observe a steep path running up its side in a northerly direction. This will lead us to Smearn Down, on reaching which we shall turn to the right and follow the road that runs over this part of it to a point where a moorland track branches off and climbs the hill on the left. The latter will bring us quite near to Boulter's Tor, a pile of rocks at the eastern end of the down, and opposite to an opening between some newtakes. Through this opening, which is known as Twyste Lane, the track runs out to the commons, and may be followed to Walkham Head. It is still a good path, and in the days when peat was the only fuel used in the border villages the traffic over it during the summer and autumn was by no means inconsiderable. Large quantities were cut round the springs of the Walkham, as the many deserted ties* to be seen in that locality amply testify. Some is still obtained there, its use in the more remote border farms being not altogether discontinued.

On the common beside the track, and about half a mile from the eastern end of Twyste Lane is a grass-covered mound marking the burial place of a suicide, and known as Stevens' Grave. There is a story in connection with it to the effect that the unfortunate young man whose remains were laid there poisoned himself in consequence of the infidelity of the girl whom he had hoped to marry. In accordance with the barbarous custom of the time Stevens was buried without any funeral rites, and a stake was driven

* The pits where the peat is cut are termed *ties*, and each farmer, or cutter, has his own.

through his body. The date of the circumstance is not given, but it is known that the mound was to be seen on the common a century ago. After a while it was said that the spot was haunted, and nobody would pass near it after nightfall. Stories became current that the ghost of the suicide had been seen sitting on the mound by more than one whom darkness had overtaken on the Moor; and it was also stated that it had visited places in the neighbourhood. The inhabitants of Peter Tavy were so disturbed that they decided to seek the aid of the parson. The offices of the good man fortunately proved effectual, and the ghost was laid, a terrific storm, it is said, raging the while. The story is related by Mrs. Bray in her *Tamar and Tavy*, and some years ago I also gathered a version of it in the neighbourhood.

Further out on the common, and to the right of the peat track, is the cradle of the little brook which we saw leaping so merrily over the rocks in the combe below. For the first mile it flows in a south-easterly direction, and then turns toward the west. It rises in a marshy part of Langstone Moor, about midway between White Tor, or Whit Tor, as it is more often called, and the Walkham, and while yet a tiny rivulet runs by the enclosure of a farm called Wedlake, which, if the stream was once known as White Lake, as old people used to declare, must have obtained its name from it. That its true appellation is as was said I have no doubt; the name of the tor so near its source is confirmatory of this. It is, however, not a little curious that this tor and the stream should each have possessed two names, and these similar, though the order in which they were borne was different. Early in the nineteenth century the tor was known as Peterstone Rock, or Peter Tor, and the stream as White Lake; now we call the stream the Peter Tavy Brook, and the rock-pile we name White Tor.

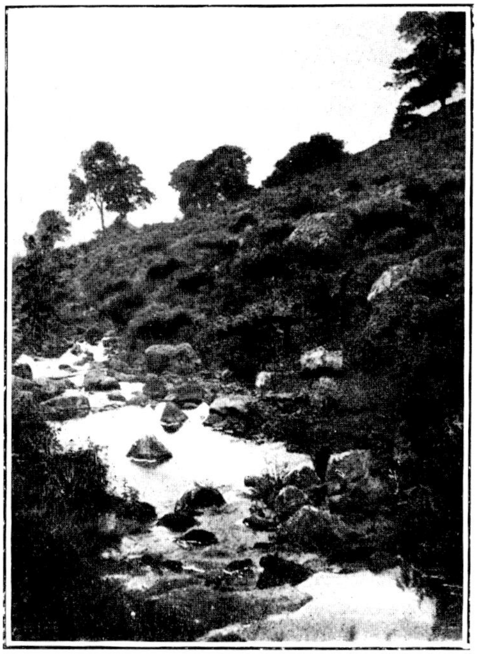

Photo by] [C. R. Rowe.

Near the Head of the Combe.

"A former haunt of the water nymphs."—*(See Page 174.)*

But the tor and the brook are not the only objects in this locality the names of which have been corrupted. The common on which the latter takes its rise is invariably referred to as Launceston Moor, and so appears on maps. But it is now considered that this should be Langstone Moor, the common, it is thought, deriving its name from the fine menhir, or long stone, under White Tor. We can hardly doubt that this is so. When the menhir was prostrate (it has been re-erected only within the past few years) the name would cease to have a meaning for the country people, and approximating in sound to that of the well-known Cornish town, would come to be regarded as being identical with it. The menhir stands by the side of the path that runs out to Walkham Head.

Having lingered thus long at Boulter's Tor in the contemplation of the various objects on the commons that neighbour the combe that has attracted us hither, we shall turn our faces westward, and make our way along the ridge of the hill. A range of crags extends throughout its whole length, and near the highest of these we shall observe a small ancient enclosure, with faint vestiges of banks near it. But what will probably prove more attractive than an examination of the few antiquities to be found on this hill is the truly magnificent view commanded from it. The beholder looks down upon a vast sweep of cultivated country, with the Cornish hills rising beyond, while in the foreground is the valley of the Tavy, which can be distinctly traced from Tavistock to the commons above Wapsworthy.

In the wide hollow below the northern side of the down is the little settlement of Cudlipp Town, which still presents some of its primitive features. In Domesday it is called Culitone, but in 1506 the name more nearly approximates to its present one, appearing in a Forester's account as Chodlype. But we fear the clerkship of some of the writers of an earlier day was not always what could be wished. A delightful freedom was exercised in the spelling of names. In the same account we find that of the parish over a part of which our ramble has extended set down as Peturspavy. Both this and Cudlipp Town are ancient vills, the venville rent received from each at the date named being 5d.

The valley of the Tavy near Cudlipp Town is exceedingly fine. From Hill Bridge, in the vicinity of Wapsworthy, to Longtimber Tor, below Mary Tavy Clam, a distance of about two miles, the right bank of the river, which is in the parish of Mary Tavy, is for the most part wooded, and from the midst of the trees several rock masses arise. The scenery is altogether of a romantic description, and takes high rank among that which the Moorland borders can show. The river valley being partly in Peter Tavy that parish is particularly happy in possessing two of Dartmoor's gems, for the beautiful stream is not less deserving of being included among them than is the combe.

Descending from the crags on Smearn Down we reach the Moor gate, whence a walk of a few minutes will bring us to Peter Tavy village.

GGS-L

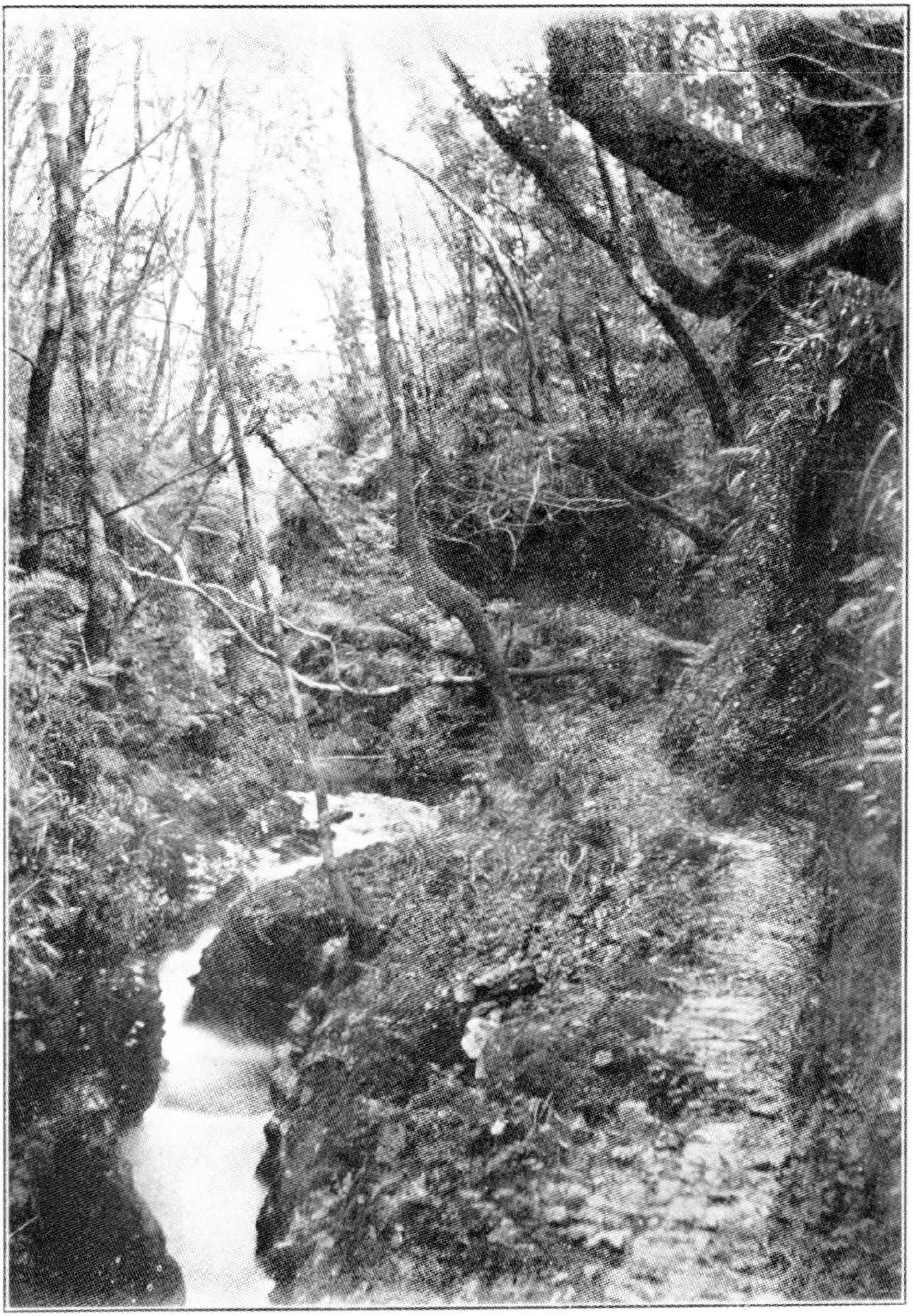

SEE PAGE 182

Above the Bridge in Lydford Gorge.

PHOTO BY C. R. ROWE

"The path by the river."

XXIII.

LYDFORD GORGE.

A Pellucid Stream——Lydford Castle and Church——Border Valleys——Hanging Woods and Distant Moor——Lydford Waterfall——The Gubbins——A Yawning Fissure——Lydford Bridge——A Terrible Leap——Story of the White Horse.

The stream
That worked its way through the green night to day.
—Rev. John Johns.

Down o'er a rock of towering height,
And black and frowning hue,
A foaming sheet of dazzling light
Its liquid radiance threw.
—Rachel Evans.

THERE is no clearer stream on Dartmoor than that which gives name to the parish in which lies so much of the great waste. This is the Lyd, the springs of which are situated below the southern slope of Corn Ridge, on the common lands of Bridestowe and Sourton, at an elevation of over sixteen hundred feet. While yet but a rivulet it is crossed by a track leading from the borders of the Moor to the valley of the Rattle Brook, whence farmers fetched their peat, for they found none by the banks of the Lyd. Never stained by amber streamlets oozing from black bogs, its water is bright and pure. Its cascades gleam like heaps of snow, and its crystal pools reveal the pebbles in its bed. Its silvery flood laves the foot of grassy hills, and sweeps by fern-covered steeps. Unseen by the grim old Forest, it runs cheerily by border heights that show some reflection of the country beyond them, and descends to the lower valleys. It reaches the plantation and the farm, and leaving the Moor, leaps towards the village with the ruined castle that fills so large a place in Dartmoor story. And then the Lyd hides itself in a deep gorge where the sun is no more its companion, but only the gloom of the narrow chasm, or of the hanging woods where the trees interweave their branches above its channel.

A humorous description of Lydford village, its surroundings, and its people, is given by Browne in his poem, *The Lydford Journey*, written in the earlier part of the seventeenth century. His remarks on Lydford Law, and his account of the castle, show that the one was then in no better repute, and the other hardly less "annoyous, contagious and detestable," than when Richard Strode, who represented Plympton in Parliament, was confined there in the time of Henry VIII. The existing remains of the building, in which transgressors of the Forest laws and Stannary prisoners were confined, consist principally of the walls of a square keep. With the decline of the power of the tinners the Castle of Dartmoor also began to decay. For some time the Duchy courts continued to be held there, but when these were removed to Princetown it became entirely neglected, and was allowed to fall into its present ruined state.*

Near the castle is the church of St. Petrock, which is interesting as being the mother

* *A Hundred Years on Dartmoor*, Chap. I.

church of the extensive parish in which the Forest is situated. But though the area of the parish is large it is needless to say the population is not so, and was considerably less before the existence of Princetown, consequently only a small church was needed. Moreover the inhabitants of the eastern part of the Forest were accustomed to attend the church of Widecombe.* It is chiefly of fifteenth century date, and consists of nave and chancel, south aisle, south porch, and tower.

Few places on the borderland of Dartmoor are better known than Lydford Gorge, which yields a rich reward to the seeker after the romantic and the beautiful. And it is unique; for while within the Moorland district there are many deep, wooded valleys, through which fretting streams force their way, there is none possessing features such as accompany this. It is only in the gorge of the Lyd that such a yawning fissure as that at its head can be seen, or a waterfall of such a height as the one formed by the Black Down stream. Lydford Gorge extends from a point near the village downward for a mile or more, when it widens somewhat, but the valley retains its features of precipitous, tree-clothed sides for a much greater distance. The gorge is easily accessible, being within half a mile of the Lydford railway station. The entrance to it at this end is at the Manor Hotel, within the grounds of which a great part of it is situated. At its upper end, and close to the bridge near the village, is another entrance.

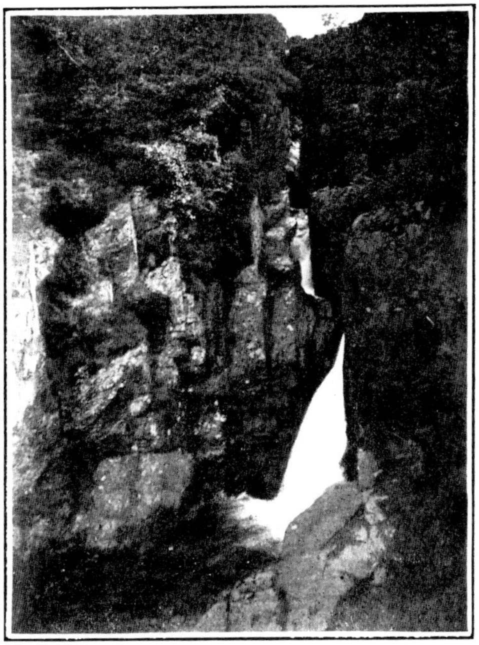

Photo by] [C. R. Rowe.

Skit Steps.

"The Lyd . . . leaps towards the village with the ruined castle."—*(See Page 179.)*

From the gardens of the hotel a narrow roadway leads to the bottom of the valley. Just where this commences to descend a green path runs from it on the left, and terminates in a small plateau. To this the visitor should on no account fail to make his way, for not only is by far the best view of the gorge obtained from it, but also one which it would not be easy to surpass in the Westcountry. Bushes grow by the green path, and nothing is seen until the little plateau is reached. Then the wide prospect bursts at once upon the sight, and the visitor looks on a picture of hill and valley, of woods and distant Moor. At his feet is the deep ravine, whence comes no sound from the Lyd, nor can it be seen, for the gorge is filled with trees. Opposite, the hill rises almost perpendicularly from the hidden brink of the stream, that here, where the valley bends, sweeps round its base. In the bosom of the woods are dark shadows, which the rays of the sun strive in vain to pierce, while uplifted on some jutting point a graceful ash here and there spreads her branches, her tremulous leaves brilliant in light. Where the eye can trace the valley no further the tower of Lydford Church is seen, and close beside it the keep of the old castle. Beyond these is the Moor, high up on which the spot where the Lyd rises can be distinguished. It is in the dip to the right of the eminence rising above a hill of a beehive

* *A Hundred Years on Dartmoor*, Chaps. II., IV.

shape; the former is Corn Ridge, the rounded hill being Great Noddon. Near this, and towering above all the others, is Great Links Tor; over the hill to the right is Hare Tor, and a small portion of Black Down. The effect of the colourings of the Moor seen beyond the mass of green in the depths of the ravine is particularly striking from this point at certain seasons, and when the atmospheric conditions are favourable. In the other direction we have a view of the valley below the gorge which is very impressive.

The descent to the bottom of the valley is not usually made by the narrow road, but by a zigzag path diverging from it on the right, which will bring the visitor directly to the cascade. The stream, which has its source near the Okehampton and Tavistock road on Black Down, here falls from a considerable height, which is given as a hundred and ten feet. It does not leap boldly out in 'the manner of most waterfalls, but slides down the precipitous face of a rock into a little pool, and immediately joins the Lyd. There is consequently no deafening roar, as when a stream falls sheer into the basin below, and is pent between walls of rock. The water glides almost silently down, broken in its course by a ledge, and produces an altogether singular and charming effect. In the wealth of foliage we see an emerald, in the cascade a pearl, set in the rocky crown of Devon, and adding to it far more beauty than any gem from the mines of Peru, or the ocean's depths, ever lent to a golden symbol of royalty.

Not far below the waterfall is a cave, but whether natural or artificial is not quite certain. If the latter it is probably a relic of old mining operations, but there is nothing near it to indicate that such were ever conducted here, nor can the marks of tools be found in the cavern itself. In Browne's poem mention is made of the cave of the Gubbins', a lawless band that once infested this part of Devon, as being near to Lydford. Fuller about the same time speaks of them as living in "Cotts (rather Holes than Houses)," and says that the "Gubbings-Land" was somewhere near Brent Tor. There is little doubt that the woods in the valley of the Lyd formed their retreat, and we may not unreasonably suppose that this cave by the waterfall, and another nearer the upper part of the gorge, were among the places in which they sought shelter and concealment. Fuller says they "multiplied, without marriage, into many hundreds," which, if it were so, must have necessitated a number of habitations.

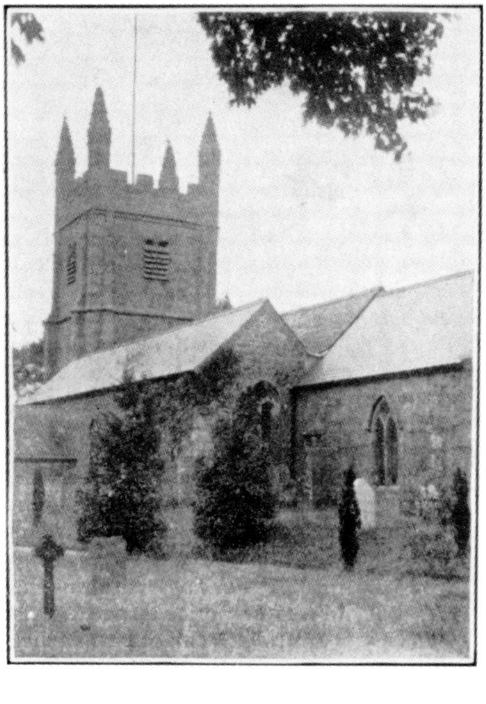

Photo by] [C. R. Rowe.

Lydford Church.

"The mother church of the extensive parish in which the Forest is situated."—(*See Pages 179-180.*)

The pool at the bottom of the waterfall is crossed by a rustic wooden bridge, which adds not a little to the picturesqueness of the scene, and from this a narrow path, carried along the margin of the stream, runs for some distance up the valley. On the opposite side is another path, reached by a bridge thrown over the Lyd below the pool, and leading the visitor through the most romantic parts of the gorge. In places the narrow way closely neighbours the river; in others it climbs some steep ascent, and the foaming waters are seen only between the branches of the trees that cover the declivity. Midway up the ravine the crags of Raven Tor thrust themselves above the leafy covering, their hoary faces turned towards the rising sun. Grey rocks and foliage, and the gleam of cascades, here mingle harmoniously: a sight pleasant to the eye. For sounds to delight the ear, the voice of the Lyd, and the soft rustling of leaves.

But the woods on this side of the river, as also those on the left bank at the upper end of the gorge, where is another footbridge, are not within the grounds of the hotel, and it is therefore not always that the public have access to them. It is at this higher part that the Lyd issues from that deep and dark fissure so unlike anything seen on the other rivers of the Moor. Into this the sunshine never penetrates, and in the gloom the happy little stream loses her smile for a time. By means of a path carried along the side of the chasm, and protected where necessary by a handrail, the visitor may make his way through it. On each side rise walls of rock; overhead the trees hide the sky, while below the stream is seen forcing its way through the narrow cleft. The lower parts of the dark precipices, wetted with spray, are smooth and shining, while higher up their sides ferns and other plants find a holding on narrow ledges. A single arch, said to be seventy feet above the bed of the stream, spans this fissure, and over this passes the road to Lydford village. Above the bridge the path by the river leads towards the waterfall bearing the name of Skit Steps, near to which are more than one deep chasm where the Lyd is almost lost to view.

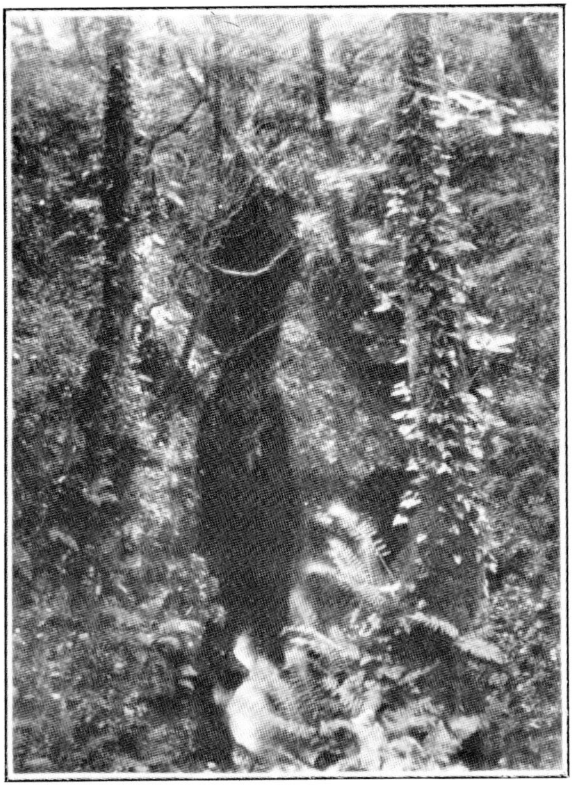

Photo by] [C. R. Rowe.

Chasm above Lydford Bridge.

"Where the Lyd is almost lost to view."

If there be any truth in the story hereafter noticed the existing Lydford Bridge replaced an earlier one, but it would be unsafe to accept as fact what may have no better foundation than tradition. Browne speaks of a bridge at Lydford in his poem, the date of which is 1644 (though some are inclined to think it was written before that time), and there is also mention of one here in 1478.

This romantic spot has been the scene of more than one tragedy. It used to be related how a young man of Exeter, some century ago, having lost his all at the gambling tables, here destroyed himself. He rode one dark and stormy night to the bridge, and endeavoured, it was supposed, to leap his steed over the parapet, which the country people said bore marks in many places of the animal's hoofs. Not succeeding in this, he dismounted and taking off the saddle and bridle, flung them over the bridge, and leapt after them into the abyss. But the measures probably taken to conceal the deed proved the means by which it was discovered, for the saddle and bridle became entangled in the branches of the trees, and this led to the body being found. It is also said that a maniac once destroyed himself here. Eluding his keepers, he ran yelling to the bridge, and before he could be overtaken plunged into the dark waters. In our own time, too, there have unfortunately been instances of individuals losing their lives in the chasm.

According to local story an adventure once befell a traveller at this spot, and was commemorated in an earlier name of the village hostelry. This is now known as the Castle Inn, but it was formerly called the White Horse, the change having been made by a relative of a recent occupier, who, perhaps overlooking the circumstance related in connection with it, or feeling no interest in such associations, saw no reason why he should retain the old name of the house, and consequently gave it one which he deemed, from its proximity to the ruined keep, to be more appropriate. The story goes that one dark night a traveller, mounted on a white horse, stopped at the door of the inn, and gave his steed in charge of the ostler. He noticed that the man, who was standing at the door as he approached, looked at him in a very strange manner, but he thought little of it at the time. After the horse had been attended to, the ostler entered the room where the traveller was sitting with the landlord and several others, and the former again saw that he was being narrowly observed.

"Which way might 'e a com', sir, makin' so bold?" asked the ostler, after a few minutes.

"Which way did I come?" said the traveller. "Why, by the Brent Tor road. What makes you ask?"

"Well, I seed 'e com' from the church way, sir," the ostler replied, "and that's what I couldn' make out."

"But the Brent Tor road lies by the church," remarked the traveller.

"I knaw he do, sir; but no man ant a travelled from Brin Tar by thackey road to-night, I knaw. He couldn' a din it, cos there bant no bridge."

"No bridge!" exclaimed the stranger. "What do you mean?"

And then it was explained that Lydford Bridge had fallen, and that communication in the direction of Brent Tor was cut off. A feeling of horror crept over the traveller at the recollection of the danger he had passed through, mingled with one of thankfulness for his preservation. Just before reaching the village he had noticed that his horse gave a sudden bound, and now he knew that the animal had leapt that yawning gulf in the darkness of the night.

XXIV.

TAVY CLEAVE.

A Wild Defile——Cleft or Cliff?——View from Ger Tor——A Group of Tors——Entrance to the Cleave——The Spectre Horseman——Rugged Rock Masses——A Narrow Pass——Watern Oke——Memories of the Moor.

What hills are those, deserted, brown and bare,
Whose mouldering crags the spoils of Time declare?
Dartmoor! thy stately presence I perceive,
Seen first at morn, and lingering last with eve;
Thy rugged pinnacles, unfolded clear,
Rising in solemn grandeur, wild and drear.
—Joseph Cottle.

At the foot of Watern Oke, a hill in the north quarter of the Forest,* the Tavy receives a tributary called the Rattle Brook, and then turning southward enters a defile so narrow that for some little distance there is room only for its waters. About three-quarters of a mile down, below a group of tors, the sides fall back, and further on the valley opens out, having the slope of Standon Hill on one side, and Nat Tor Down on the other. This defile is known as Tavy Cleave, and for wild grandeur is unsurpassed throughout the Moorland region.

The cleave may be conveniently reached from either Lydford or Mary Tavy. From the former the way is by Skit Steps to the road near Beardon, and thence by Down Lane to the commons; a track also leads from Lydford station almost directly to it, crossing the high road on Black Down, and skirting the enclosures of Redford. From Mary Tavy village a road, passing through Horndon and Zoar, runs to the Moor Gate at Lane End, from which the lower end of the cleave is only a little over half a mile distant. Those to whom a rough path and the steep banks of a stream thickly strewn with masses of granite present no obstacles will best see this romantic pass by making their way through it from Nat Tor to its head. But they ought also to ascend the tors that overhang its western side, for from them the picture of the deep and narrow valley is most impressive.

Whether we are to regard the name now borne by this valley as a corruption of *cleft*, or whether it was at first attached only to the tors on its side, and is really the word *cliff* in the Dartmoor vernacular, it is, of course, impossible to say. In the other instances where the name occurs on and around Dartmoor, the tor which may be supposed to represent the cliff is much less imposing than the valley, but in the present case the rock masses are more than ordinarily striking, and dispute the palm for grandeur with the defile above which they rise. They are placed on the brow of a declivity so steep as to form what is practically a cliff, but such a term cannot be appropriately applied to the piles of rock in the other cleaves of Dartmoor. There is therefore some ground for

* In maps drawn from the Survey of the Moor made at the beginning of the nineteenth century, Watern Oke is wrongly placed. A hill on the south side of the Tavy called Outer Standon is shown as Watern Oke. But the latter is on the north side of the Tavy, and is bounded by that river, the Rattle Brook, and a line drawn from this tributary to the Amicombe.

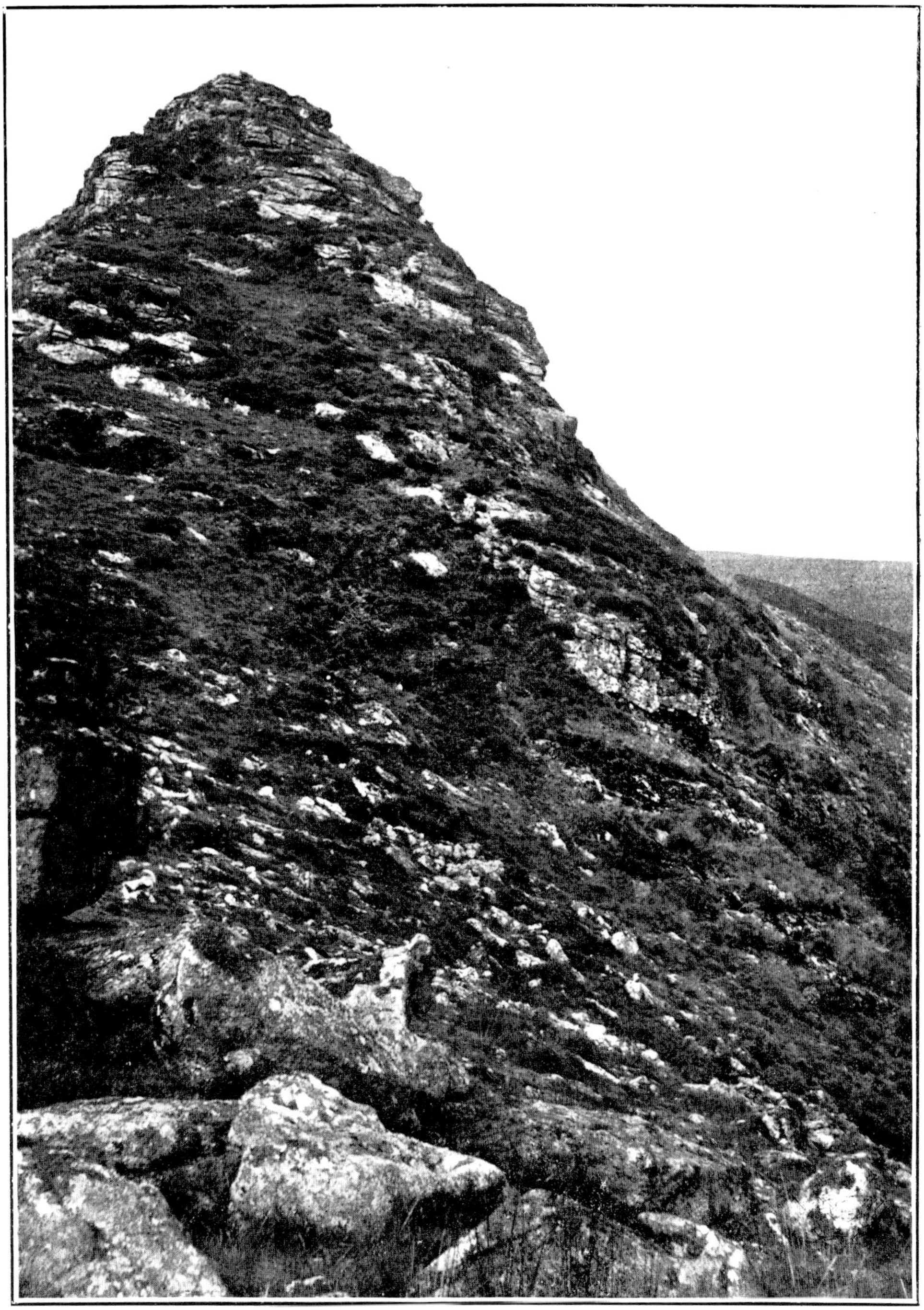

SEE PAGE 187.

Ger Tor on the Tavy.

PHOTO BY C. R. ROWE.

"The hoary crest of Nat Tor Down."

known as the Tavy Cleave Tors, only one of them bearing a distinctive title. This, the principal mass, the Moormen often call Sharp Tor, and distinguish it from another of the same name on the adjoining common by referring to the latter as Lydford Sharp. From these tors, the situation of which is such as is occupied by no others on the Moor, the best view of the cleave is obtained, much of it not seen from Ger Tor being revealed. The beholder looks into the depths of the defile as from a precipice, and so far below is the Tavy that in appearance it can be likened only to a rivulet. We have stood by these piles when the whortleberry gatherers were busy near the brink of the river; they looked like pigmies, and, but for their movements, could hardly be distinguished among the granite and the heather. Towards the west the eye roams over the far off cultivated country, but besides this little but the wild valley is in sight, for the solitary tracts of heath that roll away into the desolate recesses of the Moor are hidden by the nearer hills. Only one glimpse of the wilderness beyond is obtained. This is where the sides of the cleave at its upper end fall back, and Watern Oke is seen sloping rapidly to the meeting place of the Tavy and the Rattle Brook. Further away Great Kneeset uplifts itself from the unseen fen that covers so much of the northern part of the ancient Forest. But here at all events the book is open, and the wanderer may if he chooses turn over its leaves and read it to the end. Then he will learn of that which now lies beyond his ken, and in mastering the lesson, shall, like others have done before him, come to love the old land that hides in its broad bosom so many beauties.

Purple banks soft kissed by singing rivers,
  Moss-grown boulders 'mid the cascades' gleam,
Upland glens where bracken bends and quivers
  When the breezes brush the silvery stream.

Ancient rocks, like warriors old and hoary,
  Scarred their sides bespread with lichens grey,
In silence stand, and yet reveal their story,
  Tell of battles of a far-off day.

How the white-mantled Frost King, slowly working,
  Struck where stronger powers had hardly dared,
And his forces, in the crevice lurking,
  Spread in ruin what the earthquake spared.

Heathy hillsides seamed with deep crevasses
  That outspreading like a network lie;
Labyrinths through which the torrent passes
  When the tempest runs across the sky.

Stones that mark where ancient man is sleeping,
  Near the pile that dark and frowning towers,
Stand like sentinels their vigils keeping,
  Through the silence of the desert hours.

Land of Freedom! Land of antique story!
  Land where Nature long has held her place!
In her sterner aspect is her glory,
  Here she wears her old, primeval face.

Here her story on rude rocks is graven,
  Voices rise from out a distant day;
Here, where peace and calmness find a haven,
  On lone Dartmoor let my footsteps stray.

Having looked upon the cleave from the tors, let us now descend and make our way from Nat Tor to its head. For this purpose we shall once more turn our steps towards

Ger Tor, which, however, we shall leave a little to the left, and passing down the hill in a direction nearly due south, shall soon reach the object that is to be our starting-point. From Lane End—the appropriateness of which name will be recognised when it is explained that the road terminates here—Nat Tor is reached by following a track leading to a farm, with the enclosures on the right. Shortly before reaching this farm the visitor will strike across the common to the left, when the tor will be seen. It is small and does not rise very high above the turf, but it possesses something of interest nevertheless. On one side of it there is a small ruined enclosure, probably one of those erected in the days when the priours, or Moormen, were wont to gather their cattle at certain of the tors. The wall is in a state of dilapidation, but it can be plainly traced, and the posts forming the gateway yet remain. Not far below the Tavy bids adieu to the long and deep cleave, soon to look for the first time upon enclosed lands, and to meet with those signs of civilisation to which it has hitherto been a stranger. About half a mile down the ancient Lich Path crosses the river at Willsworthy Ford, and here, according to the story, a spectre horseman may be seen whenever the moon lights up a stormy sky, and the usually bright stream comes down from the hills a raging torrent. It is said that long ago a lady was wont to come to meet her lover secretly at the ford. Who she was is not recorded: we only know that she was young and beautiful, wore rich apparel, rode a splendid white horse, and dwelt in the neighbourhood of Lydford. We also know little about the lover, further than that he, too, was young, and also very handsome, dressed in a fashionable style, rode a magnificent black steed, and made his home in the Forest of Dartmoor. The story intimates that they met clandestinely because of the lady's father, who was so unreasonable as to wish to choose a husband for his daughter, instead of allowing her to do so herself. This is rather puzzling, because in such cases we almost invariably find that the suitor to whom the lady has given her heart is poor, whereas in the present instance the presumption is that he was wealthy. Had it been otherwise he could hardly have possessed a valuable steed, or have been able to dress in the most fashionable style, as the story says he did. How he contrived to learn the latest mode in the Forest of Dartmoor it is difficult to understand, but, as a native of the Moor once said to me, "there's no knawin' what vokes doo'd yeers agone," and so we will content ourselves with what the story relates concerning him.

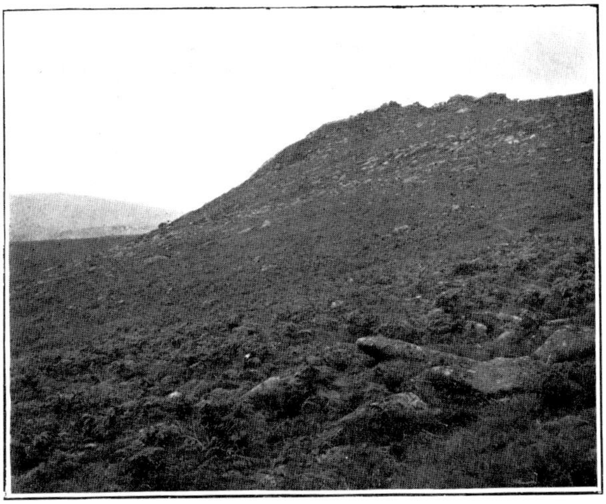

Photo by] [C. R. Rowe.

Ger Tor from the East.

"We shall once more turn our steps towards Ger Tor."—*(See Page 188.)*

The youthful lover was always the first to arrive at the ford, and there he would await the coming of the beautiful girl who had ensnared his heart, never crossing the stream until he saw her descending the rugged path that led to the bank. It was agreed that their meetings should take place towards the close of the day, and never did the lady fail to appear before the western hills hid the sun. But one evening her lover saw the rosy luminary go down behind a great bank of storm clouds, tinging the edges of the inky masses with a fierce red, and still she came not. An hour passed by, and darkness began to usher in the autumn night, but yet the youth lingered by the stream. Suddenly the moaning of the wind ceased, and the signs that had portended the coming tempest were verified. Then out of the silence, broken only by the sighs of the river that rose from the rocky cleave up the valley, came the loud crash of thunder, and presently the laden clouds poured their watery burden upon the darkened earth. Awhile the storm lasted, and then a calm fell upon all around, and a deep hush again rested over the Moor upon which the moon looked down through the swiftly fleeting vapours that partially veiled her. Soon another sound struck upon the ear of the youth who, no shelter being near, had been constrained to brave the fury of the elements. It grew louder, and by-and-bye the stream at his feet became agitated, and rose so rapidly that it speedily covered the stepping-stones near the ford. Then with a mighty rush a wall of water appeared, and in a few moments the Tavy's banks were swept by an angry flood.

The young lover succeeded in reaching a place of safety, but he had hardly done so when the dim light of the moon showed him the form of her he had come to meet. She was galloping down the old Lich Path towards the ford, but reined in her horse as she neared the bank and saw the swollen river before her. On its verge she stopped, and looked about as though to find a place where she might cross. Her lover tried to warn her of her danger, but his voice was drowned in the roar of the stream. Then two horsemen appeared, furiously riding down the ancient way by which she had come. No sooner did she perceive them than she urged her steed forward, and the white horse plunged fearlessly into the turbulent waters. But he was powerless against their mad onrush, and was rapidly carried away by the current, while his fair rider was swept from the saddle. For an instant her lover saw her pale face and one uplifted arm, and their eyes met. Then she went down beneath the surging flood, and the father who would have forced her to wed with one she could not love, and the man who would have taken her while aware that her heart was another's, knew that they had driven her to her death.

The white horse gained the bank at a point lower down the stream, and on that side of it which his mistress had hoped to reach. While yet the misty moon shed a dim light upon the Moor, a rider passed over the Lich Path, his face set towards the Forest. The steed he rode moved across the heath like a dark shadow; one which he led resembled, in that faint light, a pale ghost.

Years passed by, when one night a traveller reaching Willsworthy Ford, saw by the light of the moon that the Tavy was in flood, and not to be crossed. As he was turning away towards the bridge down the stream, he was terror stricken at seeing the shadowy figure of a young man mounted on a black horse and leading a white one, suddenly appear on the bank. The steeds moved silently along the margin of the flood, the man, who wore a richly laced coat beneath a heavy riding cloak, seeming to peer into it as though in search of something. When the traveller related his story he was not believed, but by-and-bye the spectre horseman was again seen, and more than once, but only when the moon looked down upon the Tavy and saw an angry river. Then those in the neighbourhood knew that the spirit of the youthful lover haunted the spot where the beautiful girl whose heart he had won had perished.

Leaving Nat Tor we shall make our way up the valley by a rough path on the bank of a mine leat that is here carried along the side of the hill. This will lead us through the stone encumbered ground at the foot of the rugged steep below Ger Tor, where we shall be able to more fully realise the nature of the clatter than was possible from the pile itself, while the latter is also seen from this point to the greatest advantage. Viewed from the common on its western side Ger Tor loses much of its effect, the scarp being hidden it appears as though the down surrounded it, but from the valley where its true character is revealed it presents a remarkably fine appearance.

A wall may be noticed running up the hill by the side of the clatter. It does not, however, go beyond the tor, but the intention was to carry it across the common, and thus enclose the whole of Nat Tor Down. It marks a frustrated attempt at "land-grabbing," which was often not so much the work of the farmer, or the squatter, as that of the owners of manors situated on the borders of the Moor.

From this point onward the Tavy will claim a considerable share of the rambler's attention. Many fine pools and small cascades will be passed as he proceeds. In one place a ledge of rock runs across the stream, having a narrow cleft near the centre, and through this the river falls in a sheet of foam. So smooth and square are the sides of this opening that at a first glance it has almost the appearance of having been formed by artificial means. Some of the pools, which are much larger than are usually seen on the Dartmoor streams, are very deep; in other places the river is shallow, running over a pebbly bed, or one of solid rock.*

At the foot of the clatter under Ger Tor the rocky ridge that sweeps down from the Tavy Cleave Tors to the river comes into view, but we shall not see it to the best advantage unless the sky be overcast. On a summer day, when the deep valley is steeped in light, the boulders that stream from the tors appear as one great grey mass; it is when the sun hides his face from the Moor, and the hills are wrapped in gloom, that these fields of granite blocks, hurled down from their lofty stations by the mighty forces that are ever at work, impress the beholder most powerfully. When we draw near and look up at the fallen rocks, lying in confused piles, we read the story revealed by all the clatters of the Moor. It is the story of ruin, of decay.

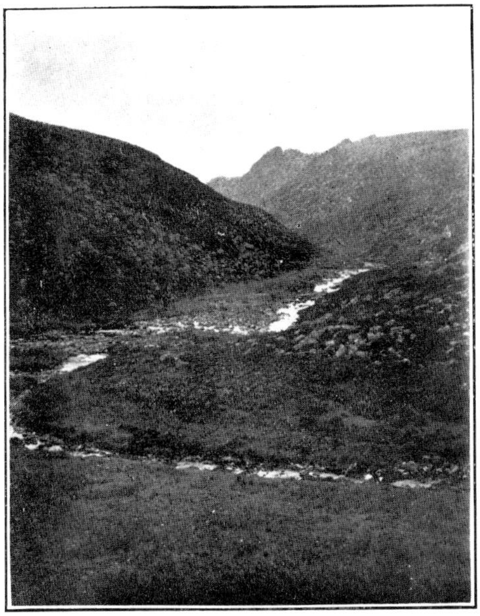

Photo by] [C. R. Rowe.

The Tavy and the Rattle Brook, looking down from Watern Oke.

"The head of the cleave is reached."—*(See Page 192.)*

We pass the river-laved foot of the ridge, and the grandest part of the ravine unfolds itself. The crags lift their fantastic forms high above the pass, one side of which is here so steep that it could only be climbed with difficulty. The defile, though narrow, yet affords ample room for a pathway on the brink of the river, where is a fine piece of turf, though the lines of wrack plainly show that when the Tavy, swollen with rain, comes sweeping down from the remote fastnesses of the Forest, it is submerged. Then it is, and when mist-wreaths partially shroud the pinnacles that lift themselves above the flood, that the cleave is seen at its grandest. What we have remarked of the clatters is true of the whole valley. The blue sky and the sunshine do not so well accord with its sternness as the leaden cloud, nor does the laughing stream find there a suitable home.

The tors on the steep are passed; let us pause and look up at them. In the masses of granite we may trace a resemblance to a ruined castle. There are the crumbling walls and the postern, the arch of which has fallen, with a narrow path appearing to lead to it. We almost look for the warder on the battlements, so like an ancient stronghold are the rocks moulded. But castles, be they never so old, are as things of yesterday compared

* A writer about 1848 happened to mention that the Tavy here "flows for some distance over a solid granite floor," and since that time this has been remarked upon as though such a thing was altogether unusual. There is, however, nothing singular in it, nor is it probable that the writer referred to supposed that there was. In many places the Dartmoor streams have a bottom of solid granite, and this is indeed only what we might expect to find in such a region.

to the citadel of Tavy Cleave. Its foundations were laid "when Time was young," and yet it has outlasted the proudest structures of man.

Further up the defile narrows; the foot of the hill on the left approaches nearer to the stream, until the level piece of turf becomes a mere strip. By-and-bye it is lost altogether, and the way is rugged. A clatter covers the steep slope and sinks down into the river. Progress can only be made by clambering over the masses of rock, many of which lie half-hidden beneath moss and whortleberry plants. Nor on the further side of the stream is it otherwise, for there, too, the hill is steep, and covered with boulders, grey granite everywhere showing itself, and creeping plants everywhere striving to hide it, while the base of the declivity is also washed by the waters. Beyond the clatter the hill above us falls back, and the Tavy making a great bend is lost to view behind the hill to the right. In front another stream comes to join it. It is the Rattle Brook, and the head of the cleave is reached.

The wild Forest now lies before the rambler. When he crosses the tributary stream, and climbs the slope of Watern Oke, the hills in the recesses of the Moor come into view. Lonely Fur Tor lifts his granite crest above the forbidding steeps, and the dark ridges behind which Cranmere hides itself are seen against the eastern sky. The Rattle Brook marks the boundary line of the Forest, on the western side of the stream being the common lands of Lydford, of Bridestowe, and of Sourton. These form a bold ridge, though its summit is not in view, and beyond this is the valley of the Lyd. In the direction whence the Rattle Brook comes down from its lofty cradle, the masses of Dunnagoat are visible, and Green Tor, on the slope of Amicombe, and one solitary building near it. This is Bleak House, but the hopes of those who reared it (modern adventurers who sought to wring wealth from the Moor) were shattered, as is now the edifice itself.

But it is the view down the valley that will attract the wanderer who reaches this spot. Truly grand is the picture of the cleave that is here presented. At the foot of the beholder the Tavy is seen struggling through a huge granite trough, above whose sides the hills, thickly dotted with grey rocks, climb to the sky. Down the narrow pass the Cleave Tors crest a hill that seems to rise almost perpendicularly from the hidden depths, and far beyond, framed by their frowning masses and the brow of Standon, is seen the Cornish eminence of Kit Hill. The scene is a most impressive one, and those who have wandered over Dartmoor, and know something of its romantic features, will admit that for rugged grandeur and sublimity it can show no other picture like this.

And now we bid farewell to the old-time region over which we have been wandering, and pass from the silence of the waste to its gemmed circlet and down into the lowlands, where the heath is no more seen, but in its place are woods and pasture lands and orchards. But though no longer before our eyes, the tor lifting its head into the still air, the rock on its cushion of heather, the gnarled trees of ancient groves, the deep valley and the waterfall, will yet live in the memory, while the notes of the lark and the whisper of the mountain breeze, and the "cry" of the far-off stream, will come back to us like the air of an old song rising out of the half-forgotten past. And how beautifully Nature has begirt her primeval home; planting a garden at the foot of its rugged hills, and lovingly giving it of her best. Stern and wild though the region be, shattered by a thousand storms its rock towers, and scarred its lichened boulders, the land of flowers greets it with a smile, and like a child climbing on its mother's knee, seeks to ascend its steeps. Far away the wanderer looks only upon blue hills, nor knows that in Devonia's crown manifold beauties hide. But he draws near, and the diadem reveals itself, and proves its fitness to be set upon such a land by the richness of its gems.

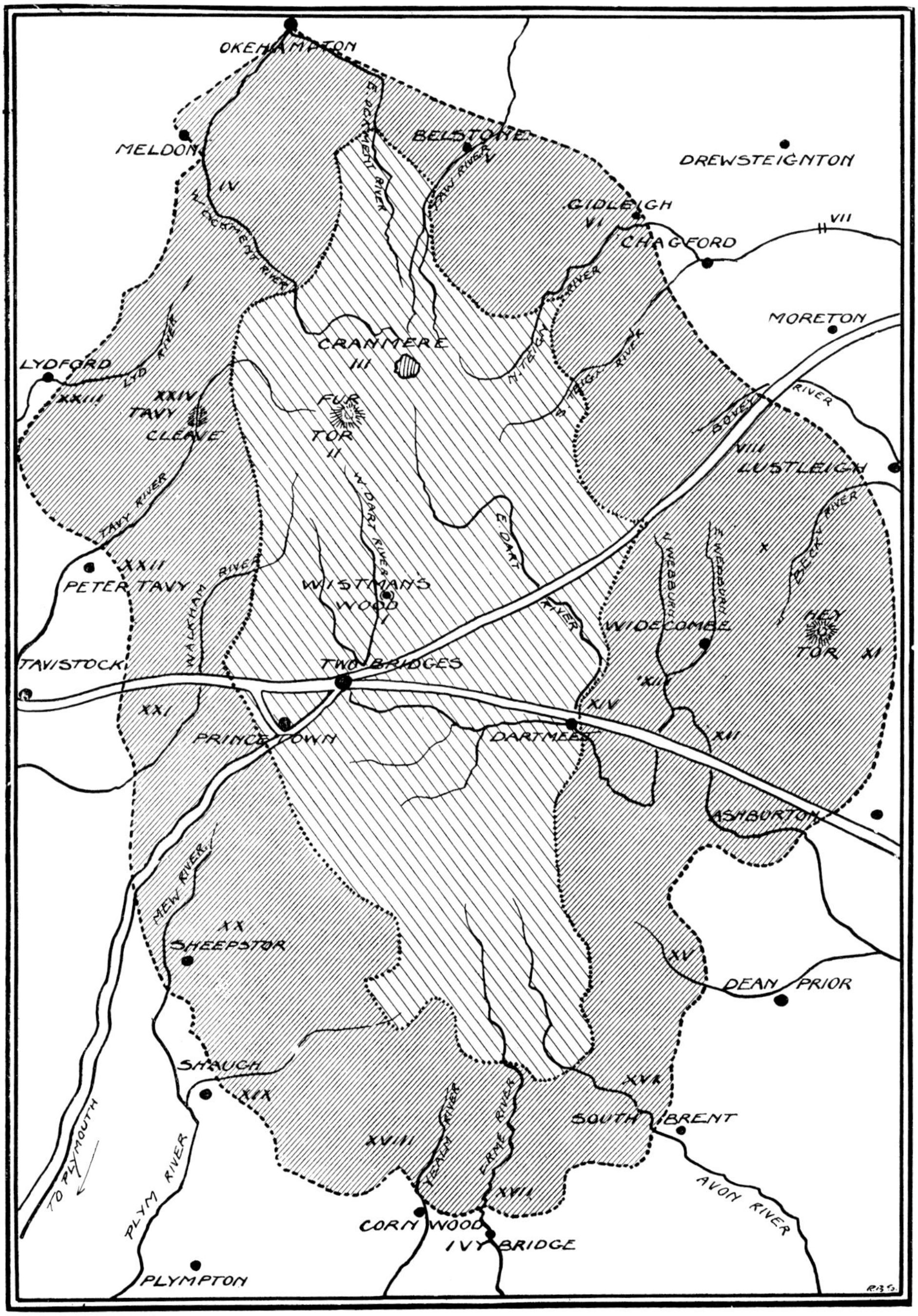

Sketch Map of Dartmoor.

The shaded portion shows the Moor; the inner dotted line represents the Boundary of the Forest. The figures refer to the Chapters.

APPENDIX.

Guide to the Places and Objects described, with Distances from the Nearest Centres.

A FEW general directions for reaching the beauty spots of Dartmoor described in the foregoing pages may perhaps prove useful. The reader is not conducted step by step over the ground, such being more within the province of a guide book, and upon this it was not desired to trench. But sufficient information is given to enable the rambler to readily reach the various places noticed from the nearest tourist centres should he desire to do so, and, where necessary, the best routes to the objects of interest in their vicinity are briefly sketched.

I. Wistman's Wood.—Two Bridges, under 1½ m. Princetown, 3 m. Tavistock to Two Bridges, 8 m. —— A path to the wood leads from the high road, the gate giving access to it being quite near to the Two Bridges Hotel. There is, however, a dispute at present as to the right of way through Crockern Farm, across which the path runs, and it is probable that another route will be provided for the visitor. Information on this point may be obtained at the hotel. The wood consists of three groups; it was in the central one that the fire of 1886 occurred. The inscription referred to in the notice of the wood is on a large triangular stone in the clatter about midway between its upper and lower verge. To reach the higher part its eastern (or upper) edge should be skirted. There is a good view of it from the hill on the Bear Down side of the Dart.

II. Fur Tor.—Two Bridges, *via* Cowsic Head, under 6 m. Lydford station, *via* Redford and Watern Oke, 6 m. Princetown, *via* Rundle Stone and Walkham Head, 7½ m. (By Walkham Head the source of the river is meant, not the hill near it marked by that name on the Ordnance Map.) Okehampton, *via* Dinger Plain and Broad Amicombe Hole, under 8 m. Tavistock, *via* Peter Tavy, Twyste Lane and Walkham Head, 10½ m. —— From Two Bridges the Cowsic may be traced to its source, the stream being approached from the Tavistock road, a short distance to the west of the starting-point; or the visitor may proceed by way of Bear Down Farm, and pursuing a northward course along the ridge behind it, reach the menhir known as Bear Down Man, from which the springs of the Cowsic are about ½ m. distant, in a direction north by west. Beyond this point the ground is very bad, the source of the stream being on the edge of the great fen that extends over so much of the north quarter of the Forest. But there is no difficulty in passing over it during a dry season, although, as it is always fatiguing walking, progress is necessarily slow. By pursuing a direction a little west of north the rambler will reach the Tavy, which is rather over ½ m. distant, Fur Tor previously coming into view. Crossing the river about ½ m. below its source under Cut Hill, and still following the same direction he will be led to the rocks. After leaving the Tavy good ground is soon gained.

The route from Lydford station to the tor passes over good, hard ground. Close to the South-Western Railway Company's cottages a gate opens on Black Down, and from this a green path runs up by the side of the common with Henscott Plantation on the left. This leads to the high road from Tavistock to Okehampton, and on reaching this it must be crossed, and the same direction followed for a short distance, when a track running from Burn Lane and Brent Tor to the Forest will be struck. This the rambler now follows, the direction being about north-east. At Forstal Cross, where is a small granite pillar, the enclosures of Redford are reached, and these are kept on the right. Near the higher end of them is Hare Tor towards which the rambler must make his way, keeping it, however, a little to the left. Continuing on the same course the hill is descended and the Tavy is reached near where it is joined by the Rattle Brook, and at the head of the Tavy Cleave defile. Crossing the Rattle Brook the rambler finds himself on Watern Oke from which hill Fur Tor is in full view. The way now lies towards the tor, keeping the Tavy on the right. Soon that river makes an abrupt turn, flowing from the south, and at the bend the Amicombe comes down to join it. The latter stream may be crossed at this point or further up, but in either case it should be followed till the rambler is nearly abreast of Fur Tor. If a bee line is struck from the confluence bad ground will be encountered. —— The route from Lydford village will be found in *III. Cranmere.*

The best route to Fur Tor from Princetown is by way of Rundle Stone and Walkham Head. From Rundle Stone, over 1½ m. from the Duchy Hotel at Princetown, the prison leat should be followed. It runs for some distance through the prison ground, but no objection is made to visitors walking that way provided that no convicts are at work on the route. If such, however, happens to be the case the rambler must make his way toward Great Mis Tor from Rundle Stone, keeping the wall of the enclosures on his right. Where this terminates he turns right, when he will soon reach the leat, which then becomes his guide to the Walkham. At the point where it is taken in from that river, or rather from a tributary of that river called Spriddle Lake, an old peat track runs north, and this he will follow to its end, when he will be close to the source of the stream, which is not far above its first bend. He must cross this where the track ends, and not go quite to the head of it, which is a little to the right. On the further side he will find himself among a number of turf ties, but they present no obstacle, having been disused for a considerable time, and are now covered with whortleberry plants. On the top of the hill in front of him is a bad piece of fen, and to avoid this it will be necessary to keep a little to the left as he passes up through the ties. Skirting the fen he will reach the Tavy, Fur Tor being in sight as he descends towards it. He will strike the river some little distance below the point where it is crossed by the route to the tor from Cowsic Head, as already described. —— If the visitor can pass through the prison ground, and the state of the Moor is suitable, he may, instead of following the leat, turn in from the road a little on the Two Bridges side of Rundle Stone to Fitz's Well, and from there follow the old tram road on the east side of the Blackabrook, and make his way to the Tavy by a line passing eastward of Walkham Head.

The route from Okehampton to Fur Tor is a very easy one. From the station a road leads up to the artillery camp on the hill, and this the visitor follows, and where it forks takes the left branch to Moor Gate. Here a rough track running south-westward immediately outside the wall of Okehampton Park will lead him between Row Tor and West Mil Tor, and on to Dinger Plain, the Moor Brook being his companion throughout its course. It seems to have been formed on the line of an ancient way, and is very plainly defined as far as Dinger Tor, being still in use as a peat track. From the tor the next point is Broad Amicombe Hole, on the further side of the West Ockment. This is an opening between Great Kneeset on the left, and Amicombe Hill on the right, and is in full view as the rambler proceeds, its direction being about south-south-west. It is a mile from Dinger Tor, Lints Tor being about midway between. A little feeder of the

West Ockment runs down the pass, and this must be followed to its head. If the Ockment cannot easily be crossed here the rambler should trace it upwards for a short distance, when he will hardly fail to find some place where he may do so by means of the boulders in its channel. When the head of the little affluent of the Ockment is reached the rambler must proceed due south through the pass, and at the distance of about $\frac{1}{4}$ m. he will come upon the springs of another stream. This is the Amicombe, which is followed for 1 m. to the point where it receives the Cut Combe Water (the second tributary on the left), when the foot of the hill which Fur Tor crowns is reached.

The rambler who desires to visit Fur Tor from Tavistock cannot do better than take the train to Lydford and follow the route already given from that place. But should he wish to make the whole of the journey on foot he will leave the town by the Okehampton road, and at the second milestone turn right to the village of Peter Tavy, which is about 1 m. further on. Passing through this little place with the church on his left, he will notice a lane just beyond it on the right. Into this he turns, and entering upon Smearn Down, follows the road that runs up by the side of the common. Near the higher end of the latter a moor track will be seen branching off to the left (*vide* Chap. XXII), and this now becomes his path. Beyond Boulters Tor it runs between some newtakes, this part of it bearing the name of Twyste Lane. On leaving the lane he passes over the common with the slope of White Tor on his left, the green path being well defined. On Langstone Moor, a little further on, he will pass quite close to the menhir mentioned in Chap. XXII, and $1\frac{1}{2}$ m. beyond this will reach the bounds of the Forest, where the track runs through a cutting. He is now on the old Lich Path, which crosses the Walkham at a ford seen below. But he does not follow it so far. Part way down the slope the road forks, the left branch being the old peat road to Walkham Head, noticed in the directions for visiting the tor from Princetown. This now becomes his path, and when its end is reached he follows the instructions given in that route.

Having penetrated so far into the recesses of the Moor the visitor will find it worth his while to slightly extend his journey, and ascend Cut Hill, from which eminence a view of the wilder parts of Dartmoor is obtained, The hill is about 1 m. from the principal pile of Fur Tor, in an east-south-easterly direction. Its summit is crowned with a low mound of turf. In walking from the tor to the hill the rambler has a good view of Cut Combe on the left.

III. Cranmere.—Lydford, Okehampton, Chagford, about 7 m. Two Bridges, about $7\frac{1}{2}$ m. (The distances given in the chapter are as the crow flies.) Princetown, *via* Two Bridges, 9 m. —— If the visitor starts from Lydford station he will follow the route to Fur Tor, already sketched, and when abreast of that tor will continue as in the route now described from Lydford village. The distance from the station is greater than from the latter point. —— From Lydford village the way lies by the Dartmoor Inn, close to which the rambler enters upon High Down. A green path leads across this to a ford and stepping-stones on the Lyd, just above where that stream receives the Doe Tor Brook, On crossing it the hill is ascended, with the Doe Tor Brook on the right hand, and Bra Tor, surmounted with a cross, on the left. When the bend on the brook is reached it must be crossed, and an easterly direction pursued to the summit of the ridge, Sharp Tor being kept a little to the right. This tor, which stands on the ridge about $\frac{1}{2}$ m. north of Hare Tor, is only a small pile. When the top of the ridge is reached the rambler will see Amicombe Hill and Watern Oke before him, on the further side of the Rattle Brook, with the rocks of Fur Tor rising beyond. To the left of Fur Tor is Black Ridge, and to the left of that a conical hill will be seen. This is Great Kneeset, and is the mark towards which the rambler should aim. Cranmere Pool lies about 1 m. beyond it, and a little to the right, and it is possible to make a direct line to it, but those who are strangers to the locality are advised to go by way of Kneeset; the distance is not much greater, and if the directions here given are followed the pool may be reached with ease, a very small portion of fen having to be crossed. On descending the ridge a point about midway between Kneeset and Fur Tor must be aimed for, as by so doing the rambler will avoid the little feeders of the Rattle Brook that run into it south of Green Tor. But when that stream is crossed, which, unless it be in flood, can be done without difficulty, a course about east-north-east should be followed, and when Kneeset comes again in sight it must be made for. The rambler here passes over the southern end of Amicombe Hill, Watern Oke, which is a continuation of the same high ground, being on his right. On approaching Kneeset it must be kept a little to the right, as the ground is rough on the side facing the visitor. At the distance of about 1 m. from the Rattle Brook the Amicombe will be reached, just below its source (*vide* route to Fur Tor from Okehampton). The summit of Kneeset ought now to be to the north-east, and is distant ¾ m. On reaching it the rambler is 1 m. from the pool, which lies nearly due east from Kneeset, Newtake, a rounded hill, one part of which is also called Hangingstone Hill, rising against the sky beyond it. But a direct course to it should not be followed, as such will lead the visitor over some very heavy and broken ground. The proper plan is to keep well to the right of the rounded hill that marks the situation of Cranmere, and cross the dip between Kneeset and Black Ridge, the direction being about east by south. On the further side of the dip the rambler will find himself on the edge of the fen, and must now turn left, the line followed from Kneeset and the one he is about to follow forming an obtuse angle. He will thus be led directly to the pool, having the fen on his right, and the dip on his left.—— Should the start be made from Bridestowe station the path leading from the Fox and Hounds Inn to Noddon Gate must be followed, and the Lyd crossed just below the latter at the stepping-stones. The ridge in front is then ascended, Arms Tor being kept a little to the left. The Rattle Brook is crossed just below Green Tor, and then the way lies over Amicombe Hill to the source of the Amicombe under Great Kneeset. When this point is reached the directions given in the preceding route must be followed. From Arms Tor to Great Kneeset the course is a trifle south of due east. Bridestowe is the nearest railway station to the pool. The distance is 6 m.

From Okehampton there are two good routes to Cranmere. The first of these will take the visitor to Dinger Plain, as already described in the route from the town to Fur Tor. From Dinger Tor the pool lies about south-east by south, and is 2 m. distant. The rambler will descend to Brim Brook, which he will cross, and make his way over the southern part of Ockment Hill. The West Ockment, the course of which can be seen, must be left about ½ m. to the right, but at the distance of rather over 1 m., and just after a shallow gully known as Vergyland Combe has been crossed, the rambler will find himself near to it, as it here runs in a direction different from that which it pursues further down. Soon after he will strike it where it is a mere rivulet, and following it to its source will be led to within a very short distance of the pool. While keeping the Ockment well to the right after leaving Brim Brook, care must be taken not to go too far to the left, as not only is the ground rather bad in that direction, near the brook, but there is a danger of missing the stream when the rambler gets further out, and in that case a stranger might fail to find the pool. If, however, he follows the directions here laid down he will be able to reach it without difficulty. —— The other route from Okehampton to Cranmere is by way of New Bridge. On reaching Moor Gate instead of turning right the rambler will cross the brook and keep straight up the hill, passing a gravel pit, which is railed in, on the right of the way, and having Row Tor also on that side some little distance in advance of him. Beyond this the road forks, but he follows the branch to the right and soon finds himself on a genuine Moor track, running in a southerly direction, and roughly parallel to the Blackaven, which he sees below him on the left. This will bring him to New Bridge, a clapper thrown over that stream, under East Mil Tor, where he will cross, and still following the path will reach the highest point of Ockment Hill, ¼ m. south-west of the springs of the East Ockment. He is now at a slightly greater elevation than Cranmere, which lies about 1¼ m. due south, and towards which there is no longer any path. Instead of following a direct line to the pool it will be better on nearing it to keep a little to the right, as by so doing he will get on to the harder ground near the source of the West Ockment. —— Cranmere can also be reached from Okehampton by tracing the West Ockment to its source, but the journey is longer. The way lies through the park to Meldon Gorge as described in *IV. The Island of Rocks.*

From Belstone there is no better plan for reaching Cranmere than to trace the Taw to its source. The rambler will first make his way along the top of the ridge southward of the village, with the Taw on the left, and will strike that river at the southern end of the hill crowned with the rocks of Steeperton Tor. Thence he follows the stream upward, still keeping it on his left, and will reach its head without difficulty. The pool is ½ mile distant, in a direction west-south-west, and care should be taken in passing over this piece of fen not to bear too much to the left. It is better to keep a little to the right, as by so doing the springs of the West Ockment will be struck. Distance 5½ m.

Cranmere is approached from Chagford by two routes, one being by way of Batworthy Corner and Watern Tor, and the other by Metherell, Fernworthy, and Teign Head Bridge. —— In the former case the road is followed to Teigncombe, and the Moor is entered at Brimestone Down. (There are two roads to Teigncombe; one by way of Waye Barton and Thorn, and the other by Leigh Bridge.) A path leads from the Moor gate at Brimestone Down to the enclosures of Batworthy, the wall of which it skirts till Batworthy Corner is reached. Here the visitor turns right, and passes down the hill, with the wall still on the right, to the North Teign, at the point where it receives the Walla Brook. There is a clapper immediately below the confluence, by means of which he will cross the stream, and another, consisting of a single stone, over the Walla Brook, a short distance above it, which will enable him to gain the right bank of that tributary. He is now between the two streams. Cranmere is about 3½ m. from this point in a direction west by south, and a straight line drawn to it would fall a little south of Watern Tor, which is seen rising on the ridge 1½ m. away. He will now make for this tor, keeping rather near the Walla Brook should he find the ground swampy, as it is in places after wet weather. On reaching the tor the visitor sees in advance of him the basin in which the Walla Brook takes its rise, and over this he must make his way, crossing that stream near its source. On the further side of the basin, in a west-south-westerly direction, and about 1 m. distant from Watern Tor, is Newtake, the rounded hill mentioned in the route to the pool from Lydford as being in sight from Great Kneeset. This is now his point, and on reaching it he will be within 1 m. of the pool. A good mark from this hill is Great Links Tor, which stands up against the sky a little north of west 4 m. away. Cranmere lies to the south of a straight line drawn from this hill to the tor. Beyond Newtake the visitor will reach the fen, but in fine weather there should be no difficulty in crossing it here. Should he find the ground bad it will be better to keep a little to the right on leaving the hill, and thus strike the head of the Taw. In any case he must be careful not to keep too much to the left, or he may miss the pool altogether. Taw Head is about ½ m. from Cranmere (see route from Belstone), and the ground between the two points is fairly good. —— There is another and more direct way to the pool from Batworthy Corner, but as this necessitates the crossing of the Teign under Manger Rock, which cannot always be accomplished, it is better for strangers to go by way of Watern Tor. —— The second route from Chagford to Cranmere, though longer than that just sketched, has the merit of being a very easy one. The way lies through Fernworthy, on the South Teign, to Teign Head Farm, to which place there is a road, so that visitors may drive thus far, and find themselves only about 2¼ m. from their objective. The Moor is entered by the gate near Metherell, which is reached from Chagford by the road passing Waye Barton. From Metherell the road is good as far as Fernworthy, but beyond that it becomes a Moor track. It can be driven over, however, without any difficulty. The North Teign is crossed just below Teign Head Farm, where there is a ford and a clapper. Cranmere lies west-north-west of the farmhouse, and if the rambler follows this course he will at the distance of rather less than $\frac{3}{4}$ m. reach a gate in the wall of the large enclosure belonging to the farm. Passing through this he finds himself on Whitehorse Hill, and very near to the source of the Varracombe Brook, which is a little in advance of him on the left. Keeping slightly to the right in order to avoid this he will reach Moute's Inn, the scanty remains of a turf-cutter's hut, exactly $\frac{1}{2}$ m. from the gate. The ground beyond this is rather heavy, but in dry weather is crossed without difficulty. The course is now west by north, which will take the rambler close to East Dart Head, $\frac{1}{2}$ m. from Moute's Inn. He leaves this on the left, and still pursuing the same course, will in another $\frac{1}{2}$ m. reach the pool. But he must steer correctly over this $\frac{1}{2}$ m. and be very careful not to keep too much to the left. The pool is not in sight from Dart Head; a low ridge of fen rises between, and until the rambler gets part way up the slope beyond the river source he has no objects to guide him. If provided with a compass he will, of course, be able to follow the correct line, and by doing so will see the pool just after he gets over the top of the ridge. If not, Great Links Tor will be his mark, as in the former route. It will come into view as he nears the top of the ridge, nearly 4 m. off, and if he steers a little to the right of it, he cannot well miss the pool. As the rambler makes his way from Moute's Inn to East Dart Head, Newtake, mentioned in the former route, is passed a short distance to the right.

From Two Bridges the best route to Cranmere is by way of the left bank of the West Dart, and the upper waters of the East Dart. —— Sometimes the route chosen is by the West Dart and Cut Hill, but this will take the rambler over some very heavy ground. —— The river is traced upwards for about 4 m., the first part of the journey being either by way of Wistman's Wood, or by the ridge to the east of it. In the latter case the rambler should, after passing Longaford Tor, make towards the river (still, however, pursuing a northerly direction), striking it between Higher White Tor on the right, and Crow Tor on the left. About $\frac{3}{4}$ m. further up he will pass Rough Tor, which is on the other side of the stream, and about the same distance beyond this, where it bends to the left, will leave it, and make his way to the East Dart. A walk of about $\frac{3}{4}$ m. in a north-north-easterly direction will bring him to this river at that part of it where it passes through a large stream work at Broad Marsh. The ground between the two streams is not very good in a wet season, but can be crossed without difficulty when the weather is fair. Care must be taken in passing over it not to bear too much to the left, or the Dart will be missed. Should the rambler keep too far to the right, it will not so much matter; he will still reach the river, only at a lower point. At the head of the Broad Marsh stream work the Dart makes an abrupt turn, and another small stream from under Cut Hill runs into it. But the Dart is the stream on the right, and this should now be traced to its source, which is 2 m. distant in a direction almost due north. It can be crossed easily here, and the ground near it being good, the rambler will be able to make his way through the fen to its head without the slightest difficulty. To reach the pool from this point the directions given in the previous route must be followed.

From Post Bridge the visitor will have the East Dart as a guide from his starting point. He will leave it where it bends to the right near Hartland Tor, and making his way over the shoulder of Broad Down will strike it again just below Sandy Hole. Above this the river runs through a narrow pass, at the head of which is the Broad Marsh stream work.

There are two or three routes by which Cranmere may be conveniently reached from Princetown, but the best is perhaps that from Two Bridges, the visitor first making his way to that place by the road. —— Another will take him nearly to the head of the Cowsic, which stream is reached from Rundle Stone by crossing the prison ground. When about $\frac{1}{2}$ m. from the source, and near Bear Down Man, he will leave it and proceeding in a north-easterly direction will at the distance of about 1 m. reach the West Dart, which he should strike about $\frac{1}{2}$ m. above Rough Tor. He will then follow the directions for reaching the pool from near that point given in the route from Two Bridges. —— An alternative route from Cowsic Head is afforded by crossing the fen to the Tavy, and making for Fur Tor. (See Route from Two Bridges to Fur Tor.) —— An easy route is by way of Rundle Stone and the prison leat to Fur Tor, which has already been described. The rambler should pass to the right of the tor and descending into Cut Combe make his way down by the right bank of the Cut Combe Water. When it bends to the left he leaves it, his course then being east of north. On his left is Little Kneeset, a hill of good hard ground, and over the eastern end of this he passes to the Black Ridge Water, the distance between the two streams being rather over ½ m. The last named is here a mere rivulet, and the rambler should strike it where two branches of it meet. Choosing the left branch he follows it to its source, the ground rising considerably. Cranmere is less than ½ m. distant across the fen, in a north-north-easterly direction. —— If the Moor is not in a good condition it will be better on leaving the Cut Combe Water to ascend Little Kneeset, and cross it in a direction north-west by north, striking the Black Ridge Water lower down than if the former line were taken. Near where the rambler should come upon it a small branch runs into it from the north, and by following this up he will reach the dip between Great Kneeset and the fen, referred to in the route from Lydford to the pool. He will then be able to reach the latter by making his way along the edge of the dip, as already described.

IV. The Island of Rocks.—Okehampton, *via* the Park, 4 m. At the bottom of the Station Road another road leads to the Workhouse, and beyond this a path runs to the lower part of Okehampton Park, and is continued to Meldon Gorge. Just beyond the viaduct the Redaven falls into the West Ockment, as mentioned in Chapter IV., and from this point the route as there sketched must be followed. From the Island of Rocks the rambler may follow the stream upwards till he reaches Black Tor Copse, and return by way of Homerton Hill. From the copse he will ascend the rocky steep, with Black Tor on his right, and steering about north-west will soon reach the hill named, with the Fishcombe Water, or, as it is sometimes called, the Homerton Brook, on his right. The northern side of Homerton Hill is very steep, and the descent is best made by keeping near to the little stream. This will lead him into the path by which he made his way upward through Meldon Gorge. —— Another way of reaching the Island of Rocks is by the road to Meldon hamlet, and on to the Moor gate above Higher Bowden Steps. This is the route to be followed if it should be desired to drive a part of the distance; on reaching the gate the carriage can be sent back to the hamlet. The old water-course referred to in Chapter IV. will be seen on the hillside not far from the gate, and this becomes the path to Vellake Corner. The Island is hardly ¼ m. above this.

V. The Belstone Cleaves.—Okehampton to Belstone, *via* Tongue End, 3¼ m.; *via* Fatherford Viaduct and Lake, 2½ m. Sufficient directions having been given in Chapter V. for reaching the objects there described, it is only necessary to sketch the route to Steeperton Tor in case the visitor should wish to take the walk referred to in that chapter. Leaving the village of Belstone by the Tors Hotel he will make his way by the road to Birchy Lake, beyond which he enters Taw Plain. Steeperton rises at the upper, or southern, end of this plain, and is easily reached by keeping the Taw on the left, the ground being good all the way up. On the western side of Steeperton the river comes down through a narrow gorge, and at the head of this, near the disused Knock Mine, is a clapper. From this point a road runs back to Belstone by way of the ridge south of the village, and by this the rambler may return, reaching the Moor gate near Watchet Hill. —— From Fatherford Viaduct, at the lower end of the West Cleave, a path leads to Okehampton station, running along the side of the hill just below the railway. —— A road also leads from the viaduct to the Bartons Hill, at the east end of the town. This road branches off to the left a short distance north of the viaduct, and forms part of the route mentioned above as running from Okehampton to Belstone by way of the viaduct and Lake. The road to Lake runs under the railway not far from the viaduct.

VI. Gidleigh Chase.—Chagford, nearest point, about 2 m.; Moretonhampstead, 6½ m. The chase not being open to the public, only the route round it is here described. —— Some excellent views of this wild valley may be obtained if the visitor makes his way by Holy Street and Leigh Bridge to Teigncombe, and thence on to the Moor gate opening on to Brimstone Down. From this point he will follow the Moor track referred to in the first route from Chagford to Cranmere, but on reaching the Round Pound, which is about ¼ m. from the gate, he will leave the track and descend the hill to the Teign, or he may make his way direct to the river on entering on the down. Here the Teign is crossed by two clams, and on the further, or northern side of it, a path runs up to Scorhill House. This he will follow, and passing the house will soon reach the stroll extending from the commons to Creaber Pound and Berry Down. At the bottom of this stroll he follows the lane to the right, passing the last-named farm, and ½ m. down will arrive at a point where a lane turns left to Gidleigh Castle. After examining this he may retrace his steps to the lane by which he descended from Berry Down, and turning left make his way to the bottom of it, crossing the Blackaton Brook at Highbury Bridge. Thence he follows the lane running through Murchington to Chagford, or he may return to the village by way of Leigh Bridge. —— If he decide upon the latter, he will turn into a lane on the right just before reaching Murchington, which will bring him to a path leading to some stepping stones, where he crosses the Teign. The bridge is just below this. —— Should it be desired to extend the walk the visitor, instead of turning aside near the Round Pound, will follow the track to Batworthy Corner, and make his way down to the clapper near the Holed Stone, as described in the route to Cranmere. Crossing the Teign, he will pass up the slope to a small leat, which he will follow for a short distance to the wall of the Scorhill property. By skirting this he will be led to the stroll down which the track runs to Berry Down. —— At a number of points on either of these routes the chase is in view, and Gidleigh Tor is also seen to advantage.

VII. Fingle Bridge.—Moreton, about 3 m.; Chagford, about 3¾ m. Few directions are needed for reaching Fingle Bridge from either of these places, as good roads lead to it. —— From Moreton the way lies by Howton, and thence by the middle road to Uppacott Down, which is about 1 m. further on. The road passes over this common, leaving Cranbrook Castle on the left, and then descends by the zig-zags mentioned in Chap. VII. to the bridge. —— From Chagford the route is by Easton, where the Whiddon Down and Moreton road is crossed, and thence up the hill to Uppacott Down, where the road from Moreton joins it. —— There is a path on the right bank of the river below the bridge, from which the rambler obtains some good views of the wooded sides of the gorge, and also of Prestonbury. —— The summit of Prestonbury is reached from the Drewsteignton road, which climbs the hill from the northern end of the bridge, with the great camp high on the right. Near the point where the road is crossed by another, which leads from Clifford Bridge, down the river, to Drewsteignton, there is a path leading to Prestonbury. —— By turning to the left at this point, and proceeding along the road for about ½ m. Drewsteignton village is reached. —— The dolmen known as the Spinsters' Rock is over 2 m. from Drewsteignton. The road to Whiddon Down is followed to a point just beyond Stone Farm, nearly 2 m., when the visitor turns into a lane on the left, soon after which the dolmen will be seen in a field, also on that side.

VIII. Grim's Pound.—Chagford, 5¼ m.; Moreton, 5¾ m.; Two Bridges, 8¾ m.; Princetown, 10¼ m. Roads lead to the pound from each of these places. —— The one from Chagford runs by Middleton Hill, and reaches the Princetown and Moreton road at a point nearly 2 m. north-east of the Warren House Inn. The way then runs a short distance back over the road to Moreton, when the road mentioned in Chap. VIII. as having been cut in 1874 is reached. This turns off to the right, and passes quite near to the pound, which is about $1\frac{1}{4}$ m. from the junction. —— From Moreton the Princetown road is followed to the junction, which is about $4\frac{1}{2}$ m. from the town. —— But there is another route from this place. This lies through North Bovey, $1\frac{3}{4}$ m. from Moreton, and over the side of East Down, or Easdon, to Easdon Farm, whence a path leads through Vogwell Farm to the common. From this point Grim's Pound is about I m. distant in a west-south-westerly direction, the route to it lying a little to the left of King Tor. By following a rivulet met soon after leaving Vogwell to its source, and continuing on the same course, the pound will shortly come in sight. —— From Two Bridges and Princetown the Moreton road is followed to the junction beyond the Warren House Inn, but if the visitor is on foot he may avoid a considerable detour by making direct for the pound from the hostelry. It lies nearly due east, and is about $1\frac{3}{4}$ m. distant. Through a break in the ridge the pound can be seen from the road near the inn. —— The various objects of interest in the vicinity of Grim's Pound having been mentioned in Chap. VIII., it is only necessary here to note their distances from the pound, and the direction in which they lie. The Challacombe stone row is about $\frac{1}{2}$ m. west by south. The stones can be seen from the pound standing up against the sky on the summit of the ridge across the valley. Hookney Tor, $\frac{1}{4}$ m. north-north-west; this is just above the pound opposite to Hameldon Tor. Shapley Tor, $\frac{3}{4}$ m. north by west; there are hut circles near the road under this pile. King's Barrow, rather more than $\frac{1}{2}$ m. north-east by east; here is a kistvaen. Berry Pound, $\frac{3}{4}$ m. east-south-east. Hameldon Cross, $\frac{1}{2}$ m. south-east by south; a fine view of the Forest is obtained from it. Southward of this are several barrows. Hameldon Tor, $\frac{1}{4}$ m. south-east, commands a good view of the pound.

IX. Lustleigh Cleave.—Lustleigh station, 1 m. Visitors will find this the best starting point. —— The way lies through the village by the church and smithy, just beyond which a lane turns up on the right. This is followed to Ellimore Farm, $\frac{1}{4}$ m. distant, through the yard of which the visitor passes. A little further on he turns to the right towards Hammerslake, but does not proceed so far, turning again at the first lane on the left. A walk of about a hundred yards will bring him to the common, and within a very short distance of Sharp Tor. Below the tor, to the south and south-west of it, a path leads down to Horsham Steps, and a little way up the stream from this crossing-place is Foxworthy. To make his way from the latter to Manaton the visitor crosses the Bovey by the clapper close to Little Silver, and climbs the path through the wood that here covers the side of the hill. This will bring him to some fields, across which the path runs to a lane. The first turning to the left will take him directly to the village. —— North Bovey is about 2 m. from Manaton; the way lies by Langstone, to which point there is a foot-path, branching from the lane near the village. —— Should the rambler desire to visit the remains of the old hill fort on the down above Lustleigh Cleave, he will, on reaching Sharp Tor, make his way along the crest of the ridge, with the enclosures on his right. Passing the fine entrance to South Harton, he follows the same course, with enclosures still on his right, for about $\frac{1}{4}$ m. when the camp will be reached. Foxworthy lies a short distance below it in a south-westerly direction.

X. Hound Tor Combe.—Bovey Tracey to Becky Fall, near the lower end of the combe, about 4 m.; Ashburton to Hemsworthy Gate, near the head of the combe, *via* Welstor Common, about $4\frac{1}{2}$ m. —— A ramble round the combe, the head of which is about 3 m. from Becky Fall, will extend over about 9 m. —— From the fall the road running near to the Becky Brook should be followed to the turning just below the bridge under Leighon, referred to in Chap. X. Striking into this lane, and keeping to the left, the rambler will reach Hound Tor Down, and will be rewarded with a fine view of the tor, to which he may make his way direct. Grea Tor, less than $\frac{1}{2}$ m. across the common in a south-easterly direction, should also be visited, not only for its own sake but also because the combe is seen to good advantage from it. The rambler will then return to the road,

road. Here the rambler turns left, and very shortly reaches Skerraton Down. He now deserts the road, and strikes over the common right, following a green path to a gate in a wall. He does not pass through this, but continues on with the wall to the left. The path will lead him across a little brook, and through a hunting-gate. The valley of Dean Burn is now below him, and on the down just above him is the ruined Lambs' Down Farm. —— This point is reached from Buckfastleigh by way of Wallaford Cross, Wallaford Down, and Cross Furzes. —— Wallaford Down may be reached from Warn Bridge by the road that branches north-west from the Buckfastleigh road quite near to it. This will bring the rambler to Wallaford Cross (nearly $\frac{3}{4}$ m.), where he turns left, and soon reaches the down.

XVI. Shipley.—South Brent to Didworthy Bridge, about $1\frac{3}{4}$m.; Shipley Bridge is $\frac{1}{2}$ m. further. —— There are two routes to Didworthy Bridge, one running through Lutton, and the other through the hamlet of Aish. —— If the former is chosen the way lies by the vicarage gate and up the hill to Lutton, whence a road runs left from the green down to Wash Gate. From this point there is a bridle path only. It runs between hedges for some distance, and then across some fields to the yard at the back of the Didworthy Sanatorium. The visitor here turns left, and will shortly reach the bridge. The gate by which the woods are entered (Chap. XVI.) is near the eastern end of the parapet, on the right. —— If the visitor goes by way of Aish he does not ascend the hill after passing the gate of the vicarage, but turns down left to Lydia Bridge. Crossing this he climbs the hill to Aish, and following the lane will be led again to the Avon, and passing along its bank will soon reach the bridge. There is not much difference in the length of these two routes. —— The path through the woods from Didworthy Bridge to Shipley Bridge is not a public one, and it will consequently be necessary to obtain permission to pass that way. But there is a path to Shipley above the woods. It runs by the farm nearly opposite to the entrance to the Sanatorium. The road at the western end of Didworthy Bridge leads directly to the Moor gate at Shipley. —— Brent Moor Villa is about $\frac{1}{2}$ m. above Shipley Bridge, the road to it running along the bank of the river. —— Shipley Tor may be reached by passing through the enclosures behind the cottage that will be seen near the bridge.

XVII. Harford.—Ivybridge to Harford Bridge by road, $2\frac{1}{2}$ m. —— From the ivy-covered bridge from which the village derives its name the road climbs the hill to Stowford, and passing onward by Lukesland, and Broomhill Farm, crosses the Butter Brook, and reaches Harford Church. The pedestrian may leave the road near Broomhill and make his way to the church by a path that runs across some fields on the right. Beyond the church the road bends to the left, and descends to Harford Bridge. —— But the route that the rambler will probably choose will be that which will lead him through Stowford Cleave by the bank of the Erme. A path runs near the river, and on this he may enter either at the turn in the road near the vicarage gate, or from a point just above the viaduct. Towards the head of the wooded valley the path is not so well defined as lower down, but there is no difficulty in following it. Where it terminates the visitor crosses a field to a gate on the left, and enters on the lane that leads to the bridge, which is quite near by. —— Close to the western end of the bridge is a Moor gate, and by passing through this and making his way up across the common, the rambler will reach Tristis Rock, or Hall Tor, as it is sometimes called. If he chooses to extend his walk to Stalldon Barrow he will find his reward in the magnificent view obtained from that lofty height. —— The return to Ivybridge from Harford may be made by way of the common. Passing up by the church to the Moor gate, the rambler will turn right to Tor Rocks, which rise close to the little Butter Brook. Then continuing on his way, and keeping near to the enclosures on the right, he will strike a track leading to a gate opening upon a lane, which will bring him down to the road at Stowford.

XVIII. Hawns and Dendles.—Cornwood station, $2\frac{1}{2}$ m. The road lies through the village, 1 m. from the station, and thence along the Harford road to the Vicarage Bridge over the Yealm. Crossing this the way lies by the side of the river, the visitor turning right a short distance up, and then taking the second turning to the left. A little further on he turns right, and passing Sweet's Wood, reaches Combe Farm. The path leads by this to the gate at which the woods are entered. These were formerly part of the Blachford property, but are now in the possession of the Misses Deare, by whose courtesy they are open to the public on Mondays, Wednesdays, and Saturdays, as formerly. —— From the higher gate visitors may pass on to Combe Waste and thence to Stall Moor, where a track running due north will bring them to the enclosed hut clusters mentioned in Chap. XVIII., and which are about 1 m. above the head of the wood.

XIX. The Dewer Stone.—Bickleigh station to Shaugh Bridge, $1\frac{1}{2}$ m. The Dewer Stone Hill being in view from Bickleigh station, and the road to it being direct, it is unnecessary to describe the route. —— Immediately above the confluence of the Plym and the Mew a clam spans the former stream, by means of which the foot of the hill is reached. A path leads to the summit, the Dewer Stone being to the right of this. —— Cadaford Bridge may be reached by way of Wigford Down, as mentioned in Chap. XIX., or by road from Shaugh village. The latter is in sight during the walk from the station to Shaugh Bridge. Those who do not mind a rough scramble will do well to make their way up to Cadaford Bridge by the river. They will then see the true character of the valley, and be rewarded with the sight of some fine bits of scenery. —— From Yelverton the Dewer Stone Hill is approached by way of Clearbrook and Hoo Meavy, or by Goodameavy and Urgles; or the road over Greenwell Down, *via* Gratton Bridge, may be followed. The distance is about 3 m. in each case.

XX. . Dean Combe.—Dousland Station to Nosworthy Bridge, $2\frac{1}{4}$ m.; Princetown to Nosworthy Bridge, *via* Black Tor and Raddick Lane, about $3\frac{1}{2}$ m. —— From Dousland the way lies up the hill to Yennadon Cross where the visitor turns right, and making his way across the common, takes the left branch of the road where it forks. This will lead him down to Lowery, and thence to Higher Lowery, where the road runs by the side of the Devonport leat. Less than $\frac{1}{4}$ m. beyond this is Cross Gate, approached by a bridge over the water-course. Passing through this the visitor follows the road between the enclosures and over a piece of open ground to his objective. —— From Princetown the Plymouth road is followed to Double Waters, a short distance beyond Devil's Bridge, when the visitor strikes over the common left towards Black Tor, which he will see not far off. Just below this he crosses the Mew by the blowing-houses, and passing down the left bank soon reaches the tributary brook that comes from beyond Hart Tor. This he also crosses, and still proceeding down by the Mew, but keeping high above its bank, reaches Iron Bridge, where he can pass over the Devonport leat. His course is then by the side of Raddick Hill, with the enclosures on his right, and the Mew in the valley below them. About $\frac{3}{4}$ m. on a track runs between the enclosures. This is Raddick Lane, and it will bring him into the road running out from Lowery to the Forest. Here he may either turn right to Lether Tor Bridge, and make his way to Nosworthy Bridge by road, *via* Cross Gate, or by the enclosures below the road near Lether Tor Farm,—or he may turn left and then strike into another lane a few yards on to the right. This leads direct to Nosworthy Farm and the bridge.

XXI. The Walkham below Merivale.—Princetown to Long Ash Farm, near Merivale Bridge, 3 m.; Tavistock to Pu Tor, $3\frac{1}{4}$ m.; to Merivale Bridge, $4\frac{1}{4}$ m.; Yelverton to Ward Bridge, about 4 m. —— From Princetown the way lies by Rundle Stone, the Tavistock road being followed from that point. The lane running past Long Ash Farm branches from the road near the foot of the hill, just before Merivale Bridge is reached. —— Visitors from Two Bridges also pass Rundle Stone. —— From Tavistock to Pu Tor the road running across Whitchurch Down must be followed to Quarry Lane. This road leaves the town by way of Vigo Bridge, but it may be reached by the path leading to the down opposite to the entrance to the G.W.R. station. Quarry Lane runs eastward, down the slope, from the eastern end of Whitchurch Down, branching from the road that there runs approximately north (to Harford Bridge and Peter Tavy) and south (to Horrabridge). It is $\frac{3}{4}$ m. long, and leads to the commons at the entrance to Moortown, from which point Pu Tor is less than $\frac{1}{2}$ m. distant in a south-easterly direction. —— Merivale Bridge is on the direct road from Tavistock to Princetown. Vixen Tor is seen on the common to the right soon after the third milestone is passed, and can be easily approached from the road at a point about $3\frac{1}{2}$ m. from Tavistock. —— The road from Yelverton to Ward Bridge lies through Walkhampton; the road to Huckworthy Bridge is then followed for less than $\frac{1}{2}$ m., when the turning on the right is taken. The rambler keeps straight on, with the Walkham in the valley on his left, for about $1\frac{3}{4}$ m., when the road is crossed by another coming down from the commons. Here he turns left and descends to the bridge. —— From each of the points forming the termination of these routes the examination of the valley can be commenced. —— The route from Horrabridge to Pu Tor is given in Chap. XXI. The distance from that place to the tor is about 3 m.

XXII. Peter Tavy Combe.—Tavistock to Peter Tavy, 3 m. —— The Okehampton road is followed to the second milestone from the town, which is at the foot of Wringworthy Hill. Immediately opposite to this a road turns off to Peter Tavy. It crosses the Tavy at Harford Bridge, and $\frac{1}{4}$ m. further on turns left, and runs northward to the village. The combe is reached by turning into the road that branches from the main one near the bridge, and then turning left above the school. The mill is only a short distance from the latter. The best way of seeing the combe and its surroundings having been described in Chap. XXII., it is not necessary to give any directions here. The visitor may return from Boulters Tor by way of Cudlipp Town, instead of Smearn Down, by a path leading from that common to Broad Moor. This he will find a little to the north of the eastern end of Twyste Lane. On reaching Broad Moor he will turn to the left, and follow the track down the hill, at the bottom of which he will enter upon a lane that will bring him to the little settlement, and will return to Peter Tavy by the road that runs through it. —— Mary Tavy Clam is reached from Peter Tavy by the lane that passes to the south of the church, and by the village inn. A few yards beyond the latter there is a gate on the right giving access to another lane, and this will take the visitor direct to the clam. The surroundings are no longer as formerly, the opening of a mine a little way up the stream having greatly marred their beauty. Above this, however, the attractions of the valley are still as they were.

XXIII. Lydford Gorge.—The cascade, and that part of the gorge near it, can be visited at any time by obtaining a ticket (3d.) at the Manor Hotel, near the station. The higher part of the gorge, including the chasm under the bridge, is only open to visitors on Mondays (tickets 3d.). The entrance to this part is quite close to Lydford Bridge. —— The ruined castle may be viewed at any time; the caretaker lives close by. —— Skit Steps are not far from Lydford village. The spot is reached by a lane branching off by the chapel. This leads to Lake, where the visitor turns right to the old mill, whence a path runs upward by the side of the river, here crossed by a rustic bridge.

XXIV. Tavy Cleave.—Lydford village to the Tavy Cleave Tors, about 3 m.; Lydford station to do., $3\frac{1}{2}$ m.; Mary Tavy station to Lane End, 4 m. —— From Lydford village the way will lead the visitor to Skit Steps (as in the last route), and on passing the waterfall he will follow the path up through the brake, with the river below him on the left. This will bring him into the Tavistock and Okehampton highway, which he will reach at the seventh milestone from the first named town. Turning right he will follow this road past Beardon, and a little further on will see a lane branching left. This is an approach to the common appropriately called Down Lane, and now becomes his path. When he enters on the common he only follows it for a short distance, and then strikes left over White Hill, passing a little to the south of the summit. His course here is east by south, and this he pursues for a distance of about 1 m. from Down Lane, when he will find himself not far from the wall of the Redford enclosures. These are on his right, Hare Tor being in advance of him to the left. Keeping the same course as before he soon comes in sight of the Tavy Cleave Tors—straight ahead of him. Ger Tor is a prominent object across the common to the right. —— From Lydford station the route is the same as that given for reaching Fur Tor and Cranmere, as far as the northern end of the enclosures of Redford, on reaching which point the visitor will follow the directions just given. —— The route from Mary Tavy station to Lane End is by way of Horndon and Zoar. The road is followed to the Mary Tavy post-office, opposite to which another runs down through the old workings of Wheal Friendship Mine. On reaching the top of the ascent on the further side of these workings the road runs along a level for a short distance, when another runs off left. This is the Horndon road, and a walk of about 1¼ m. will bring the visitor to that hamlet. Keeping straight on he crosses the edge of Black Lion Down, and a little further on reaches the smaller hamlet of Zoar, placed on the verge of the down of that name. The road runs over this and again enters on enclosed land, this part of it being known as Buddla Lane. At its end another lane runs across at right angles, and here the visitor turns right. A short distance down it forks, the branch to the left being the one to be followed. This will take him by Will Farm, and not far beyond this he will cross the Willsworthy Brook, close to which is an ancient manor pound. A little further on he passes Willsworthy Farm on the right, and in another ½ m. reaches the Moor gate at Lane End. —— If he desires to visit Ger Tor from this point he will make his way up the common towards it, the rocks being in sight from the gate, crossing the mine leat at a bridge. —— Nat Tor Farm is reached by a Moor road running to the right inside the gate, and if desirous of making his way up through the valley from Nat Tor, he will follow this to within a short distance of the farm, when striking left he will reach a bridge that will enable him to cross the leat near by, when he will find himself close to Nat Tor.

Railway Stations around Dartmoor.—The Roman figures refer to chapters, and follow the names of stations from which the objects described in them are most conveniently reached. —— Okehampton (S.W.), II., III., IV., V. Moretonhampstead (G.W.), VI., VII., VIII. Lustleigh (G.W.), IX., X. Bovey Tracey (G.W.), X., XI. Ashburton (G.W.), X., XI., XII., XIII., XIV. Buckfastleigh (G.W.), XV. Brent (G.W.), XV., XVI. Wrangaton (G.W.), Ivybridge (G.W.), XVII. Cornwood (G.W.), XVIII. Plympton (G.W.), Bickleigh (G.W.), XIX. Yelverton (G.W.), XXI. Dousland (G.W.), XX., XXI. Princetown (G.W.), I., II., III., XX., XXI. Horrabridge (G.W.), XXI. Tavistock (S.W. and G.W.), XXI., XXII. Mary Tavy (G.W.), XXII. Brent Tor (S.W.), Lydford (S.W. and G.W.), II., III., XXIII., XXIV. Bridestowe (S.W.), II., III.

ILLUSTRATIONS.

From photographs taken expressly for this work by MRS. ERNEST CROFT, ERNEST CROFT, A. EDMUND SPENDER, and C. R. ROWE.

PLATES.

INDEX.

ERRATA.

Frontispiece, for *Heytor* read *Hey Tor ;*
for *Ripon* read *Rippon.*
P. 57, line 13 from top, for *and* read *or.*
P. 88, line 6 from top, for *and* read *are.*
Pp. 100, 103, 105, for *Leusden* read *Leusdon.*